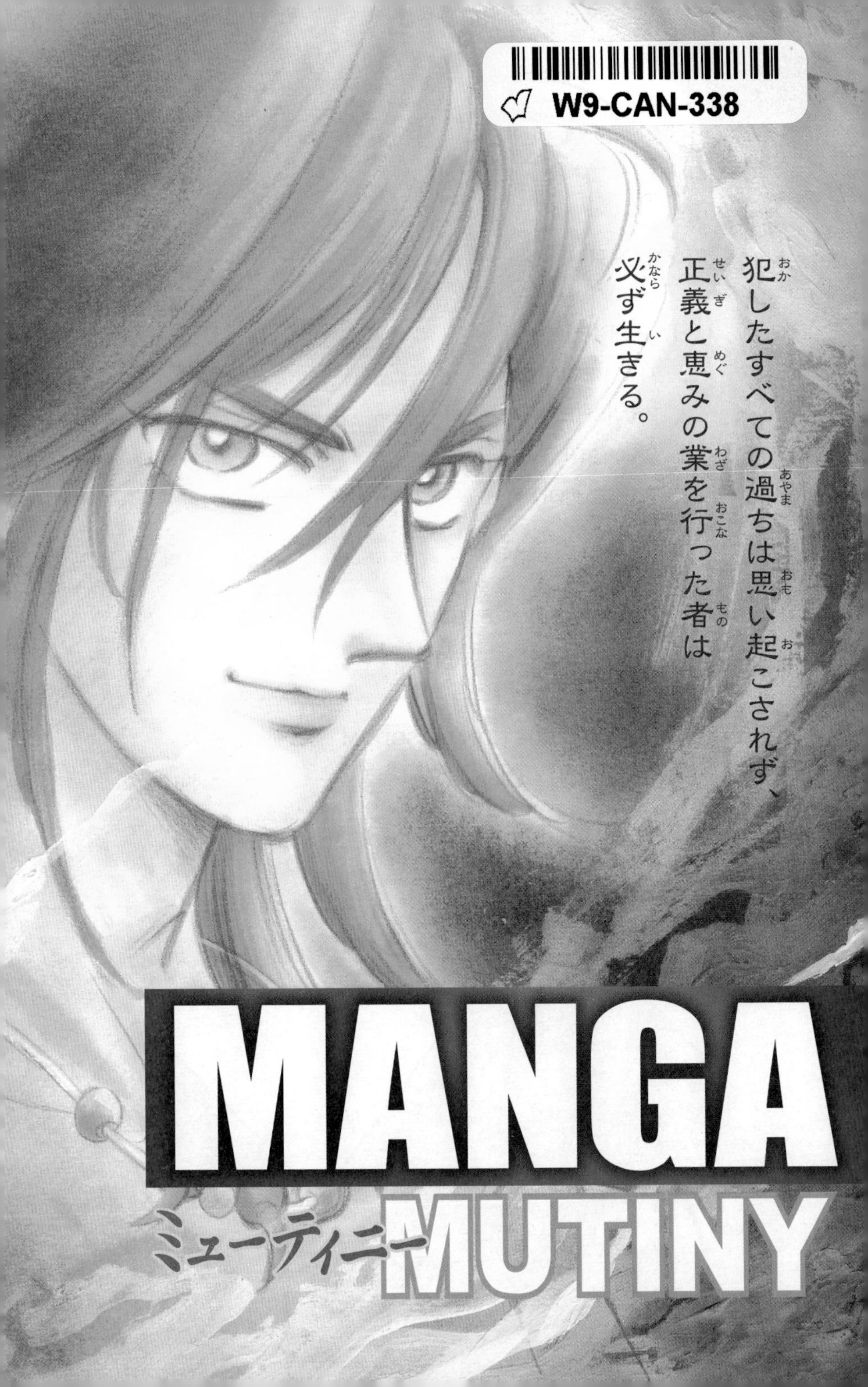
犯したすべての過ちは思い起こされず、
正義と恵みの業を行った者は
必ず生きる。
MANGA
ミューティニー
MUTINY

CONTENTS

CHAPTER 3

CHAPTER 4

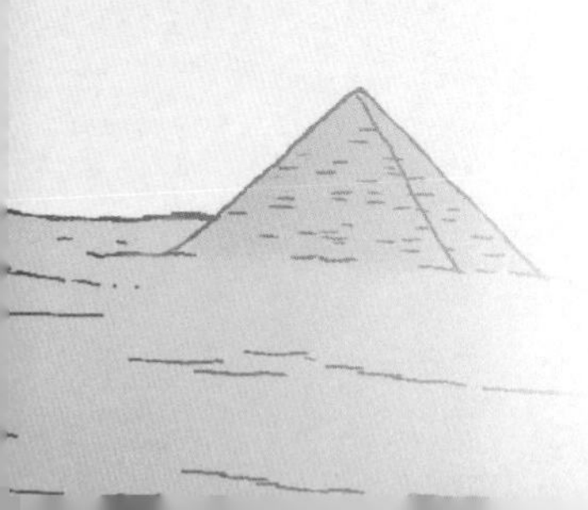

PROLOGUE

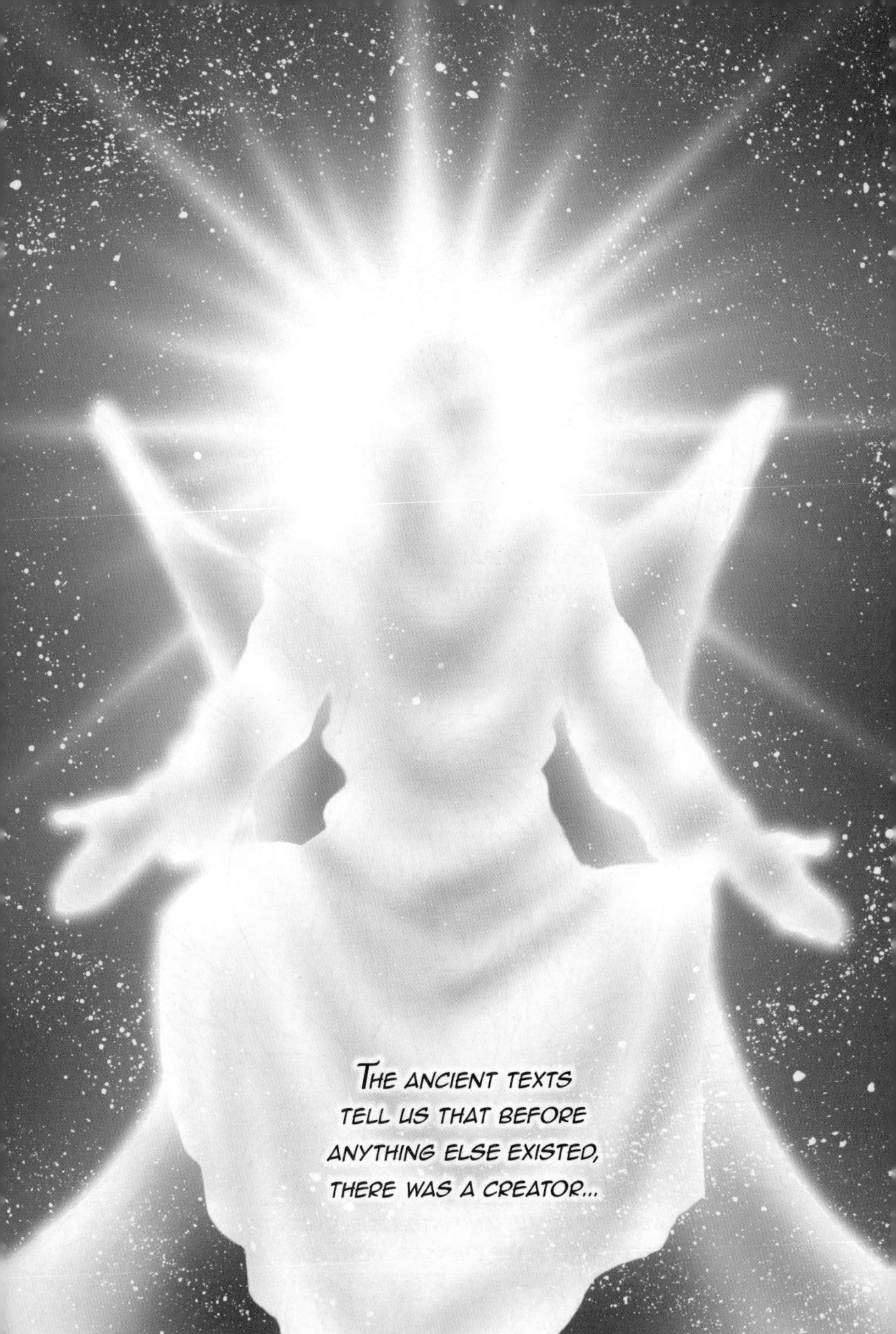
THE ANCIENT TEXTS TELL US THAT BEFORE ANYTHING ELSE EXISTED, THERE WAS A CREATOR...

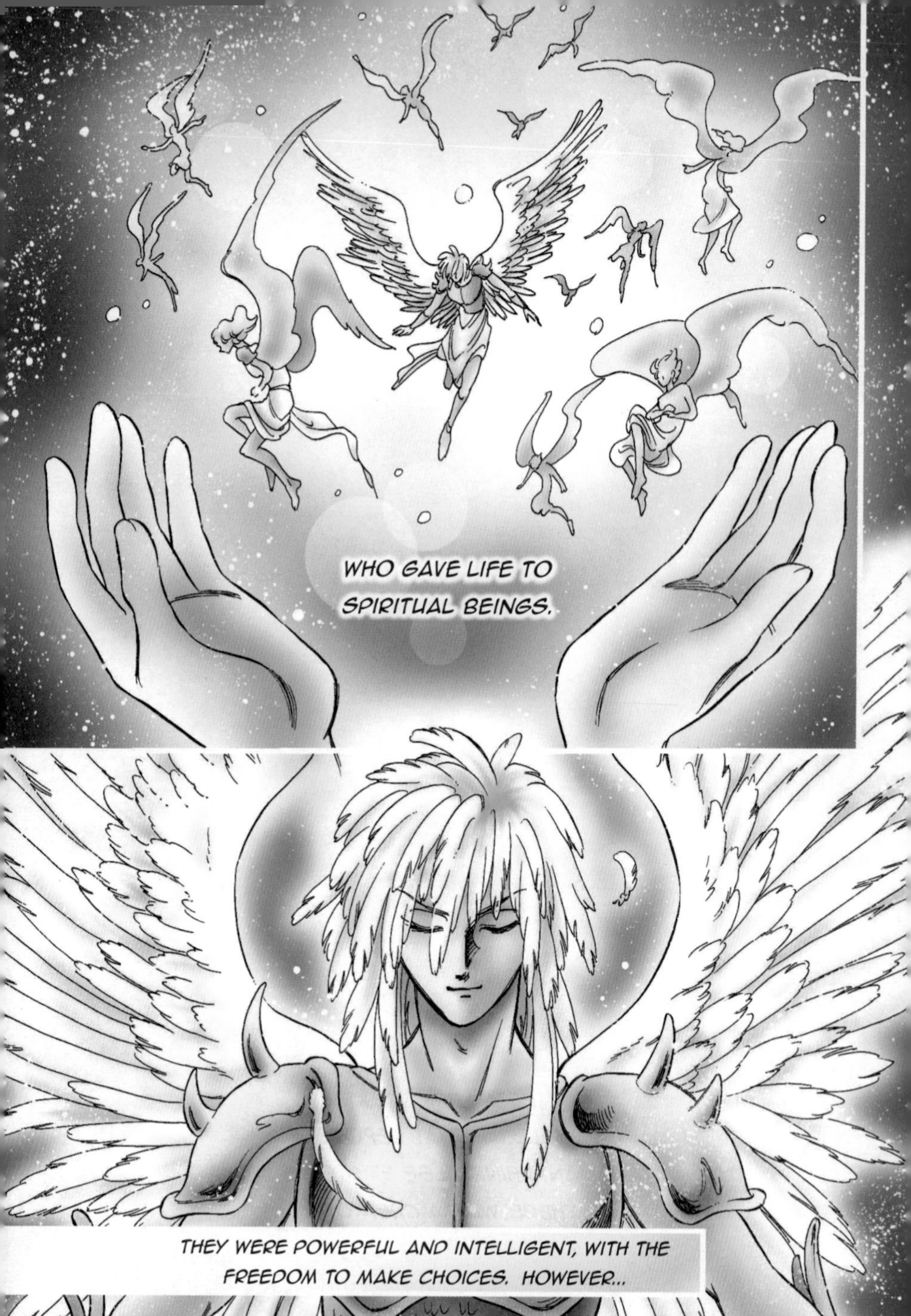
WHO GAVE LIFE TO
SPIRITUAL BEINGS.
THEY WERE POWERFUL AND INTELLIGENT, WITH THE
FREEDOM TO MAKE CHOICES. HOWEVER...

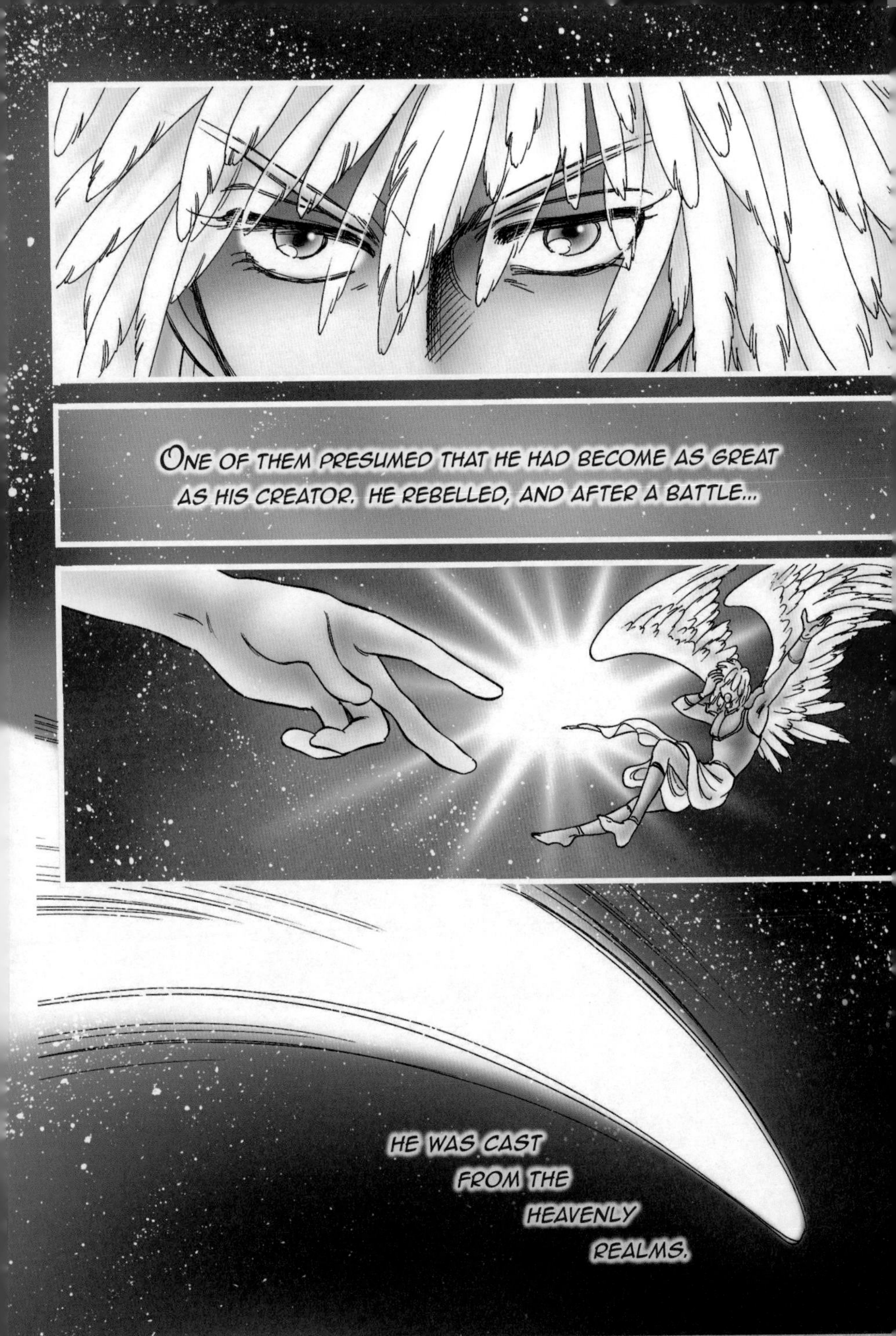
ONE OF THEM PRESUMED THAT HE HAD BECOME AS GREAT AS HIS CREATOR. HE REBELLED, AND AFTER A BATTLE...
HE WAS CAST FROM THE HEAVENLY REALMS.

Isaiah 14:12–15, Revelation 12:7–9

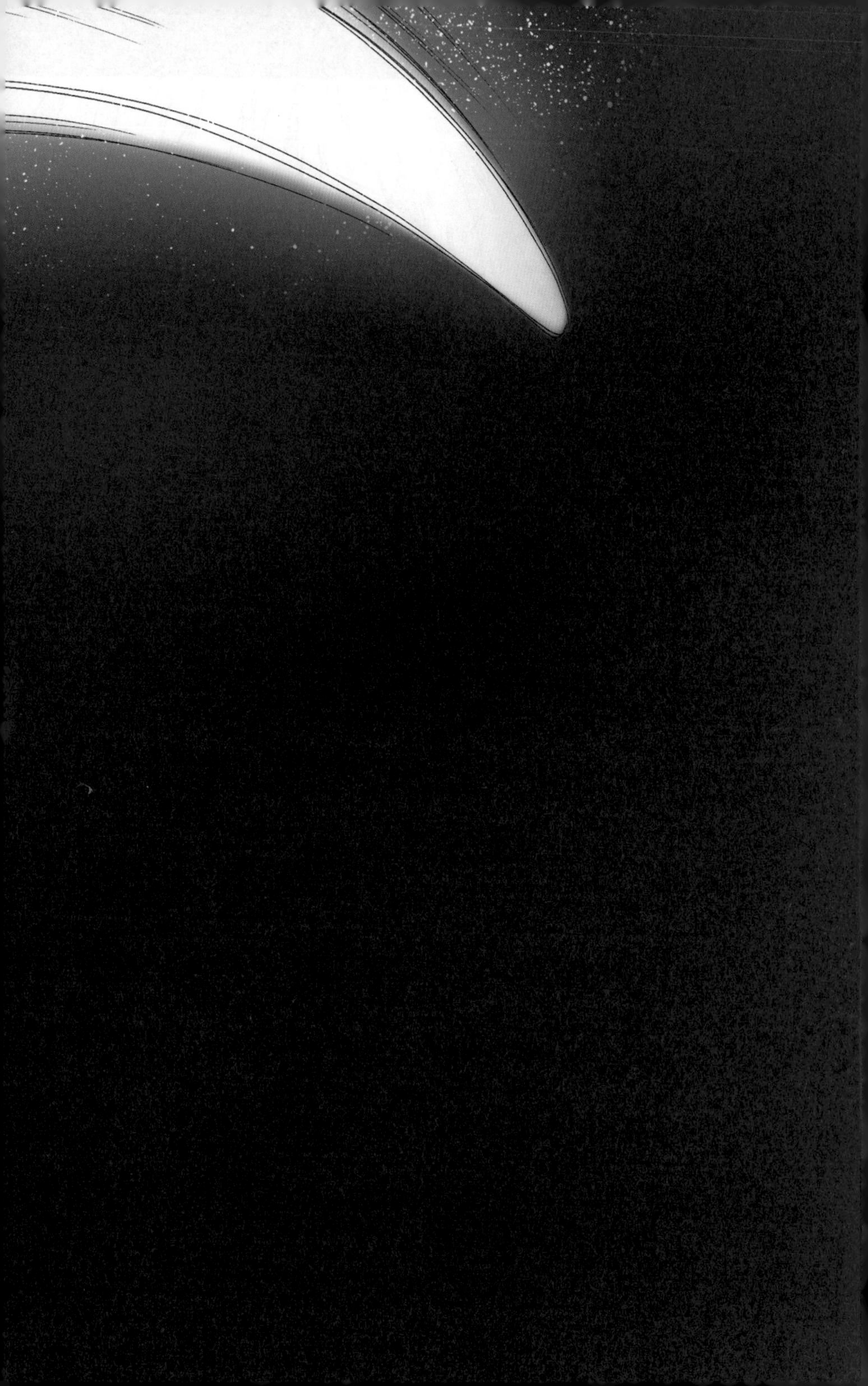

CHAPTER 1

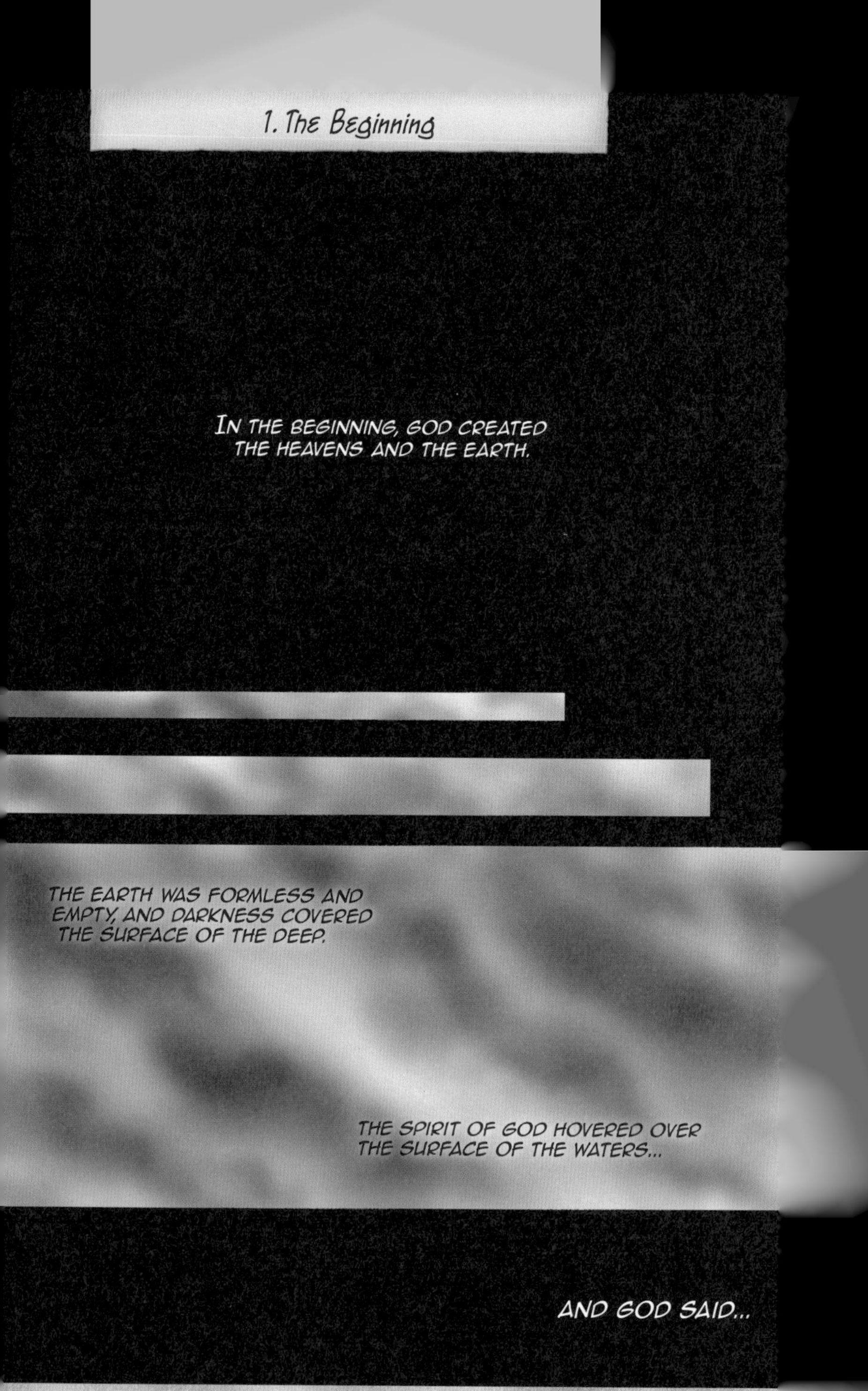
1. The Beginning
IN THE BEGINNING, GOD CREATED THE HEAVENS AND THE EARTH.
THE EARTH WAS FORMLESS AND EMPTY, AND DARKNESS COVERED THE SURFACE OF THE DEEP.
THE SPIRIT OF GOD HOVERED OVER THE SURFACE OF THE WATERS...
AND GOD SAID...

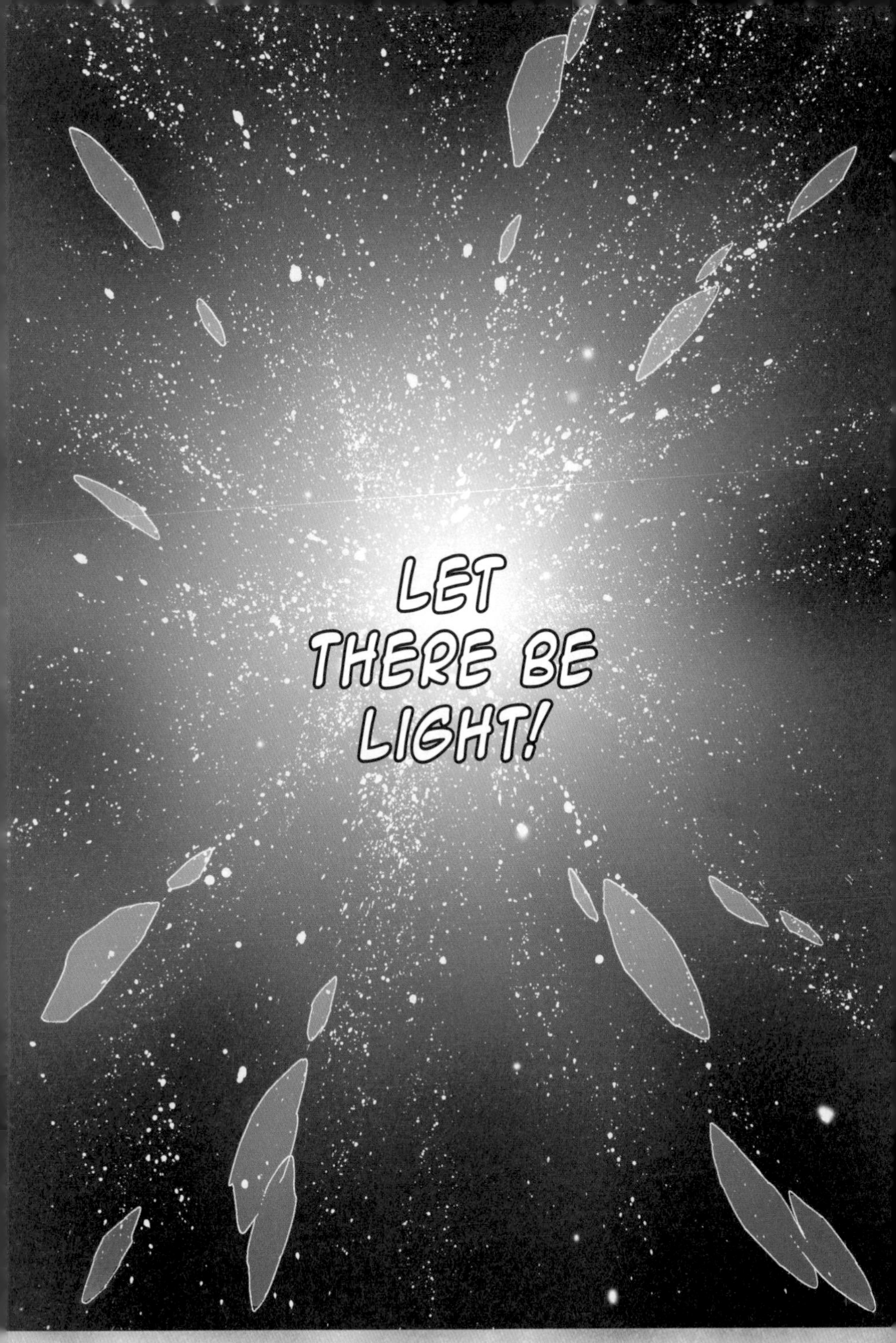
LET THERE BE LIGHT!

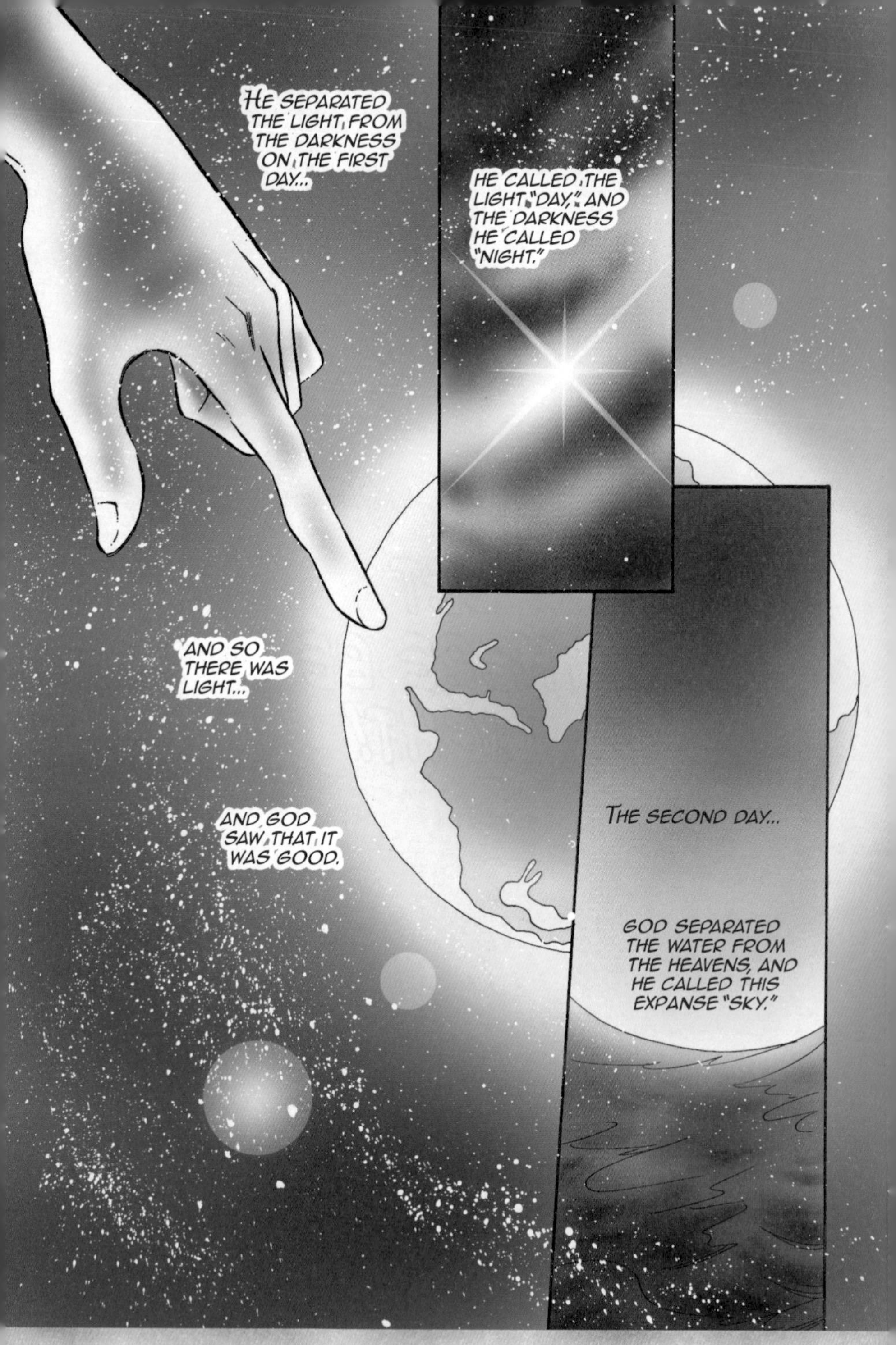
HE SEPARATED THE LIGHT FROM THE DARKNESS ON THE FIRST DAY...
HE CALLED THE LIGHT "DAY," AND THE DARKNESS HE CALLED "NIGHT."
AND SO THERE WAS LIGHT...
AND GOD SAW THAT IT WAS GOOD.
THE SECOND DAY...
GOD SEPARATED THE WATER FROM THE HEAVENS, AND HE CALLED THIS EXPANSE "SKY."

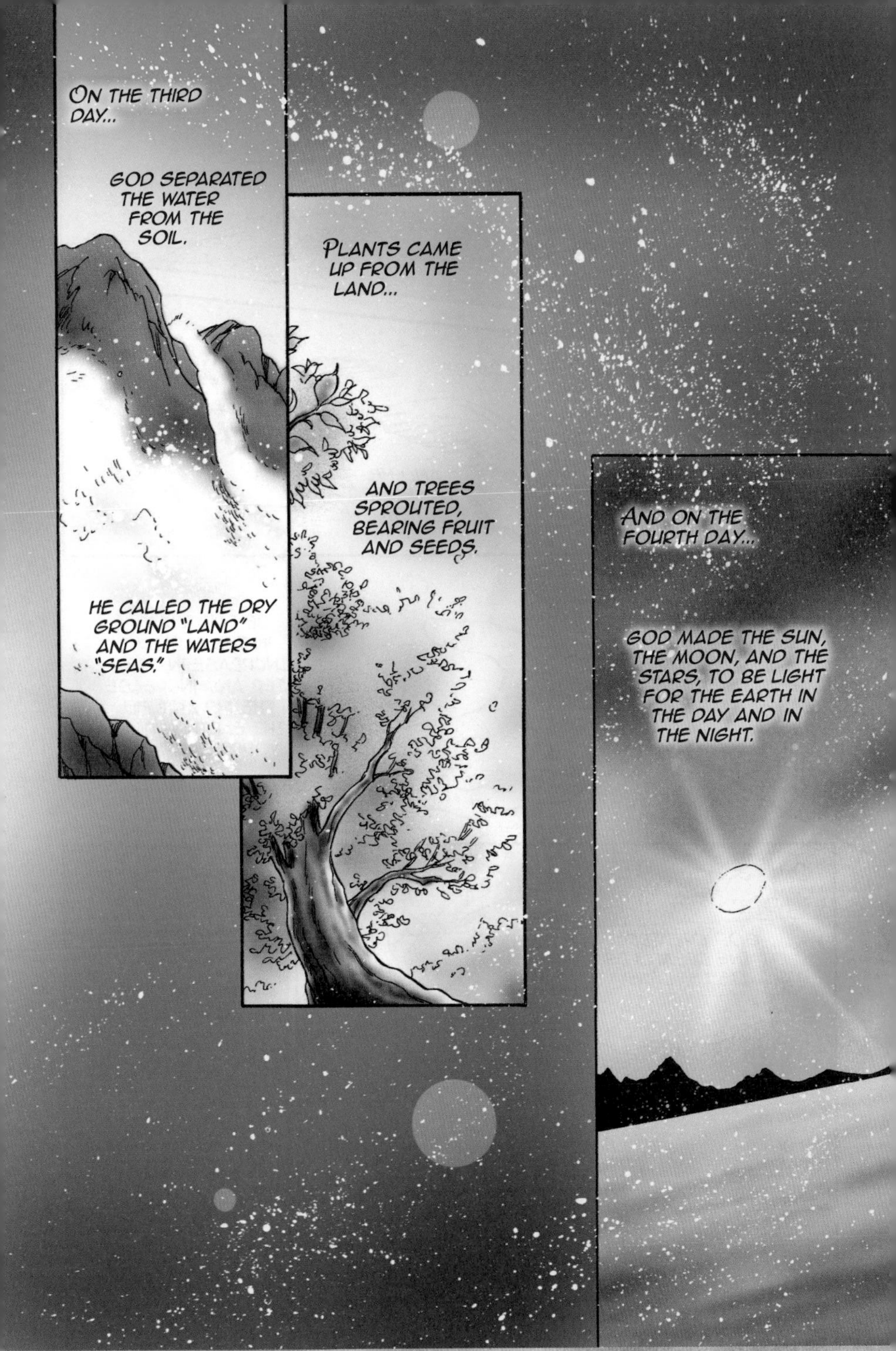
ON THE THIRD DAY...
GOD SEPARATED THE WATER FROM THE SOIL.
HE CALLED THE DRY GROUND "LAND" AND THE WATERS "SEAS."
PLANTS CAME UP FROM THE LAND...
AND TREES SPROUTED, BEARING FRUIT AND SEEDS.
AND ON THE FOURTH DAY...
GOD MADE THE SUN, THE MOON, AND THE STARS, TO BE LIGHT FOR THE EARTH IN THE DAY AND IN THE NIGHT.

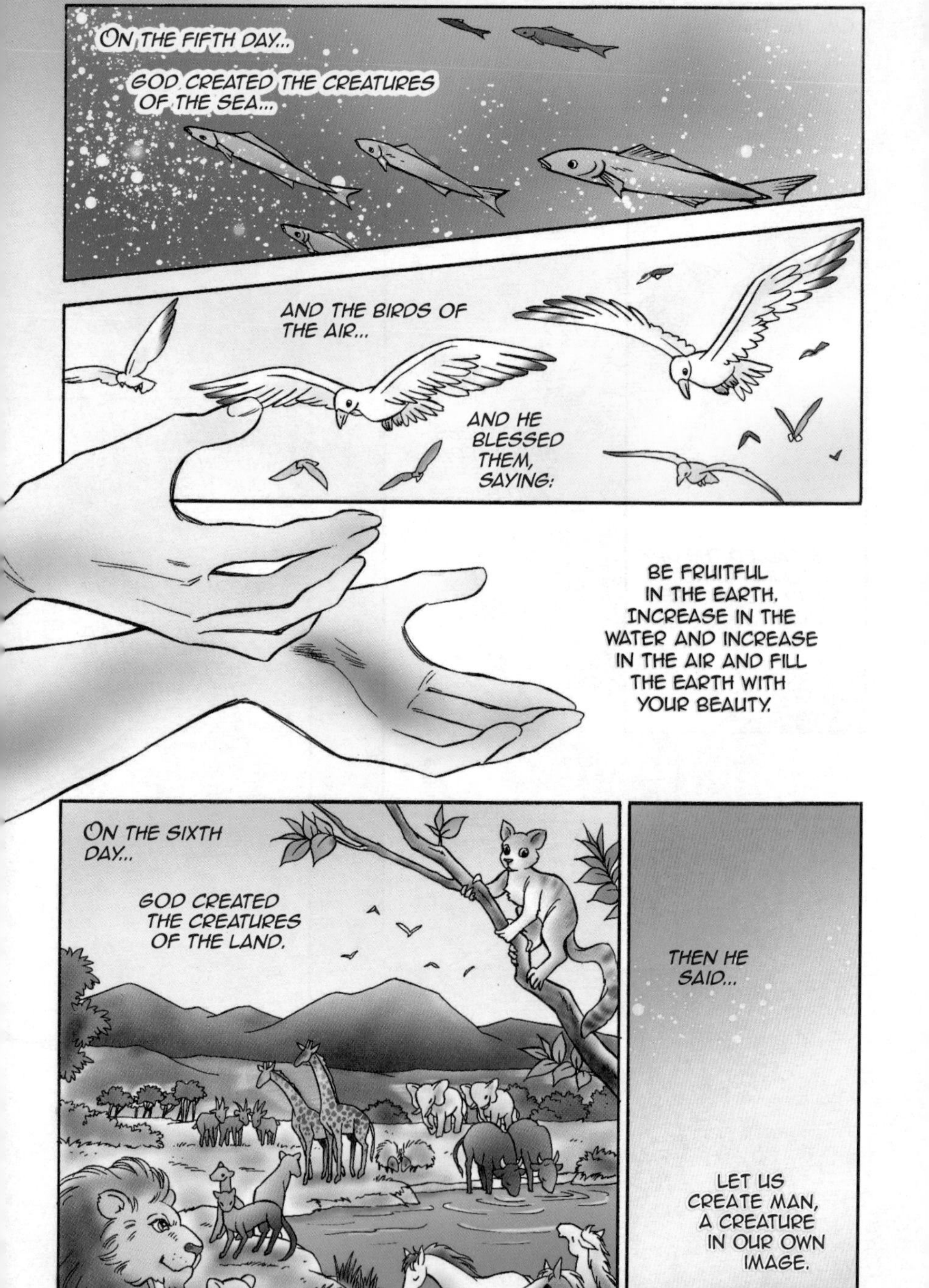
ON THE FIFTH DAY...
GOD CREATED THE CREATURES OF THE SEA...
AND THE BIRDS OF THE AIR...
AND HE BLESSED THEM, SAYING:
BE FRUITFUL IN THE EARTH. INCREASE IN THE WATER AND INCREASE IN THE AIR AND FILL THE EARTH WITH YOUR BEAUTY.
ON THE SIXTH DAY...
GOD CREATED THE CREATURES OF THE LAND.
THEN HE SAID...
LET US CREATE MAN, A CREATURE IN OUR OWN IMAGE.

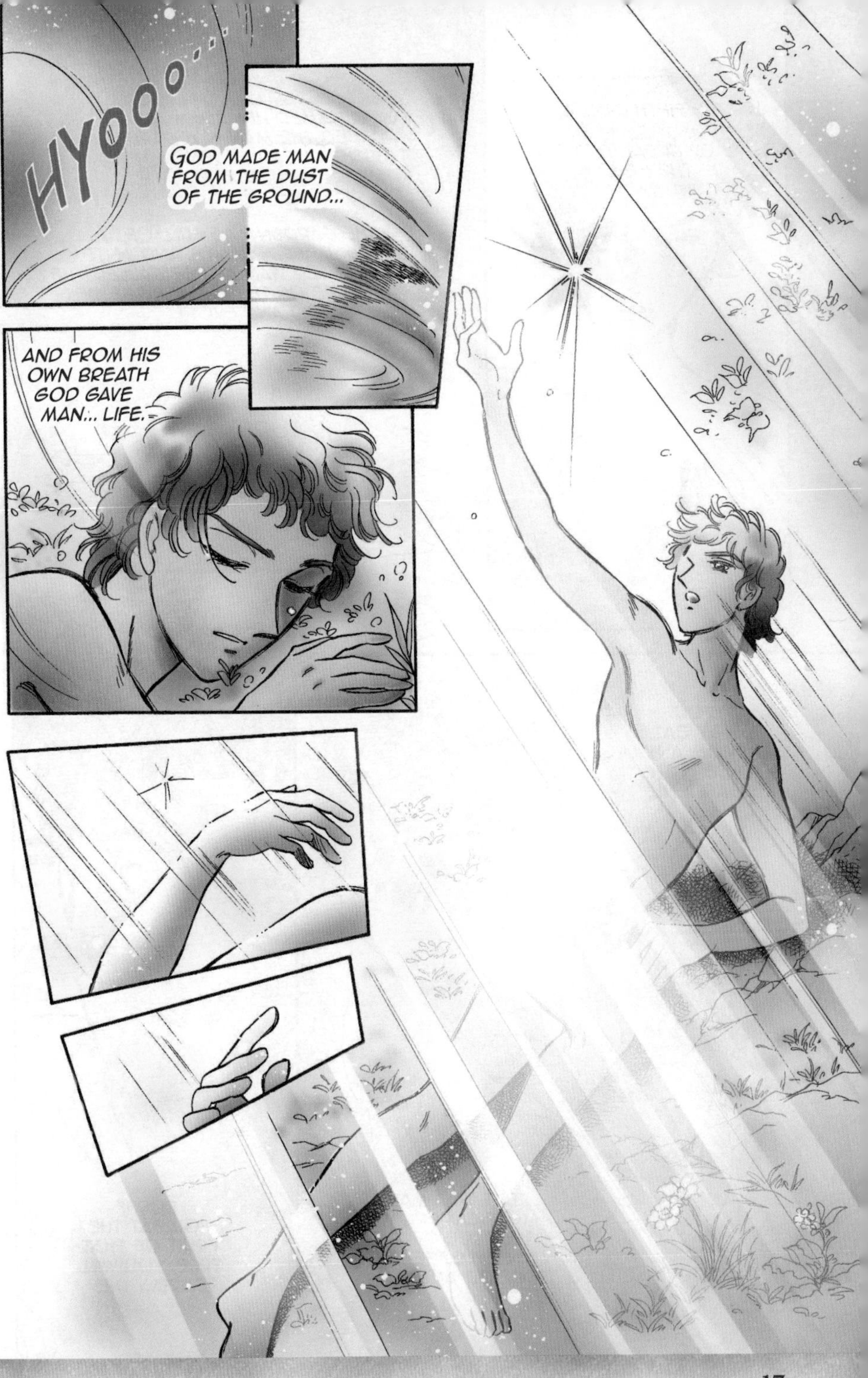
HYOOO...
GOD MADE MAN FROM THE DUST OF THE GROUND...
AND FROM HIS OWN BREATH GOD GAVE MAN... LIFE.

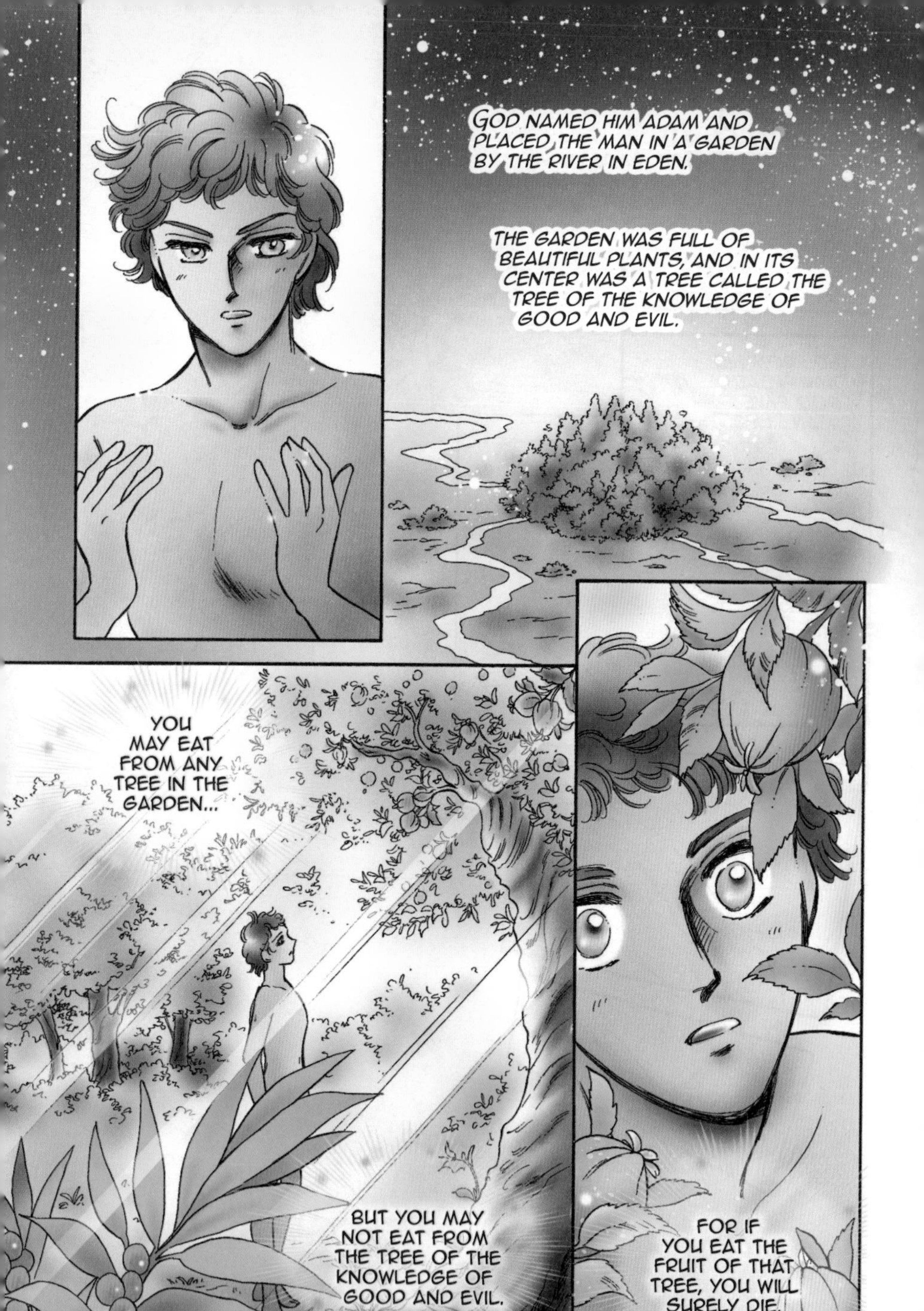
GOD NAMED HIM ADAM AND PLACED THE MAN IN A GARDEN BY THE RIVER IN EDEN.
THE GARDEN WAS FULL OF BEAUTIFUL PLANTS, AND IN ITS CENTER WAS A TREE CALLED THE TREE OF THE KNOWLEDGE OF GOOD AND EVIL.
YOU MAY EAT FROM ANY TREE IN THE GARDEN...
BUT YOU MAY NOT EAT FROM THE TREE OF THE KNOWLEDGE OF GOOD AND EVIL.
FOR IF YOU EAT THE FRUIT OF THAT TREE, YOU WILL SURELY DIE.

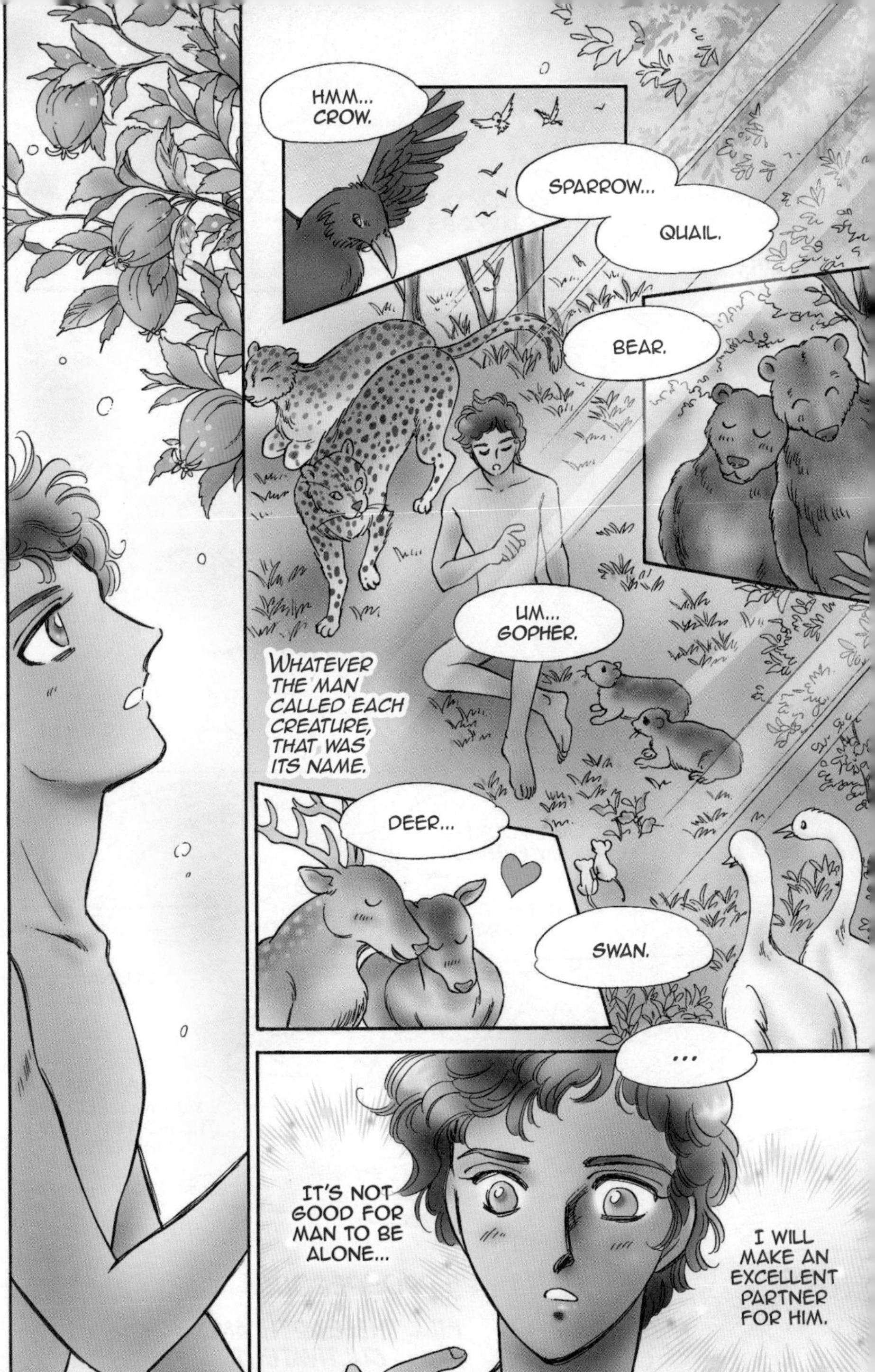
HMM... CROW.
SPARROW...
QUAIL.
BEAR.
UM... GOPHER.
WHATEVER THE MAN CALLED EACH CREATURE, THAT WAS ITS NAME.
DEER...
SWAN.
...
IT'S NOT GOOD FOR MAN TO BE ALONE...
I WILL MAKE AN EXCELLENT PARTNER FOR HIM.

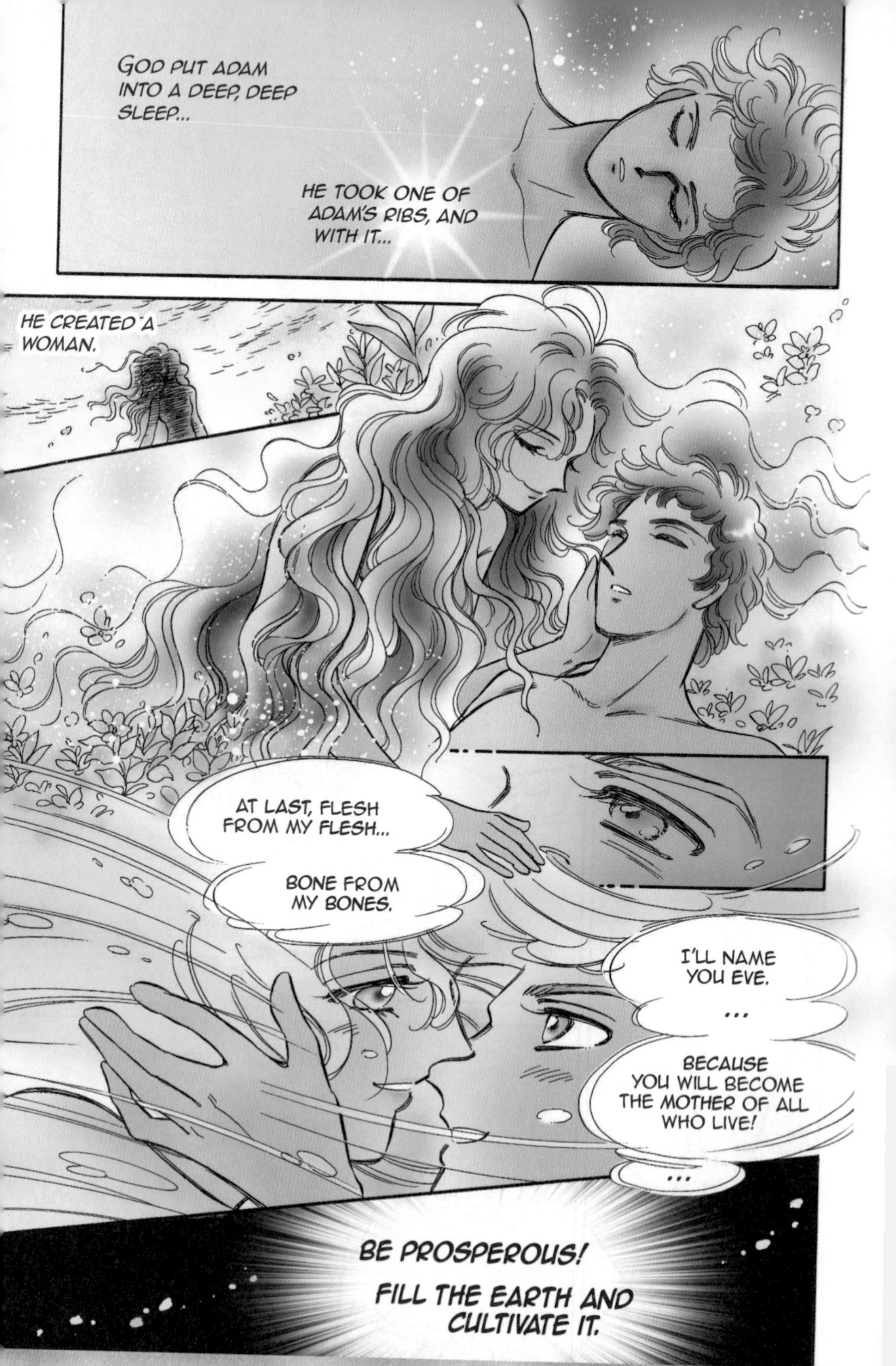
GOD PUT ADAM INTO A DEEP, DEEP SLEEP...
HE TOOK ONE OF ADAM'S RIBS, AND WITH IT...
HE CREATED A WOMAN.
AT LAST, FLESH FROM MY FLESH...
BONE FROM MY BONES.
I'LL NAME YOU EVE.
...
BECAUSE YOU WILL BECOME THE MOTHER OF ALL WHO LIVE!
...
BE PROSPEROUS!
FILL THE EARTH AND CULTIVATE IT.

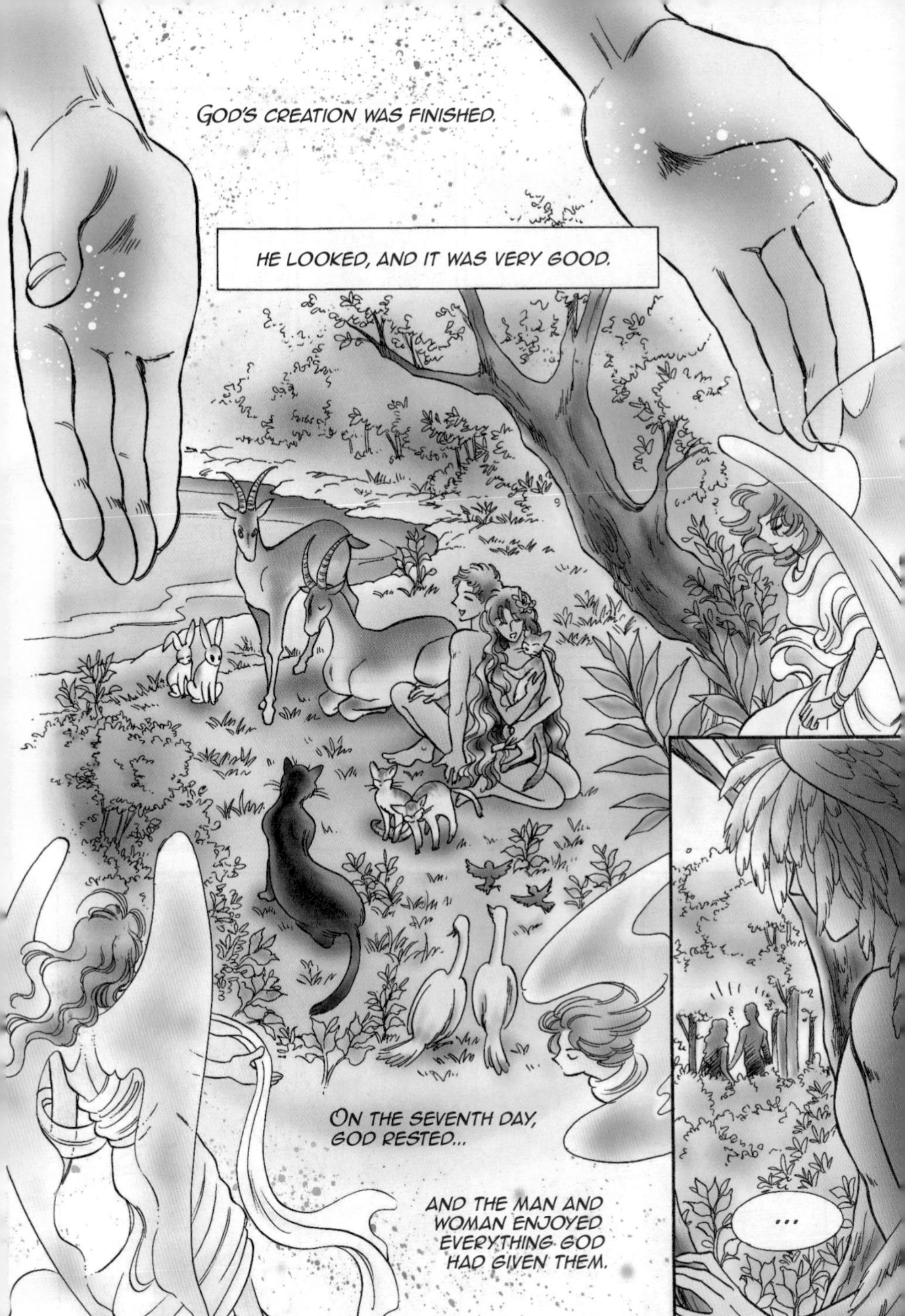
GOD'S CREATION WAS FINISHED.
HE LOOKED, AND IT WAS VERY GOOD.
ON THE SEVENTH DAY, GOD RESTED...
AND THE MAN AND WOMAN ENJOYED EVERYTHING GOD HAD GIVEN THEM.
...

2. Banished

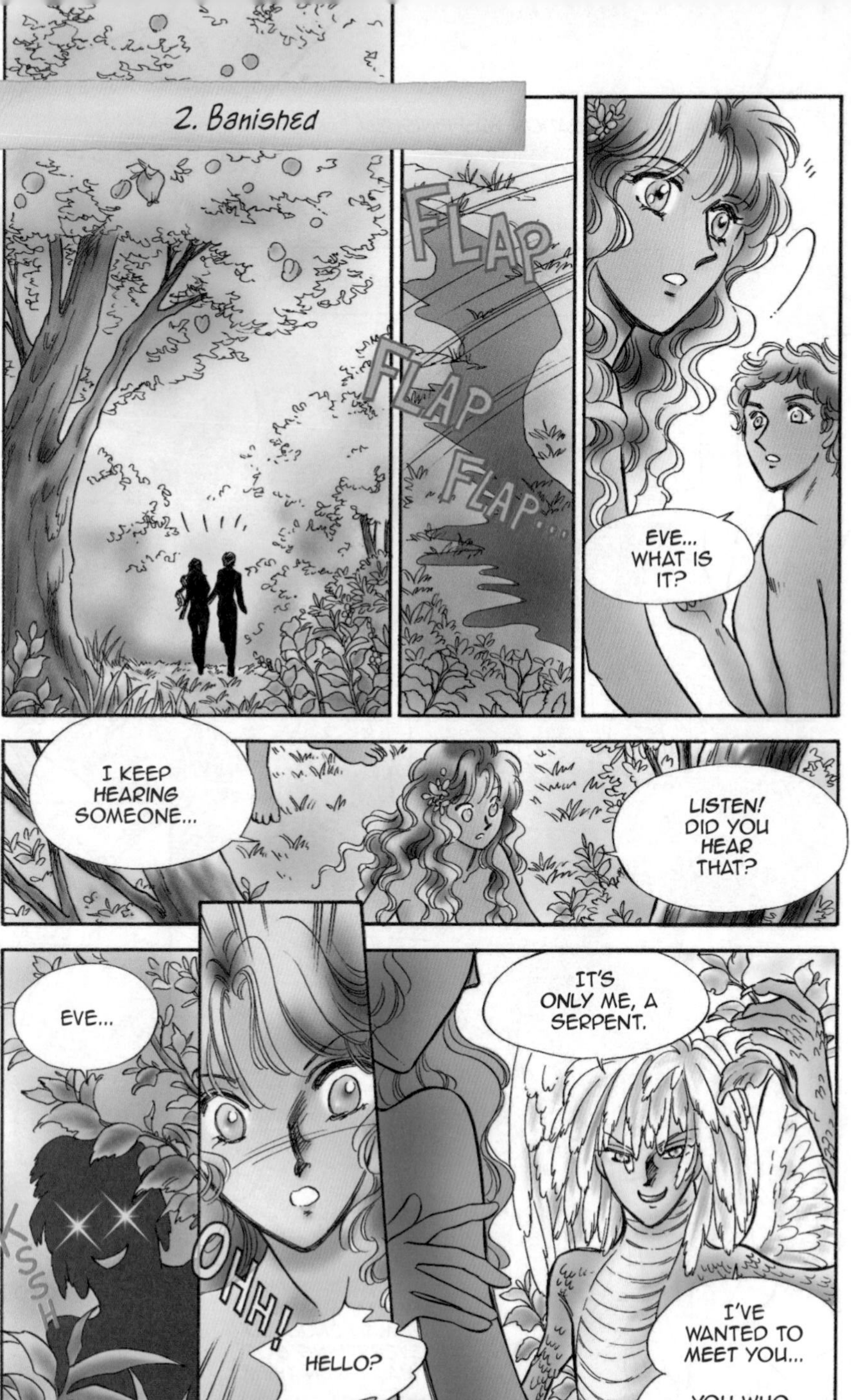
FLAP
FLAP
FLAP...
EVE... WHAT IS IT?
I KEEP HEARING SOMEONE...
LISTEN! DID YOU HEAR THAT?
EVE...
KSSH
OHH!
HELLO?
IT'S ONLY ME, A SERPENT.
I'VE WANTED TO MEET YOU...
YOU WHO ARE FAVORED BY GOD...

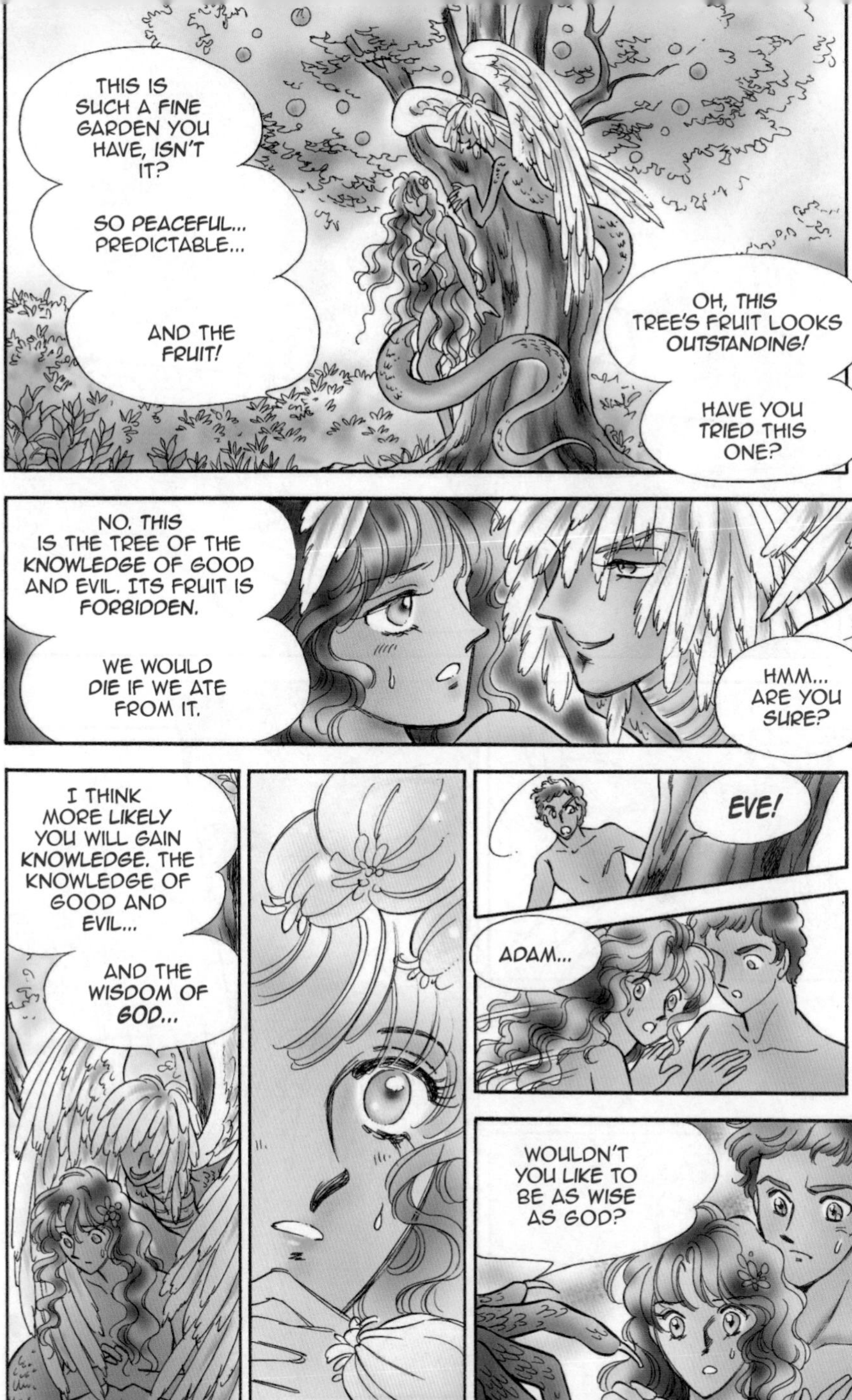
THIS IS SUCH A FINE GARDEN YOU HAVE, ISN'T IT?
SO PEACEFUL... PREDICTABLE...
AND THE FRUIT!
OH, THIS TREE'S FRUIT LOOKS OUTSTANDING!
HAVE YOU TRIED THIS ONE?
NO. THIS IS THE TREE OF THE KNOWLEDGE OF GOOD AND EVIL. ITS FRUIT IS FORBIDDEN.
WE WOULD DIE IF WE ATE FROM IT.
HMM... ARE YOU SURE?
I THINK MORE LIKELY YOU WILL GAIN KNOWLEDGE. THE KNOWLEDGE OF GOOD AND EVIL...
AND THE WISDOM OF GOD...
EVE!
ADAM...
WOULDN'T YOU LIKE TO BE AS WISE AS GOD?

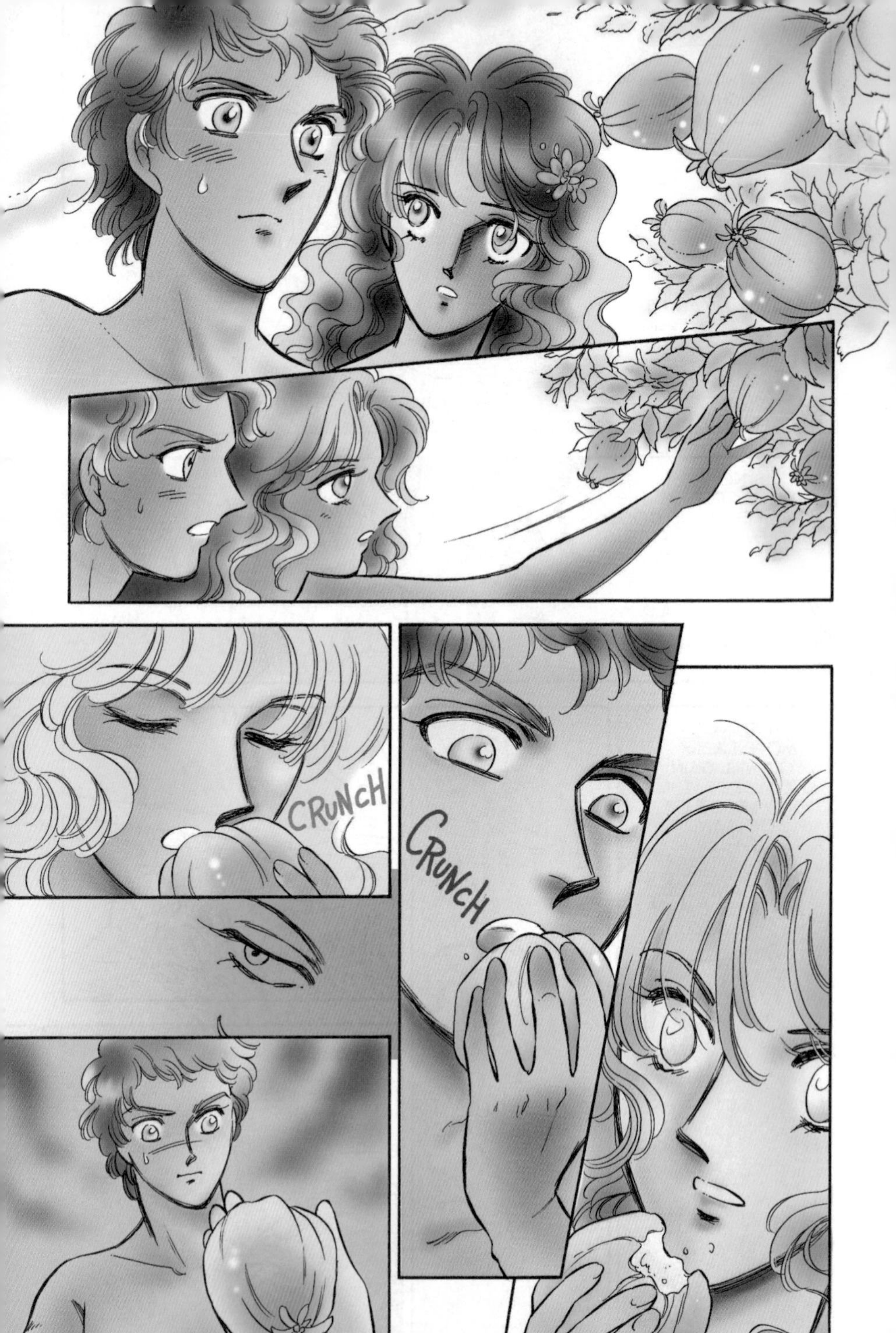
CRUNCH
CRUNCH

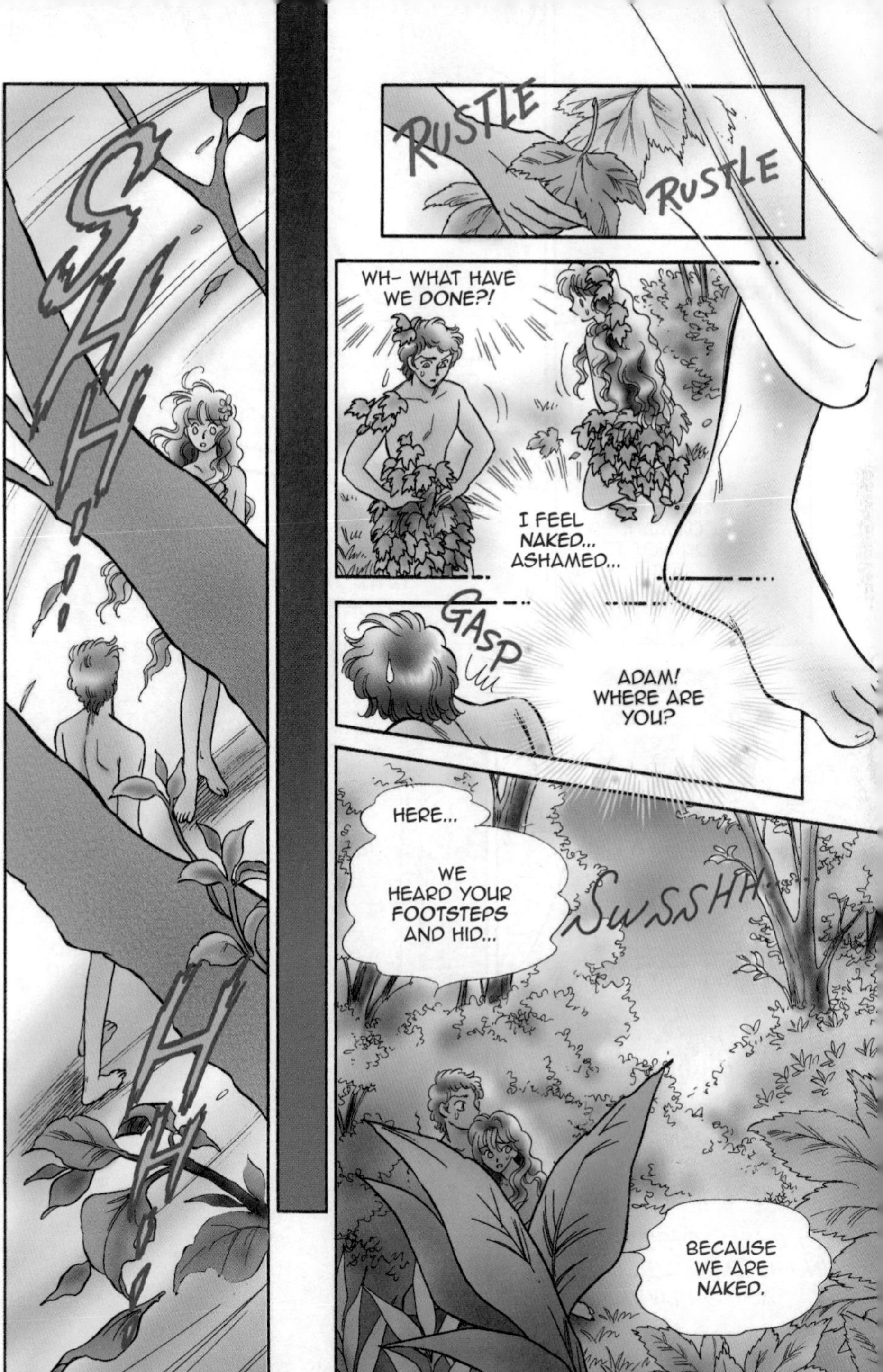
SHHH...
RUSTLE
RUSTLE
WH- WHAT HAVE WE DONE?!
I FEEL NAKED... ASHAMED...
GASP
ADAM! WHERE ARE YOU?
HERE...
WE HEARD YOUR FOOTSTEPS AND HID...
SWSSHH
BECAUSE WE ARE NAKED.

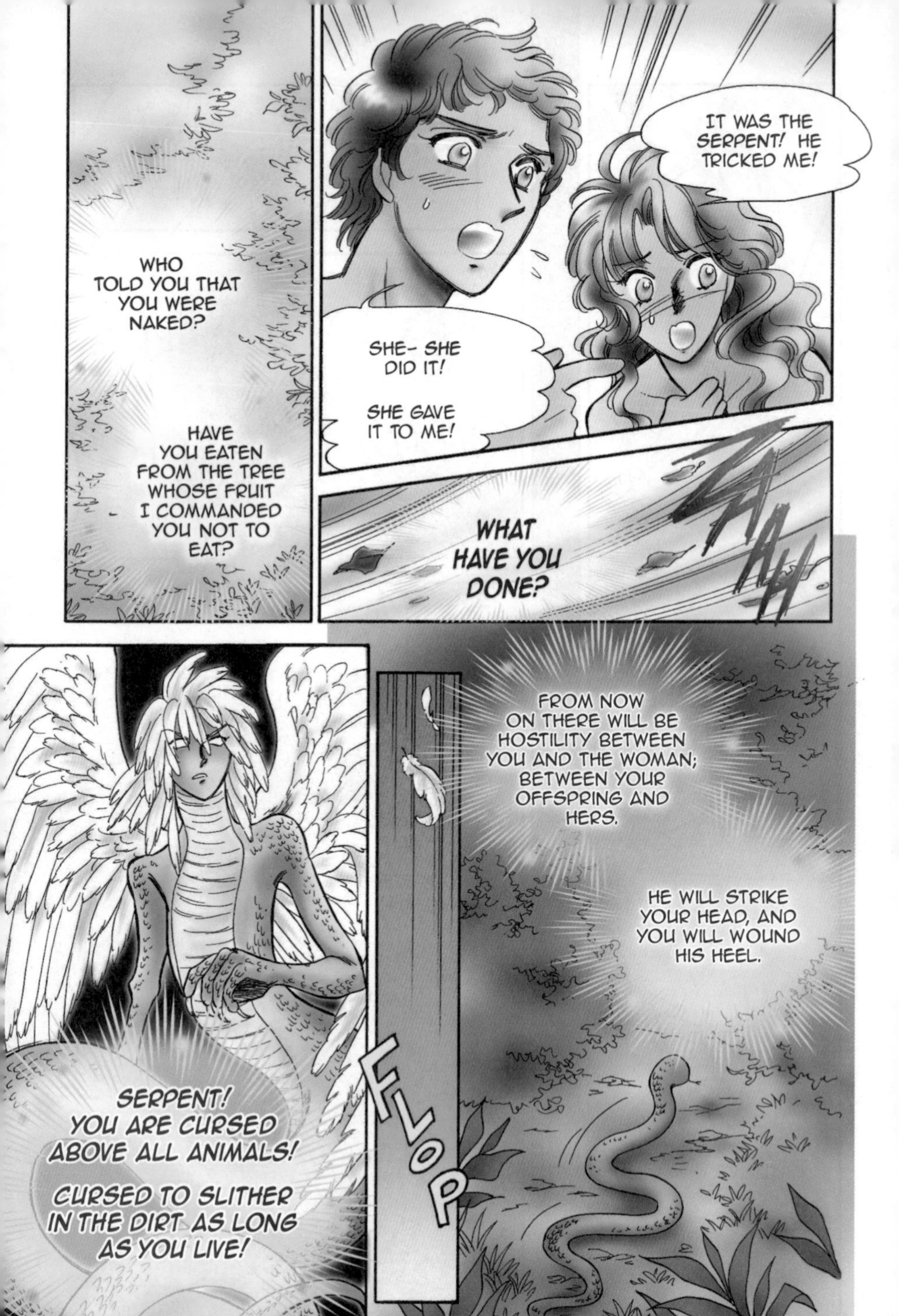
WHO TOLD YOU THAT YOU WERE NAKED?
HAVE YOU EATEN FROM THE TREE WHOSE FRUIT I COMMANDED YOU NOT TO EAT?
SHE- SHE DID IT!
SHE GAVE IT TO ME!
IT WAS THE SERPENT! HE TRICKED ME!
WHAT HAVE YOU DONE?
ZAAH
SERPENT! YOU ARE CURSED ABOVE ALL ANIMALS!
CURSED TO SLITHER IN THE DIRT AS LONG AS YOU LIVE!
FLOP
FROM NOW ON THERE WILL BE HOSTILITY BETWEEN YOU AND THE WOMAN; BETWEEN YOUR OFFSPRING AND HERS.
HE WILL STRIKE YOUR HEAD, AND YOU WILL WOUND HIS HEEL.

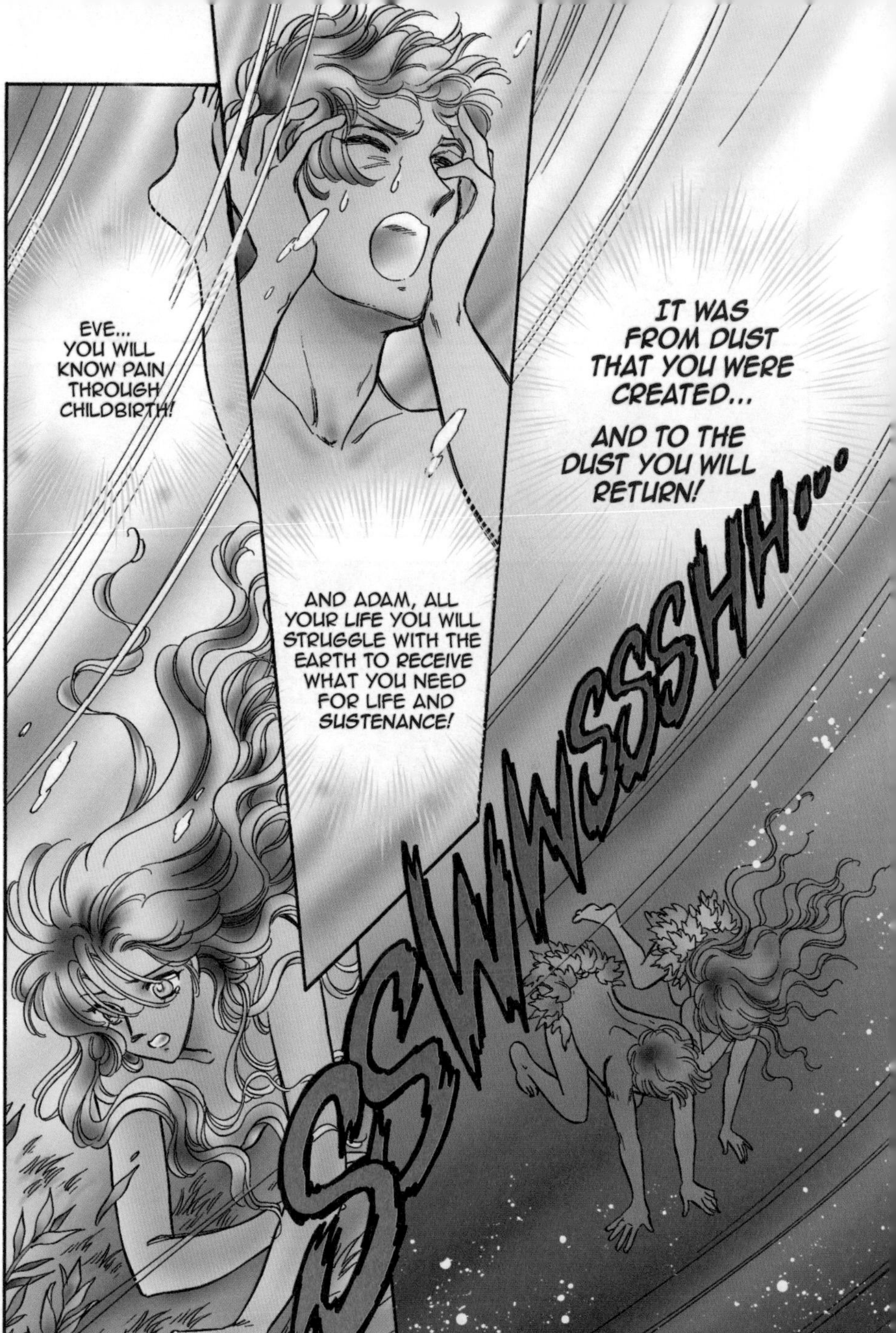
EVE... YOU WILL KNOW PAIN THROUGH CHILDBIRTH!
AND ADAM, ALL YOUR LIFE YOU WILL STRUGGLE WITH THE EARTH TO RECEIVE WHAT YOU NEED FOR LIFE AND SUSTENANCE!
IT WAS FROM DUST THAT YOU WERE CREATED...
AND TO THE DUST YOU WILL RETURN!
SSWWSSSHH...

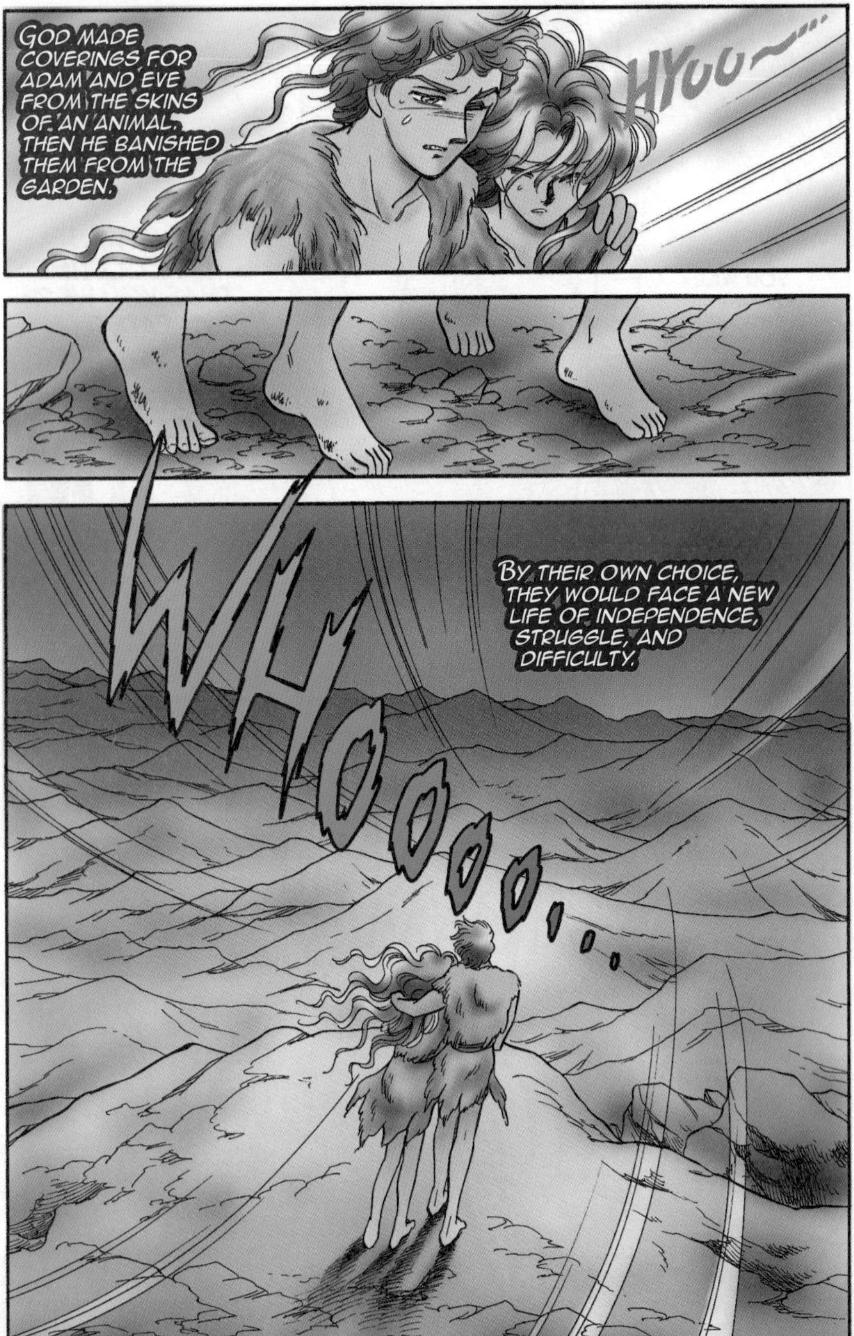
GOD MADE COVERINGS FOR ADAM AND EVE FROM THE SKINS OF AN ANIMAL. THEN HE BANISHED THEM FROM THE GARDEN.
HYUU~...
WHOOOO...
BY THEIR OWN CHOICE, THEY WOULD FACE A NEW LIFE OF INDEPENDENCE, STRUGGLE, AND DIFFICULTY.

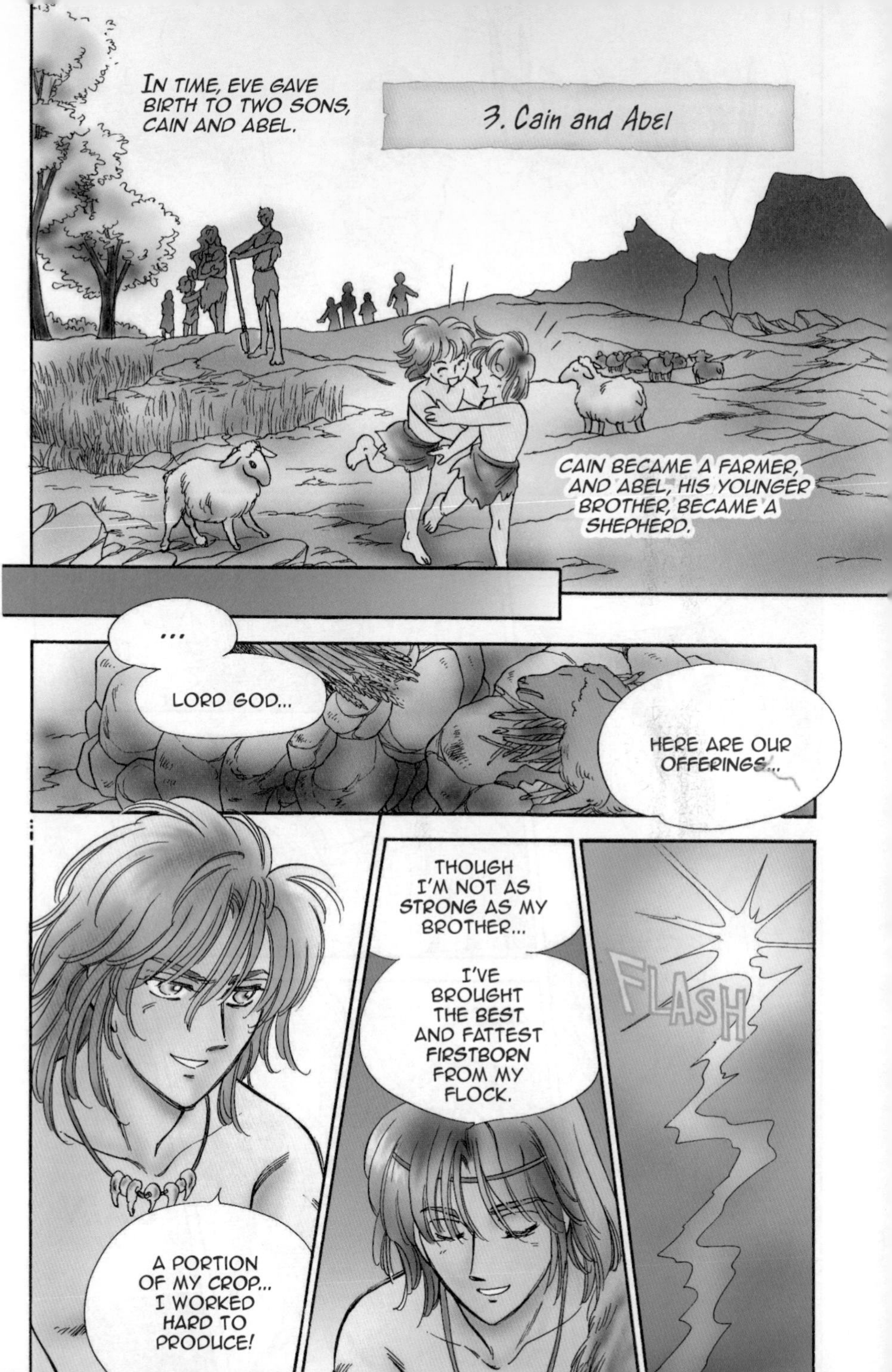
IN TIME, EVE GAVE BIRTH TO TWO SONS, CAIN AND ABEL.
3. Cain and Abel
CAIN BECAME A FARMER, AND ABEL, HIS YOUNGER BROTHER, BECAME A SHEPHERD.
...
LORD GOD...
HERE ARE OUR OFFERINGS...
A PORTION OF MY CROP... I WORKED HARD TO PRODUCE!
THOUGH I'M NOT AS STRONG AS MY BROTHER...
I'VE BROUGHT THE BEST AND FATTEST FIRSTBORN FROM MY FLOCK.
FLASH

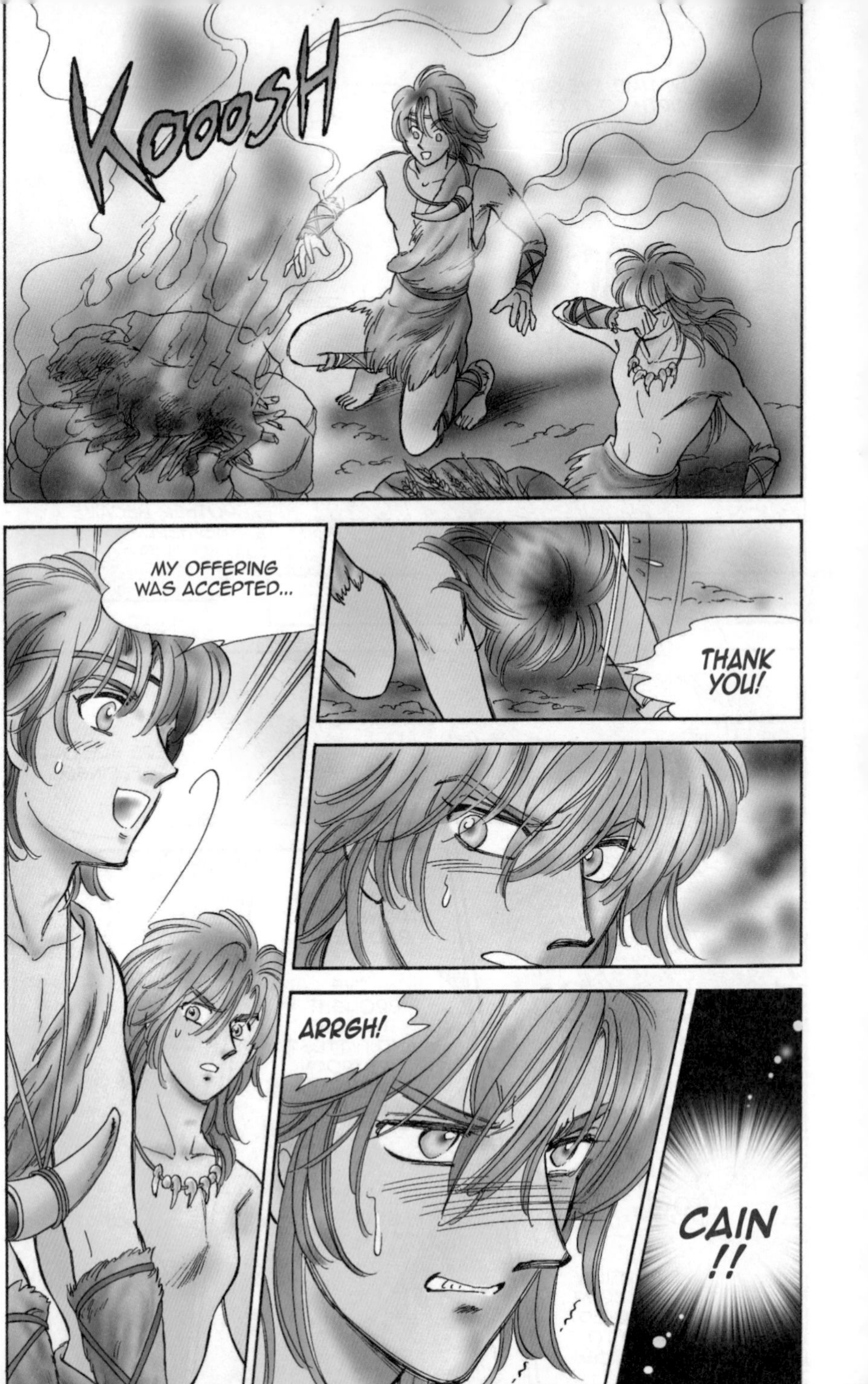
KOOOSH
MY OFFERING WAS ACCEPTED...
THANK YOU!
ARRGH!
CAIN !!

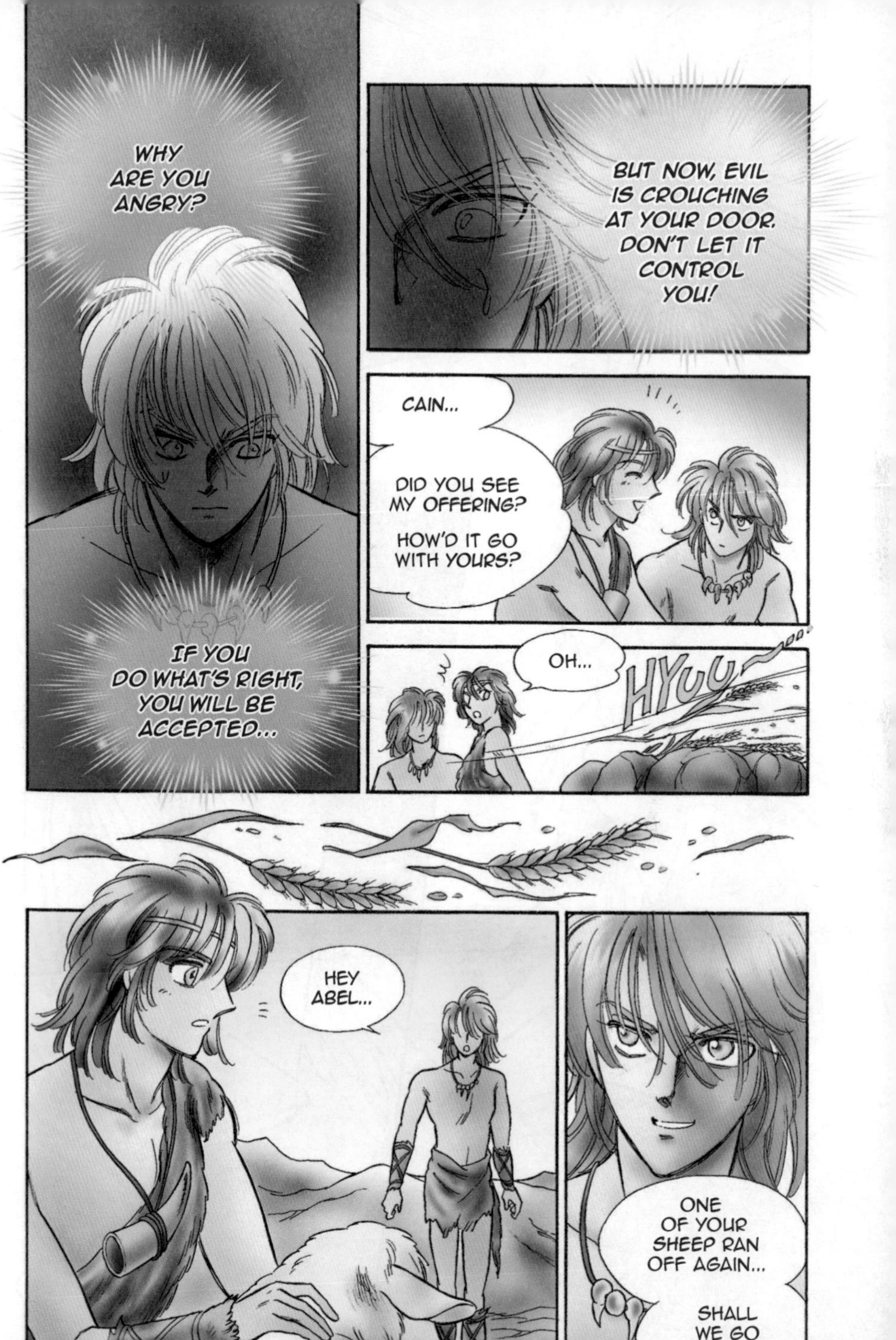

WHY ARE YOU ANGRY?
IF YOU DO WHAT'S RIGHT, YOU WILL BE ACCEPTED...
BUT NOW, EVIL IS CROUCHING AT YOUR DOOR. DON'T LET IT CONTROL YOU!
CAIN...
DID YOU SEE MY OFFERING?
HOW'D IT GO WITH YOURS?
OH...
HYUU~
HEY ABEL...
ONE OF YOUR SHEEP RAN OFF AGAIN...
SHALL WE GO FIND IT?

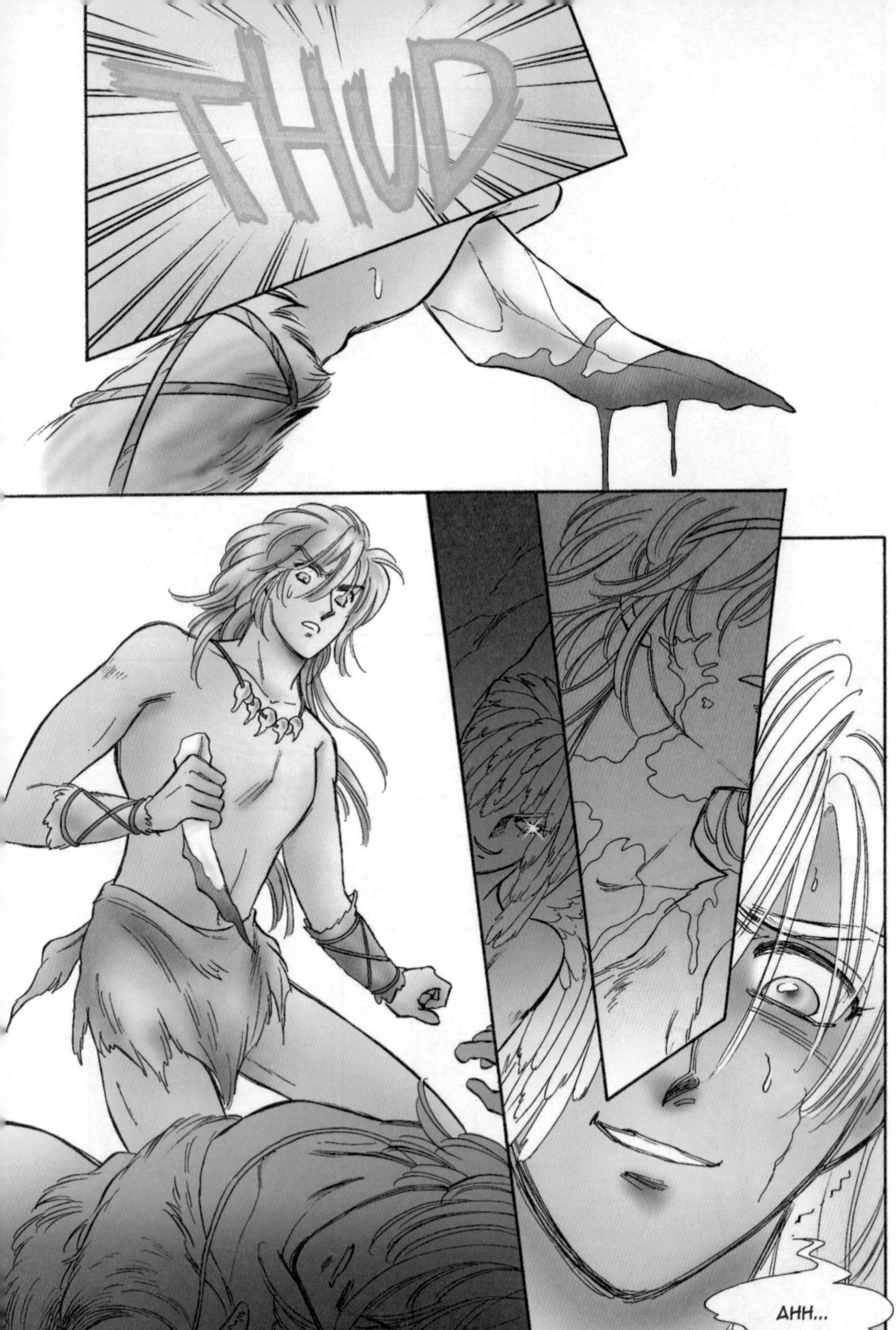
THUD
AHH...

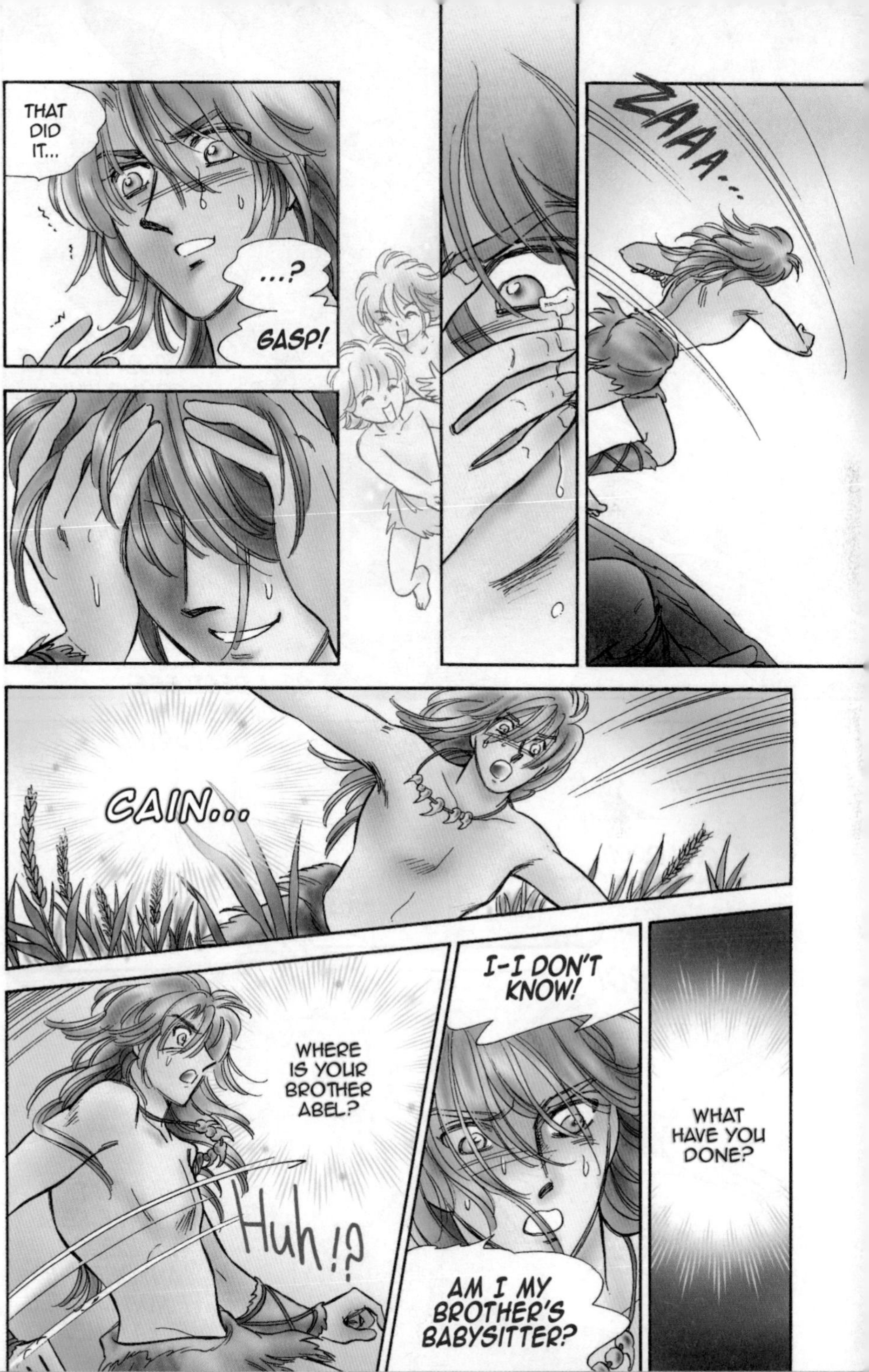

THAT DID IT...
...?
GASP!
ZAAA...
CAIN...
I-I DON'T KNOW!
WHERE IS YOUR BROTHER ABEL?
Huh!?
AM I MY BROTHER'S BABYSITTER?
WHAT HAVE YOU DONE?

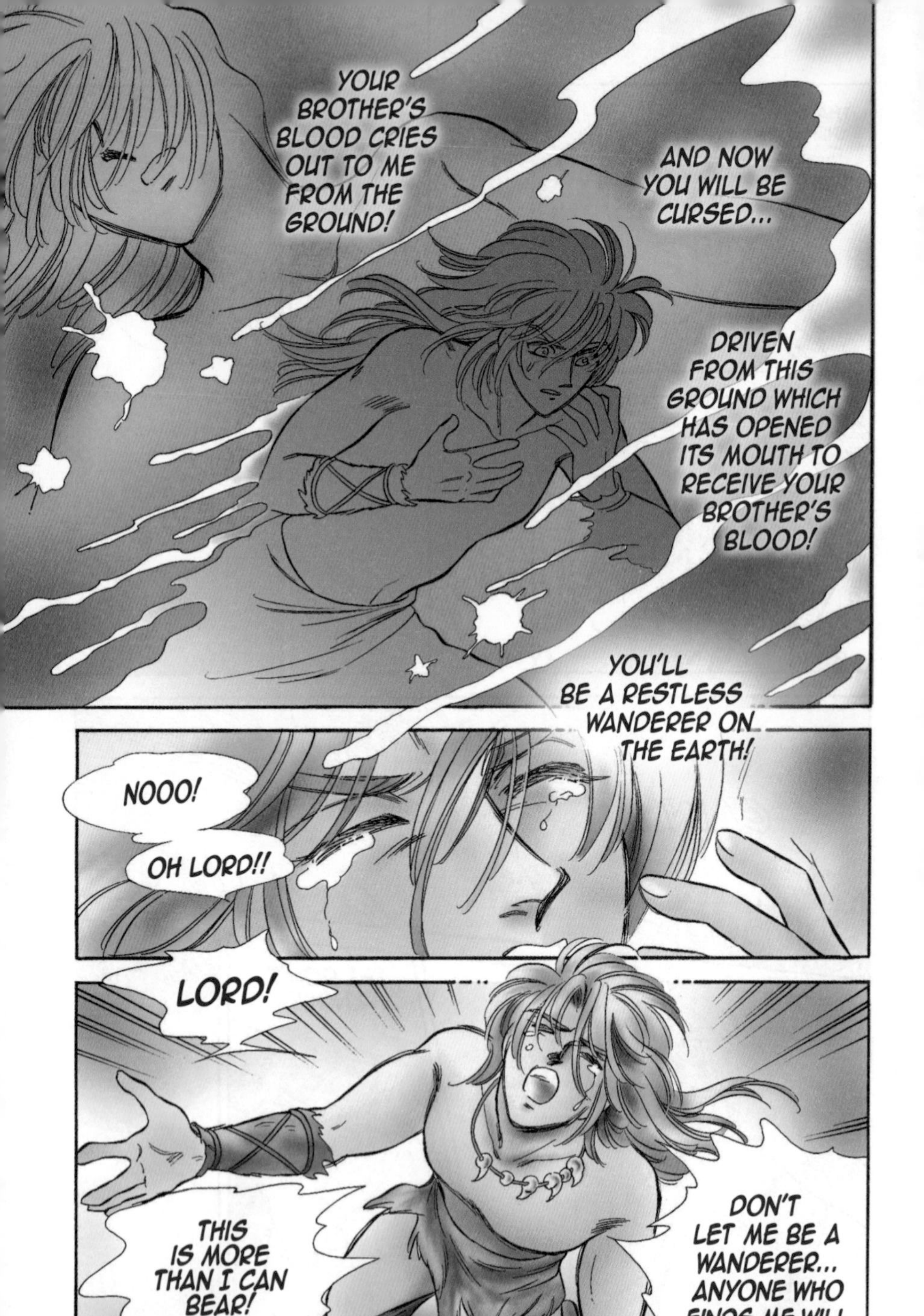
YOUR BROTHER'S BLOOD CRIES OUT TO ME FROM THE GROUND!
AND NOW YOU WILL BE CURSED...
DRIVEN FROM THIS GROUND WHICH HAS OPENED ITS MOUTH TO RECEIVE YOUR BROTHER'S BLOOD!
YOU'LL BE A RESTLESS WANDERER ON THE EARTH!
NOOO!
OH LORD!!
LORD!
DON'T LET ME BE A WANDERER... ANYONE WHO FINDS ME WILL KILL ME!
THIS IS MORE THAN I CAN BEAR!

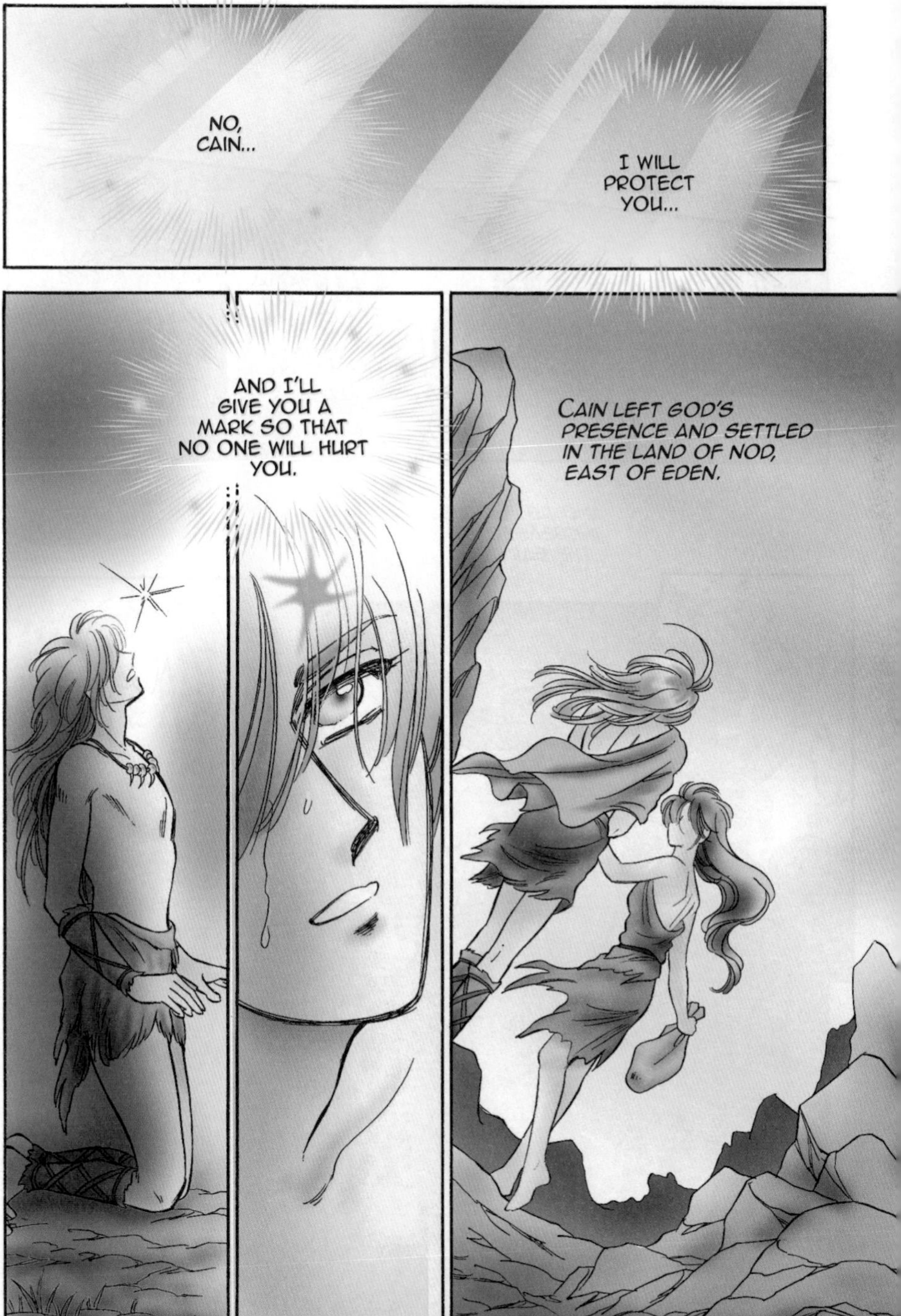
NO, CAIN...
I WILL PROTECT YOU...
AND I'LL GIVE YOU A MARK SO THAT NO ONE WILL HURT YOU.
CAIN LEFT GOD'S PRESENCE AND SETTLED IN THE LAND OF NOD, EAST OF EDEN.

ADAM AND EVE HAD ANOTHER SON NAMED SETH...

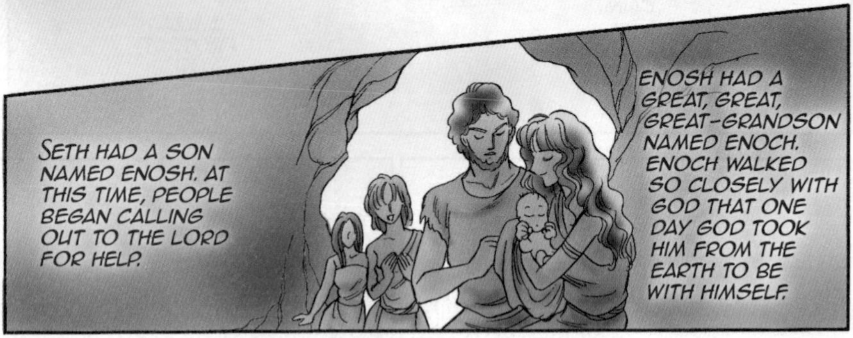
SETH HAD A SON NAMED ENOSH. AT THIS TIME, PEOPLE BEGAN CALLING OUT TO THE LORD FOR HELP.
ENOSH HAD A GREAT, GREAT, GREAT-GRANDSON NAMED ENOCH. ENOCH WALKED SO CLOSELY WITH GOD THAT ONE DAY GOD TOOK HIM FROM THE EARTH TO BE WITH HIMSELF.

AND AS PEOPLE INCREASED ON THE EARTH...

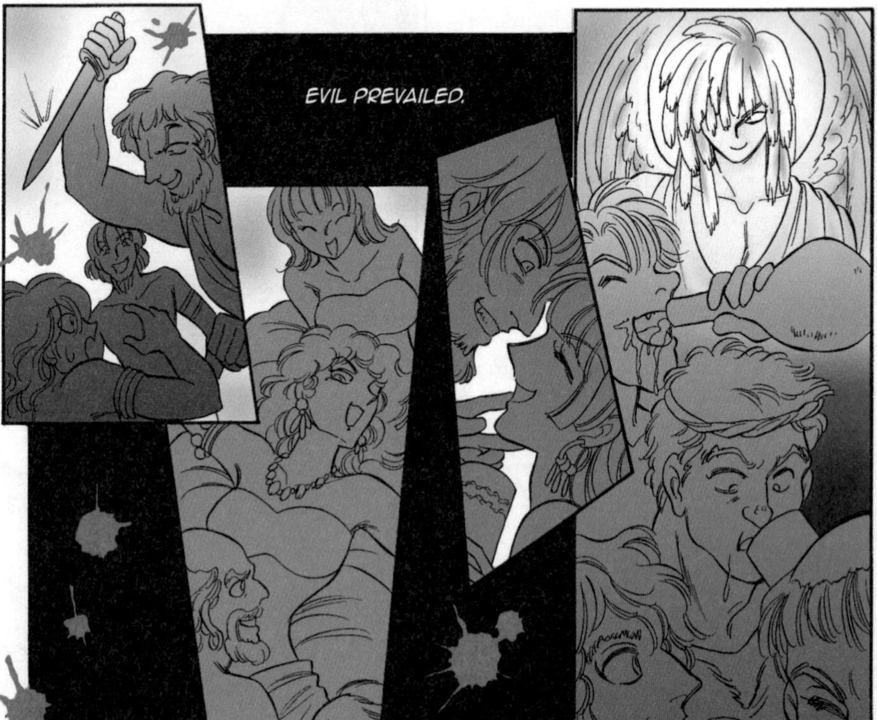
EVIL PREVAILED.

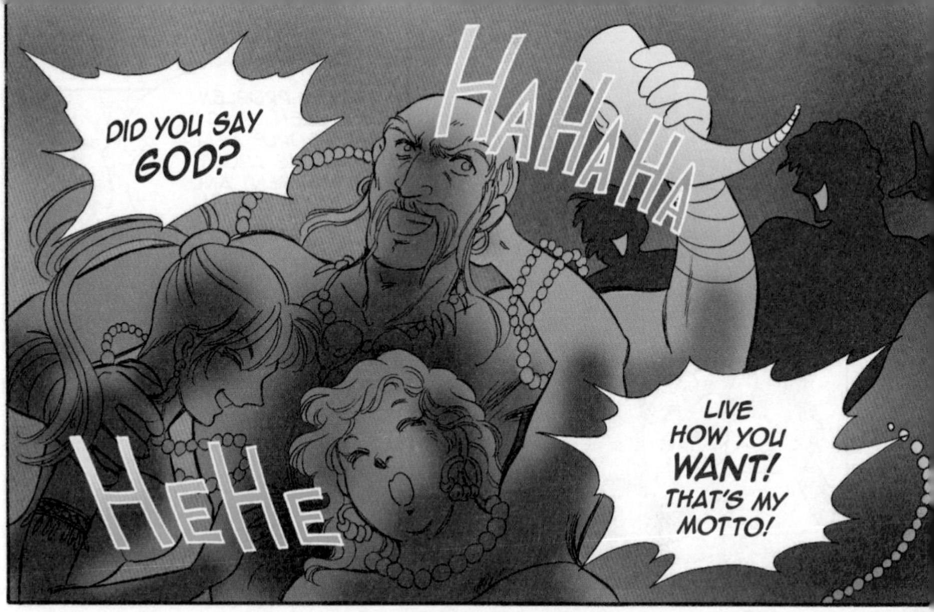
DID YOU SAY GOD?
HAHAHAHA
HEHE
LIVE HOW YOU WANT! THAT'S MY MOTTO!

4. The Flood

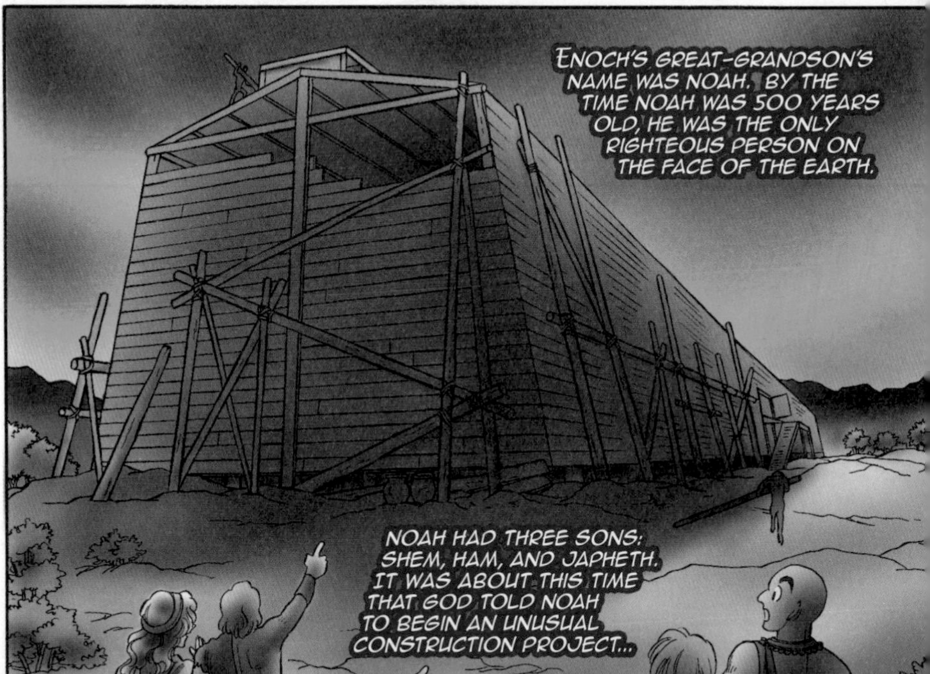
ENOCH'S GREAT-GRANDSON'S NAME WAS NOAH. BY THE TIME NOAH WAS 500 YEARS OLD, HE WAS THE ONLY RIGHTEOUS PERSON ON THE FACE OF THE EARTH.
NOAH HAD THREE SONS: SHEM, HAM, AND JAPHETH. IT WAS ABOUT THIS TIME THAT GOD TOLD NOAH TO BEGIN AN UNUSUAL CONSTRUCTION PROJECT...

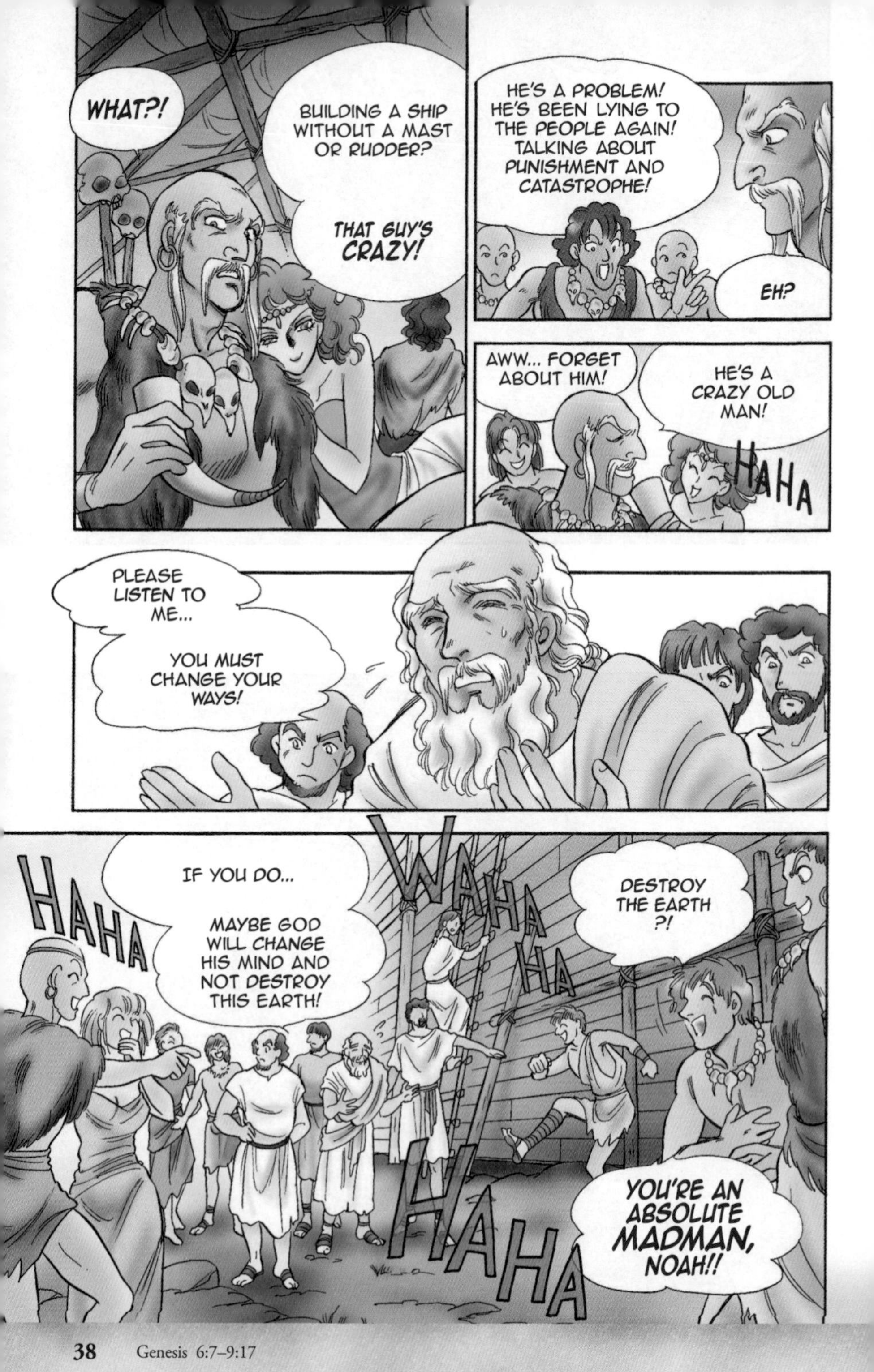
WHAT?!
BUILDING A SHIP WITHOUT A MAST OR RUDDER?
THAT GUY'S CRAZY!
HE'S A PROBLEM! HE'S BEEN LYING TO THE PEOPLE AGAIN! TALKING ABOUT PUNISHMENT AND CATASTROPHE!
EH?
AWW... FORGET ABOUT HIM!
HE'S A CRAZY OLD MAN!
HAHA
PLEASE LISTEN TO ME...
YOU MUST CHANGE YOUR WAYS!
HAHA
IF YOU DO...
MAYBE GOD WILL CHANGE HIS MIND AND NOT DESTROY THIS EARTH!
WAHAHA HA
DESTROY THE EARTH ?!
HAHA
YOU'RE AN ABSOLUTE MADMAN, NOAH!!

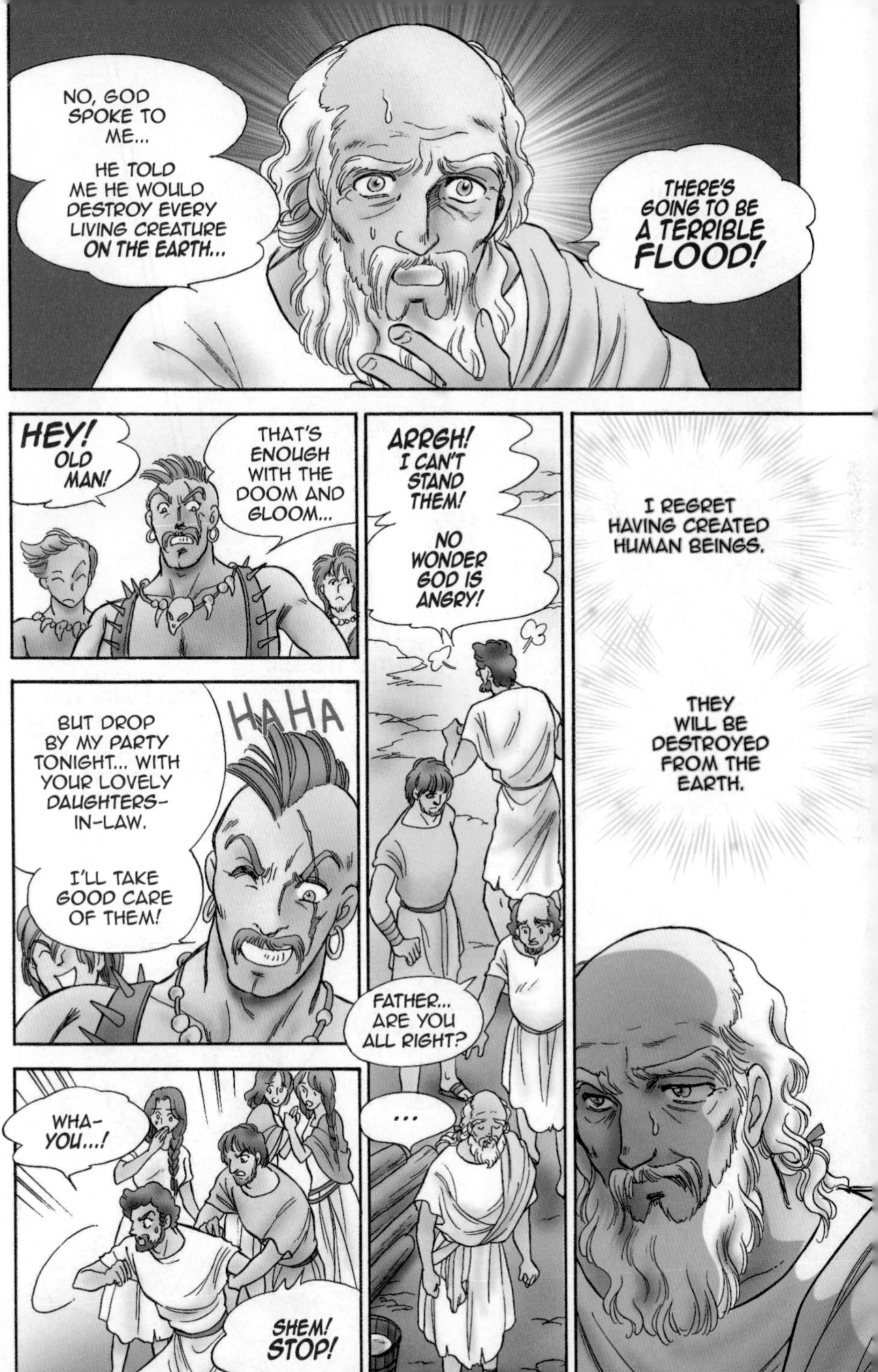
NO, GOD SPOKE TO ME...
HE TOLD ME HE WOULD DESTROY EVERY LIVING CREATURE ON THE EARTH...
THERE'S GOING TO BE A TERRIBLE FLOOD!
HEY! OLD MAN!
THAT'S ENOUGH WITH THE DOOM AND GLOOM...
BUT DROP BY MY PARTY TONIGHT... WITH YOUR LOVELY DAUGHTERS-IN-LAW.
I'LL TAKE GOOD CARE OF THEM!
HAHA
WHA- YOU...!
SHEM! STOP!
ARRGH! I CAN'T STAND THEM!
NO WONDER GOD IS ANGRY!
FATHER... ARE YOU ALL RIGHT?
...
I REGRET HAVING CREATED HUMAN BEINGS.
THEY WILL BE DESTROYED FROM THE EARTH.

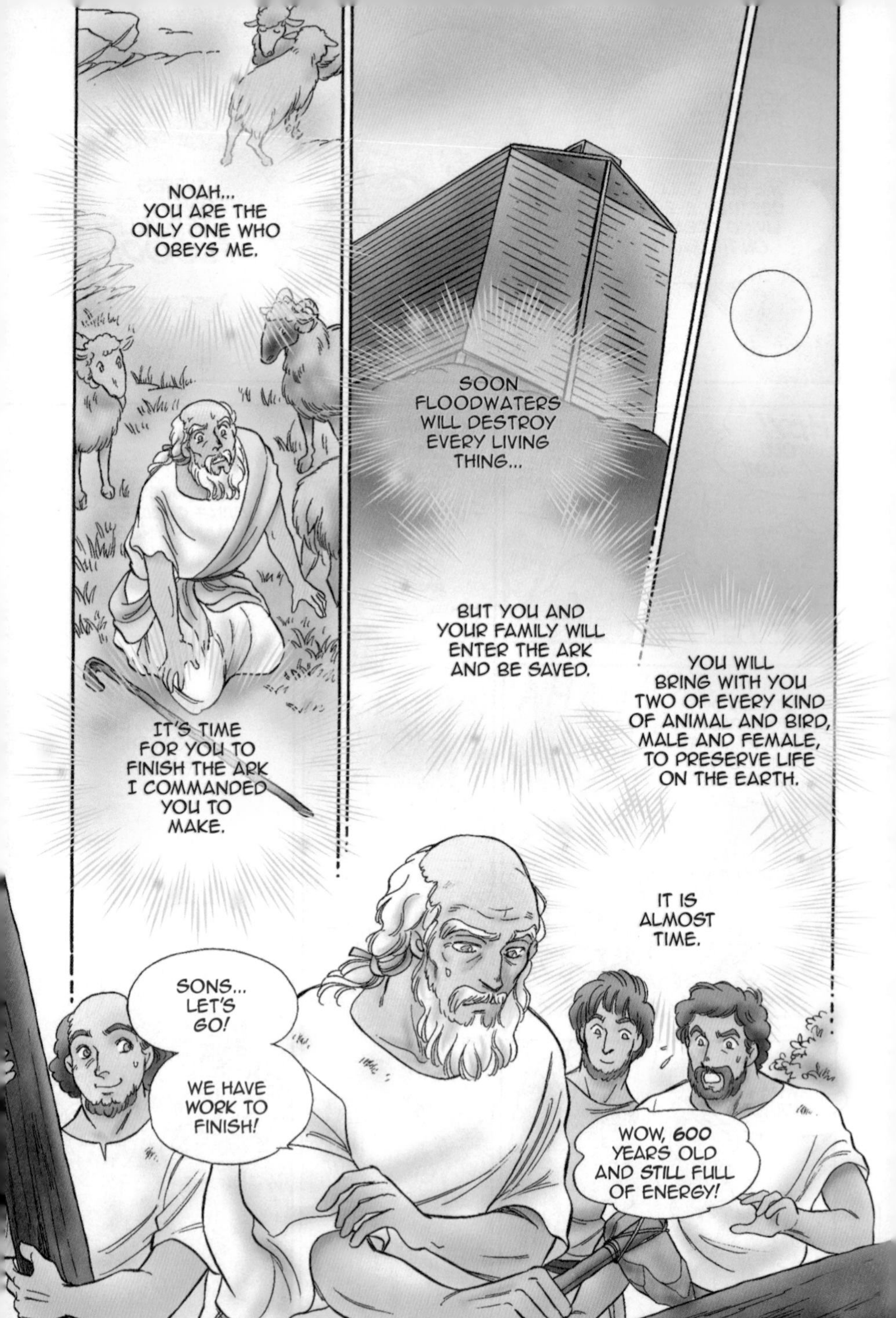
NOAH... YOU ARE THE ONLY ONE WHO OBEYS ME.
SOON FLOODWATERS WILL DESTROY EVERY LIVING THING...
IT'S TIME FOR YOU TO FINISH THE ARK I COMMANDED YOU TO MAKE.
BUT YOU AND YOUR FAMILY WILL ENTER THE ARK AND BE SAVED.
YOU WILL BRING WITH YOU TWO OF EVERY KIND OF ANIMAL AND BIRD, MALE AND FEMALE, TO PRESERVE LIFE ON THE EARTH.
IT IS ALMOST TIME.
SONS... LET'S GO!
WE HAVE WORK TO FINISH!
WOW, 600 YEARS OLD AND STILL FULL OF ENERGY!

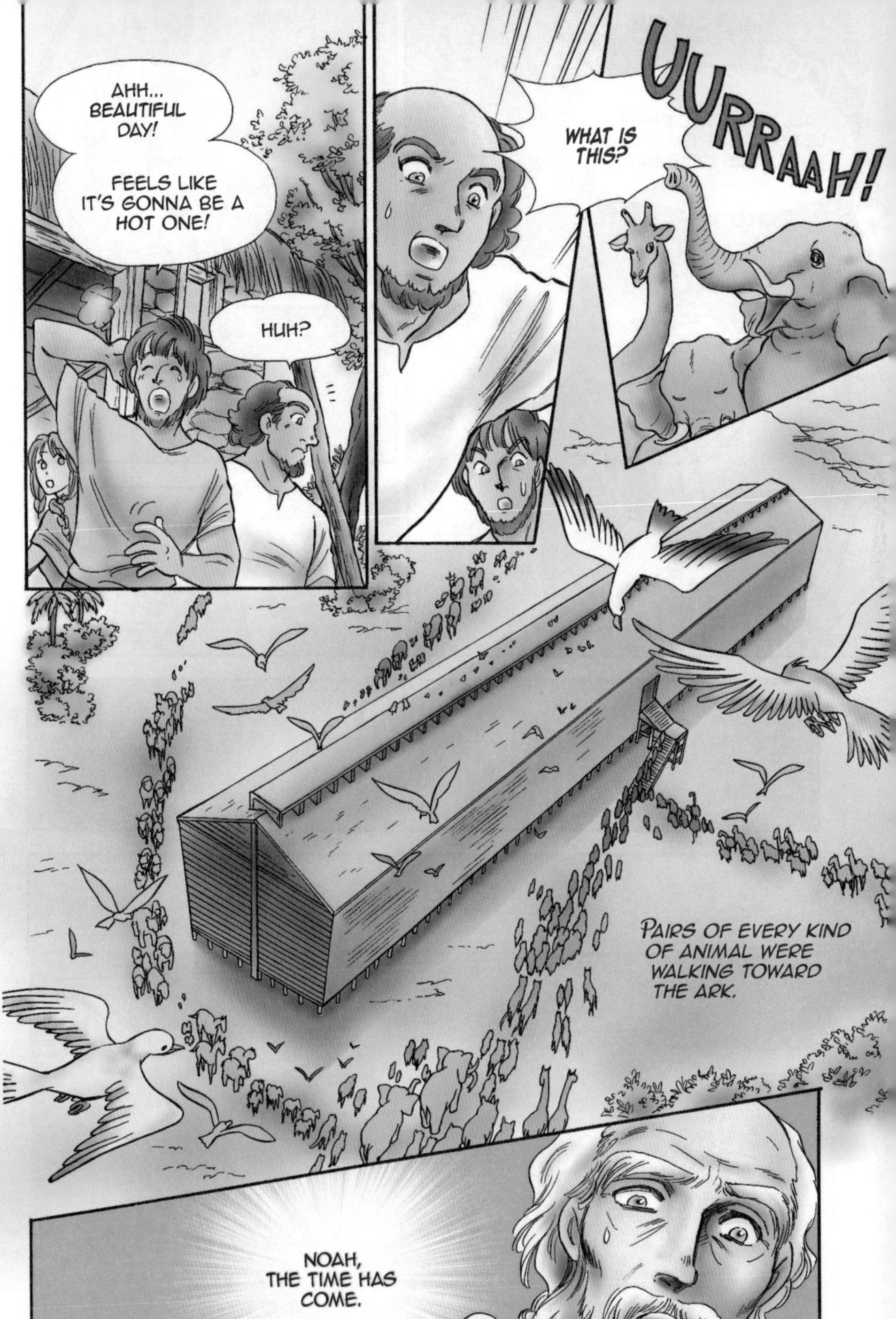
AHH... BEAUTIFUL DAY!
FEELS LIKE IT'S GONNA BE A HOT ONE!
HUH?
WHAT IS THIS?
UURRAAH!
PAIRS OF EVERY KIND OF ANIMAL WERE WALKING TOWARD THE ARK.
NOAH, THE TIME HAS COME.

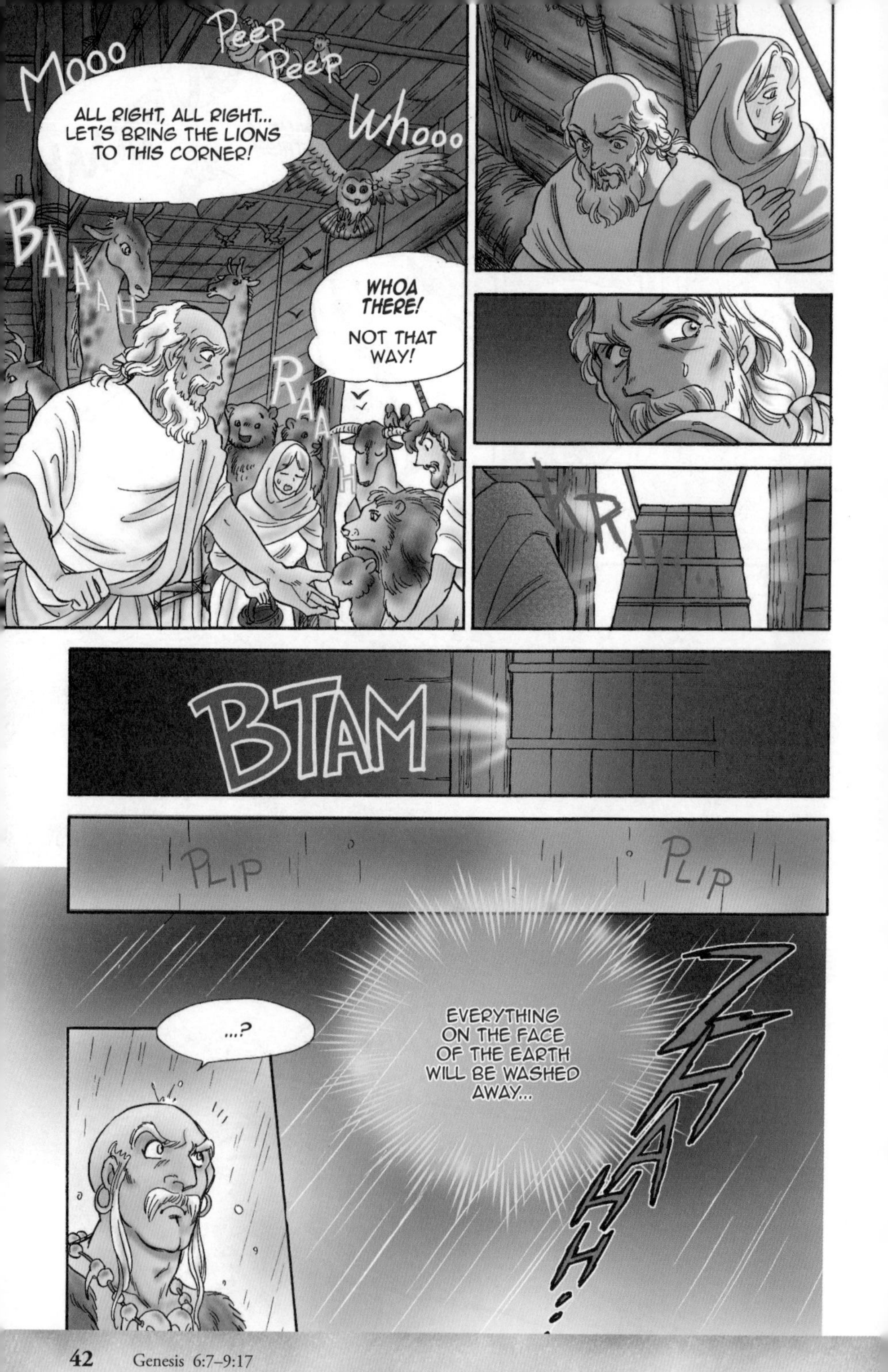

Mooo
Peep Peep
ALL RIGHT, ALL RIGHT... LET'S BRING THE LIONS TO THIS CORNER!
Whooo
BAAAAH
WHOA THERE!
NOT THAT WAY!
RAAAAH
KRI...
BTAM
PLIP
PLIP
...?
EVERYTHING ON THE FACE OF THE EARTH WILL BE WASHED AWAY...
ZHAHHH...

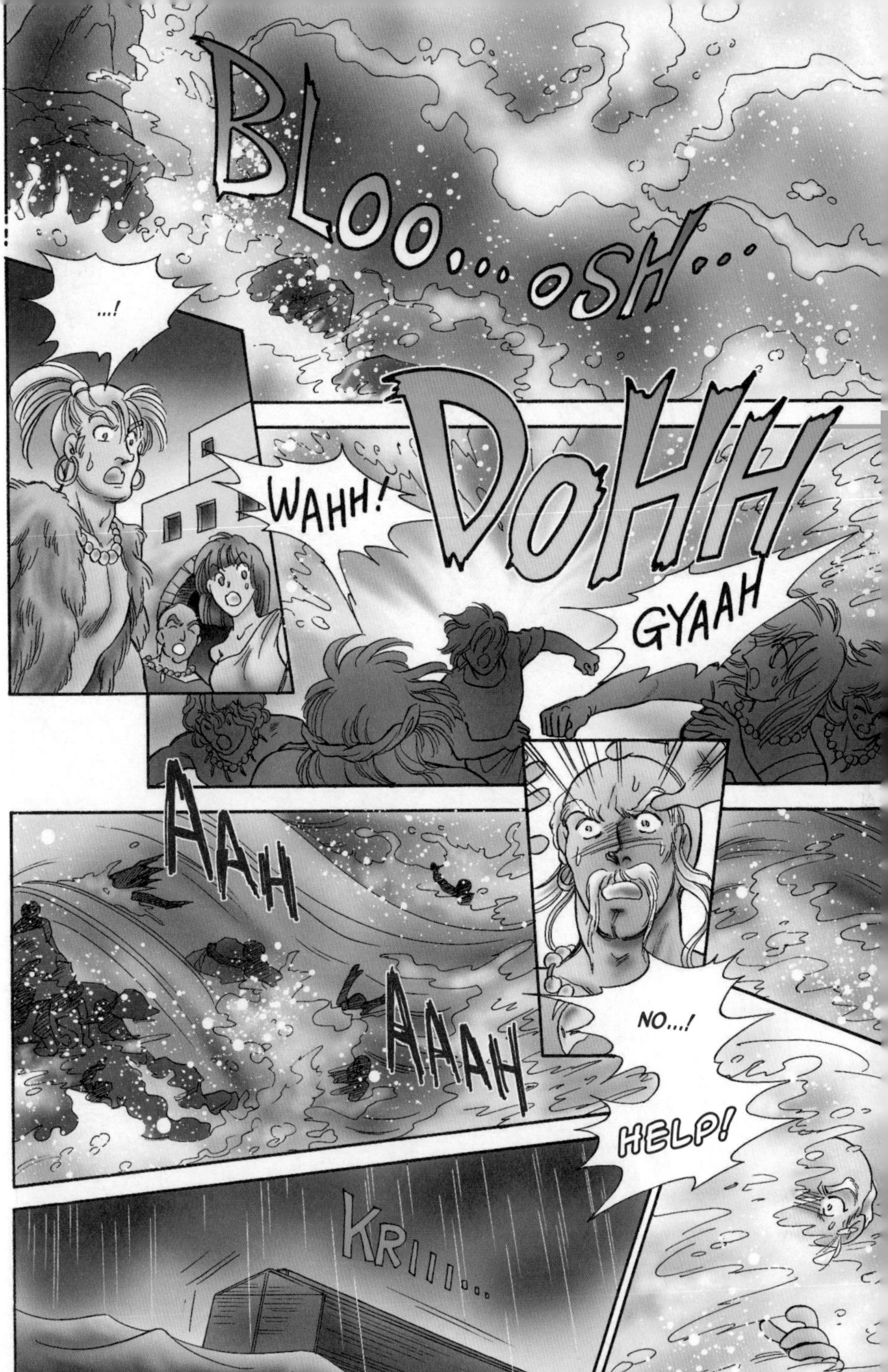
BLOO... OSH...
...!
WAHH!
DOHH
GYAAH
AAH
AAAH
NO...!
HELP!
KRIII...

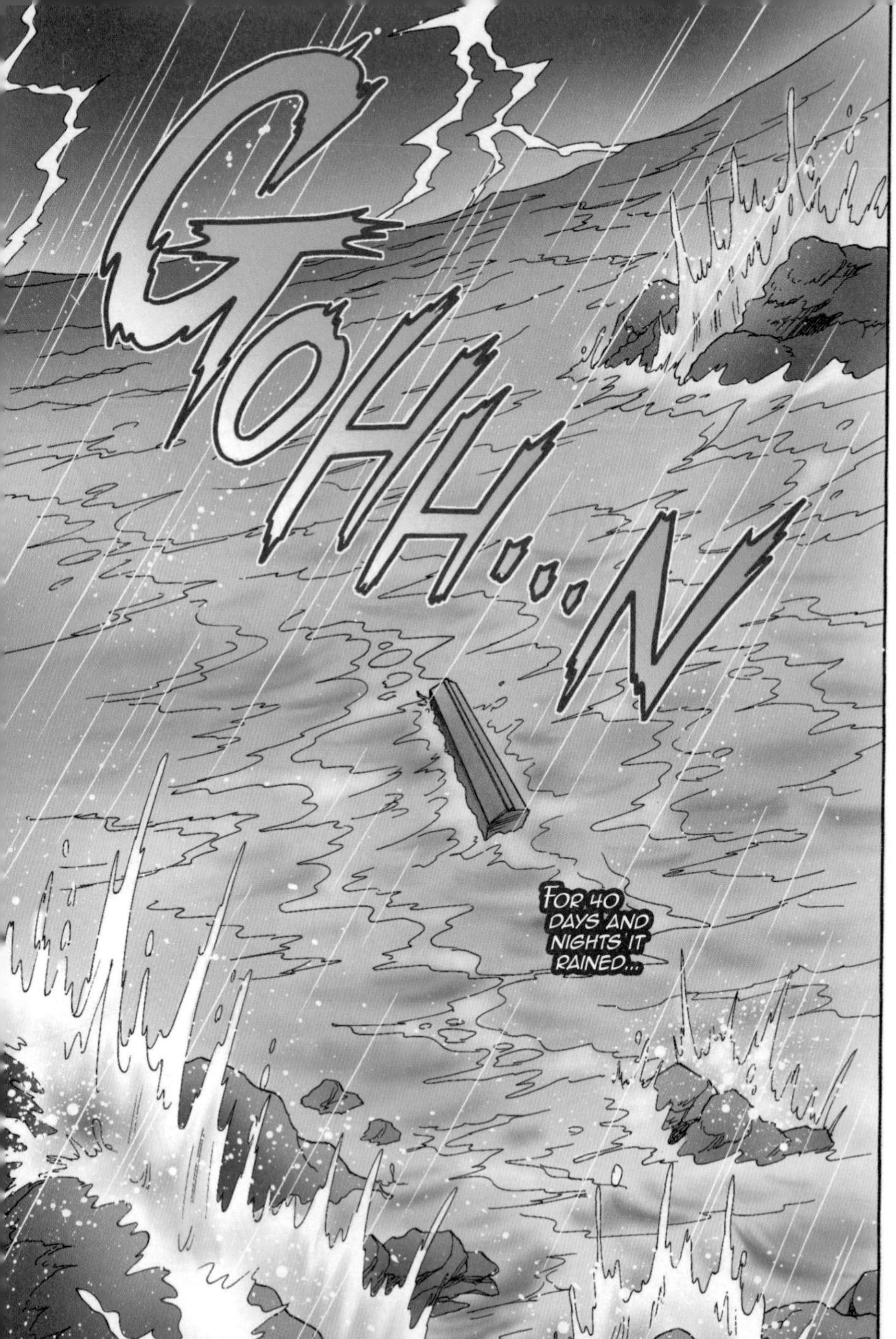
GOHH..N
FOR 40 DAYS AND NIGHTS IT RAINED...

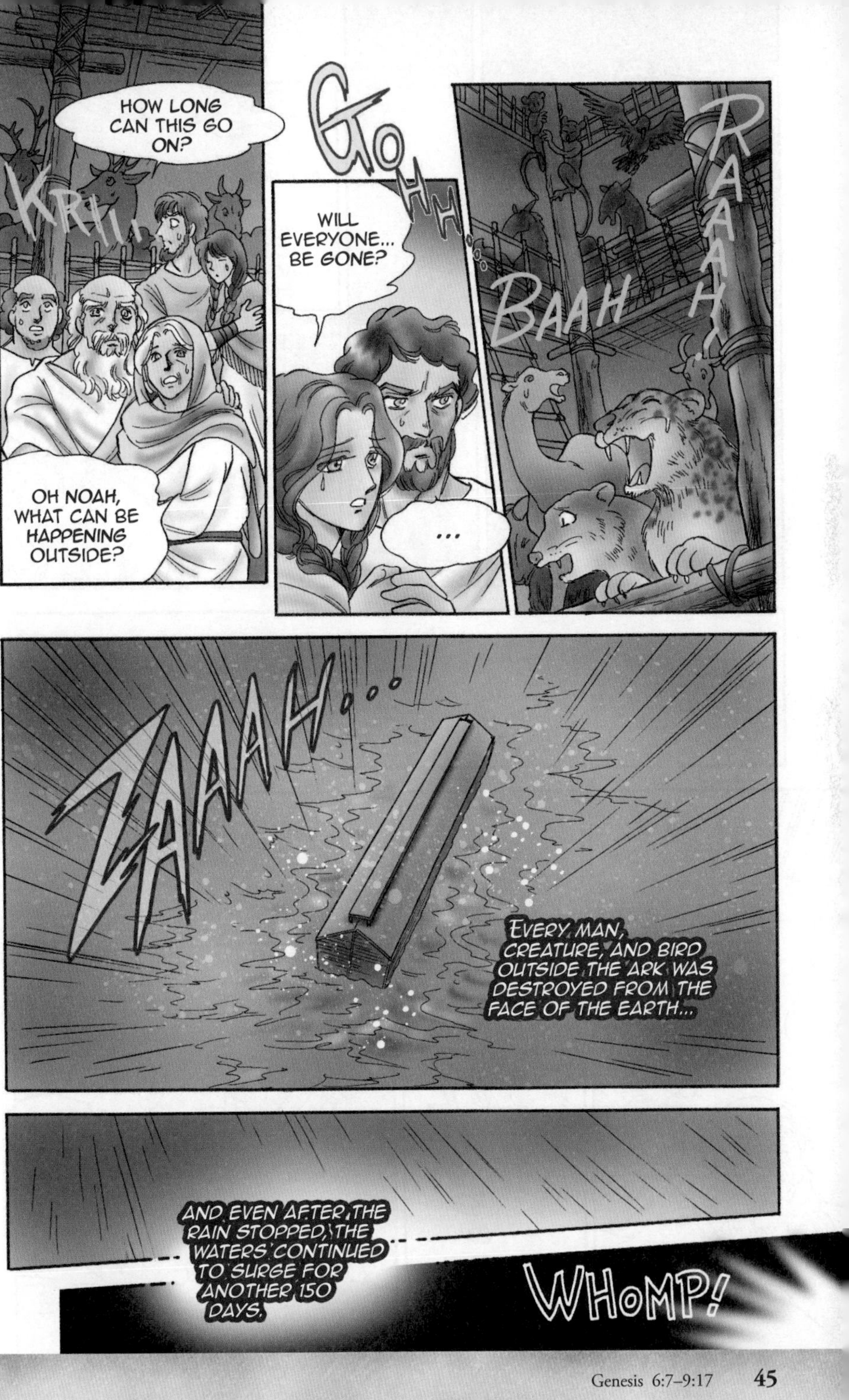
HOW LONG CAN THIS GO ON?
KRIII
OH NOAH, WHAT CAN BE HAPPENING OUTSIDE?
GOHH
WILL EVERYONE... BE GONE?
...
RAAAAH!
BAAH
ZAAAAH
EVERY MAN, CREATURE, AND BIRD OUTSIDE THE ARK WAS DESTROYED FROM THE FACE OF THE EARTH...
AND EVEN AFTER THE RAIN STOPPED, THE WATERS CONTINUED TO SURGE FOR ANOTHER 150 DAYS.
WHOMP!

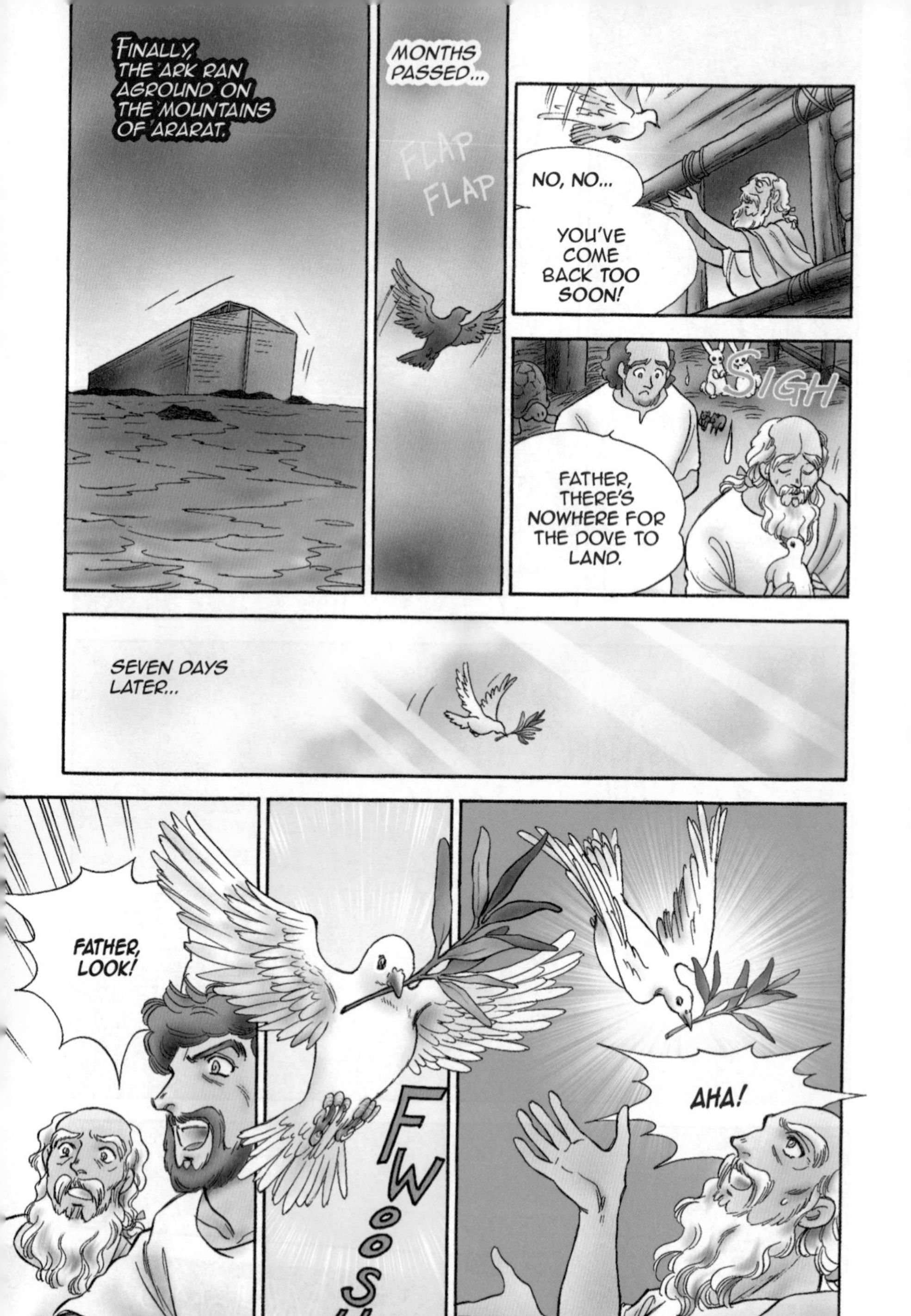
FINALLY, THE ARK RAN AGROUND ON THE MOUNTAINS OF ARARAT.
MONTHS PASSED...
FLAP FLAP
NO, NO...
YOU'VE COME BACK TOO SOON!
SIGH
FATHER, THERE'S NOWHERE FOR THE DOVE TO LAND.
SEVEN DAYS LATER...
FATHER, LOOK!
FWOOSH
AHA!

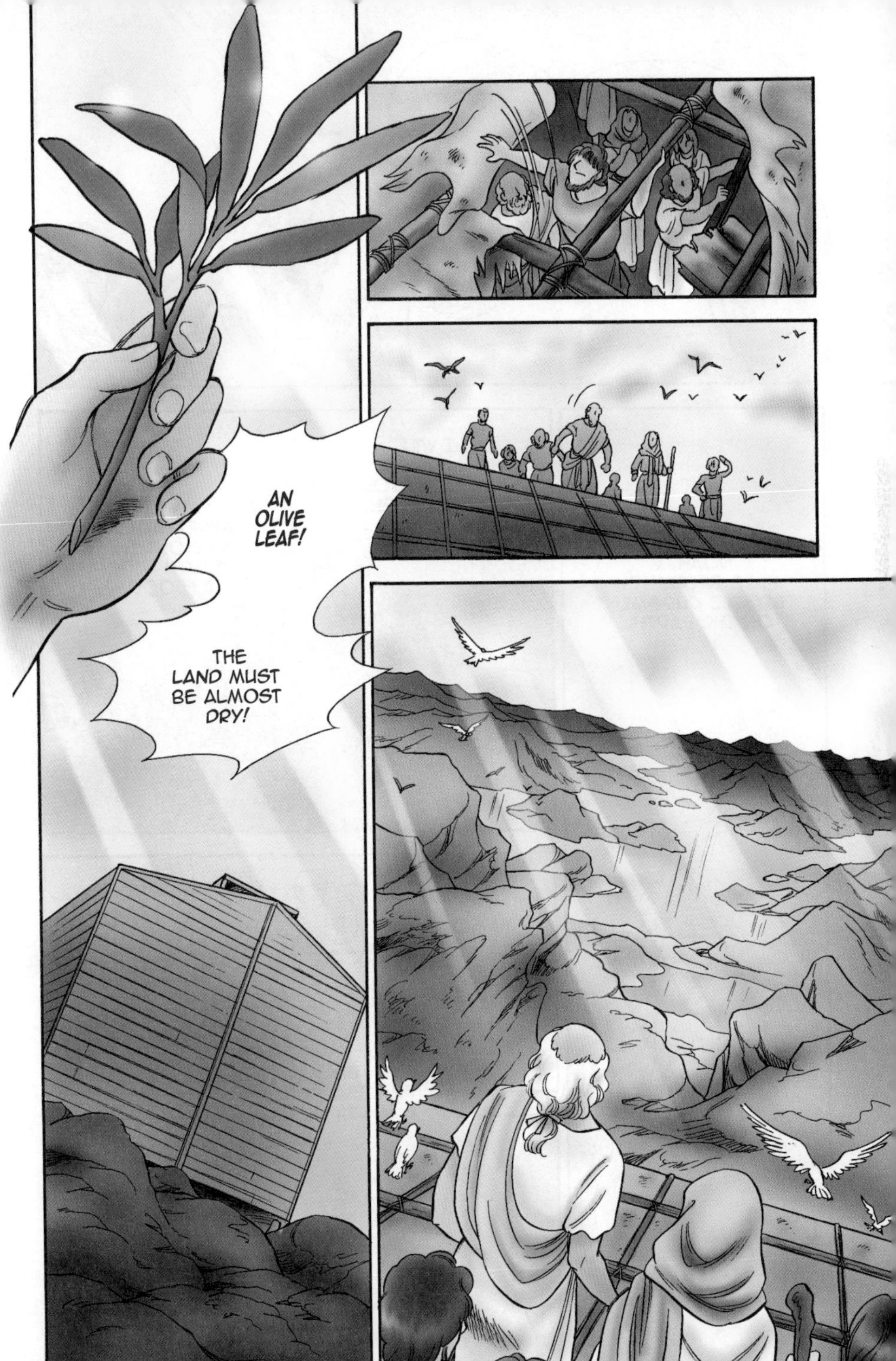
AN OLIVE LEAF!
THE LAND MUST BE ALMOST DRY!

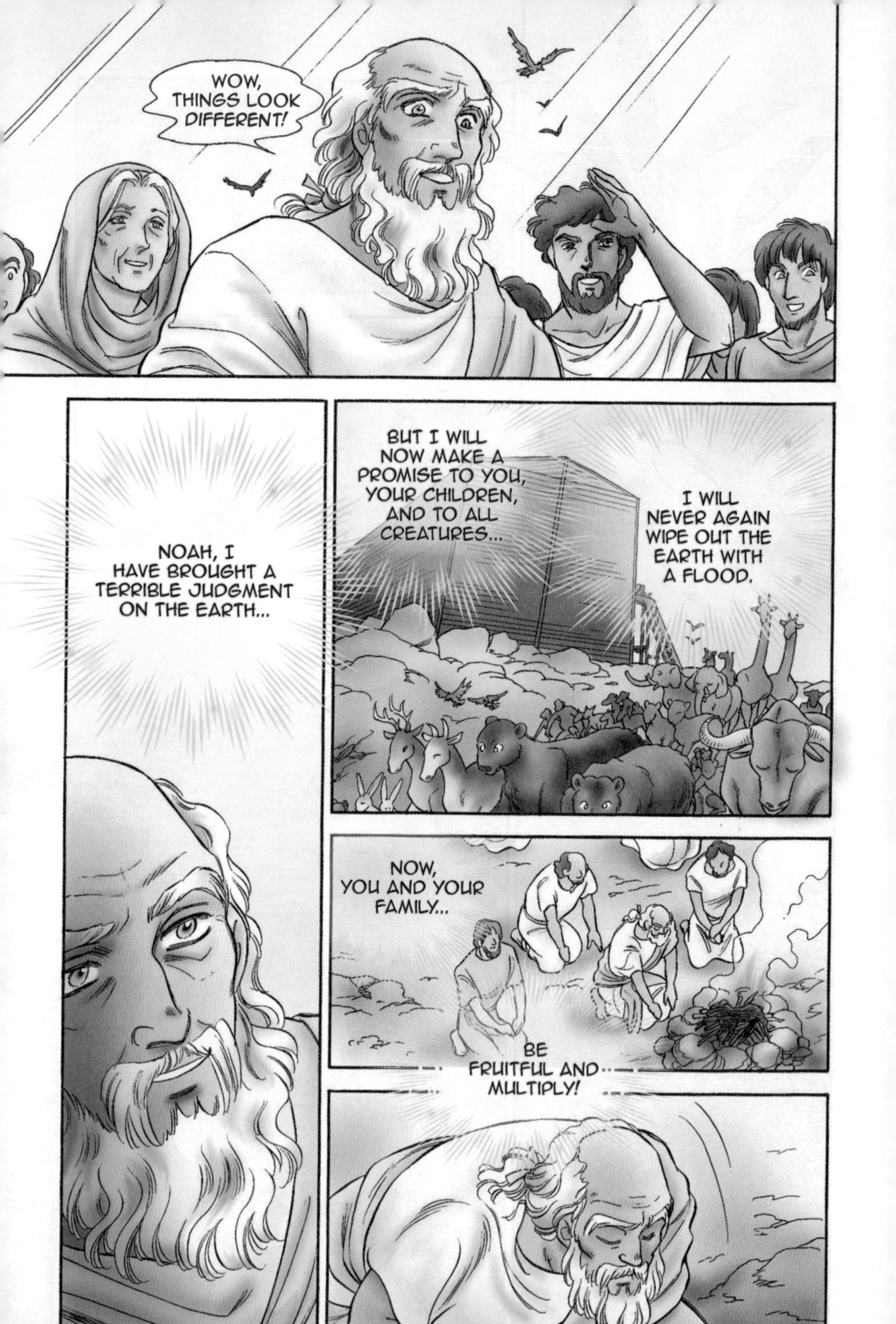
WOW, THINGS LOOK DIFFERENT!
NOAH, I HAVE BROUGHT A TERRIBLE JUDGMENT ON THE EARTH...
BUT I WILL NOW MAKE A PROMISE TO YOU, YOUR CHILDREN, AND TO ALL CREATURES...
I WILL NEVER AGAIN WIPE OUT THE EARTH WITH A FLOOD.
NOW, YOU AND YOUR FAMILY...
BE FRUITFUL AND MULTIPLY!

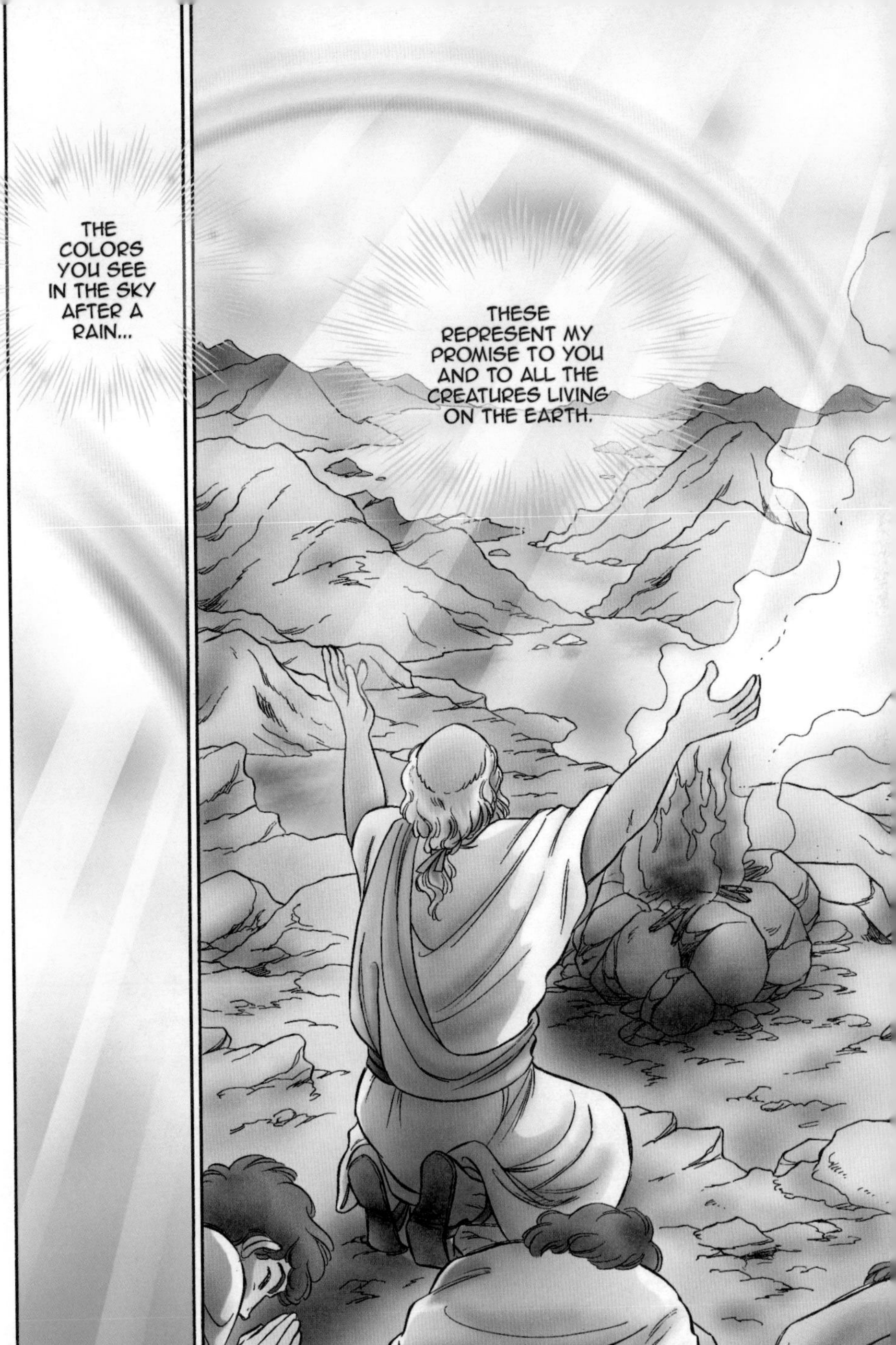
THE COLORS YOU SEE IN THE SKY AFTER A RAIN...
THESE REPRESENT MY PROMISE TO YOU AND TO ALL THE CREATURES LIVING ON THE EARTH.

CHAPTER 2

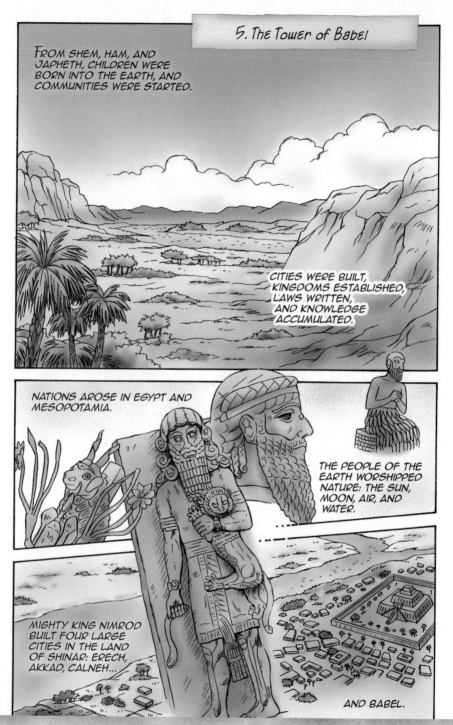

FROM SHEM, HAM, AND JAPHETH, CHILDREN WERE BORN INTO THE EARTH, AND COMMUNITIES WERE STARTED.

CITIES WERE BUILT, KINGDOMS ESTABLISHED, LAWS WRITTEN, AND KNOWLEDGE ACCUMULATED.

NATIONS AROSE IN EGYPT AND MESOPOTAMIA.

THE PEOPLE OF THE EARTH WORSHIPPED NATURE: THE SUN, MOON, AIR, AND WATER.

MIGHTY KING NIMROD BUILT FOUR LARGE CITIES IN THE LAND OF SHINAR: ERECH, AKKAD, CALNEH...

AND BABEL.

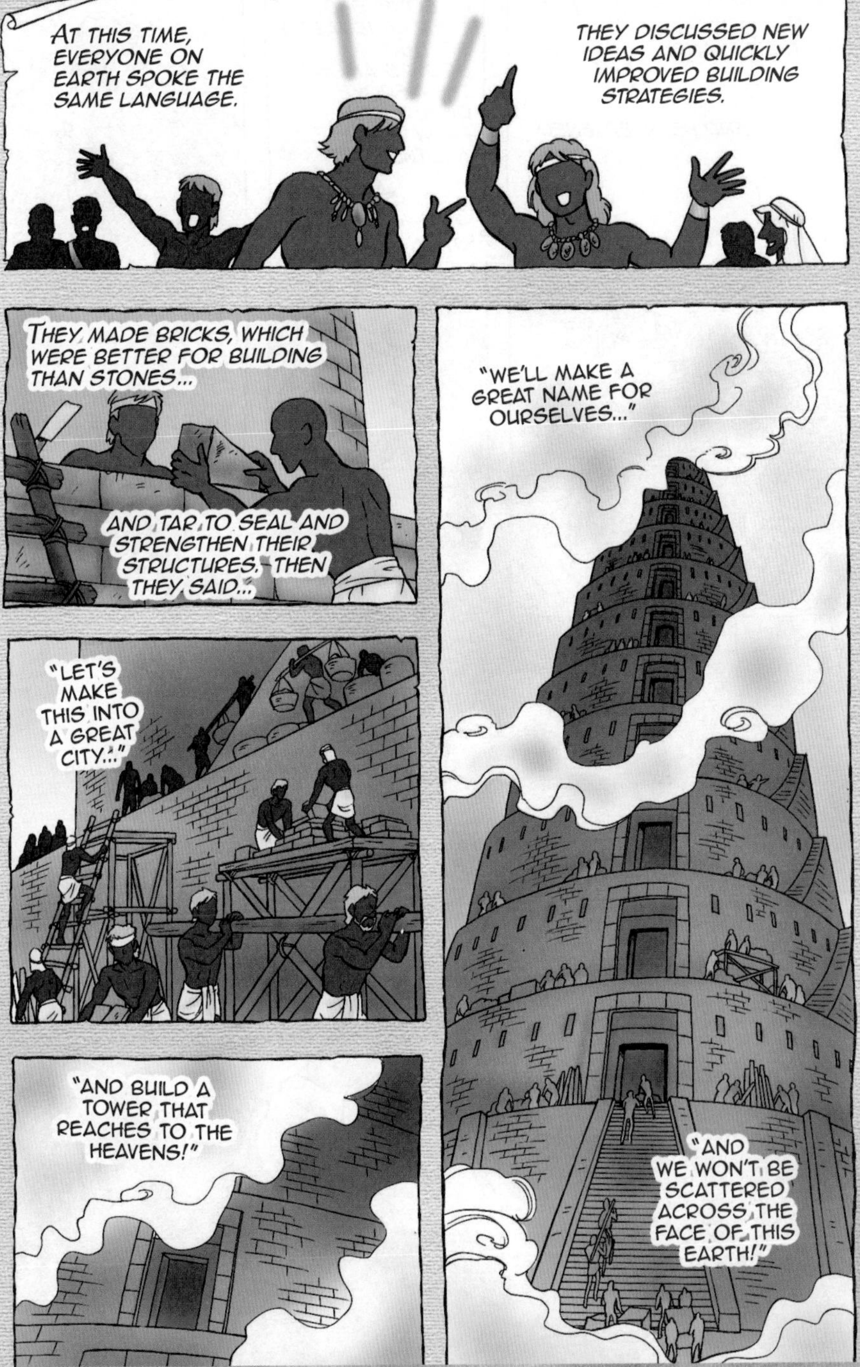
AT THIS TIME, EVERYONE ON EARTH SPOKE THE SAME LANGUAGE.
THEY DISCUSSED NEW IDEAS AND QUICKLY IMPROVED BUILDING STRATEGIES.
THEY MADE BRICKS, WHICH WERE BETTER FOR BUILDING THAN STONES...
AND TAR TO SEAL AND STRENGTHEN THEIR STRUCTURES. THEN THEY SAID...
"LET'S MAKE THIS INTO A GREAT CITY..."
"AND BUILD A TOWER THAT REACHES TO THE HEAVENS!"
"WE'LL MAKE A GREAT NAME FOR OURSELVES..."
"AND WE WON'T BE SCATTERED ACROSS THE FACE OF THIS EARTH!"

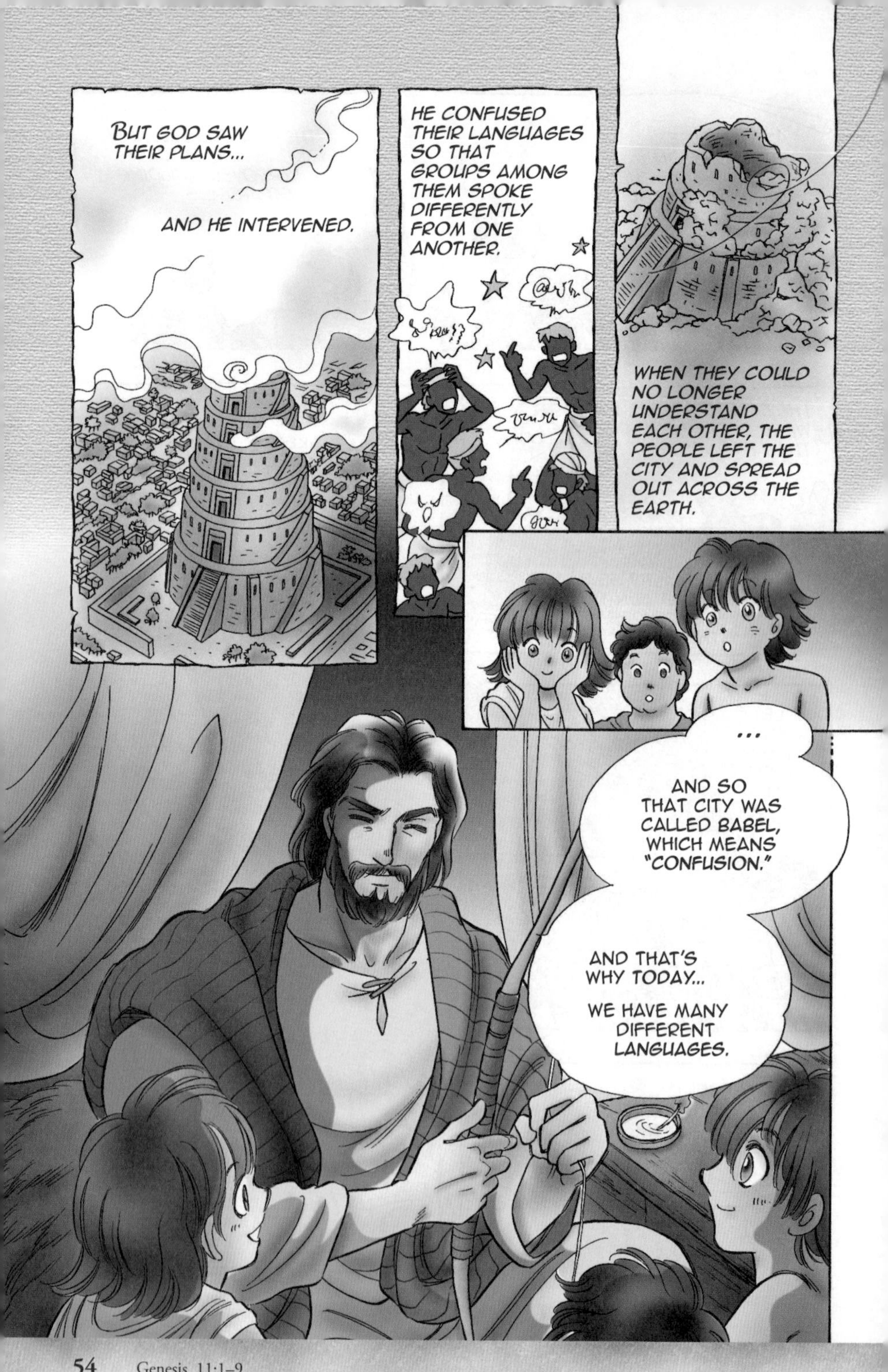
BUT GOD SAW THEIR PLANS...
AND HE INTERVENED.
HE CONFUSED THEIR LANGUAGES SO THAT GROUPS AMONG THEM SPOKE DIFFERENTLY FROM ONE ANOTHER.
WHEN THEY COULD NO LONGER UNDERSTAND EACH OTHER, THE PEOPLE LEFT THE CITY AND SPREAD OUT ACROSS THE EARTH.
...
AND SO THAT CITY WAS CALLED BABEL, WHICH MEANS "CONFUSION."
AND THAT'S WHY TODAY...
WE HAVE MANY DIFFERENT LANGUAGES.

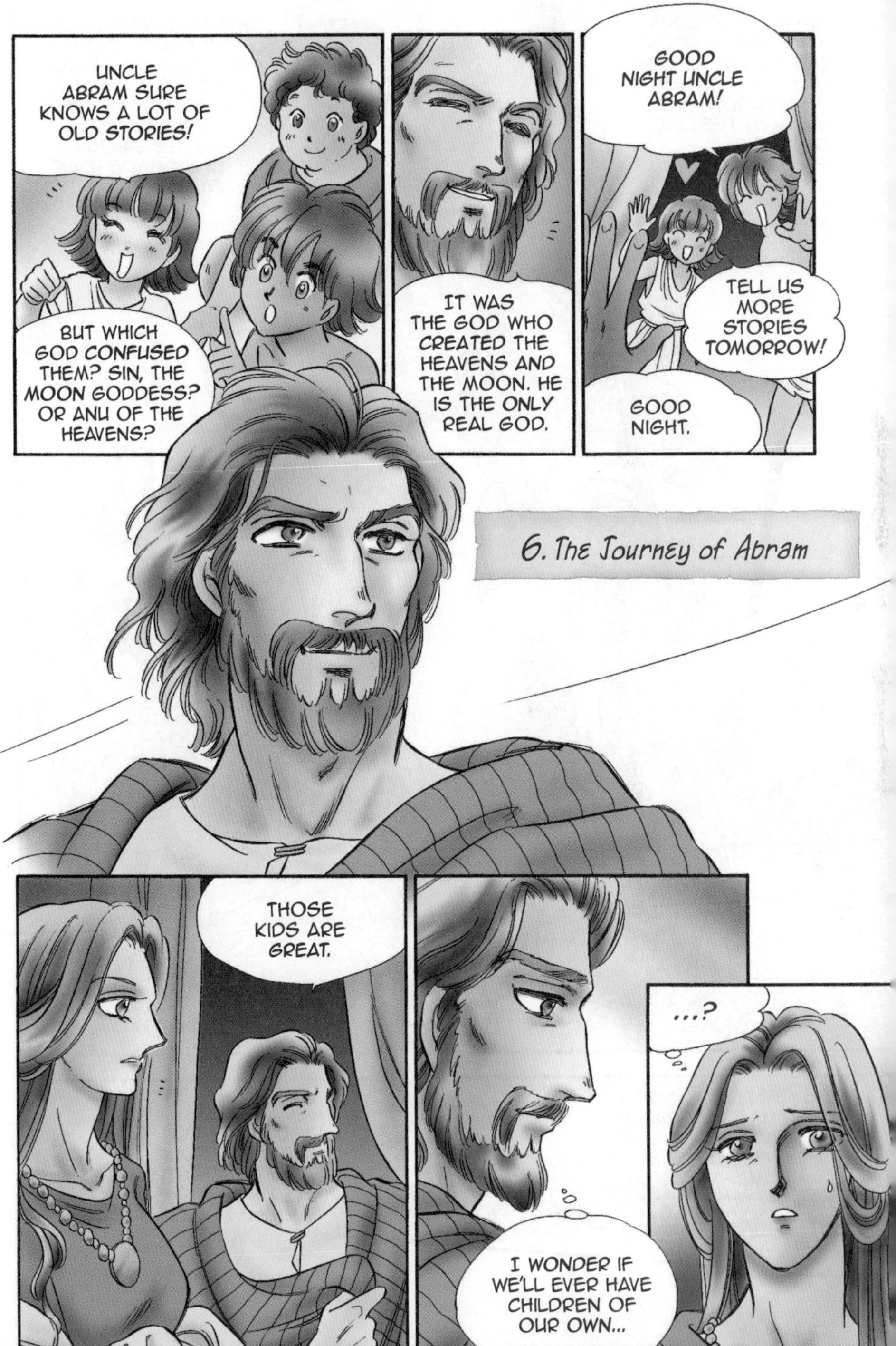
UNCLE ABRAM SURE KNOWS A LOT OF OLD STORIES!
BUT WHICH GOD CONFUSED THEM? SIN, THE MOON GODDESS? OR ANU OF THE HEAVENS?
IT WAS THE GOD WHO CREATED THE HEAVENS AND THE MOON. HE IS THE ONLY REAL GOD.
GOOD NIGHT UNCLE ABRAM!
TELL US MORE STORIES TOMORROW!
GOOD NIGHT.
6. The Journey of Abram
THOSE KIDS ARE GREAT.
I WONDER IF WE'LL EVER HAVE CHILDREN OF OUR OWN...
...?

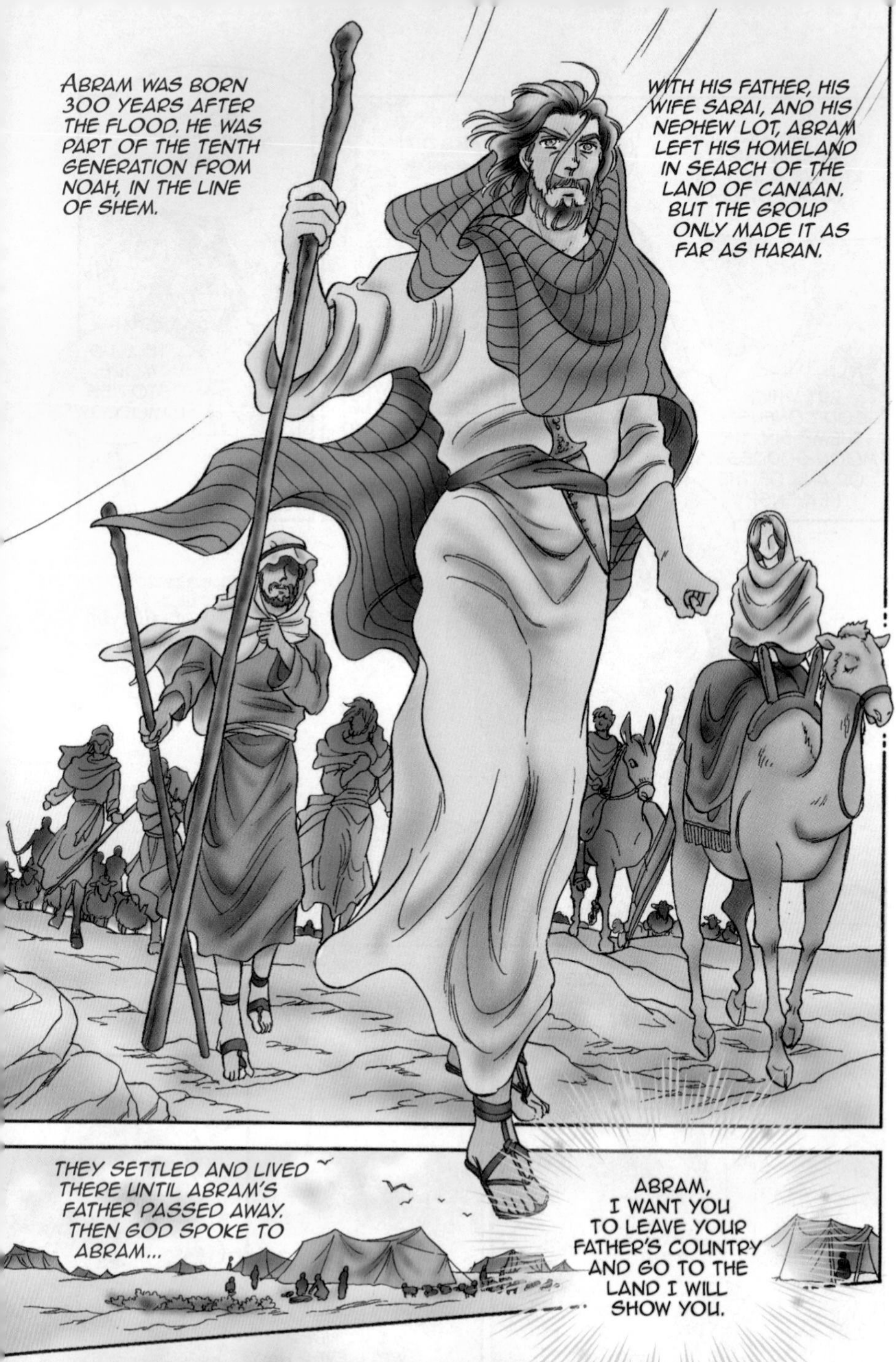
ABRAM WAS BORN 300 YEARS AFTER THE FLOOD. HE WAS PART OF THE TENTH GENERATION FROM NOAH, IN THE LINE OF SHEM.
WITH HIS FATHER, HIS WIFE SARAI, AND HIS NEPHEW LOT, ABRAM LEFT HIS HOMELAND IN SEARCH OF THE LAND OF CANAAN. BUT THE GROUP ONLY MADE IT AS FAR AS HARAN.
THEY SETTLED AND LIVED THERE UNTIL ABRAM'S FATHER PASSED AWAY. THEN GOD SPOKE TO ABRAM...
ABRAM, I WANT YOU TO LEAVE YOUR FATHER'S COUNTRY AND GO TO THE LAND I WILL SHOW YOU.

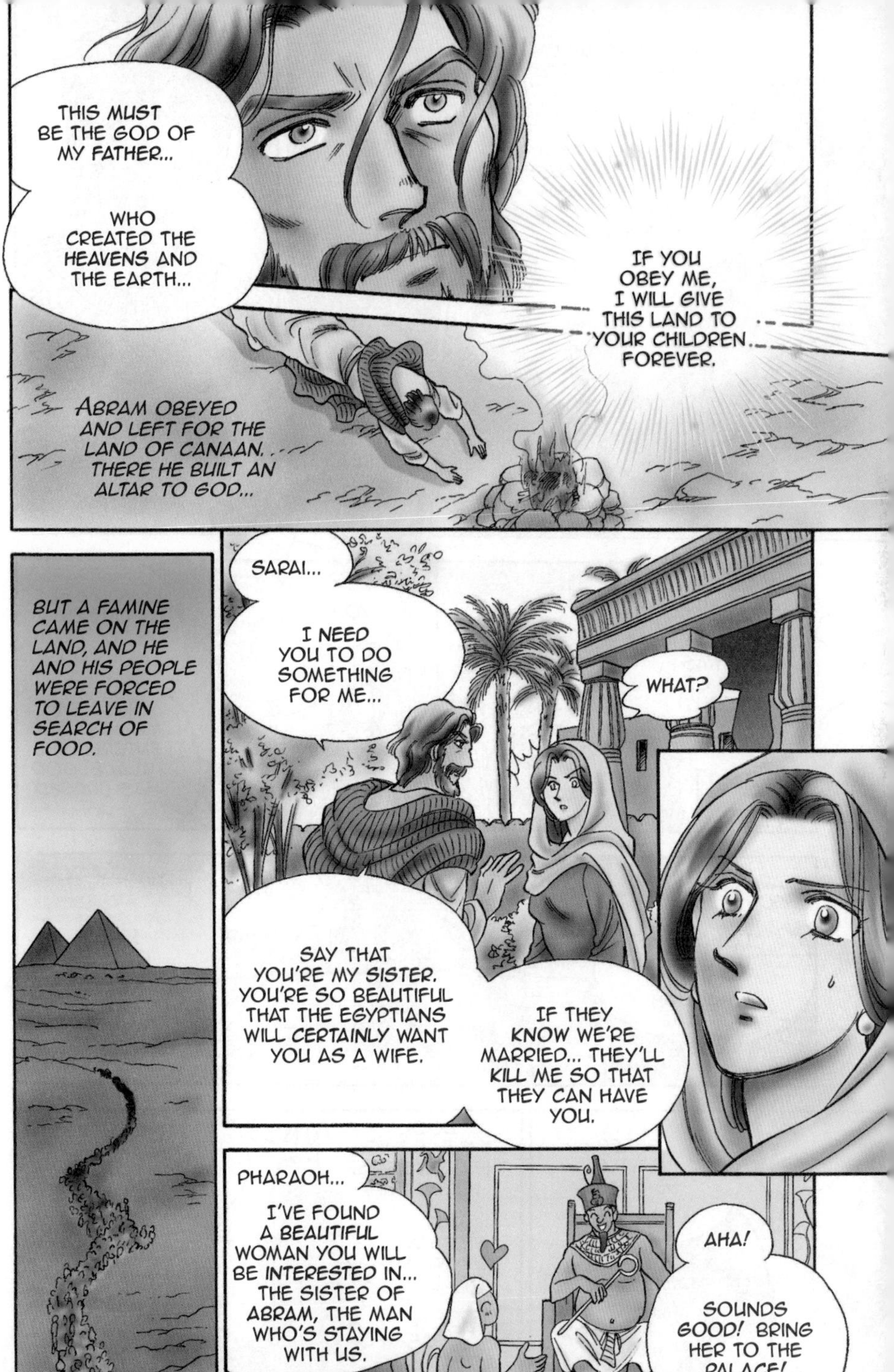
THIS MUST BE THE GOD OF MY FATHER...
WHO CREATED THE HEAVENS AND THE EARTH...
IF YOU OBEY ME, I WILL GIVE THIS LAND TO YOUR CHILDREN FOREVER.
ABRAM OBEYED AND LEFT FOR THE LAND OF CANAAN. THERE HE BUILT AN ALTAR TO GOD...
BUT A FAMINE CAME ON THE LAND, AND HE AND HIS PEOPLE WERE FORCED TO LEAVE IN SEARCH OF FOOD.
SARAI...
I NEED YOU TO DO SOMETHING FOR ME...
WHAT?
SAY THAT YOU'RE MY SISTER. YOU'RE SO BEAUTIFUL THAT THE EGYPTIANS WILL CERTAINLY WANT YOU AS A WIFE.
IF THEY KNOW WE'RE MARRIED... THEY'LL KILL ME SO THAT THEY CAN HAVE YOU.
PHARAOH...
I'VE FOUND A BEAUTIFUL WOMAN YOU WILL BE INTERESTED IN... THE SISTER OF ABRAM, THE MAN WHO'S STAYING WITH US.
AHA!
SOUNDS GOOD! BRING HER TO THE PALACE!

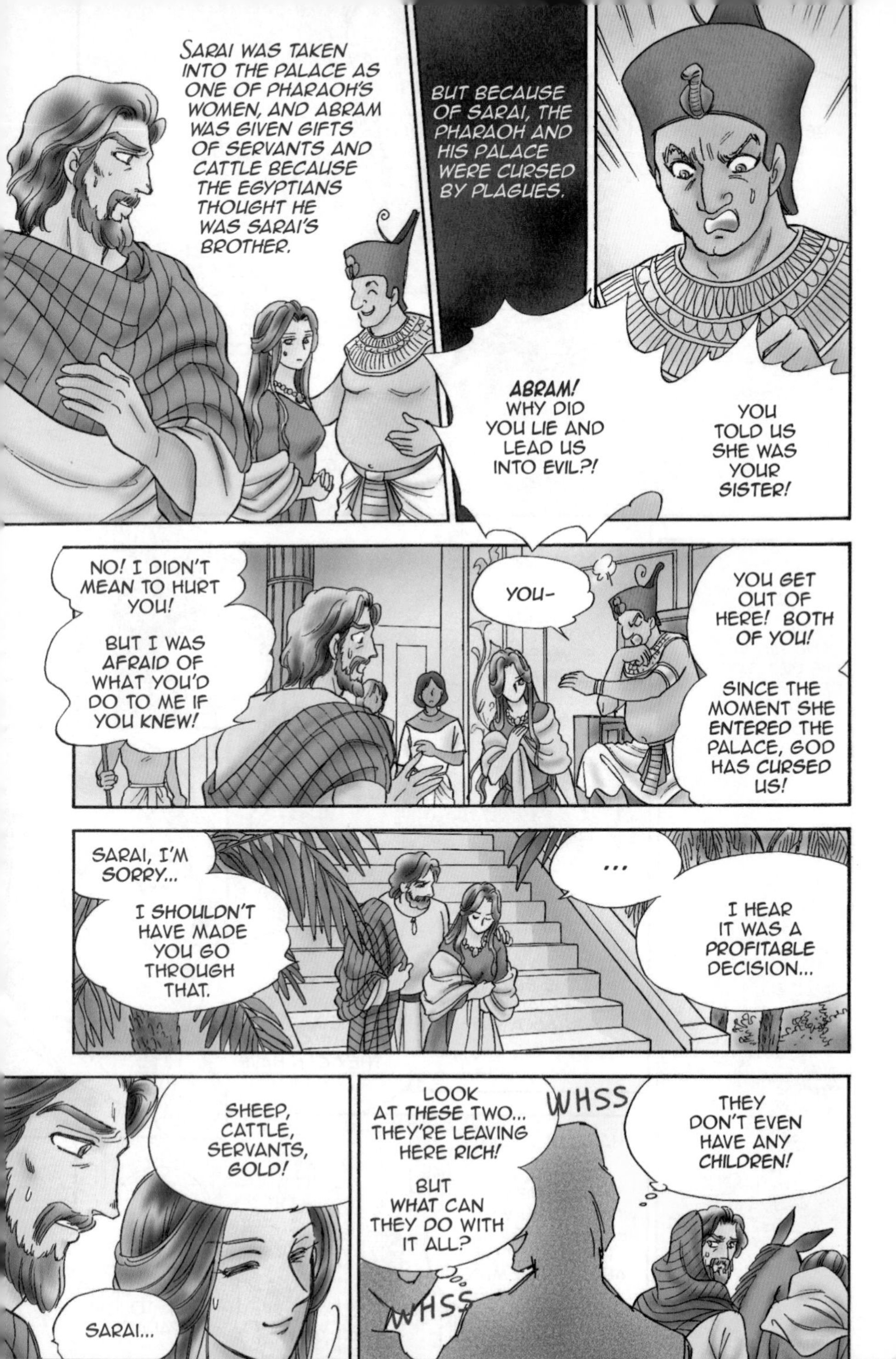

SARAI WAS TAKEN INTO THE PALACE AS ONE OF PHARAOH'S WOMEN, AND ABRAM WAS GIVEN GIFTS OF SERVANTS AND CATTLE BECAUSE THE EGYPTIANS THOUGHT HE WAS SARAI'S BROTHER.
BUT BECAUSE OF SARAI, THE PHARAOH AND HIS PALACE WERE CURSED BY PLAGUES.
ABRAM! WHY DID YOU LIE AND LEAD US INTO EVIL?!
YOU TOLD US SHE WAS YOUR SISTER!
NO! I DIDN'T MEAN TO HURT YOU!
BUT I WAS AFRAID OF WHAT YOU'D DO TO ME IF YOU KNEW!
YOU-
YOU GET OUT OF HERE! BOTH OF YOU!
SINCE THE MOMENT SHE ENTERED THE PALACE, GOD HAS CURSED US!
SARAI, I'M SORRY...
I SHOULDN'T HAVE MADE YOU GO THROUGH THAT.
...
I HEAR IT WAS A PROFITABLE DECISION...
SHEEP, CATTLE, SERVANTS, GOLD!
SARAI...
LOOK AT THESE TWO... THEY'RE LEAVING HERE RICH!
BUT WHAT CAN THEY DO WITH IT ALL?
WHSS
THEY DON'T EVEN HAVE ANY CHILDREN!
WHSS

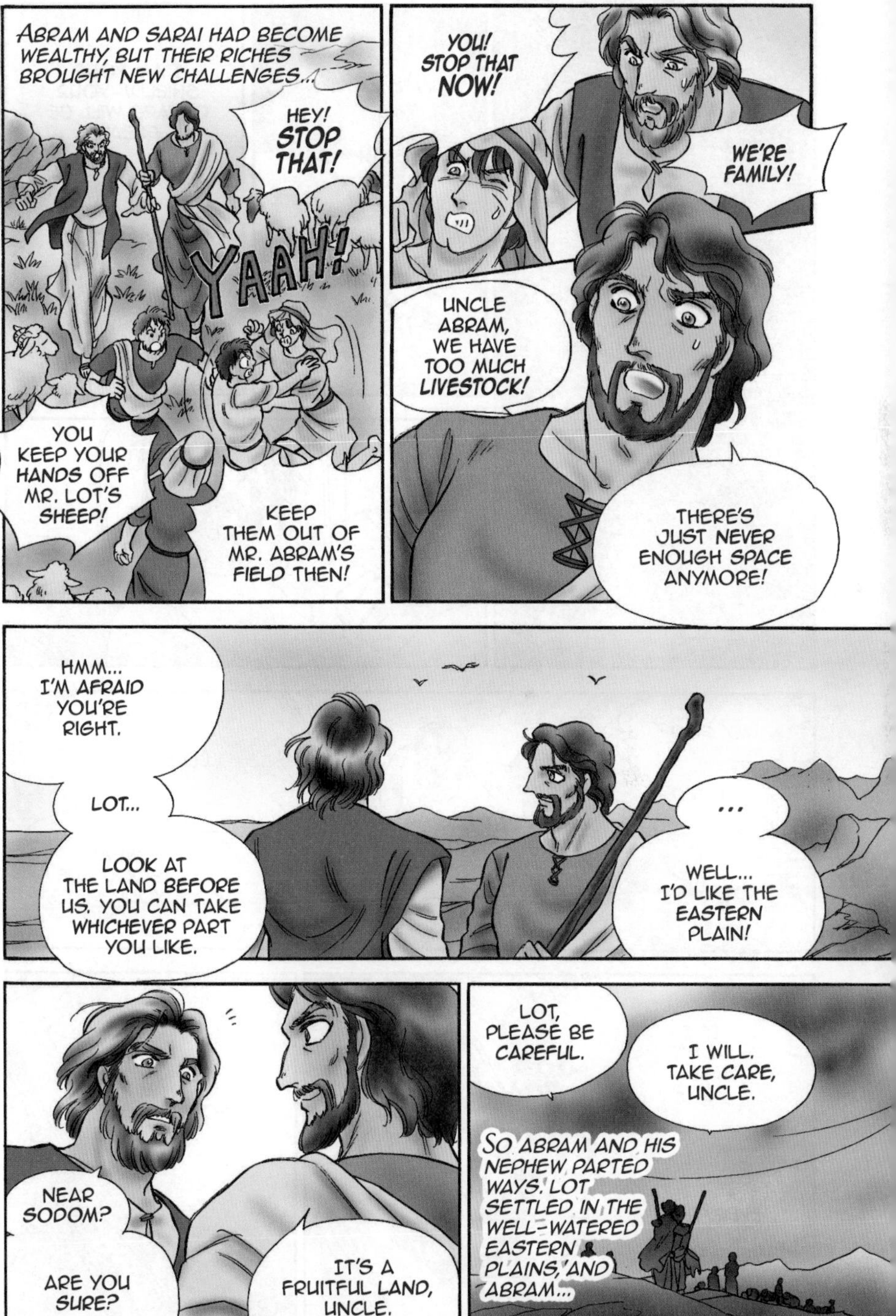

ABRAM AND SARAI HAD BECOME WEALTHY, BUT THEIR RICHES BROUGHT NEW CHALLENGES...
HEY! STOP THAT!
YAAH!
YOU KEEP YOUR HANDS OFF MR. LOT'S SHEEP!
KEEP THEM OUT OF MR. ABRAM'S FIELD THEN!
YOU! STOP THAT NOW!
WE'RE FAMILY!
UNCLE ABRAM, WE HAVE TOO MUCH LIVESTOCK!
THERE'S JUST NEVER ENOUGH SPACE ANYMORE!
HMM... I'M AFRAID YOU'RE RIGHT.
LOT...
LOOK AT THE LAND BEFORE US. YOU CAN TAKE WHICHEVER PART YOU LIKE.
...
WELL... I'D LIKE THE EASTERN PLAIN!
NEAR SODOM?
ARE YOU SURE?
IT'S A FRUITFUL LAND, UNCLE.
LOT, PLEASE BE CAREFUL.
I WILL. TAKE CARE, UNCLE.
SO ABRAM AND HIS NEPHEW PARTED WAYS. LOT SETTLED IN THE WELL-WATERED EASTERN PLAINS, AND ABRAM...

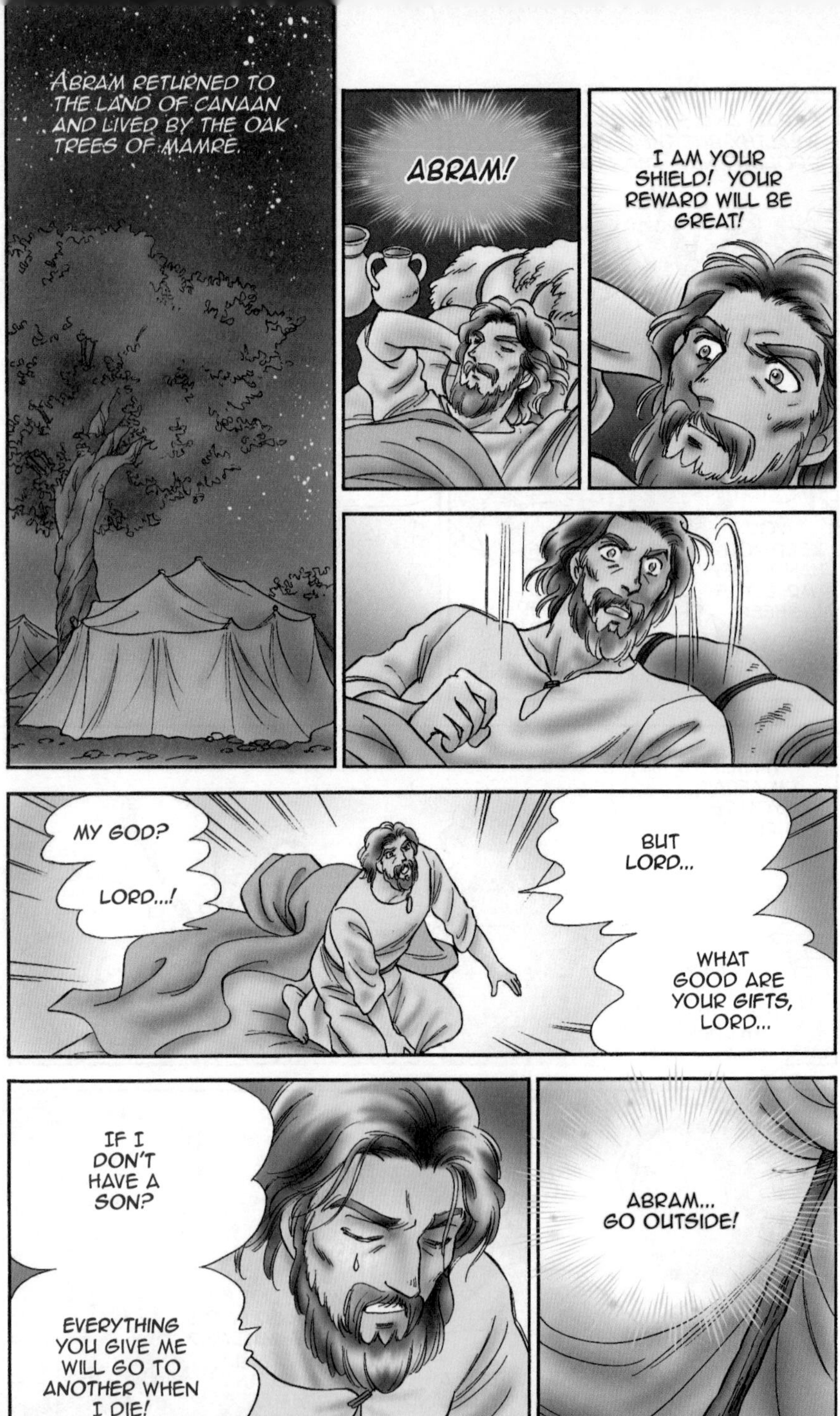
ABRAM RETURNED TO THE LAND OF CANAAN AND LIVED BY THE OAK TREES OF MAMRE.
ABRAM!
I AM YOUR SHIELD! YOUR REWARD WILL BE GREAT!
MY GOD?
LORD...!
BUT LORD...
WHAT GOOD ARE YOUR GIFTS, LORD...
IF I DON'T HAVE A SON?
EVERYTHING YOU GIVE ME WILL GO TO ANOTHER WHEN I DIE!
ABRAM... GO OUTSIDE!

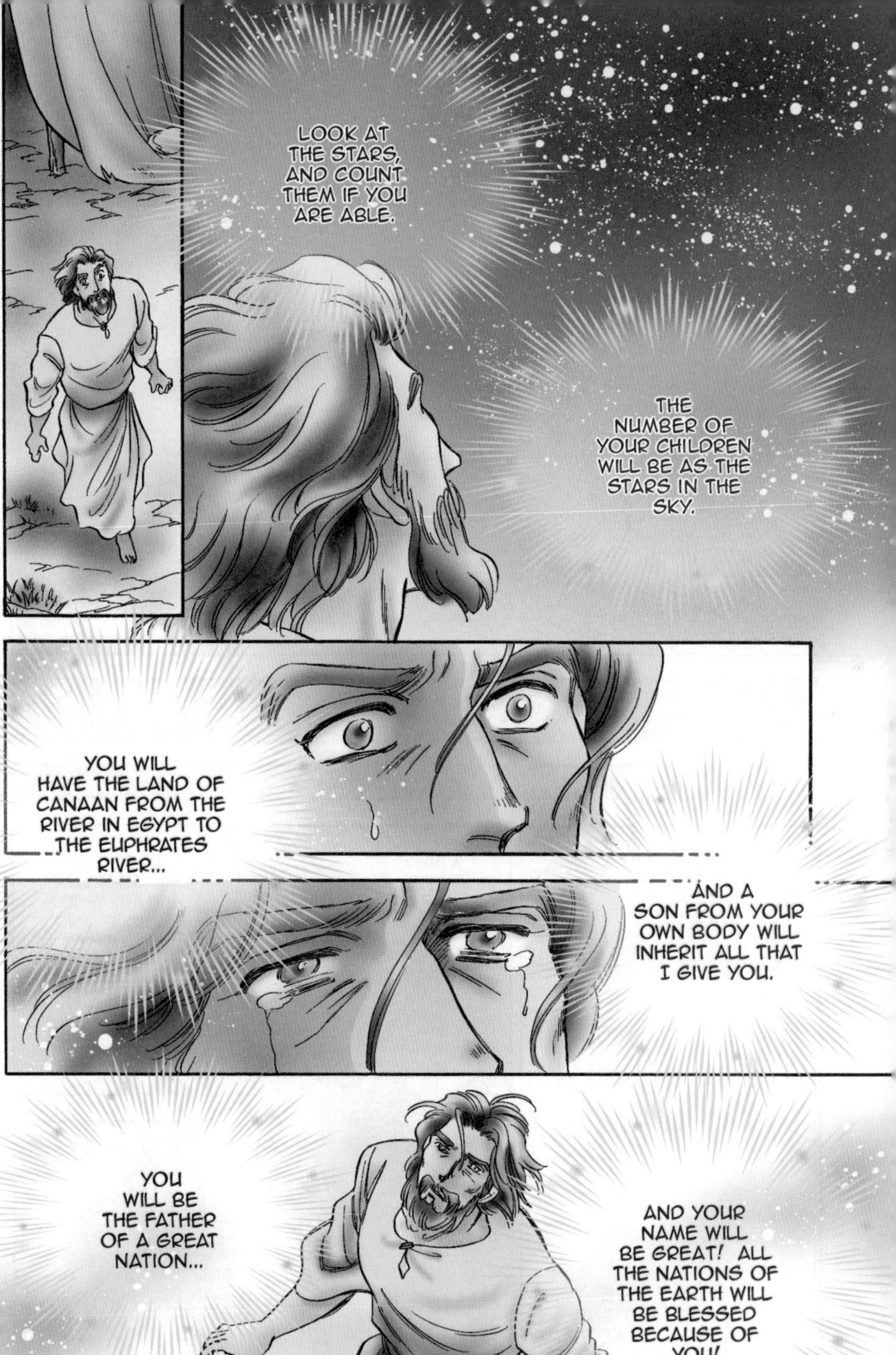
LOOK AT THE STARS, AND COUNT THEM IF YOU ARE ABLE.
THE NUMBER OF YOUR CHILDREN WILL BE AS THE STARS IN THE SKY.
YOU WILL HAVE THE LAND OF CANAAN FROM THE RIVER IN EGYPT TO THE EUPHRATES RIVER...
AND A SON FROM YOUR OWN BODY WILL INHERIT ALL THAT I GIVE YOU.
YOU WILL BE THE FATHER OF A GREAT NATION...
AND YOUR NAME WILL BE GREAT! ALL THE NATIONS OF THE EARTH WILL BE BLESSED BECAUSE OF YOU!

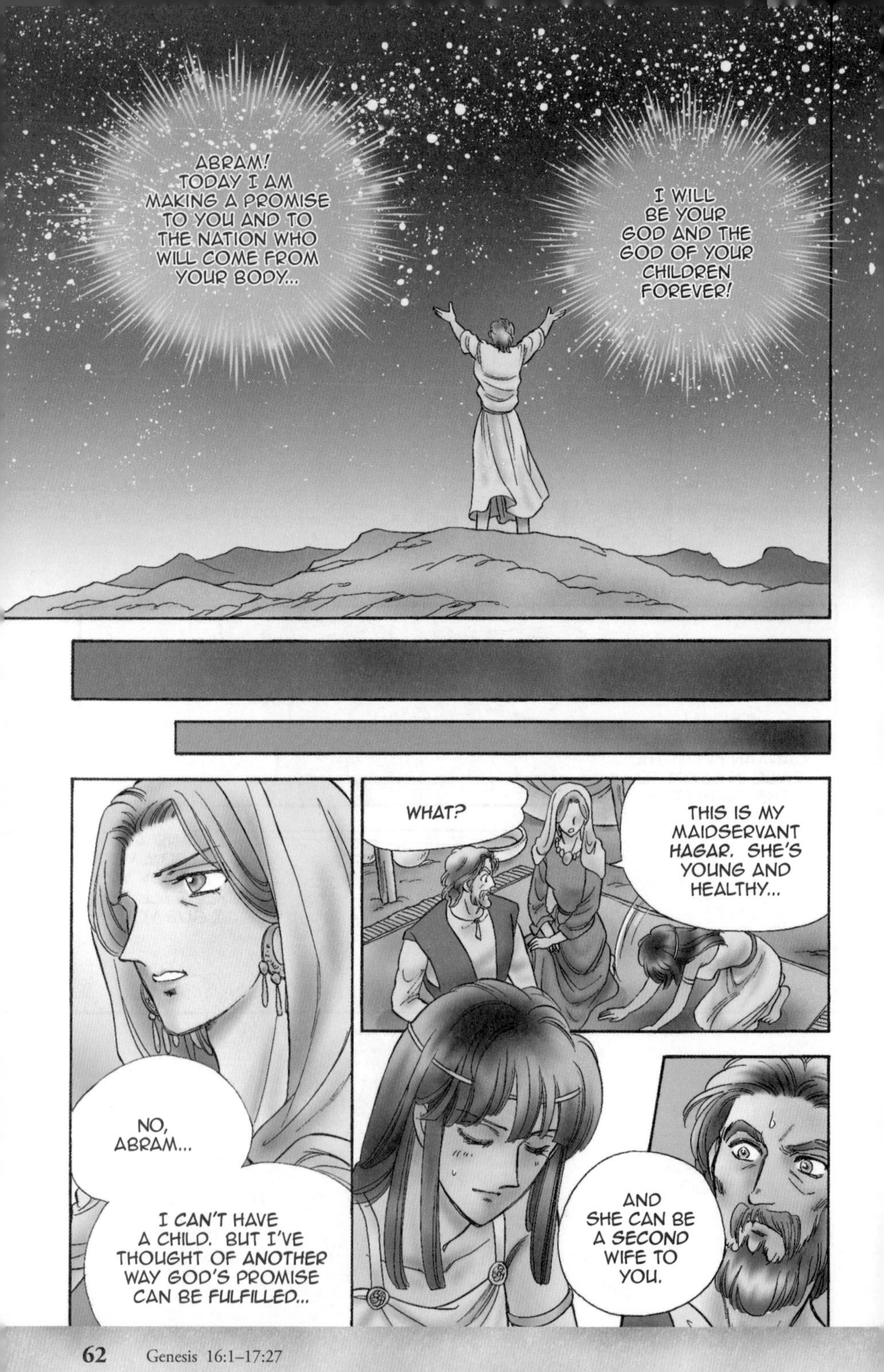
ABRAM! TODAY I AM MAKING A PROMISE TO YOU AND TO THE NATION WHO WILL COME FROM YOUR BODY...
I WILL BE YOUR GOD AND THE GOD OF YOUR CHILDREN FOREVER!
WHAT?
THIS IS MY MAIDSERVANT HAGAR. SHE'S YOUNG AND HEALTHY...
NO, ABRAM...
I CAN'T HAVE A CHILD. BUT I'VE THOUGHT OF ANOTHER WAY GOD'S PROMISE CAN BE FULFILLED...
AND SHE CAN BE A SECOND WIFE TO YOU.

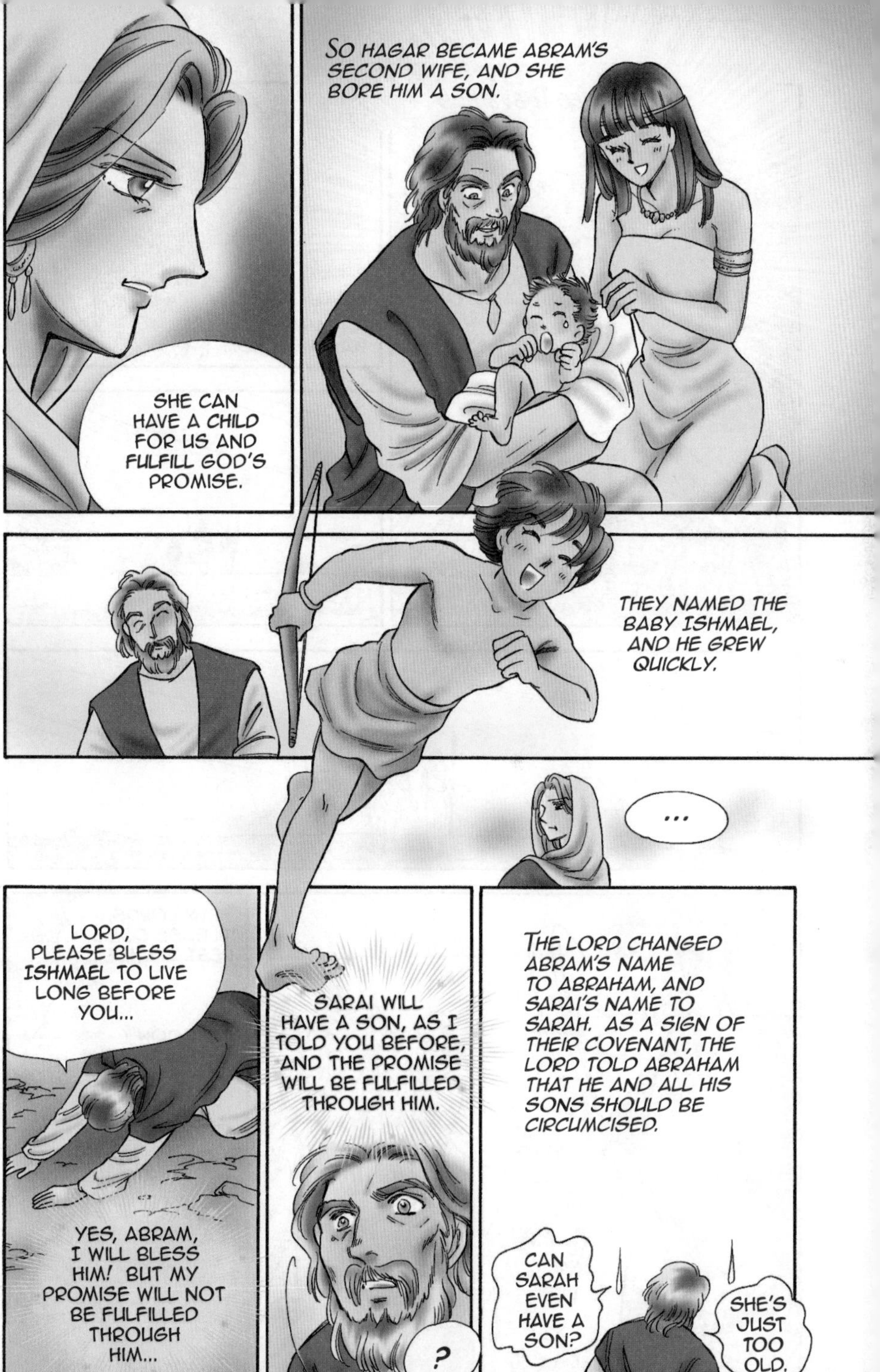
SHE CAN HAVE A CHILD FOR US AND FULFILL GOD'S PROMISE.
SO HAGAR BECAME ABRAM'S SECOND WIFE, AND SHE BORE HIM A SON.
THEY NAMED THE BABY ISHMAEL, AND HE GREW QUICKLY.
...
LORD, PLEASE BLESS ISHMAEL TO LIVE LONG BEFORE YOU...
YES, ABRAM, I WILL BLESS HIM! BUT MY PROMISE WILL NOT BE FULFILLED THROUGH HIM...
SARAI WILL HAVE A SON, AS I TOLD YOU BEFORE, AND THE PROMISE WILL BE FULFILLED THROUGH HIM.
?
THE LORD CHANGED ABRAM'S NAME TO ABRAHAM, AND SARAI'S NAME TO SARAH. AS A SIGN OF THEIR COVENANT, THE LORD TOLD ABRAHAM THAT HE AND ALL HIS SONS SHOULD BE CIRCUMCISED.
CAN SARAH EVEN HAVE A SON?
SHE'S JUST TOO OLD.

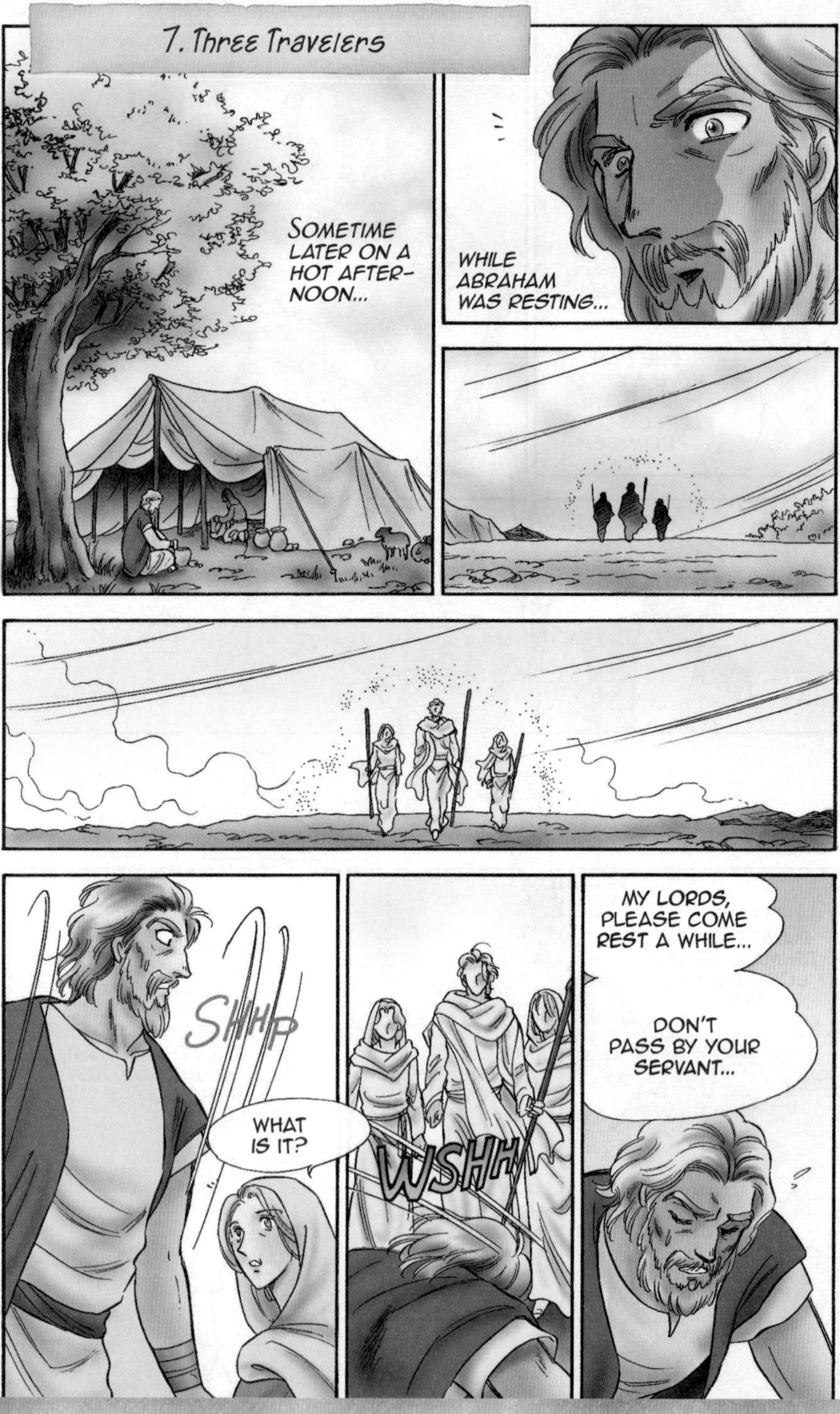
7. Three Travelers
SOMETIME LATER ON A HOT AFTER-NOON...
WHILE ABRAHAM WAS RESTING...
SHHP
WHAT IS IT?
WSHH
MY LORDS, PLEASE COME REST A WHILE...
DON'T PASS BY YOUR SERVANT...

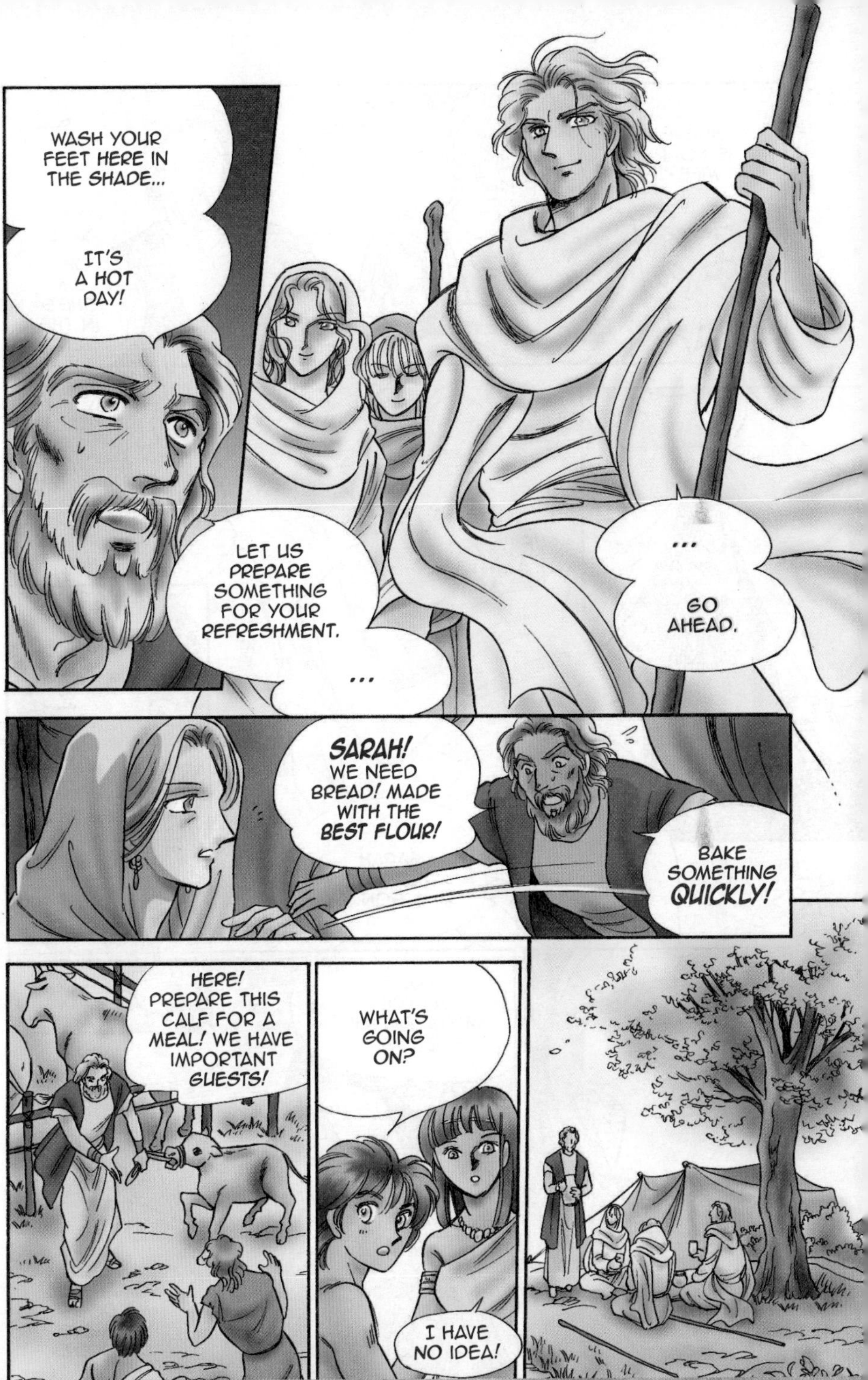
WASH YOUR FEET HERE IN THE SHADE...
IT'S A HOT DAY!
LET US PREPARE SOMETHING FOR YOUR REFRESHMENT.
...
...
GO AHEAD.
SARAH! WE NEED BREAD! MADE WITH THE BEST FLOUR!
BAKE SOMETHING QUICKLY!
HERE! PREPARE THIS CALF FOR A MEAL! WE HAVE IMPORTANT GUESTS!
WHAT'S GOING ON?
I HAVE NO IDEA!

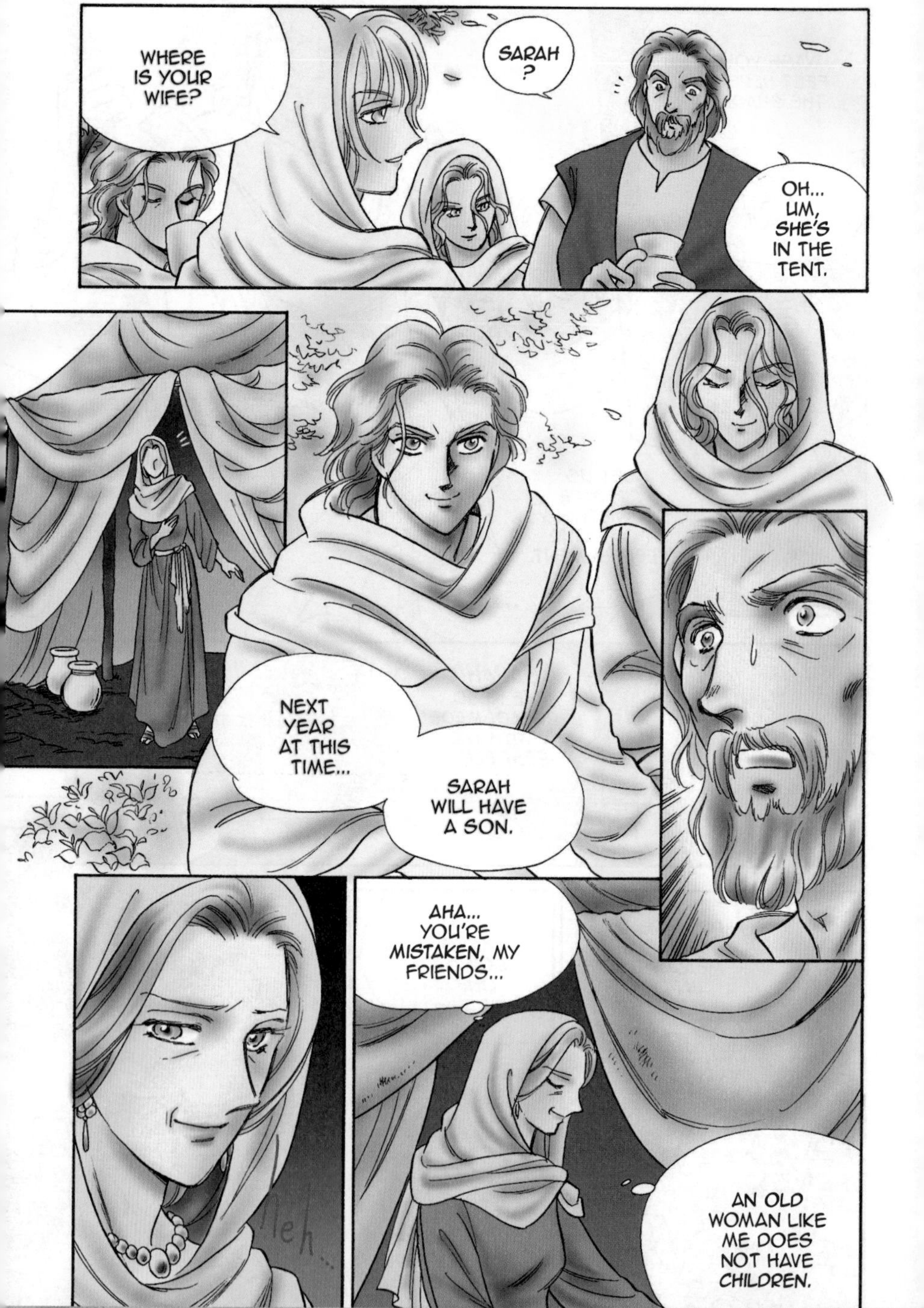
WHERE IS YOUR WIFE?
SARAH?
OH... UM, SHE'S IN THE TENT.
NEXT YEAR AT THIS TIME...
SARAH WILL HAVE A SON.
AHA... YOU'RE MISTAKEN, MY FRIENDS...
AN OLD WOMAN LIKE ME DOES NOT HAVE CHILDREN.

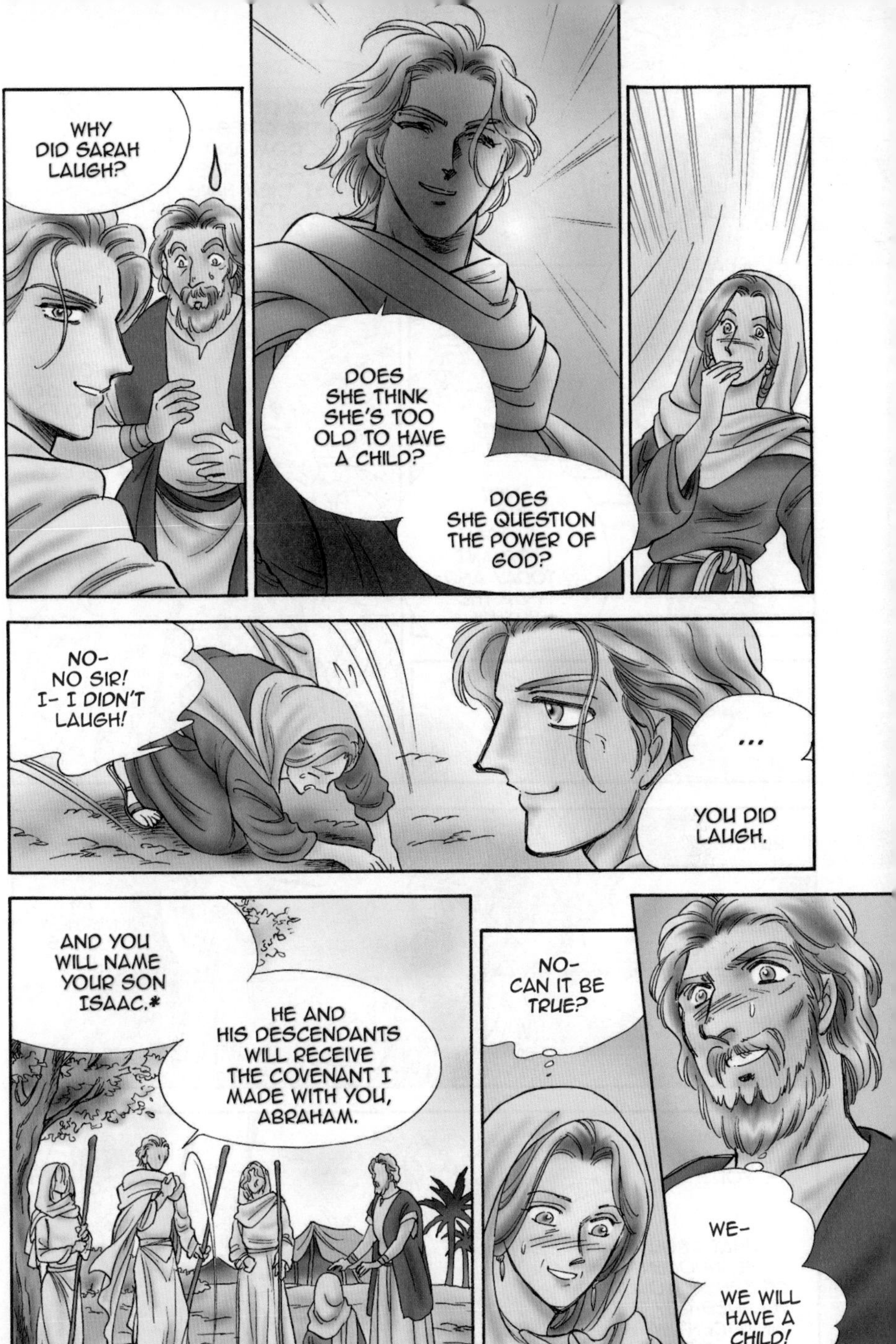
WHY DID SARAH LAUGH?
DOES SHE THINK SHE'S TOO OLD TO HAVE A CHILD?
DOES SHE QUESTION THE POWER OF GOD?
NO- NO SIR! I- I DIDN'T LAUGH!
...
YOU DID LAUGH.
AND YOU WILL NAME YOUR SON ISAAC.*
HE AND HIS DESCENDANTS WILL RECEIVE THE COVENANT I MADE WITH YOU, ABRAHAM.
*The name Isaac means "laughter."
NO- CAN IT BE TRUE?
WE-
WE WILL HAVE A CHILD!

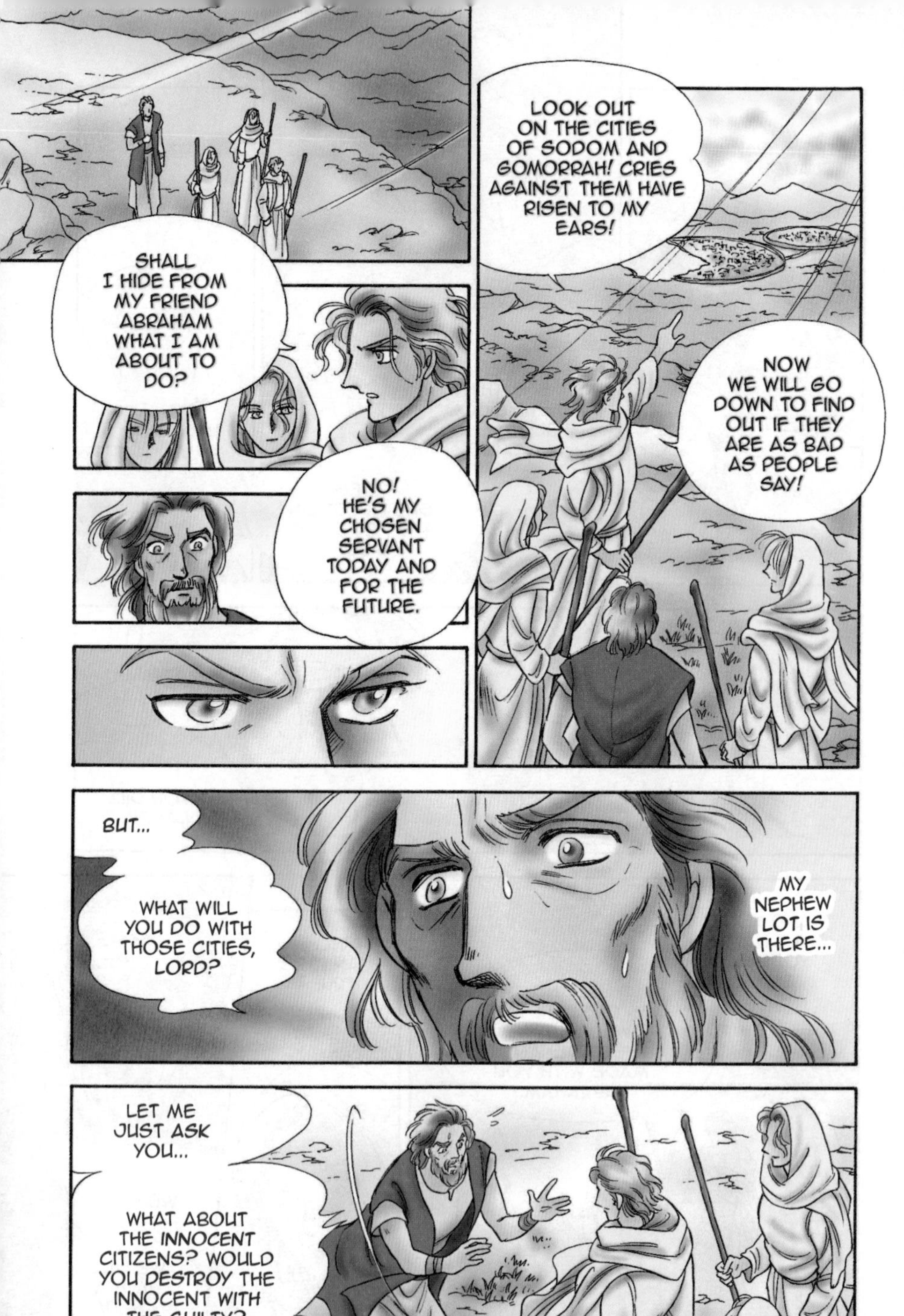
SHALL I HIDE FROM MY FRIEND ABRAHAM WHAT I AM ABOUT TO DO?
NO! HE'S MY CHOSEN SERVANT TODAY AND FOR THE FUTURE.
LOOK OUT ON THE CITIES OF SODOM AND GOMORRAH! CRIES AGAINST THEM HAVE RISEN TO MY EARS!
NOW WE WILL GO DOWN TO FIND OUT IF THEY ARE AS BAD AS PEOPLE SAY!
BUT...
WHAT WILL YOU DO WITH THOSE CITIES, LORD?
MY NEPHEW LOT IS THERE...
LET ME JUST ASK YOU...
WHAT ABOUT THE INNOCENT CITIZENS? WOULD YOU DESTROY THE INNOCENT WITH THE GUILTY?

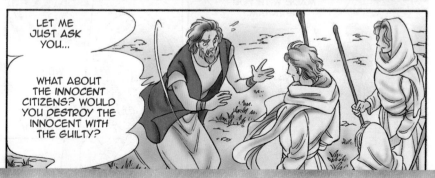

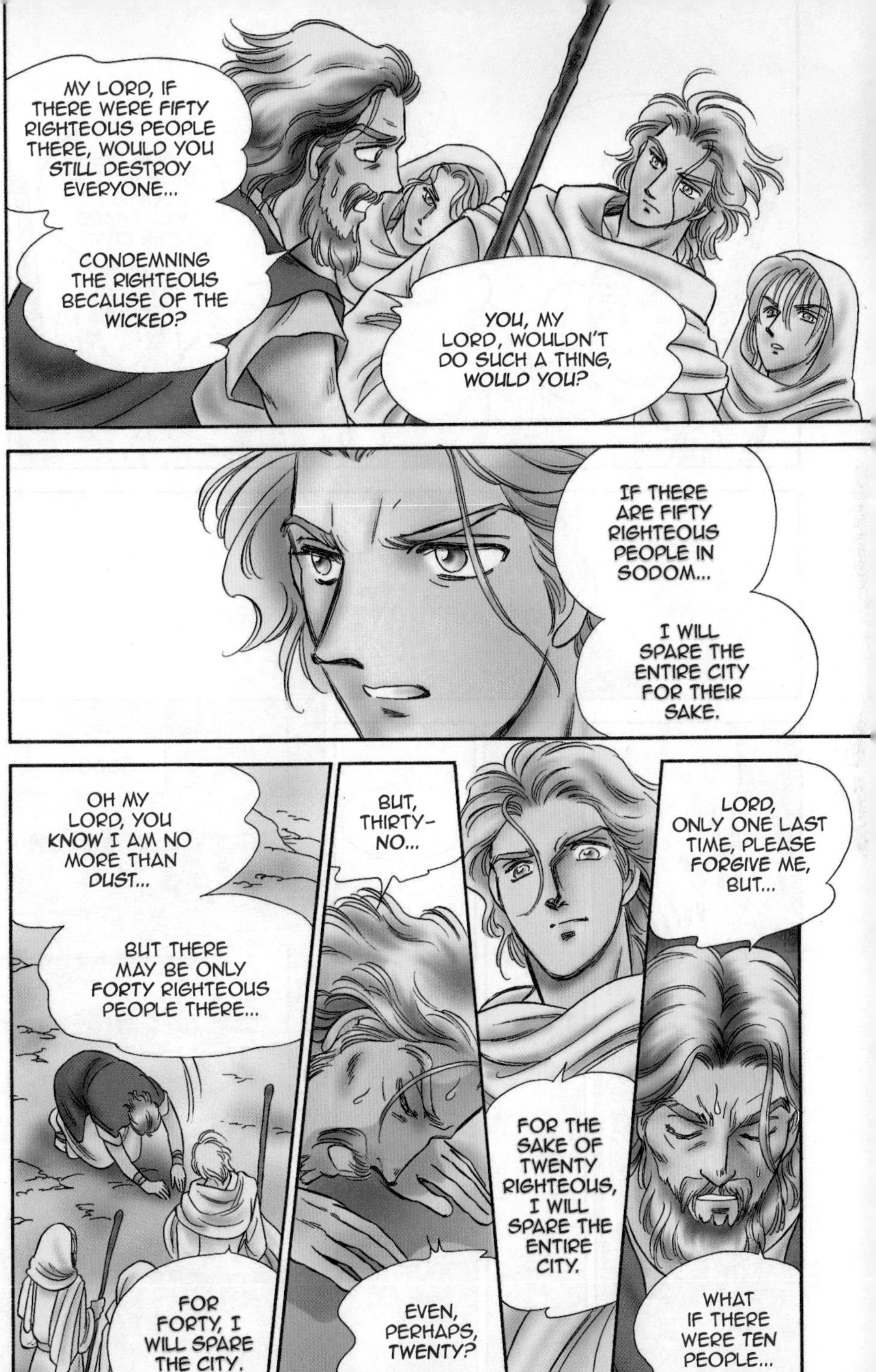
MY LORD, IF THERE WERE FIFTY RIGHTEOUS PEOPLE THERE, WOULD YOU STILL DESTROY EVERYONE...
CONDEMNING THE RIGHTEOUS BECAUSE OF THE WICKED?
YOU, MY LORD, WOULDN'T DO SUCH A THING, WOULD YOU?
IF THERE ARE FIFTY RIGHTEOUS PEOPLE IN SODOM...
I WILL SPARE THE ENTIRE CITY FOR THEIR SAKE.
OH MY LORD, YOU KNOW I AM NO MORE THAN DUST...
BUT THERE MAY BE ONLY FORTY RIGHTEOUS PEOPLE THERE...
FOR FORTY, I WILL SPARE THE CITY.
BUT, THIRTY-NO...
EVEN, PERHAPS, TWENTY?
FOR THE SAKE OF TWENTY RIGHTEOUS, I WILL SPARE THE ENTIRE CITY.
LORD, ONLY ONE LAST TIME, PLEASE FORGIVE ME, BUT...
WHAT IF THERE WERE TEN PEOPLE...

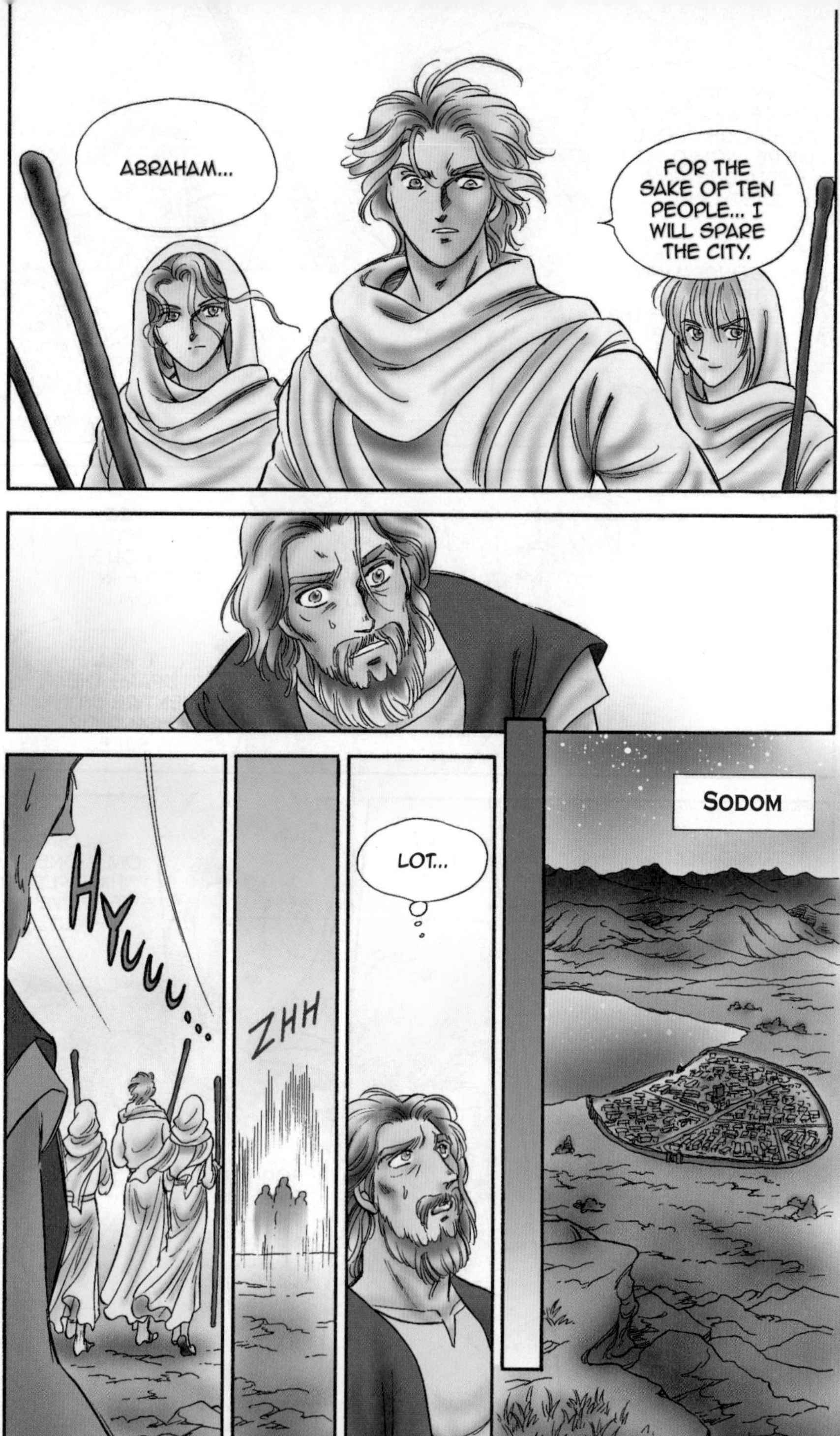
ABRAHAM...
FOR THE SAKE OF TEN PEOPLE... I WILL SPARE THE CITY.
HYUUU...
ZHH
LOT...
SODOM

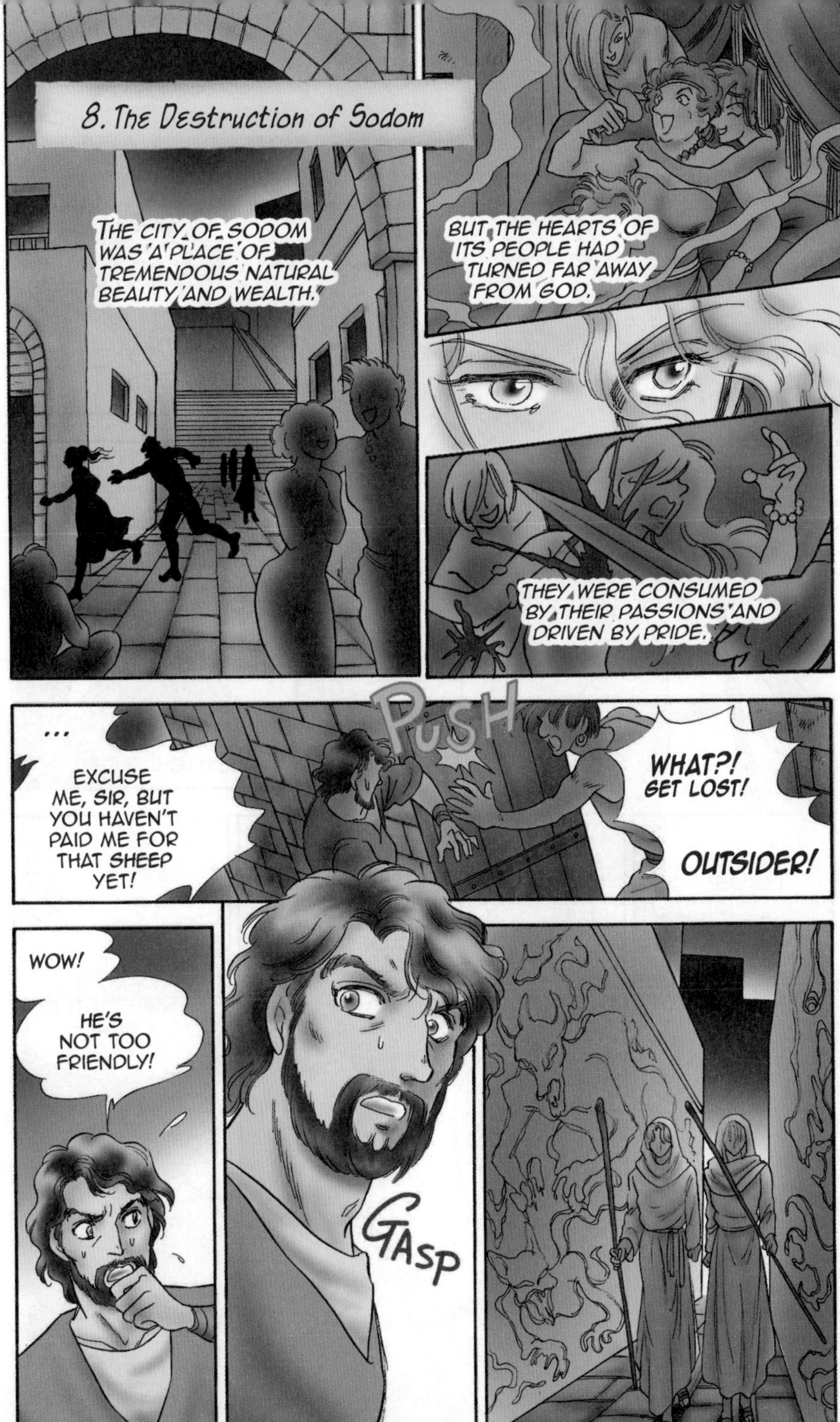
8. The Destruction of Sodom
THE CITY OF SODOM WAS A PLACE OF TREMENDOUS NATURAL BEAUTY AND WEALTH.
BUT THE HEARTS OF ITS PEOPLE HAD TURNED FAR AWAY FROM GOD.
THEY WERE CONSUMED BY THEIR PASSIONS AND DRIVEN BY PRIDE.
PUSH
...
EXCUSE ME, SIR, BUT YOU HAVEN'T PAID ME FOR THAT SHEEP YET!
WHAT?! GET LOST!
OUTSIDER!
WOW!
HE'S NOT TOO FRIENDLY!
GASP

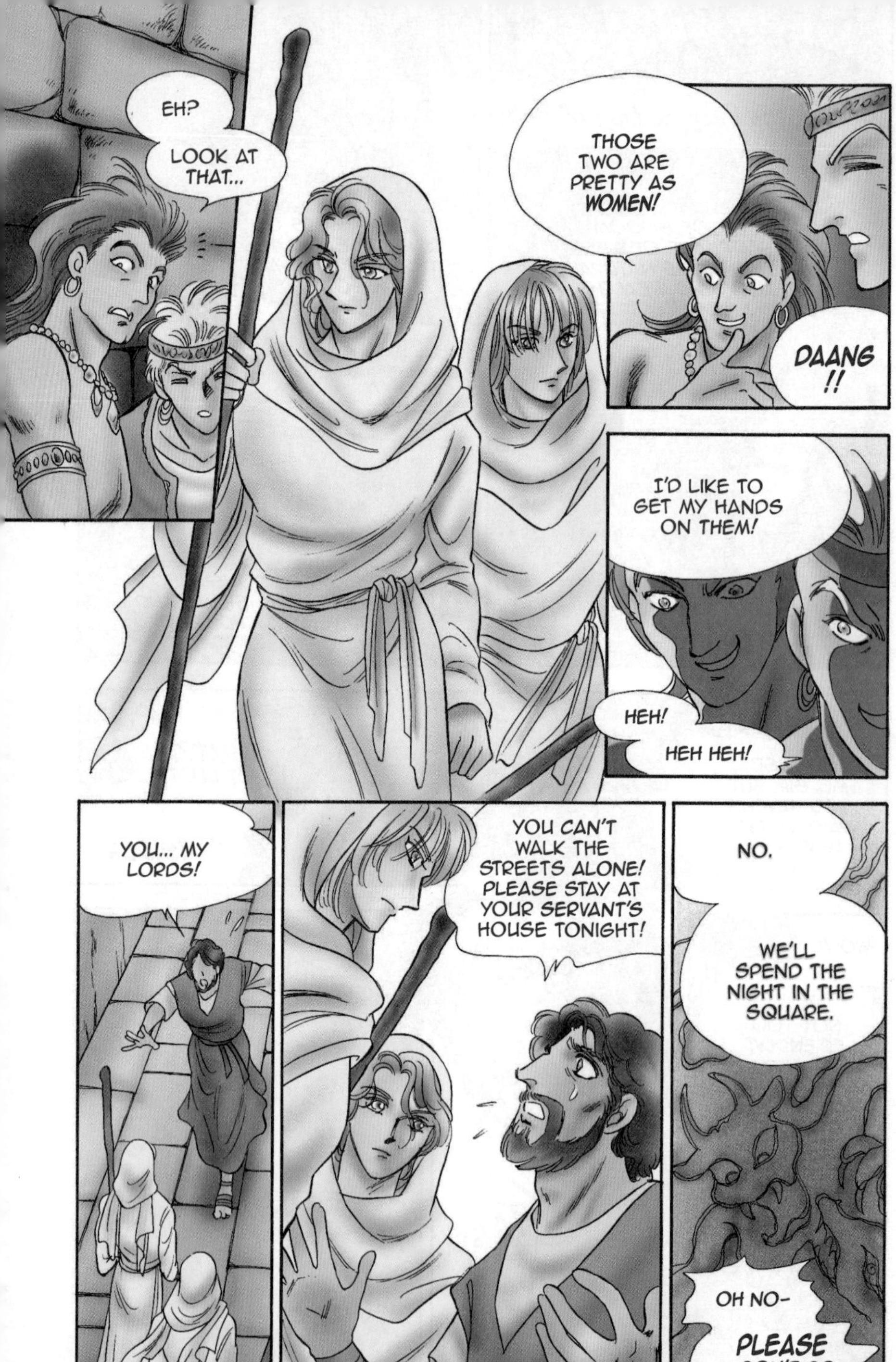
EH?
LOOK AT THAT...
THOSE TWO ARE PRETTY AS WOMEN!
DAANG !!
I'D LIKE TO GET MY HANDS ON THEM!
HEH!
HEH HEH!
YOU... MY LORDS!
YOU CAN'T WALK THE STREETS ALONE! PLEASE STAY AT YOUR SERVANT'S HOUSE TONIGHT!
NO.
WE'LL SPEND THE NIGHT IN THE SQUARE.
OH NO-
PLEASE DON'T DO THAT!

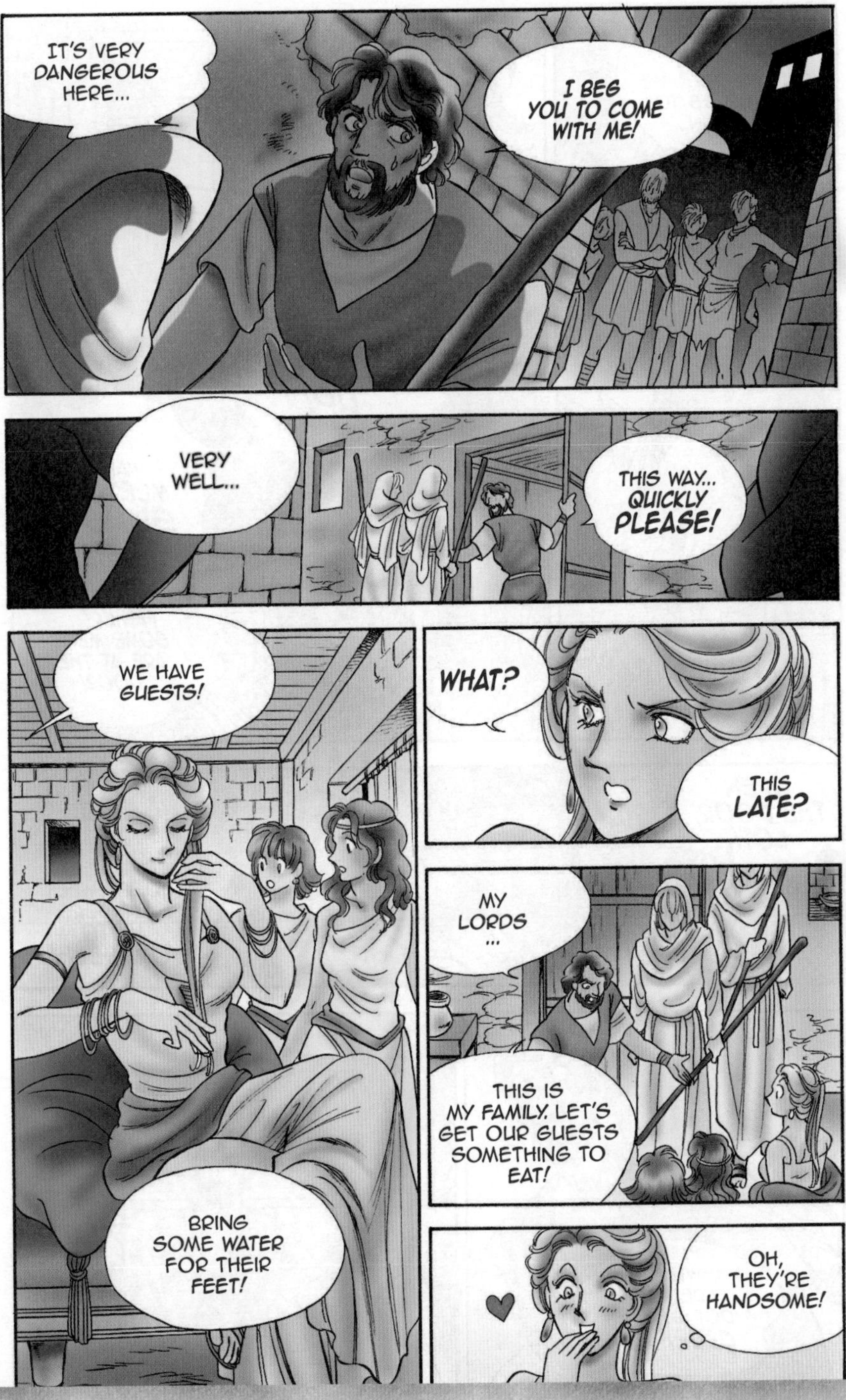
IT'S VERY DANGEROUS HERE...
I BEG YOU TO COME WITH ME!
VERY WELL...
THIS WAY... QUICKLY PLEASE!
WE HAVE GUESTS!
WHAT?
THIS LATE?
BRING SOME WATER FOR THEIR FEET!
MY LORDS ...
THIS IS MY FAMILY. LET'S GET OUR GUESTS SOMETHING TO EAT!
OH, THEY'RE HANDSOME!

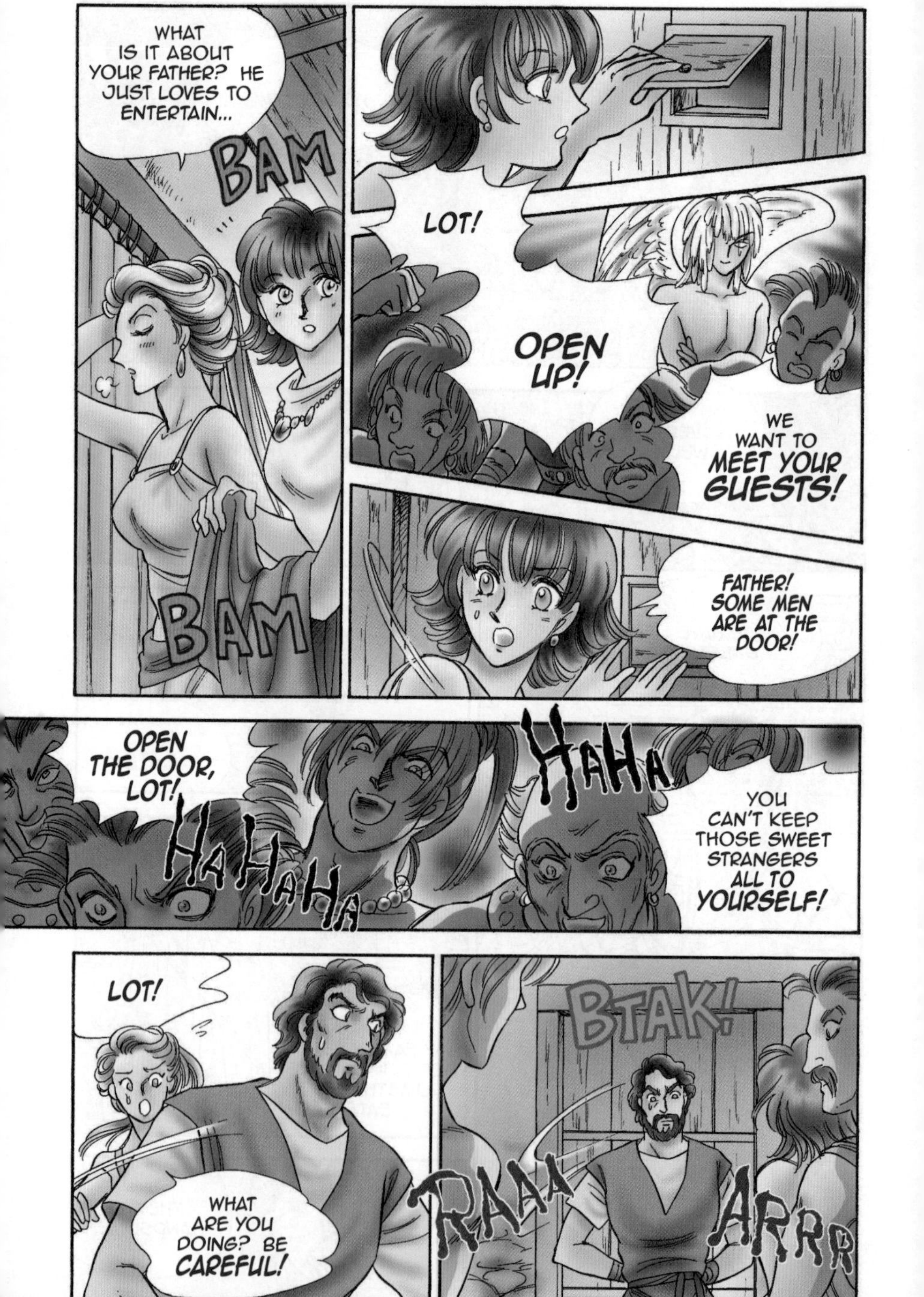
WHAT IS IT ABOUT YOUR FATHER? HE JUST LOVES TO ENTERTAIN...
BAM
BAM
LOT!
OPEN UP!
WE WANT TO MEET YOUR GUESTS!
FATHER! SOME MEN ARE AT THE DOOR!
OPEN THE DOOR, LOT!
HAHAHAHA
HAHA
YOU CAN'T KEEP THOSE SWEET STRANGERS ALL TO YOURSELF!
LOT!
WHAT ARE YOU DOING? BE CAREFUL!
BTAK!
RAAAARRR

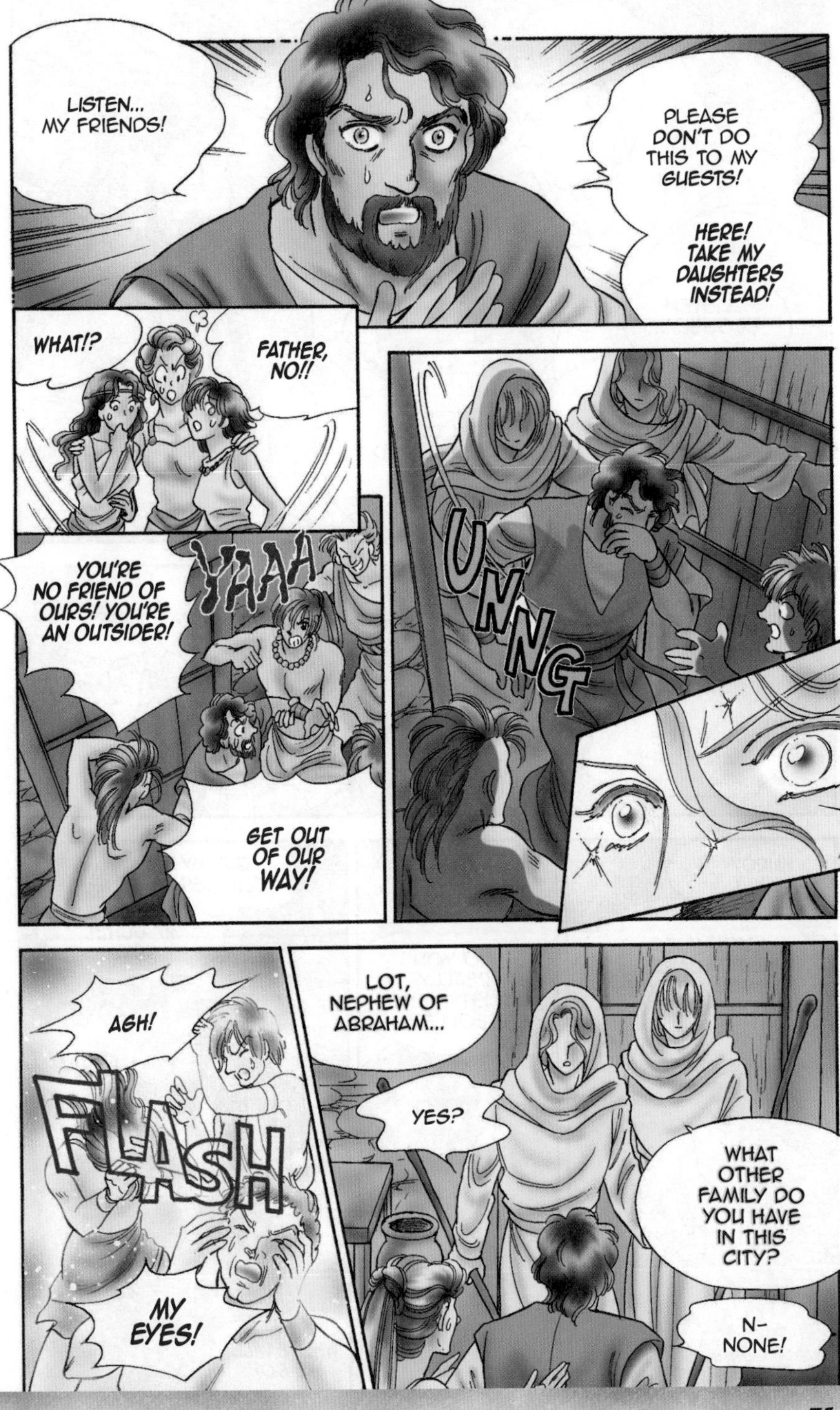
LISTEN... MY FRIENDS!
PLEASE DON'T DO THIS TO MY GUESTS!
HERE! TAKE MY DAUGHTERS INSTEAD!
WHAT!?
FATHER, NO!!
YOU'RE NO FRIEND OF OURS! YOU'RE AN OUTSIDER!
YAAA
GET OUT OF OUR WAY!
UNNG
AGH!
FLASH
MY EYES!
LOT, NEPHEW OF ABRAHAM...
YES?
WHAT OTHER FAMILY DO YOU HAVE IN THIS CITY?
N- NONE!

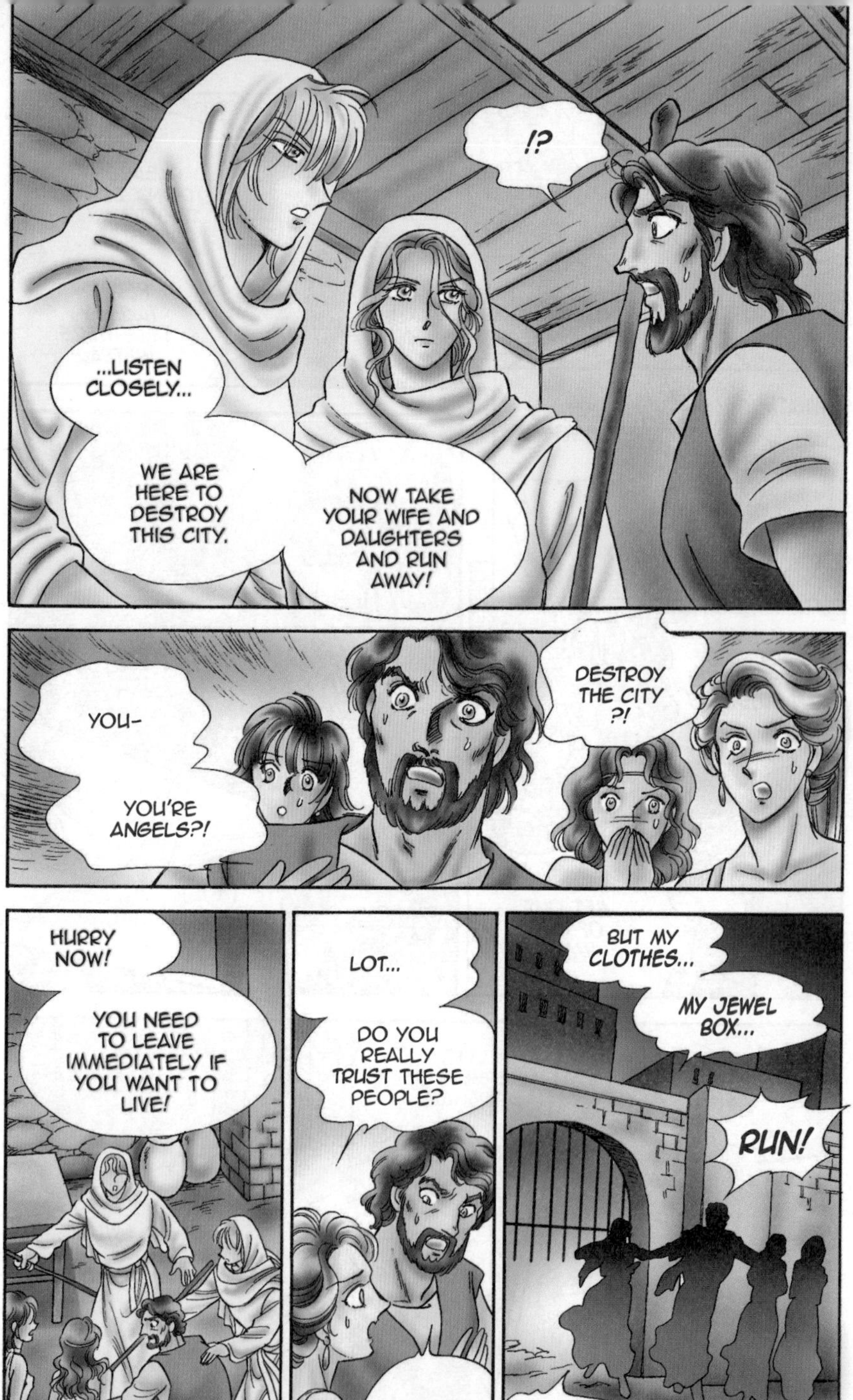
!?
...LISTEN CLOSELY...
WE ARE HERE TO DESTROY THIS CITY.
NOW TAKE YOUR WIFE AND DAUGHTERS AND RUN AWAY!
YOU-
YOU'RE ANGELS?!
DESTROY THE CITY ?!
HURRY NOW!
YOU NEED TO LEAVE IMMEDIATELY IF YOU WANT TO LIVE!
LOT...
DO YOU REALLY TRUST THESE PEOPLE?
COME ON!
BUT MY CLOTHES...
MY JEWEL BOX...
RUN!
WHERE WILL WE GO?

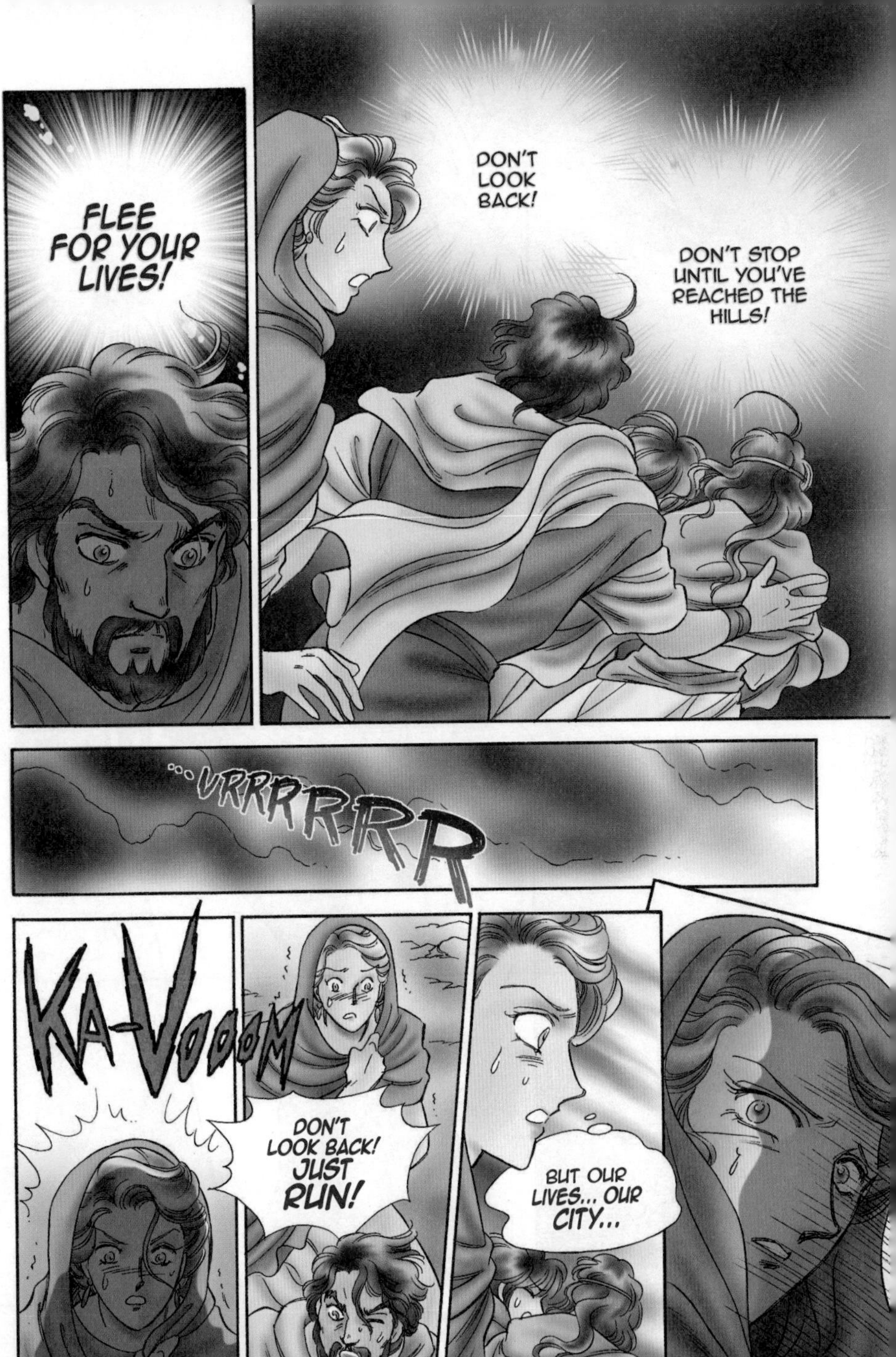
FLEE FOR YOUR LIVES!
DON'T LOOK BACK!
DON'T STOP UNTIL YOU'VE REACHED THE HILLS!
...URRRRRRR
KA-VOOOM
DON'T LOOK BACK! JUST RUN!
BUT OUR LIVES... OUR CITY...

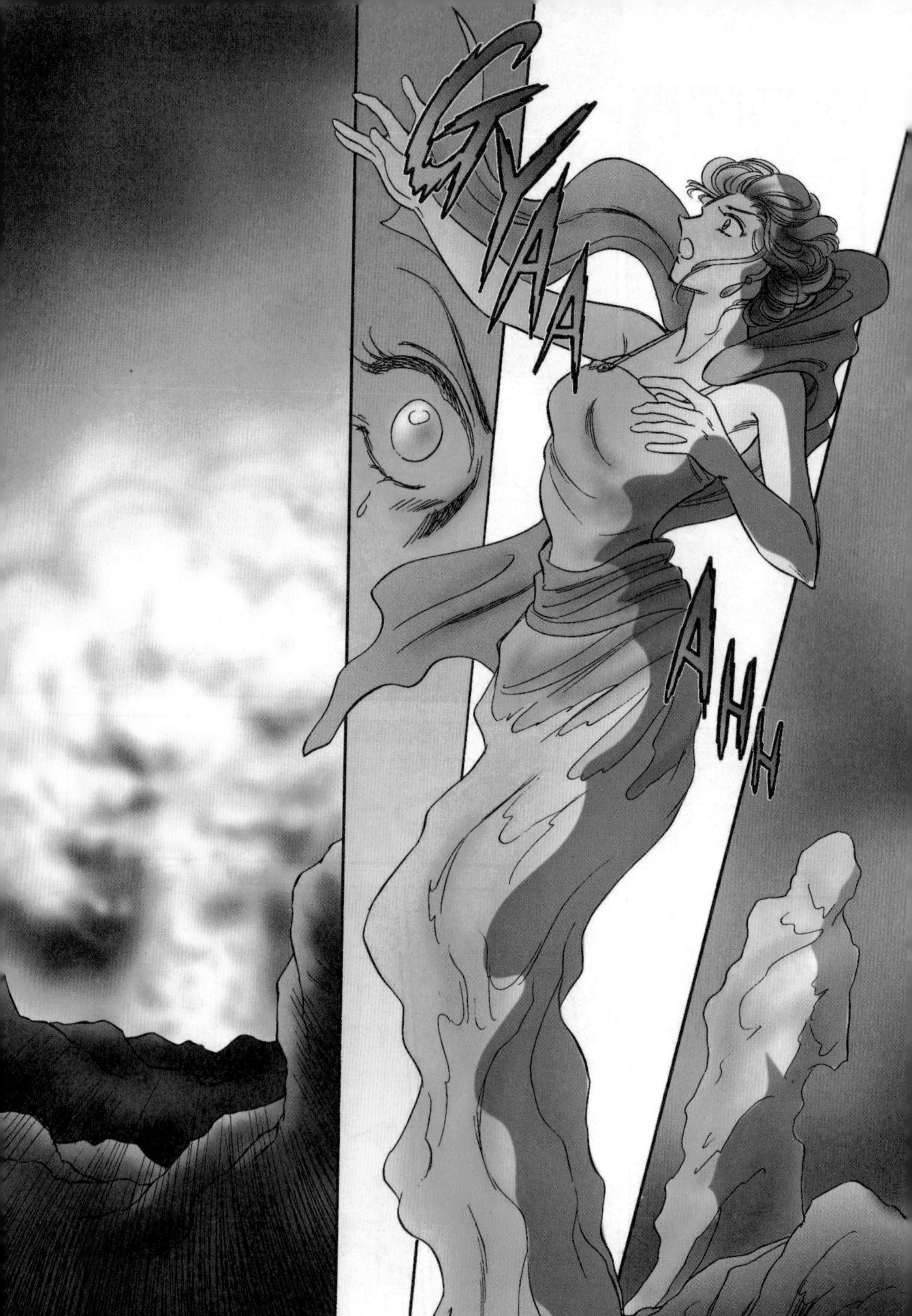
GYAAA
AHH

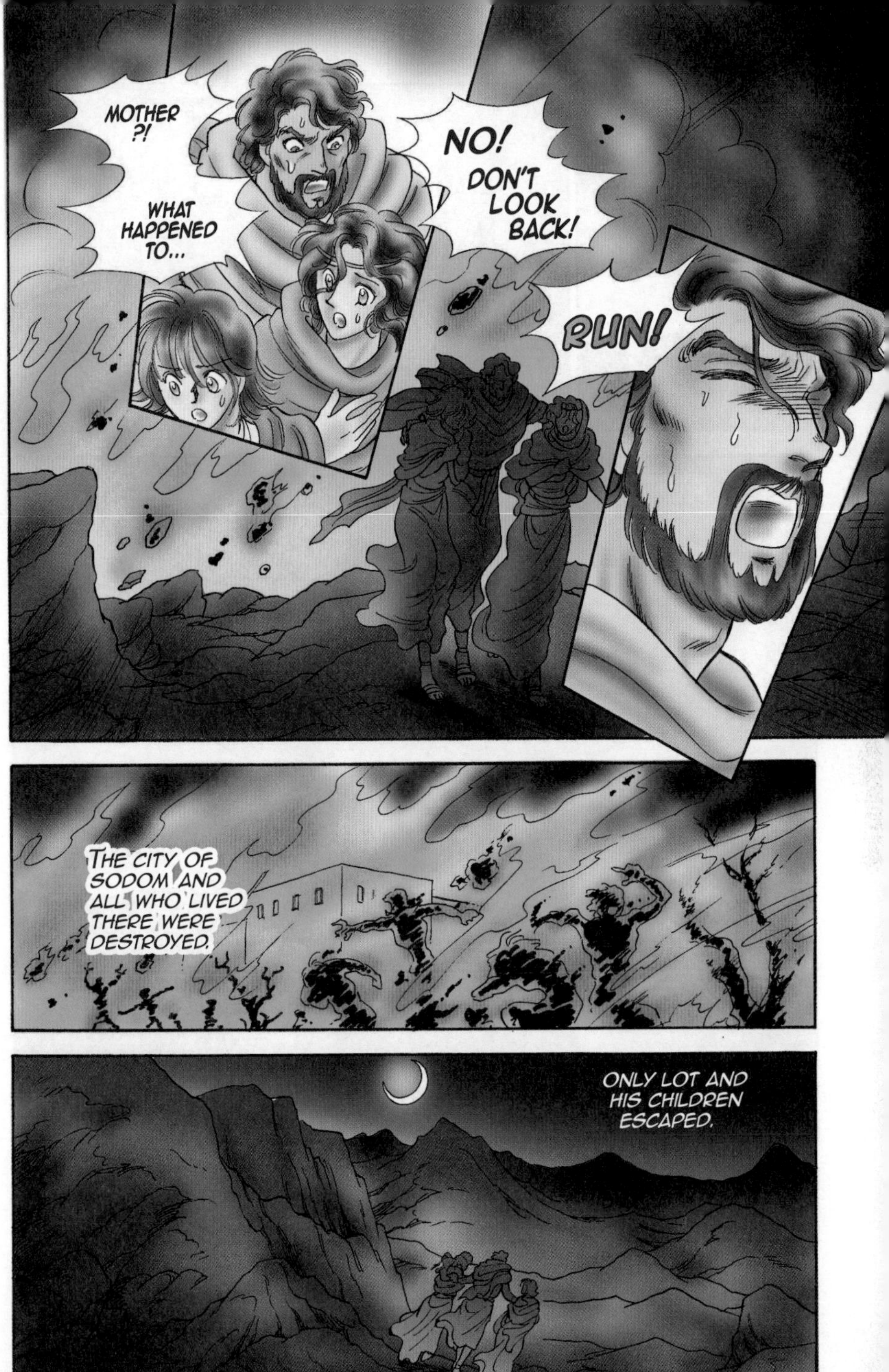
MOTHER ?!
WHAT HAPPENED TO...
NO! DON'T LOOK BACK!
RUN!
THE CITY OF SODOM AND ALL WHO LIVED THERE WERE DESTROYED.
ONLY LOT AND HIS CHILDREN ESCAPED.

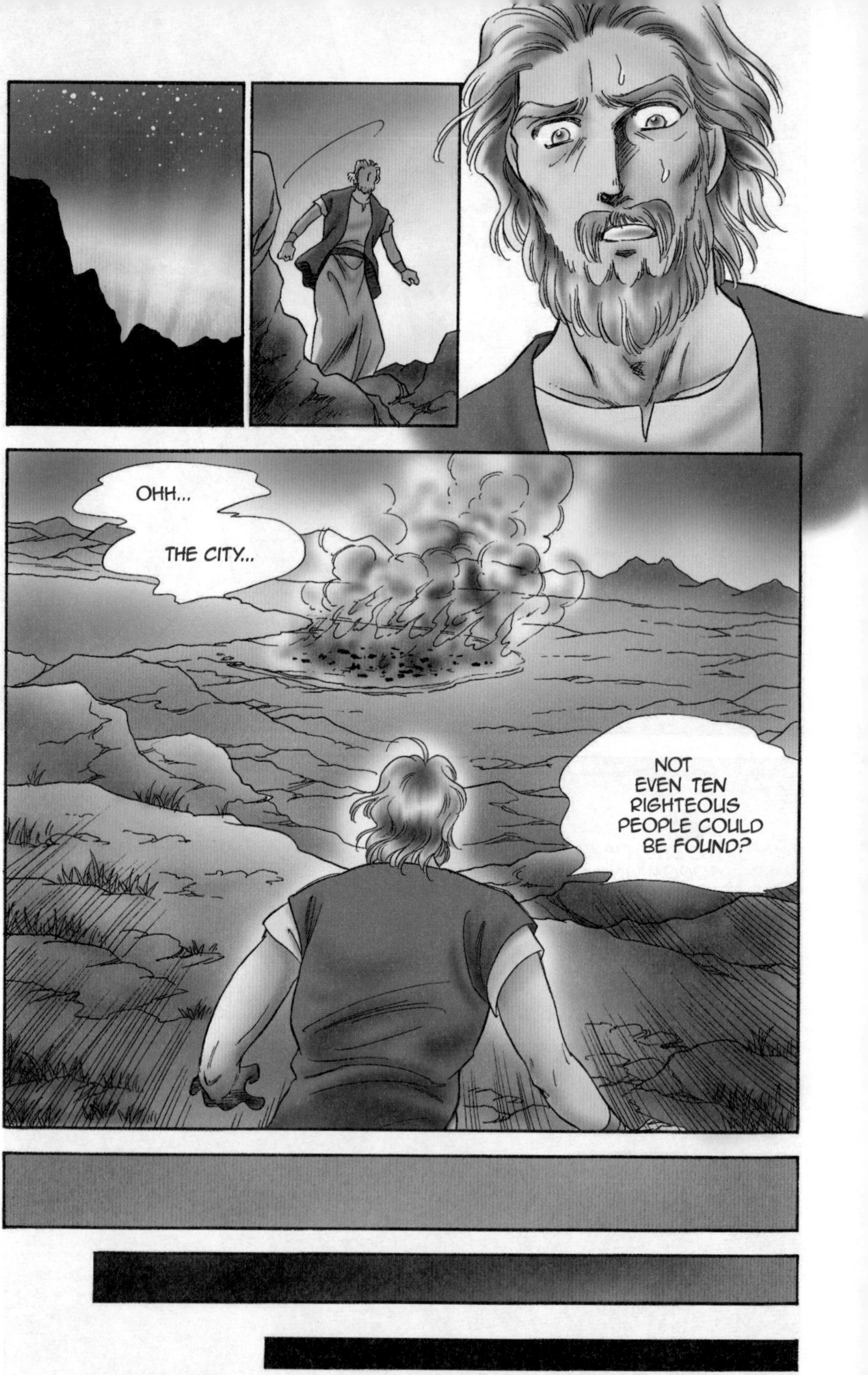
OHH...
THE CITY...
NOT EVEN TEN RIGHTEOUS PEOPLE COULD BE FOUND?

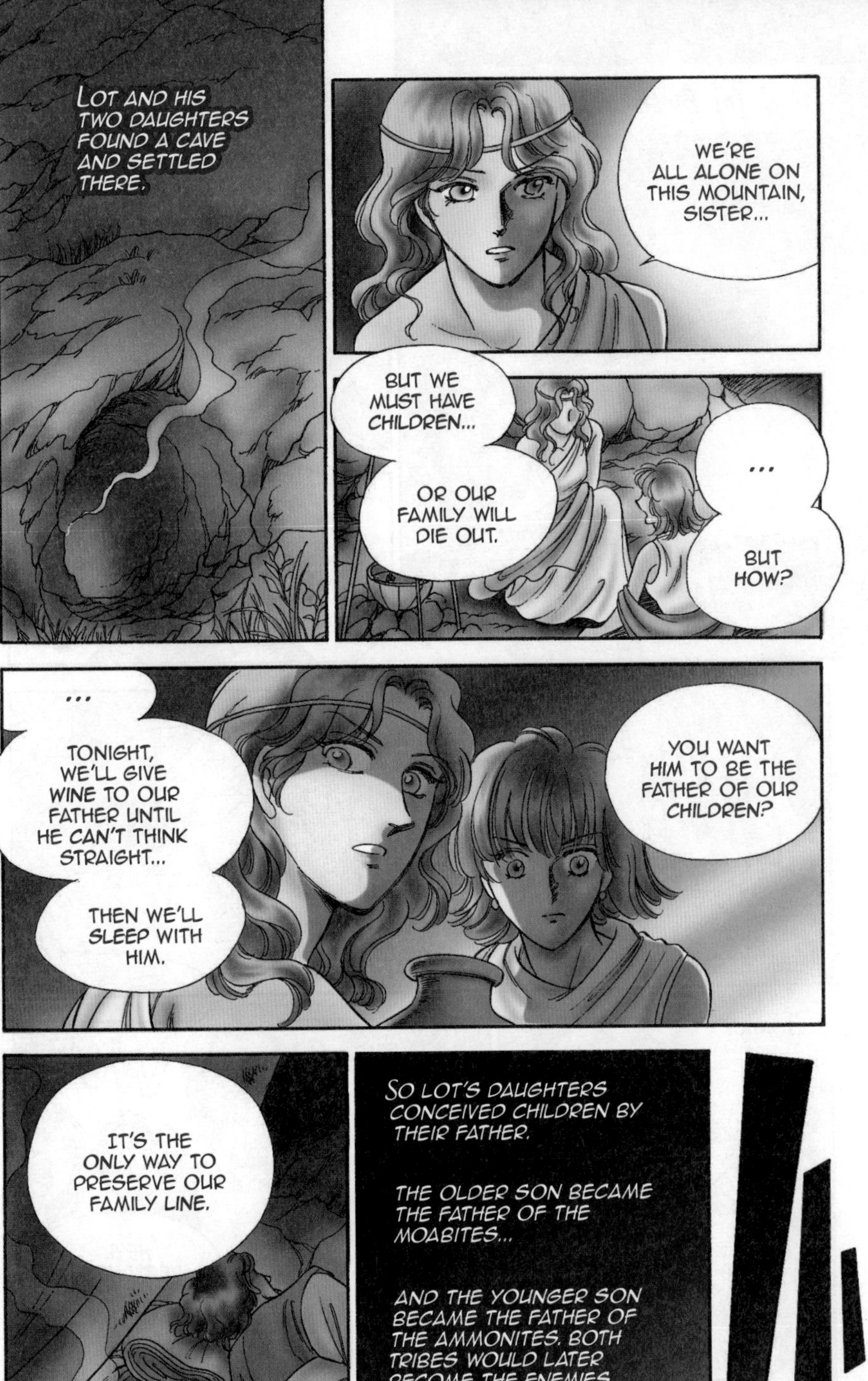
LOT AND HIS TWO DAUGHTERS FOUND A CAVE AND SETTLED THERE.
WE'RE ALL ALONE ON THIS MOUNTAIN, SISTER...
BUT WE MUST HAVE CHILDREN...
OR OUR FAMILY WILL DIE OUT.
...
BUT HOW?
...
TONIGHT, WE'LL GIVE WINE TO OUR FATHER UNTIL HE CAN'T THINK STRAIGHT...
THEN WE'LL SLEEP WITH HIM.
YOU WANT HIM TO BE THE FATHER OF OUR CHILDREN?
IT'S THE ONLY WAY TO PRESERVE OUR FAMILY LINE.
SO LOT'S DAUGHTERS CONCEIVED CHILDREN BY THEIR FATHER.
THE OLDER SON BECAME THE FATHER OF THE MOABITES...
AND THE YOUNGER SON BECAME THE FATHER OF THE AMMONITES. BOTH TRIBES WOULD LATER BECOME THE ENEMIES OF ISRAEL.

9. The Birth of Isaac

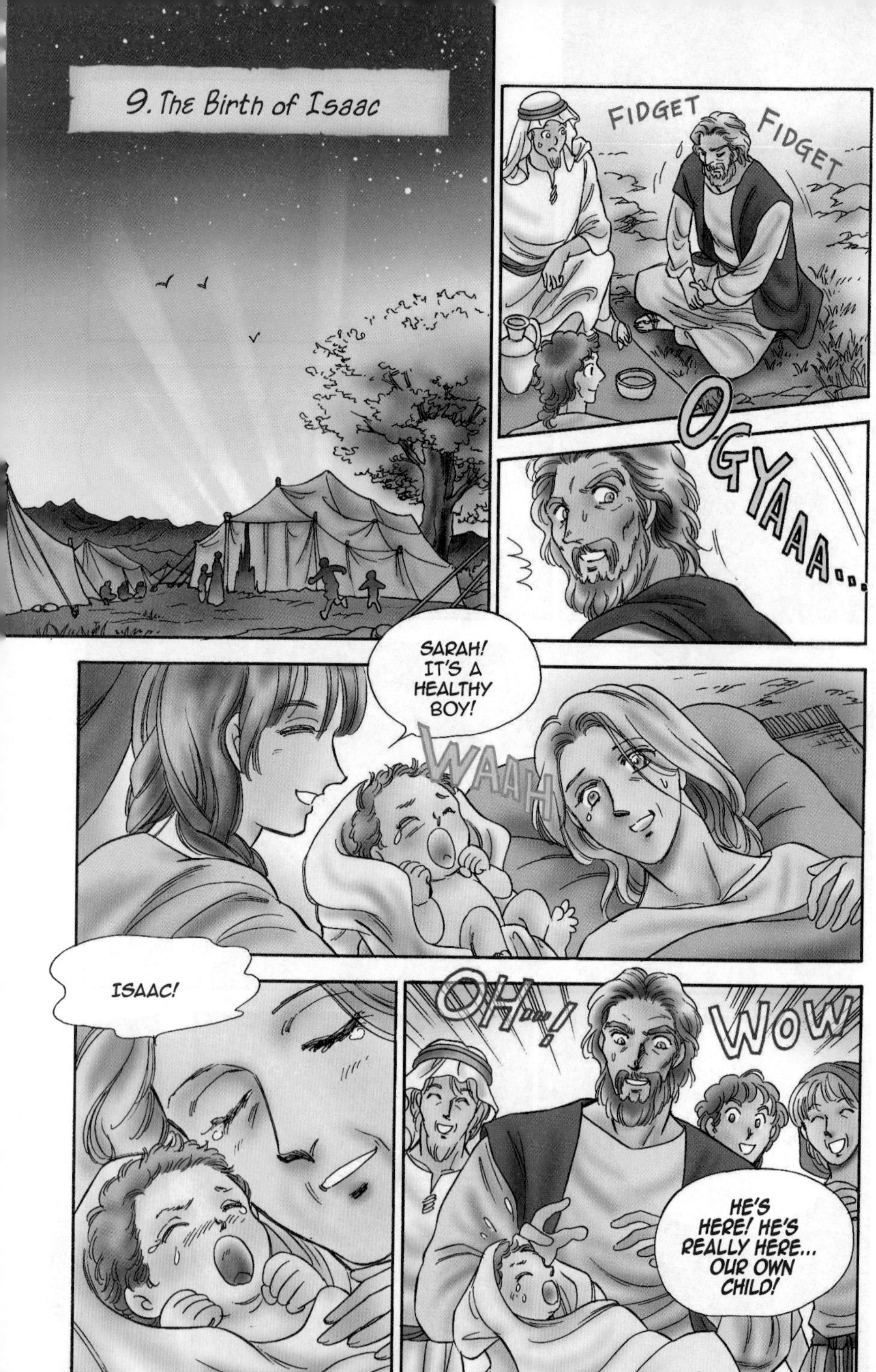

FIDGET
FIDGET
OGYAAA...
SARAH! IT'S A HEALTHY BOY!
WAAH
ISAAC!
OH...!
WOW
HE'S HERE! HE'S REALLY HERE... OUR OWN CHILD!

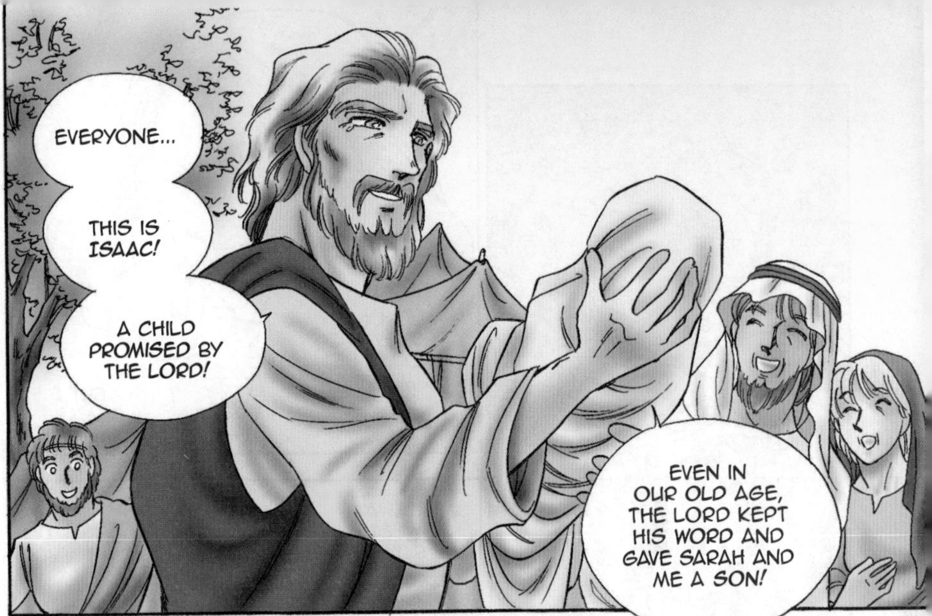
EVERYONE...
THIS IS ISAAC!
A CHILD PROMISED BY THE LORD!
EVEN IN OUR OLD AGE, THE LORD KEPT HIS WORD AND GAVE SARAH AND ME A SON!

ABRAHAM WAS 100 YEARS OLD WHEN ISAAC WAS BORN.

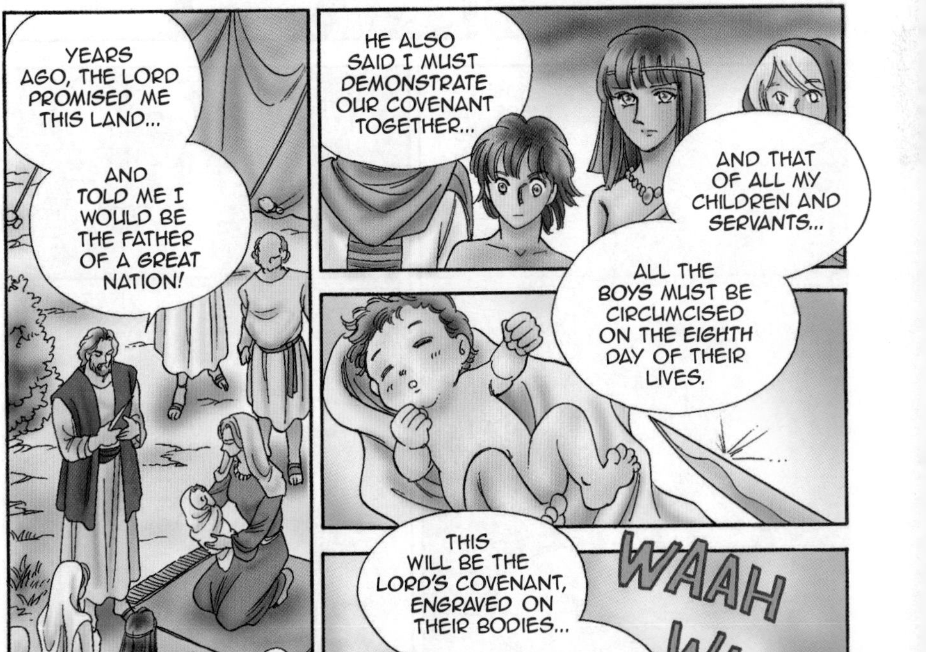
YEARS AGO, THE LORD PROMISED ME THIS LAND...
AND TOLD ME I WOULD BE THE FATHER OF A GREAT NATION!
HE ALSO SAID I MUST DEMONSTRATE OUR COVENANT TOGETHER...
AND THAT OF ALL MY CHILDREN AND SERVANTS...
ALL THE BOYS MUST BE CIRCUMCISED ON THE EIGHTH DAY OF THEIR LIVES.
THIS WILL BE THE LORD'S COVENANT, ENGRAVED ON THEIR BODIES...
A COVENANT THAT WILL LAST FOREVER!
WAAH
WAAHH

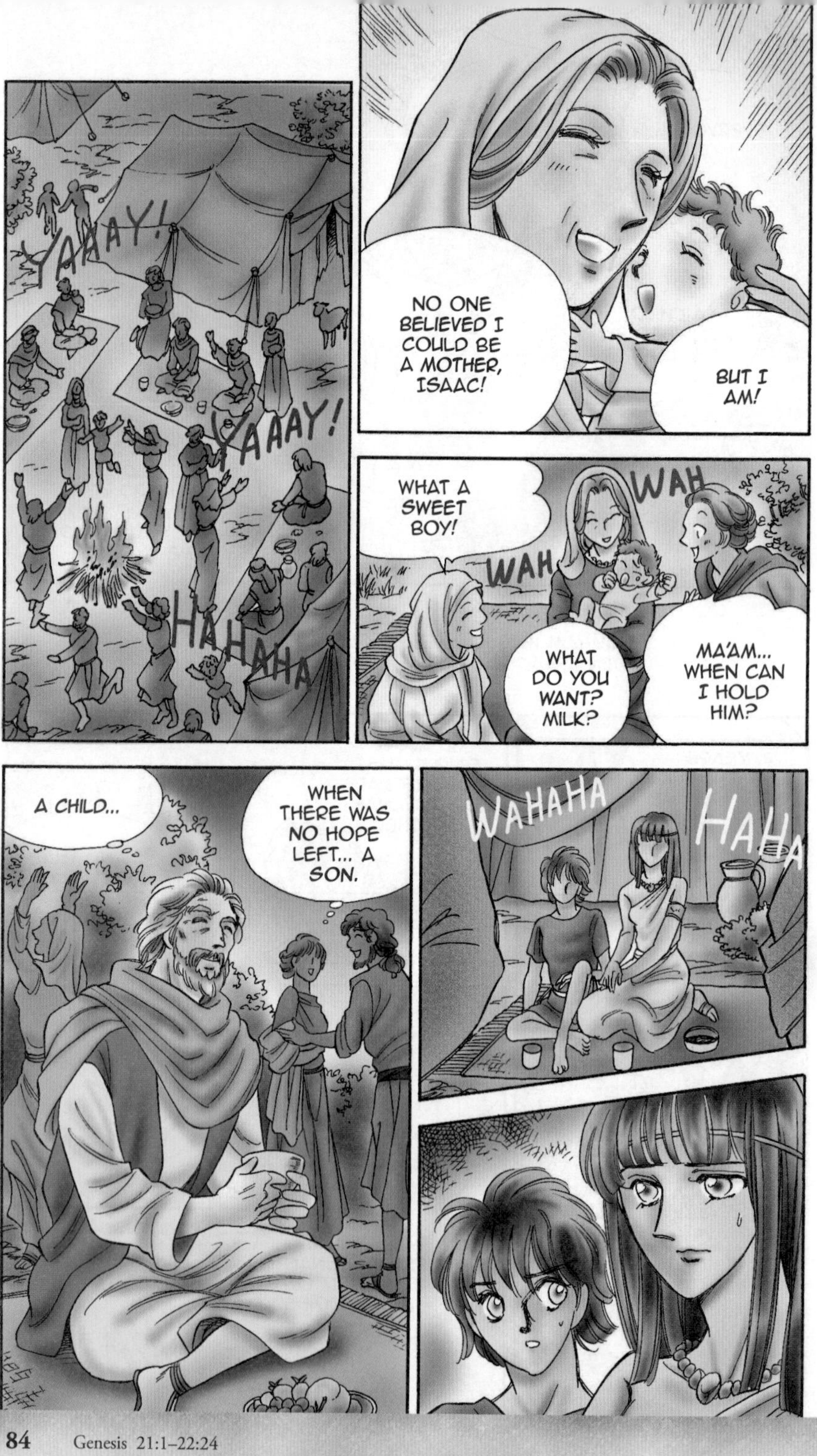
YAAAY!
YAAAY!
HAHAHA
NO ONE BELIEVED I COULD BE A MOTHER, ISAAC!
BUT I AM!
WHAT A SWEET BOY!
WAH
WAH
WHAT DO YOU WANT? MILK?
MA'AM... WHEN CAN I HOLD HIM?
A CHILD...
WHEN THERE WAS NO HOPE LEFT... A SON.
WAHAHA
HAHA

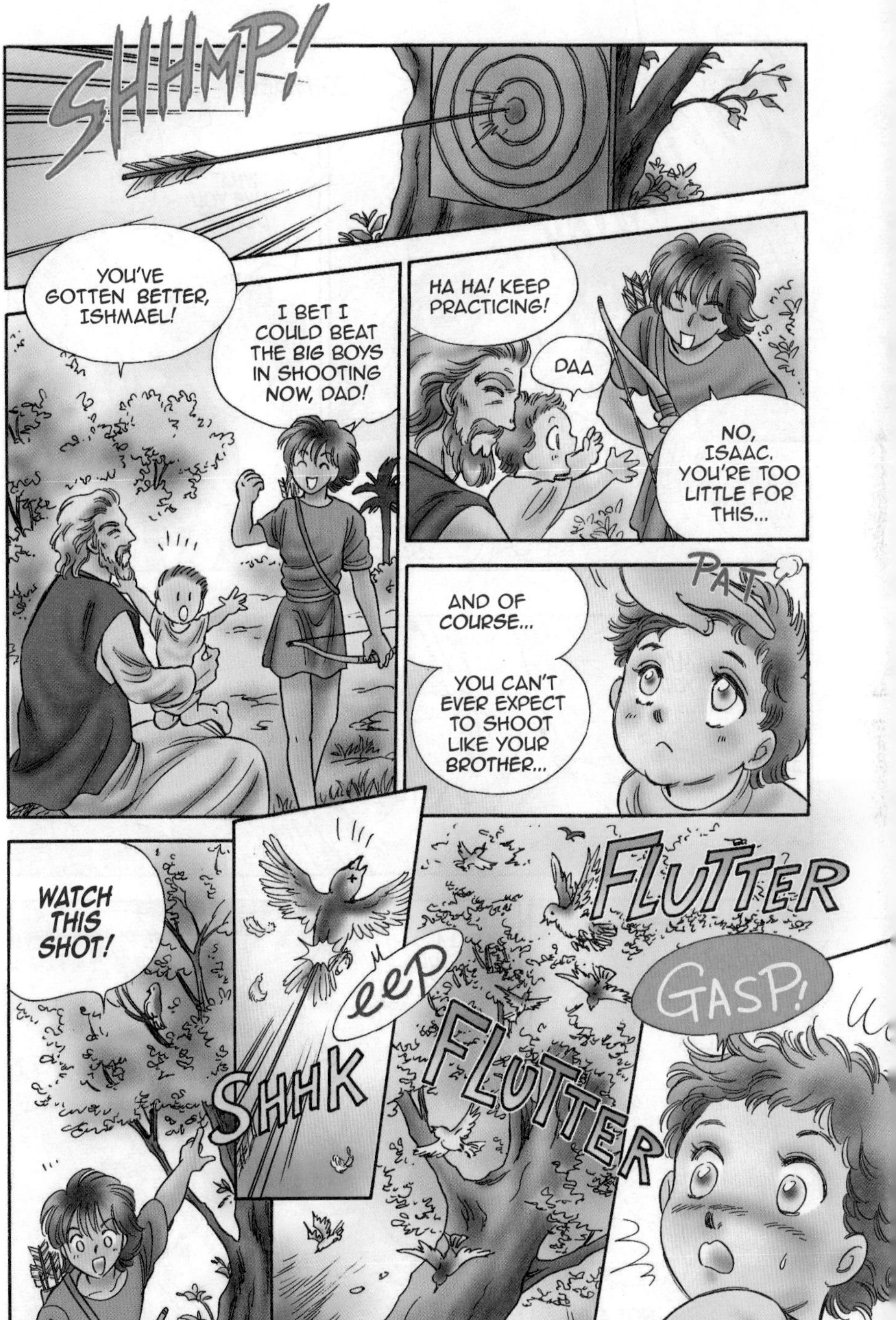
SHHMP!
YOU'VE GOTTEN BETTER, ISHMAEL!
I BET I COULD BEAT THE BIG BOYS IN SHOOTING NOW, DAD!
HA HA! KEEP PRACTICING!
DAA
NO, ISAAC. YOU'RE TOO LITTLE FOR THIS...
PAT
AND OF COURSE...
YOU CAN'T EVER EXPECT TO SHOOT LIKE YOUR BROTHER...
WATCH THIS SHOT!
SHHK
eep
FLUTTER
FLUTTER
GASP!

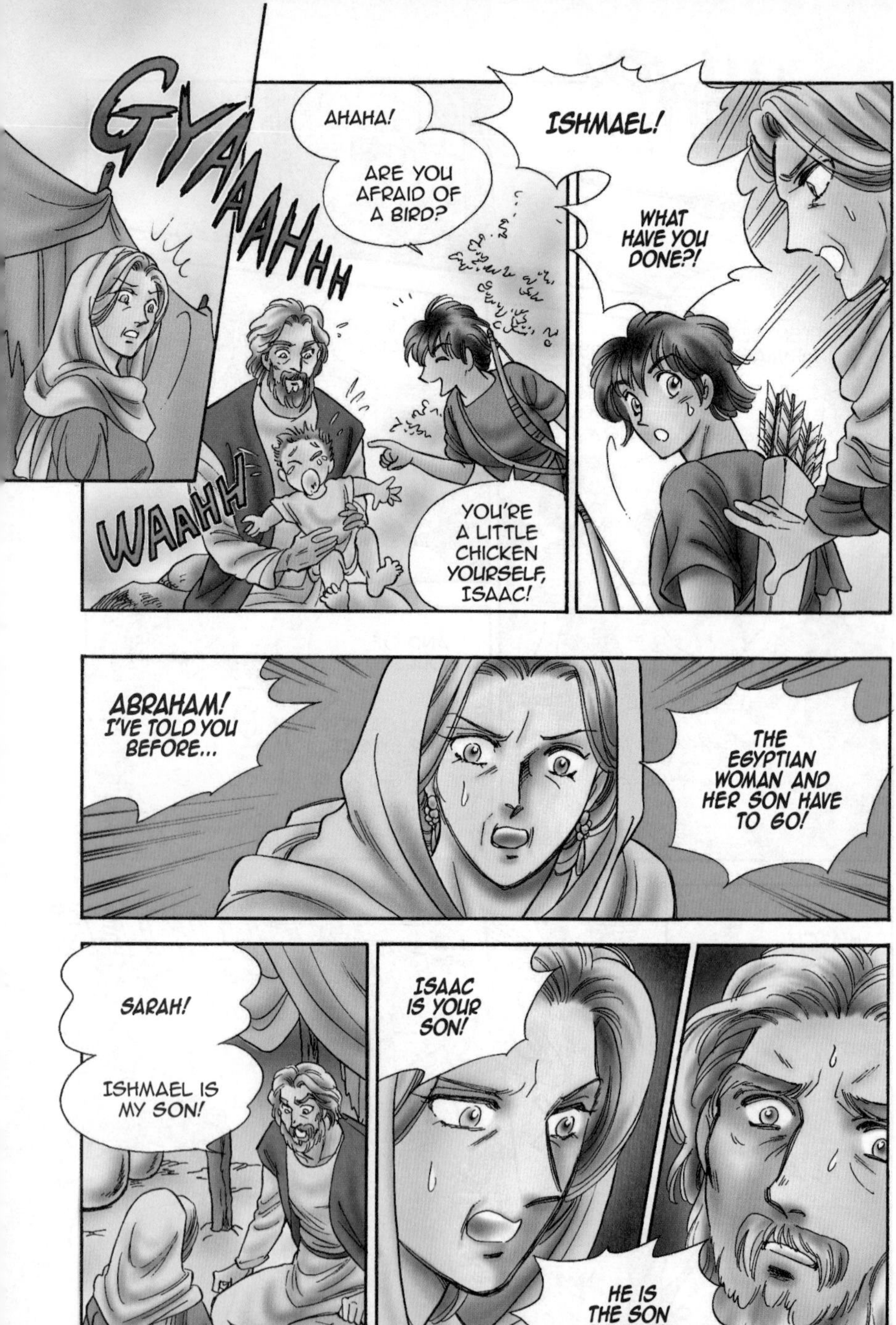
GYAAAAHHH
AHAHA!
ARE YOU AFRAID OF A BIRD?
WAAHH
YOU'RE A LITTLE CHICKEN YOURSELF, ISAAC!
ISHMAEL!
WHAT HAVE YOU DONE?!
ABRAHAM! I'VE TOLD YOU BEFORE...
THE EGYPTIAN WOMAN AND HER SON HAVE TO GO!
SARAH!
ISHMAEL IS MY SON!
NOT ANY MORE!
ISAAC IS YOUR SON!
HE IS THE SON OF GOD'S PROMISE!

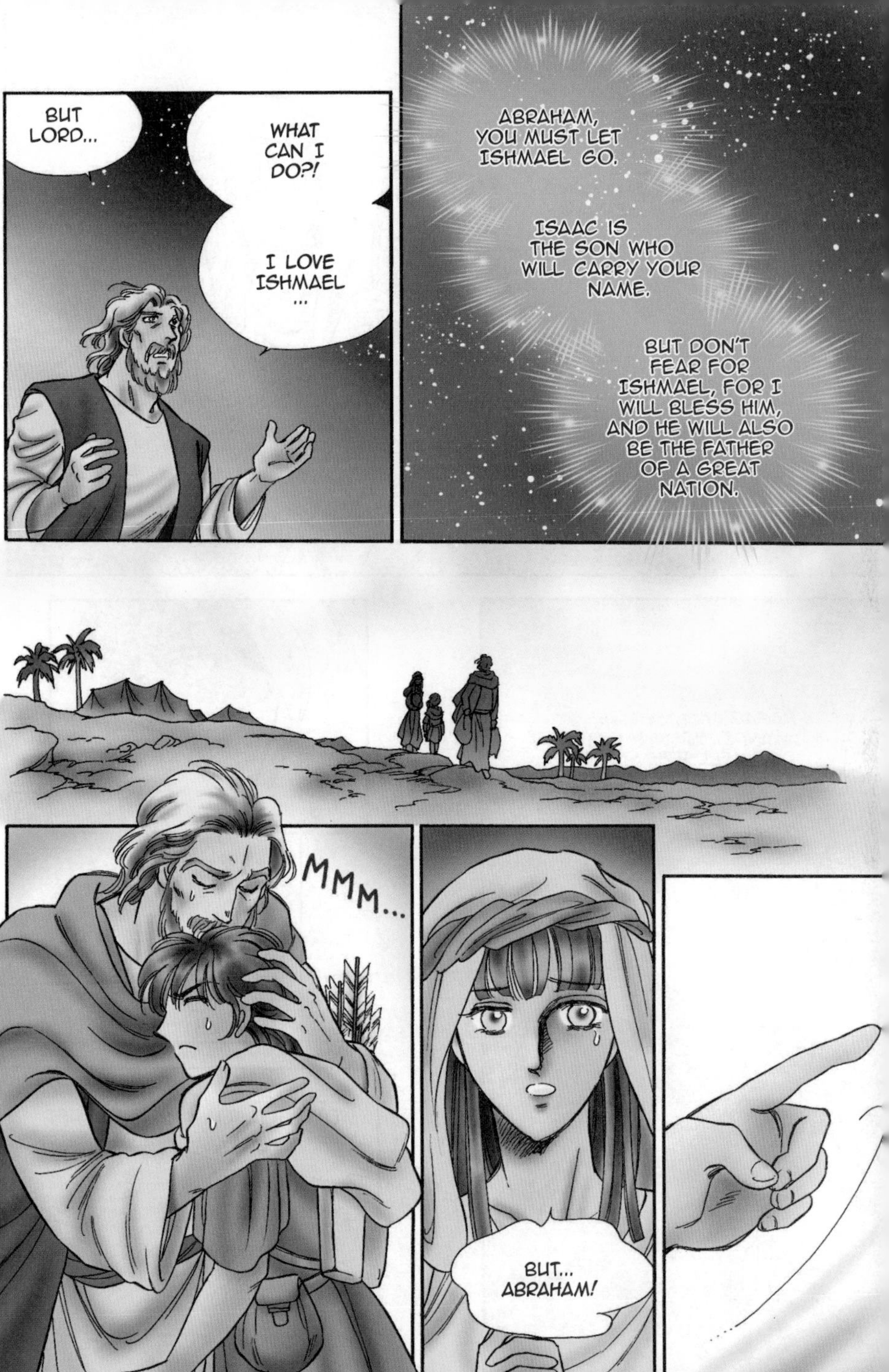
BUT LORD...
WHAT CAN I DO?!
I LOVE ISHMAEL ...
ABRAHAM, YOU MUST LET ISHMAEL GO.
ISAAC IS THE SON WHO WILL CARRY YOUR NAME.
BUT DON'T FEAR FOR ISHMAEL, FOR I WILL BLESS HIM, AND HE WILL ALSO BE THE FATHER OF A GREAT NATION.
MMM...
BUT... ABRAHAM!
...

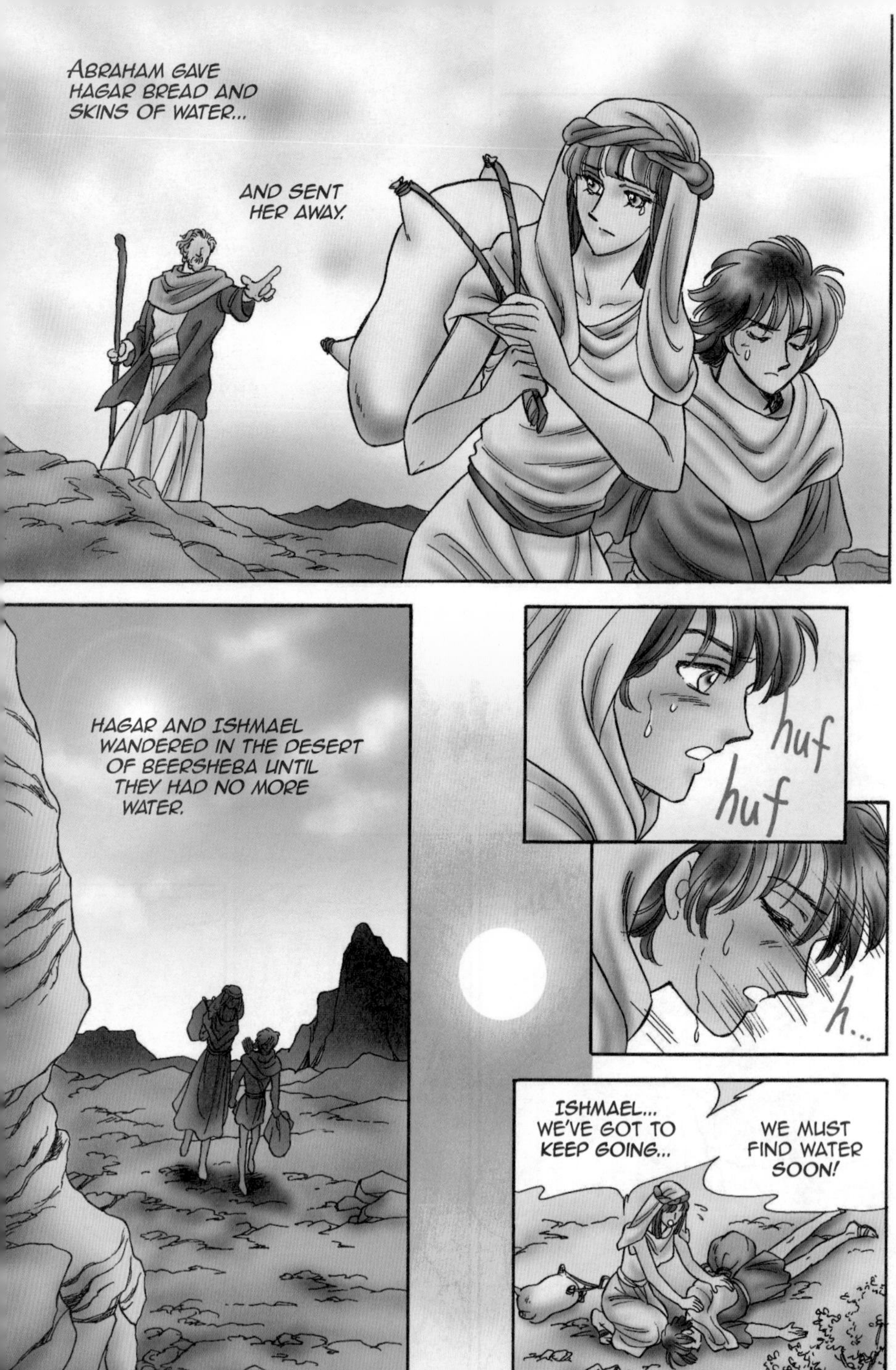
ABRAHAM GAVE HAGAR BREAD AND SKINS OF WATER...
AND SENT HER AWAY.
HAGAR AND ISHMAEL WANDERED IN THE DESERT OF BEERSHEBA UNTIL THEY HAD NO MORE WATER.
huf huf
h...
ISHMAEL... WE'VE GOT TO KEEP GOING...
WE MUST FIND WATER SOON!

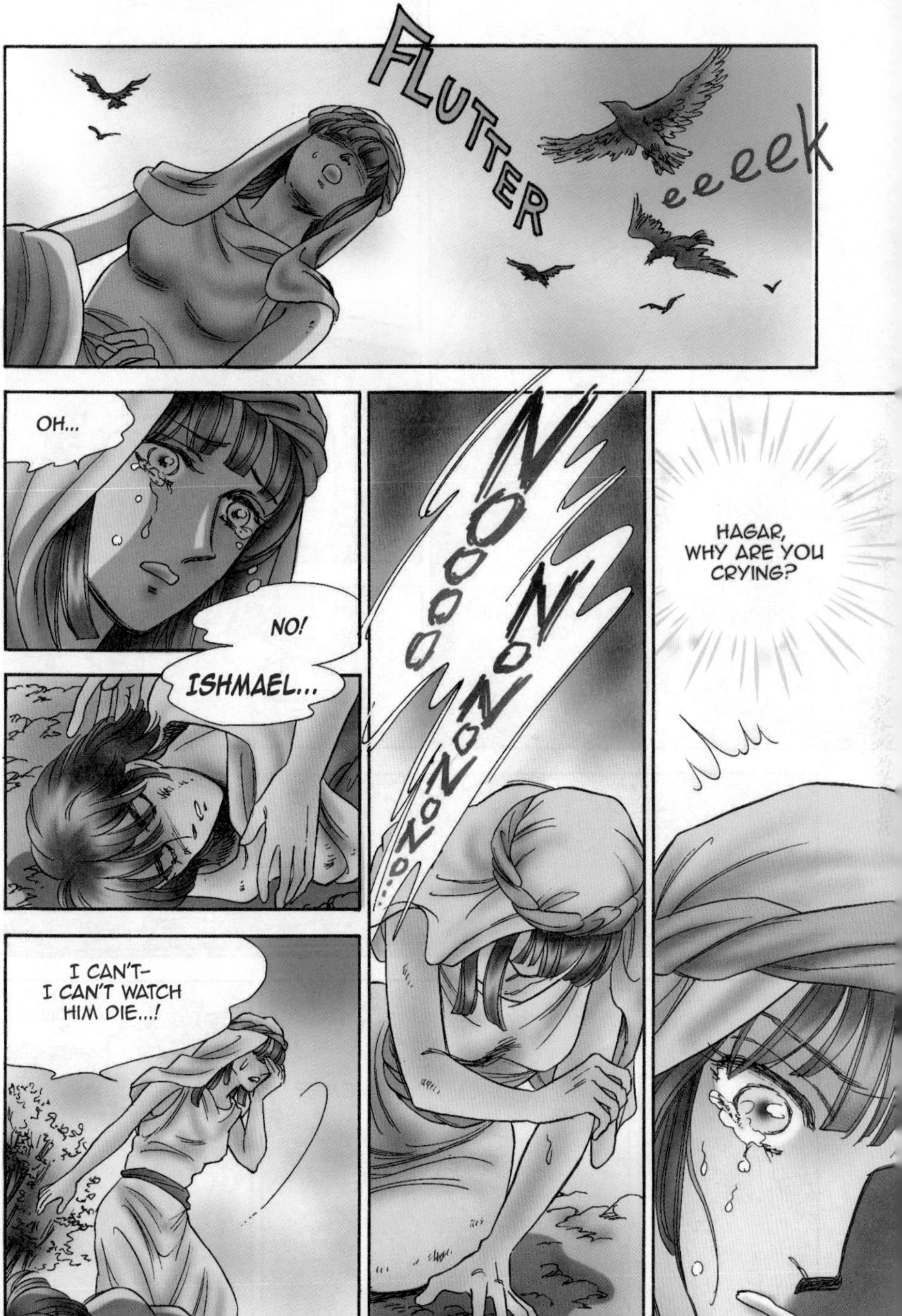
FLUTTER
eeeek
OH...
NO!
ISHMAEL...
I CAN'T-
I CAN'T WATCH
HIM DIE...!
NOOOOOOONONONONONONONO
HAGAR,
WHY ARE YOU
CRYING?

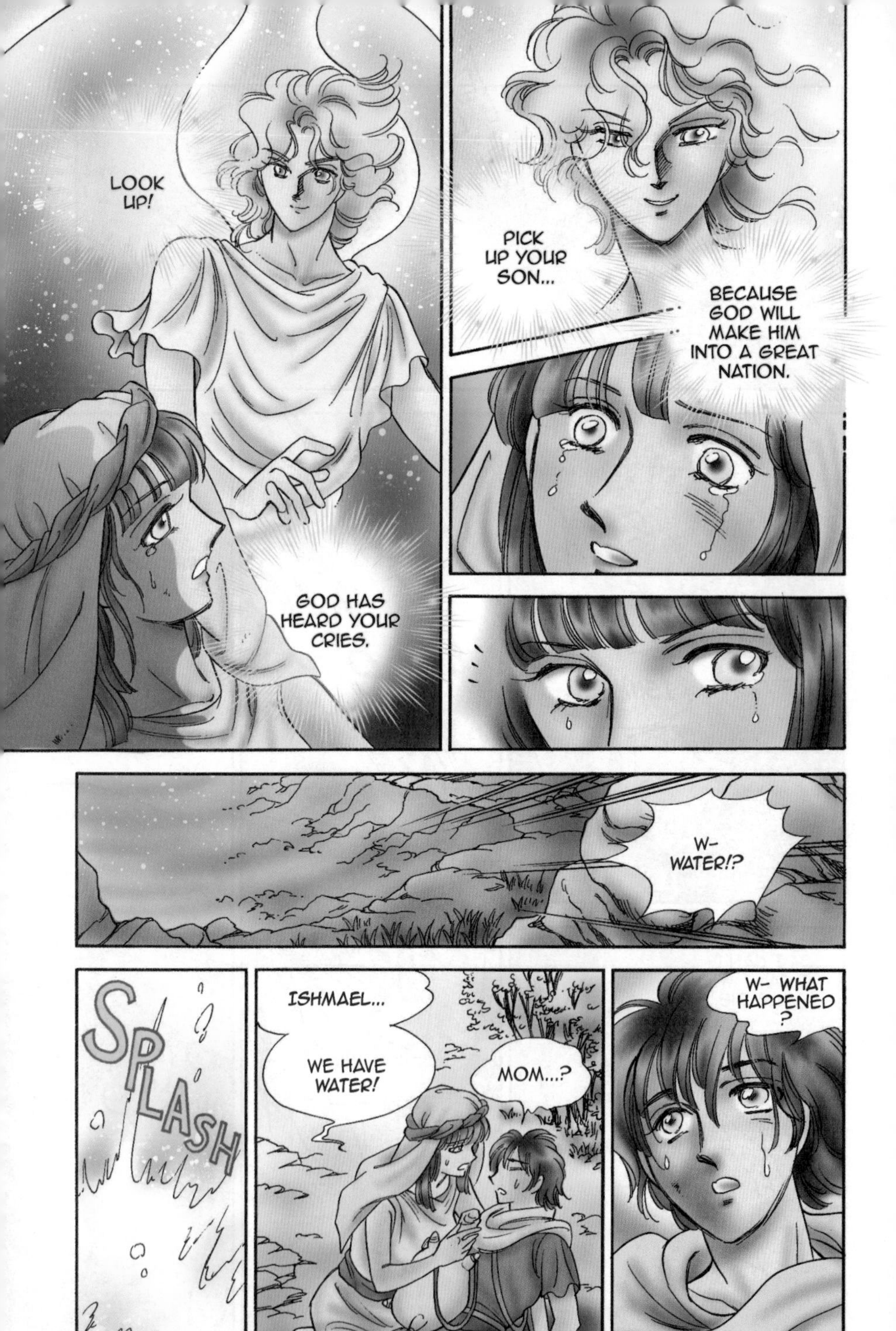
LOOK UP!
GOD HAS HEARD YOUR CRIES.
PICK UP YOUR SON...
BECAUSE GOD WILL MAKE HIM INTO A GREAT NATION.
W- WATER!?
SPLASH
ISHMAEL...
WE HAVE WATER!
MOM...?
W- WHAT HAPPENED ?

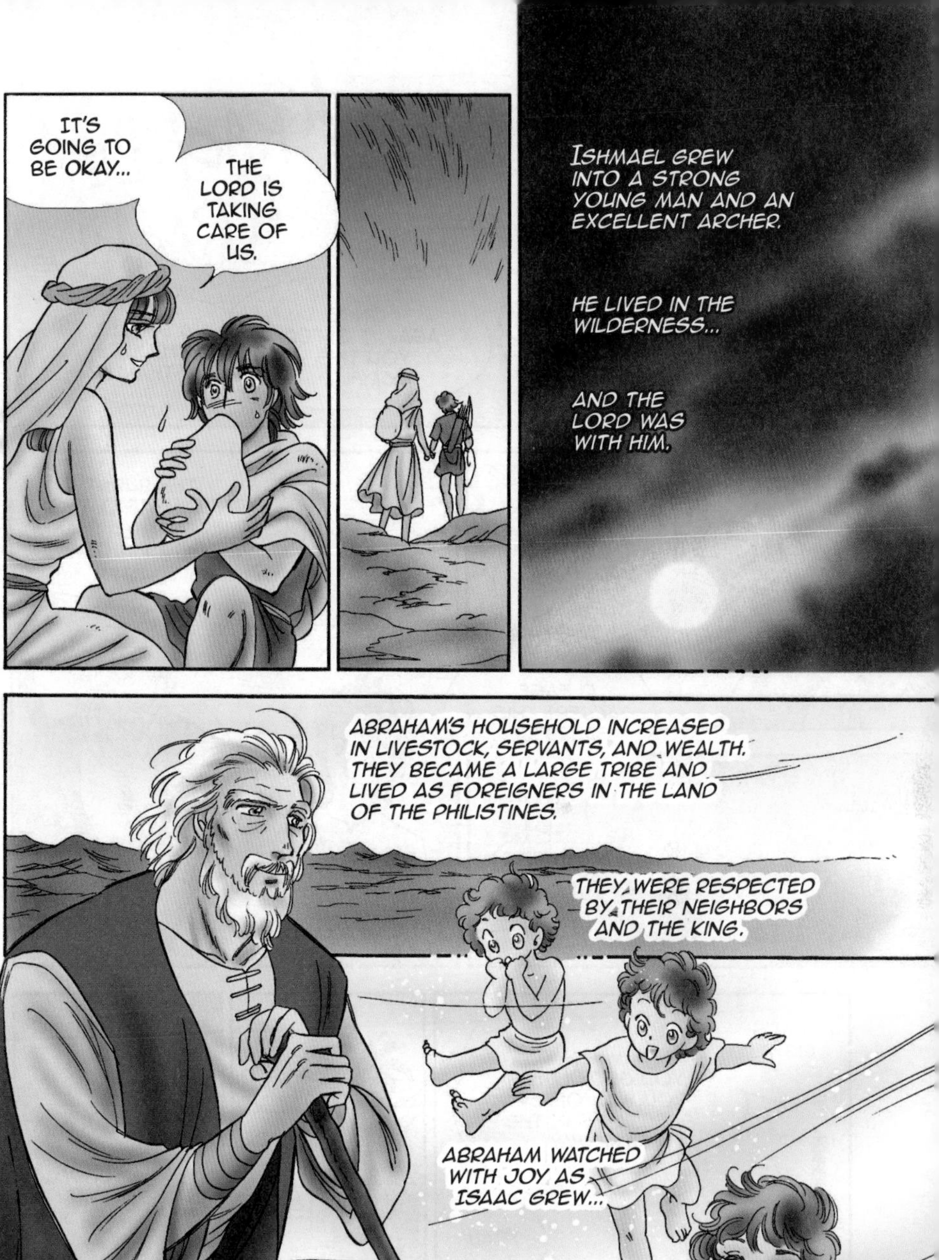

IT'S GOING TO BE OKAY...
THE LORD IS TAKING CARE OF US.
ISHMAEL GREW INTO A STRONG YOUNG MAN AND AN EXCELLENT ARCHER.
HE LIVED IN THE WILDERNESS...
AND THE LORD WAS WITH HIM.
ABRAHAM'S HOUSEHOLD INCREASED IN LIVESTOCK, SERVANTS, AND WEALTH. THEY BECAME A LARGE TRIBE AND LIVED AS FOREIGNERS IN THE LAND OF THE PHILISTINES.
THEY WERE RESPECTED BY THEIR NEIGHBORS AND THE KING.
ABRAHAM WATCHED WITH JOY AS ISAAC GREW...
INTO A YOUNG MAN.

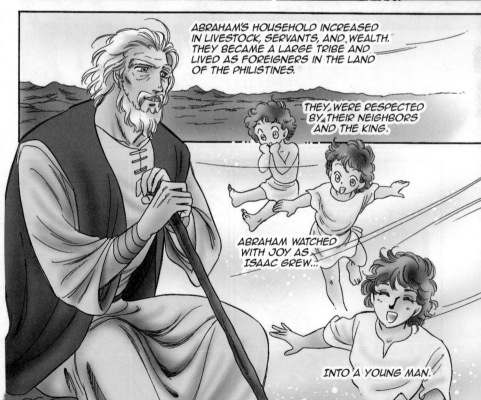

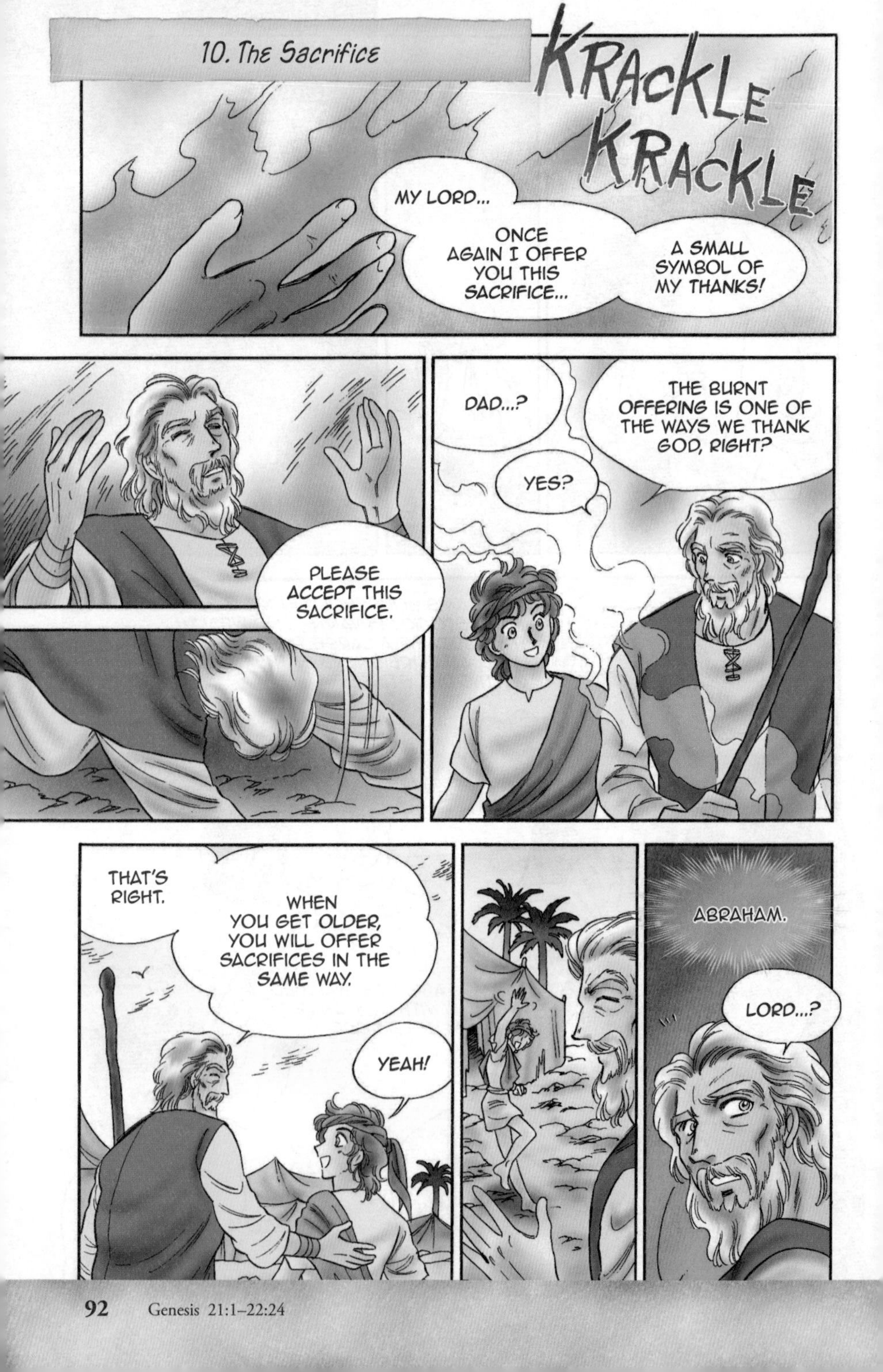
10. The Sacrifice
KRACKLE
KRACKLE
KRACKLE
MY LORD...
ONCE AGAIN I OFFER YOU THIS SACRIFICE...
A SMALL SYMBOL OF MY THANKS!
PLEASE ACCEPT THIS SACRIFICE.
DAD...?
YES?
THE BURNT OFFERING IS ONE OF THE WAYS WE THANK GOD, RIGHT?
THAT'S RIGHT.
WHEN YOU GET OLDER, YOU WILL OFFER SACRIFICES IN THE SAME WAY.
YEAH!
ABRAHAM.
LORD...?

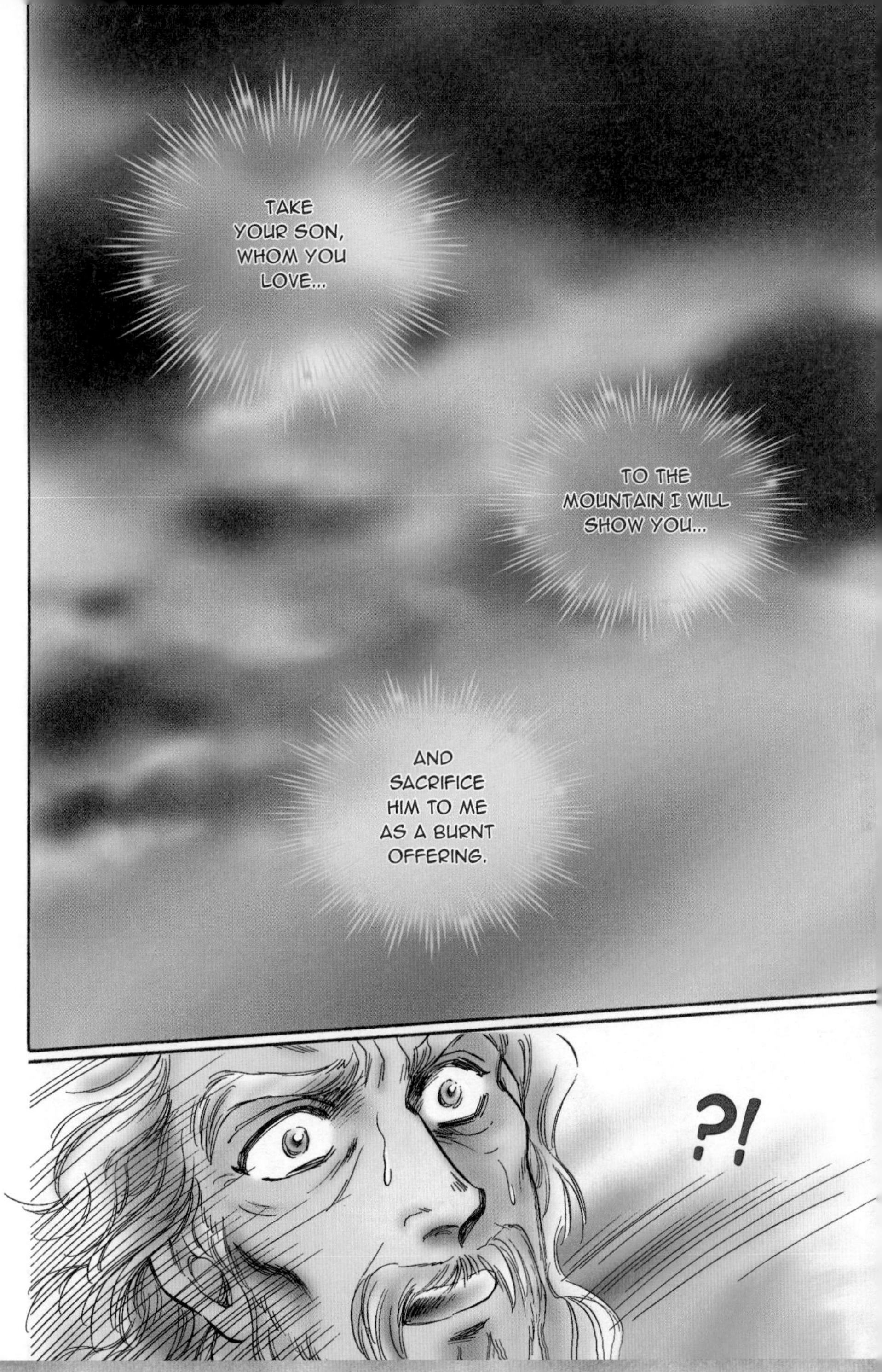
TAKE YOUR SON, WHOM YOU LOVE...
TO THE MOUNTAIN I WILL SHOW YOU...
AND SACRIFICE HIM TO ME AS A BURNT OFFERING.
?!

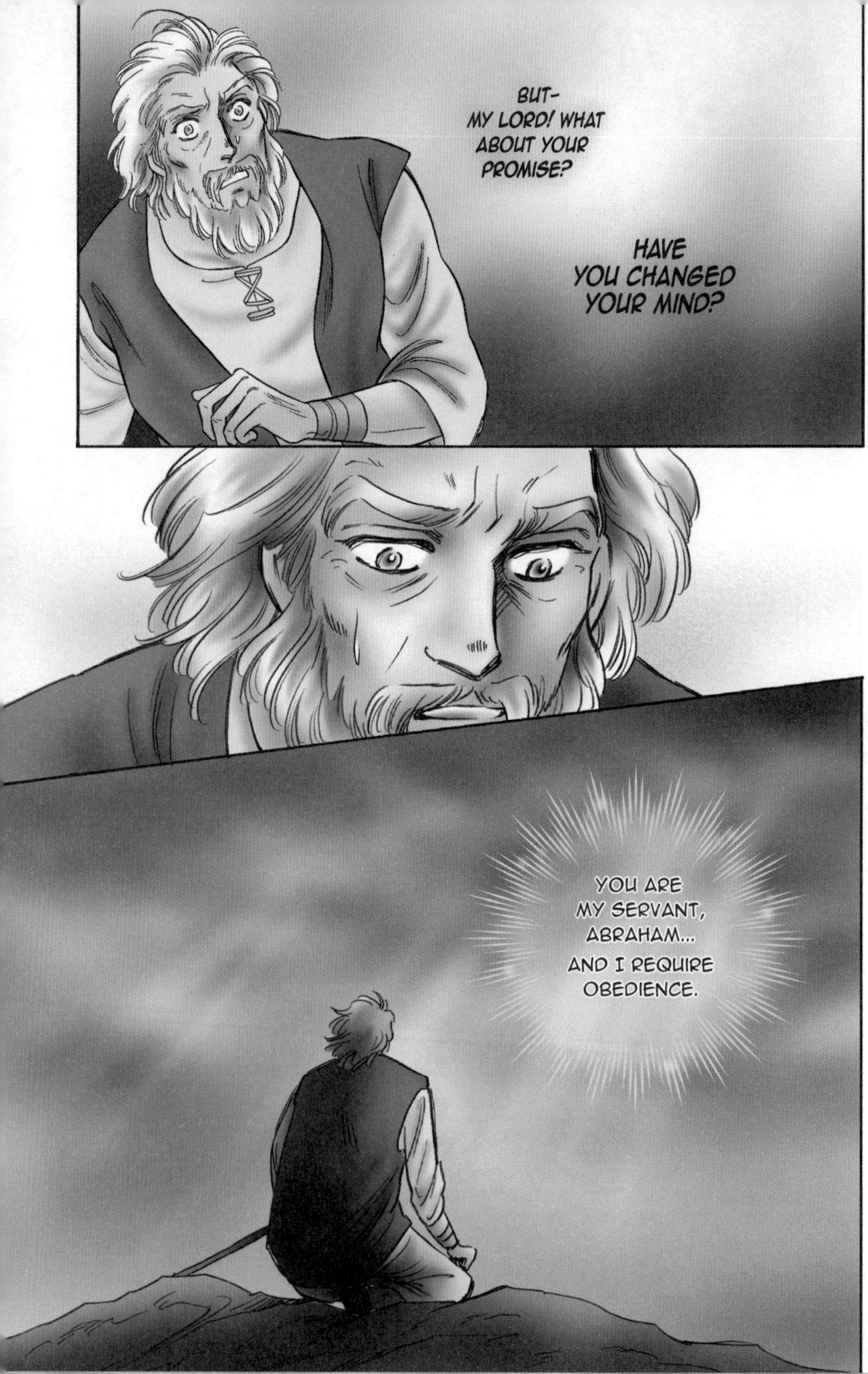
BUT- MY LORD! WHAT ABOUT YOUR PROMISE?
HAVE YOU CHANGED YOUR MIND?
YOU ARE MY SERVANT, ABRAHAM...
AND I REQUIRE OBEDIENCE.

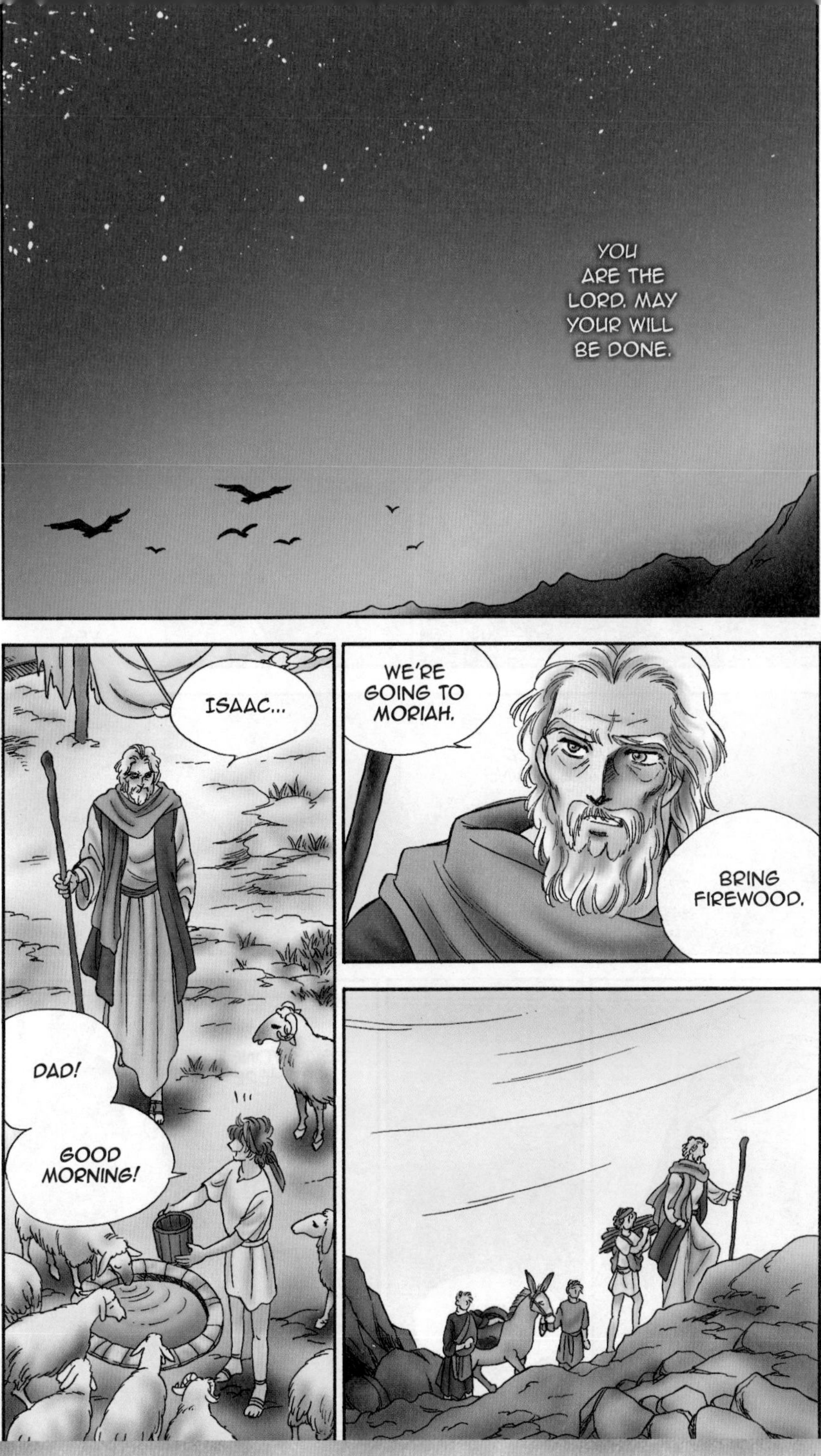
YOU ARE THE LORD. MAY YOUR WILL BE DONE.
ISAAC...
WE'RE GOING TO MORIAH.
BRING FIREWOOD.
DAD!
GOOD MORNING!

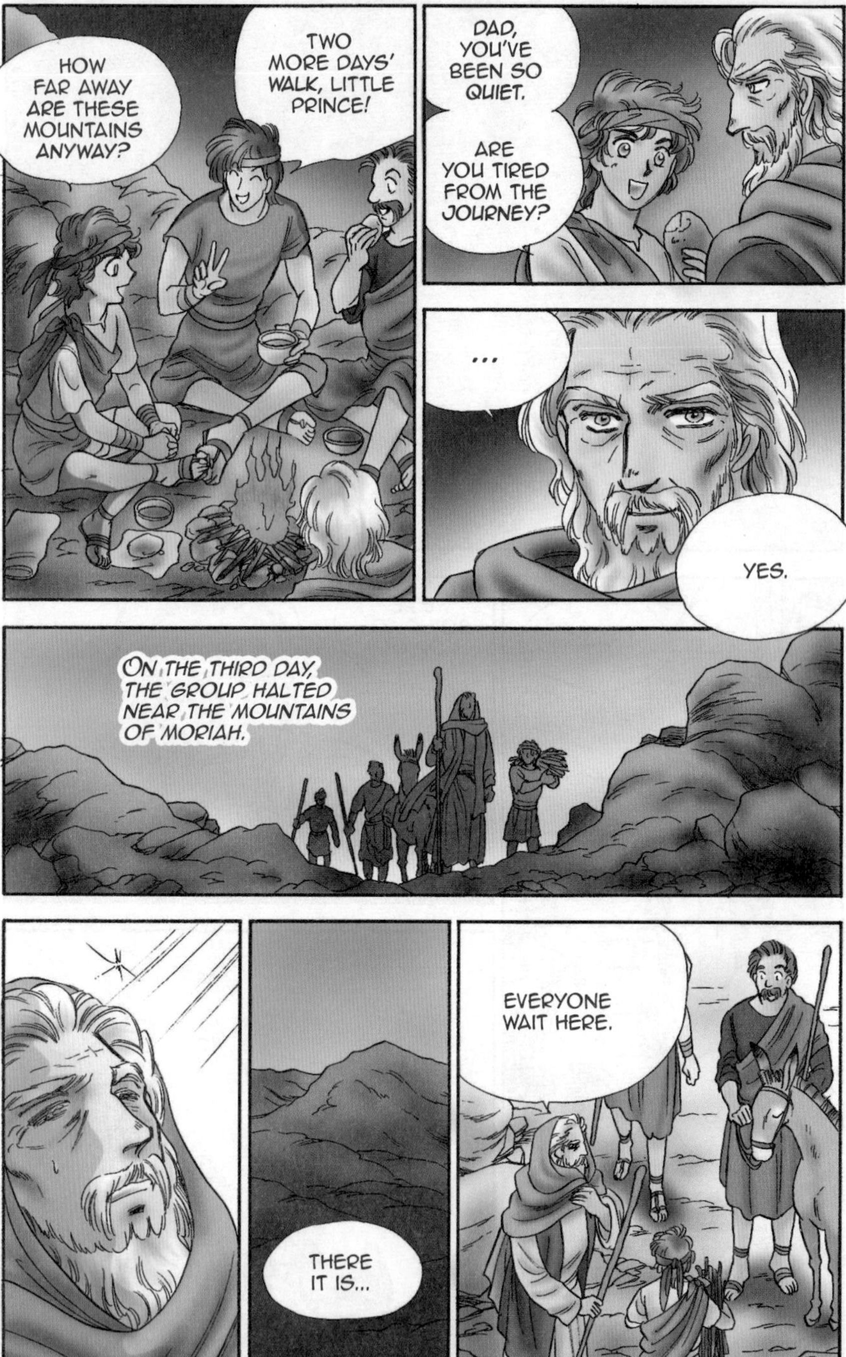
HOW FAR AWAY ARE THESE MOUNTAINS ANYWAY?
TWO MORE DAYS' WALK, LITTLE PRINCE!
DAD, YOU'VE BEEN SO QUIET.
ARE YOU TIRED FROM THE JOURNEY?
...
YES.
ON THE THIRD DAY, THE GROUP HALTED NEAR THE MOUNTAINS OF MORIAH.
THERE IT IS...
EVERYONE WAIT HERE.

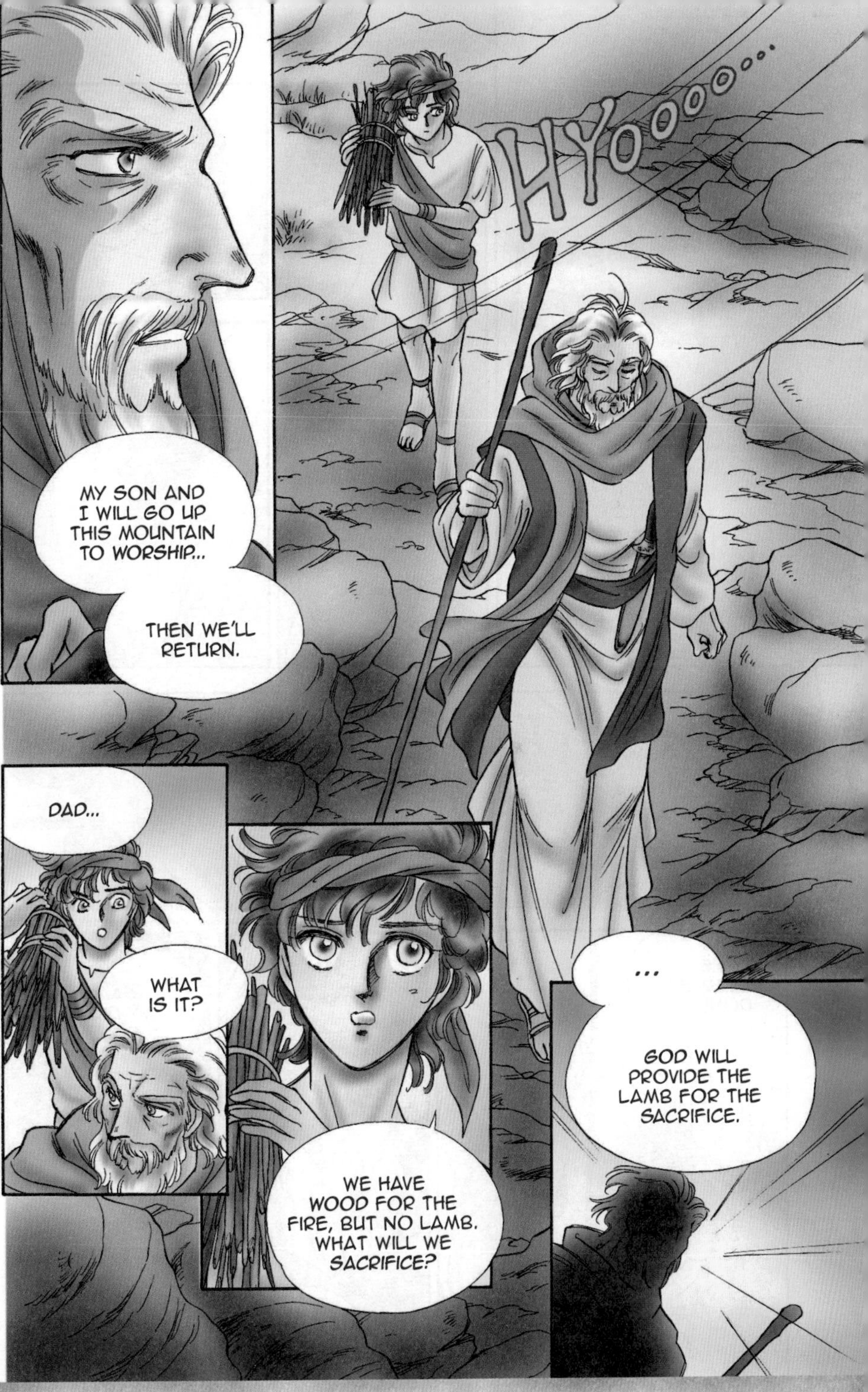
HYOOOO...
MY SON AND I WILL GO UP THIS MOUNTAIN TO WORSHIP...
THEN WE'LL RETURN.
DAD...
WHAT IS IT?
WE HAVE WOOD FOR THE FIRE, BUT NO LAMB. WHAT WILL WE SACRIFICE?
...
GOD WILL PROVIDE THE LAMB FOR THE SACRIFICE.

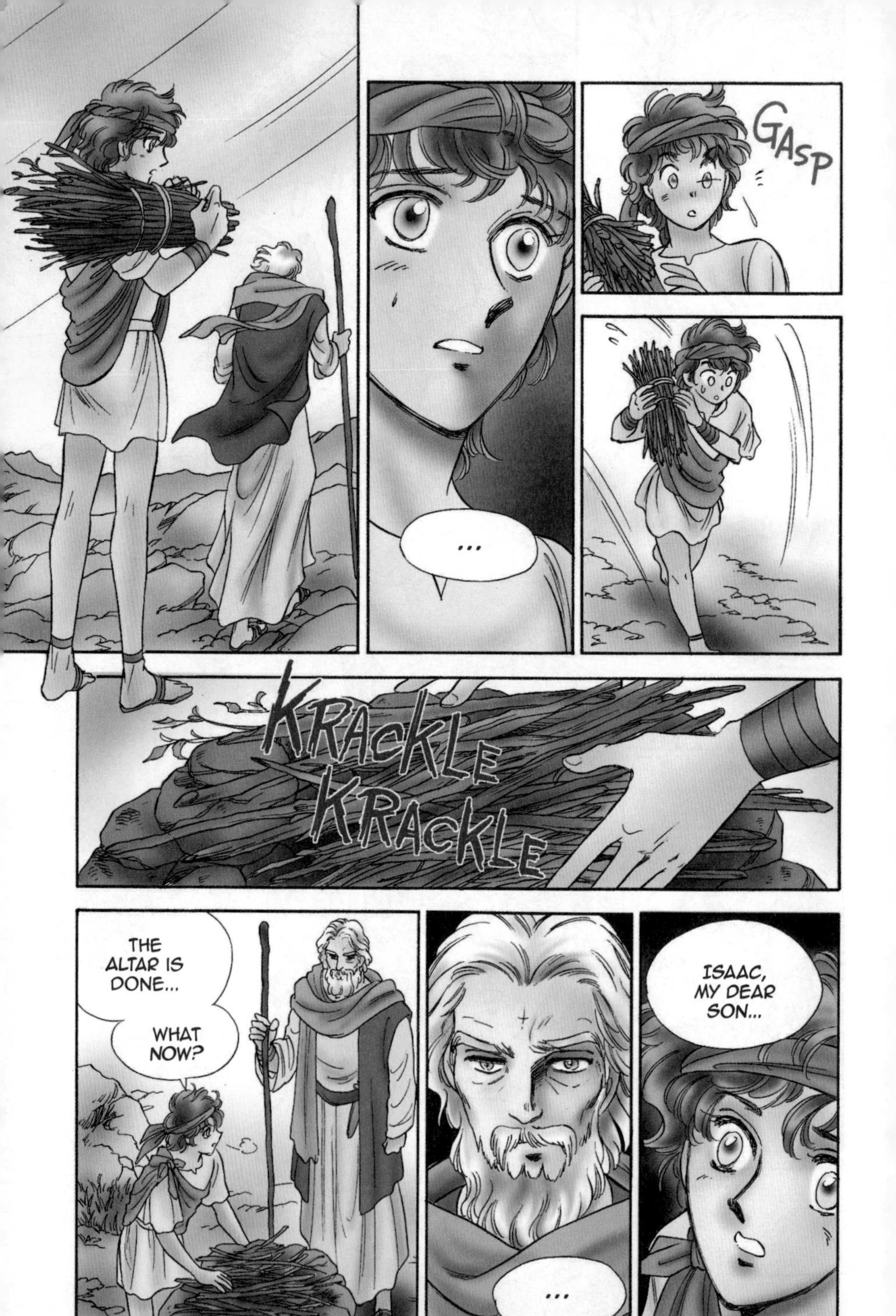
GASP
...
KRACKLE KRACKLE
THE ALTAR IS DONE...
WHAT NOW?
...
ISAAC, MY DEAR SON...

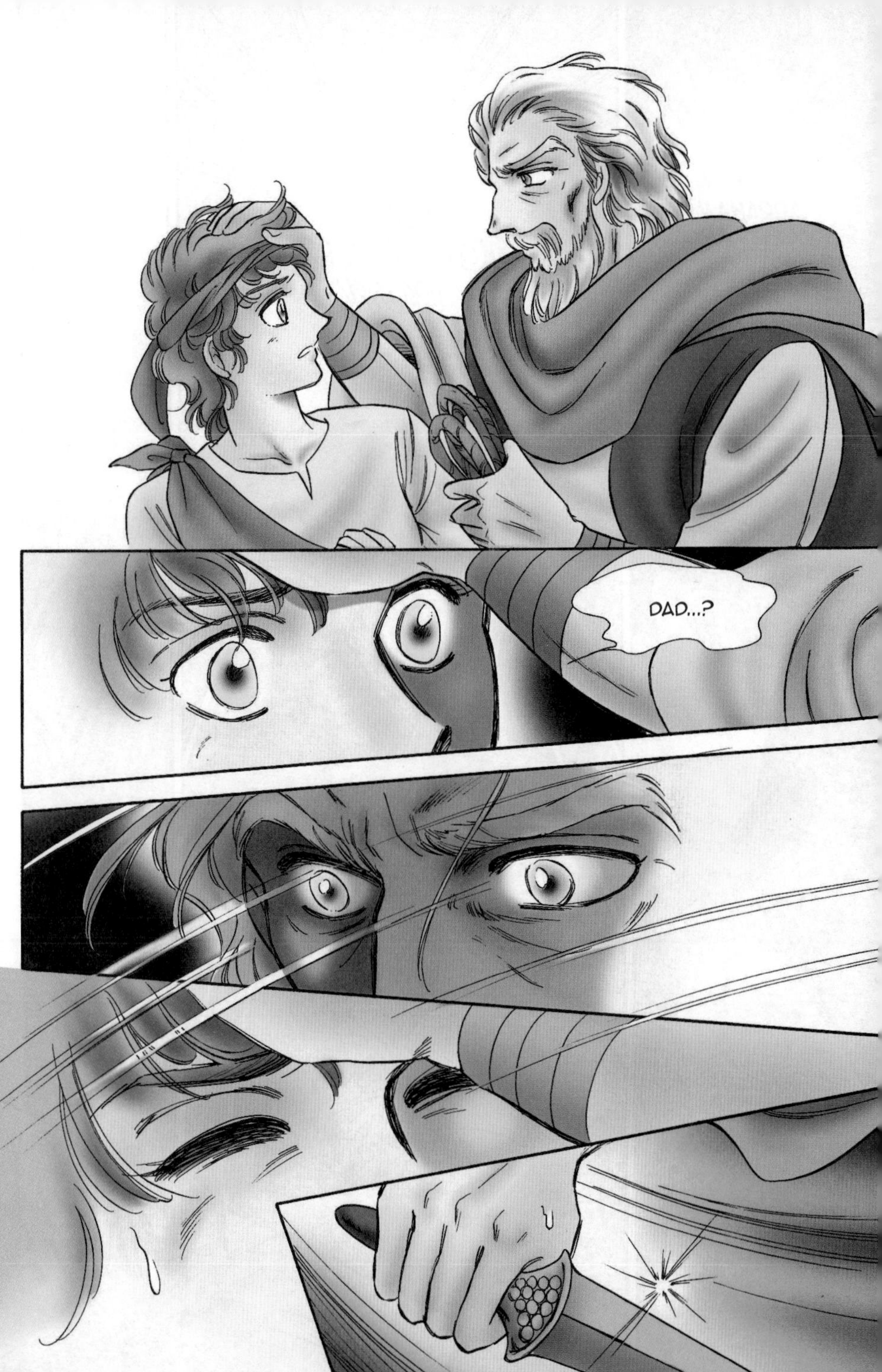
DAD...?

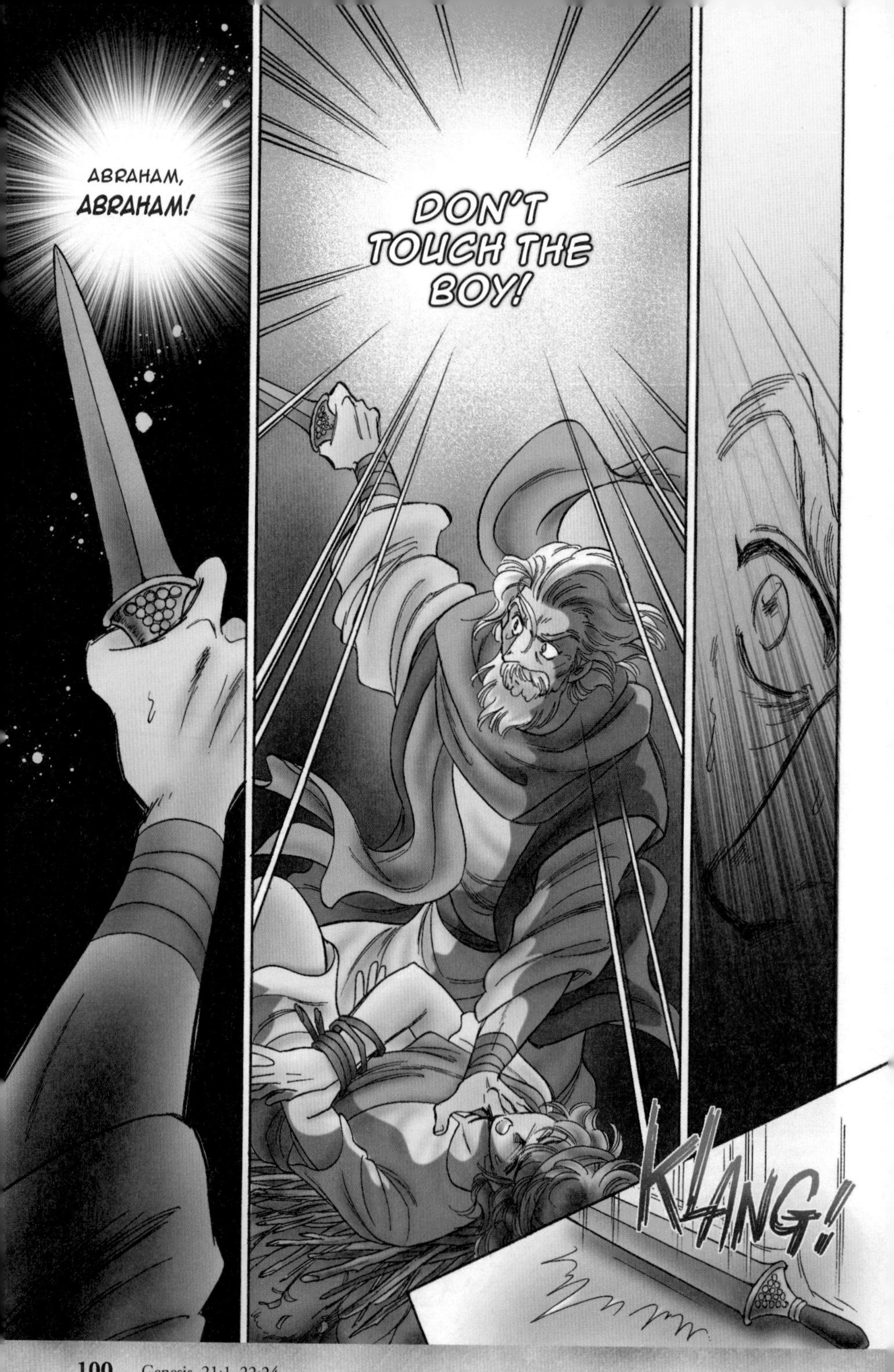
ABRAHAM, ABRAHAM!
DON'T TOUCH THE BOY!
KLANG!

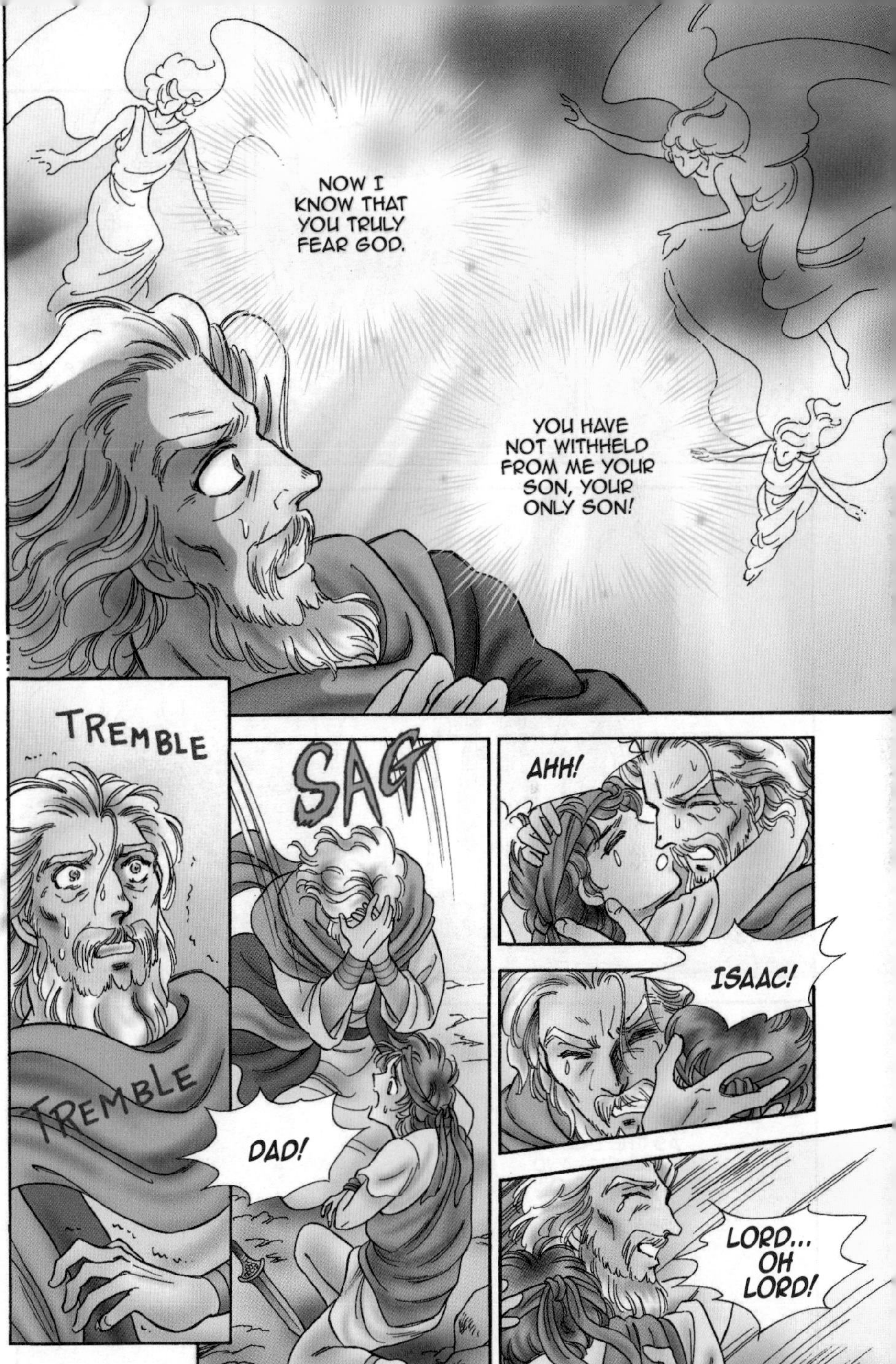
NOW I KNOW THAT YOU TRULY FEAR GOD.
YOU HAVE NOT WITHHELD FROM ME YOUR SON, YOUR ONLY SON!
TREMBLE
TREMBLE
SAG
DAD!
AHH!
ISAAC!
LORD... OH LORD!

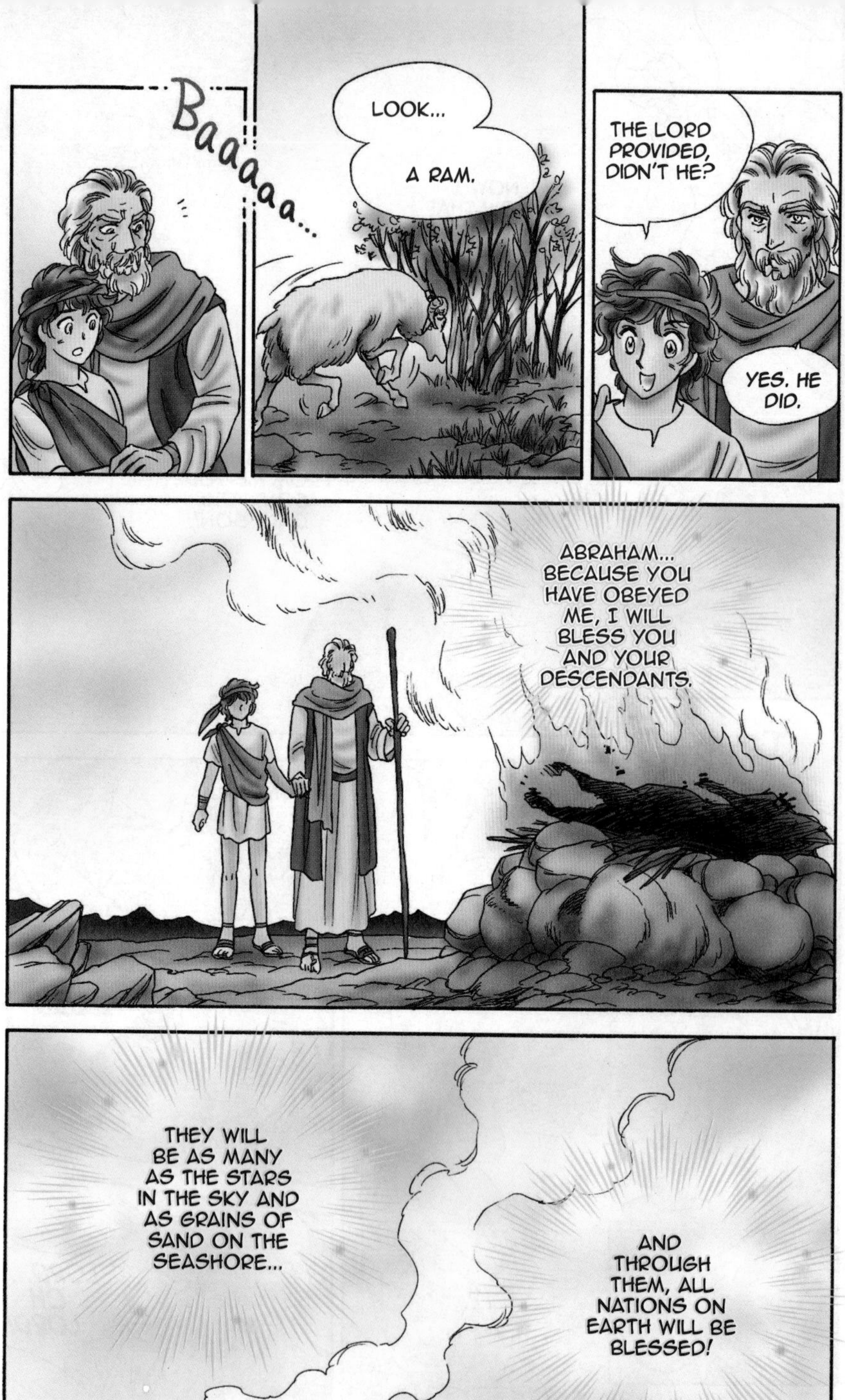
Baaaaaa...
LOOK...
A RAM.
THE LORD PROVIDED, DIDN'T HE?
YES. HE DID.
ABRAHAM... BECAUSE YOU HAVE OBEYED ME, I WILL BLESS YOU AND YOUR DESCENDANTS.
THEY WILL BE AS MANY AS THE STARS IN THE SKY AND AS GRAINS OF SAND ON THE SEASHORE...
AND THROUGH THEM, ALL NATIONS ON EARTH WILL BE BLESSED!

11. Death and Marriage

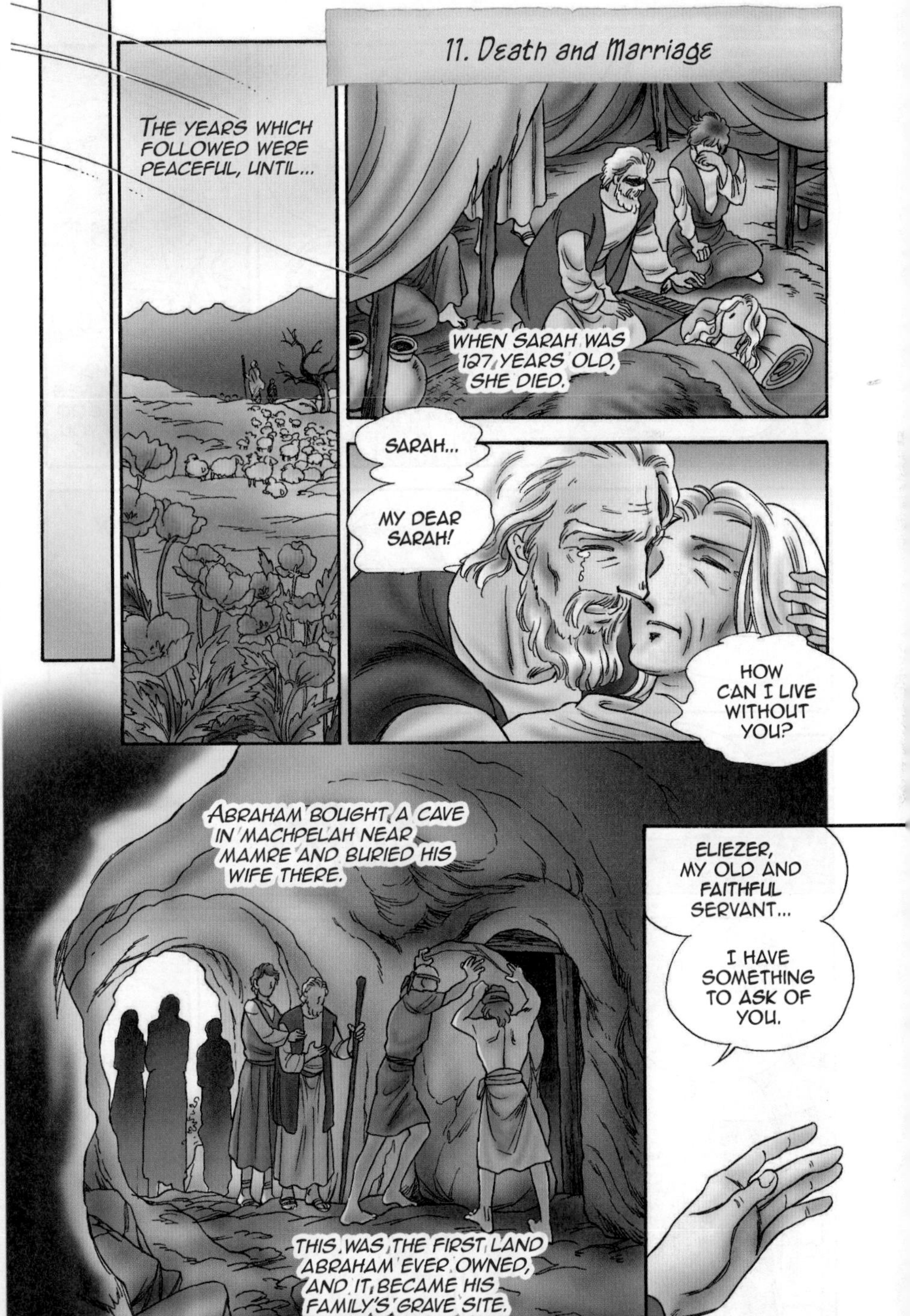
THE YEARS WHICH FOLLOWED WERE PEACEFUL, UNTIL...
WHEN SARAH WAS 127 YEARS OLD, SHE DIED.
SARAH...
MY DEAR SARAH!
HOW CAN I LIVE WITHOUT YOU?
ABRAHAM BOUGHT A CAVE IN MACHPELAH NEAR MAMRE AND BURIED HIS WIFE THERE.
THIS WAS THE FIRST LAND ABRAHAM EVER OWNED, AND IT BECAME HIS FAMILY'S GRAVE SITE.
ELIEZER, MY OLD AND FAITHFUL SERVANT...
I HAVE SOMETHING TO ASK OF YOU.

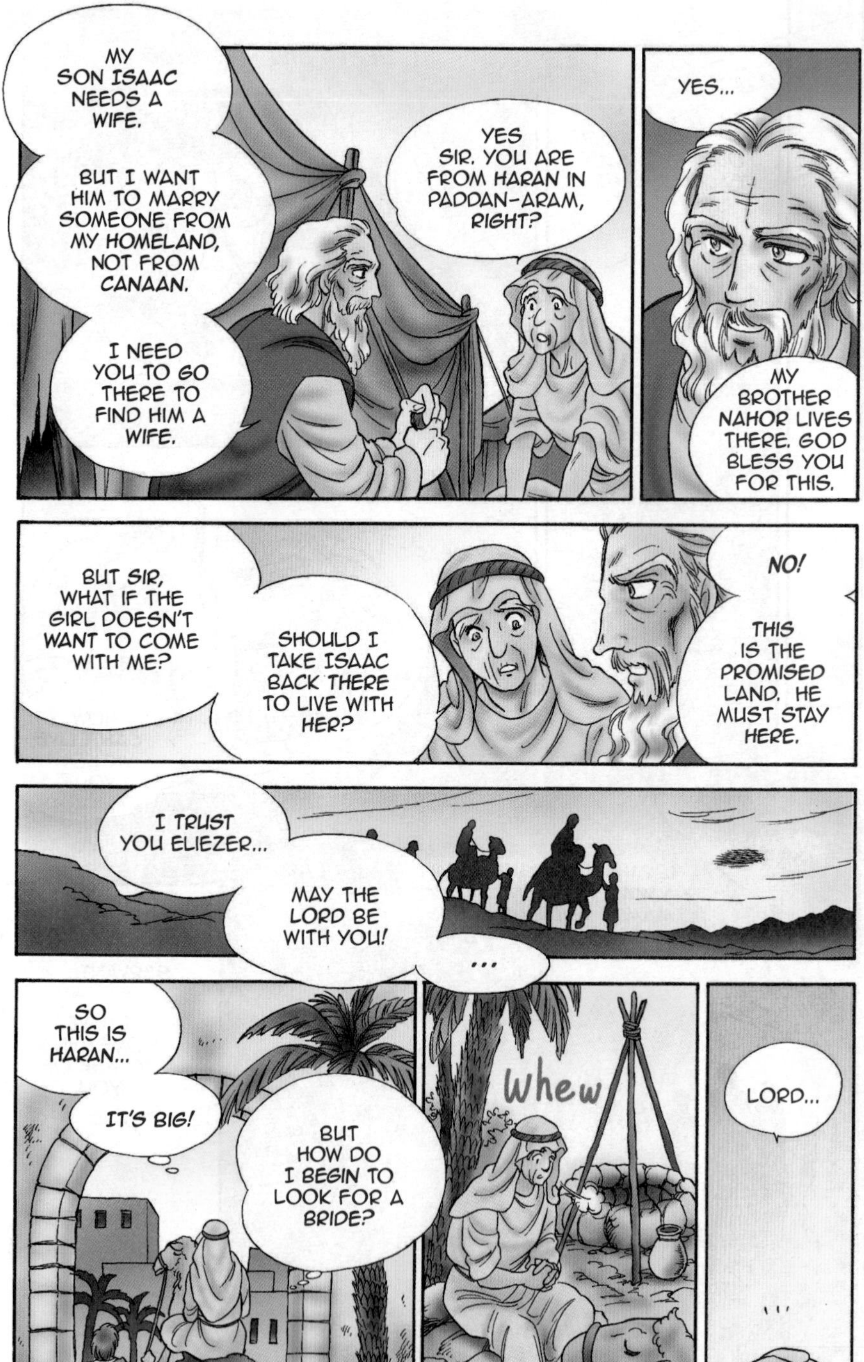
MY SON ISAAC NEEDS A WIFE.
BUT I WANT HIM TO MARRY SOMEONE FROM MY HOMELAND, NOT FROM CANAAN.
I NEED YOU TO GO THERE TO FIND HIM A WIFE.
YES SIR. YOU ARE FROM HARAN IN PADDAN-ARAM, RIGHT?
YES...
MY BROTHER NAHOR LIVES THERE. GOD BLESS YOU FOR THIS.
BUT SIR, WHAT IF THE GIRL DOESN'T WANT TO COME WITH ME?
SHOULD I TAKE ISAAC BACK THERE TO LIVE WITH HER?
NO!
THIS IS THE PROMISED LAND. HE MUST STAY HERE.
I TRUST YOU ELIEZER...
MAY THE LORD BE WITH YOU!
...
SO THIS IS HARAN...
IT'S BIG!
BUT HOW DO I BEGIN TO LOOK FOR A BRIDE?
Whew
LORD...

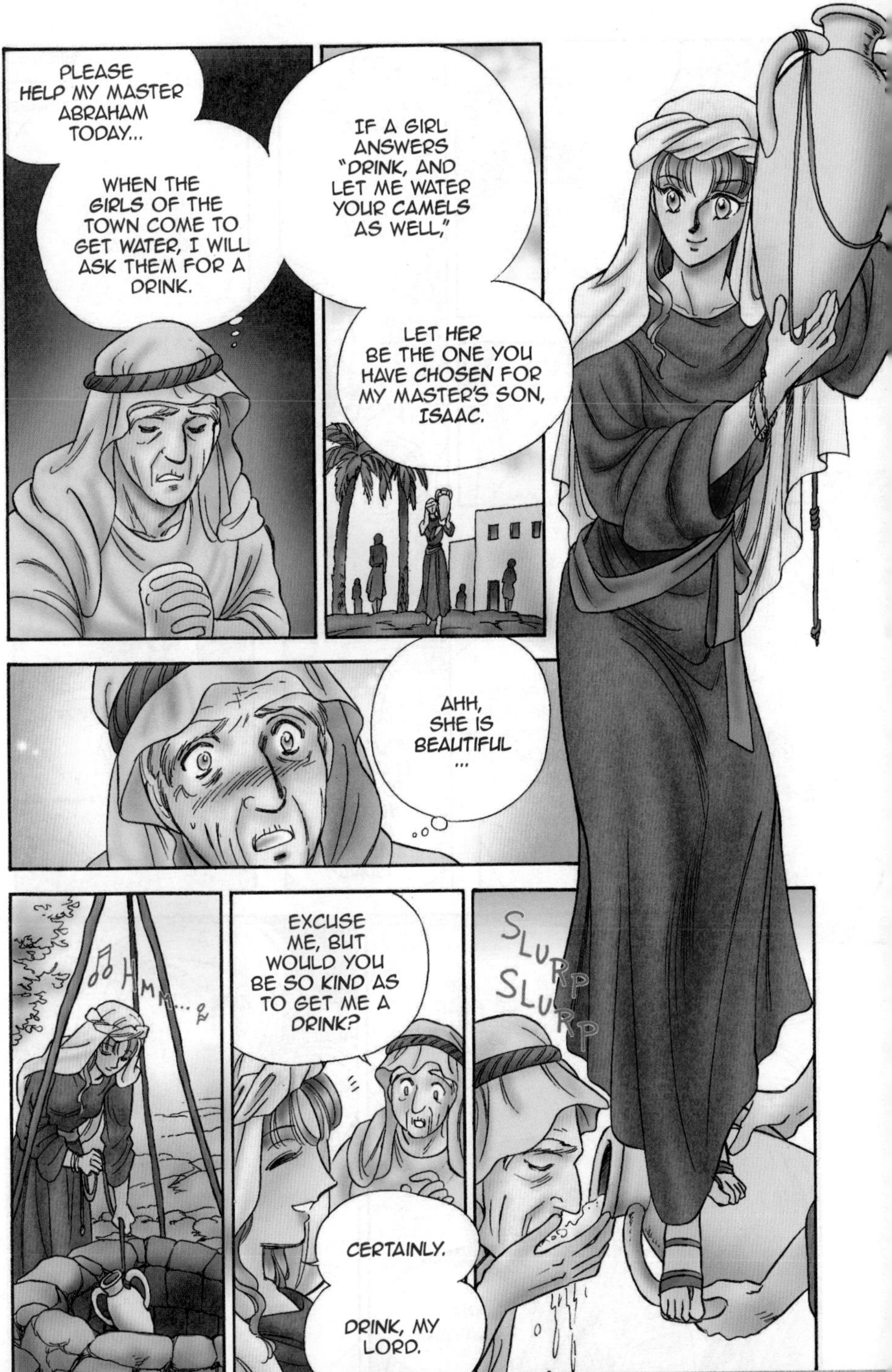
PLEASE HELP MY MASTER ABRAHAM TODAY...
WHEN THE GIRLS OF THE TOWN COME TO GET WATER, I WILL ASK THEM FOR A DRINK.
IF A GIRL ANSWERS "DRINK, AND LET ME WATER YOUR CAMELS AS WELL,"
LET HER BE THE ONE YOU HAVE CHOSEN FOR MY MASTER'S SON, ISAAC.
AHH, SHE IS BEAUTIFUL ...
HMM...
EXCUSE ME, BUT WOULD YOU BE SO KIND AS TO GET ME A DRINK?
CERTAINLY.
DRINK, MY LORD.
SLURP SLURP

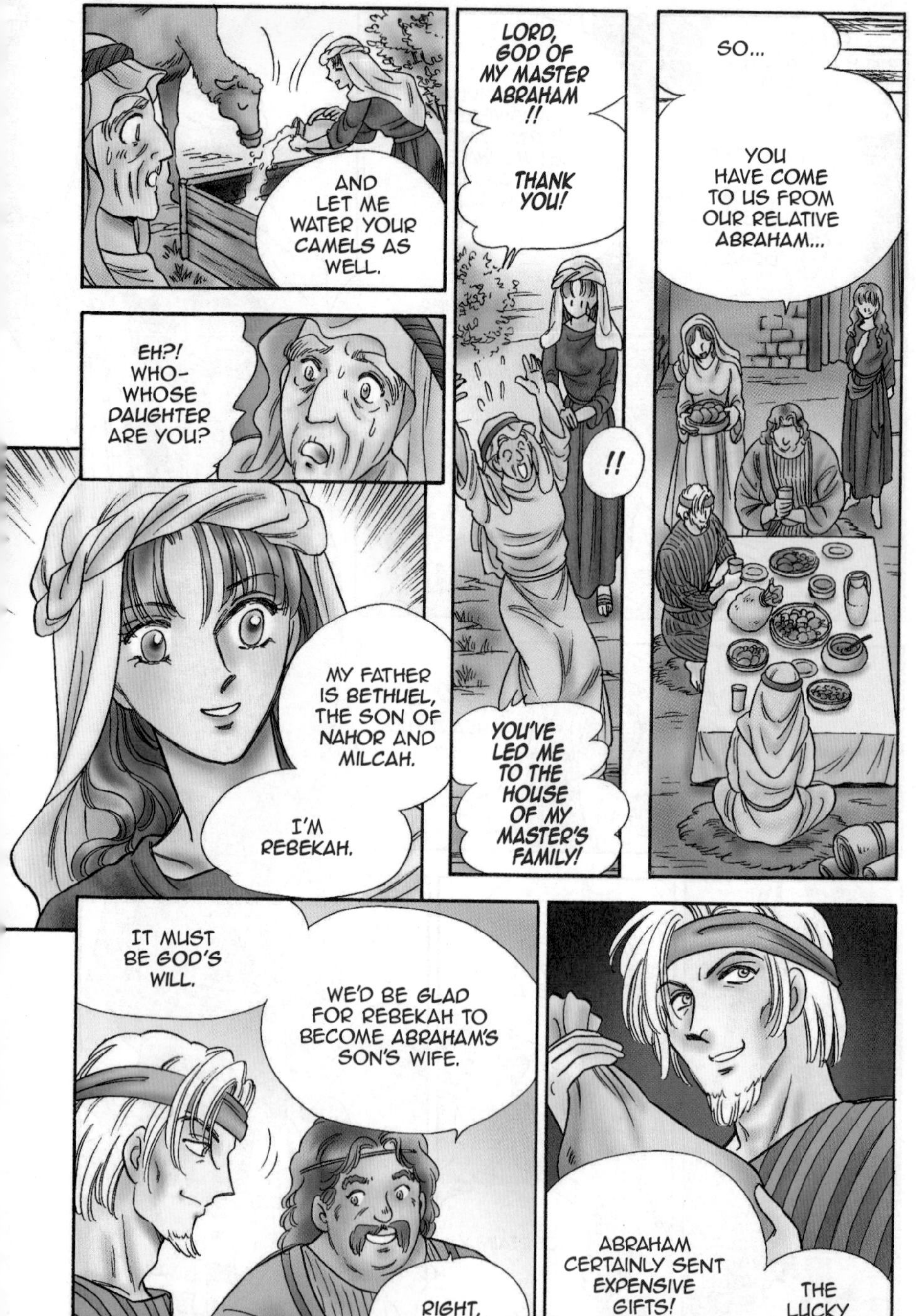
AND LET ME WATER YOUR CAMELS AS WELL.
LORD, GOD OF MY MASTER ABRAHAM !!
THANK YOU!
SO...
YOU HAVE COME TO US FROM OUR RELATIVE ABRAHAM...
EH?! WHO- WHOSE DAUGHTER ARE YOU?
!!
MY FATHER IS BETHUEL, THE SON OF NAHOR AND MILCAH.
I'M REBEKAH.
YOU'VE LED ME TO THE HOUSE OF MY MASTER'S FAMILY!
IT MUST BE GOD'S WILL.
WE'D BE GLAD FOR REBEKAH TO BECOME ABRAHAM'S SON'S WIFE.
RIGHT, LABAN?
ABRAHAM CERTAINLY SENT EXPENSIVE GIFTS!
THE LUCKY DOG MUST BE RICH!

WITH FINAL FAREWELLS TO HER FAMILY, REBEKAH LEFT HER HOME FOR CANAAN.

WHO IS THAT COMING TOWARD US?

THAT IS MY MASTER, ISAAC.

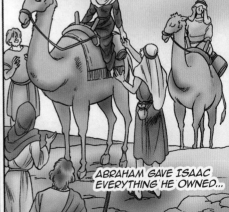

AND SO ISAAC MARRIED REBEKAH, AND HE LOVED HER.

ABRAHAM GAVE ISAAC EVERYTHING HE OWNED...

WSSH

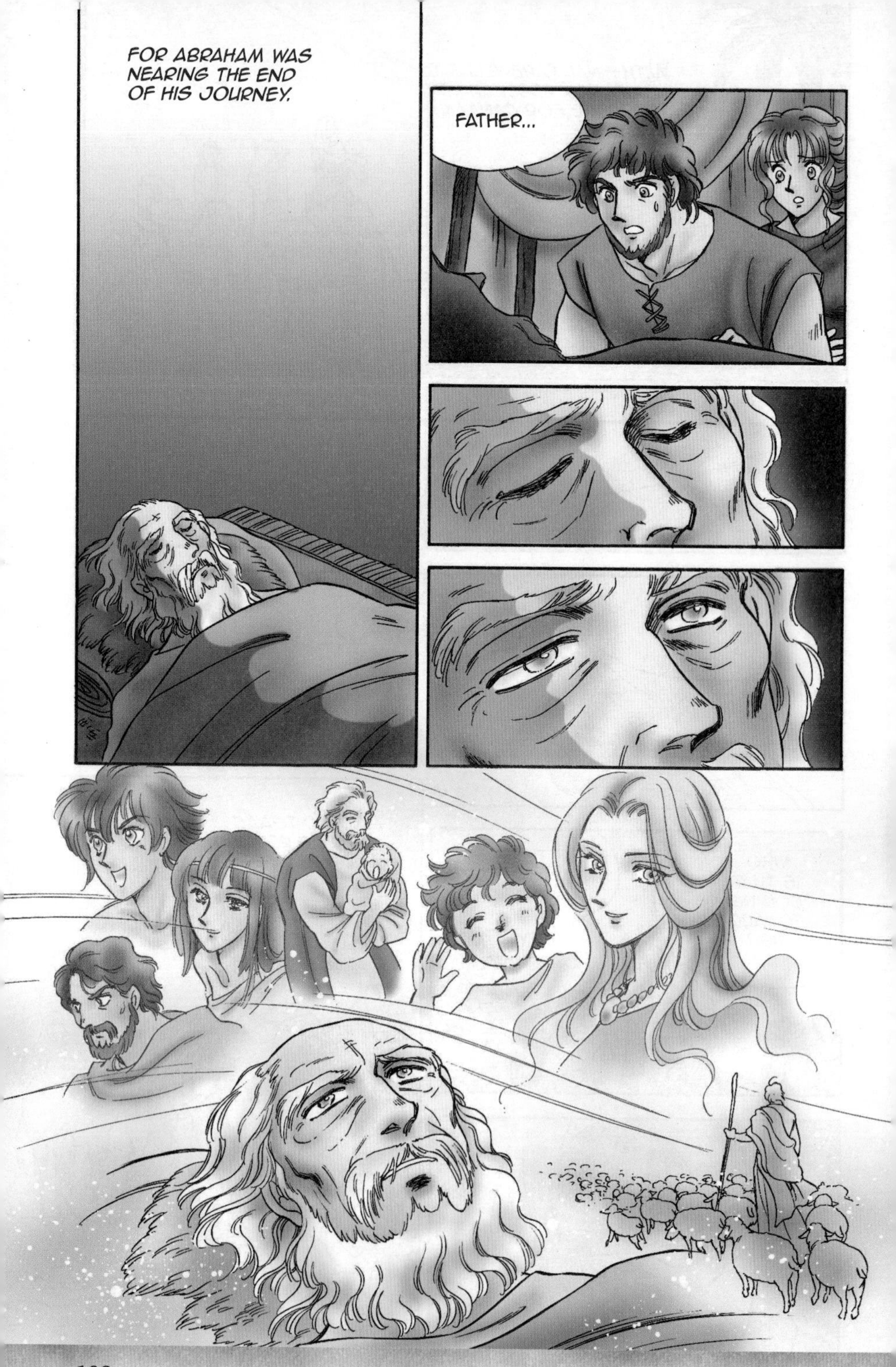
FOR ABRAHAM WAS NEARING THE END OF HIS JOURNEY.
FATHER...

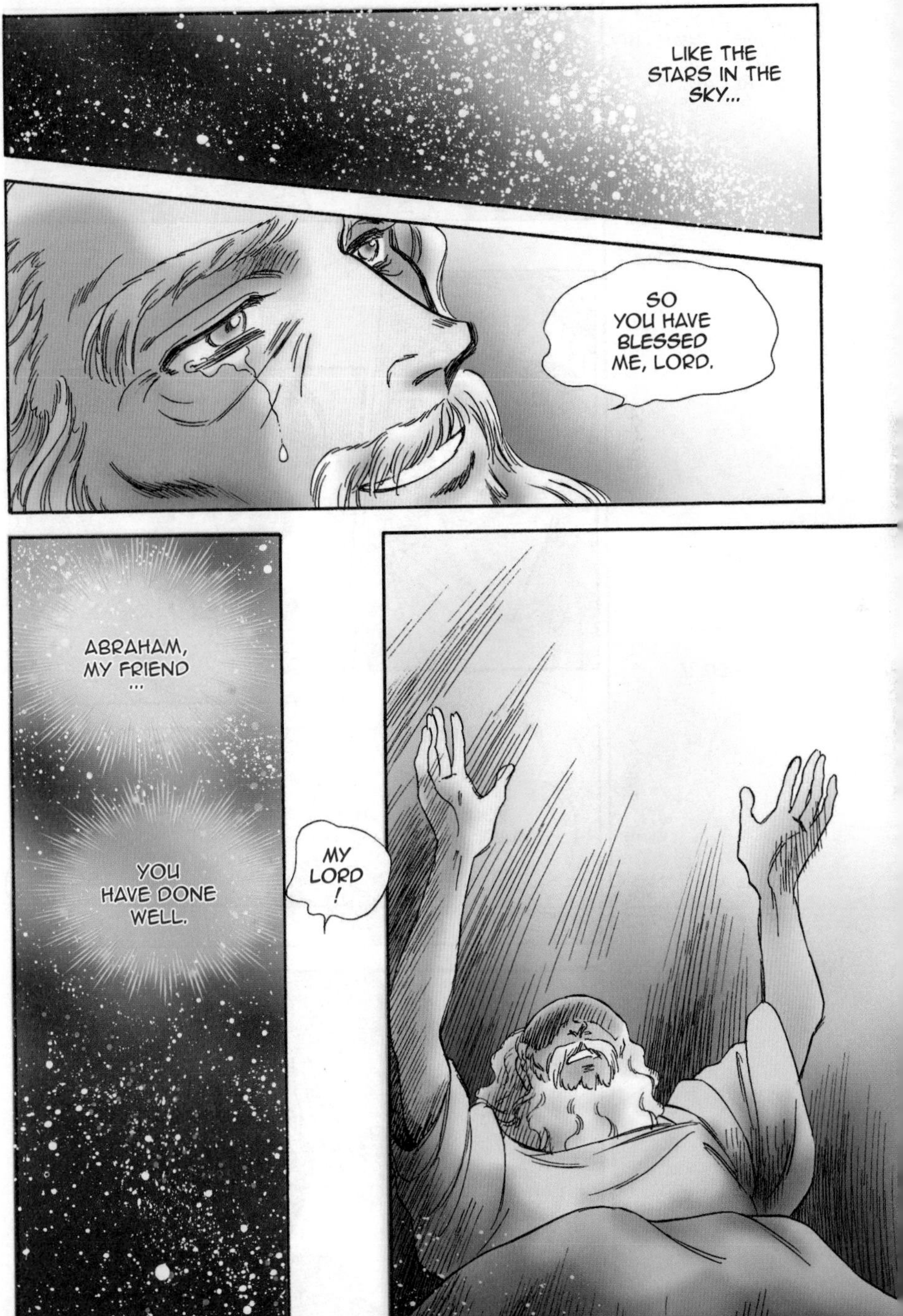
LIKE THE STARS IN THE SKY...
SO YOU HAVE BLESSED ME, LORD.
ABRAHAM, MY FRIEND ...
YOU HAVE DONE WELL.
MY LORD!

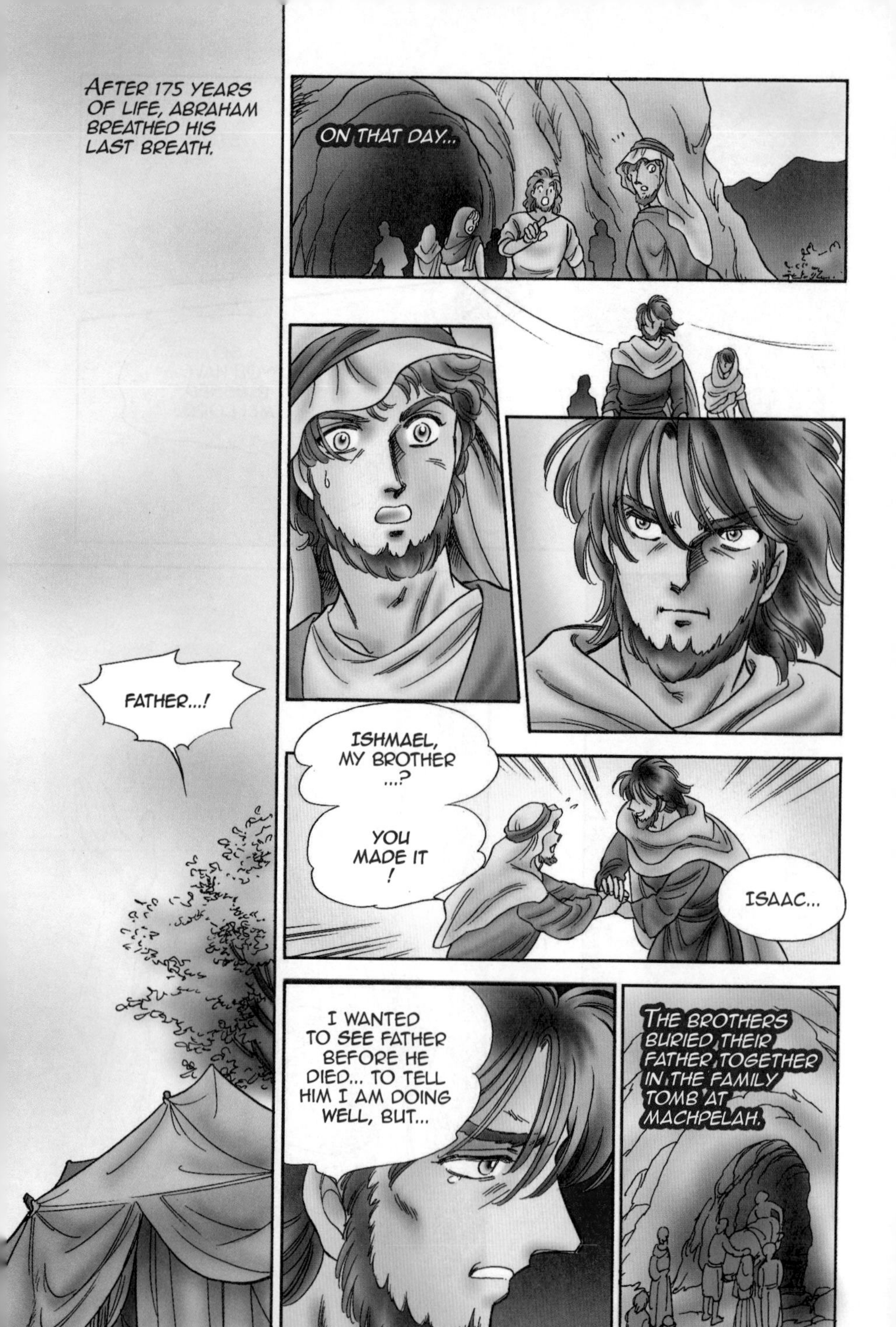
AFTER 175 YEARS OF LIFE, ABRAHAM BREATHED HIS LAST BREATH.
ON THAT DAY...
FATHER...!
ISHMAEL, MY BROTHER ...?
YOU MADE IT !
ISAAC...
I WANTED TO SEE FATHER BEFORE HE DIED... TO TELL HIM I AM DOING WELL, BUT...
THE BROTHERS BURIED THEIR FATHER TOGETHER IN THE FAMILY TOMB AT MACHPELAH.

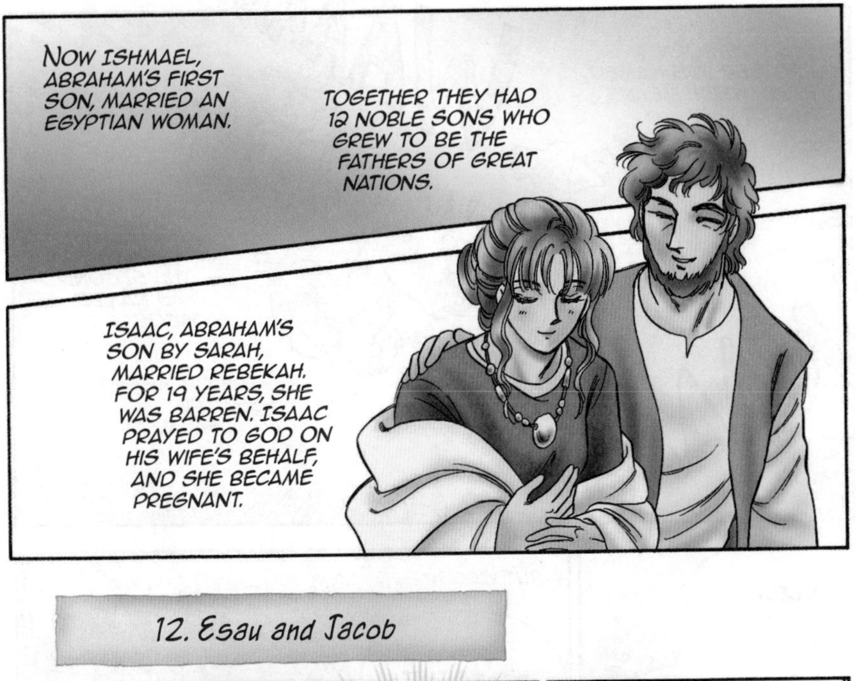
NOW ISHMAEL, ABRAHAM'S FIRST SON, MARRIED AN EGYPTIAN WOMAN.
TOGETHER THEY HAD 12 NOBLE SONS WHO GREW TO BE THE FATHERS OF GREAT NATIONS.
ISAAC, ABRAHAM'S SON BY SARAH, MARRIED REBEKAH. FOR 19 YEARS, SHE WAS BARREN. ISAAC PRAYED TO GOD ON HIS WIFE'S BEHALF, AND SHE BECAME PREGNANT.

12. Esau and Jacob

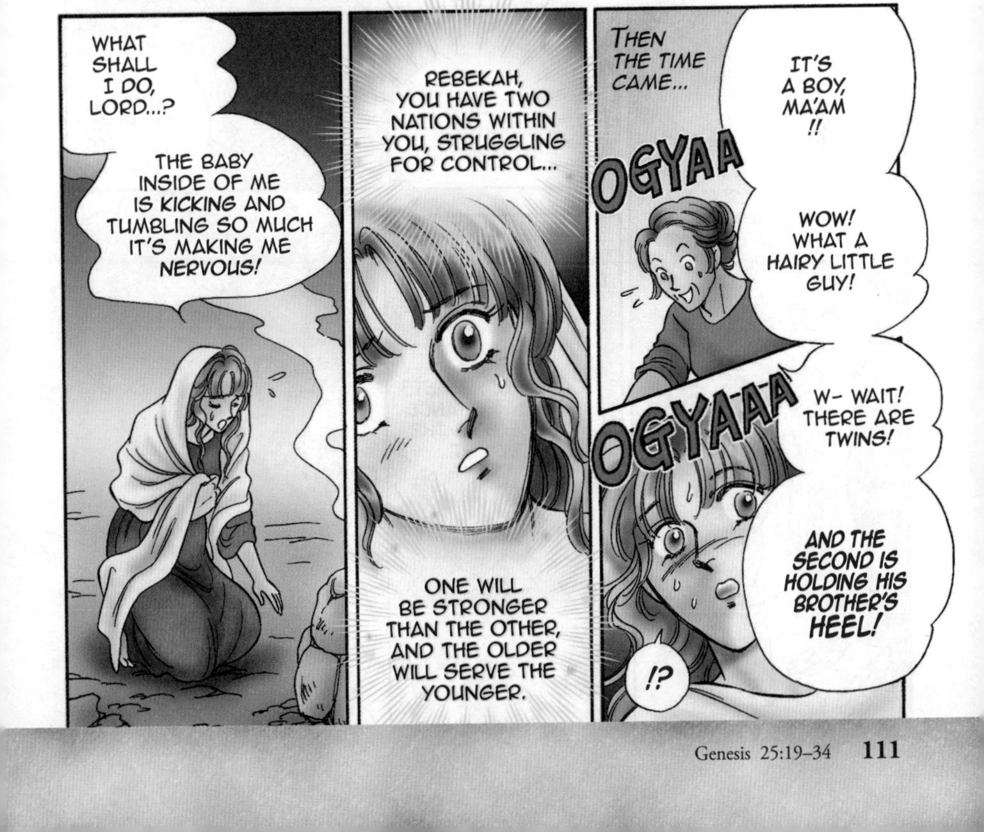
WHAT SHALL I DO, LORD...?
THE BABY INSIDE OF ME IS KICKING AND TUMBLING SO MUCH IT'S MAKING ME NERVOUS!
REBEKAH, YOU HAVE TWO NATIONS WITHIN YOU, STRUGGLING FOR CONTROL...
ONE WILL BE STRONGER THAN THE OTHER, AND THE OLDER WILL SERVE THE YOUNGER.
THEN THE TIME CAME...
IT'S A BOY, MA'AM !!
OGYAA
WOW! WHAT A HAIRY LITTLE GUY!
OGYAAA
W- WAIT! THERE ARE TWINS!
AND THE SECOND IS HOLDING HIS BROTHER'S HEEL!
!?

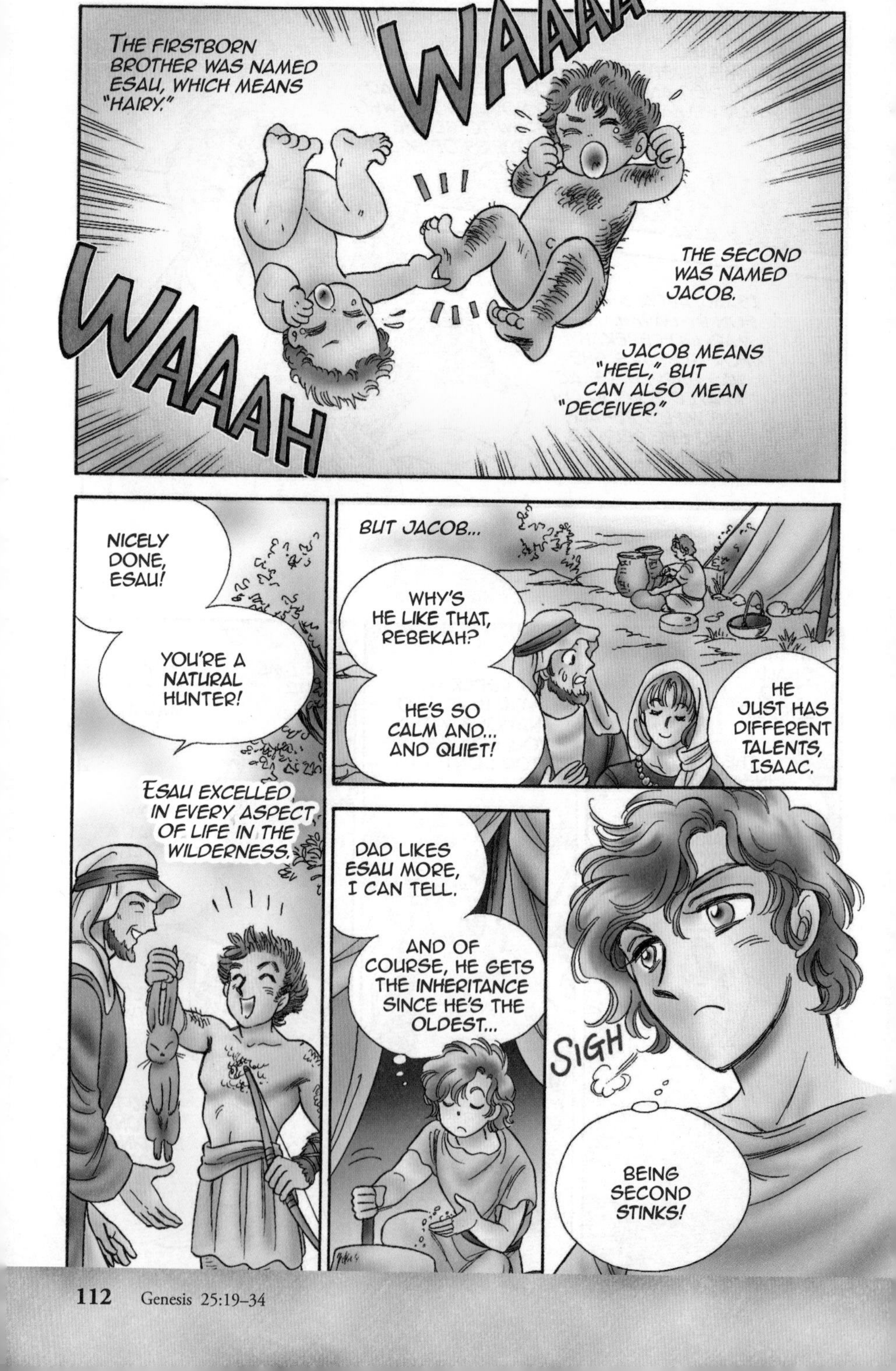
THE FIRSTBORN BROTHER WAS NAMED ESAU, WHICH MEANS "HAIRY."
WAAAA
WAAAAH
THE SECOND WAS NAMED JACOB.
JACOB MEANS "HEEL," BUT CAN ALSO MEAN "DECEIVER."
NICELY DONE, ESAU!
YOU'RE A NATURAL HUNTER!
ESAU EXCELLED IN EVERY ASPECT OF LIFE IN THE WILDERNESS.
BUT JACOB...
WHY'S HE LIKE THAT, REBEKAH?
HE'S SO CALM AND... AND QUIET!
HE JUST HAS DIFFERENT TALENTS, ISAAC.
DAD LIKES ESAU MORE, I CAN TELL.
AND OF COURSE, HE GETS THE INHERITANCE SINCE HE'S THE OLDEST...
SIGH
BEING SECOND STINKS!

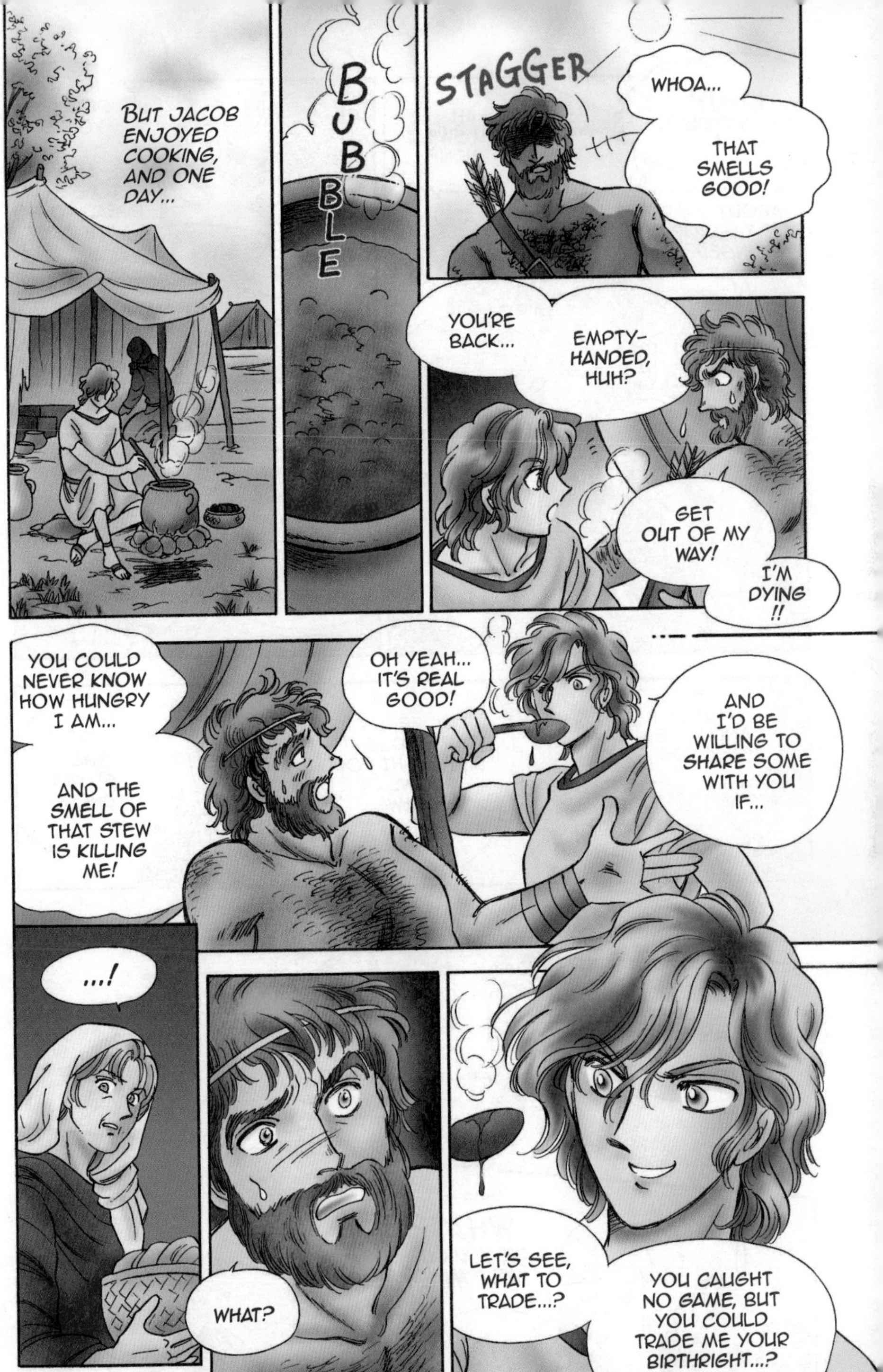
BUT JACOB ENJOYED COOKING, AND ONE DAY...
BUBBLE
STAGGER
WHOA...
THAT SMELLS GOOD!
YOU'RE BACK...
EMPTY-HANDED, HUH?
GET OUT OF MY WAY!
I'M DYING !!
YOU COULD NEVER KNOW HOW HUNGRY I AM...
AND THE SMELL OF THAT STEW IS KILLING ME!
OH YEAH... IT'S REAL GOOD!
AND I'D BE WILLING TO SHARE SOME WITH YOU IF...
...!
WHAT?
LET'S SEE, WHAT TO TRADE...?
YOU CAUGHT NO GAME, BUT YOU COULD TRADE ME YOUR BIRTHRIGHT...?

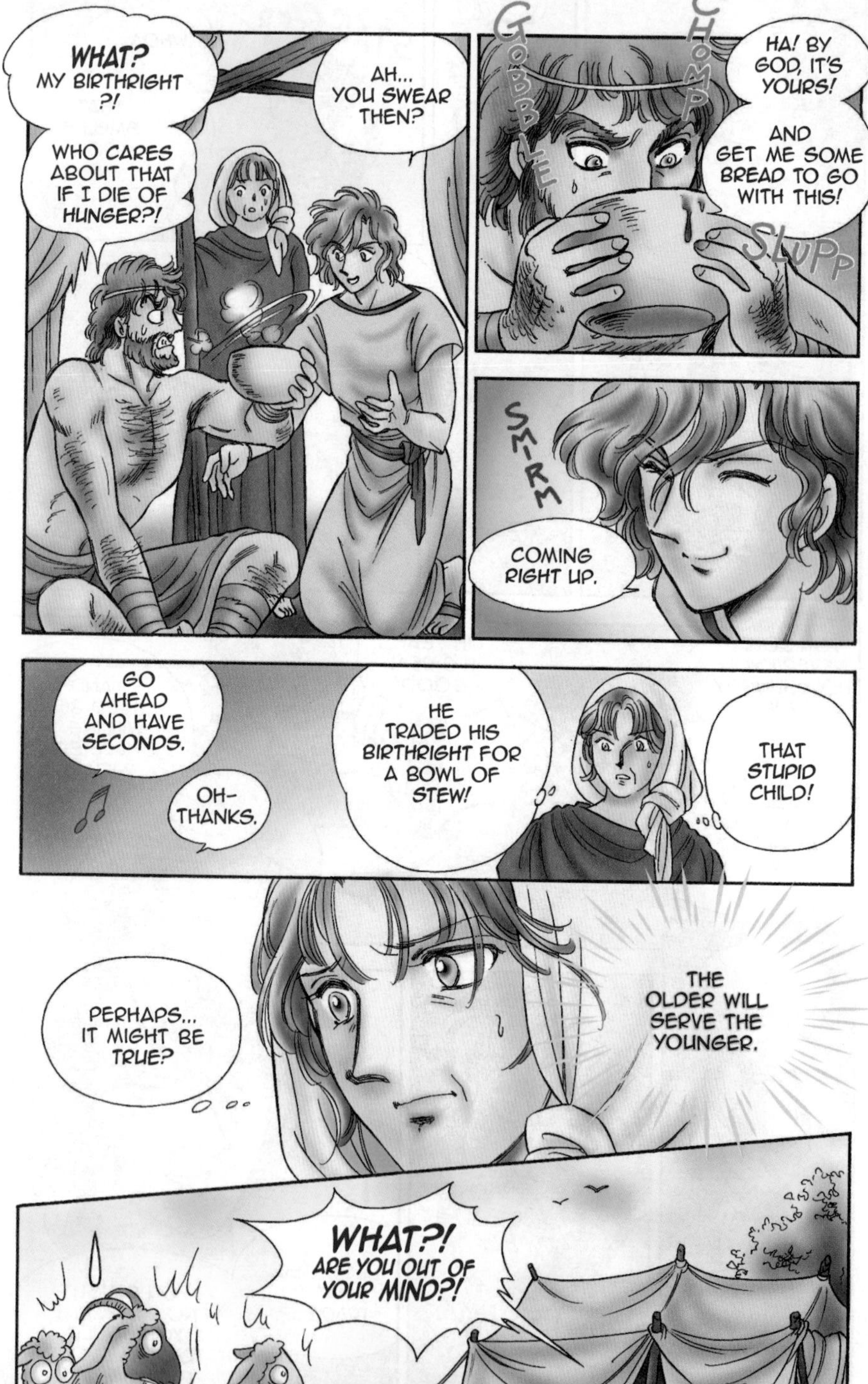
WHAT? MY BIRTHRIGHT ?!
WHO CARES ABOUT THAT IF I DIE OF HUNGER?!
AH... YOU SWEAR THEN?
GOBBLE
CHOMP
HA! BY GOD, IT'S YOURS!
AND GET ME SOME BREAD TO GO WITH THIS!
SLUPP
SMIRM
COMING RIGHT UP.
GO AHEAD AND HAVE SECONDS.
OH- THANKS.
HE TRADED HIS BIRTHRIGHT FOR A BOWL OF STEW!
THAT STUPID CHILD!
PERHAPS... IT MIGHT BE TRUE?
THE OLDER WILL SERVE THE YOUNGER.
WHAT?! ARE YOU OUT OF YOUR MIND?!

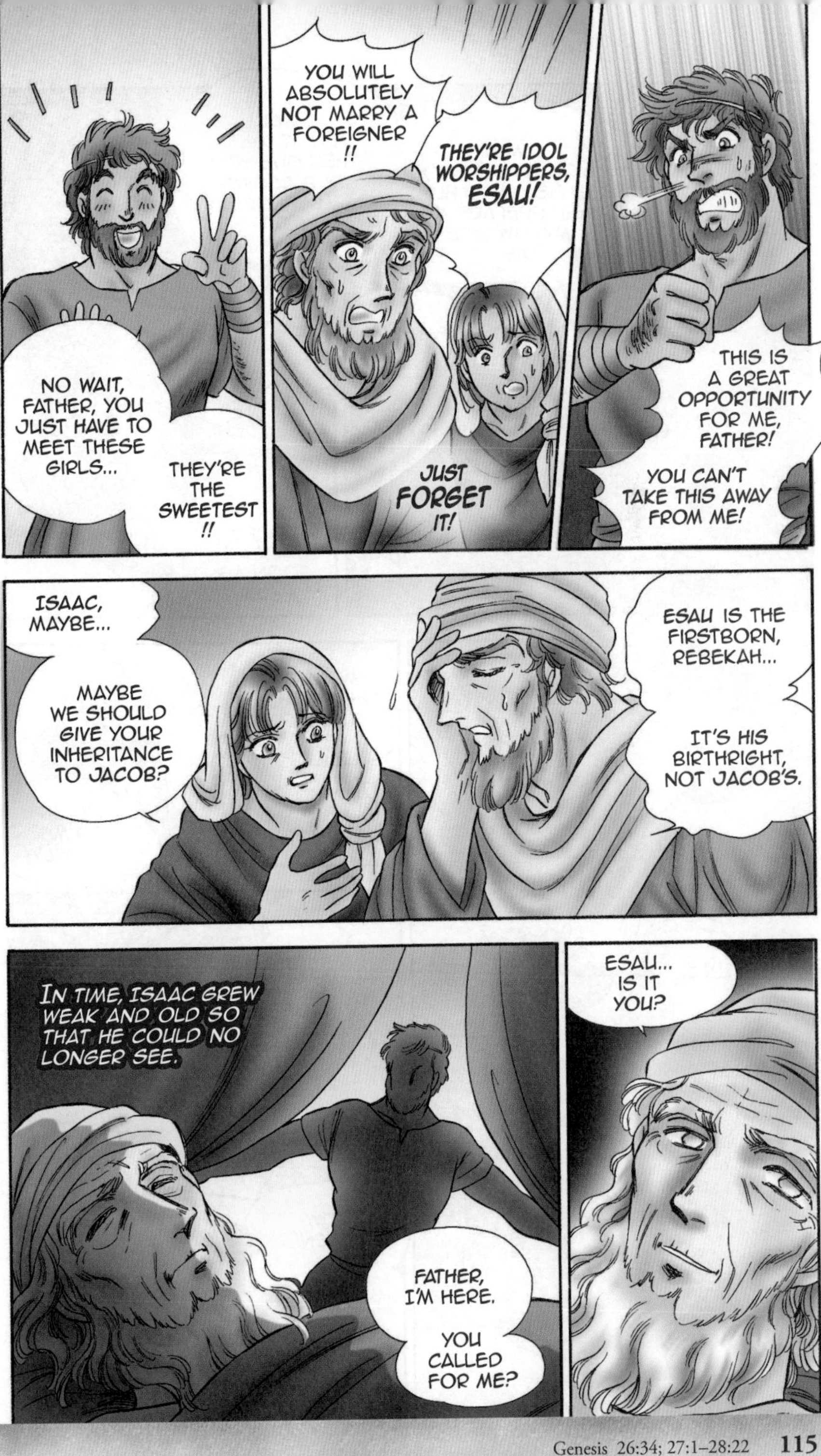
NO WAIT, FATHER, YOU JUST HAVE TO MEET THESE GIRLS...
THEY'RE THE SWEETEST !!
YOU WILL ABSOLUTELY NOT MARRY A FOREIGNER !!
THEY'RE IDOL WORSHIPPERS, ESAU!
JUST FORGET IT!
THIS IS A GREAT OPPORTUNITY FOR ME, FATHER!
YOU CAN'T TAKE THIS AWAY FROM ME!
ISAAC, MAYBE...
MAYBE WE SHOULD GIVE YOUR INHERITANCE TO JACOB?
ESAU IS THE FIRSTBORN, REBEKAH...
IT'S HIS BIRTHRIGHT, NOT JACOB'S.
IN TIME, ISAAC GREW WEAK AND OLD SO THAT HE COULD NO LONGER SEE.
FATHER, I'M HERE.
YOU CALLED FOR ME?
ESAU... IS IT YOU?

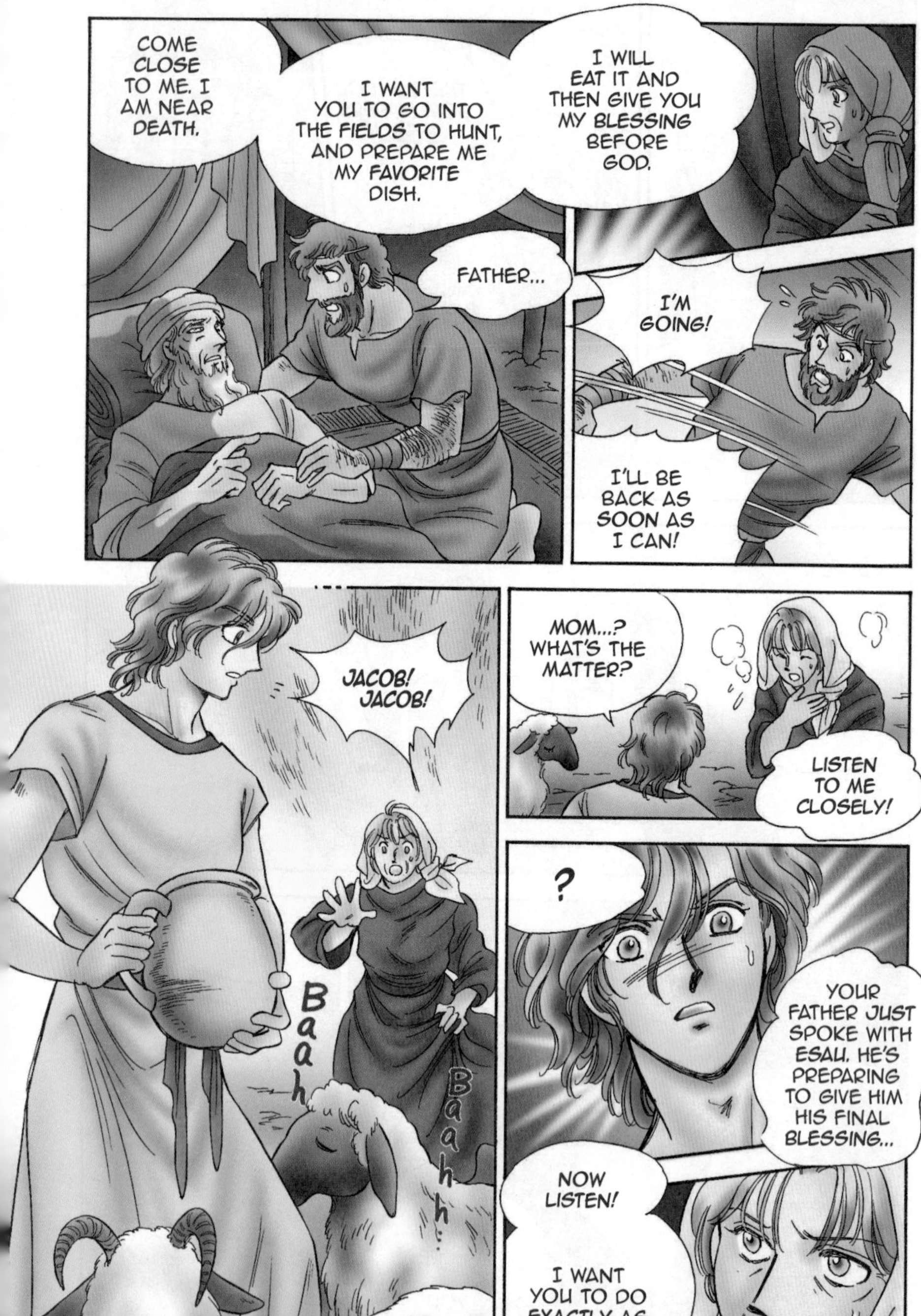
COME CLOSE TO ME. I AM NEAR DEATH.
I WANT YOU TO GO INTO THE FIELDS TO HUNT, AND PREPARE ME MY FAVORITE DISH.
I WILL EAT IT AND THEN GIVE YOU MY BLESSING BEFORE GOD.
FATHER...
I'M GOING!
I'LL BE BACK AS SOON AS I CAN!
JACOB! JACOB!
Baah
Baahh...
MOM...? WHAT'S THE MATTER?
LISTEN TO ME CLOSELY!
?
YOUR FATHER JUST SPOKE WITH ESAU. HE'S PREPARING TO GIVE HIM HIS FINAL BLESSING...
NOW LISTEN!
I WANT YOU TO DO EXACTLY AS I SAY...

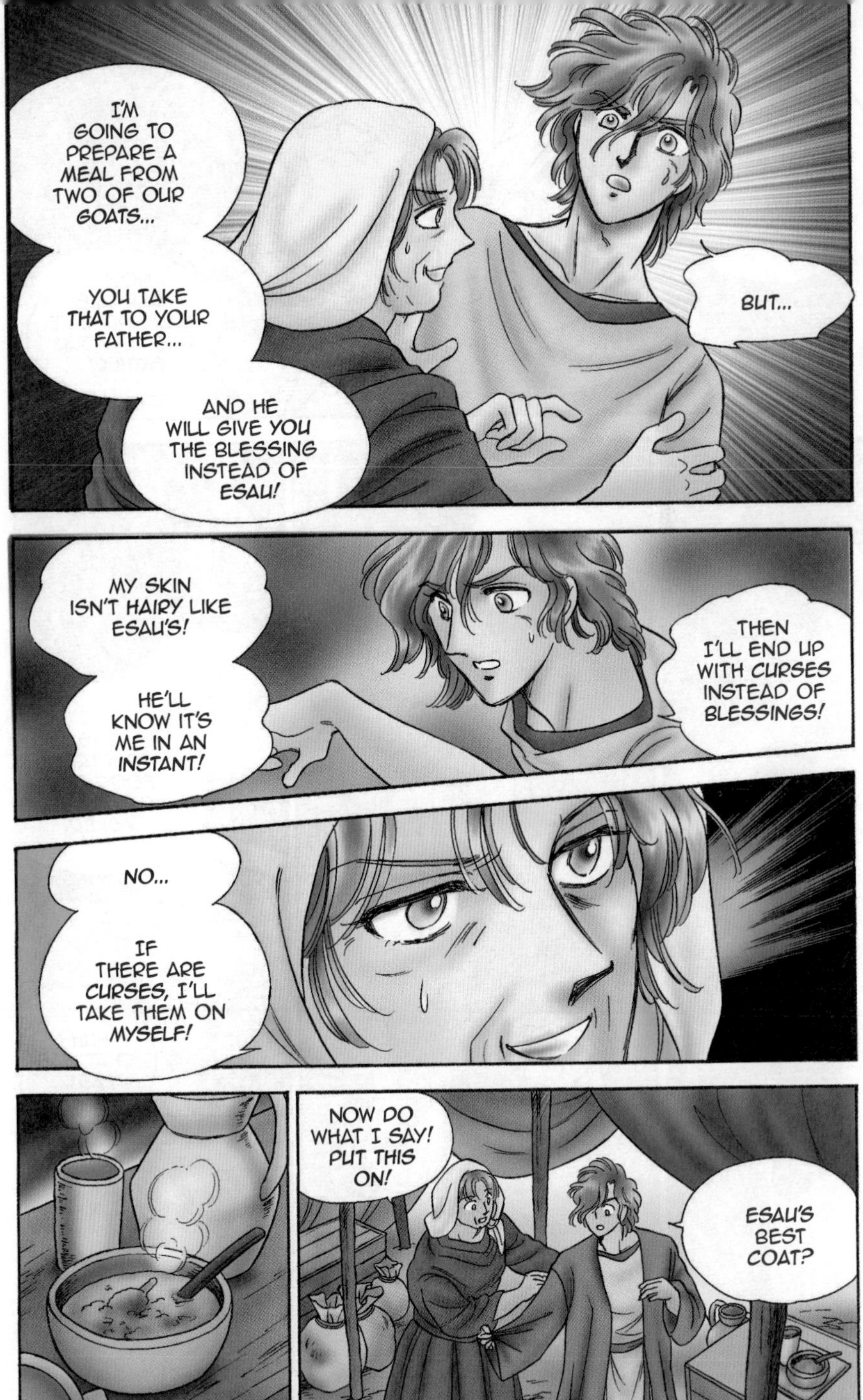
I'M GOING TO PREPARE A MEAL FROM TWO OF OUR GOATS...
YOU TAKE THAT TO YOUR FATHER...
AND HE WILL GIVE YOU THE BLESSING INSTEAD OF ESAU!
BUT...
MY SKIN ISN'T HAIRY LIKE ESAU'S!
HE'LL KNOW IT'S ME IN AN INSTANT!
THEN I'LL END UP WITH CURSES INSTEAD OF BLESSINGS!
NO...
IF THERE ARE CURSES, I'LL TAKE THEM ON MYSELF!
NOW DO WHAT I SAY! PUT THIS ON!
ESAU'S BEST COAT?

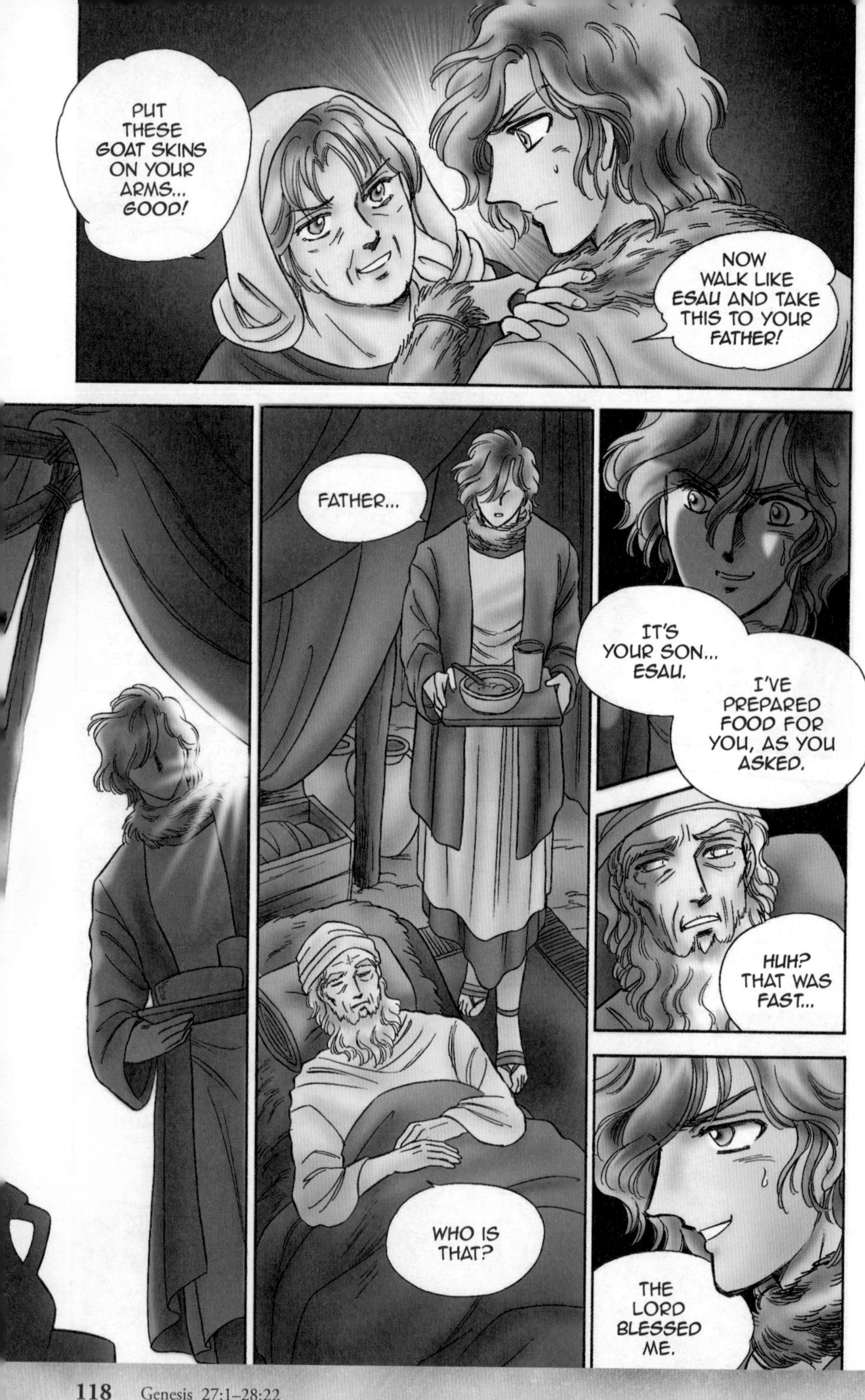
PUT THESE GOAT SKINS ON YOUR ARMS... GOOD!
NOW WALK LIKE ESAU AND TAKE THIS TO YOUR FATHER!
FATHER...
WHO IS THAT?
IT'S YOUR SON... ESAU.
I'VE PREPARED FOOD FOR YOU, AS YOU ASKED.
HUH? THAT WAS FAST...
THE LORD BLESSED ME.

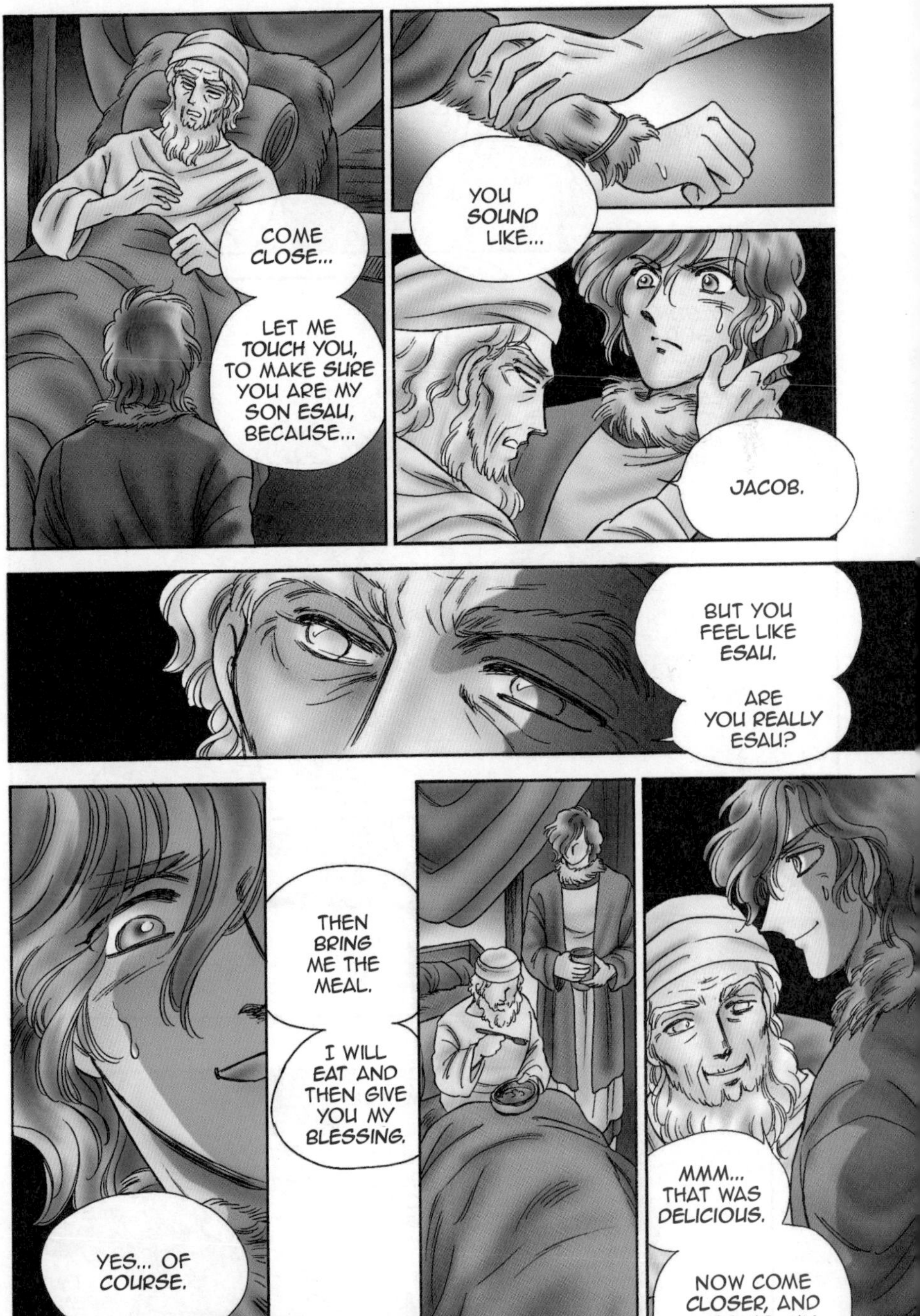
COME CLOSE...
LET ME TOUCH YOU, TO MAKE SURE YOU ARE MY SON ESAU, BECAUSE...
YOU SOUND LIKE...
JACOB.
BUT YOU FEEL LIKE ESAU.
ARE YOU REALLY ESAU?
THEN BRING ME THE MEAL.
I WILL EAT AND THEN GIVE YOU MY BLESSING.
YES... OF COURSE.
MMM... THAT WAS DELICIOUS.
NOW COME CLOSER, AND KISS ME, MY SON...

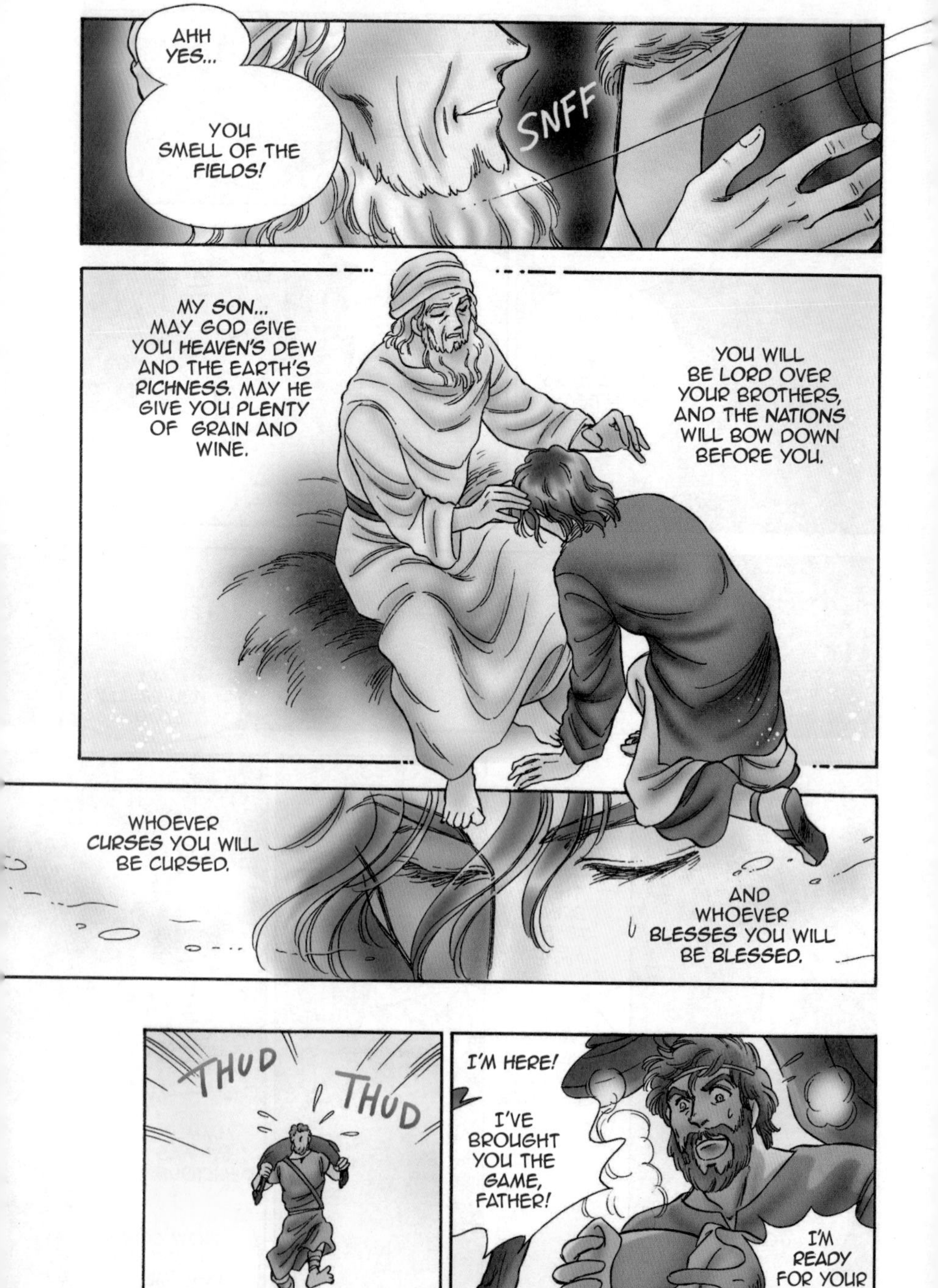
AHH YES...
YOU SMELL OF THE FIELDS!
SNFF
MY SON... MAY GOD GIVE YOU HEAVEN'S DEW AND THE EARTH'S RICHNESS. MAY HE GIVE YOU PLENTY OF GRAIN AND WINE.
YOU WILL BE LORD OVER YOUR BROTHERS, AND THE NATIONS WILL BOW DOWN BEFORE YOU.
WHOEVER CURSES YOU WILL BE CURSED.
AND WHOEVER BLESSES YOU WILL BE BLESSED.
THUD
THUD
I'M HERE!
I'VE BROUGHT YOU THE GAME, FATHER!
I'M READY FOR YOUR BLESSING !!

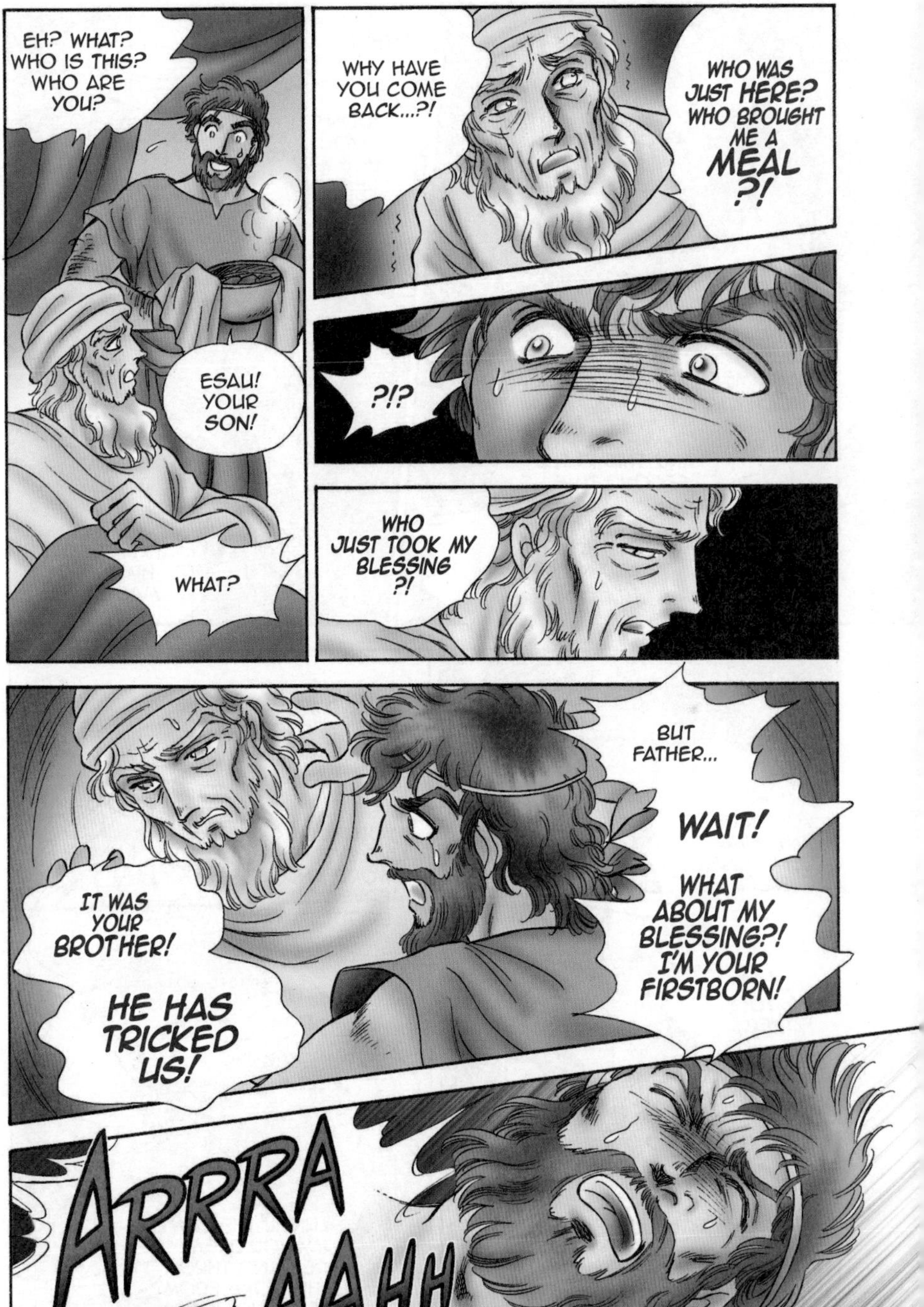

EH? WHAT? WHO IS THIS? WHO ARE YOU?
ESAU! YOUR SON!
WHAT?
WHY HAVE YOU COME BACK...?!
WHO WAS JUST HERE? WHO BROUGHT ME A MEAL?!
?!?
WHO JUST TOOK MY BLESSING?!
IT WAS YOUR BROTHER!
HE HAS TRICKED US!
BUT FATHER...
WAIT!
WHAT ABOUT MY BLESSING?! I'M YOUR FIRSTBORN!
ARRRA AAHH

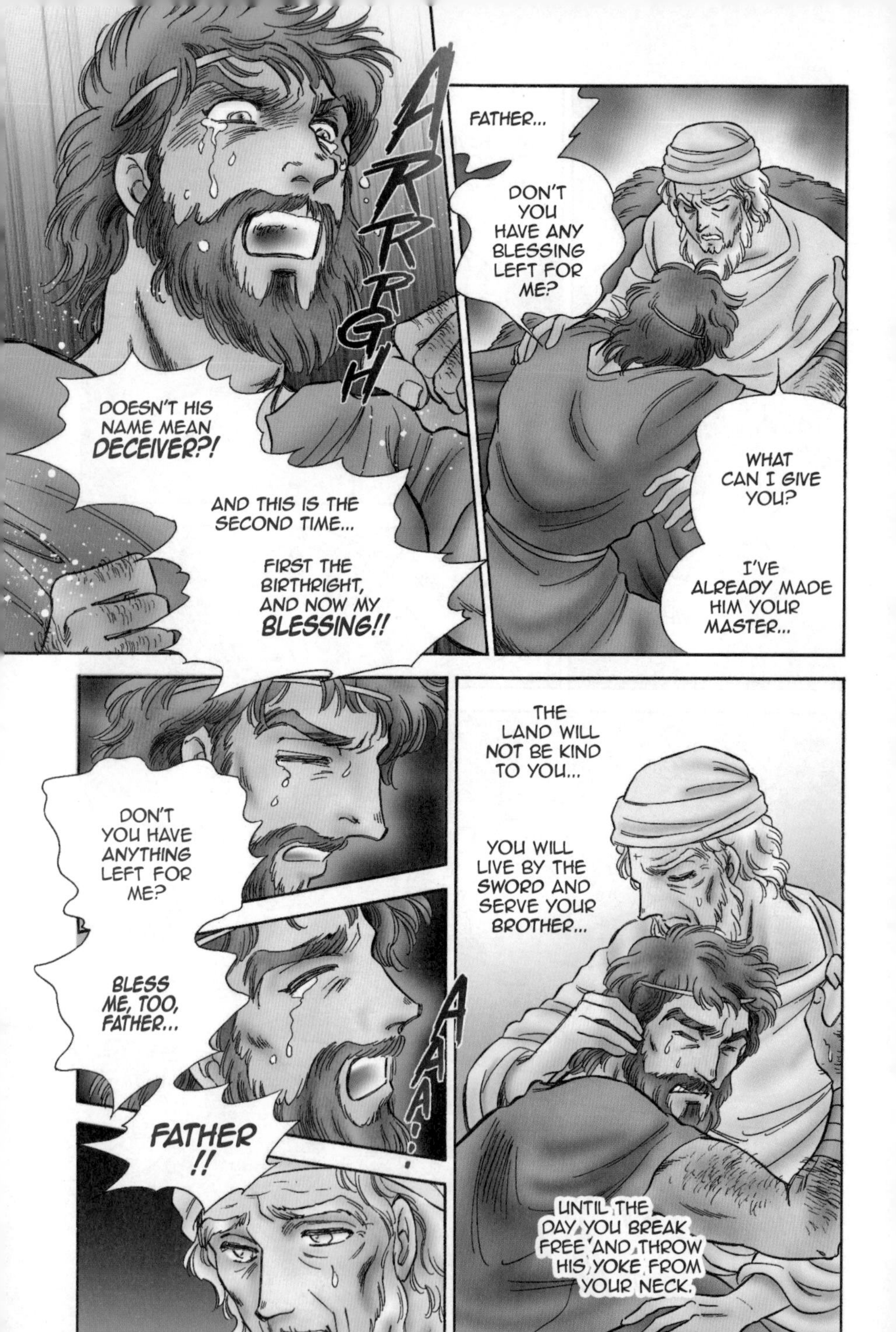
ARRRGH
DOESN'T HIS NAME MEAN DECEIVER?!
AND THIS IS THE SECOND TIME...
FIRST THE BIRTHRIGHT, AND NOW MY BLESSING!!
FATHER...
DON'T YOU HAVE ANY BLESSING LEFT FOR ME?
WHAT CAN I GIVE YOU?
I'VE ALREADY MADE HIM YOUR MASTER...
DON'T YOU HAVE ANYTHING LEFT FOR ME?
BLESS ME, TOO, FATHER...
FATHER !!
AAAA!
THE LAND WILL NOT BE KIND TO YOU...
YOU WILL LIVE BY THE SWORD AND SERVE YOUR BROTHER...
UNTIL THE DAY YOU BREAK FREE AND THROW HIS YOKE FROM YOUR NECK.

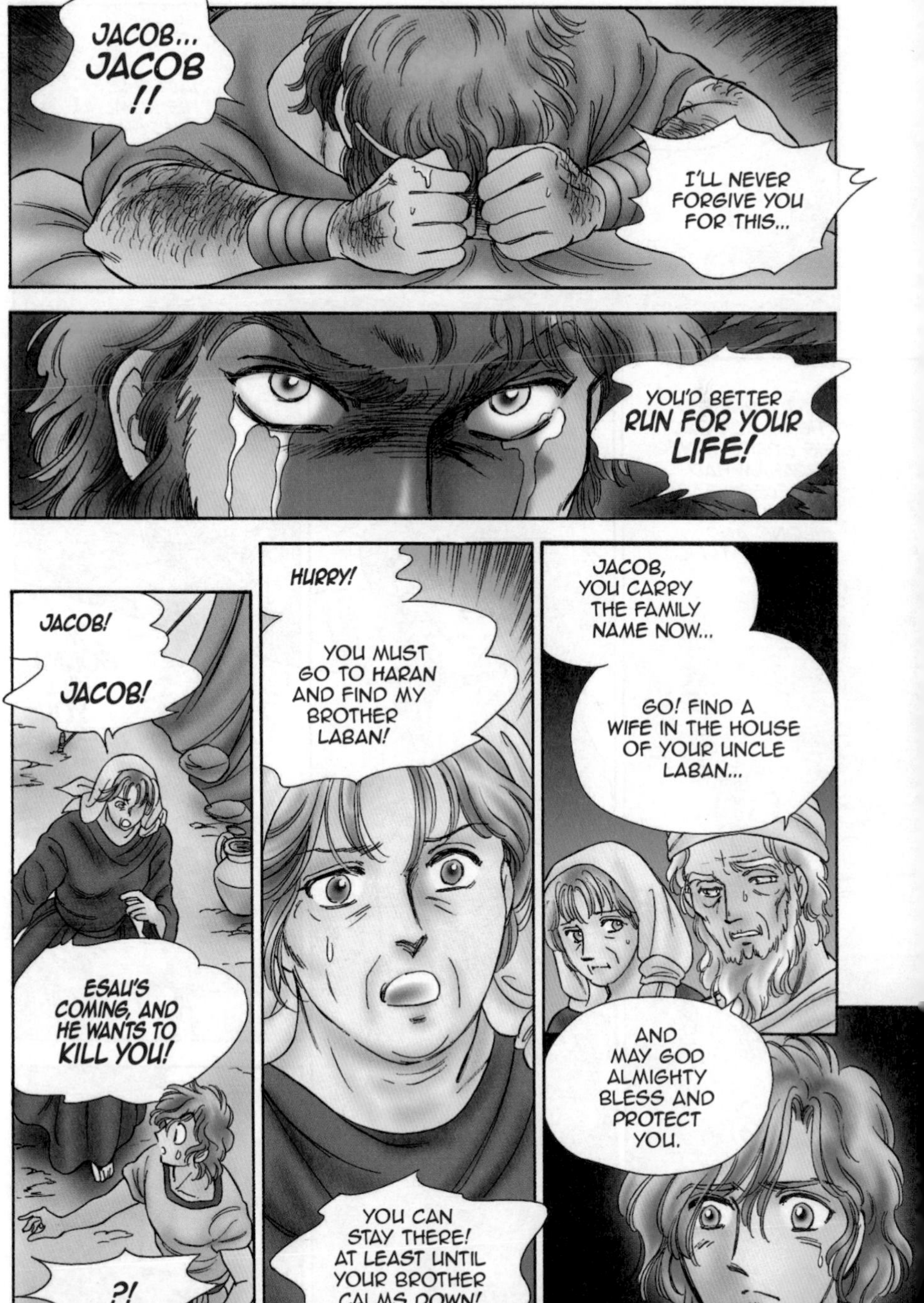
JACOB... JACOB !!
I'LL NEVER FORGIVE YOU FOR THIS...
YOU'D BETTER RUN FOR YOUR LIFE!
JACOB!
JACOB!
ESAU'S COMING, AND HE WANTS TO KILL YOU!
?!
HURRY!
YOU MUST GO TO HARAN AND FIND MY BROTHER LABAN!
YOU CAN STAY THERE! AT LEAST UNTIL YOUR BROTHER CALMS DOWN!
JACOB, YOU CARRY THE FAMILY NAME NOW...
GO! FIND A WIFE IN THE HOUSE OF YOUR UNCLE LABAN...
AND MAY GOD ALMIGHTY BLESS AND PROTECT YOU.

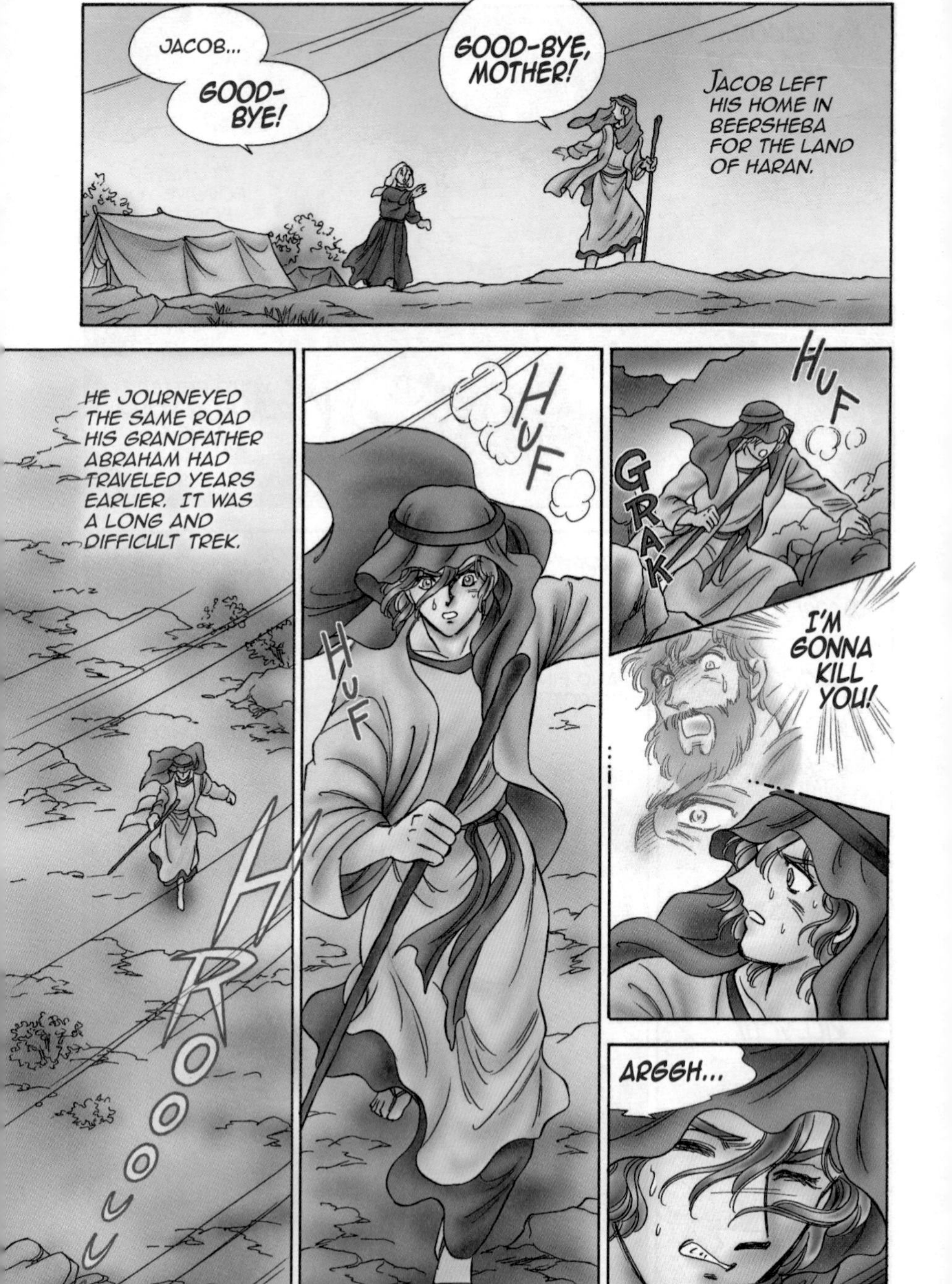
JACOB... GOOD-BYE!
GOOD-BYE, MOTHER!
JACOB LEFT HIS HOME IN BEERSHEBA FOR THE LAND OF HARAN.
HE JOURNEYED THE SAME ROAD HIS GRANDFATHER ABRAHAM HAD TRAVELED YEARS EARLIER. IT WAS A LONG AND DIFFICULT TREK.
HROOOUU
HUF
HUF
HUF
GRAK
I'M GONNA KILL YOU!
ARGGH...

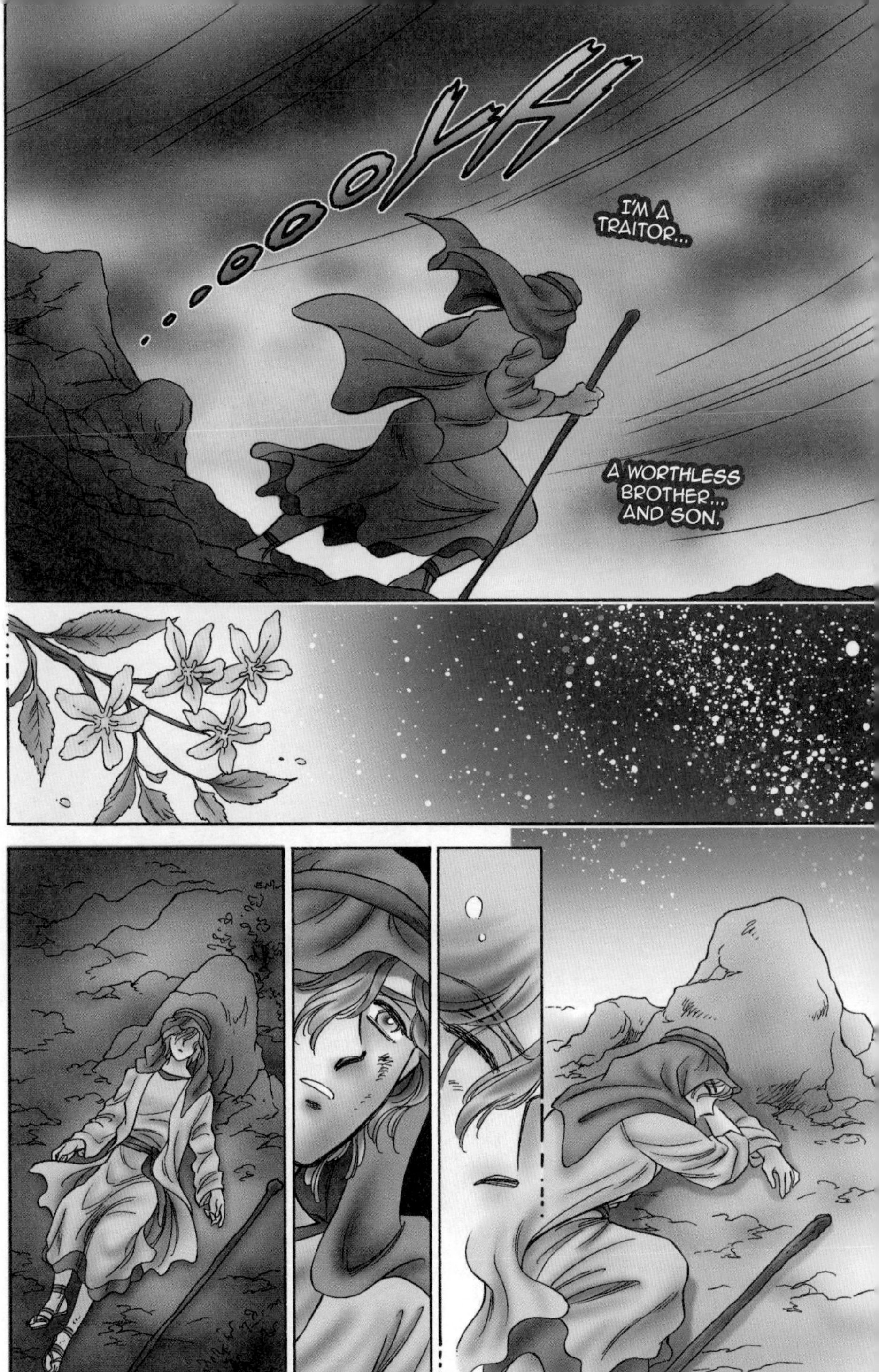
...OOOOYH
I'M A TRAITOR...
A WORTHLESS BROTHER... AND SON.

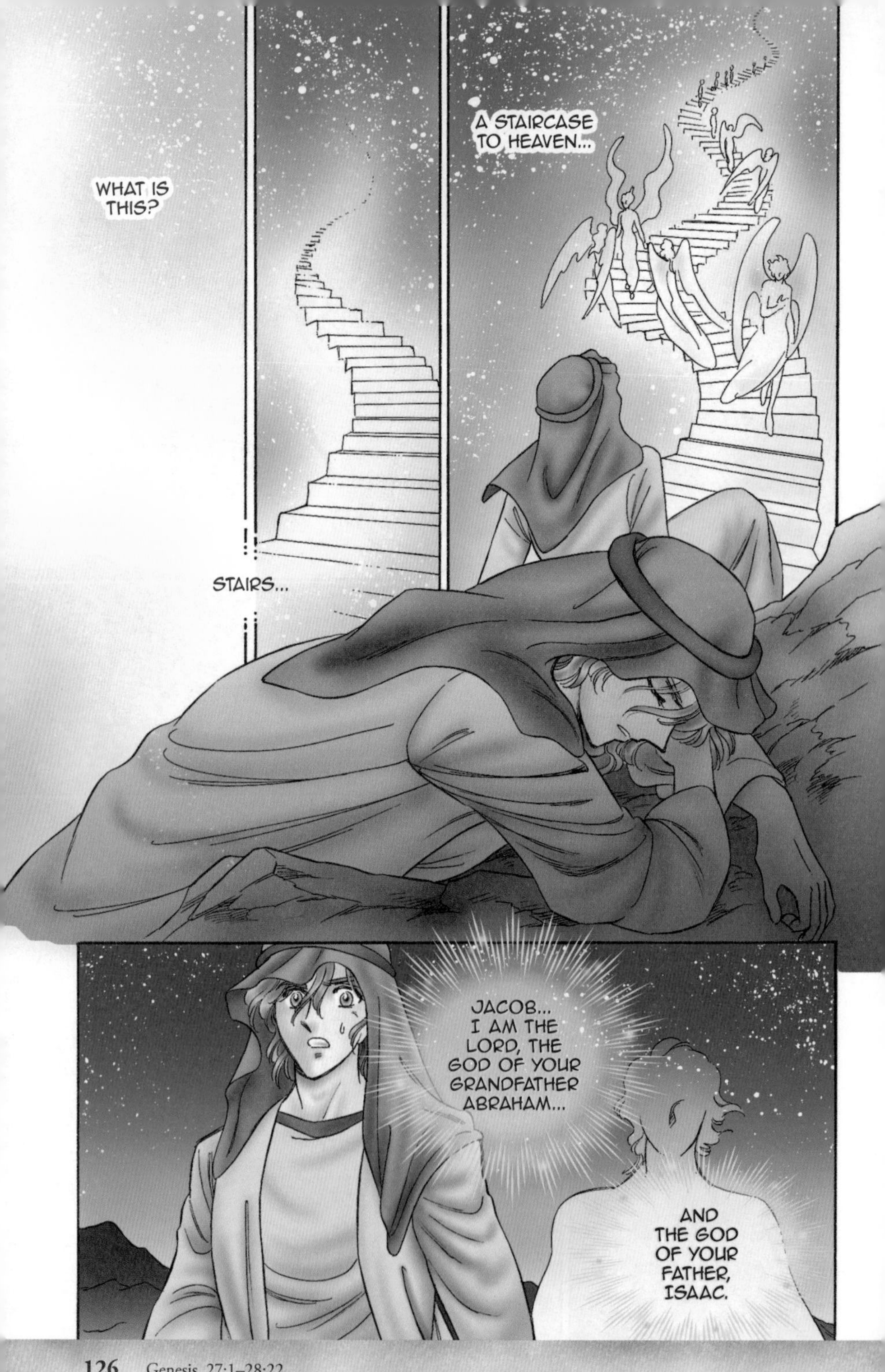
WHAT IS
THIS?
STAIRS...
A STAIRCASE
TO HEAVEN...
JACOB...
I AM THE
LORD, THE
GOD OF YOUR
GRANDFATHER
ABRAHAM...
AND
THE GOD
OF YOUR
FATHER,
ISAAC.

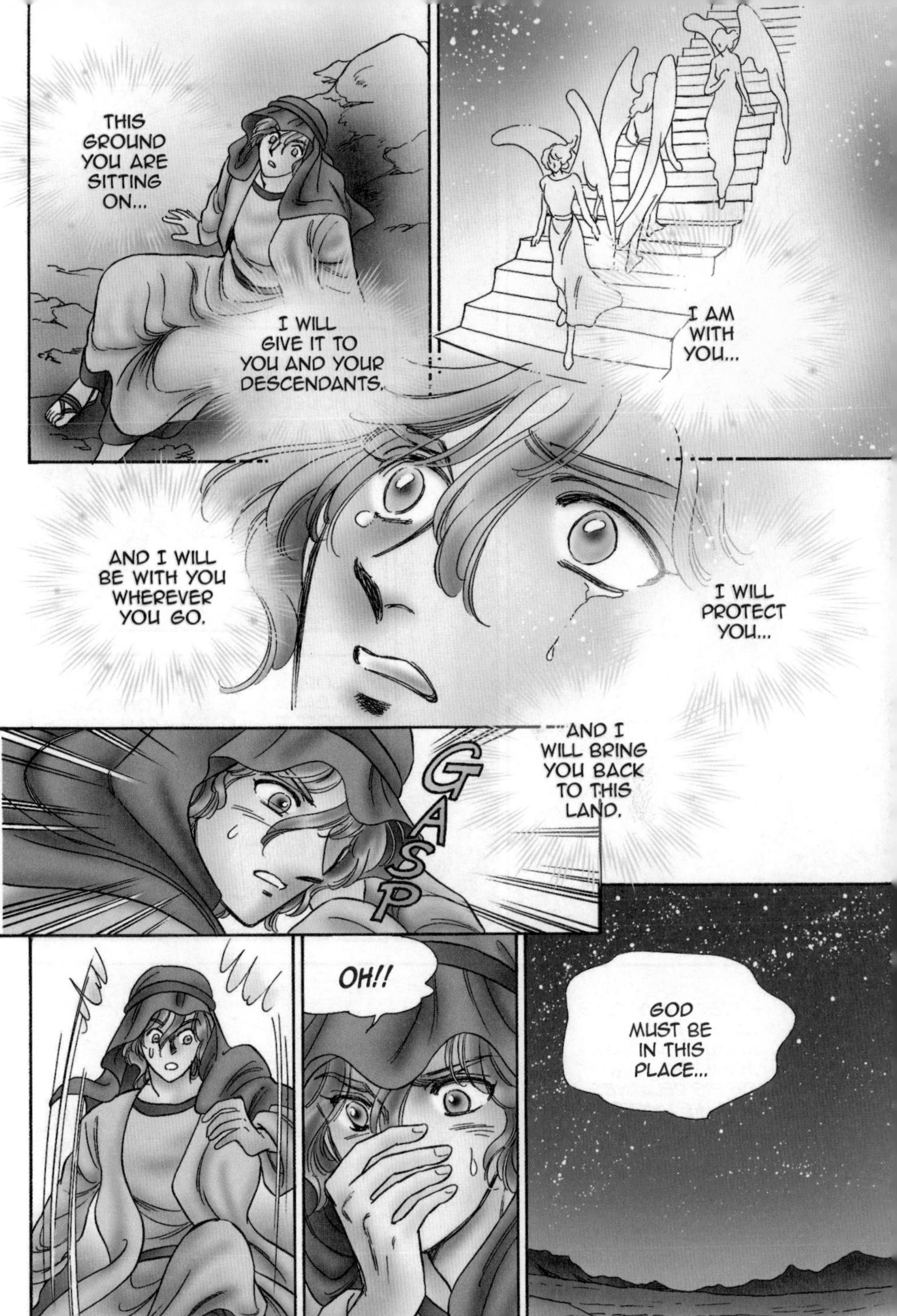
THIS GROUND YOU ARE SITTING ON...
I WILL GIVE IT TO YOU AND YOUR DESCENDANTS.
I AM WITH YOU...
AND I WILL BE WITH YOU WHEREVER YOU GO.
I WILL PROTECT YOU...
AND I WILL BRING YOU BACK TO THIS LAND.
GASP
OH!!
GOD MUST BE IN THIS PLACE...

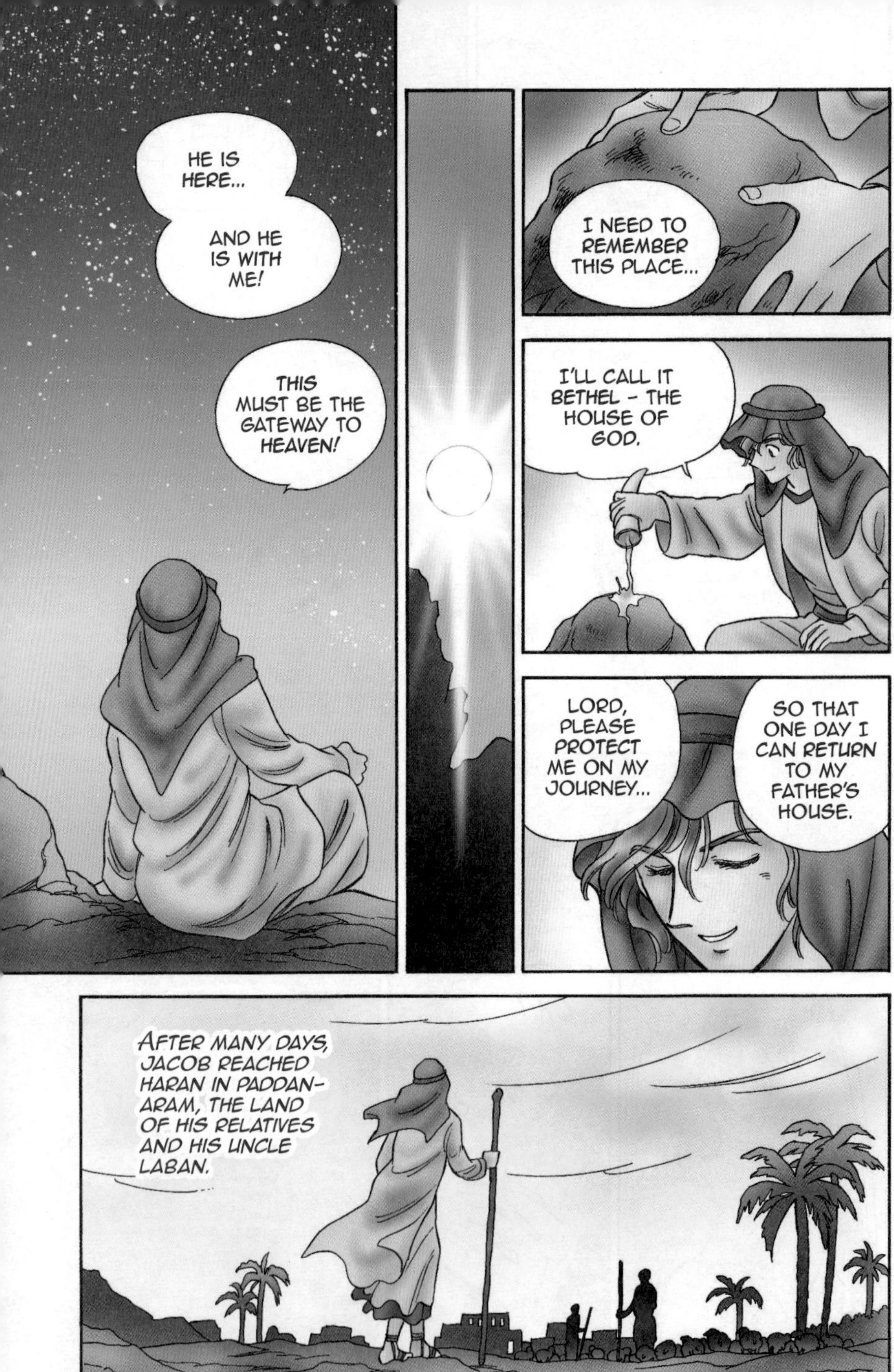
HE IS HERE...
AND HE IS WITH ME!
THIS MUST BE THE GATEWAY TO HEAVEN!
I NEED TO REMEMBER THIS PLACE...
I'LL CALL IT BETHEL - THE HOUSE OF GOD.
LORD, PLEASE PROTECT ME ON MY JOURNEY...
SO THAT ONE DAY I CAN RETURN TO MY FATHER'S HOUSE.
AFTER MANY DAYS, JACOB REACHED HARAN IN PADDAN-ARAM, THE LAND OF HIS RELATIVES AND HIS UNCLE LABAN.

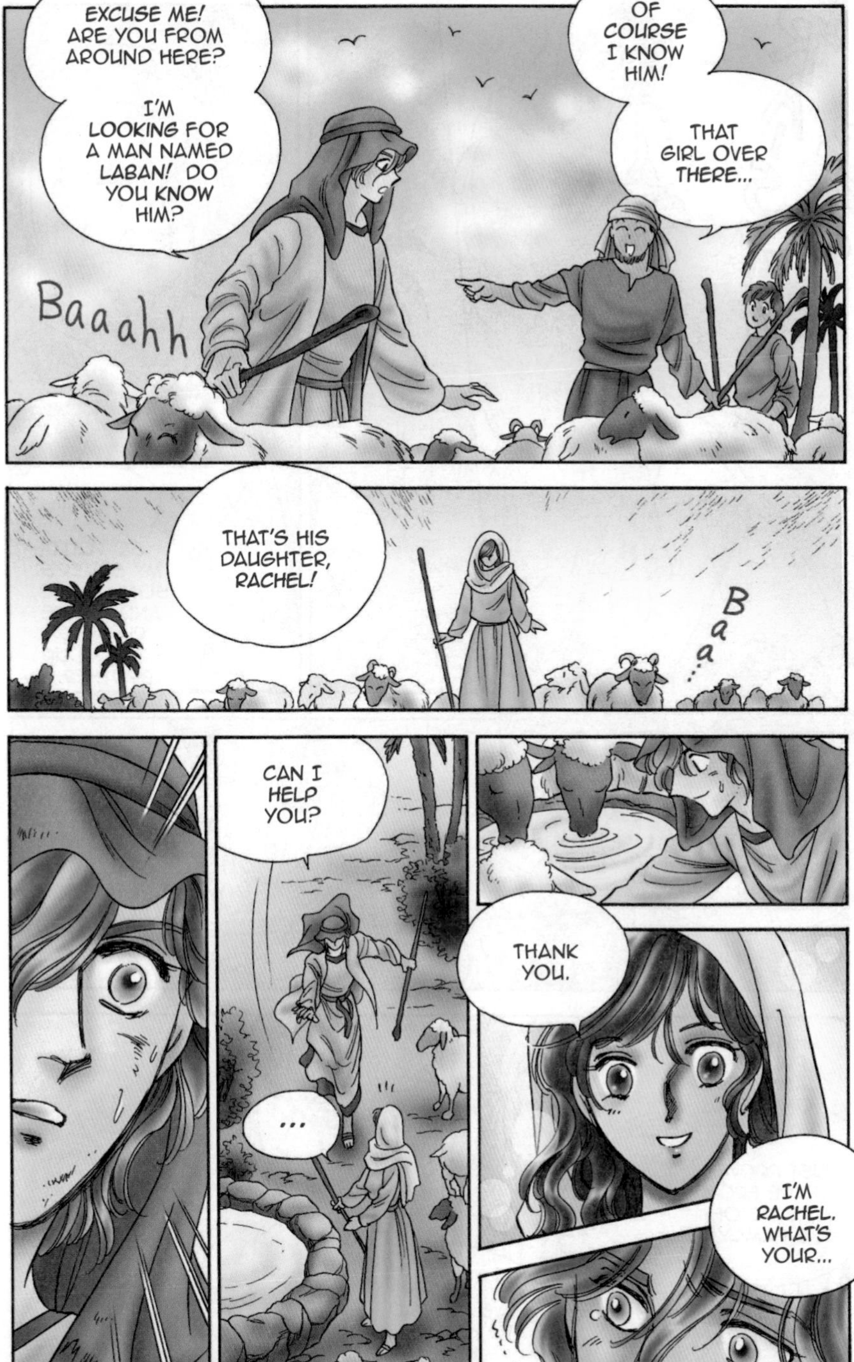
EXCUSE ME! ARE YOU FROM AROUND HERE?
I'M LOOKING FOR A MAN NAMED LABAN! DO YOU KNOW HIM?
OF COURSE I KNOW HIM!
THAT GIRL OVER THERE...
Baaahh
THAT'S HIS DAUGHTER, RACHEL!
Baa...
CAN I HELP YOU?
...
THANK YOU.
I'M RACHEL. WHAT'S YOUR...

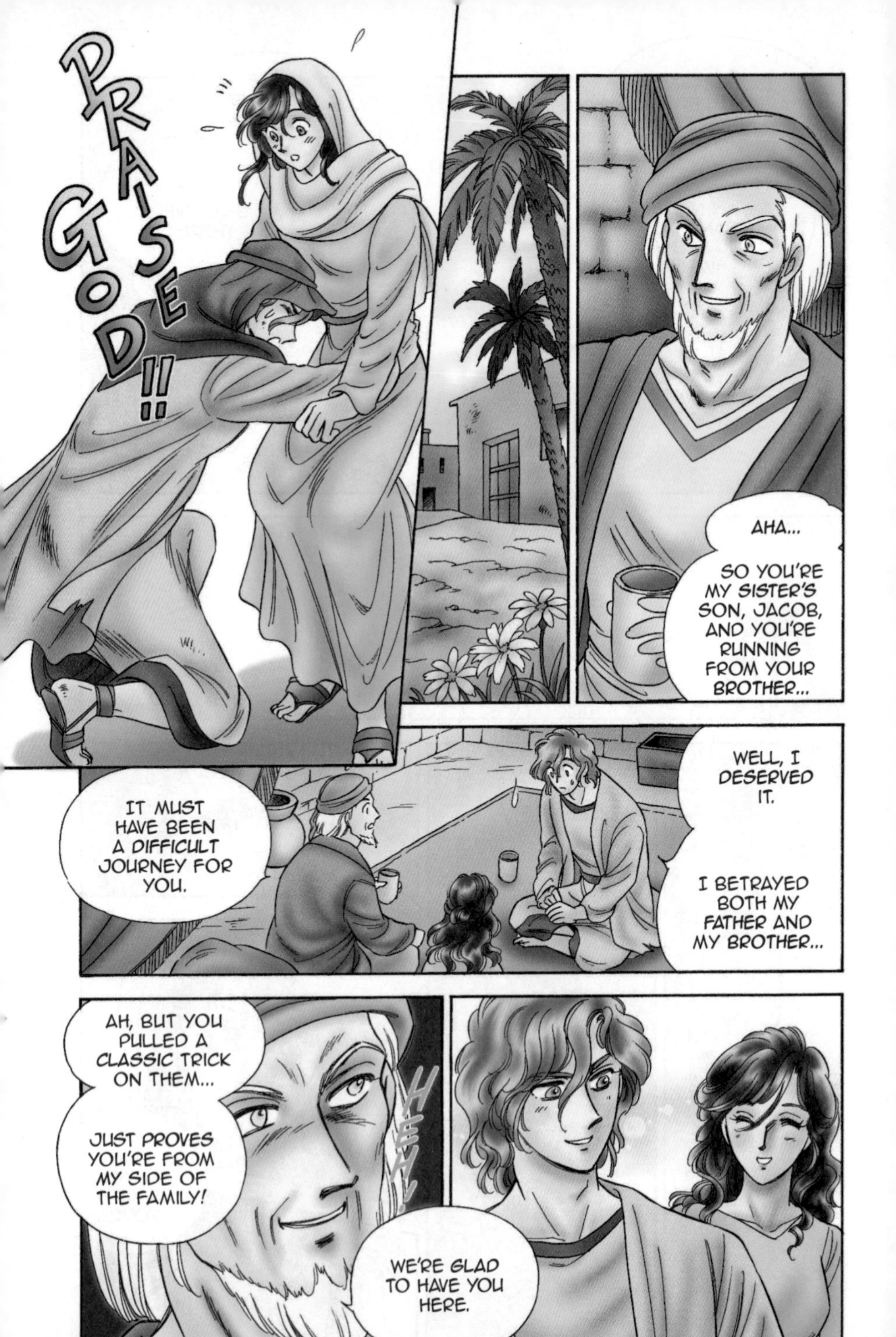
PRAISE GOD!!
AHA...
SO YOU'RE MY SISTER'S SON, JACOB, AND YOU'RE RUNNING FROM YOUR BROTHER...
IT MUST HAVE BEEN A DIFFICULT JOURNEY FOR YOU.
WELL, I DESERVED IT.
I BETRAYED BOTH MY FATHER AND MY BROTHER...
AH, BUT YOU PULLED A CLASSIC TRICK ON THEM...
JUST PROVES YOU'RE FROM MY SIDE OF THE FAMILY!
HEH!
WE'RE GLAD TO HAVE YOU HERE.

13. In the House of Laban

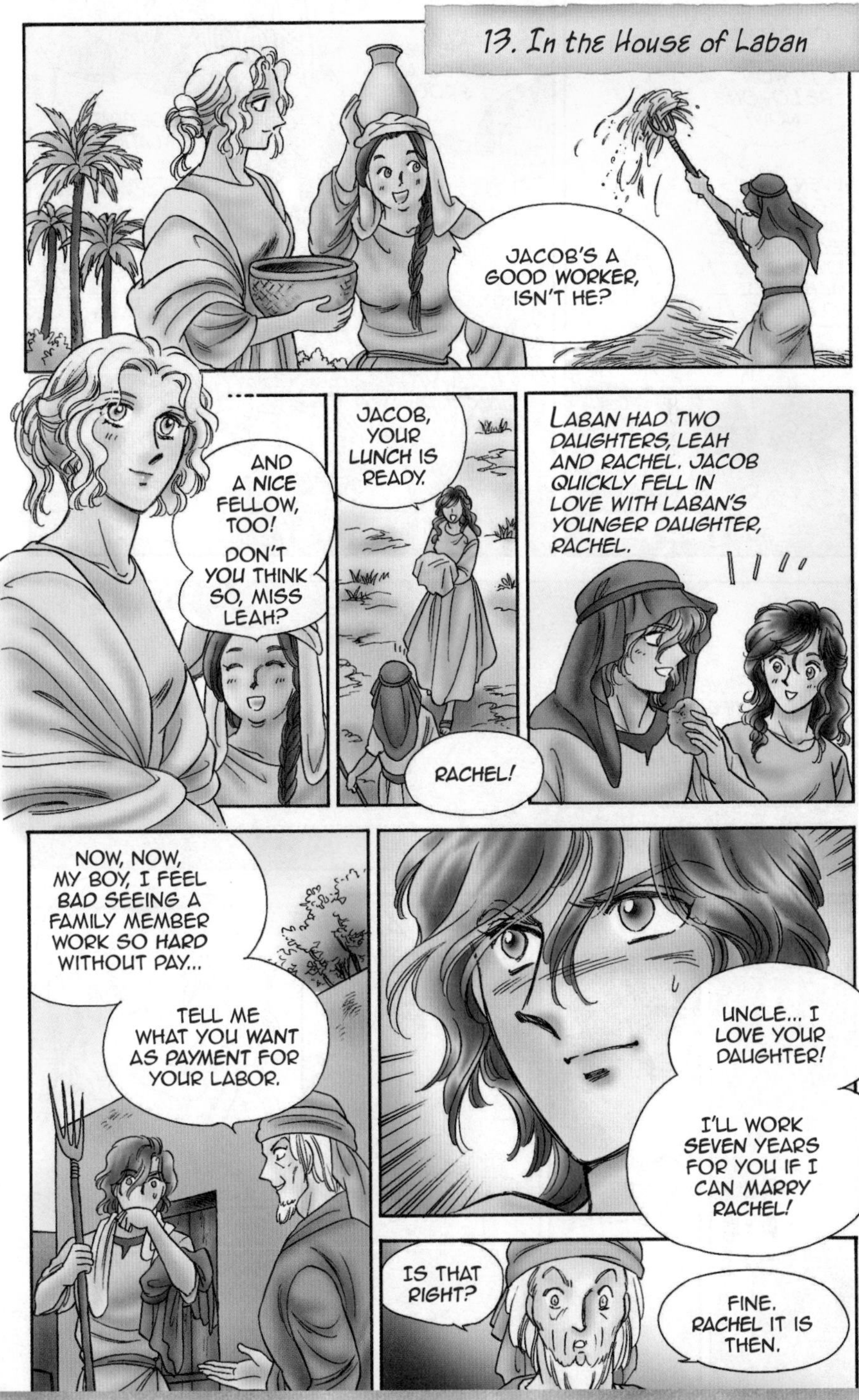
JACOB'S A GOOD WORKER, ISN'T HE?
...
AND A NICE FELLOW, TOO!
DON'T YOU THINK SO, MISS LEAH?
JACOB, YOUR LUNCH IS READY.
RACHEL!
LABAN HAD TWO DAUGHTERS, LEAH AND RACHEL. JACOB QUICKLY FELL IN LOVE WITH LABAN'S YOUNGER DAUGHTER, RACHEL.
NOW, NOW, MY BOY, I FEEL BAD SEEING A FAMILY MEMBER WORK SO HARD WITHOUT PAY...
TELL ME WHAT YOU WANT AS PAYMENT FOR YOUR LABOR.
UNCLE... I LOVE YOUR DAUGHTER!
I'LL WORK SEVEN YEARS FOR YOU IF I CAN MARRY RACHEL!
IS THAT RIGHT?
FINE. RACHEL IT IS THEN.

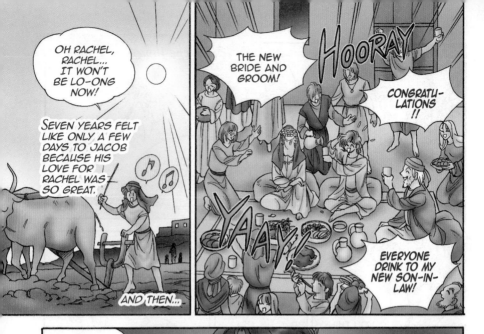

OH RACHEL, RACHEL... IT WON'T BE LO-ONG NOW!

SEVEN YEARS FELT LIKE ONLY A FEW DAYS TO JACOB BECAUSE HIS LOVE FOR RACHEL WAS SO GREAT.

AND THEN...

HOORAY

THE NEW BRIDE AND GROOM!

CONGRATU-LATIONS!!

YAAY!

EVERYONE DRINK TO MY NEW SON-IN-LAW!

OH RACHEL... MY SWEET WIFE!

TO FINALLY BE WITH YOU!

CHIRP

CHIRP

HUH?

AAAH!!

GOOD MORNING, JACOB.

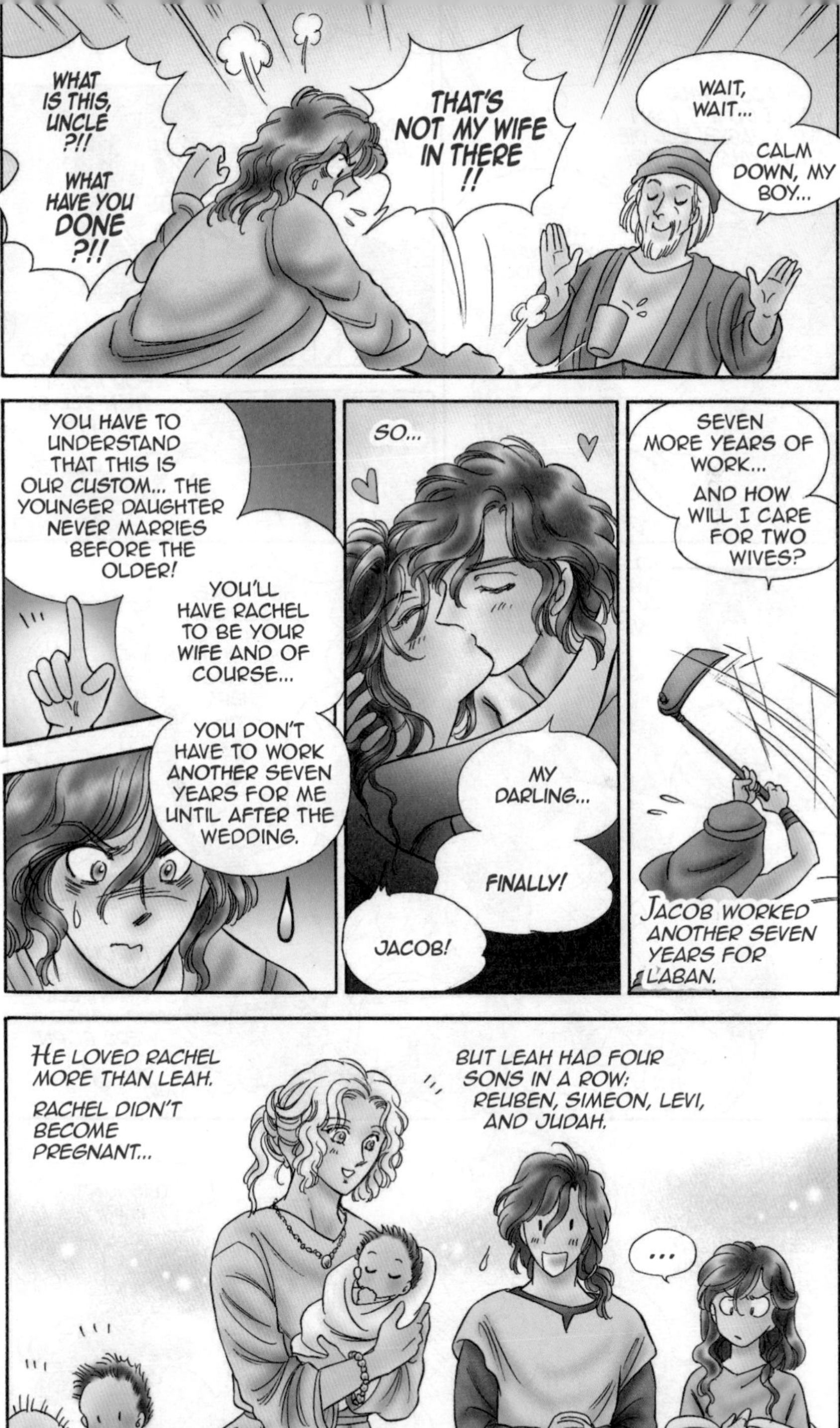
WHAT IS THIS, UNCLE ?!!
WHAT HAVE YOU DONE ?!!
THAT'S NOT MY WIFE IN THERE !!
WAIT, WAIT...
CALM DOWN, MY BOY...
YOU HAVE TO UNDERSTAND THAT THIS IS OUR CUSTOM... THE YOUNGER DAUGHTER NEVER MARRIES BEFORE THE OLDER!
YOU'LL HAVE RACHEL TO BE YOUR WIFE AND OF COURSE...
YOU DON'T HAVE TO WORK ANOTHER SEVEN YEARS FOR ME UNTIL AFTER THE WEDDING.
SO...
MY DARLING...
FINALLY!
JACOB!
SEVEN MORE YEARS OF WORK...
AND HOW WILL I CARE FOR TWO WIVES?
JACOB WORKED ANOTHER SEVEN YEARS FOR LABAN.
HE LOVED RACHEL MORE THAN LEAH.
RACHEL DIDN'T BECOME PREGNANT...
BUT LEAH HAD FOUR SONS IN A ROW: REUBEN, SIMEON, LEVI, AND JUDAH.
...

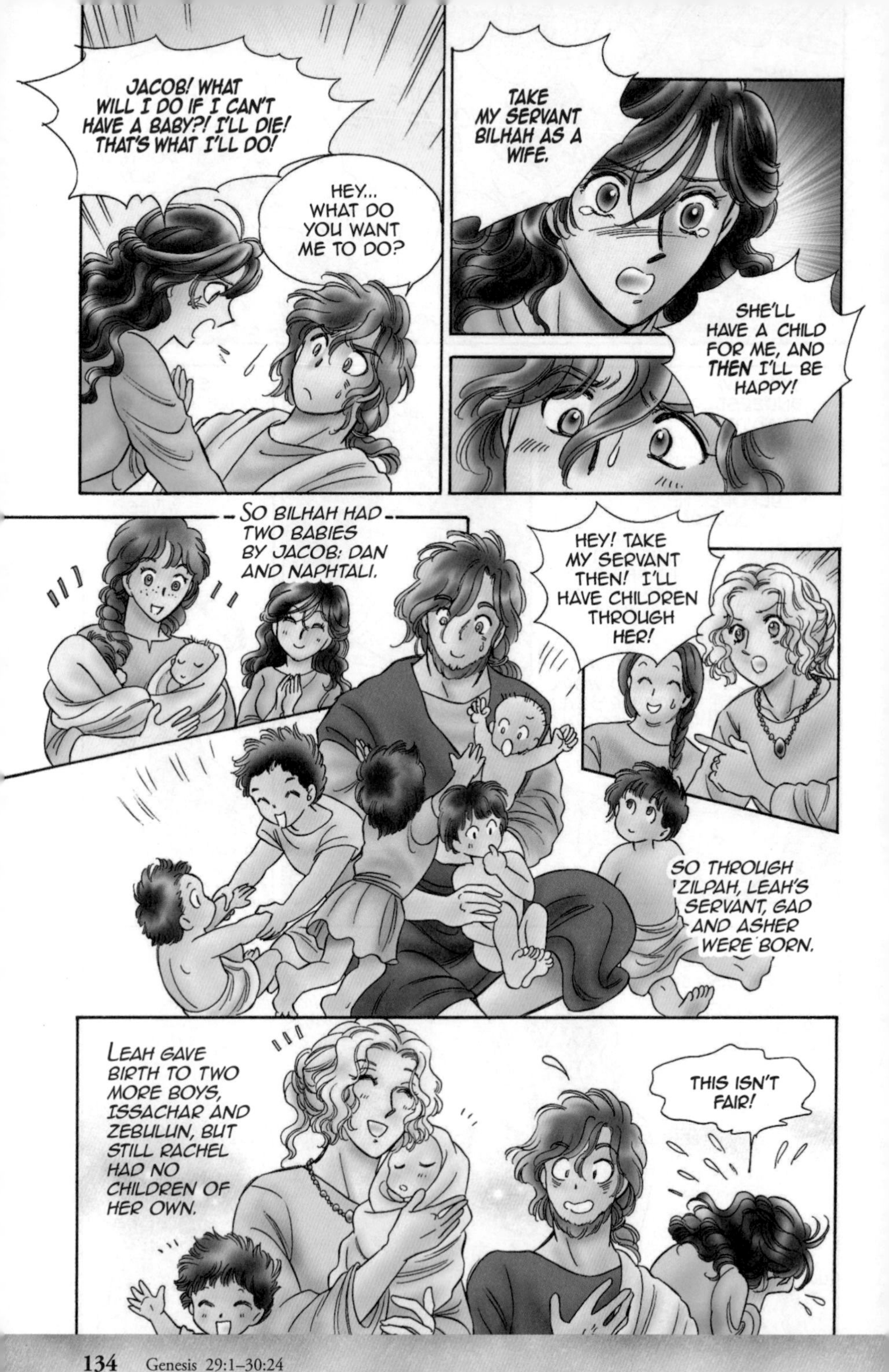
JACOB! WHAT WILL I DO IF I CAN'T HAVE A BABY?! I'LL DIE! THAT'S WHAT I'LL DO!
HEY... WHAT DO YOU WANT ME TO DO?
TAKE MY SERVANT BILHAH AS A WIFE.
SHE'LL HAVE A CHILD FOR ME, AND THEN I'LL BE HAPPY!
SO BILHAH HAD TWO BABIES BY JACOB: DAN AND NAPHTALI.
HEY! TAKE MY SERVANT THEN! I'LL HAVE CHILDREN THROUGH HER!
SO THROUGH ZILPAH, LEAH'S SERVANT, GAD AND ASHER WERE BORN.
LEAH GAVE BIRTH TO TWO MORE BOYS, ISSACHAR AND ZEBULUN, BUT STILL RACHEL HAD NO CHILDREN OF HER OWN.
THIS ISN'T FAIR!

OH GOD, PLEASE...

PLEASE LET ME HAVE A CHILD, TOO!

AND FINALLY...

RACHEL DID HAVE A CHILD, JACOB'S ELEVENTH SON...

AND SHE NAMED HIM JOSEPH.

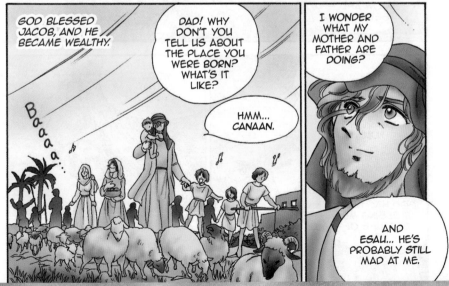

GOD BLESSED JACOB, AND HE BECAME WEALTHY.

DAD! WHY DON'T YOU TELL US ABOUT THE PLACE YOU WERE BORN? WHAT'S IT LIKE?

HMM... CANAAN.

Baaaa...♪

I WONDER WHAT MY MOTHER AND FATHER ARE DOING?

AND ESAU... HE'S PROBABLY STILL MAD AT ME.

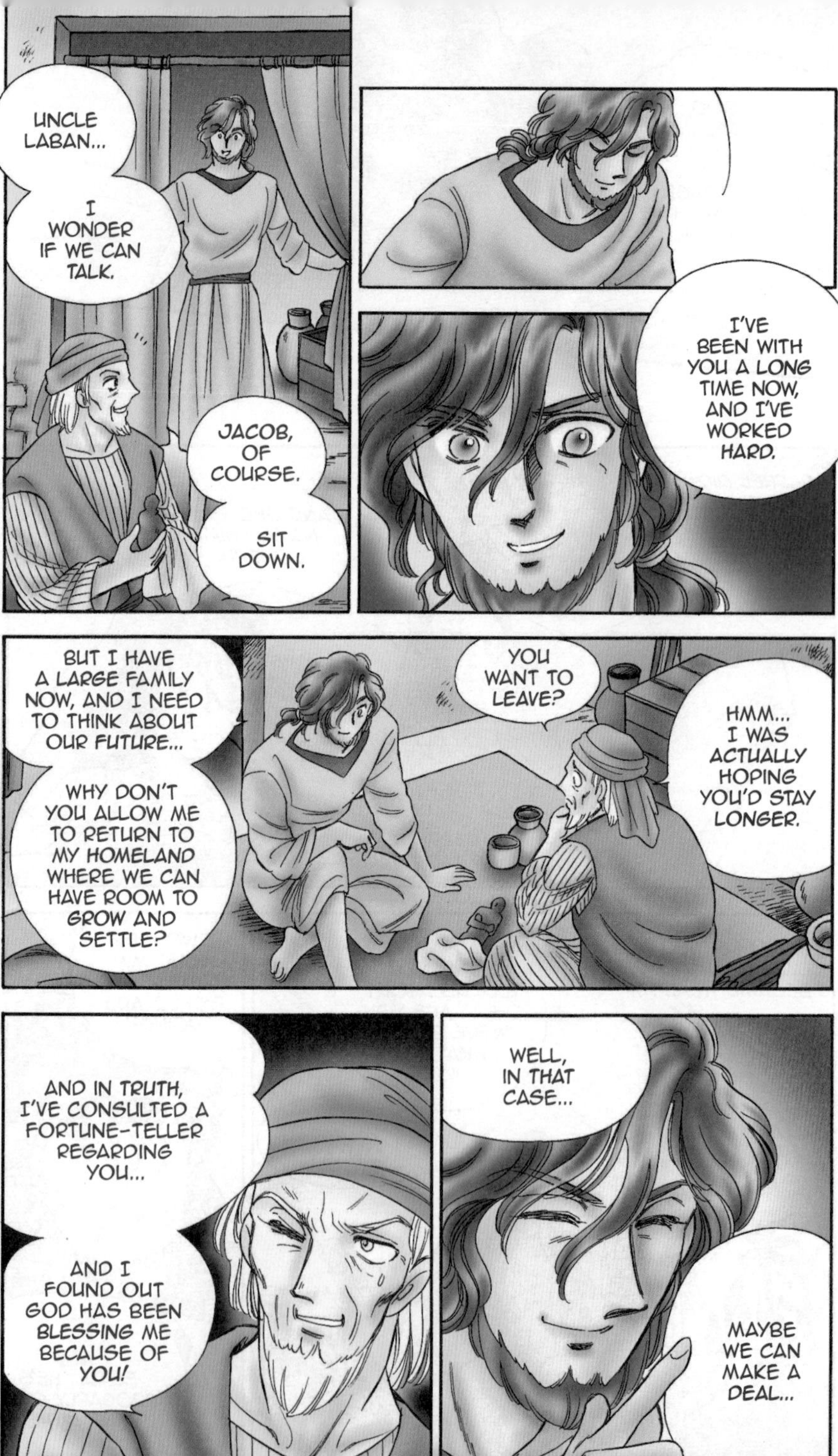
UNCLE LABAN...
I WONDER IF WE CAN TALK.
JACOB, OF COURSE.
SIT DOWN.
I'VE BEEN WITH YOU A LONG TIME NOW, AND I'VE WORKED HARD.
BUT I HAVE A LARGE FAMILY NOW, AND I NEED TO THINK ABOUT OUR FUTURE...
WHY DON'T YOU ALLOW ME TO RETURN TO MY HOMELAND WHERE WE CAN HAVE ROOM TO GROW AND SETTLE?
YOU WANT TO LEAVE?
HMM... I WAS ACTUALLY HOPING YOU'D STAY LONGER.
AND IN TRUTH, I'VE CONSULTED A FORTUNE-TELLER REGARDING YOU...
AND I FOUND OUT GOD HAS BEEN BLESSING ME BECAUSE OF YOU!
WELL, IN THAT CASE...
MAYBE WE CAN MAKE A DEAL...

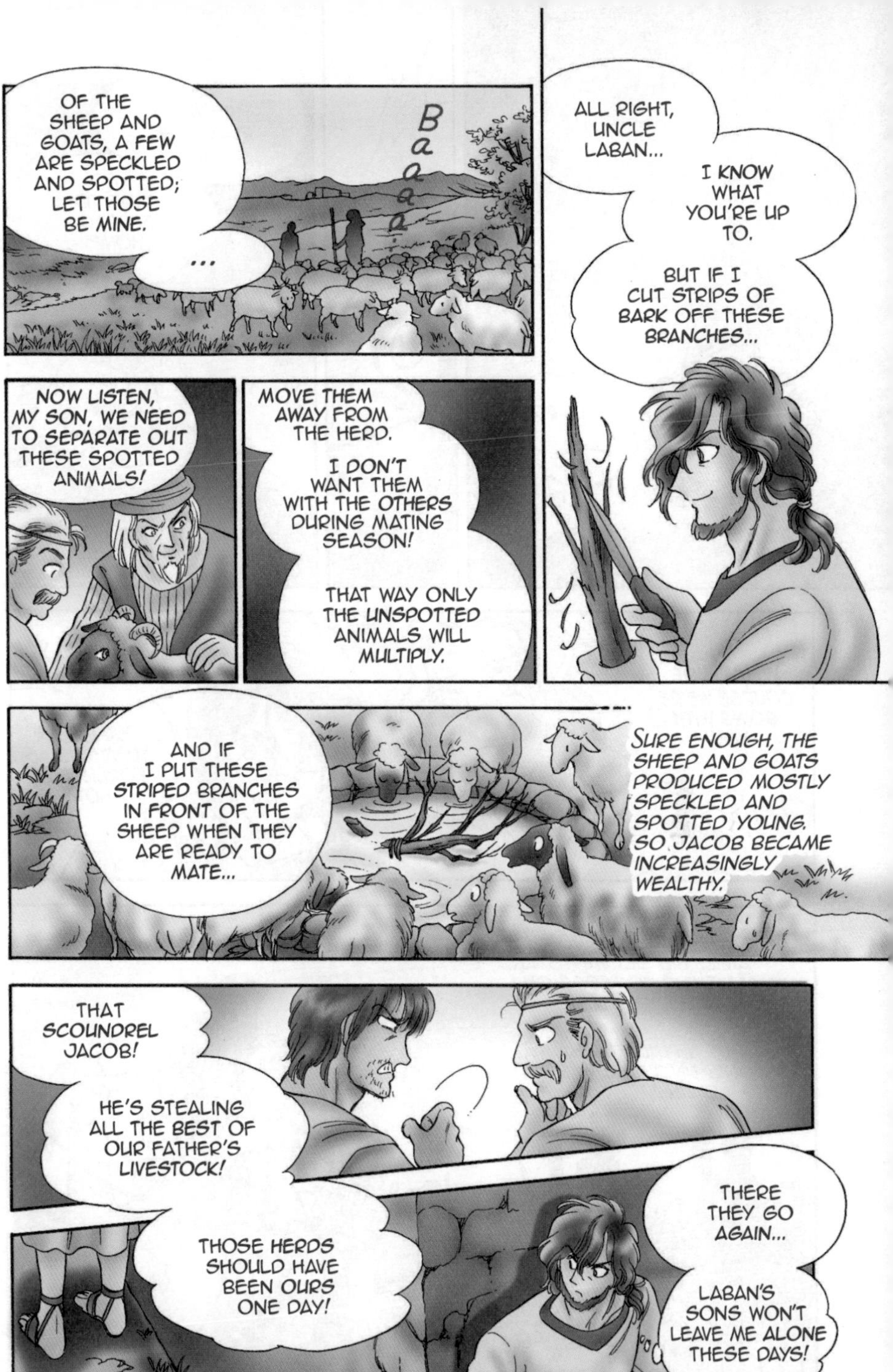
OF THE SHEEP AND GOATS, A FEW ARE SPECKLED AND SPOTTED; LET THOSE BE MINE.
Baaaaa
...
NOW LISTEN, MY SON, WE NEED TO SEPARATE OUT THESE SPOTTED ANIMALS!
MOVE THEM AWAY FROM THE HERD.
I DON'T WANT THEM WITH THE OTHERS DURING MATING SEASON!
THAT WAY ONLY THE UNSPOTTED ANIMALS WILL MULTIPLY.
ALL RIGHT, UNCLE LABAN...
I KNOW WHAT YOU'RE UP TO.
BUT IF I CUT STRIPS OF BARK OFF THESE BRANCHES...
AND IF I PUT THESE STRIPED BRANCHES IN FRONT OF THE SHEEP WHEN THEY ARE READY TO MATE...
SURE ENOUGH, THE SHEEP AND GOATS PRODUCED MOSTLY SPECKLED AND SPOTTED YOUNG. SO JACOB BECAME INCREASINGLY WEALTHY.
THAT SCOUNDREL JACOB!
HE'S STEALING ALL THE BEST OF OUR FATHER'S LIVESTOCK!
THOSE HERDS SHOULD HAVE BEEN OURS ONE DAY!
THERE THEY GO AGAIN...
LABAN'S SONS WON'T LEAVE ME ALONE THESE DAYS!

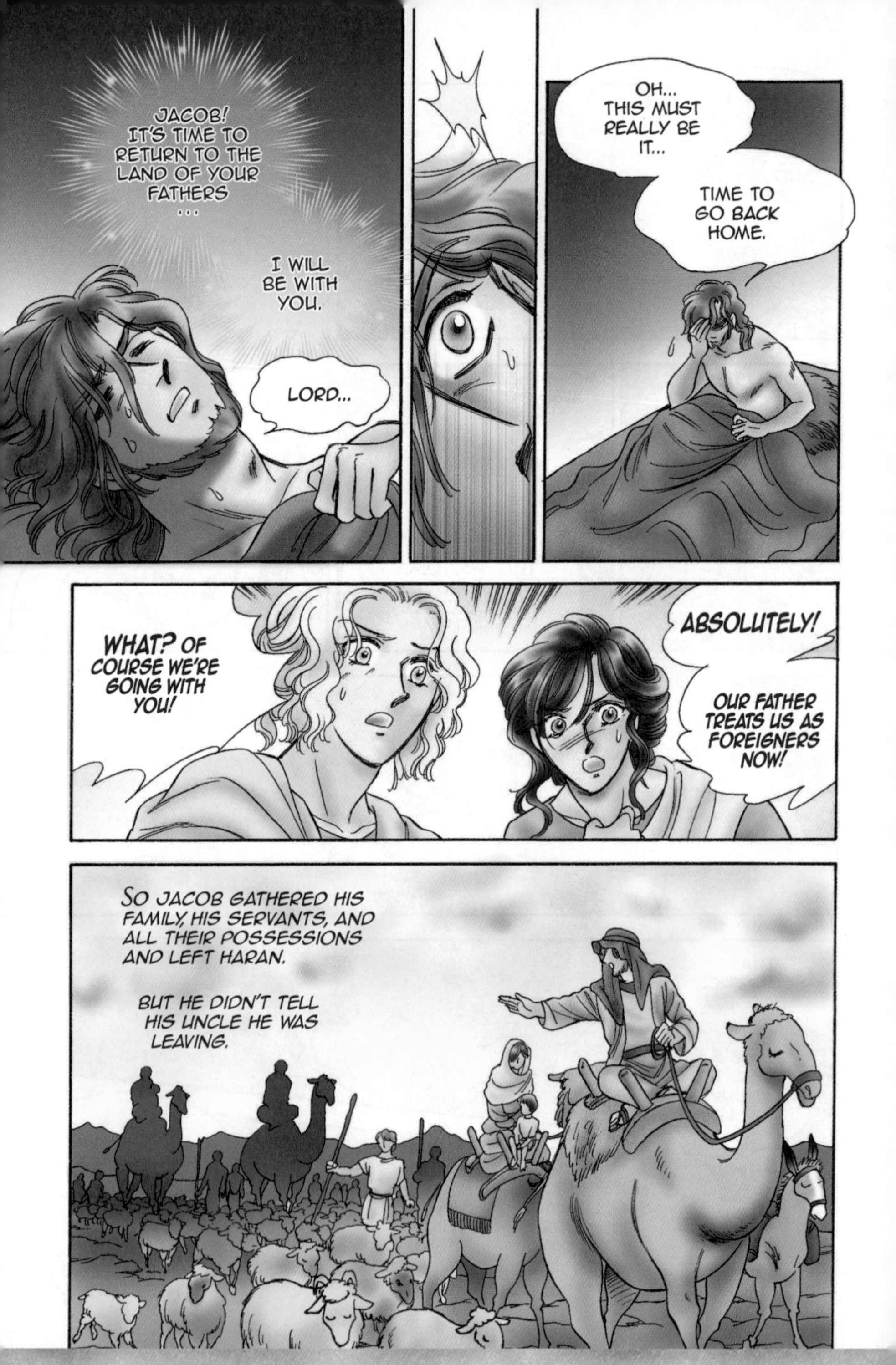
JACOB! IT'S TIME TO RETURN TO THE LAND OF YOUR FATHERS ...
I WILL BE WITH YOU.
LORD...
OH... THIS MUST REALLY BE IT...
TIME TO GO BACK HOME.
WHAT? OF COURSE WE'RE GOING WITH YOU!
ABSOLUTELY!
OUR FATHER TREATS US AS FOREIGNERS NOW!
SO JACOB GATHERED HIS FAMILY, HIS SERVANTS, AND ALL THEIR POSSESSIONS AND LEFT HARAN.
BUT HE DIDN'T TELL HIS UNCLE HE WAS LEAVING.

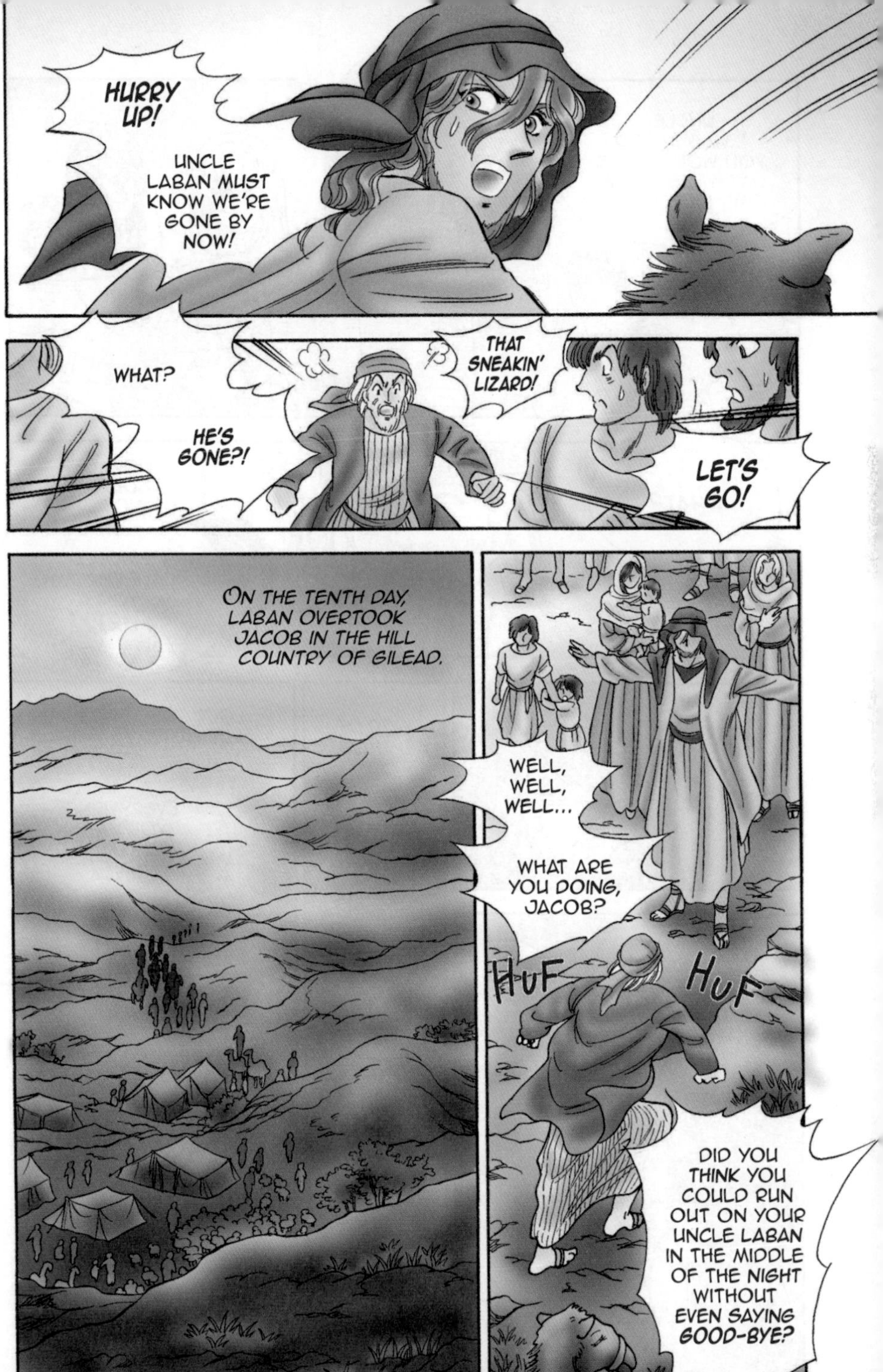
HURRY UP!
UNCLE LABAN MUST KNOW WE'RE GONE BY NOW!
WHAT?
HE'S GONE?!
THAT SNEAKIN' LIZARD!
LET'S GO!
ON THE TENTH DAY, LABAN OVERTOOK JACOB IN THE HILL COUNTRY OF GILEAD.
WELL, WELL, WELL...
WHAT ARE YOU DOING, JACOB?
HUF HUF
DID YOU THINK YOU COULD RUN OUT ON YOUR UNCLE LABAN IN THE MIDDLE OF THE NIGHT WITHOUT EVEN SAYING GOOD-BYE?

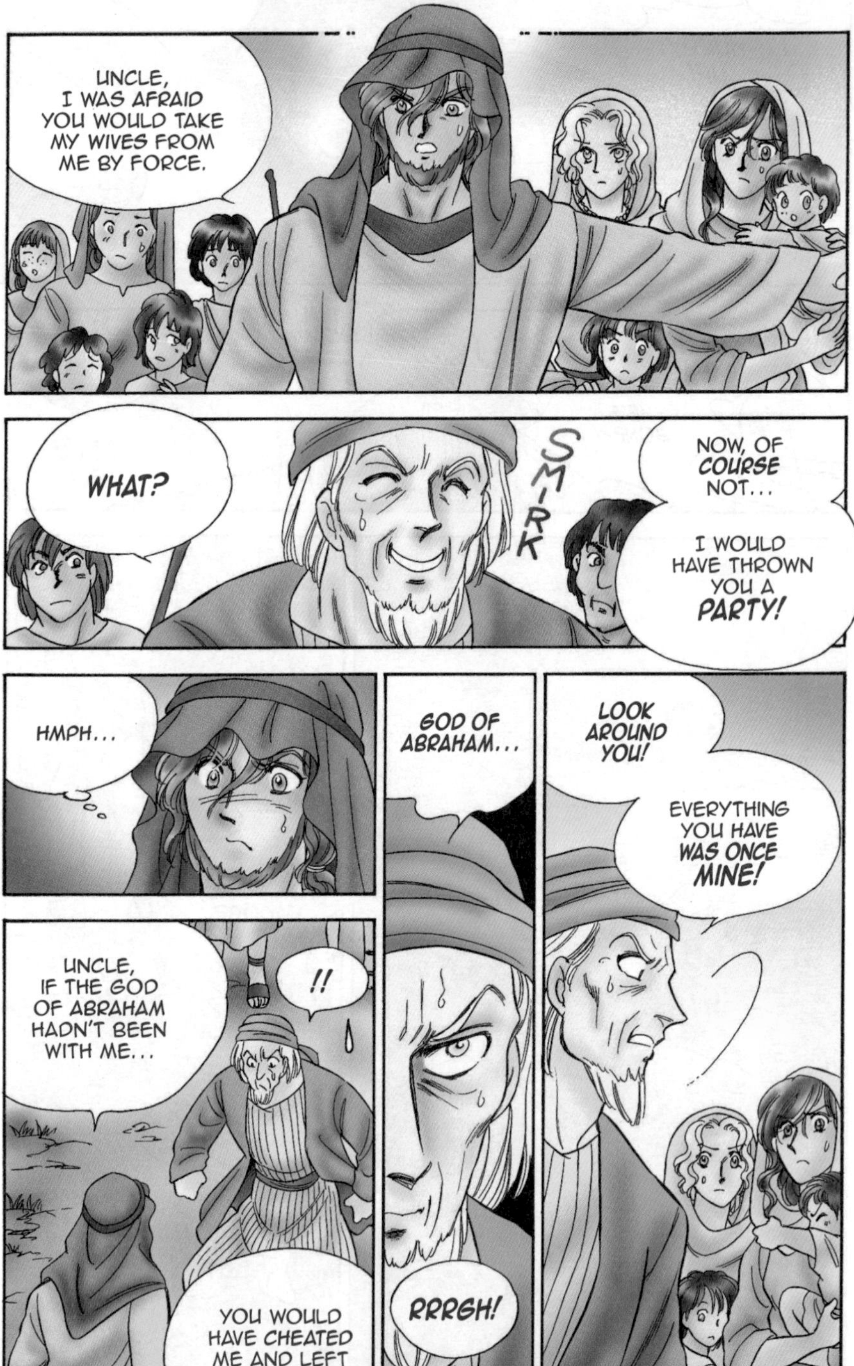
UNCLE, I WAS AFRAID YOU WOULD TAKE MY WIVES FROM ME BY FORCE.
WHAT?
SMIRK
NOW, OF COURSE NOT...
I WOULD HAVE THROWN YOU A PARTY!
HMPH...
GOD OF ABRAHAM...
LOOK AROUND YOU!
EVERYTHING YOU HAVE WAS ONCE MINE!
UNCLE, IF THE GOD OF ABRAHAM HADN'T BEEN WITH ME...
!!
YOU WOULD HAVE CHEATED ME AND LEFT ME WITH NOTHING!
RRRGH!

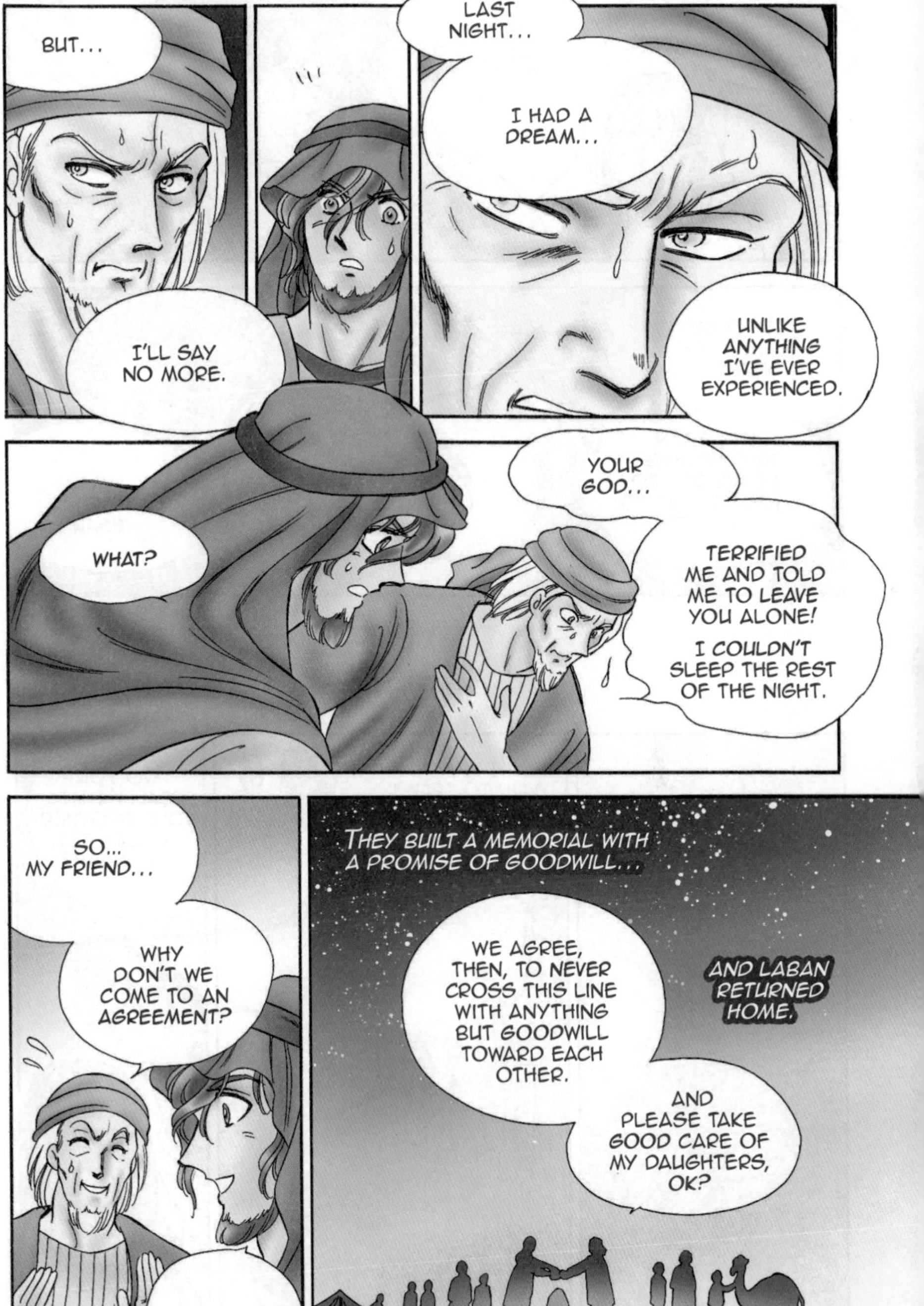
BUT...
I'LL SAY NO MORE.
LAST NIGHT...
I HAD A DREAM...
UNLIKE ANYTHING I'VE EVER EXPERIENCED.
WHAT?
YOUR GOD...
TERRIFIED ME AND TOLD ME TO LEAVE YOU ALONE!
I COULDN'T SLEEP THE REST OF THE NIGHT.
SO... MY FRIEND...
WHY DON'T WE COME TO AN AGREEMENT?
...
THEY BUILT A MEMORIAL WITH A PROMISE OF GOODWILL...
WE AGREE, THEN, TO NEVER CROSS THIS LINE WITH ANYTHING BUT GOODWILL TOWARD EACH OTHER.
AND PLEASE TAKE GOOD CARE OF MY DAUGHTERS, OK?
AND LABAN RETURNED HOME.

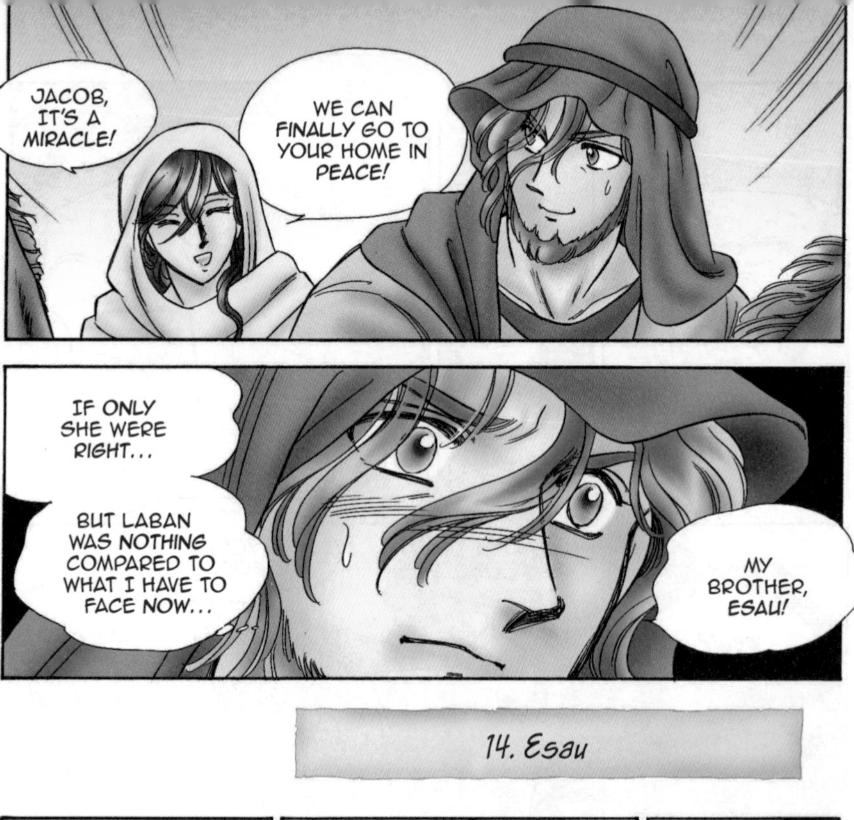
JACOB, IT'S A MIRACLE!
WE CAN FINALLY GO TO YOUR HOME IN PEACE!
IF ONLY SHE WERE RIGHT...
BUT LABAN WAS NOTHING COMPARED TO WHAT I HAVE TO FACE NOW...
MY BROTHER, ESAU!

14. Esau

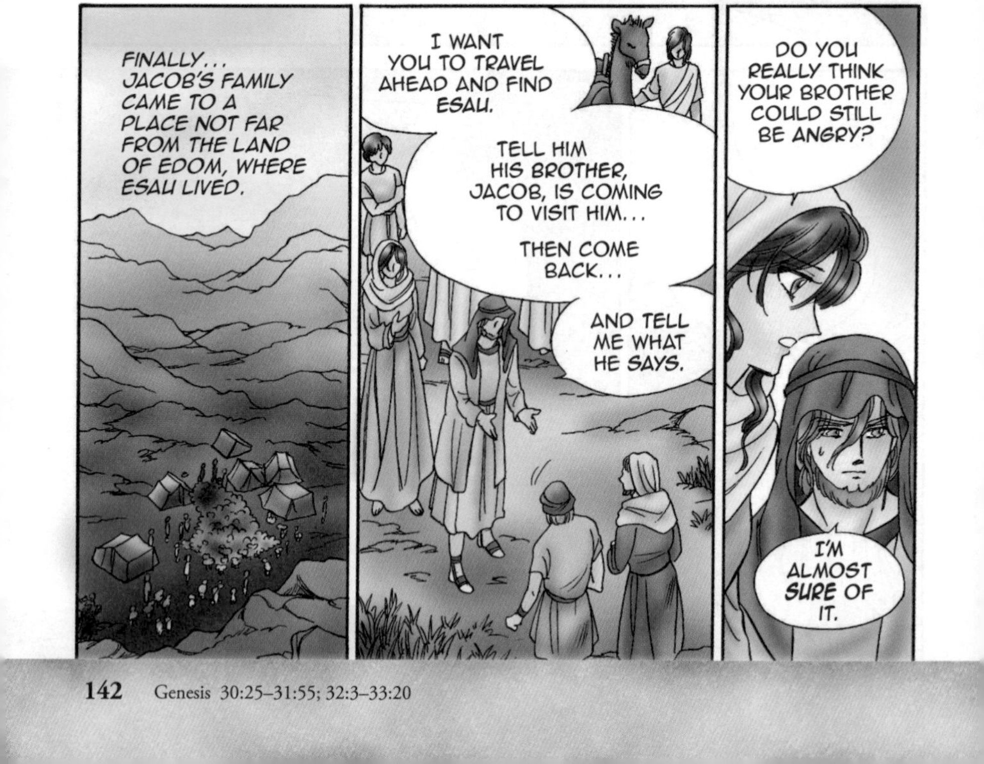
FINALLY... JACOB'S FAMILY CAME TO A PLACE NOT FAR FROM THE LAND OF EDOM, WHERE ESAU LIVED.
I WANT YOU TO TRAVEL AHEAD AND FIND ESAU.
TELL HIM HIS BROTHER, JACOB, IS COMING TO VISIT HIM...
THEN COME BACK...
AND TELL ME WHAT HE SAYS.
DO YOU REALLY THINK YOUR BROTHER COULD STILL BE ANGRY?
I'M ALMOST SURE OF IT.

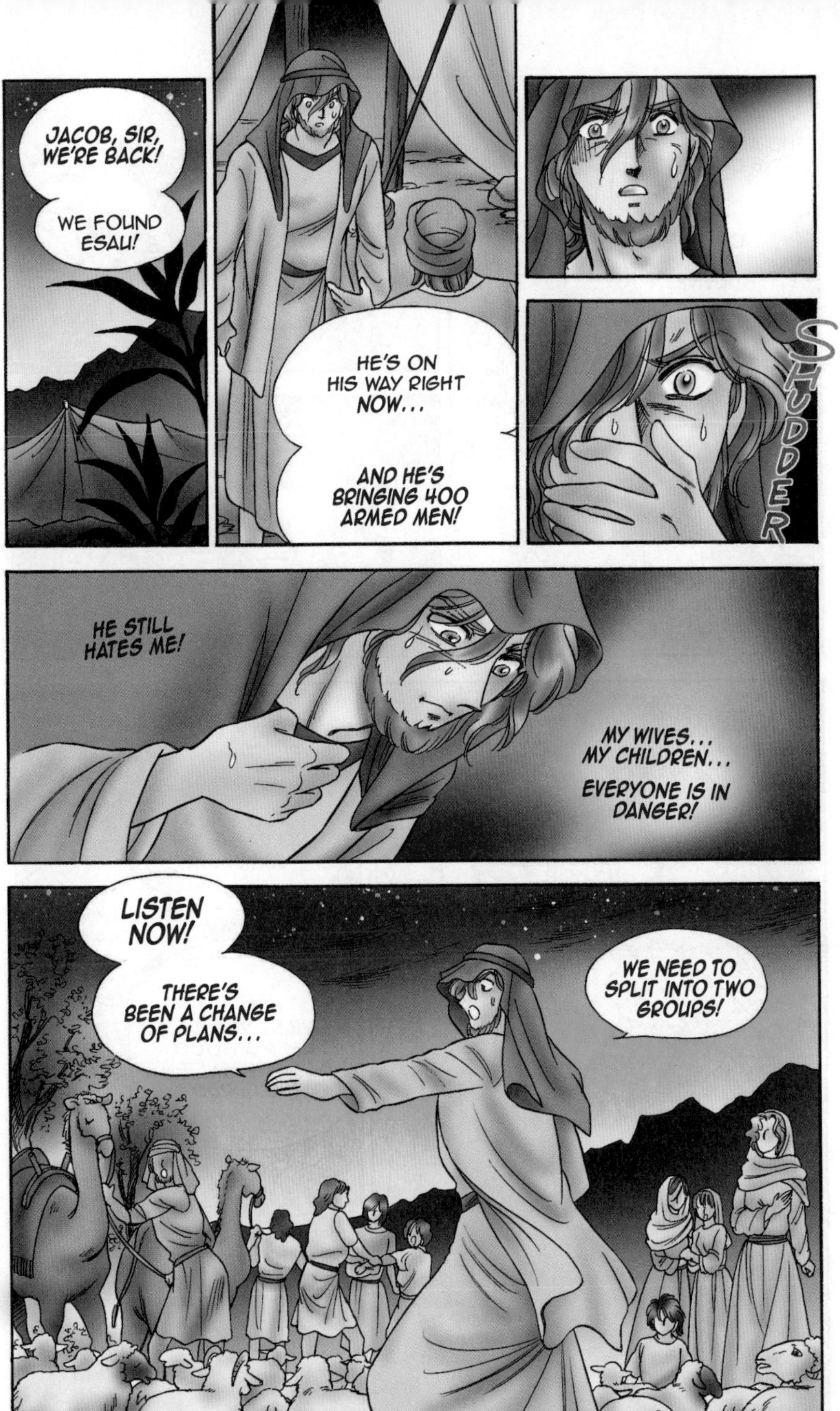
JACOB, SIR, WE'RE BACK!
WE FOUND ESAU!
HE'S ON HIS WAY RIGHT NOW...
AND HE'S BRINGING 400 ARMED MEN!
SHUDDER
HE STILL HATES ME!
MY WIVES... MY CHILDREN...
EVERYONE IS IN DANGER!
LISTEN NOW!
THERE'S BEEN A CHANGE OF PLANS...
WE NEED TO SPLIT INTO TWO GROUPS!

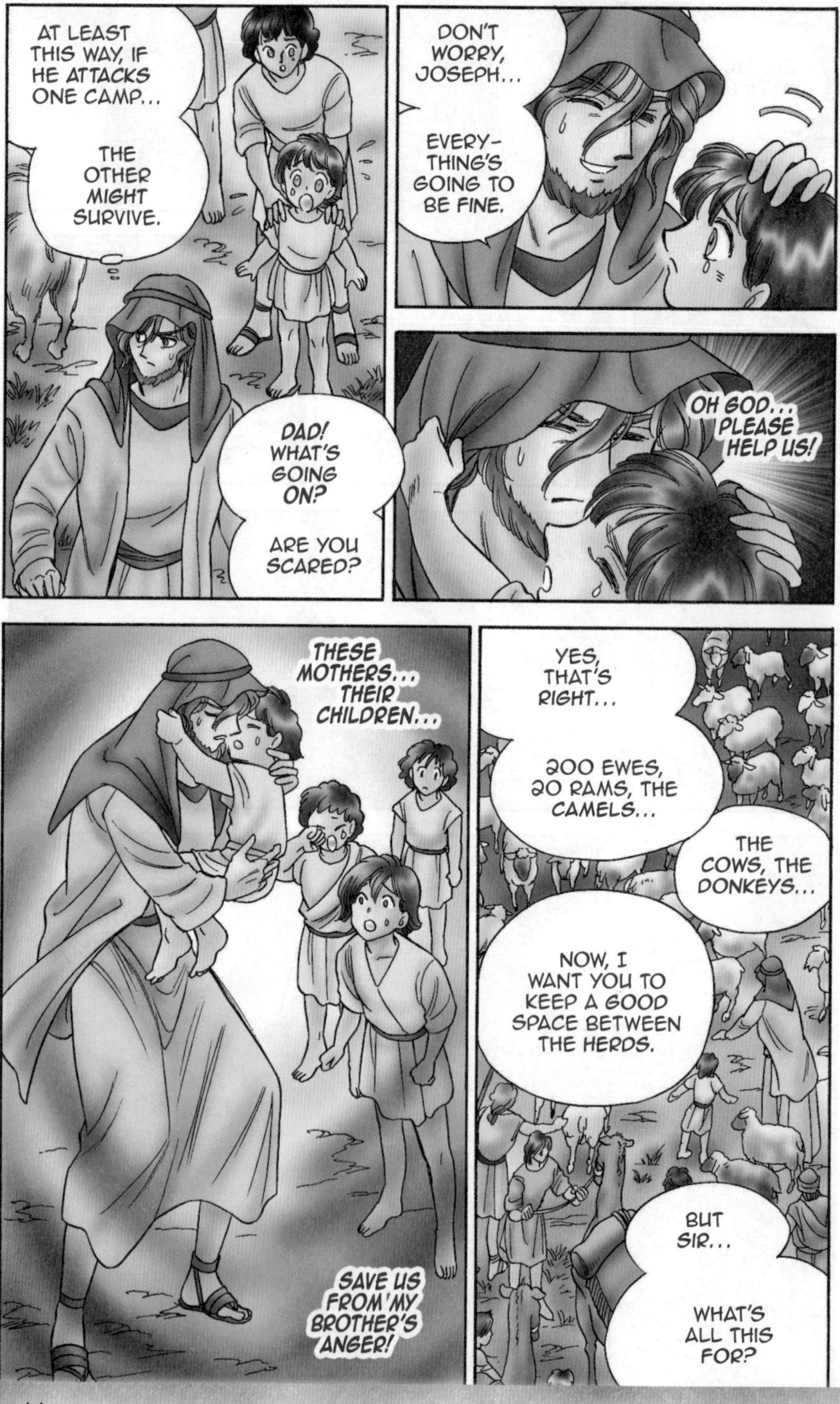
AT LEAST THIS WAY, IF HE ATTACKS ONE CAMP...
THE OTHER MIGHT SURVIVE.
DAD! WHAT'S GOING ON?
ARE YOU SCARED?
DON'T WORRY, JOSEPH...
EVERY-THING'S GOING TO BE FINE.
OH GOD... PLEASE HELP US!
THESE MOTHERS... THEIR CHILDREN...
SAVE US FROM MY BROTHER'S ANGER!
YES, THAT'S RIGHT...
200 EWES, 20 RAMS, THE CAMELS...
THE COWS, THE DONKEYS...
NOW, I WANT YOU TO KEEP A GOOD SPACE BETWEEN THE HERDS.
BUT SIR...
WHAT'S ALL THIS FOR?

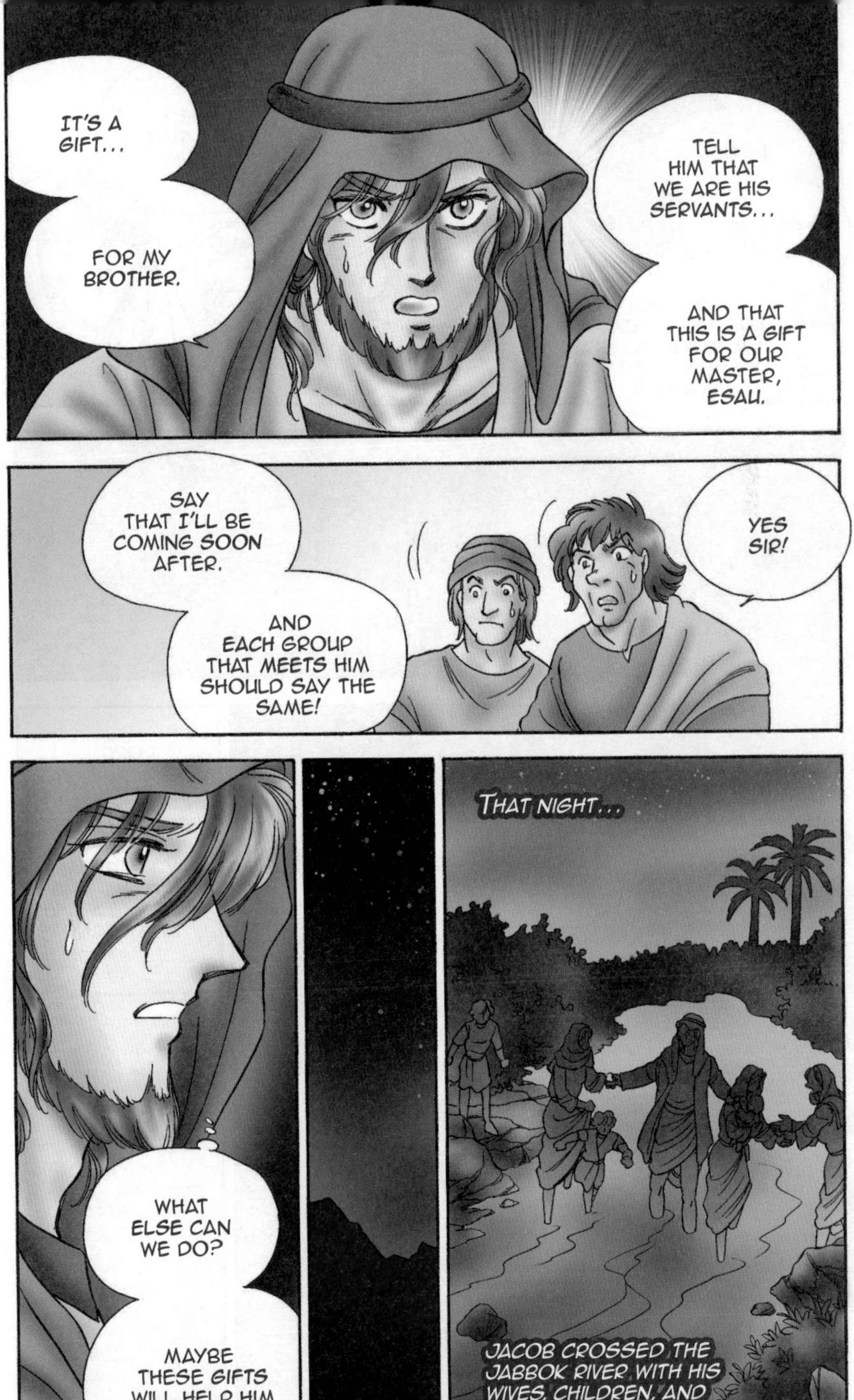
IT'S A GIFT...
FOR MY BROTHER.
TELL HIM THAT WE ARE HIS SERVANTS...
AND THAT THIS IS A GIFT FOR OUR MASTER, ESAU.
SAY THAT I'LL BE COMING SOON AFTER.
AND EACH GROUP THAT MEETS HIM SHOULD SAY THE SAME!
YES SIR!
WHAT ELSE CAN WE DO?
MAYBE THESE GIFTS WILL HELP HIM FORGIVE ME.
THAT NIGHT...
JACOB CROSSED THE JABBOK RIVER WITH HIS WIVES, CHILDREN, AND POSSESSIONS.

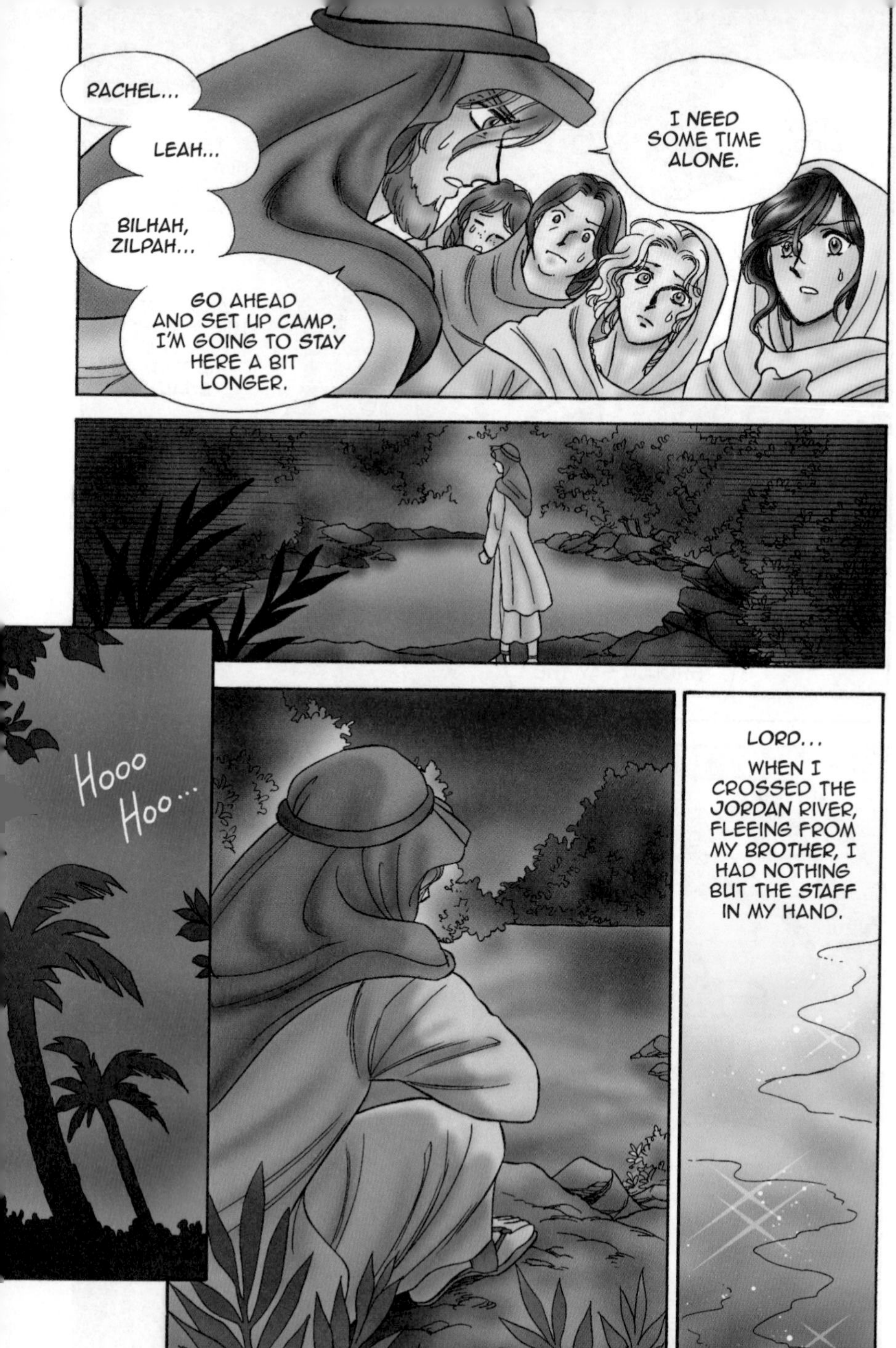
RACHEL...
LEAH...
BILHAH, ZILPAH...
GO AHEAD AND SET UP CAMP. I'M GOING TO STAY HERE A BIT LONGER.
I NEED SOME TIME ALONE.
Hooo Hoo...
LORD...
WHEN I CROSSED THE JORDAN RIVER, FLEEING FROM MY BROTHER, I HAD NOTHING BUT THE STAFF IN MY HAND.

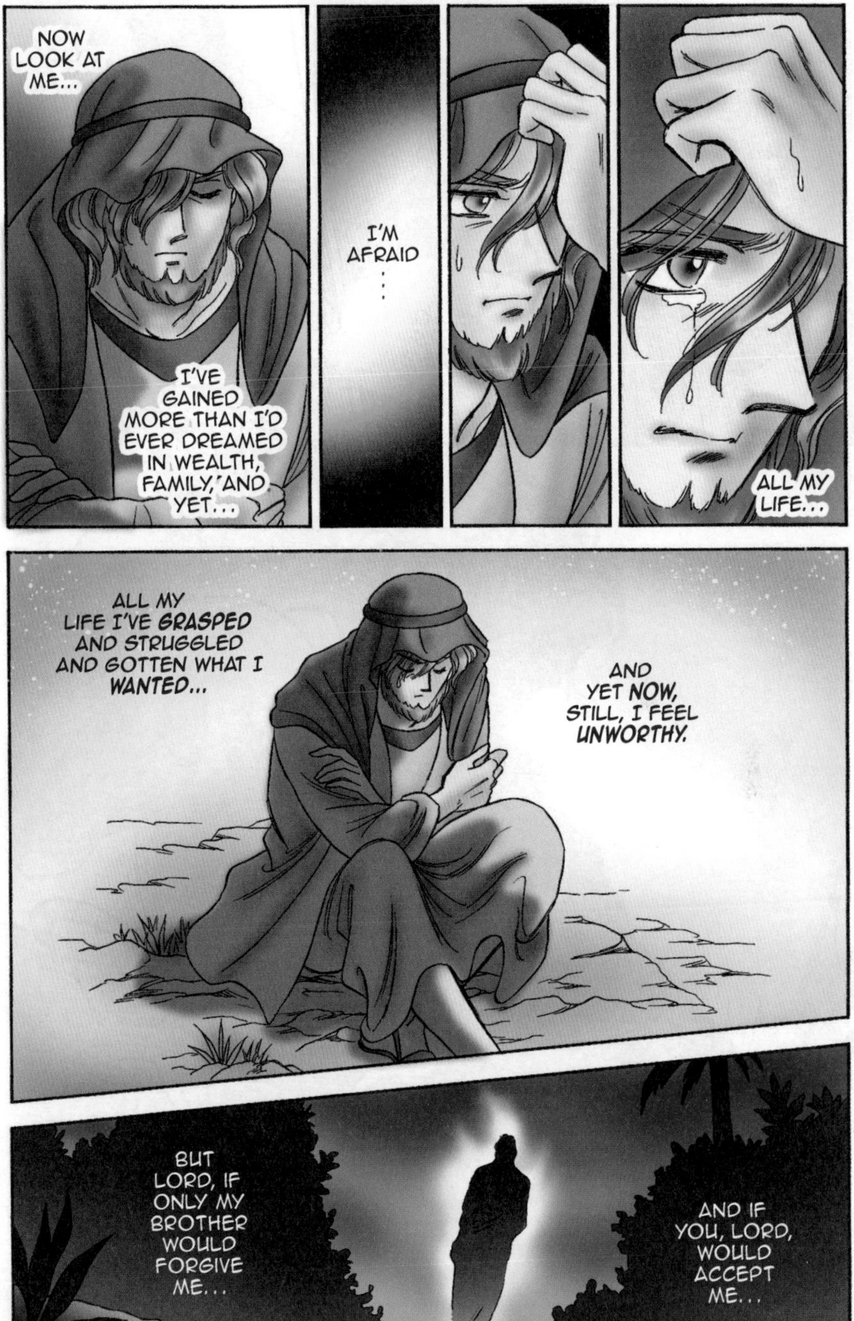
NOW LOOK AT ME...
I'VE GAINED MORE THAN I'D EVER DREAMED IN WEALTH, FAMILY, AND YET...
I'M AFRAID
...
ALL MY LIFE...
ALL MY LIFE I'VE GRASPED AND STRUGGLED AND GOTTEN WHAT I WANTED...
AND YET NOW, STILL, I FEEL UNWORTHY.
BUT LORD, IF ONLY MY BROTHER WOULD FORGIVE ME...
AND IF YOU, LORD, WOULD ACCEPT ME...

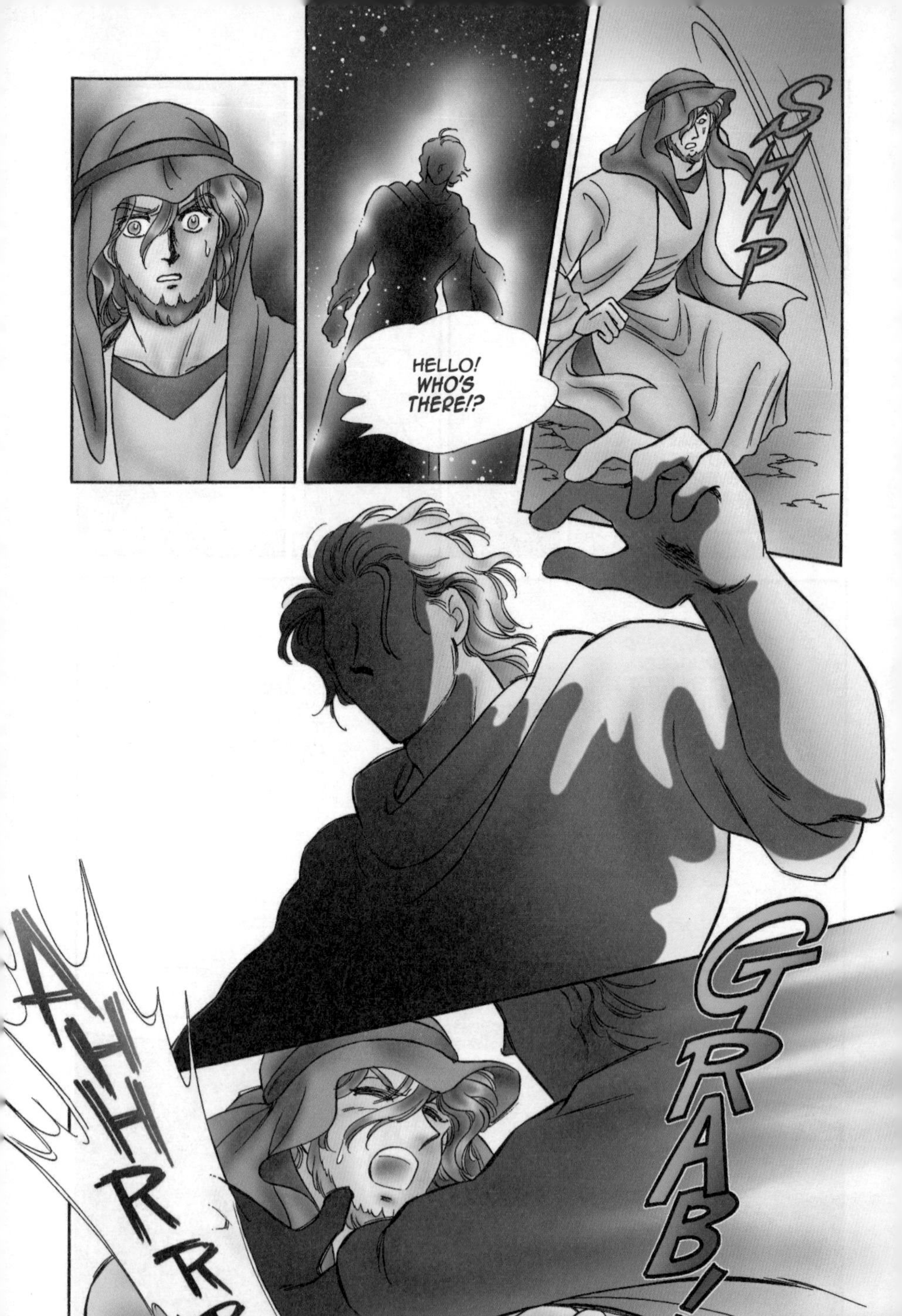
HELLO! WHO'S THERE!?
SHHP
GRAB!
AHHRRRR

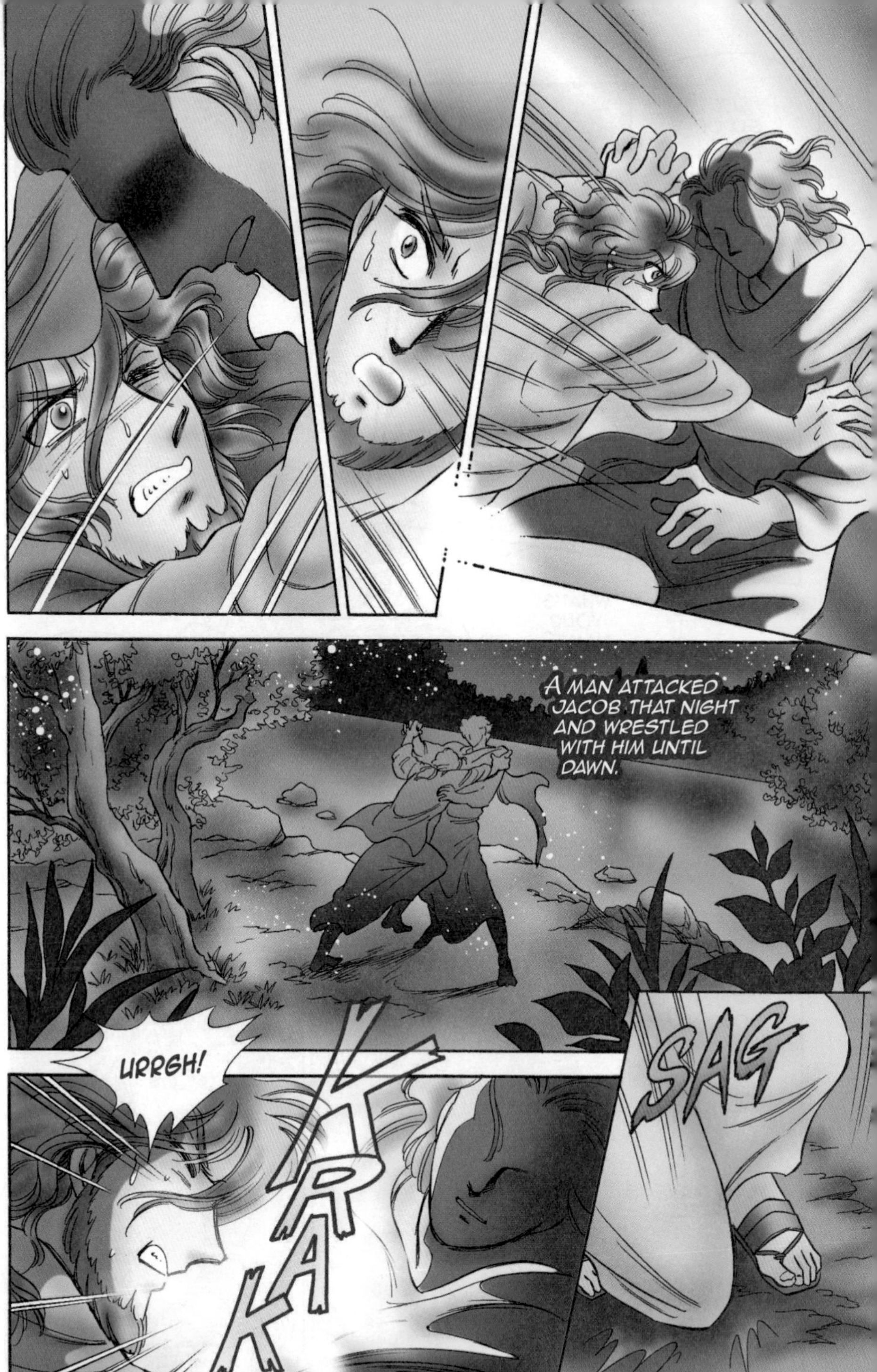
A MAN ATTACKED JACOB THAT NIGHT AND WRESTLED WITH HIM UNTIL DAWN.
URRGH!
KRAK
SAG

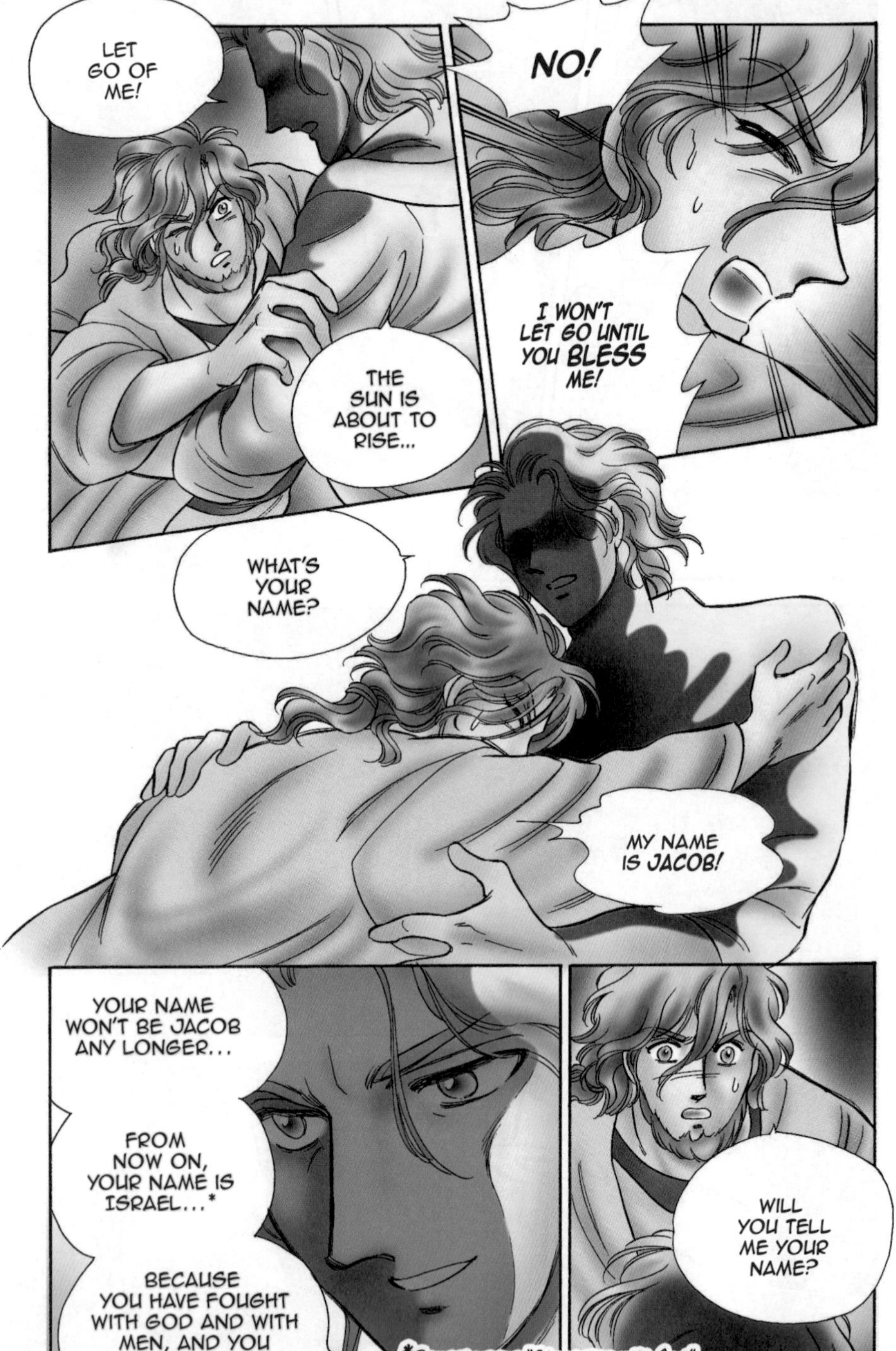
LET GO OF ME!
NO!
I WON'T LET GO UNTIL YOU BLESS ME!
THE SUN IS ABOUT TO RISE...
WHAT'S YOUR NAME?
MY NAME IS JACOB!
YOUR NAME WON'T BE JACOB ANY LONGER...
FROM NOW ON, YOUR NAME IS ISRAEL...*
BECAUSE YOU HAVE FOUGHT WITH GOD AND WITH MEN, AND YOU HAVE WON!
WILL YOU TELL ME YOUR NAME?
*Israel means "Struggles with God."

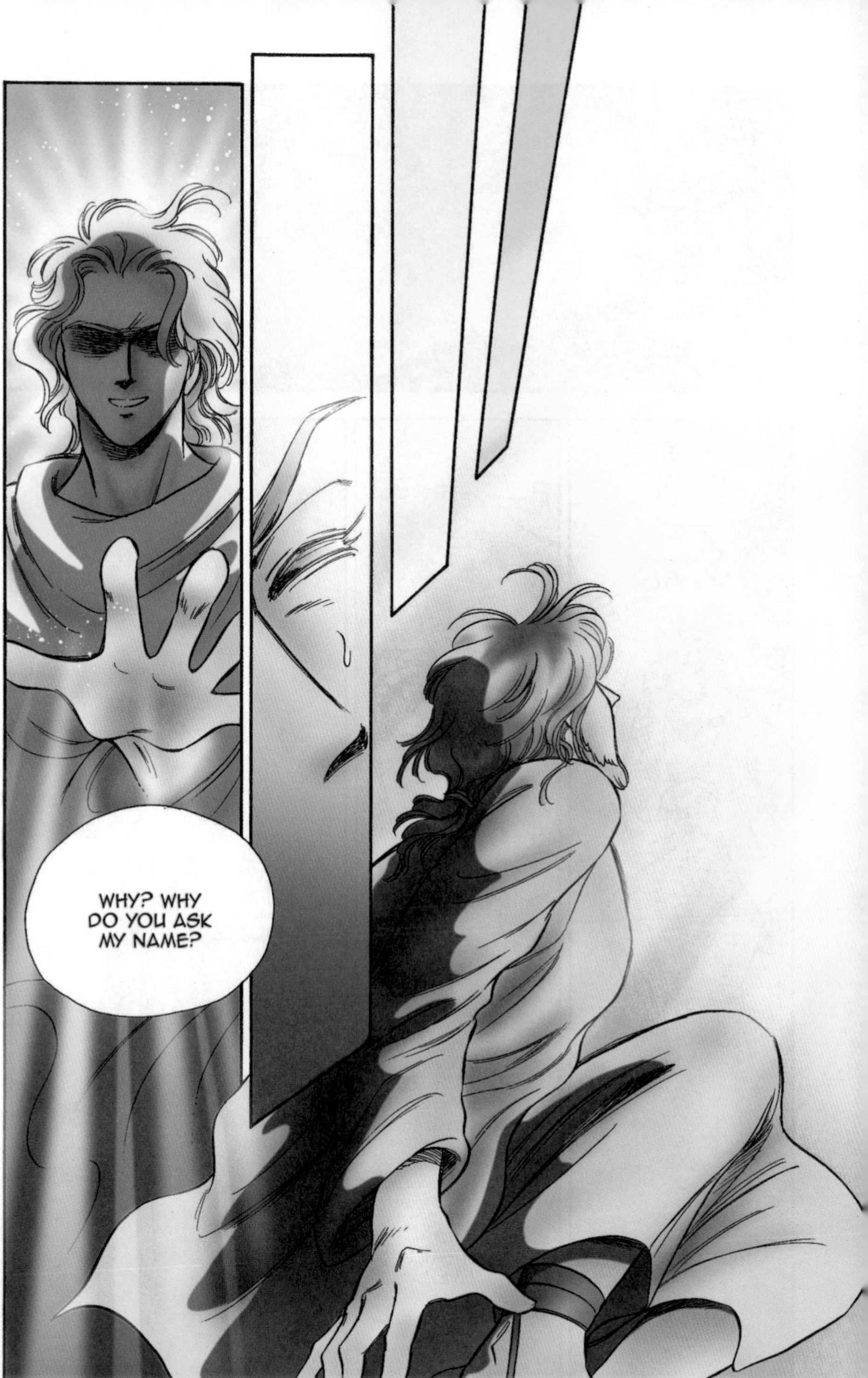
WHY? WHY DO YOU ASK MY NAME?

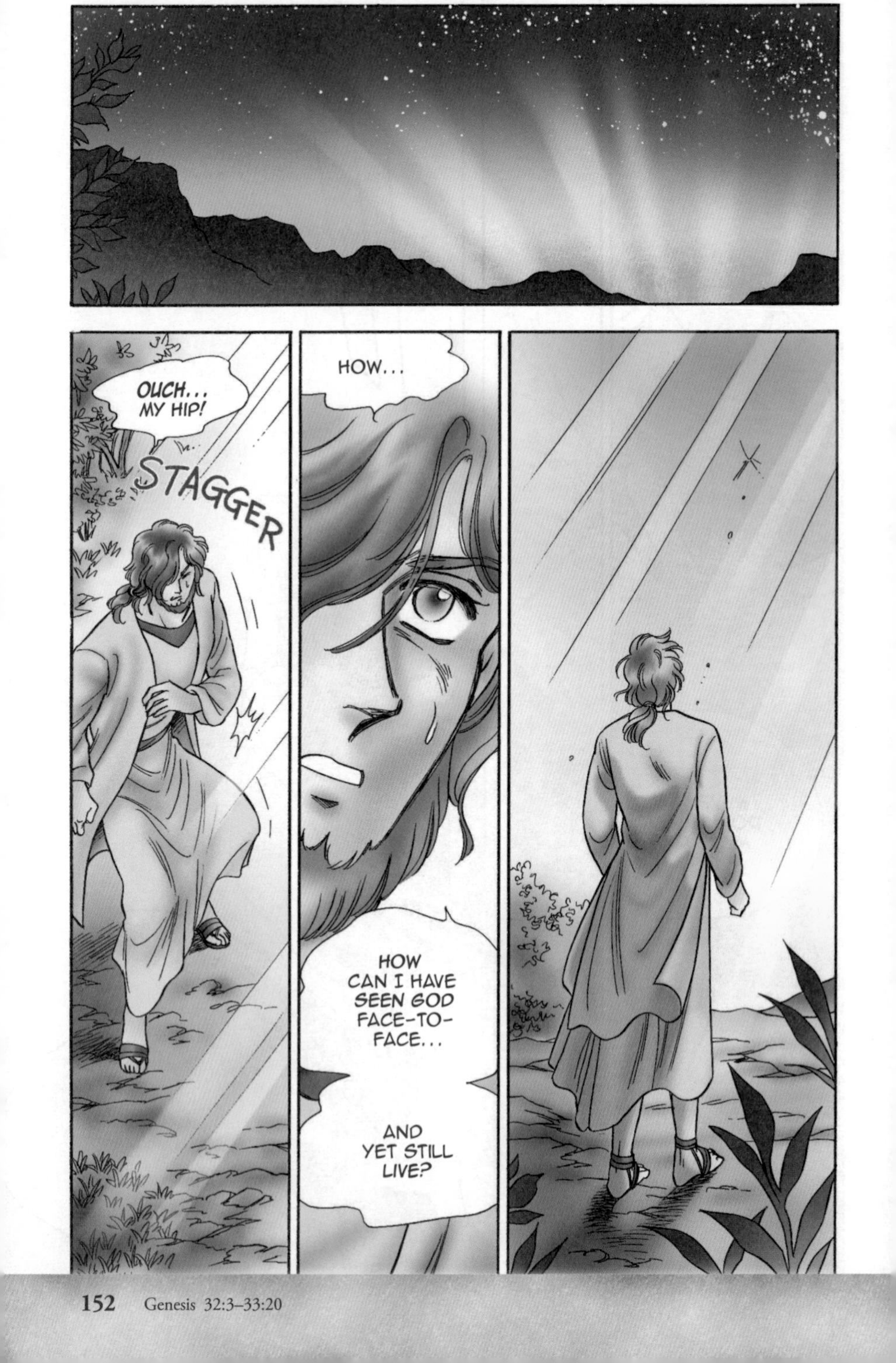
OUCH... MY HIP!
STAGGER
HOW...
HOW CAN I HAVE SEEN GOD FACE-TO-FACE...
AND YET STILL LIVE?

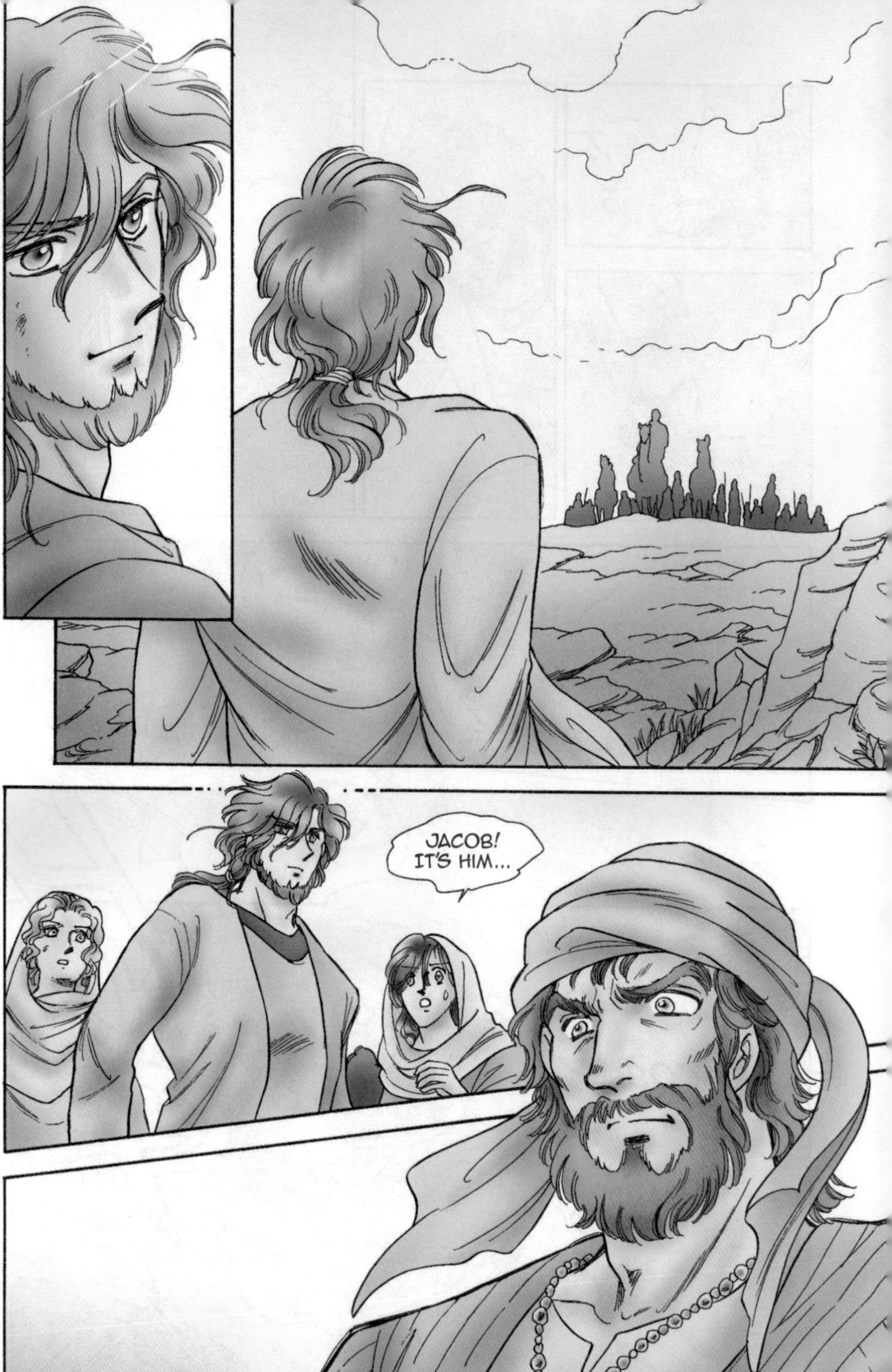
JACOB!
IT'S HIM...

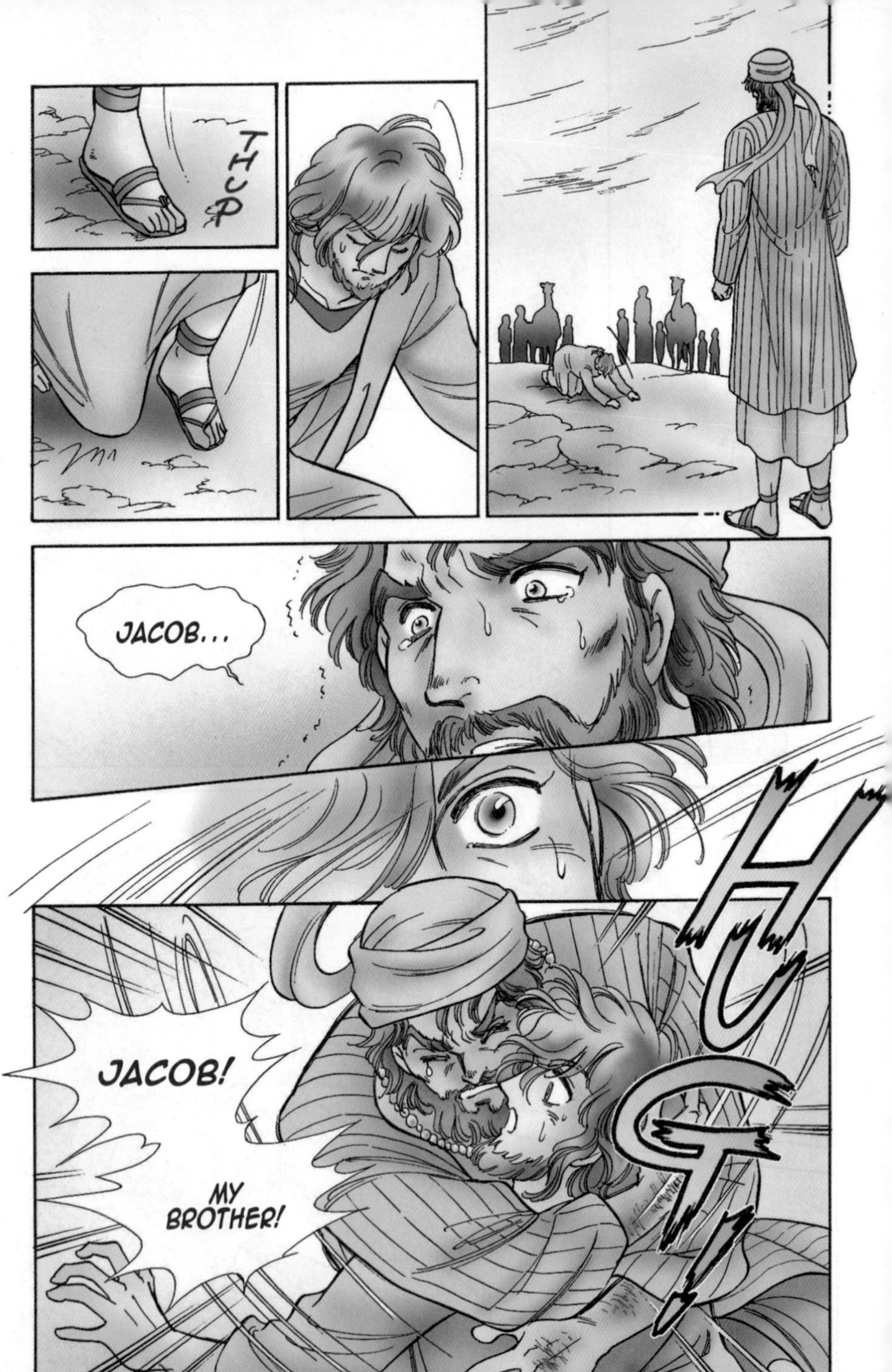
THUP
JACOB...
HUG!
JACOB!
MY BROTHER!

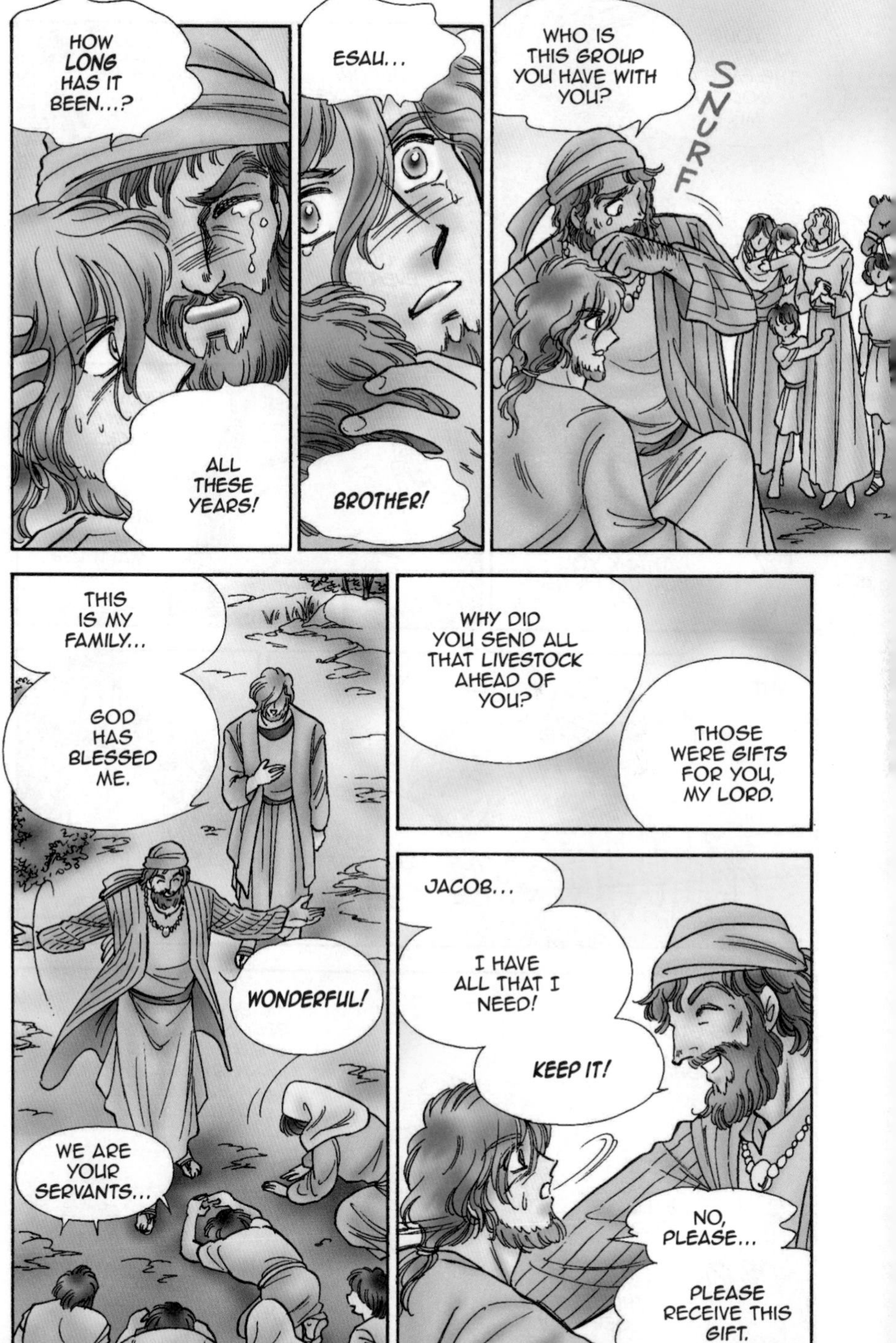

HOW LONG HAS IT BEEN...?
ALL THESE YEARS!
ESAU...
BROTHER!
WHO IS THIS GROUP YOU HAVE WITH YOU?
SNURF
THIS IS MY FAMILY...
GOD HAS BLESSED ME.
WONDERFUL!
WE ARE YOUR SERVANTS...
WHY DID YOU SEND ALL THAT LIVESTOCK AHEAD OF YOU?
THOSE WERE GIFTS FOR YOU, MY LORD.
JACOB...
I HAVE ALL THAT I NEED!
KEEP IT!
NO, PLEASE...
PLEASE RECEIVE THIS GIFT.

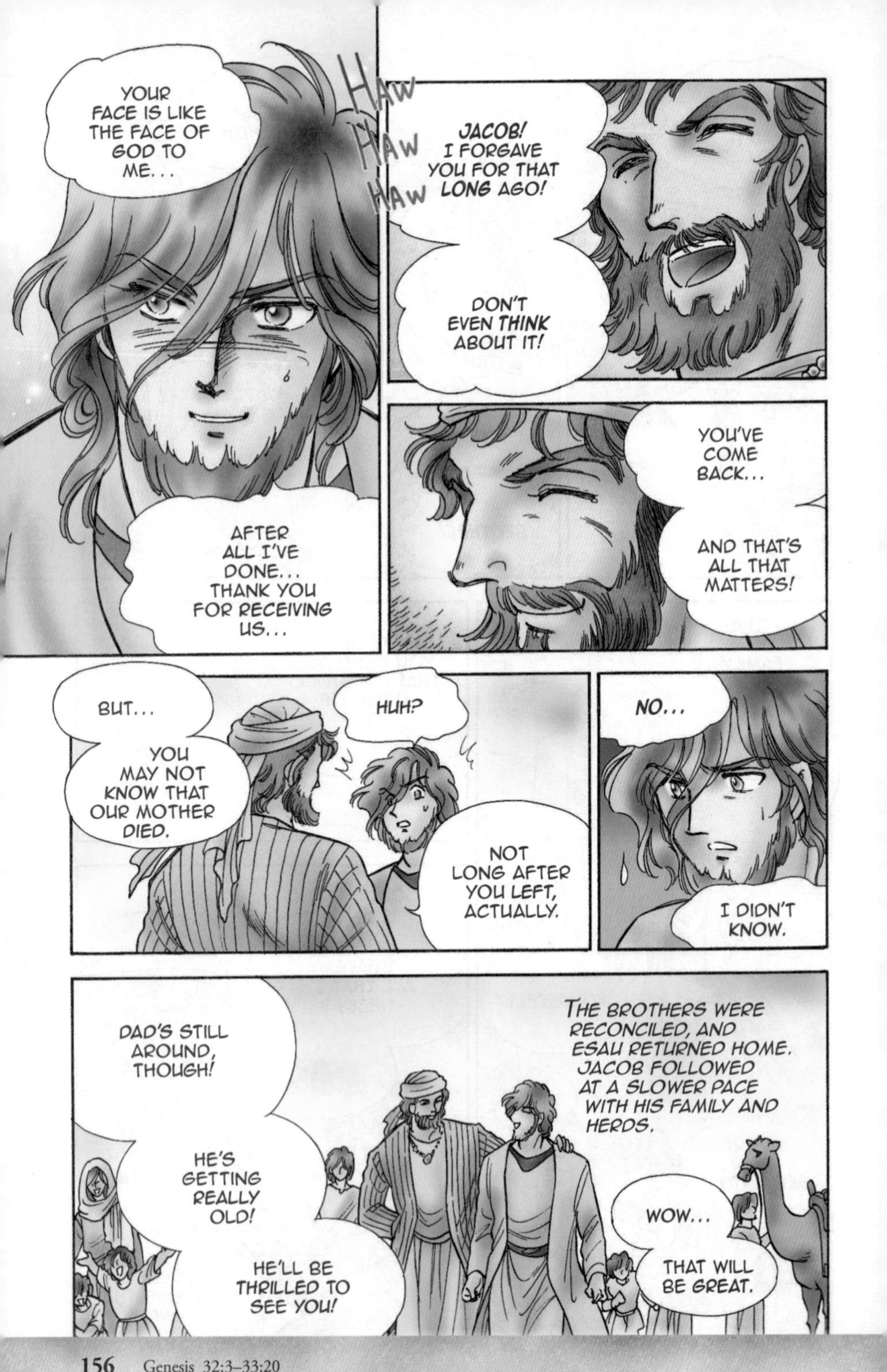
YOUR FACE IS LIKE THE FACE OF GOD TO ME...
AFTER ALL I'VE DONE... THANK YOU FOR RECEIVING US...
HAW HAW HAW
JACOB! I FORGAVE YOU FOR THAT LONG AGO!
DON'T EVEN THINK ABOUT IT!
YOU'VE COME BACK...
AND THAT'S ALL THAT MATTERS!
BUT...
YOU MAY NOT KNOW THAT OUR MOTHER DIED.
HUH?
NOT LONG AFTER YOU LEFT, ACTUALLY.
NO...
I DIDN'T KNOW.
DAD'S STILL AROUND, THOUGH!
HE'S GETTING REALLY OLD!
HE'LL BE THRILLED TO SEE YOU!
THE BROTHERS WERE RECONCILED, AND ESAU RETURNED HOME. JACOB FOLLOWED AT A SLOWER PACE WITH HIS FAMILY AND HERDS.
WOW...
THAT WILL BE GREAT.

AT BETHEL, WHERE JACOB HAD FIRST HEARD THE VOICE OF GOD, HE BUILT AN ALTAR.

ISRAEL, I AM GOD ALMIGHTY. BE FRUITFUL AND INCREASE IN NUMBER.

A COMMUNITY OF NATIONS WILL COME FROM YOUR BODY.

THE LAND I GAVE TO ABRAHAM AND ISAAC I ALSO GIVE TO YOU AND TO YOUR DESCENDANTS AFTER YOU.

RACHEL DIED WHILE GIVING BIRTH TO JACOB'S TWELFTH SON.

JACOB NAMED THE BOY BENJAMIN.

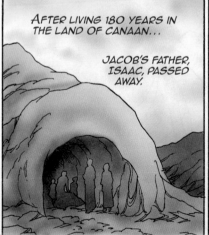

AFTER LIVING 180 YEARS IN THE LAND OF CANAAN...

JACOB'S FATHER, ISAAC, PASSED AWAY.

ESAU AND JACOB LIVED TOGETHER UNTIL THE LAND BECAME TOO CROWDED WITH THEIR HERDS OF LIVESTOCK. THEN THEY SEPARATED. ESAU BECAME THE FATHER OF THE EDOMITES.

YEARS PASSED, AND JACOB'S SONS GREW STRONG AND WORKED IN THE FIELDS.

JOSEPH, RACHEL'S OLDEST SON, BECAME JACOB'S FAVORITE.

CHAPTER 3

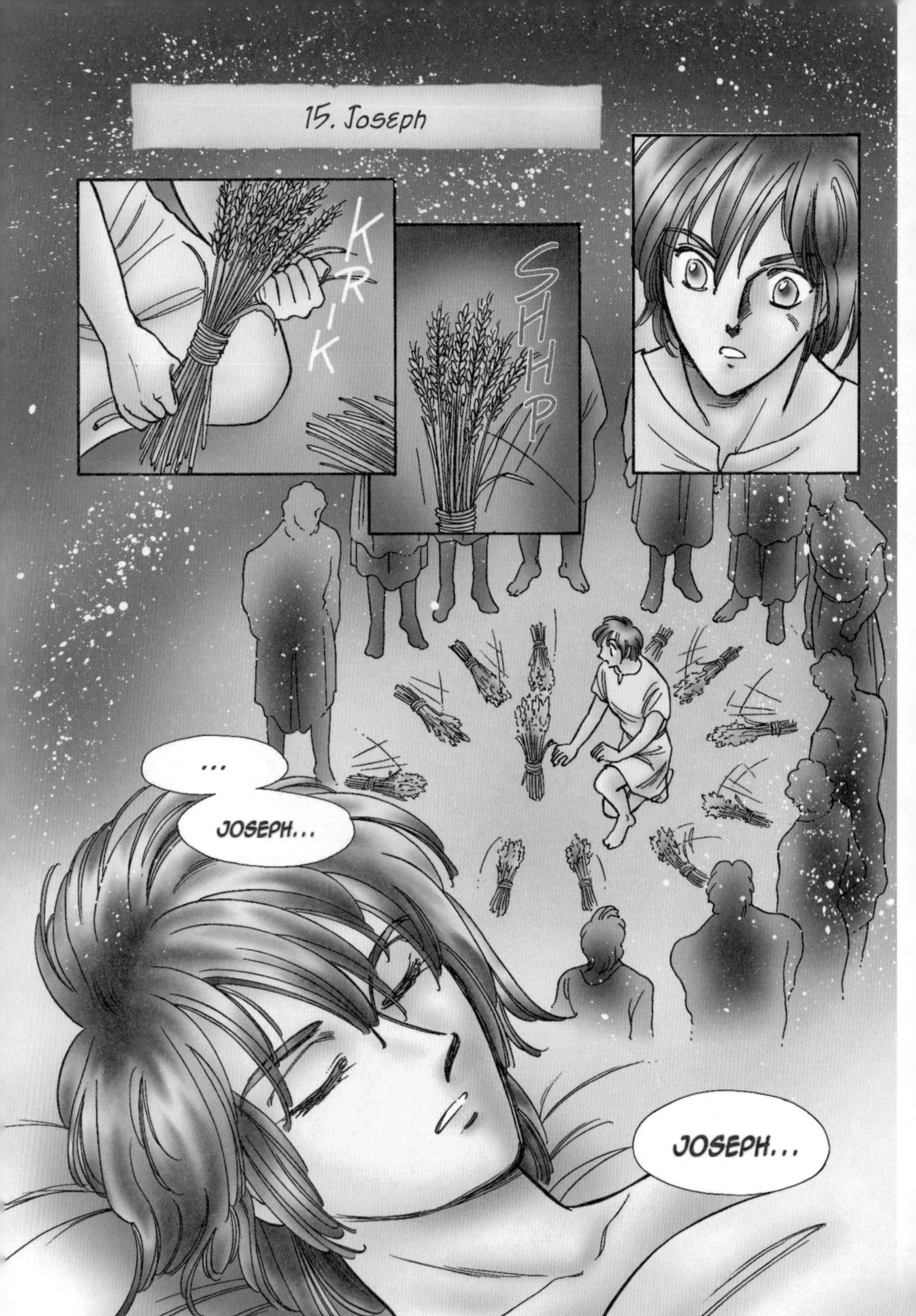

15. Joseph
KRIK
SHHP
...
JOSEPH...
JOSEPH...

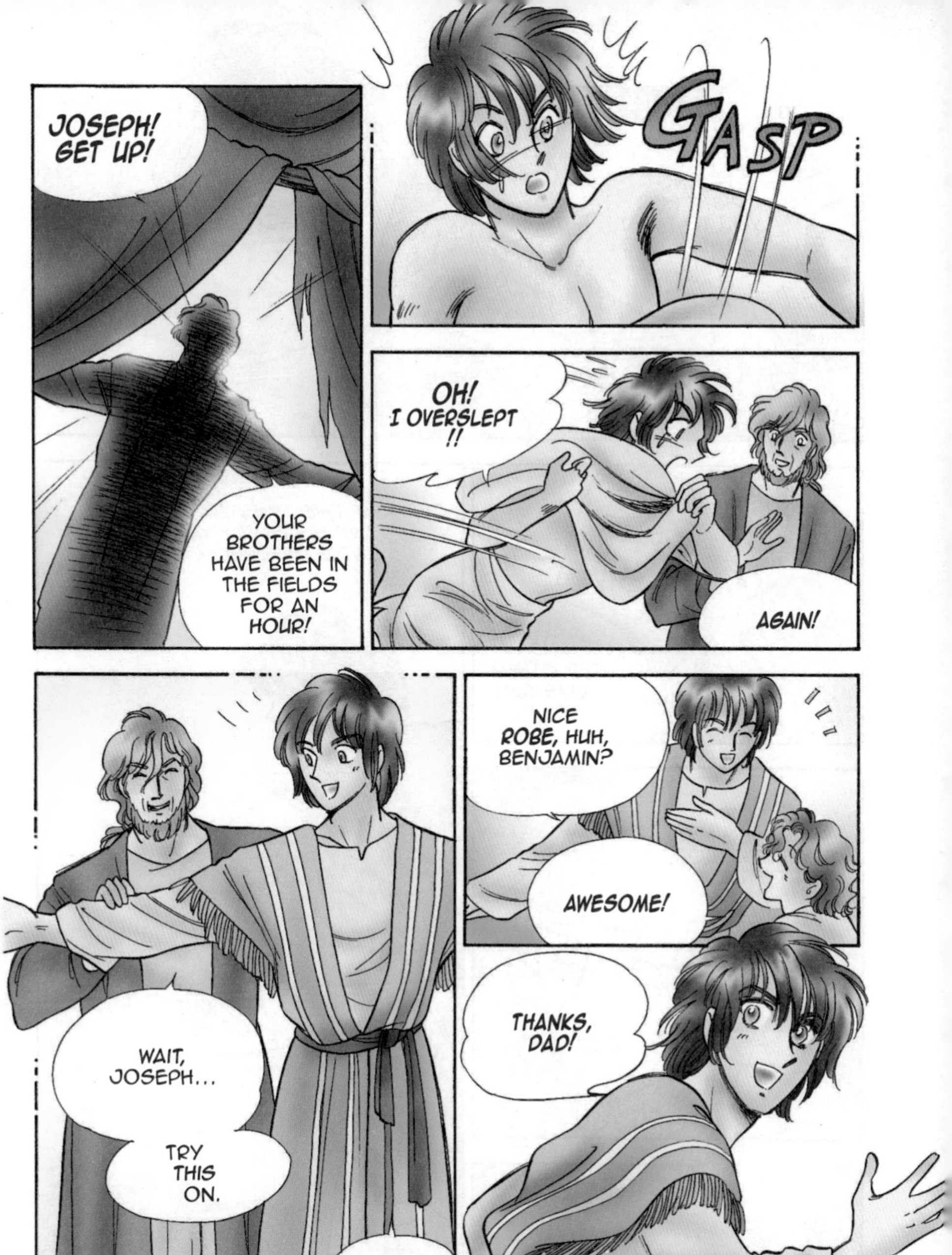
JOSEPH! GET UP!
GASP
YOUR BROTHERS HAVE BEEN IN THE FIELDS FOR AN HOUR!
OH! I OVERSLEPT !!
AGAIN!
WAIT, JOSEPH...
TRY THIS ON.
WOW...
NICE ROBE, HUH, BENJAMIN?
AWESOME!
THANKS, DAD!
GOTTA RUN!

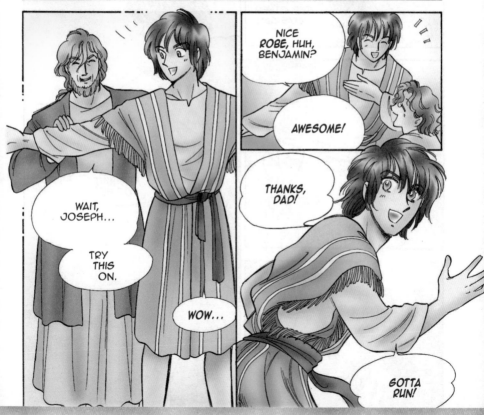

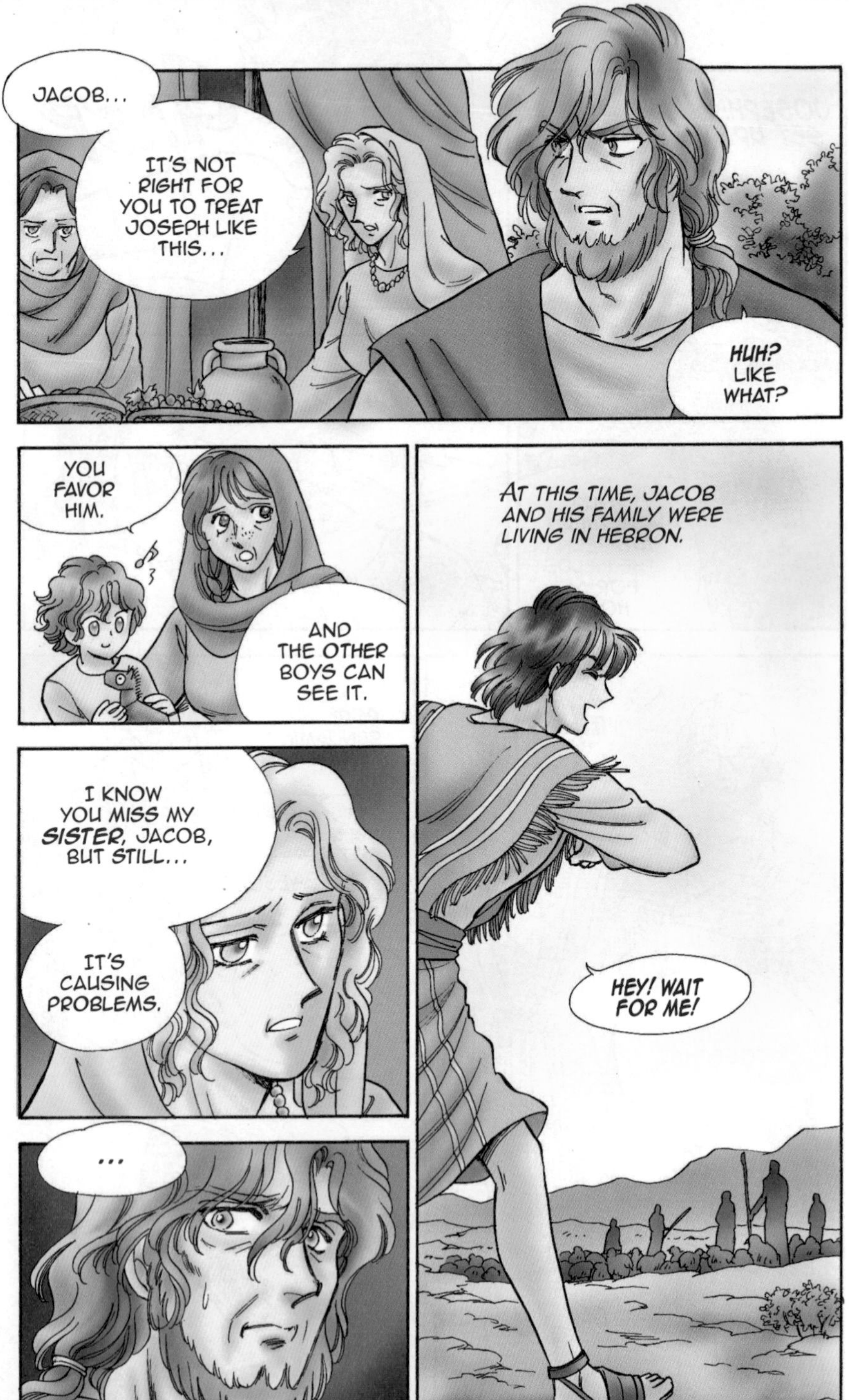
JACOB...
IT'S NOT RIGHT FOR YOU TO TREAT JOSEPH LIKE THIS...
HUH? LIKE WHAT?
YOU FAVOR HIM.
AND THE OTHER BOYS CAN SEE IT.
I KNOW YOU MISS MY SISTER, JACOB, BUT STILL...
IT'S CAUSING PROBLEMS.
...
AT THIS TIME, JACOB AND HIS FAMILY WERE LIVING IN HEBRON.
HEY! WAIT FOR ME!

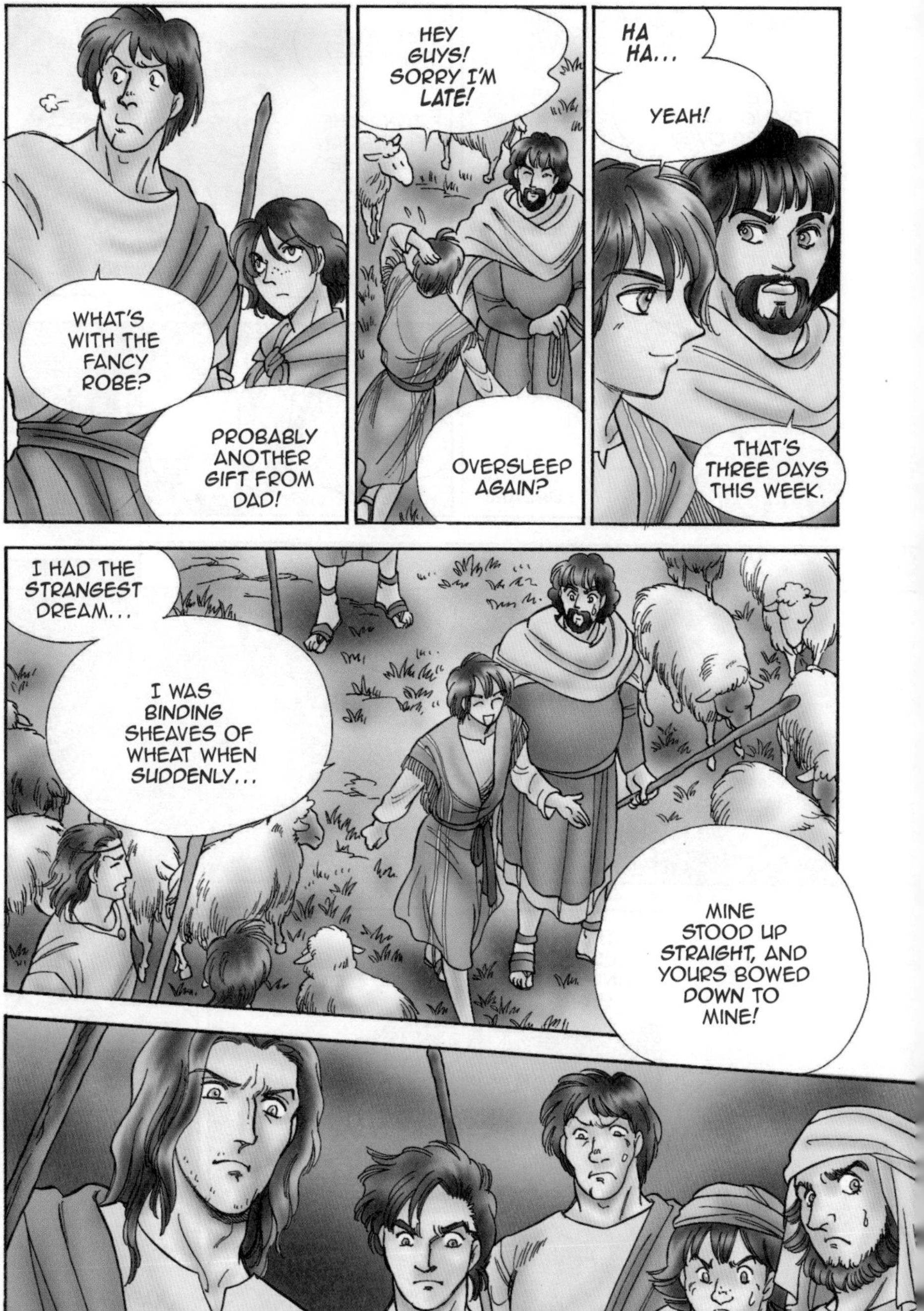
WHAT'S WITH THE FANCY ROBE?
PROBABLY ANOTHER GIFT FROM DAD!
HEY GUYS! SORRY I'M LATE!
OVERSLEEP AGAIN?
HA HA...
YEAH!
THAT'S THREE DAYS THIS WEEK.
I HAD THE STRANGEST DREAM...
I WAS BINDING SHEAVES OF WHEAT WHEN SUDDENLY...
MINE STOOD UP STRAIGHT, AND YOURS BOWED DOWN TO MINE!

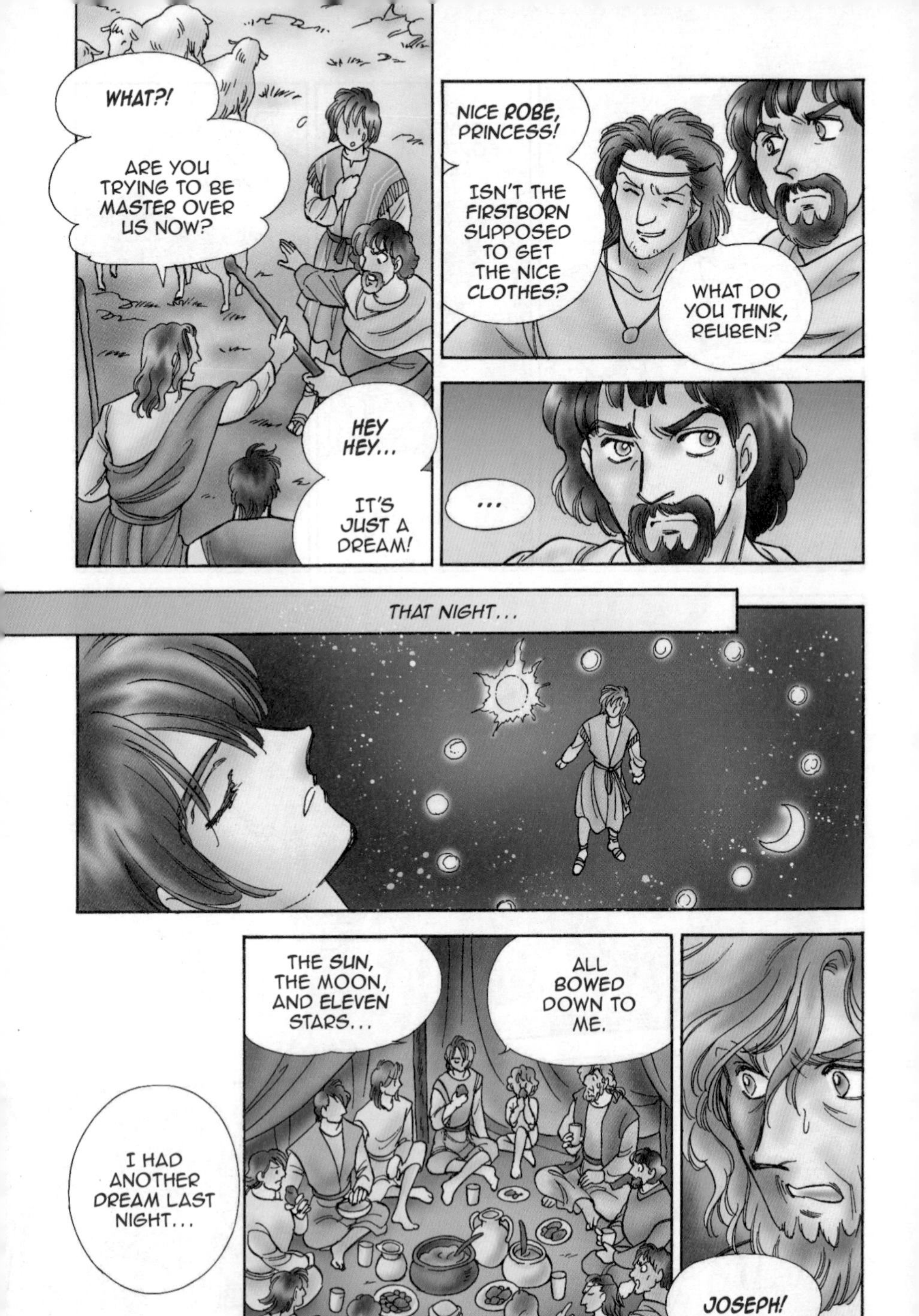
WHAT?!
ARE YOU TRYING TO BE MASTER OVER US NOW?
HEY HEY...
IT'S JUST A DREAM!
NICE ROBE, PRINCESS!
ISN'T THE FIRSTBORN SUPPOSED TO GET THE NICE CLOTHES?
WHAT DO YOU THINK, REUBEN?
...
THAT NIGHT...
I HAD ANOTHER DREAM LAST NIGHT...
THE SUN, THE MOON, AND ELEVEN STARS...
ALL BOWED DOWN TO ME.
JOSEPH!

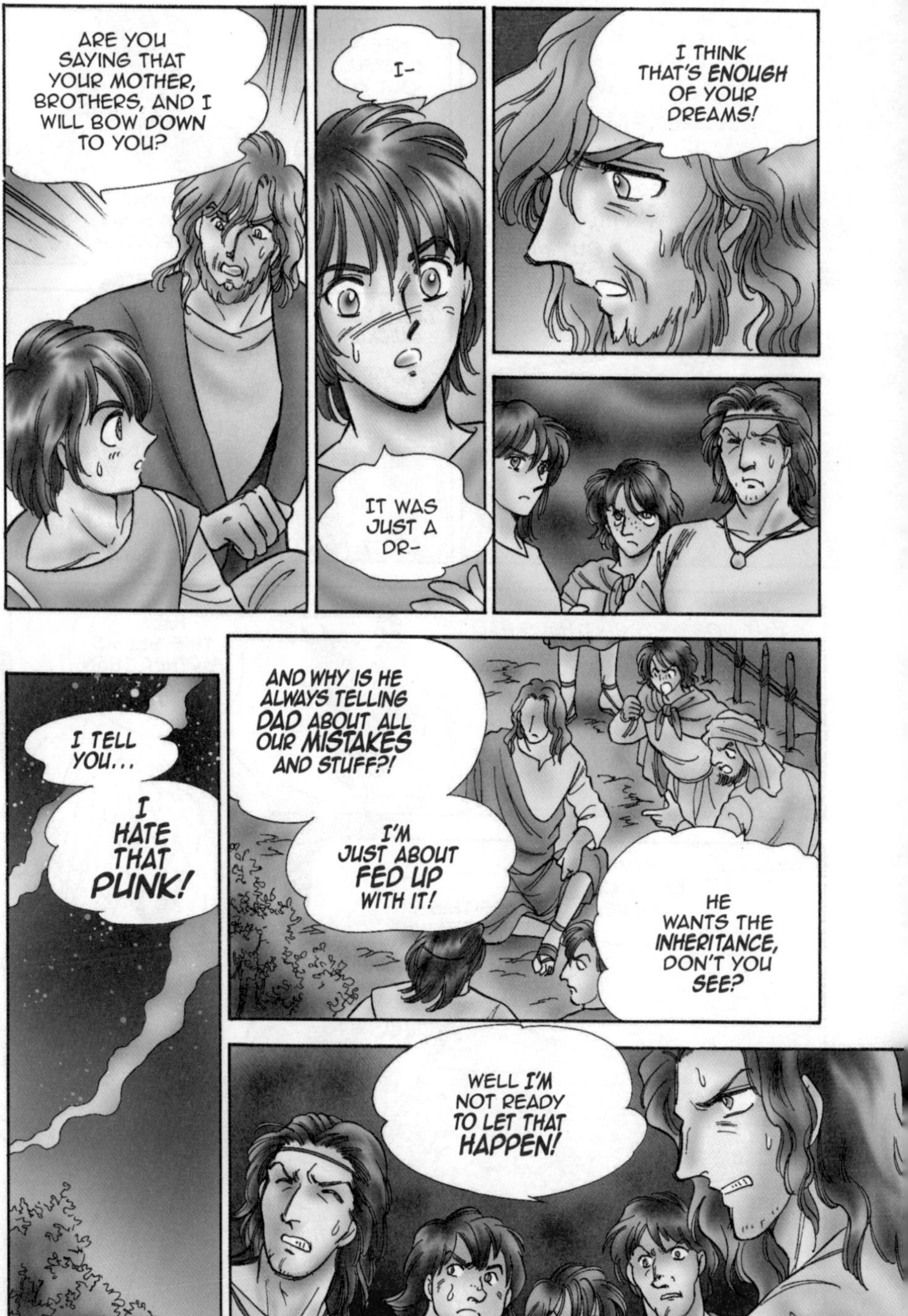
ARE YOU SAYING THAT YOUR MOTHER, BROTHERS, AND I WILL BOW DOWN TO YOU?
I-
IT WAS JUST A DR-
I THINK THAT'S ENOUGH OF YOUR DREAMS!
I TELL YOU...
I HATE THAT PUNK!
AND WHY IS HE ALWAYS TELLING DAD ABOUT ALL OUR MISTAKES AND STUFF?!
I'M JUST ABOUT FED UP WITH IT!
HE WANTS THE INHERITANCE, DON'T YOU SEE?
WELL I'M NOT READY TO LET THAT HAPPEN!

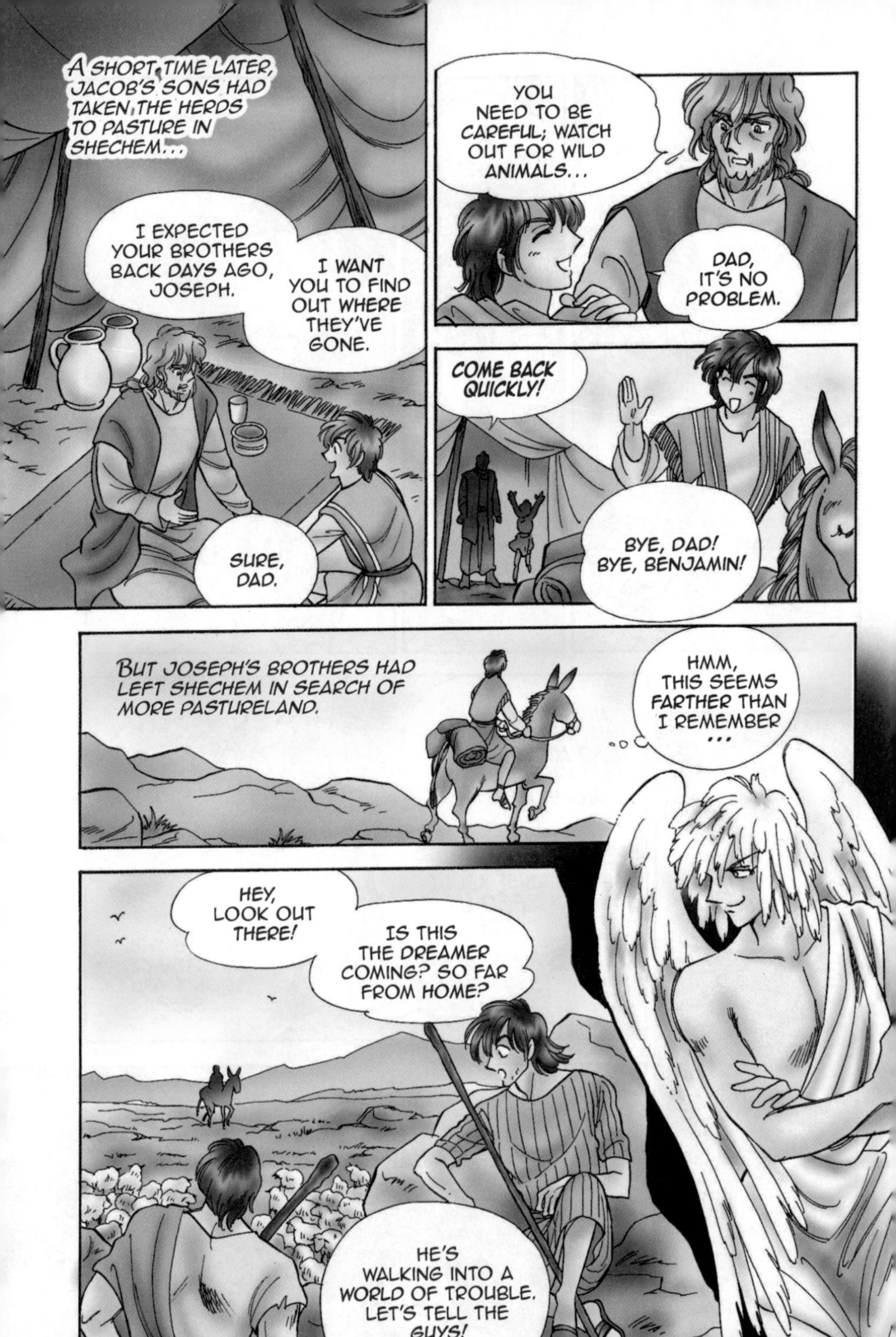
A SHORT TIME LATER, JACOB'S SONS HAD TAKEN THE HERDS TO PASTURE IN SHECHEM...
I EXPECTED YOUR BROTHERS BACK DAYS AGO, JOSEPH.
I WANT YOU TO FIND OUT WHERE THEY'VE GONE.
SURE, DAD.
YOU NEED TO BE CAREFUL; WATCH OUT FOR WILD ANIMALS...
DAD, IT'S NO PROBLEM.
COME BACK QUICKLY!
BYE, DAD! BYE, BENJAMIN!
BUT JOSEPH'S BROTHERS HAD LEFT SHECHEM IN SEARCH OF MORE PASTURELAND.
HMM, THIS SEEMS FARTHER THAN I REMEMBER...
HEY, LOOK OUT THERE!
IS THIS THE DREAMER COMING? SO FAR FROM HOME?
HE'S WALKING INTO A WORLD OF TROUBLE. LET'S TELL THE GUYS!

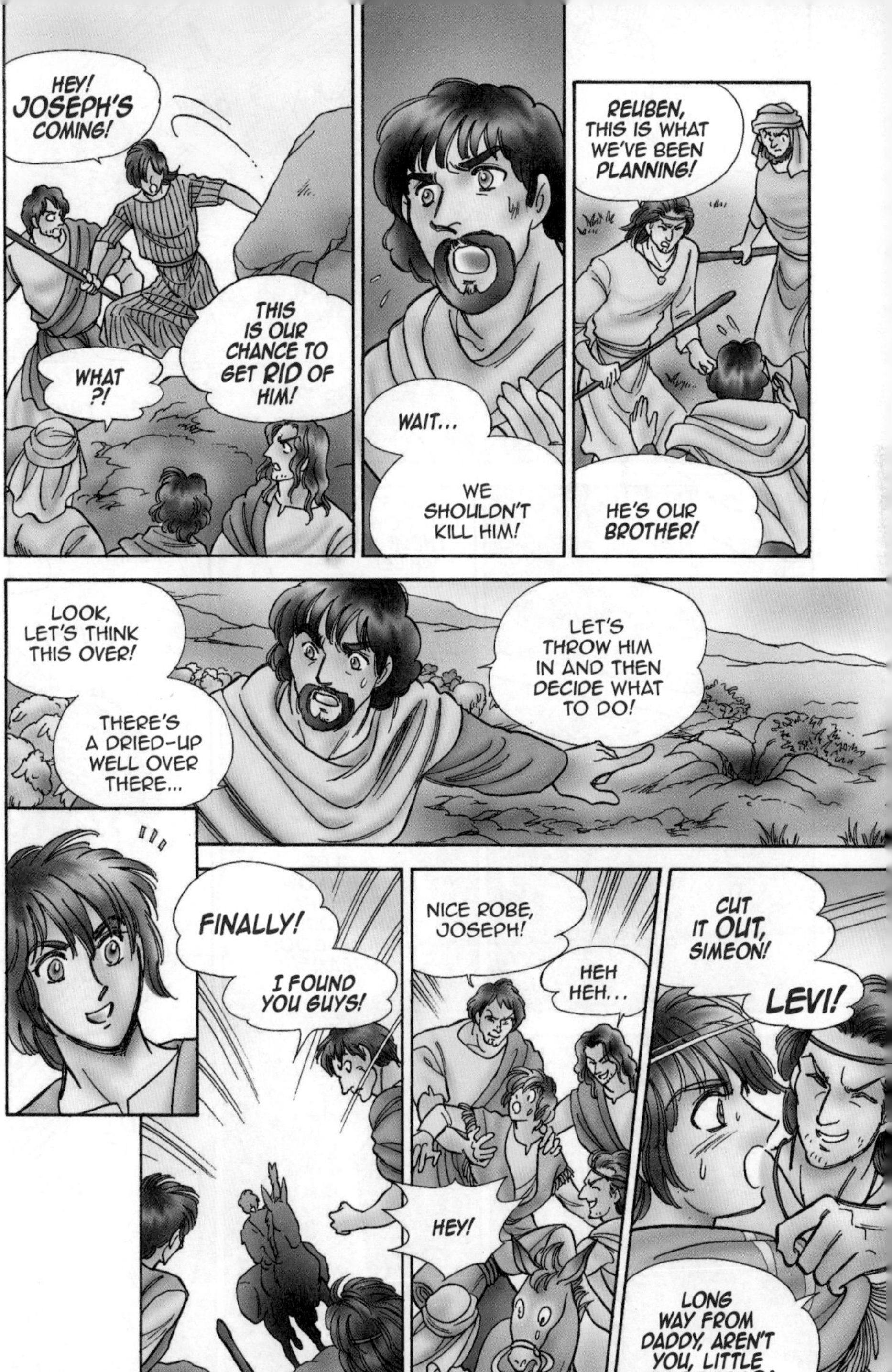
HEY! JOSEPH'S COMING!
WHAT ?!
THIS IS OUR CHANCE TO GET RID OF HIM!
WAIT...
WE SHOULDN'T KILL HIM!
REUBEN, THIS IS WHAT WE'VE BEEN PLANNING!
HE'S OUR BROTHER!
LOOK, LET'S THINK THIS OVER!
THERE'S A DRIED-UP WELL OVER THERE...
LET'S THROW HIM IN AND THEN DECIDE WHAT TO DO!
FINALLY!
I FOUND YOU GUYS!
NICE ROBE, JOSEPH!
HEH HEH...
HEY!
CUT IT OUT, SIMEON!
LEVI!
LONG WAY FROM DADDY, AREN'T YOU, LITTLE BROTHER?!

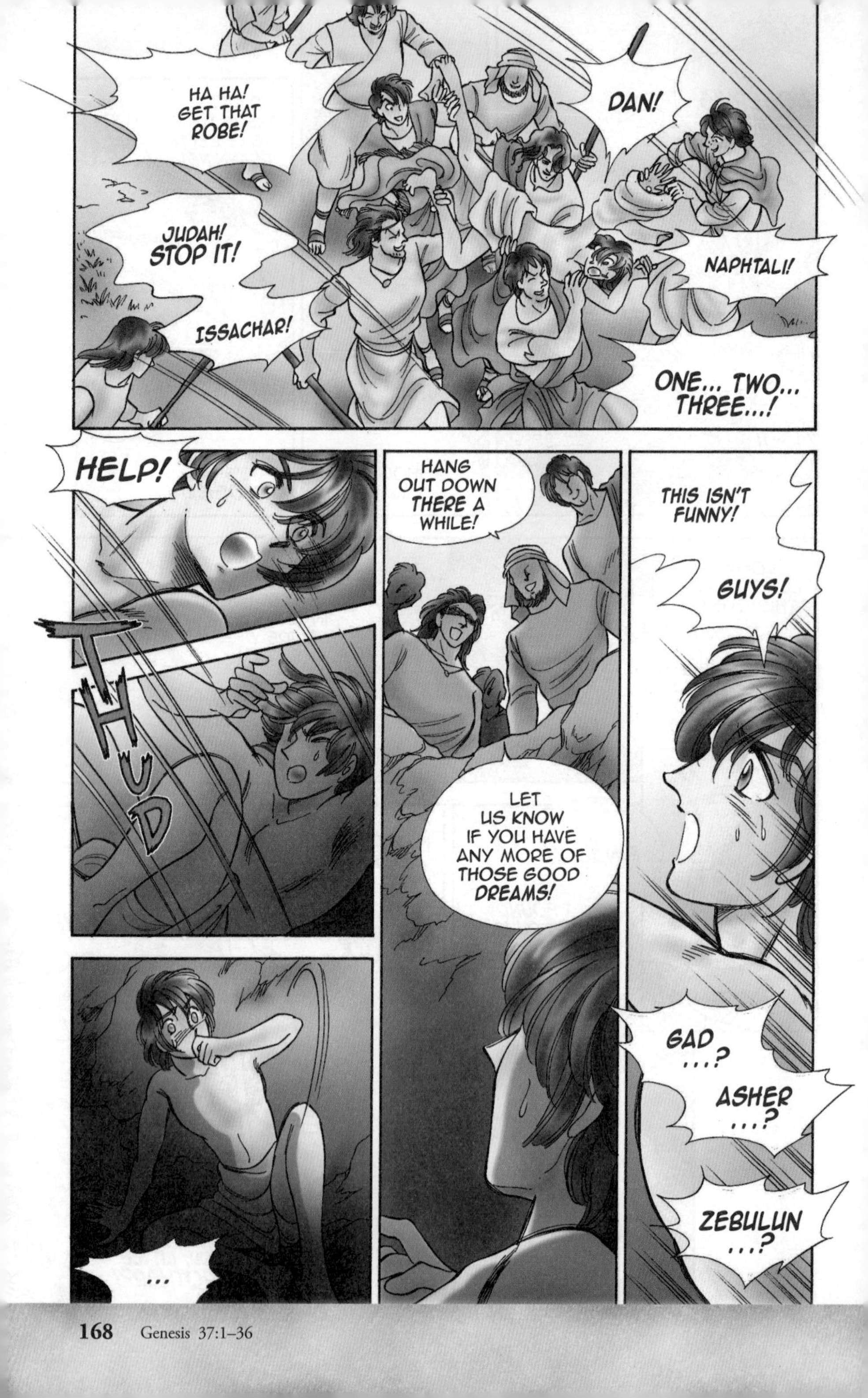
HA HA! GET THAT ROBE!
DAN!
JUDAH! STOP IT!
NAPHTALI!
ISSACHAR!
ONE... TWO... THREE...!
HELP!
THUD
HANG OUT DOWN THERE A WHILE!
LET US KNOW IF YOU HAVE ANY MORE OF THOSE GOOD DREAMS!
THIS ISN'T FUNNY!
GUYS!
...
GAD ...?
ASHER ...?
ZEBULUN ...?

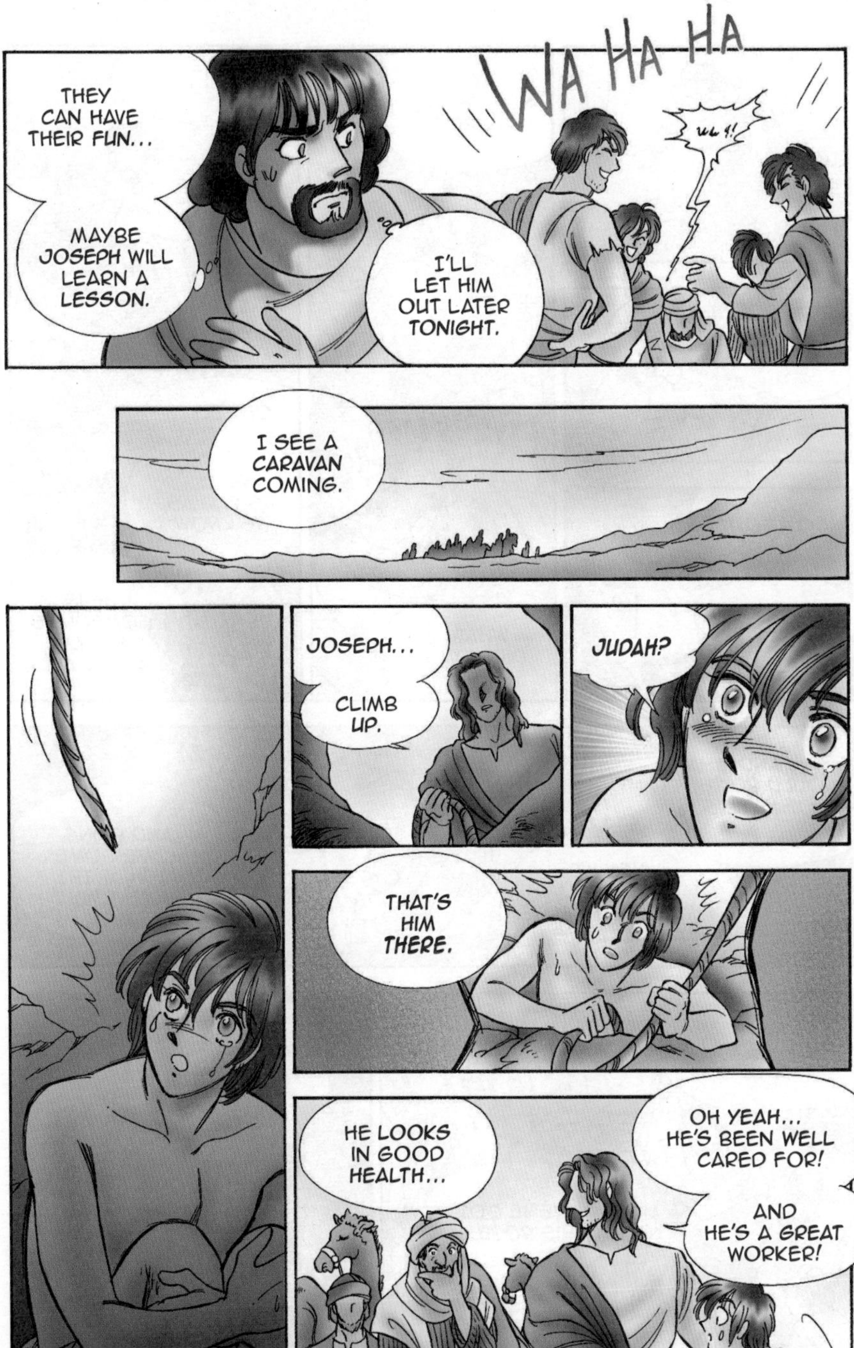
THEY CAN HAVE THEIR FUN...
MAYBE JOSEPH WILL LEARN A LESSON.
WA HA HA
I'LL LET HIM OUT LATER TONIGHT.
I SEE A CARAVAN COMING.
JOSEPH...
CLIMB UP.
JUDAH?
THAT'S HIM THERE.
HE LOOKS IN GOOD HEALTH...
OH YEAH... HE'S BEEN WELL CARED FOR!
AND HE'S A GREAT WORKER!

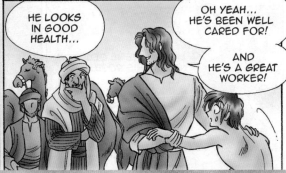

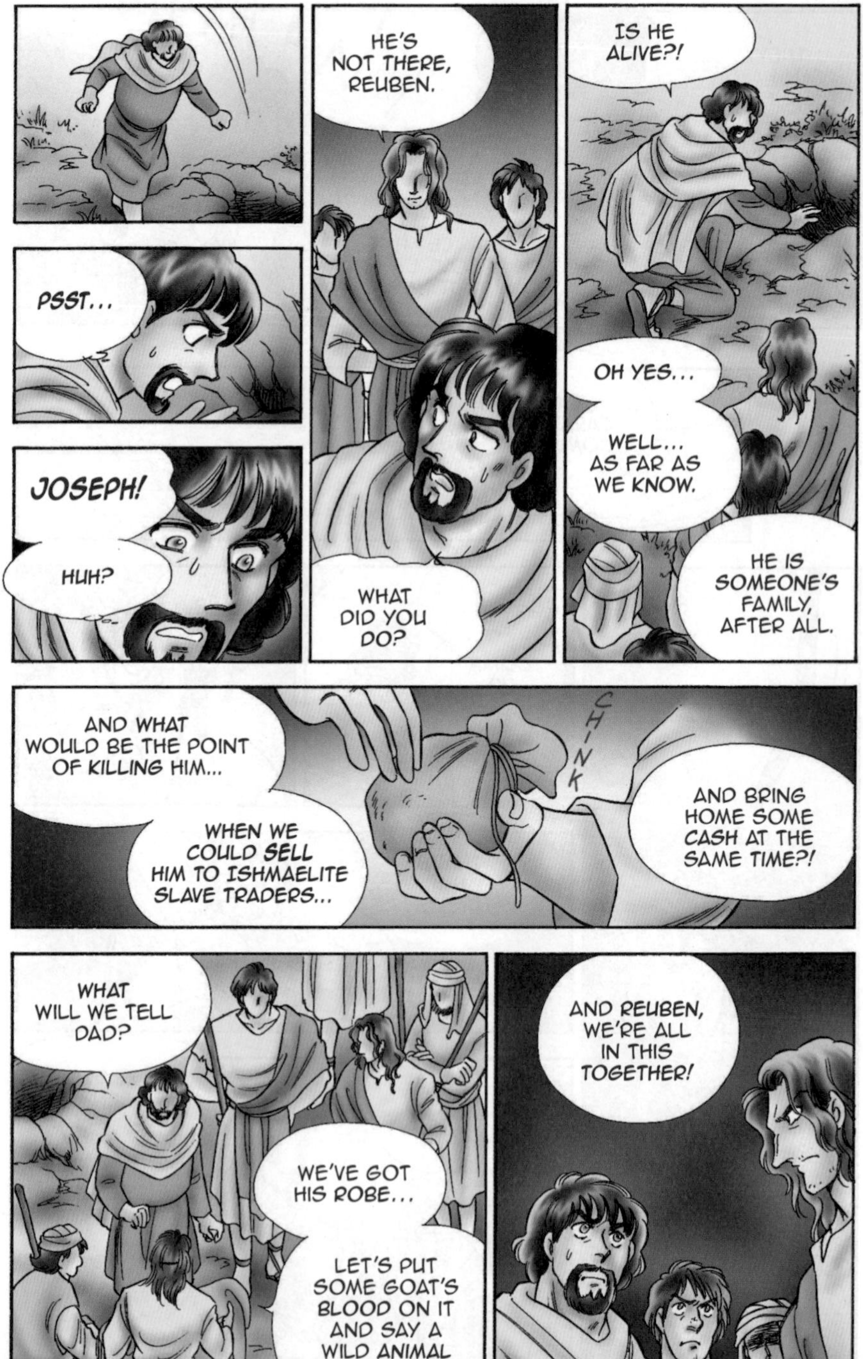
PSST...
JOSEPH!
HUH?
HE'S NOT THERE, REUBEN.
WHAT DID YOU DO?
IS HE ALIVE?!
OH YES...
WELL... AS FAR AS WE KNOW.
HE IS SOMEONE'S FAMILY, AFTER ALL.
AND WHAT WOULD BE THE POINT OF KILLING HIM...
WHEN WE COULD SELL HIM TO ISHMAELITE SLAVE TRADERS...
CHINK
AND BRING HOME SOME CASH AT THE SAME TIME?!
WHAT WILL WE TELL DAD?
WE'VE GOT HIS ROBE...
LET'S PUT SOME GOAT'S BLOOD ON IT AND SAY A WILD ANIMAL GOT HIM!
AND REUBEN, WE'RE ALL IN THIS TOGETHER!

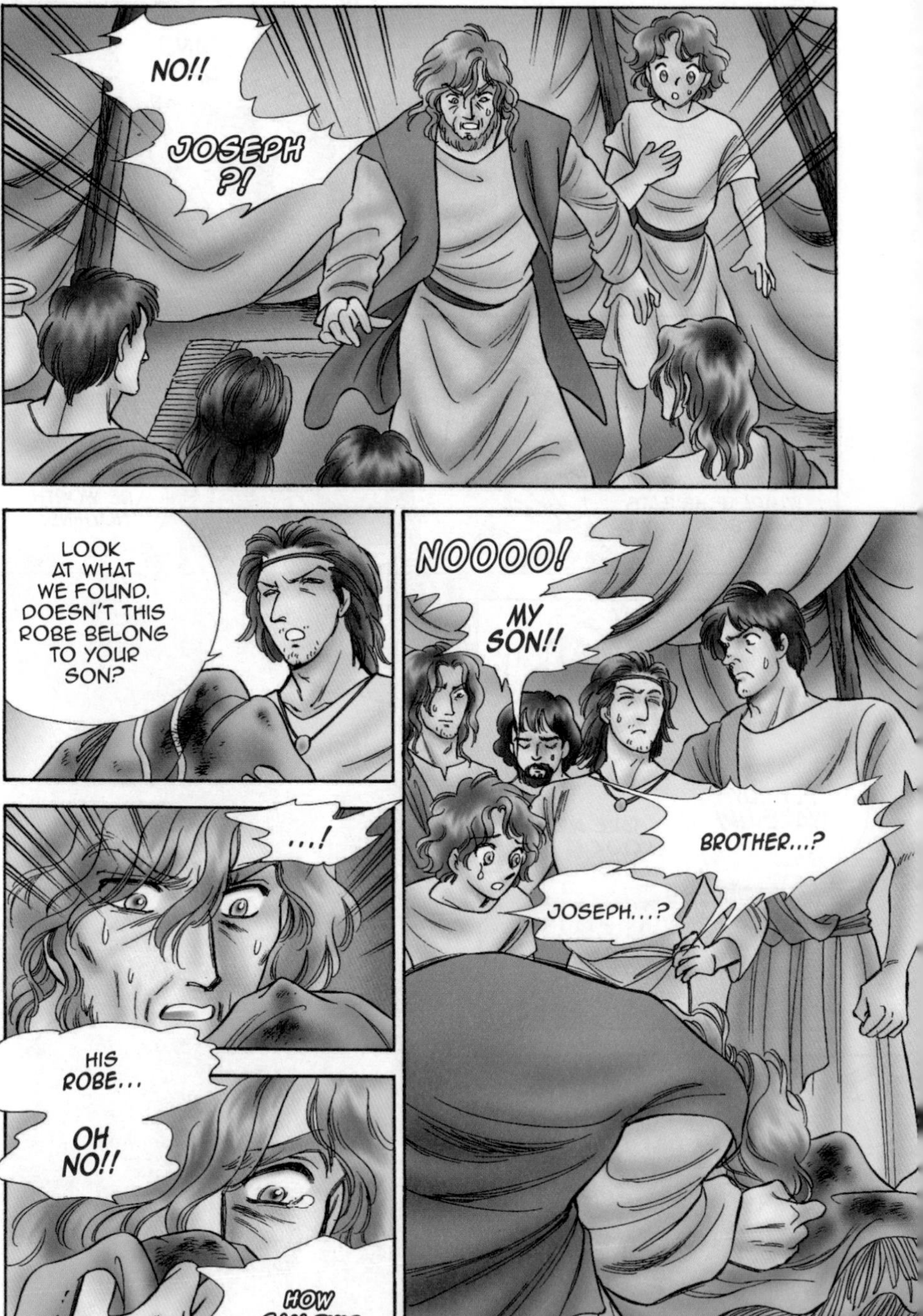
NO!!
JOSEPH ?!
LOOK AT WHAT WE FOUND. DOESN'T THIS ROBE BELONG TO YOUR SON?
NOOOO!
MY SON!!
...!
BROTHER...?
JOSEPH...?
HIS ROBE...
OH NO!!
HOW CAN THIS BE?!

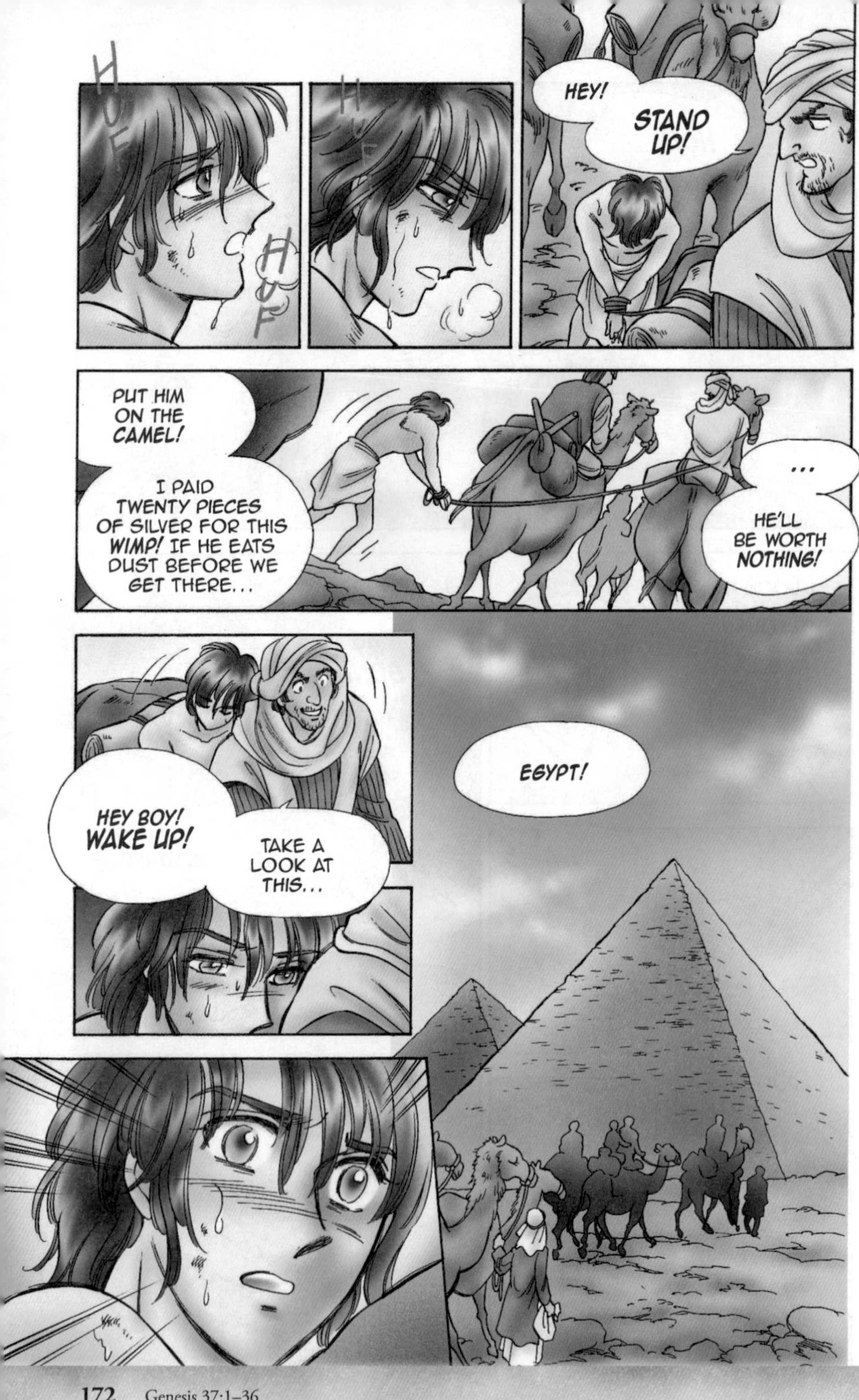
HUF
HUF
HUF HUF
HEY!
STAND UP!
PUT HIM ON THE CAMEL!
I PAID TWENTY PIECES OF SILVER FOR THIS WIMP! IF HE EATS DUST BEFORE WE GET THERE...
...
HE'LL BE WORTH NOTHING!
HEY BOY! WAKE UP!
TAKE A LOOK AT THIS...
EGYPT!

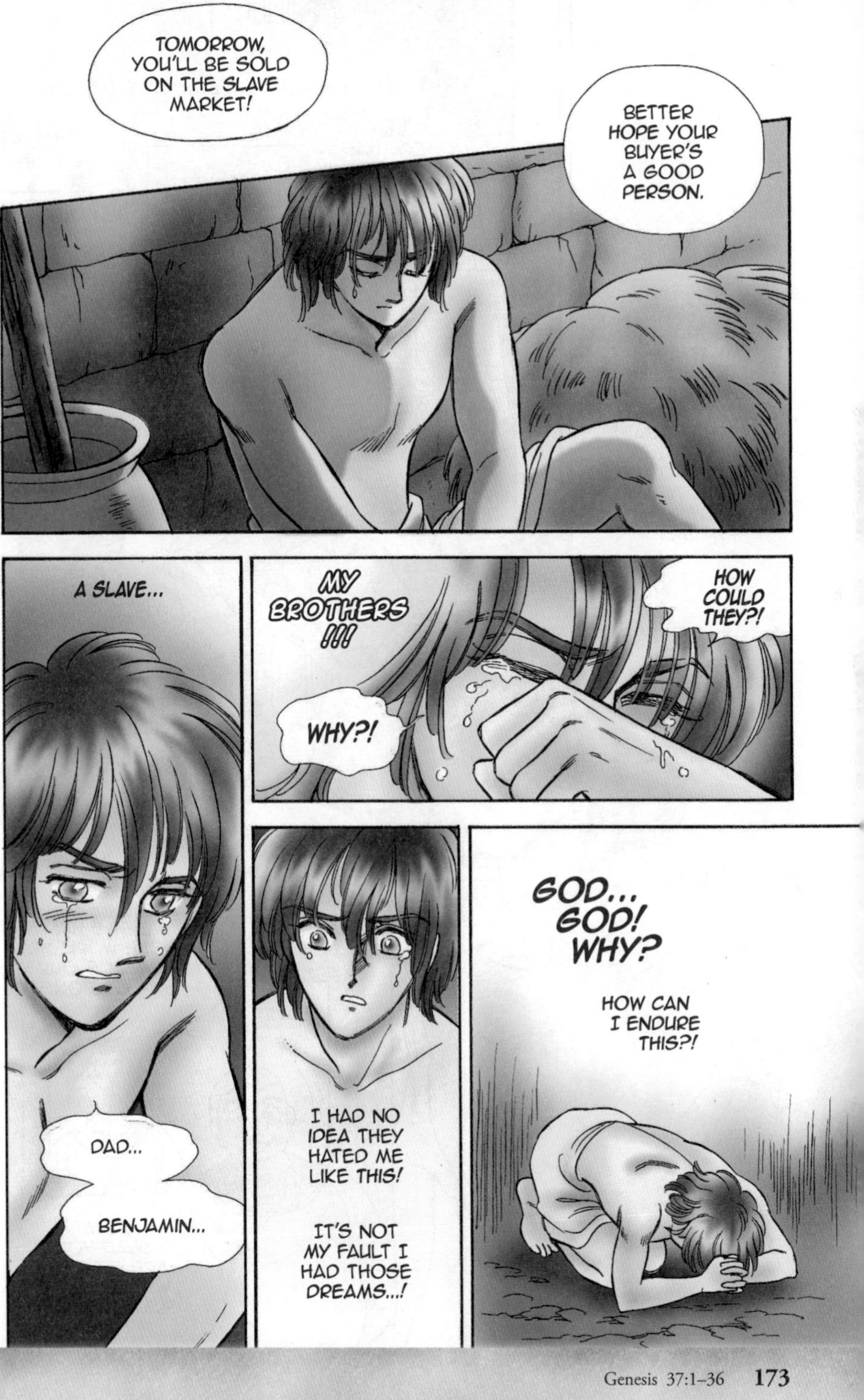
TOMORROW, YOU'LL BE SOLD ON THE SLAVE MARKET!
BETTER HOPE YOUR BUYER'S A GOOD PERSON.
A SLAVE...
MY BROTHERS!!!
HOW COULD THEY?!
WHY?!
DAD...
BENJAMIN...
I HAD NO IDEA THEY HATED ME LIKE THIS!
IT'S NOT MY FAULT I HAD THOSE DREAMS...!
GOD... GOD! WHY?
HOW CAN I ENDURE THIS?!

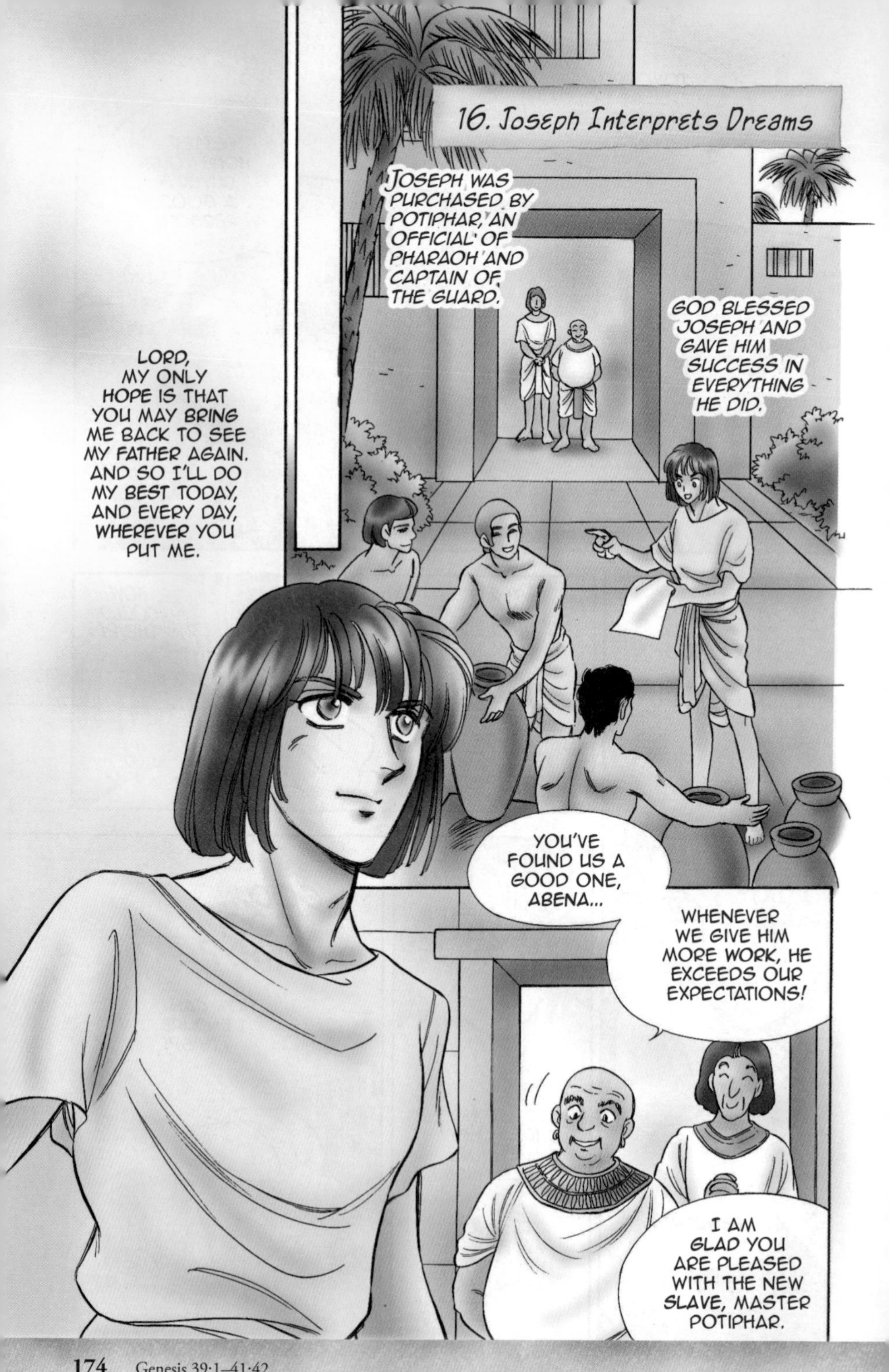
16. Joseph Interprets Dreams
JOSEPH WAS PURCHASED BY POTIPHAR, AN OFFICIAL OF PHARAOH AND CAPTAIN OF THE GUARD.
GOD BLESSED JOSEPH AND GAVE HIM SUCCESS IN EVERYTHING HE DID.
LORD, MY ONLY HOPE IS THAT YOU MAY BRING ME BACK TO SEE MY FATHER AGAIN. AND SO I'LL DO MY BEST TODAY, AND EVERY DAY, WHEREVER YOU PUT ME.
YOU'VE FOUND US A GOOD ONE, ABENA...
WHENEVER WE GIVE HIM MORE WORK, HE EXCEEDS OUR EXPECTATIONS!
I AM GLAD YOU ARE PLEASED WITH THE NEW SLAVE, MASTER POTIPHAR.

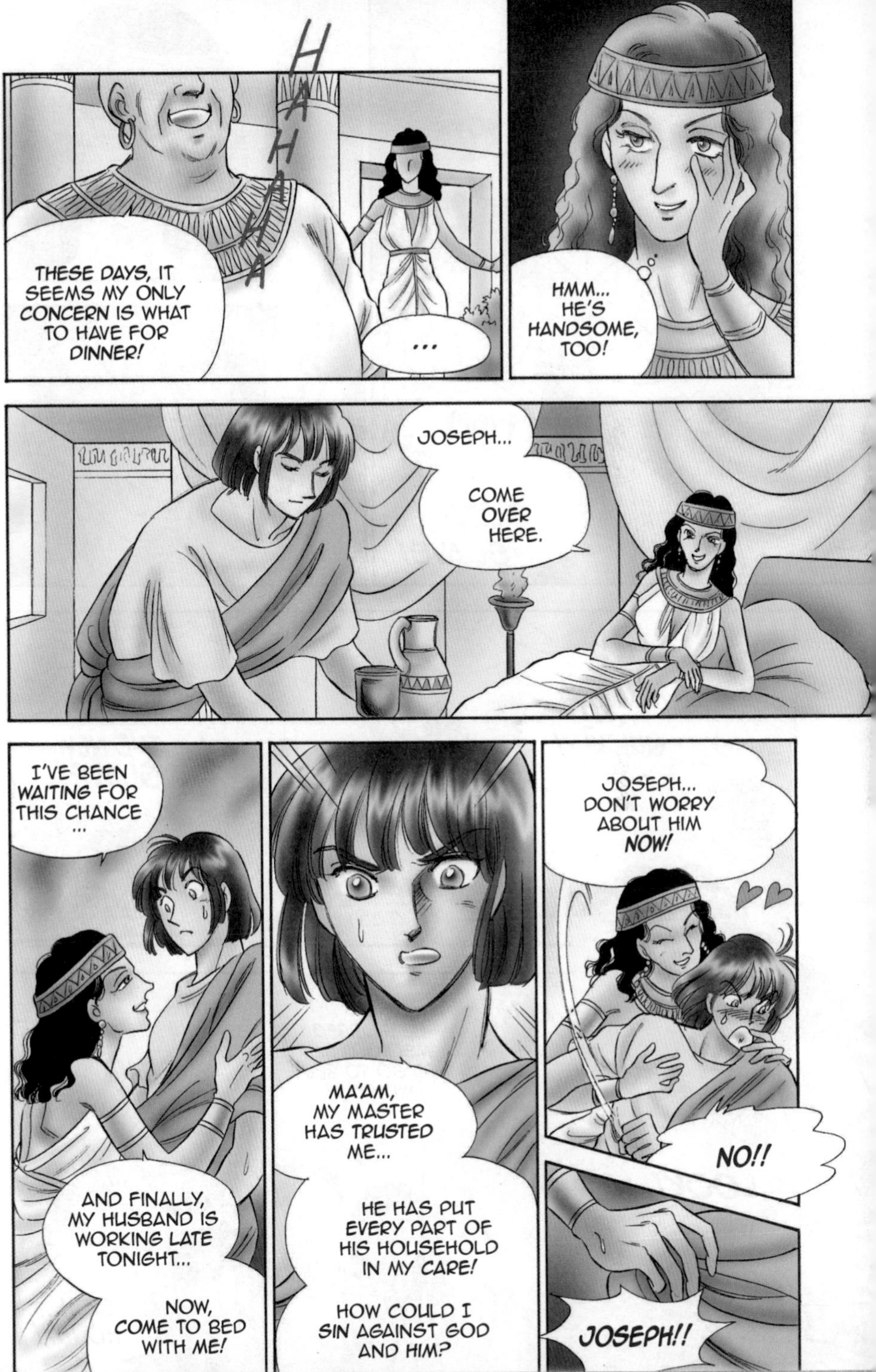
HAHAHAHA
THESE DAYS, IT SEEMS MY ONLY CONCERN IS WHAT TO HAVE FOR DINNER!
...
HMM... HE'S HANDSOME, TOO!
JOSEPH...
COME OVER HERE.
I'VE BEEN WAITING FOR THIS CHANCE ...
AND FINALLY, MY HUSBAND IS WORKING LATE TONIGHT...
NOW, COME TO BED WITH ME!
MA'AM, MY MASTER HAS TRUSTED ME...
HE HAS PUT EVERY PART OF HIS HOUSEHOLD IN MY CARE!
HOW COULD I SIN AGAINST GOD AND HIM?
JOSEPH... DON'T WORRY ABOUT HIM NOW!
NO!!
JOSEPH!!

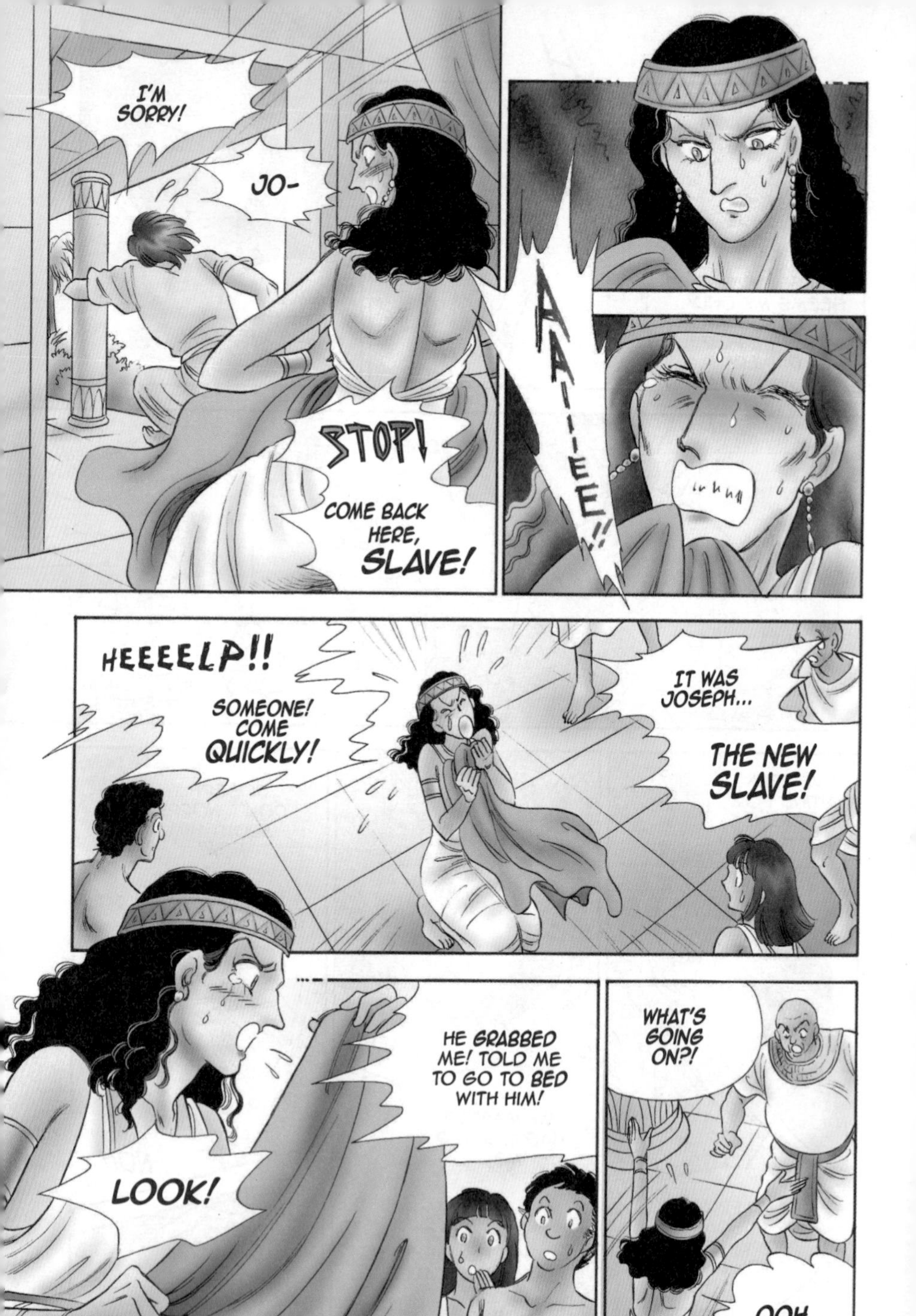
I'M SORRY!
JO-
STOP!
COME BACK HERE, SLAVE!
AAIIIEE!!
HEEEELP!!
SOMEONE! COME QUICKLY!
IT WAS JOSEPH...
THE NEW SLAVE!
HE GRABBED ME! TOLD ME TO GO TO BED WITH HIM!
LOOK!
WHAT'S GOING ON?!
OOH... HONEY!

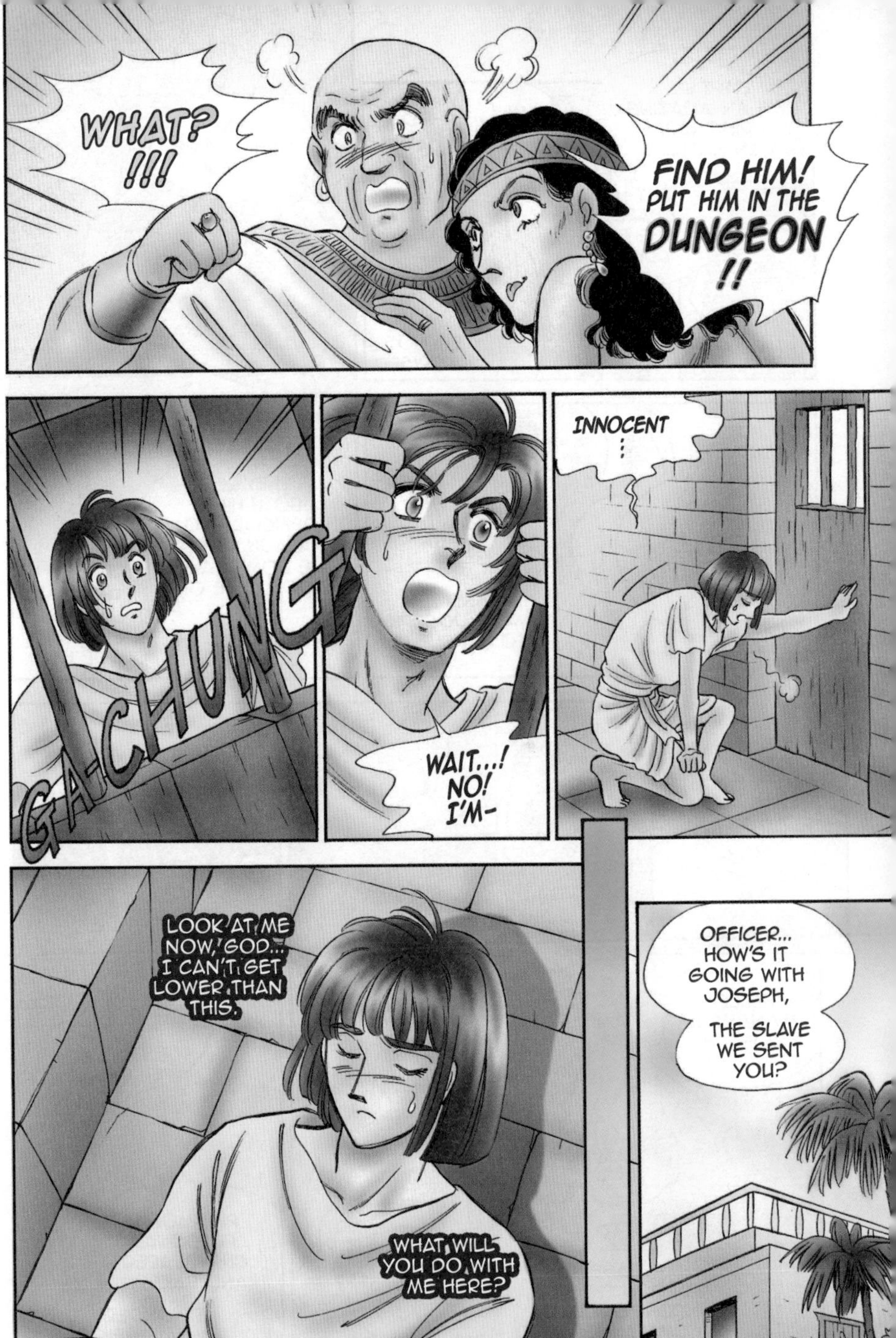
WHAT? !!!
FIND HIM! PUT HIM IN THE DUNGEON !!
GA-CHUNG
WAIT...! NO! I'M-
INNOCENT :
LOOK AT ME NOW, GOD... I CAN'T GET LOWER THAN THIS.
WHAT WILL YOU DO WITH ME HERE?
OFFICER... HOW'S IT GOING WITH JOSEPH,
THE SLAVE WE SENT YOU?

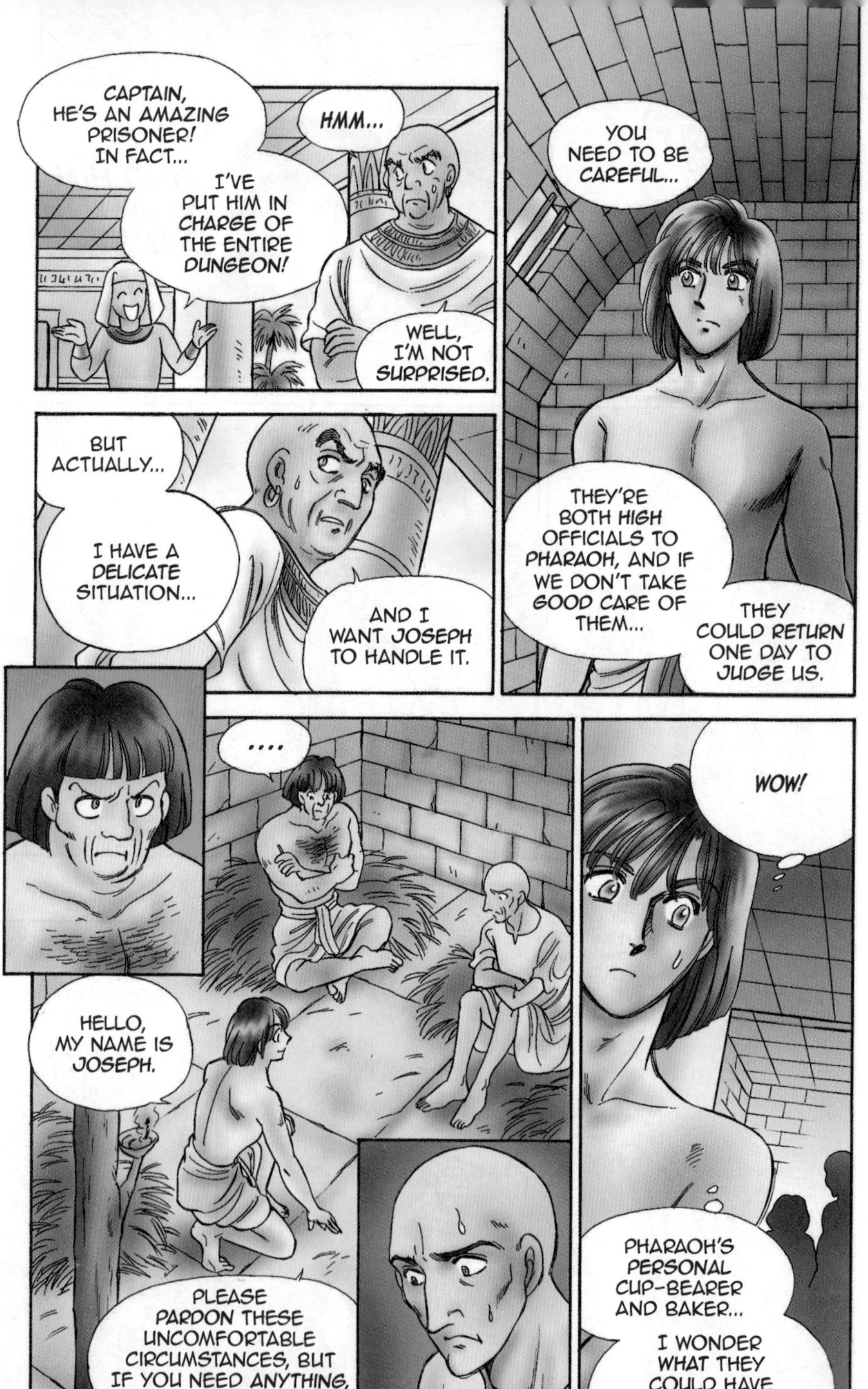
CAPTAIN, HE'S AN AMAZING PRISONER! IN FACT...
I'VE PUT HIM IN CHARGE OF THE ENTIRE DUNGEON!
HMM...
WELL, I'M NOT SURPRISED.
BUT ACTUALLY...
I HAVE A DELICATE SITUATION...
AND I WANT JOSEPH TO HANDLE IT.
YOU NEED TO BE CAREFUL...
THEY'RE BOTH HIGH OFFICIALS TO PHARAOH, AND IF WE DON'T TAKE GOOD CARE OF THEM...
THEY COULD RETURN ONE DAY TO JUDGE US.
....
HELLO, MY NAME IS JOSEPH.
PLEASE PARDON THESE UNCOMFORTABLE CIRCUMSTANCES, BUT IF YOU NEED ANYTHING, I WILL BE AT YOUR SERVICE.
WOW!
PHARAOH'S PERSONAL CUP-BEARER AND BAKER...
I WONDER WHAT THEY COULD HAVE DONE TO END UP DOWN HERE!

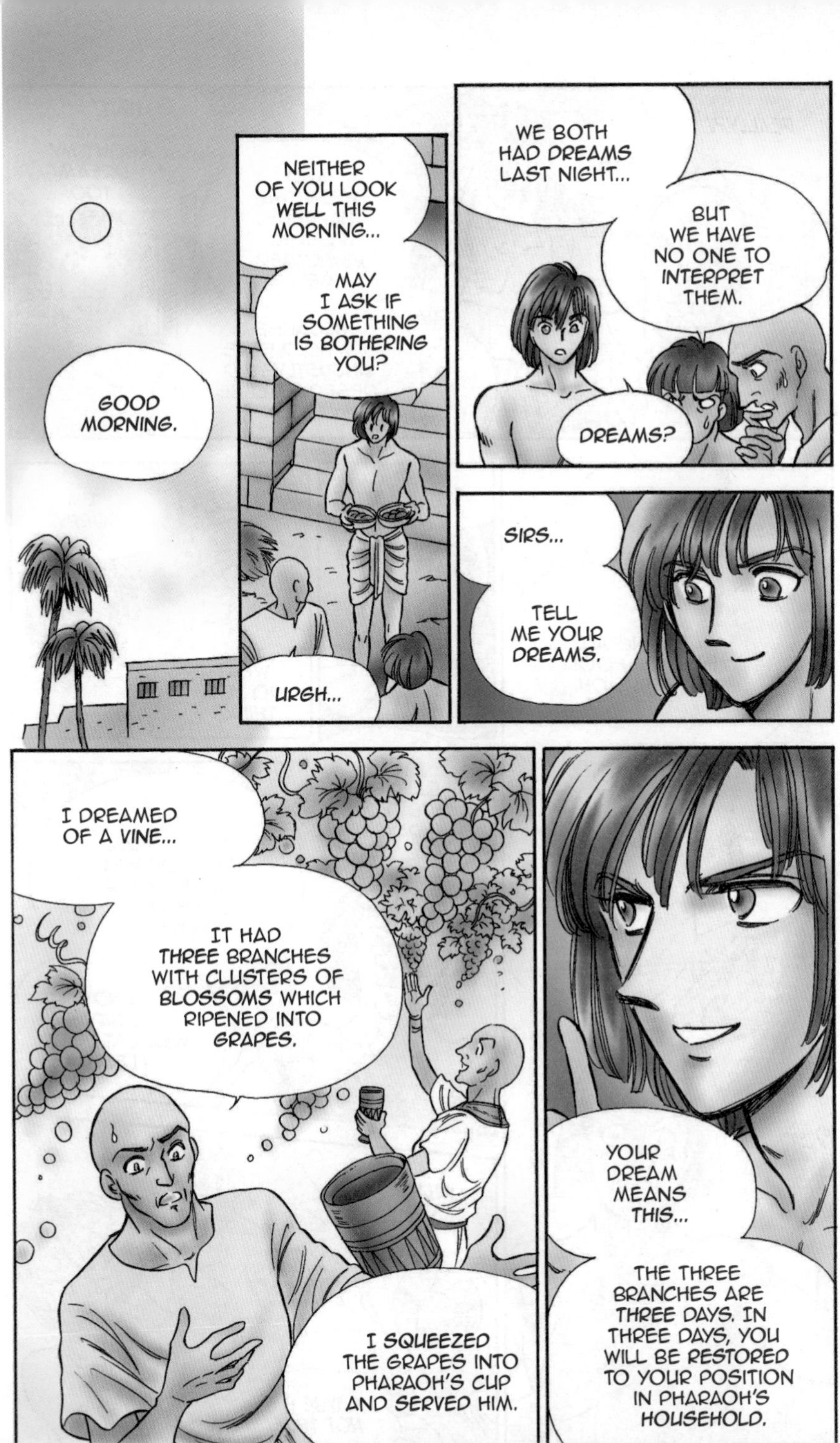
GOOD MORNING.
NEITHER OF YOU LOOK WELL THIS MORNING...
MAY I ASK IF SOMETHING IS BOTHERING YOU?
URGH...
WE BOTH HAD DREAMS LAST NIGHT...
BUT WE HAVE NO ONE TO INTERPRET THEM.
DREAMS?
SIRS...
TELL ME YOUR DREAMS.
I DREAMED OF A VINE...
IT HAD THREE BRANCHES WITH CLUSTERS OF BLOSSOMS WHICH RIPENED INTO GRAPES.
I SQUEEZED THE GRAPES INTO PHARAOH'S CUP AND SERVED HIM.
YOUR DREAM MEANS THIS...
THE THREE BRANCHES ARE THREE DAYS. IN THREE DAYS, YOU WILL BE RESTORED TO YOUR POSITION IN PHARAOH'S HOUSEHOLD.

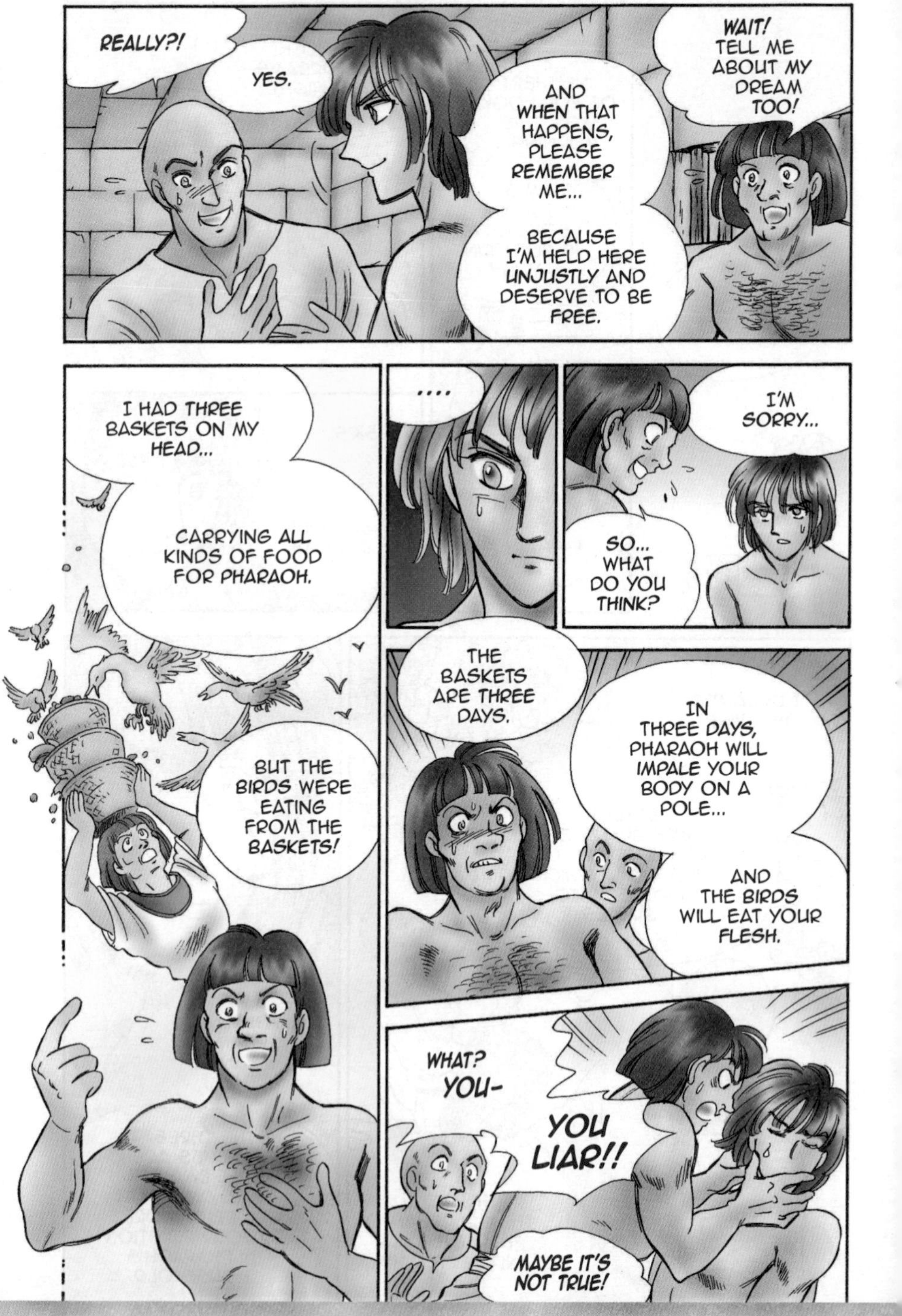
REALLY?!
YES.
AND WHEN THAT HAPPENS, PLEASE REMEMBER ME...
BECAUSE I'M HELD HERE UNJUSTLY AND DESERVE TO BE FREE.
WAIT! TELL ME ABOUT MY DREAM TOO!
I HAD THREE BASKETS ON MY HEAD...
CARRYING ALL KINDS OF FOOD FOR PHARAOH.
BUT THE BIRDS WERE EATING FROM THE BASKETS!
....
I'M SORRY...
SO... WHAT DO YOU THINK?
THE BASKETS ARE THREE DAYS.
IN THREE DAYS, PHARAOH WILL IMPALE YOUR BODY ON A POLE...
AND THE BIRDS WILL EAT YOUR FLESH.
WHAT? YOU-
YOU LIAR!!
MAYBE IT'S NOT TRUE!

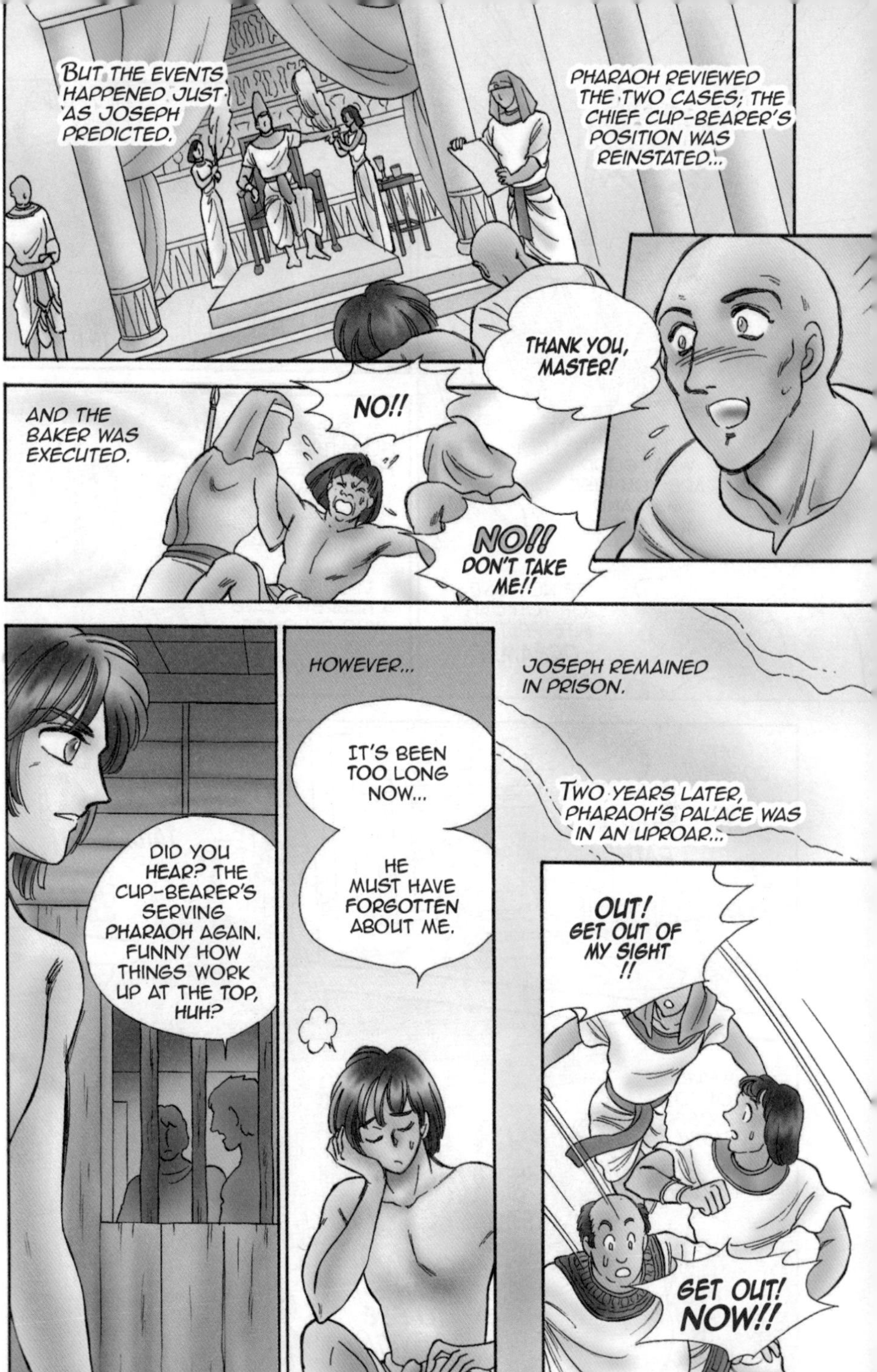

BUT THE EVENTS HAPPENED JUST AS JOSEPH PREDICTED.
PHARAOH REVIEWED THE TWO CASES; THE CHIEF CUP-BEARER'S POSITION WAS REINSTATED...
THANK YOU, MASTER!
AND THE BAKER WAS EXECUTED.
NO!!
NO!! DON'T TAKE ME!!
DID YOU HEAR? THE CUP-BEARER'S SERVING PHARAOH AGAIN. FUNNY HOW THINGS WORK UP AT THE TOP, HUH?
HOWEVER...
IT'S BEEN TOO LONG NOW...
HE MUST HAVE FORGOTTEN ABOUT ME.
JOSEPH REMAINED IN PRISON.
TWO YEARS LATER, PHARAOH'S PALACE WAS IN AN UPROAR...
OUT! GET OUT OF MY SIGHT !!
GET OUT! NOW!!

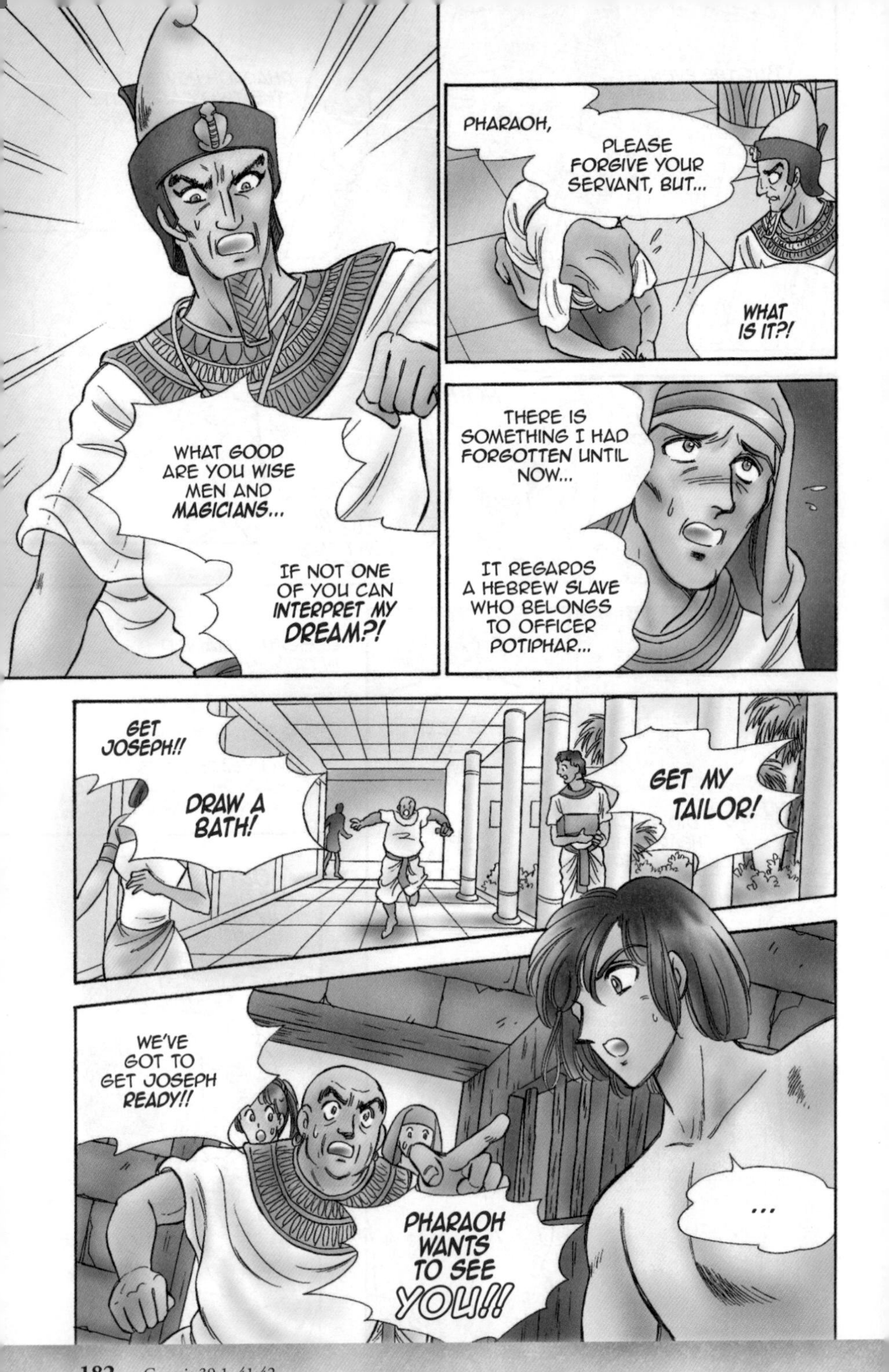
WHAT GOOD ARE YOU WISE MEN AND MAGICIANS...
IF NOT ONE OF YOU CAN INTERPRET MY DREAM?!
PHARAOH,
PLEASE FORGIVE YOUR SERVANT, BUT...
WHAT IS IT?!
THERE IS SOMETHING I HAD FORGOTTEN UNTIL NOW...
IT REGARDS A HEBREW SLAVE WHO BELONGS TO OFFICER POTIPHAR...
GET JOSEPH!!
DRAW A BATH!
GET MY TAILOR!
WE'VE GOT TO GET JOSEPH READY!!
PHARAOH WANTS TO SEE YOU!!
...

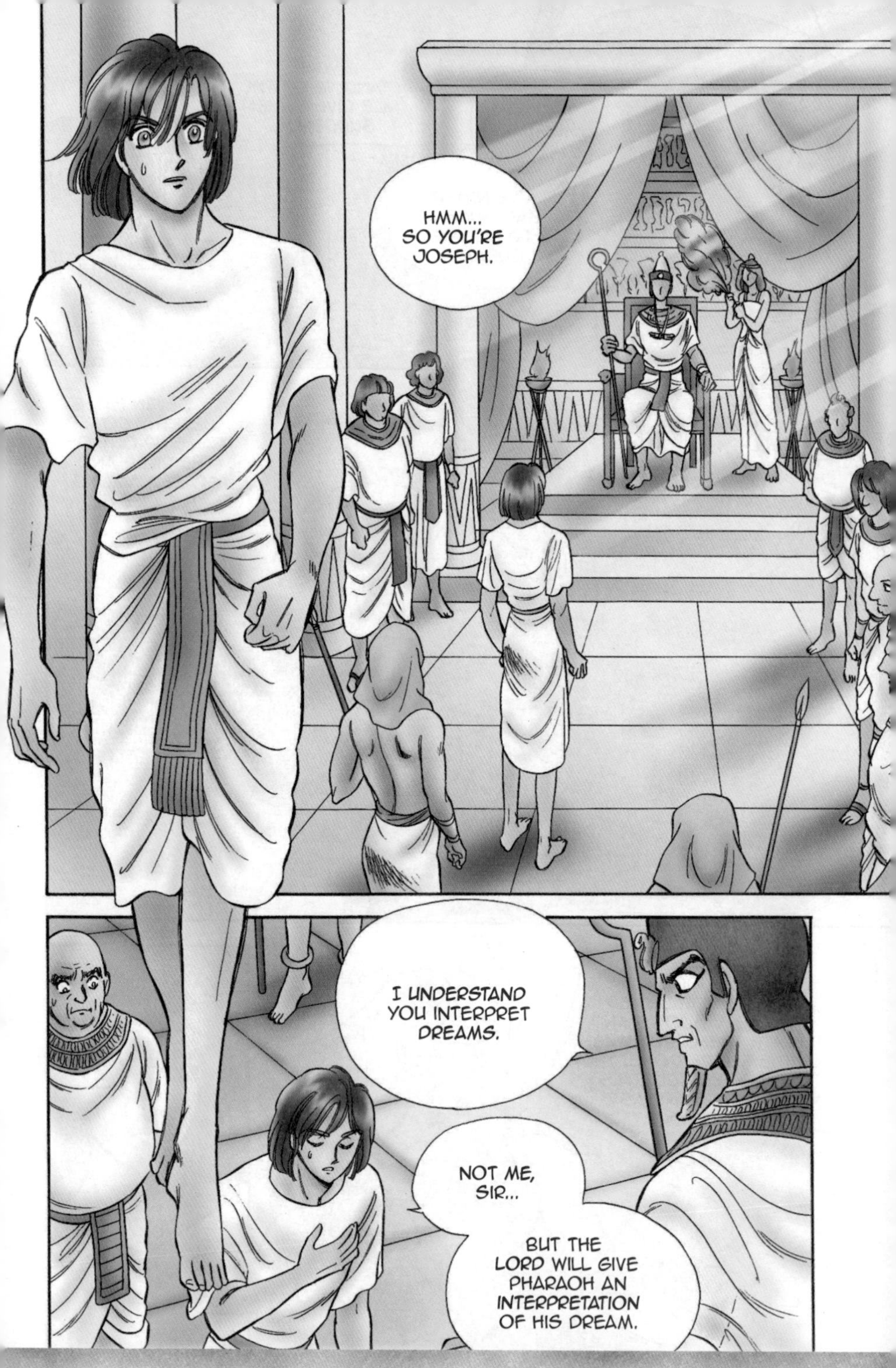
HMM... SO YOU'RE JOSEPH.
I UNDERSTAND YOU INTERPRET DREAMS.
NOT ME, SIR...
BUT THE LORD WILL GIVE PHARAOH AN INTERPRETATION OF HIS DREAM.

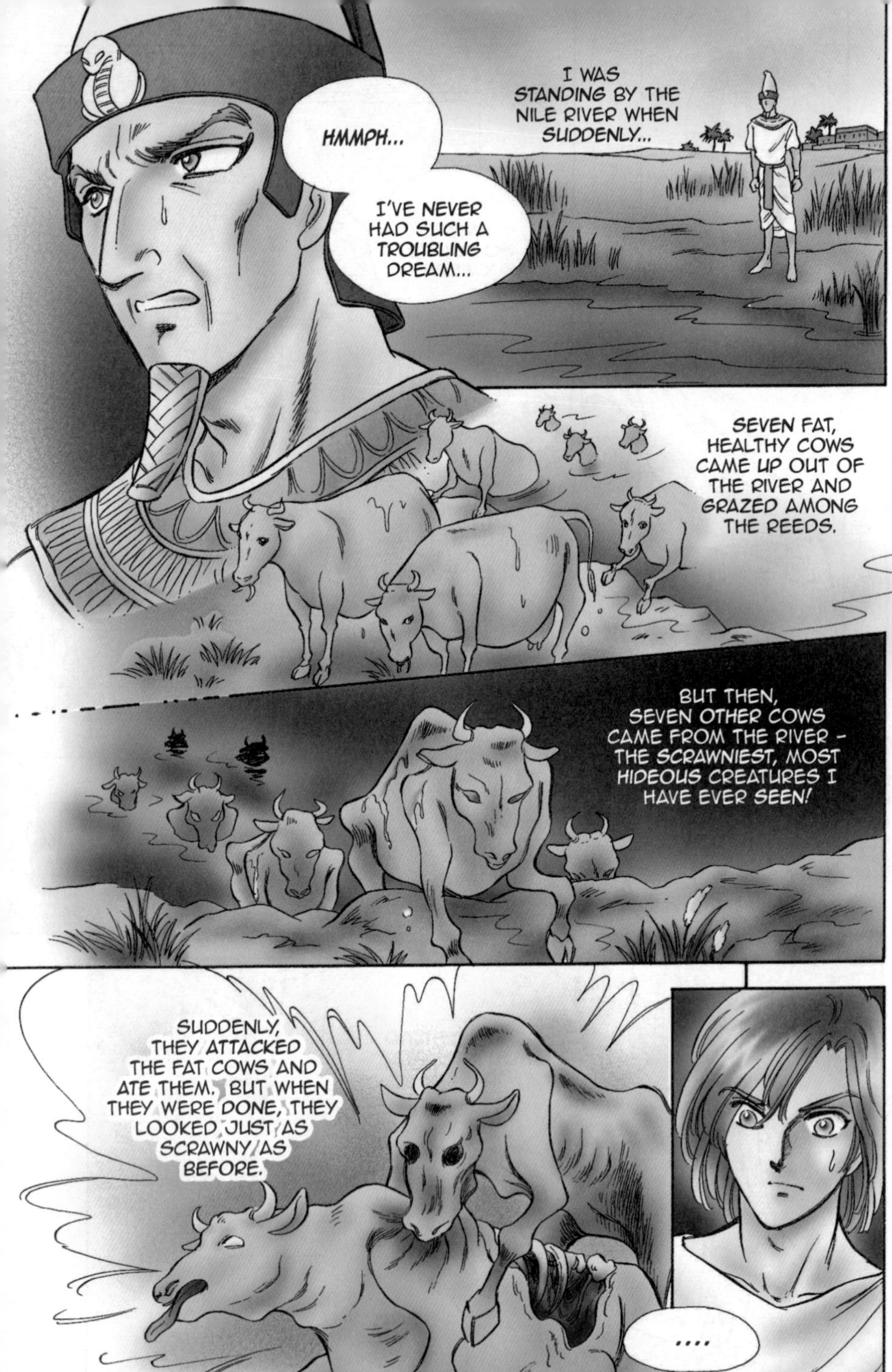
HMMPH...
I'VE NEVER HAD SUCH A TROUBLING DREAM...
I WAS STANDING BY THE NILE RIVER WHEN SUDDENLY...
SEVEN FAT, HEALTHY COWS CAME UP OUT OF THE RIVER AND GRAZED AMONG THE REEDS.
BUT THEN, SEVEN OTHER COWS CAME FROM THE RIVER - THE SCRAWNIEST, MOST HIDEOUS CREATURES I HAVE EVER SEEN!
SUDDENLY, THEY ATTACKED THE FAT COWS AND ATE THEM. BUT WHEN THEY WERE DONE, THEY LOOKED JUST AS SCRAWNY AS BEFORE.
....

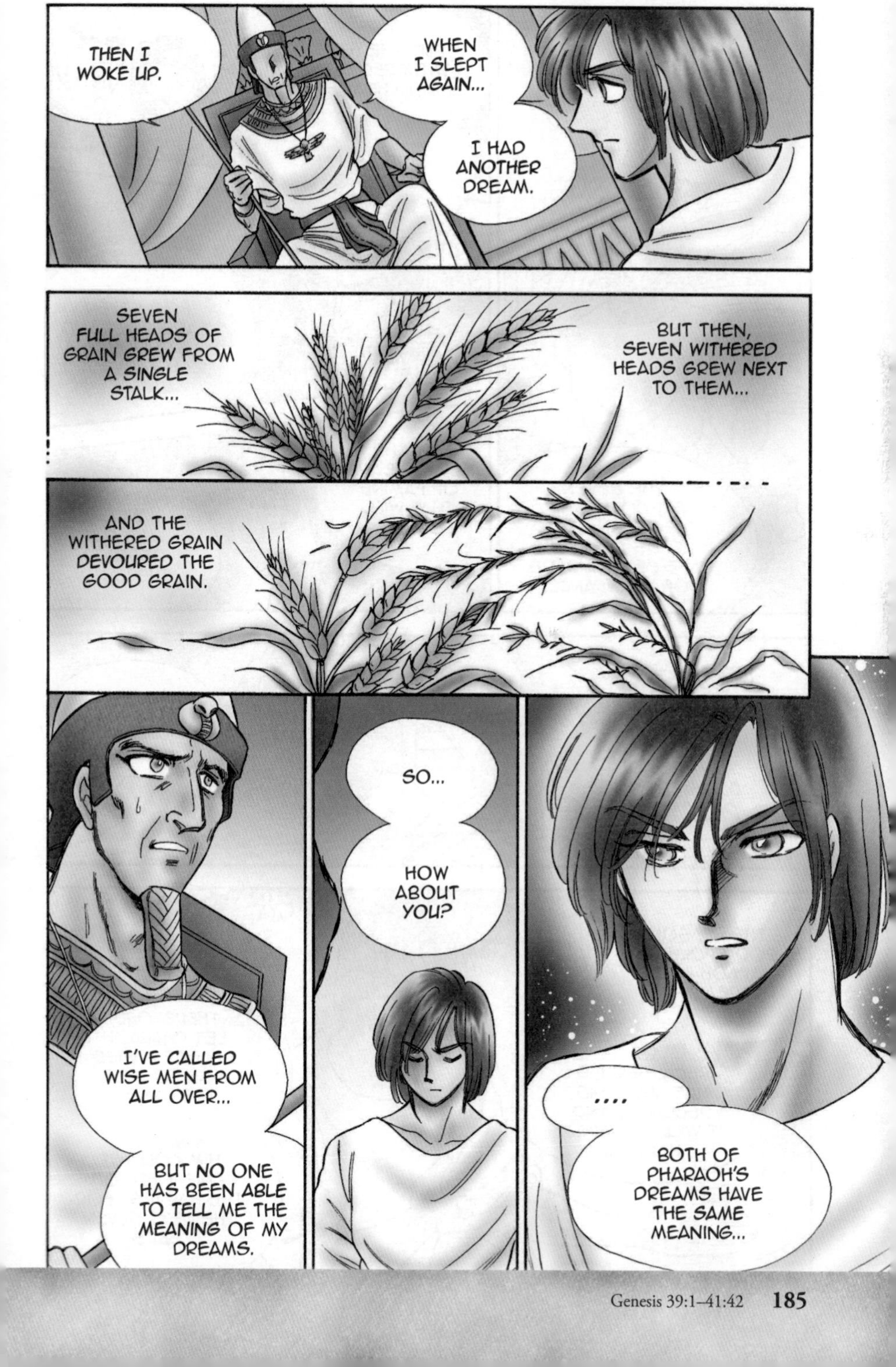

THEN I WOKE UP.
WHEN I SLEPT AGAIN...
I HAD ANOTHER DREAM.
SEVEN FULL HEADS OF GRAIN GREW FROM A SINGLE STALK...
BUT THEN, SEVEN WITHERED HEADS GREW NEXT TO THEM...
AND THE WITHERED GRAIN DEVOURED THE GOOD GRAIN.
I'VE CALLED WISE MEN FROM ALL OVER...
BUT NO ONE HAS BEEN ABLE TO TELL ME THE MEANING OF MY DREAMS.
SO...
HOW ABOUT YOU?
....
BOTH OF PHARAOH'S DREAMS HAVE THE SAME MEANING...

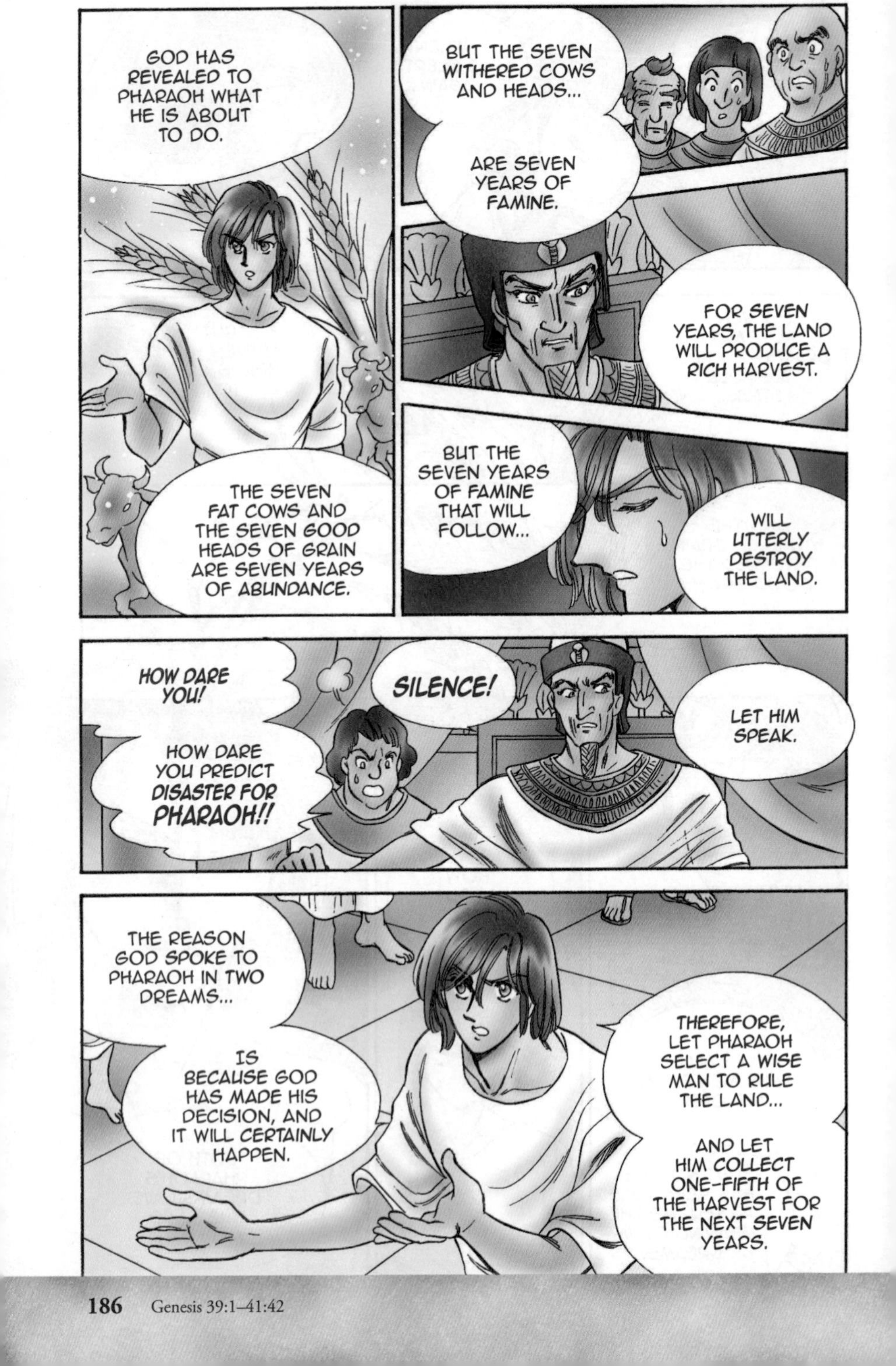
GOD HAS REVEALED TO PHARAOH WHAT HE IS ABOUT TO DO.
THE SEVEN FAT COWS AND THE SEVEN GOOD HEADS OF GRAIN ARE SEVEN YEARS OF ABUNDANCE.
BUT THE SEVEN WITHERED COWS AND HEADS...
ARE SEVEN YEARS OF FAMINE.
FOR SEVEN YEARS, THE LAND WILL PRODUCE A RICH HARVEST.
BUT THE SEVEN YEARS OF FAMINE THAT WILL FOLLOW...
WILL UTTERLY DESTROY THE LAND.
HOW DARE YOU!
HOW DARE YOU PREDICT DISASTER FOR PHARAOH!!
SILENCE!
LET HIM SPEAK.
THE REASON GOD SPOKE TO PHARAOH IN TWO DREAMS...
IS BECAUSE GOD HAS MADE HIS DECISION, AND IT WILL CERTAINLY HAPPEN.
THEREFORE, LET PHARAOH SELECT A WISE MAN TO RULE THE LAND...
AND LET HIM COLLECT ONE-FIFTH OF THE HARVEST FOR THE NEXT SEVEN YEARS.

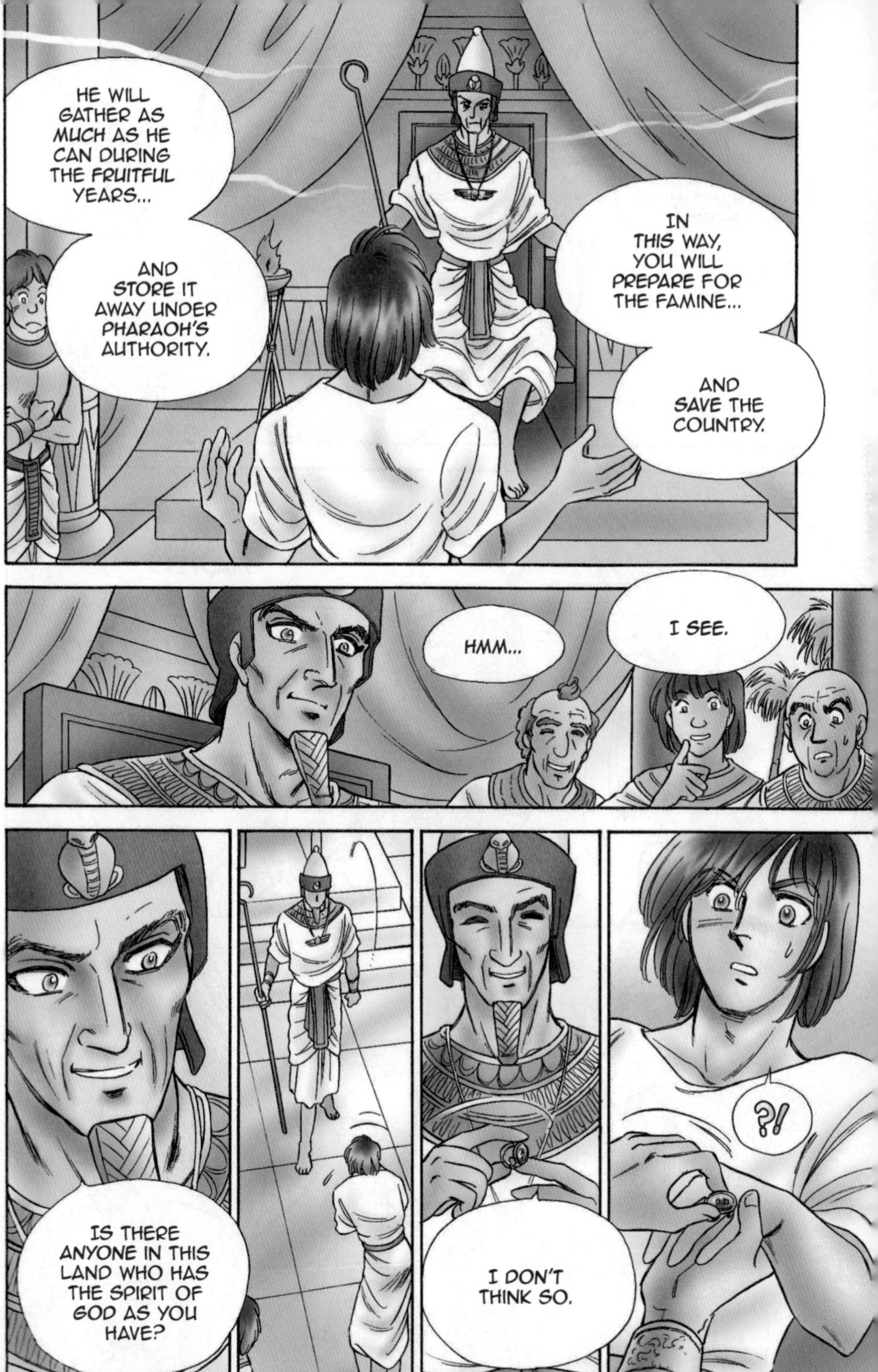
HE WILL GATHER AS MUCH AS HE CAN DURING THE FRUITFUL YEARS...
AND STORE IT AWAY UNDER PHARAOH'S AUTHORITY.
IN THIS WAY, YOU WILL PREPARE FOR THE FAMINE...
AND SAVE THE COUNTRY.
HMM...
I SEE.
IS THERE ANYONE IN THIS LAND WHO HAS THE SPIRIT OF GOD AS YOU HAVE?
I DON'T THINK SO.
?!

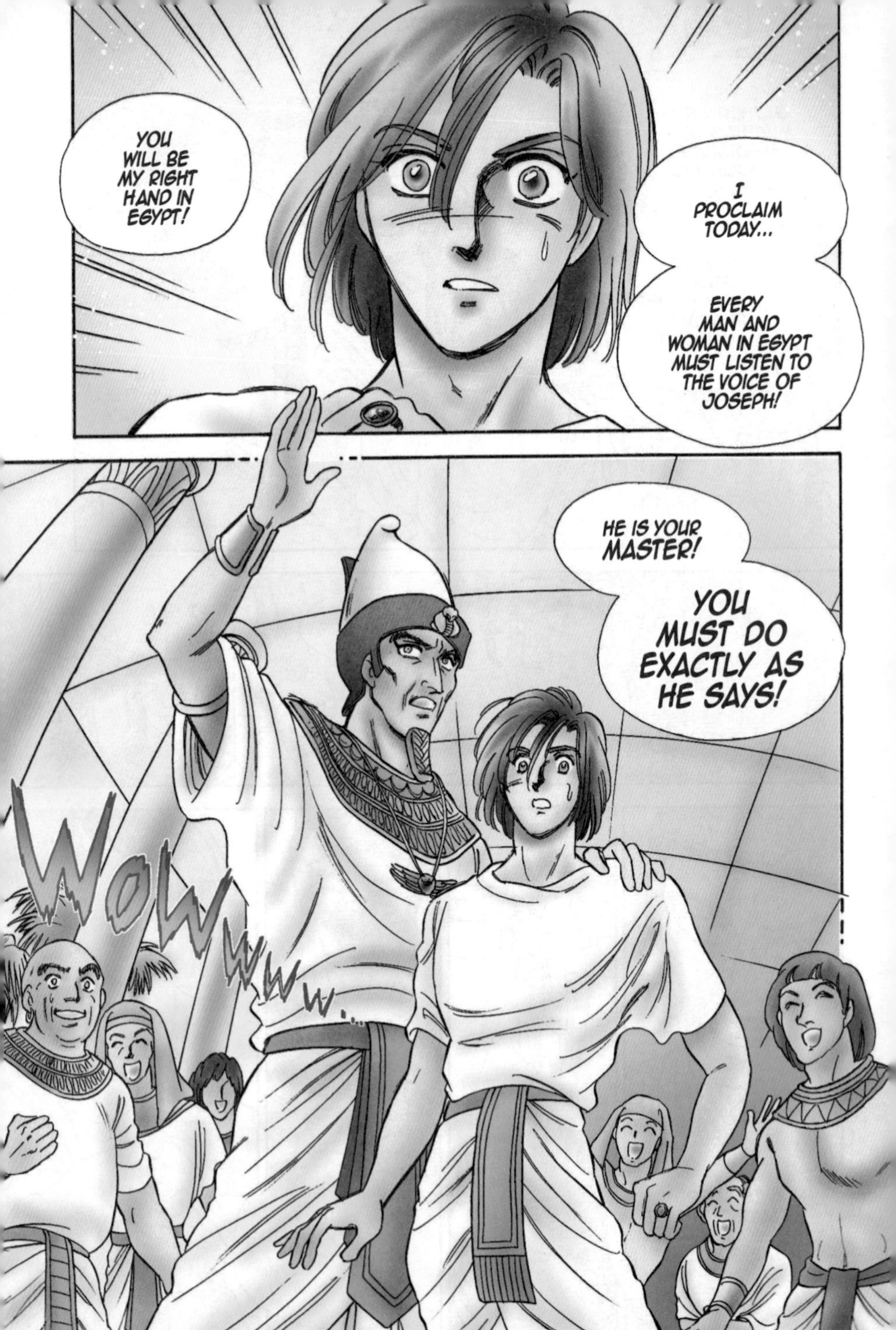
YOU WILL BE MY RIGHT HAND IN EGYPT!
I PROCLAIM TODAY...
EVERY MAN AND WOMAN IN EGYPT MUST LISTEN TO THE VOICE OF JOSEPH!
WOWWWW...
HE IS YOUR MASTER!
YOU MUST DO EXACTLY AS HE SAYS!

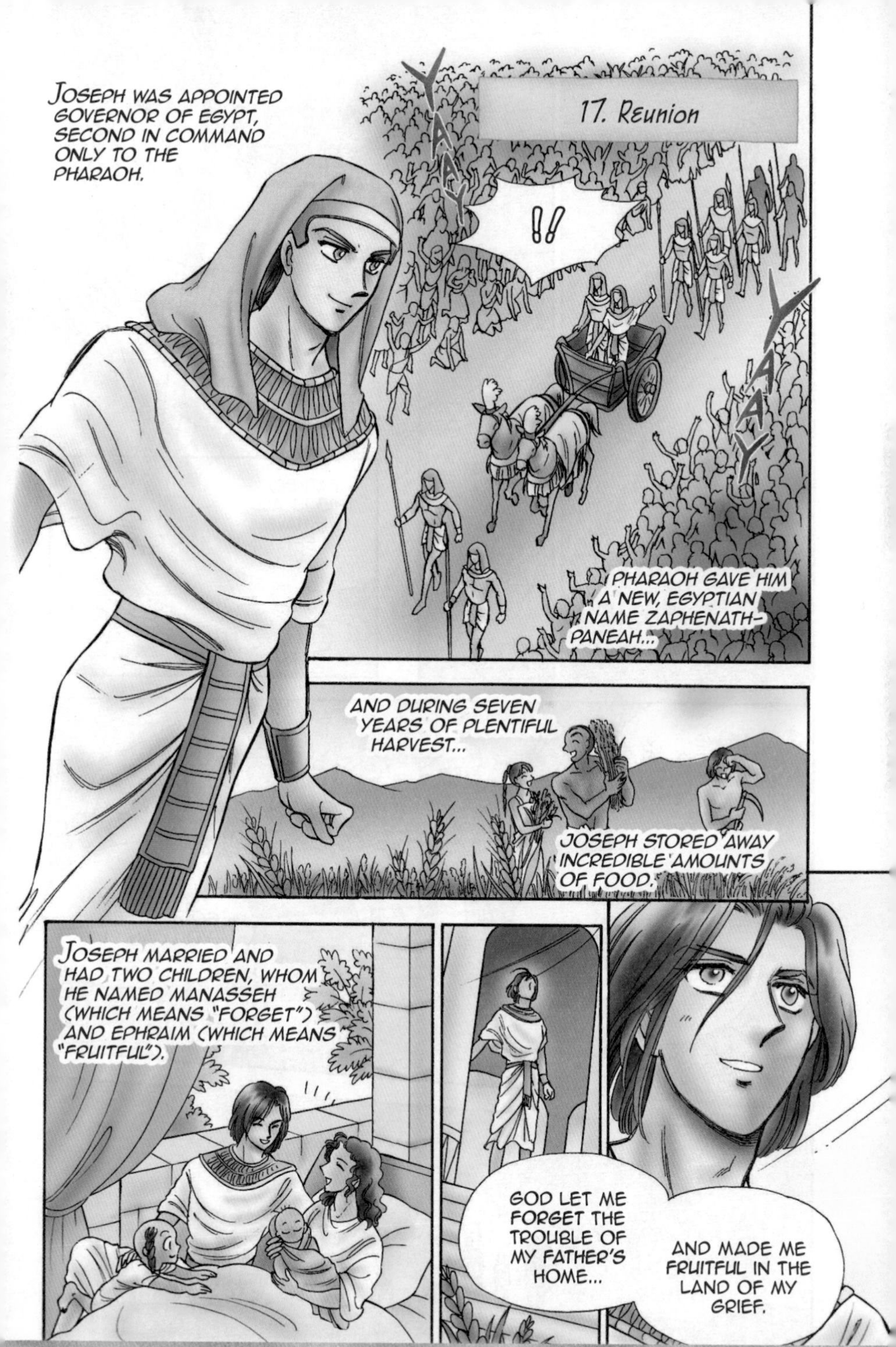
17. Reunion
JOSEPH WAS APPOINTED GOVERNOR OF EGYPT, SECOND IN COMMAND ONLY TO THE PHARAOH.
YAAAY
!!
YAAAY
PHARAOH GAVE HIM A NEW, EGYPTIAN NAME ZAPHENATH-PANEAH...
AND DURING SEVEN YEARS OF PLENTIFUL HARVEST...
JOSEPH STORED AWAY INCREDIBLE AMOUNTS OF FOOD.
JOSEPH MARRIED AND HAD TWO CHILDREN, WHOM HE NAMED MANASSEH (WHICH MEANS "FORGET") AND EPHRAIM (WHICH MEANS "FRUITFUL").
GOD LET ME FORGET THE TROUBLE OF MY FATHER'S HOME...
AND MADE ME FRUITFUL IN THE LAND OF MY GRIEF.

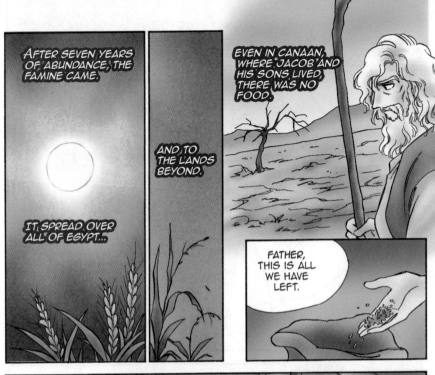

AFTER SEVEN YEARS OF ABUNDANCE, THE FAMINE CAME.

IT SPREAD OVER ALL OF EGYPT...

AND, TO THE LANDS BEYOND.

EVEN IN CANAAN, WHERE JACOB AND HIS SONS LIVED, THERE WAS NO FOOD.

FATHER, THIS IS ALL WE HAVE LEFT.

IF WE DON'T DO SOMETHING, OUR FAMILIES WILL DIE.

BUT I'VE HEARD THERE IS GRAIN IN EGYPT.

YES, YOU SHOULD GO AND SEE IF YOU CAN BUY US FOOD.

SO THE SONS OF JACOB PACKED UP AND JOURNEYED TO EGYPT.

BUT BENJAMIN, JACOB'S YOUNGEST SON, STAYED HOME WITH HIS FATHER.

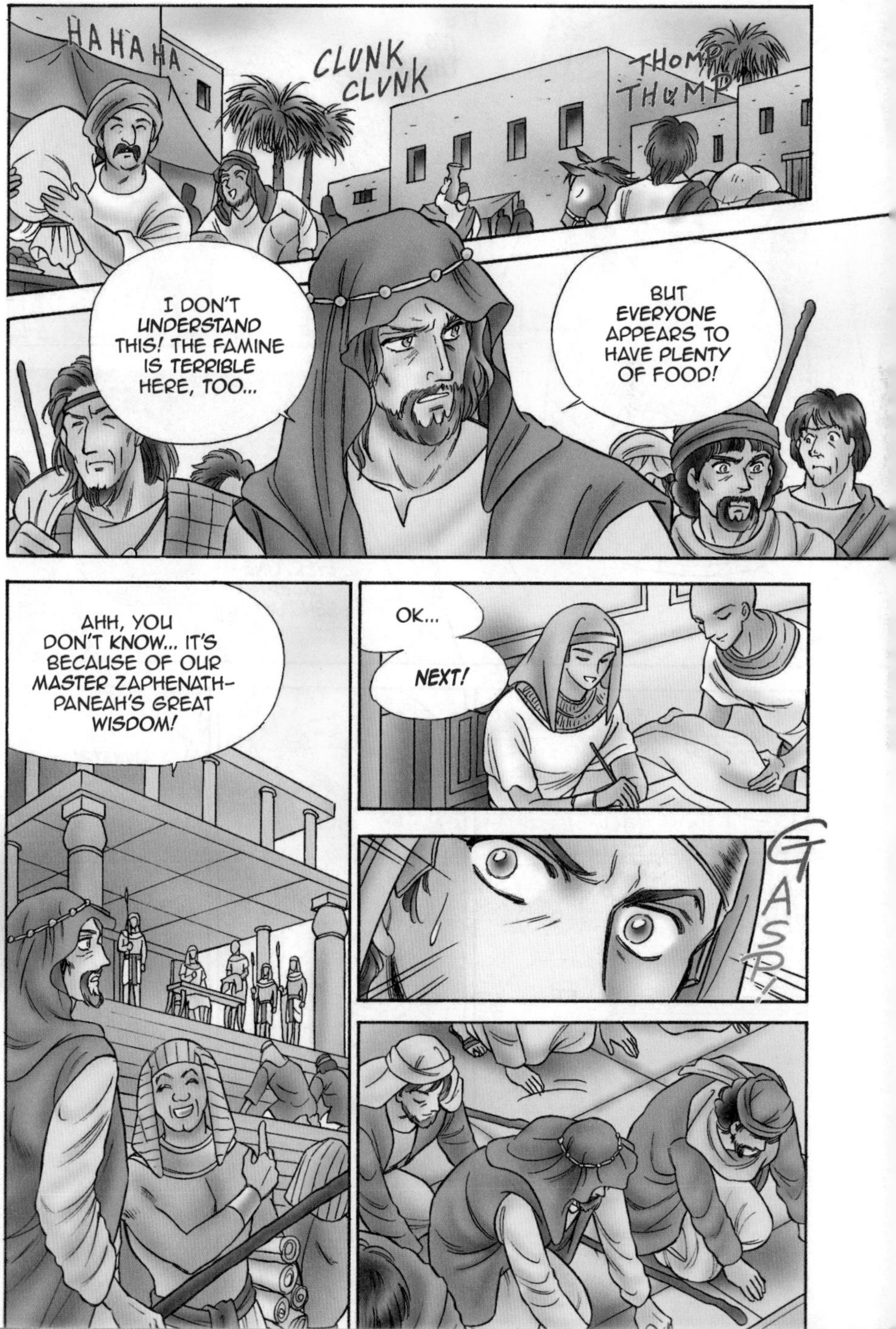
HAHAHA
CLUNK CLUNK
THUMP THUMP
I DON'T UNDERSTAND THIS! THE FAMINE IS TERRIBLE HERE, TOO...
BUT EVERYONE APPEARS TO HAVE PLENTY OF FOOD!
AHH, YOU DON'T KNOW... IT'S BECAUSE OF OUR MASTER ZAPHENATH-PANEAH'S GREAT WISDOM!
OK...
NEXT!
GASP!

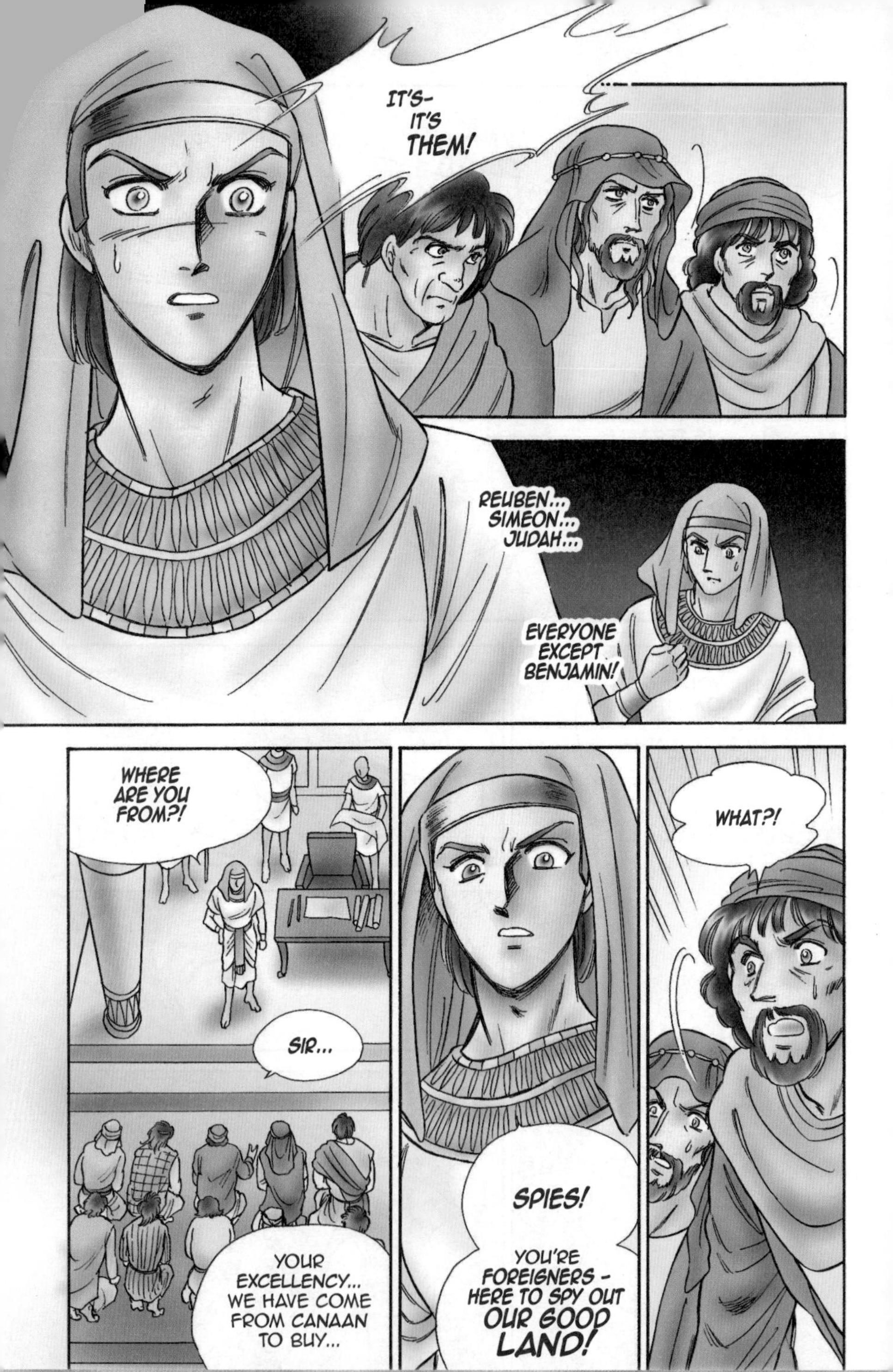
IT'S- IT'S THEM!
REUBEN... SIMEON... JUDAH...
EVERYONE EXCEPT BENJAMIN!
WHERE ARE YOU FROM?!
SIR...
YOUR EXCELLENCY... WE HAVE COME FROM CANAAN TO BUY...
SPIES!
YOU'RE FOREIGNERS - HERE TO SPY OUT OUR GOOD LAND!
WHAT?!

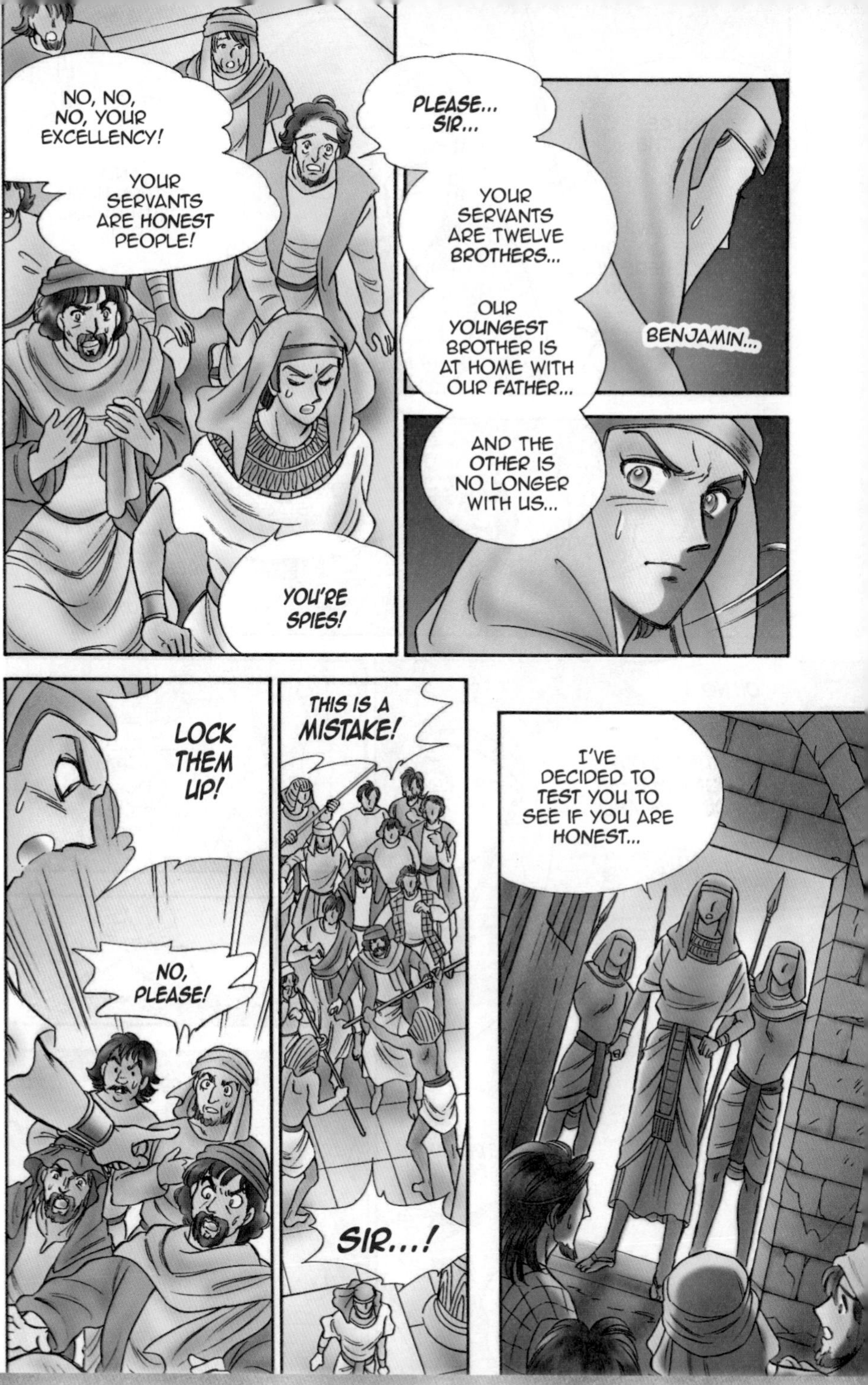
NO, NO, NO, YOUR EXCELLENCY!
YOUR SERVANTS ARE HONEST PEOPLE!
YOU'RE SPIES!
PLEASE... SIR...
YOUR SERVANTS ARE TWELVE BROTHERS...
OUR YOUNGEST BROTHER IS AT HOME WITH OUR FATHER...
BENJAMIN...
AND THE OTHER IS NO LONGER WITH US...
LOCK THEM UP!
NO, PLEASE!
THIS IS A MISTAKE!
SIR...!
I'VE DECIDED TO TEST YOU TO SEE IF YOU ARE HONEST...

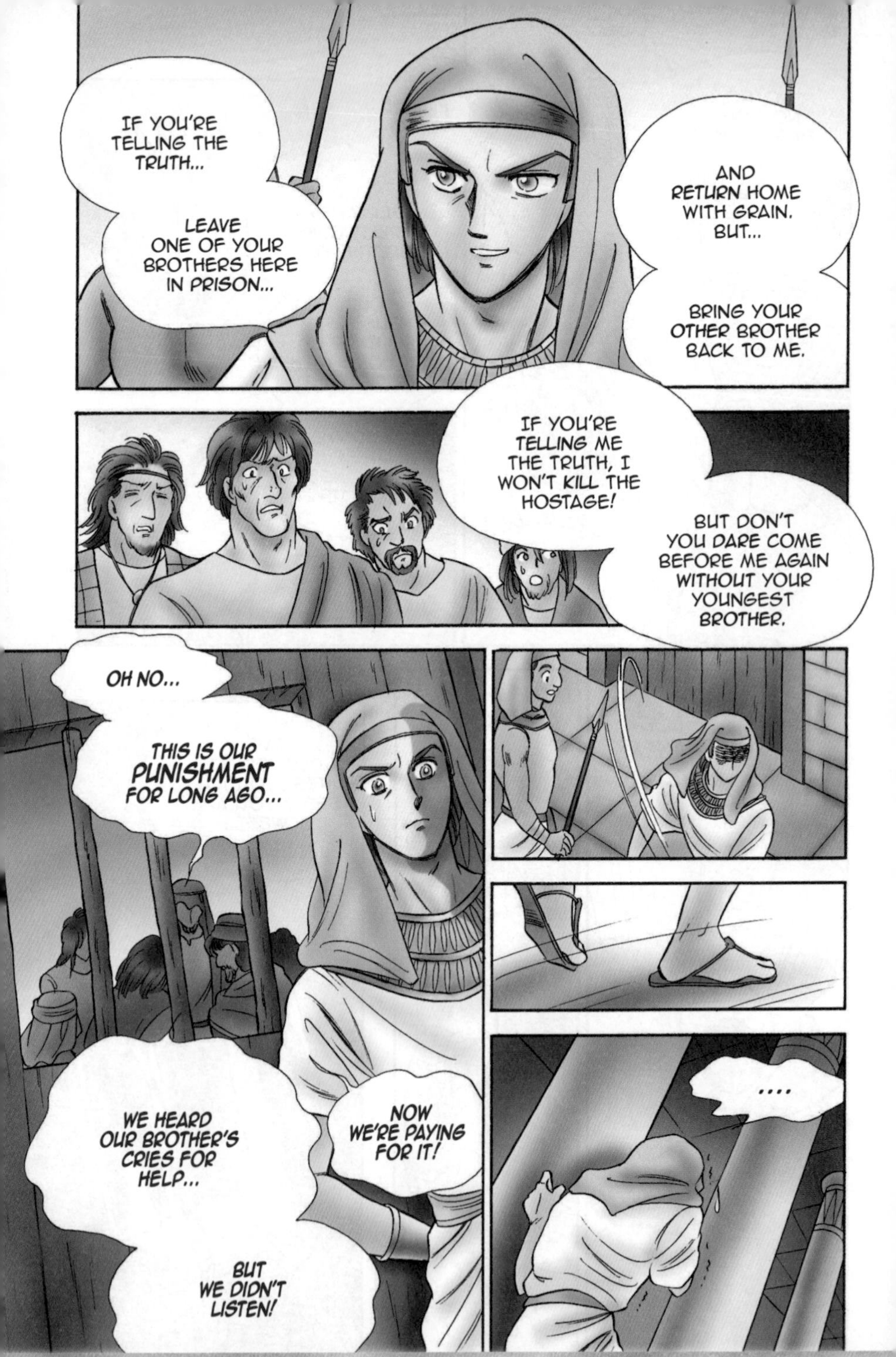
IF YOU'RE TELLING THE TRUTH...
LEAVE ONE OF YOUR BROTHERS HERE IN PRISON...
AND RETURN HOME WITH GRAIN. BUT...
BRING YOUR OTHER BROTHER BACK TO ME.
IF YOU'RE TELLING ME THE TRUTH, I WON'T KILL THE HOSTAGE!
BUT DON'T YOU DARE COME BEFORE ME AGAIN WITHOUT YOUR YOUNGEST BROTHER.
OH NO...
THIS IS OUR PUNISHMENT FOR LONG AGO...
WE HEARD OUR BROTHER'S CRIES FOR HELP...
BUT WE DIDN'T LISTEN!
NOW WE'RE PAYING FOR IT!
....

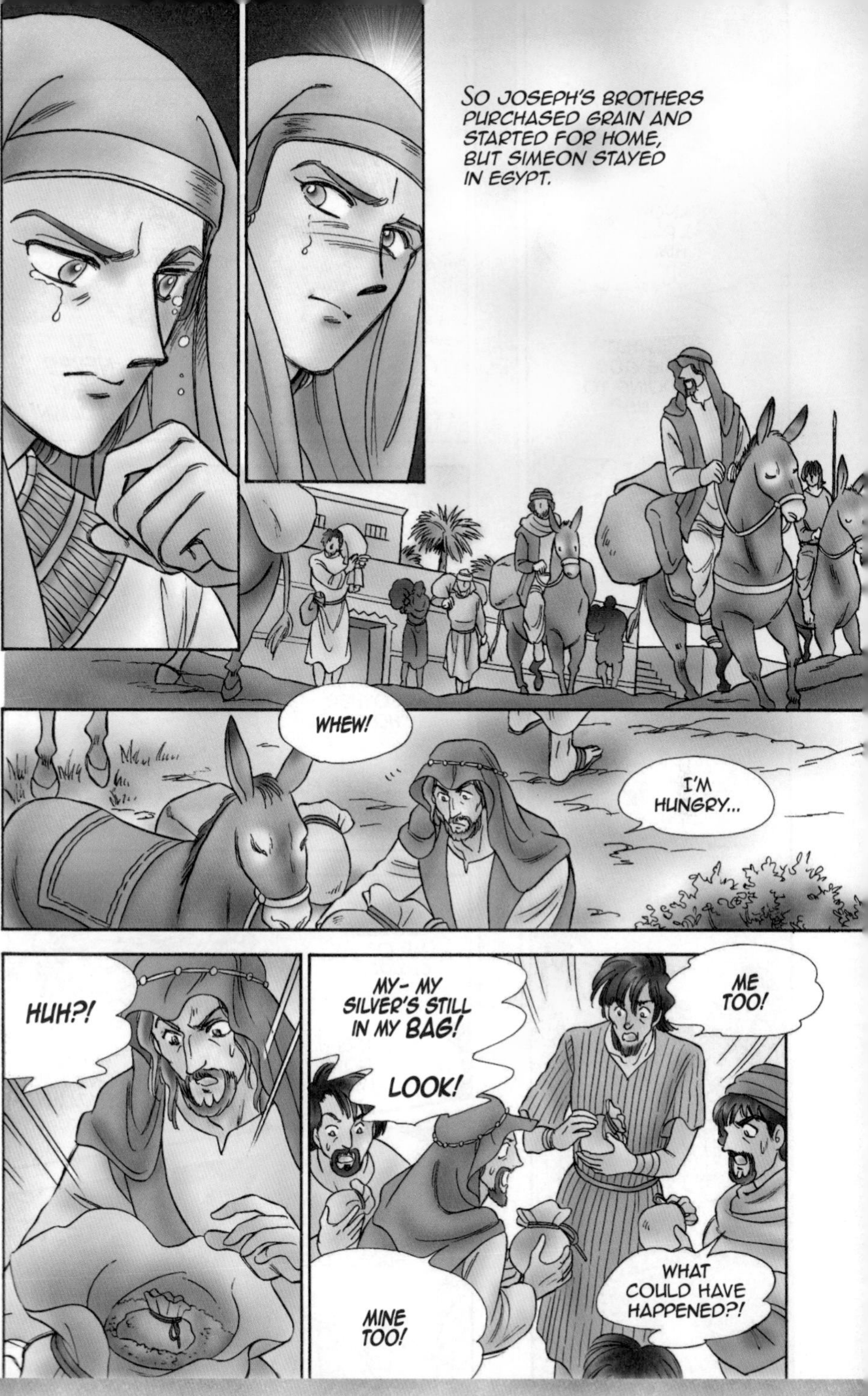
SO JOSEPH'S BROTHERS PURCHASED GRAIN AND STARTED FOR HOME, BUT SIMEON STAYED IN EGYPT.
WHEW!
I'M HUNGRY...
HUH?!
MY- MY SILVER'S STILL IN MY BAG!
ME TOO!
LOOK!
WHAT COULD HAVE HAPPENED?!
MINE TOO!

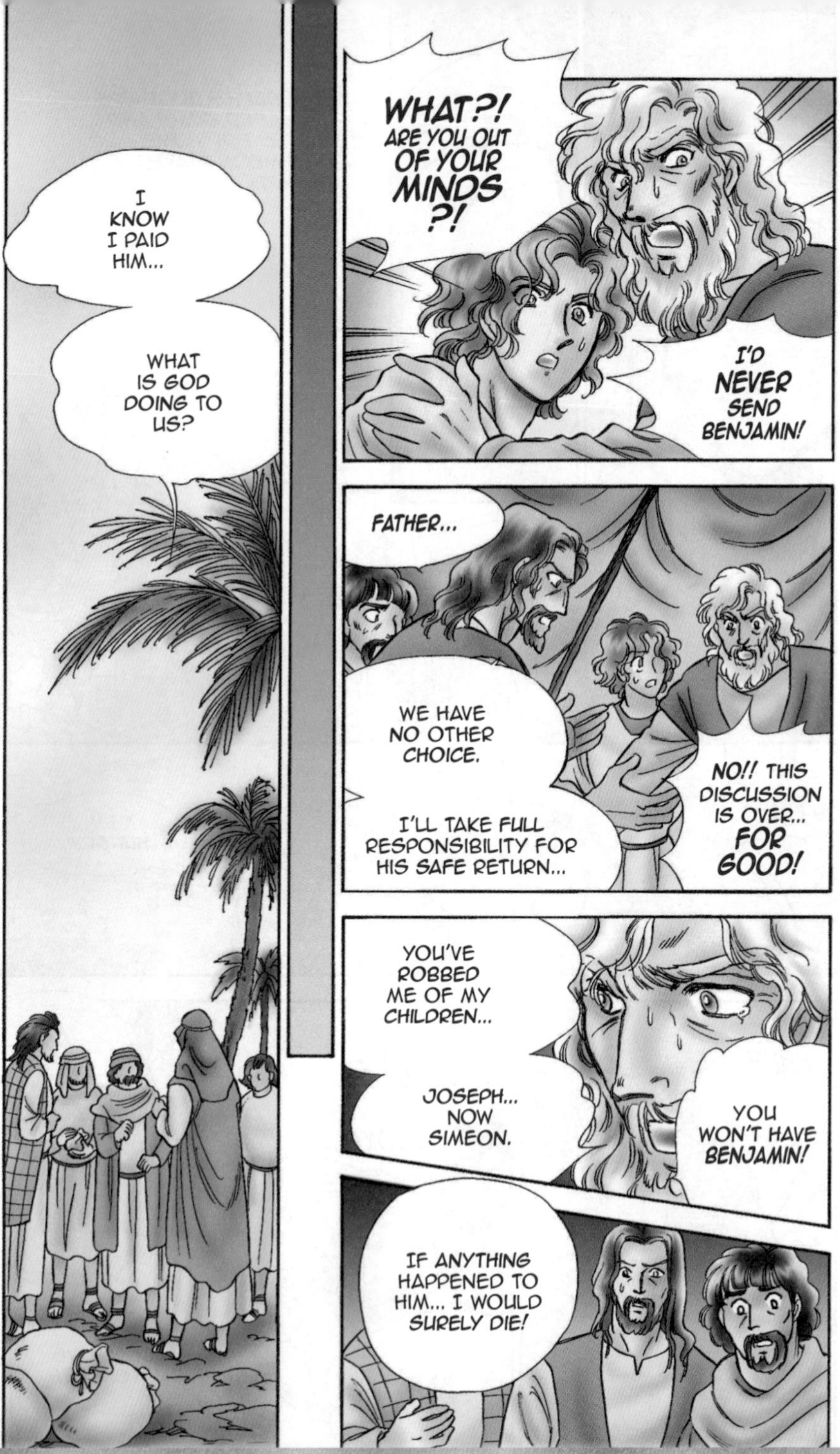
I KNOW I PAID HIM...
WHAT IS GOD DOING TO US?
WHAT?! ARE YOU OUT OF YOUR MINDS ?!
I'D NEVER SEND BENJAMIN!
FATHER...
WE HAVE NO OTHER CHOICE.
I'LL TAKE FULL RESPONSIBILITY FOR HIS SAFE RETURN...
NO!! THIS DISCUSSION IS OVER... FOR GOOD!
YOU'VE ROBBED ME OF MY CHILDREN...
JOSEPH... NOW SIMEON.
YOU WON'T HAVE BENJAMIN!
IF ANYTHING HAPPENED TO HIM... I WOULD SURELY DIE!

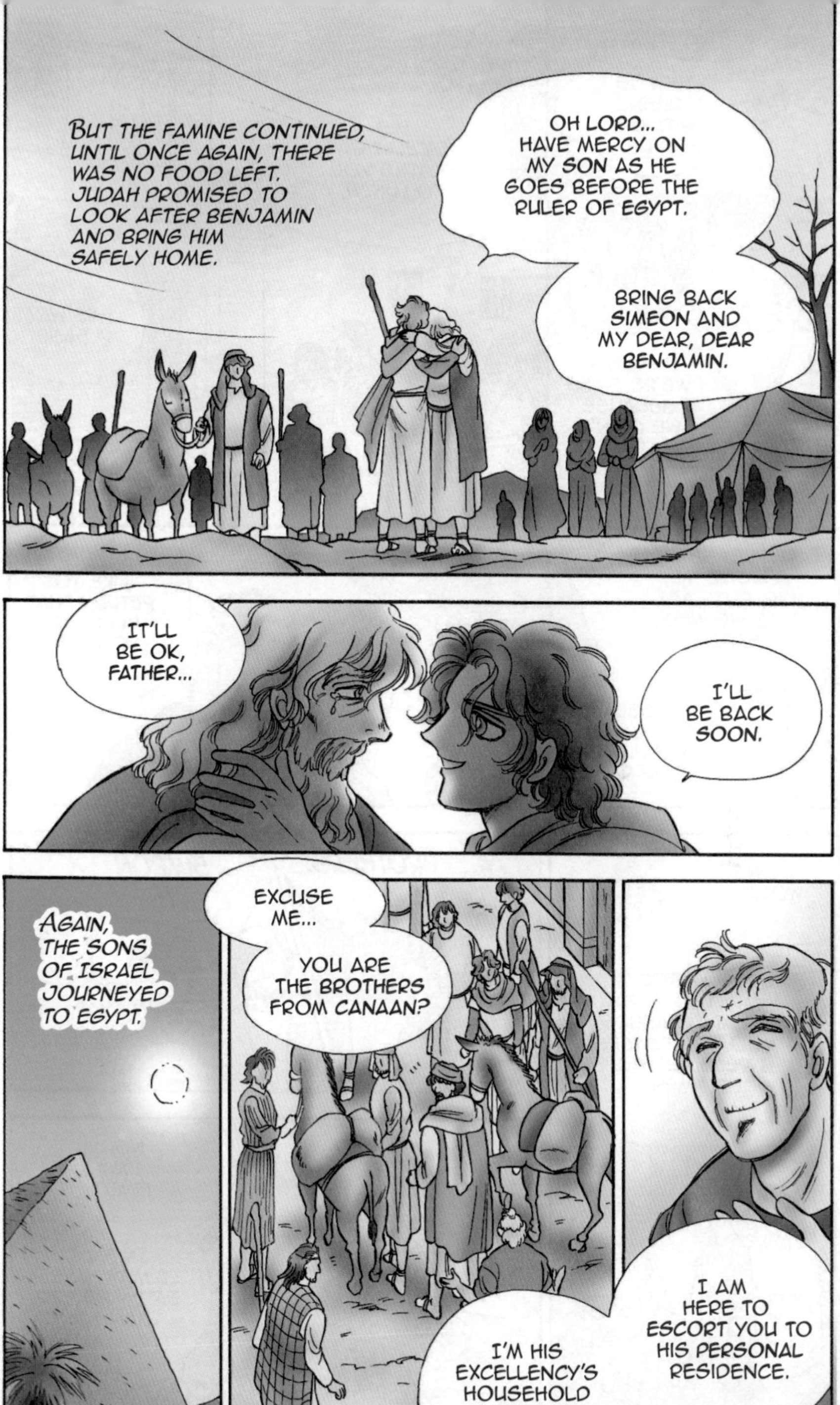
BUT THE FAMINE CONTINUED, UNTIL ONCE AGAIN, THERE WAS NO FOOD LEFT. JUDAH PROMISED TO LOOK AFTER BENJAMIN AND BRING HIM SAFELY HOME.
OH LORD... HAVE MERCY ON MY SON AS HE GOES BEFORE THE RULER OF EGYPT.
BRING BACK SIMEON AND MY DEAR, DEAR BENJAMIN.
IT'LL BE OK, FATHER...
I'LL BE BACK SOON.
AGAIN, THE SONS OF ISRAEL JOURNEYED TO EGYPT.
EXCUSE ME...
YOU ARE THE BROTHERS FROM CANAAN?
I'M HIS EXCELLENCY'S HOUSEHOLD MANAGER...
I AM HERE TO ESCORT YOU TO HIS PERSONAL RESIDENCE.

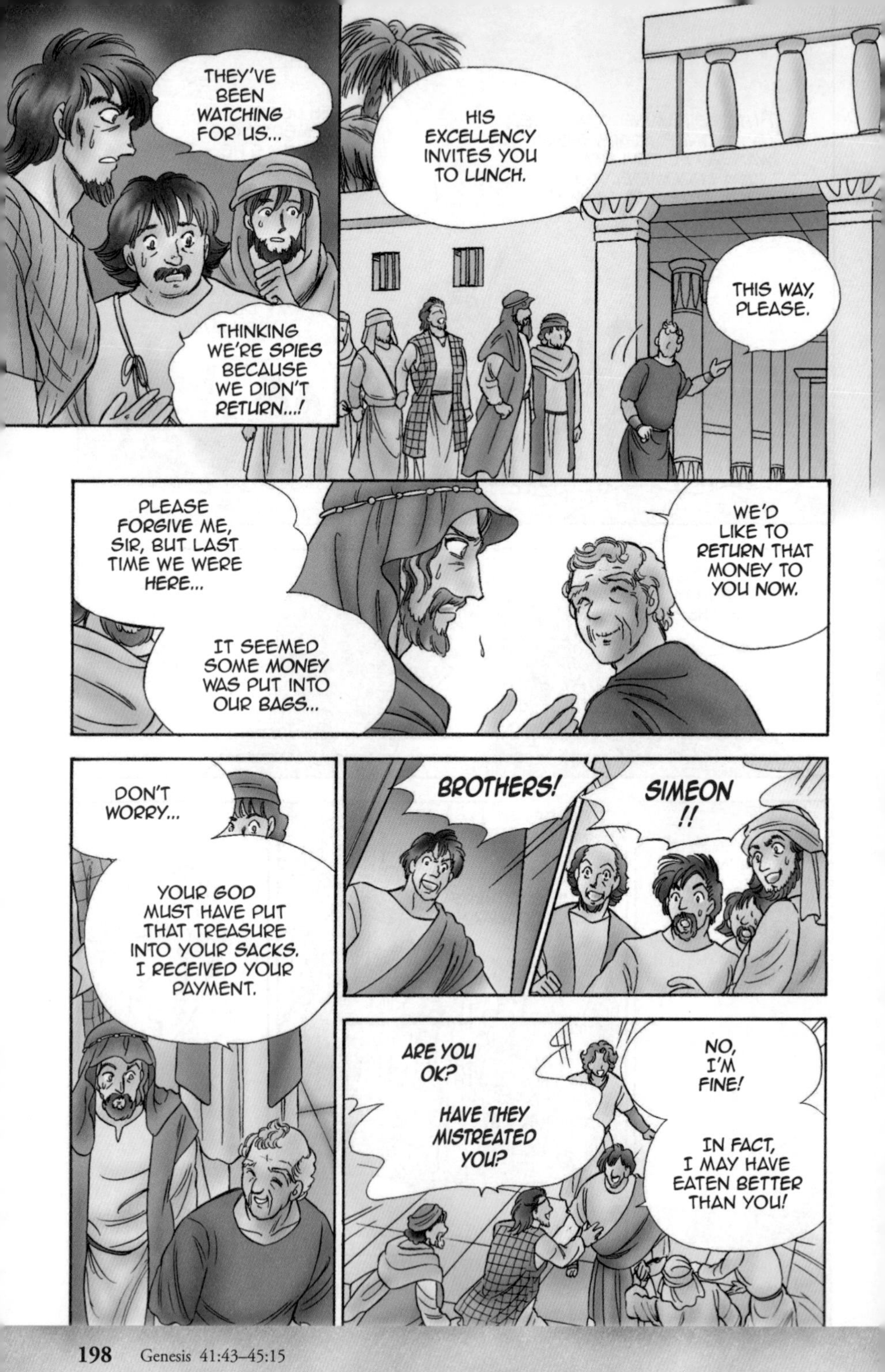
THEY'VE BEEN WATCHING FOR US...
THINKING WE'RE SPIES BECAUSE WE DIDN'T RETURN...!
HIS EXCELLENCY INVITES YOU TO LUNCH.
THIS WAY, PLEASE.
PLEASE FORGIVE ME, SIR, BUT LAST TIME WE WERE HERE...
IT SEEMED SOME MONEY WAS PUT INTO OUR BAGS...
WE'D LIKE TO RETURN THAT MONEY TO YOU NOW.
DON'T WORRY...
YOUR GOD MUST HAVE PUT THAT TREASURE INTO YOUR SACKS. I RECEIVED YOUR PAYMENT.
BROTHERS!
SIMEON !!
ARE YOU OK?
HAVE THEY MISTREATED YOU?
NO, I'M FINE!
IN FACT, I MAY HAVE EATEN BETTER THAN YOU!

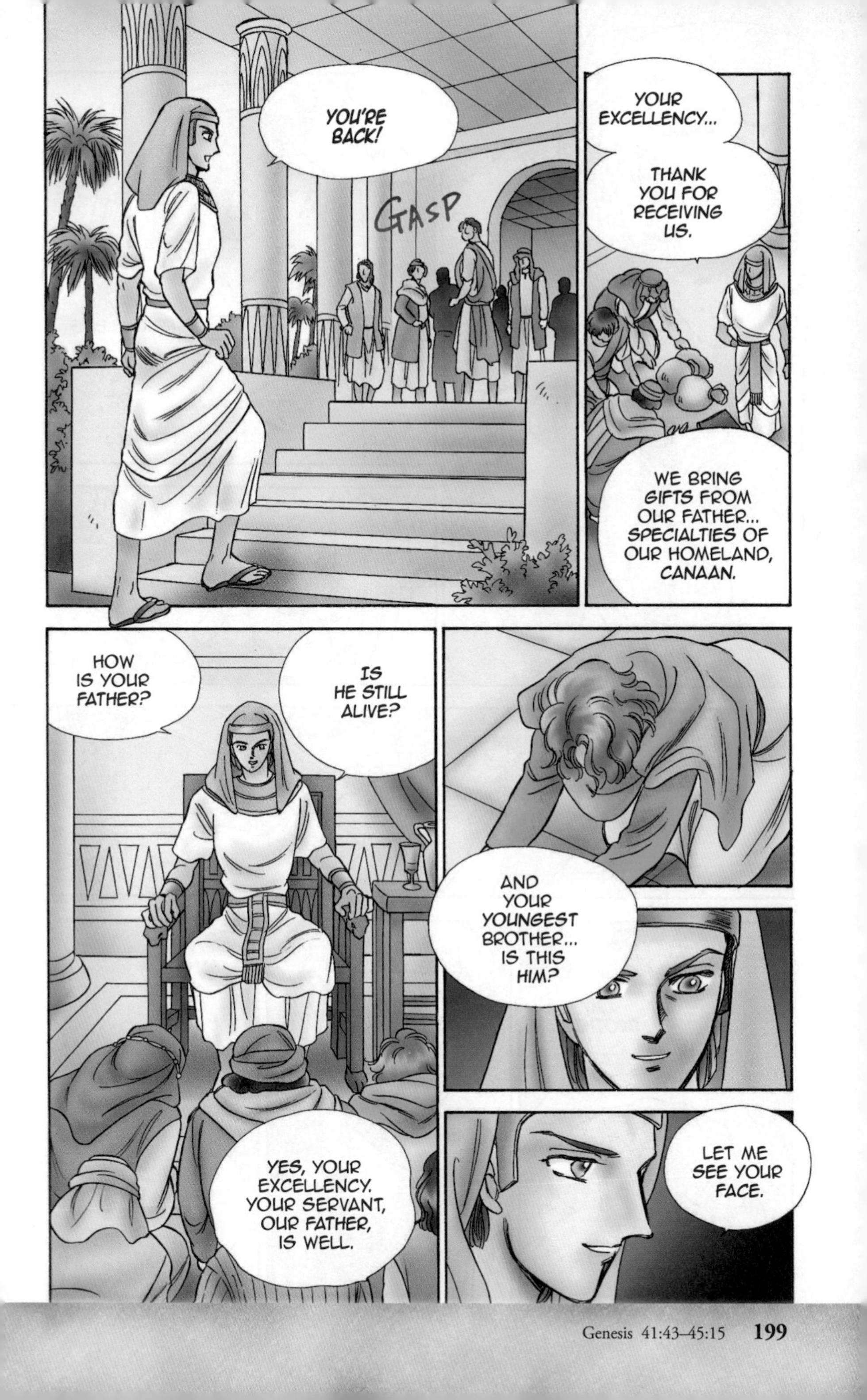
YOU'RE BACK!
GASP
YOUR EXCELLENCY...
THANK YOU FOR RECEIVING US.
WE BRING GIFTS FROM OUR FATHER... SPECIALTIES OF OUR HOMELAND, CANAAN.
HOW IS YOUR FATHER?
IS HE STILL ALIVE?
YES, YOUR EXCELLENCY. YOUR SERVANT, OUR FATHER, IS WELL.
AND YOUR YOUNGEST BROTHER... IS THIS HIM?
LET ME SEE YOUR FACE.

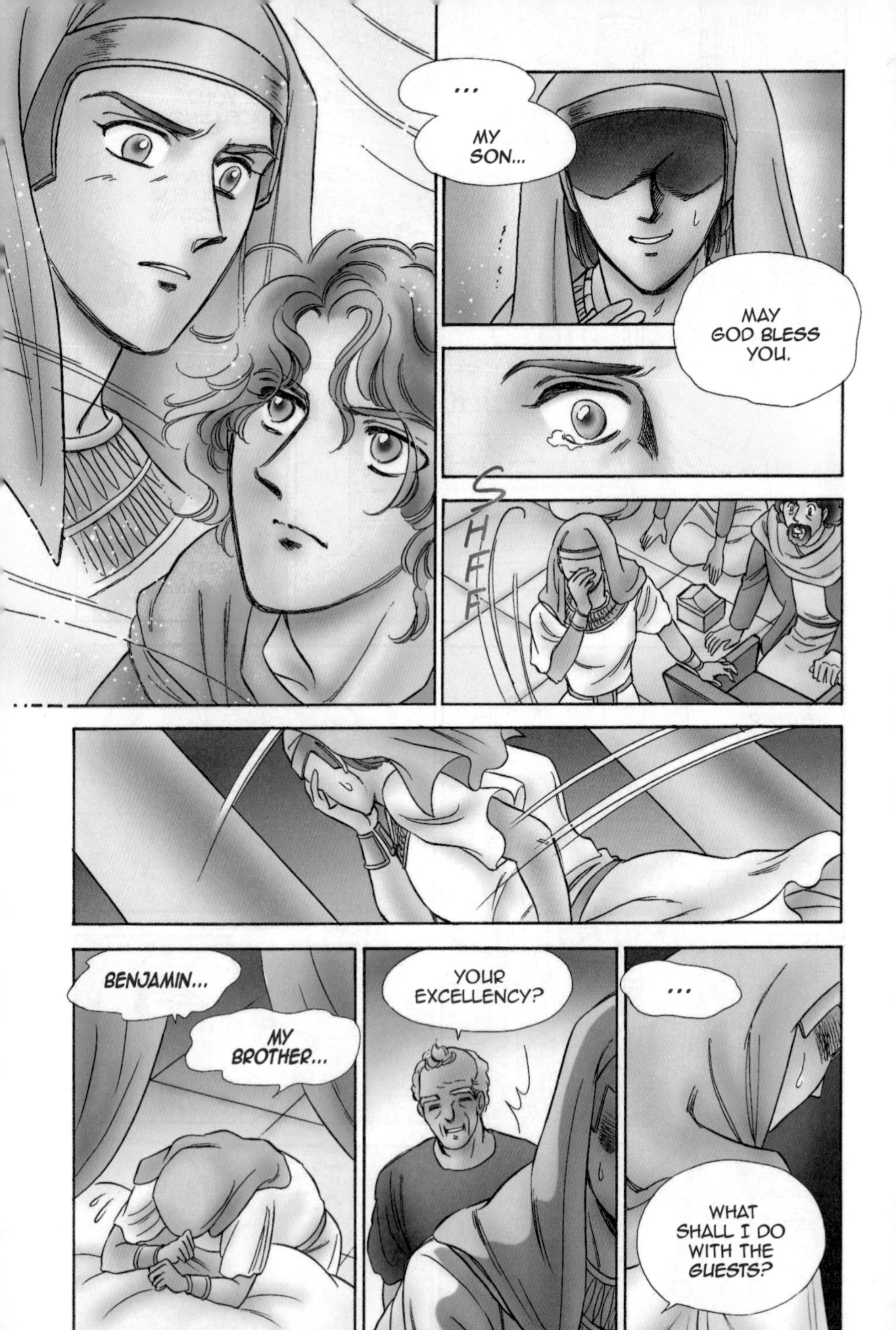
...
MY SON...
MAY GOD BLESS YOU.
SHFFF
BENJAMIN...
MY BROTHER...
YOUR EXCELLENCY?
...
WHAT SHALL I DO WITH THE GUESTS?

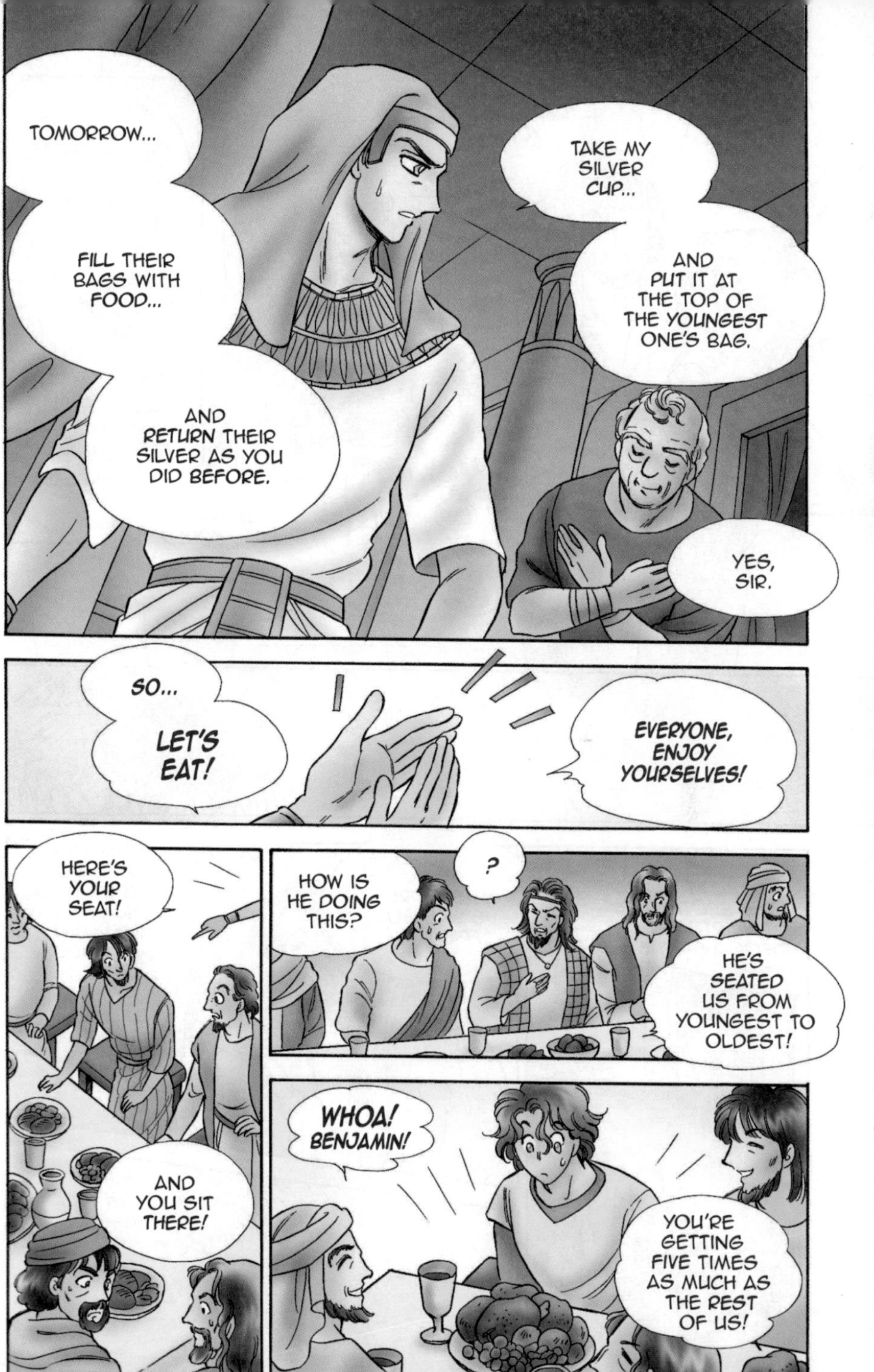
TOMORROW...
FILL THEIR BAGS WITH FOOD...
AND RETURN THEIR SILVER AS YOU DID BEFORE.
TAKE MY SILVER CUP...
AND PUT IT AT THE TOP OF THE YOUNGEST ONE'S BAG.
YES, SIR.
SO...
LET'S EAT!
EVERYONE, ENJOY YOURSELVES!
HERE'S YOUR SEAT!
AND YOU SIT THERE!
HOW IS HE DOING THIS?
?
HE'S SEATED US FROM YOUNGEST TO OLDEST!
WHOA! BENJAMIN!
YOU'RE GETTING FIVE TIMES AS MUCH AS THE REST OF US!

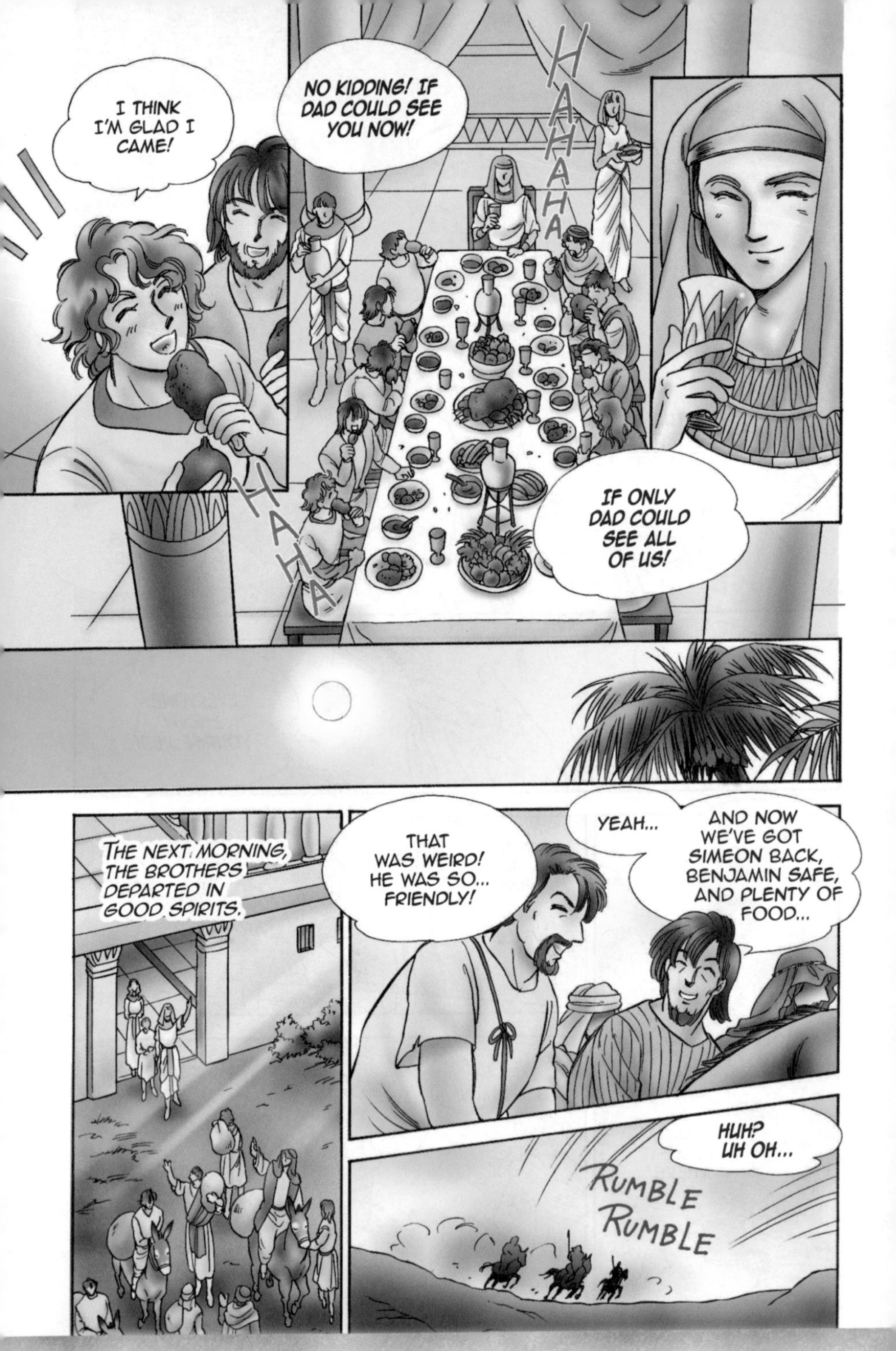
I THINK I'M GLAD I CAME!
NO KIDDING! IF DAD COULD SEE YOU NOW!
HAHAHAHA
HAHAHA
IF ONLY DAD COULD SEE ALL OF US!
THE NEXT MORNING, THE BROTHERS DEPARTED IN GOOD SPIRITS.
THAT WAS WEIRD! HE WAS SO... FRIENDLY!
YEAH...
AND NOW WE'VE GOT SIMEON BACK, BENJAMIN SAFE, AND PLENTY OF FOOD...
HUH? UH OH...
RUMBLE RUMBLE

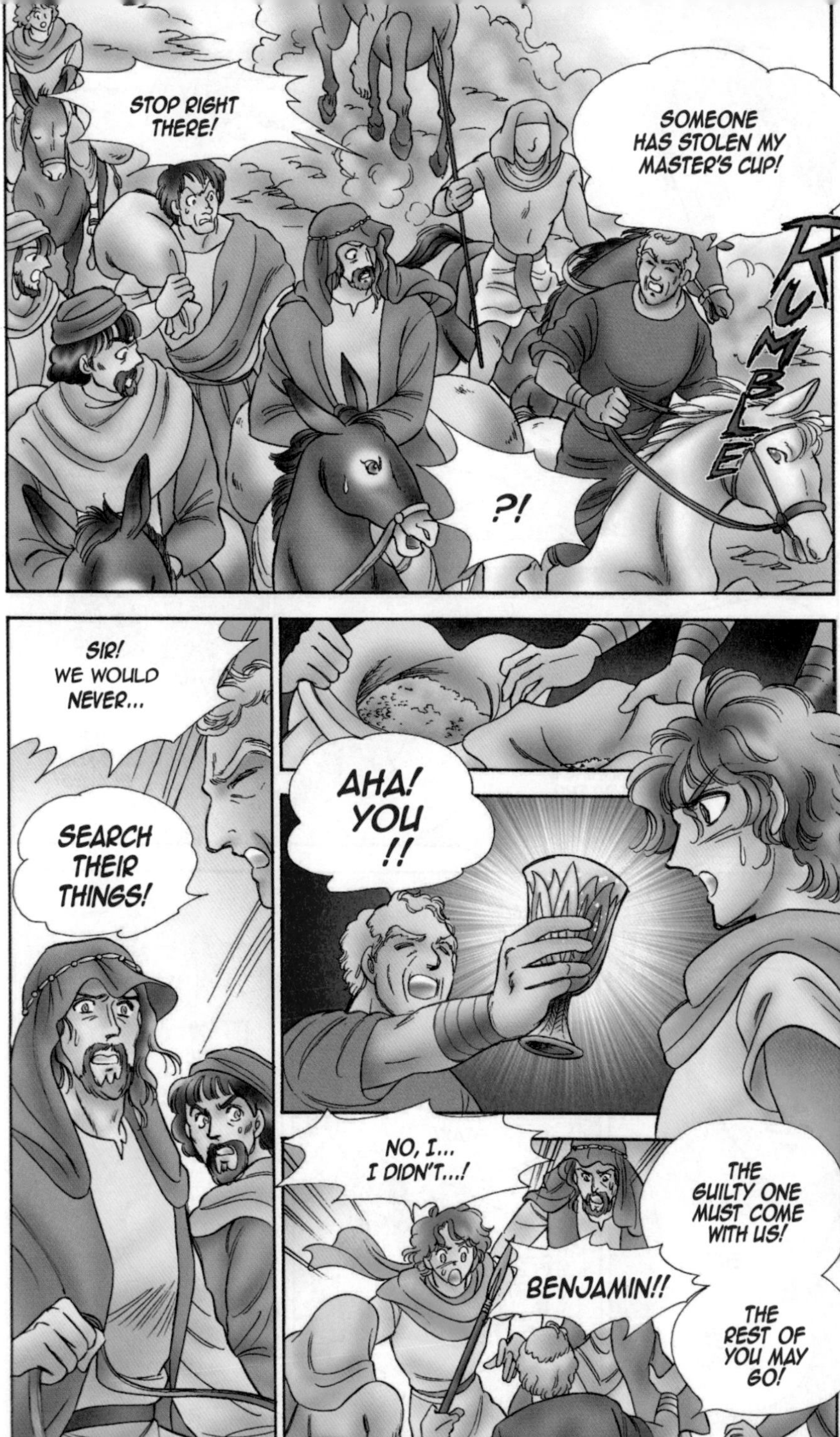
STOP RIGHT THERE!
SOMEONE HAS STOLEN MY MASTER'S CUP!
RUMBLE
?!
SIR! WE WOULD NEVER...
SEARCH THEIR THINGS!
AHA! YOU !!
NO, I... I DIDN'T...!
THE GUILTY ONE MUST COME WITH US!
BENJAMIN!!
THE REST OF YOU MAY GO!

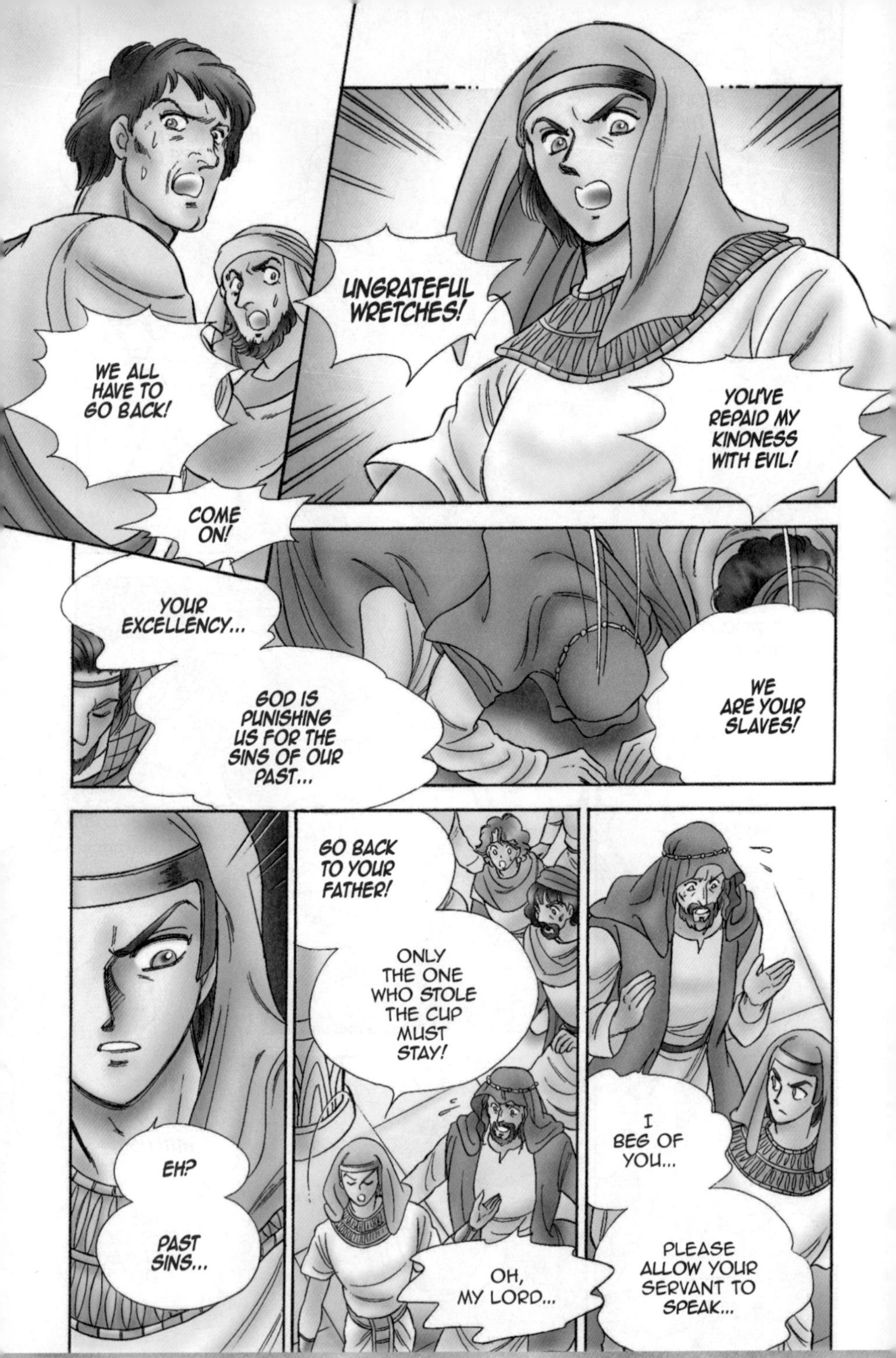
UNGRATEFUL WRETCHES!
YOU'VE REPAID MY KINDNESS WITH EVIL!
WE ALL HAVE TO GO BACK!
COME ON!
YOUR EXCELLENCY...
GOD IS PUNISHING US FOR THE SINS OF OUR PAST...
WE ARE YOUR SLAVES!
EH?
PAST SINS...
GO BACK TO YOUR FATHER!
ONLY THE ONE WHO STOLE THE CUP MUST STAY!
OH, MY LORD...
I BEG OF YOU...
PLEASE ALLOW YOUR SERVANT TO SPEAK...

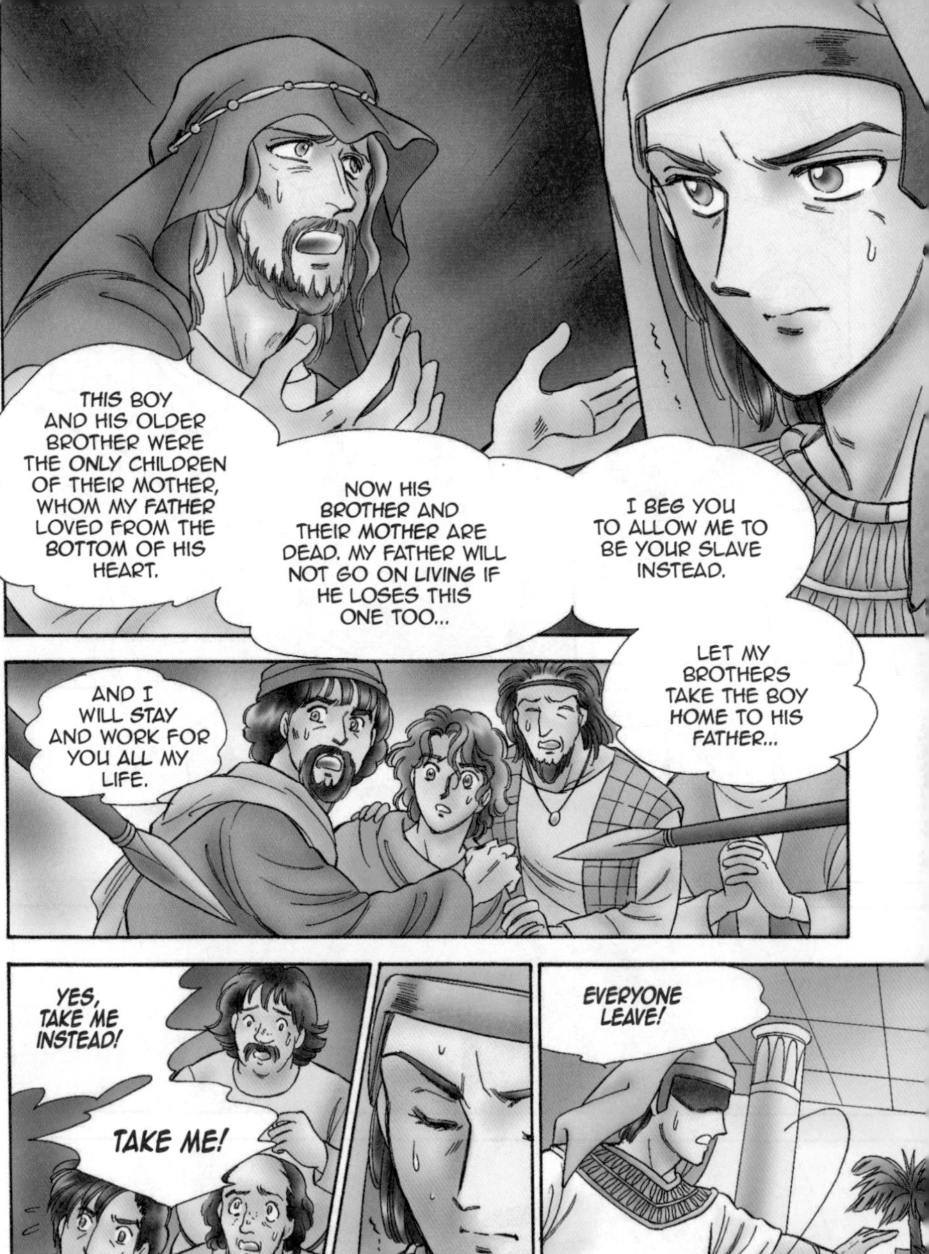
THIS BOY AND HIS OLDER BROTHER WERE THE ONLY CHILDREN OF THEIR MOTHER, WHOM MY FATHER LOVED FROM THE BOTTOM OF HIS HEART.
NOW HIS BROTHER AND THEIR MOTHER ARE DEAD. MY FATHER WILL NOT GO ON LIVING IF HE LOSES THIS ONE TOO...
I BEG YOU TO ALLOW ME TO BE YOUR SLAVE INSTEAD.
LET MY BROTHERS TAKE THE BOY HOME TO HIS FATHER...
AND I WILL STAY AND WORK FOR YOU ALL MY LIFE.
YES, TAKE ME INSTEAD!
TAKE ME!
I'LL STAY!
SPARE OUR BROTHER!
EVERYONE LEAVE!
I WISH TO SPEAK WITH THESE MEN ALONE!

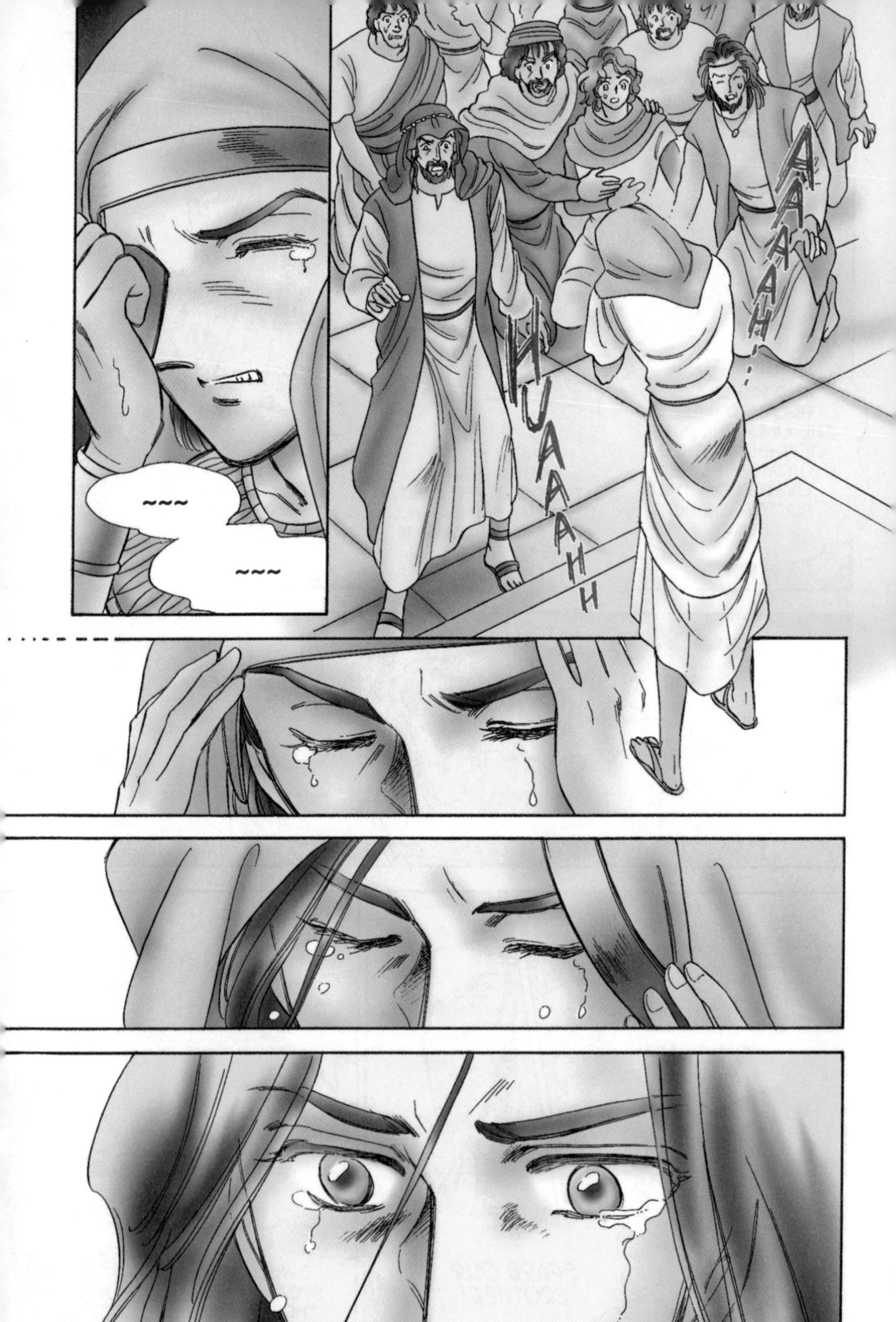
~~~
~~~
HUAAAAHH
AAAAAH...

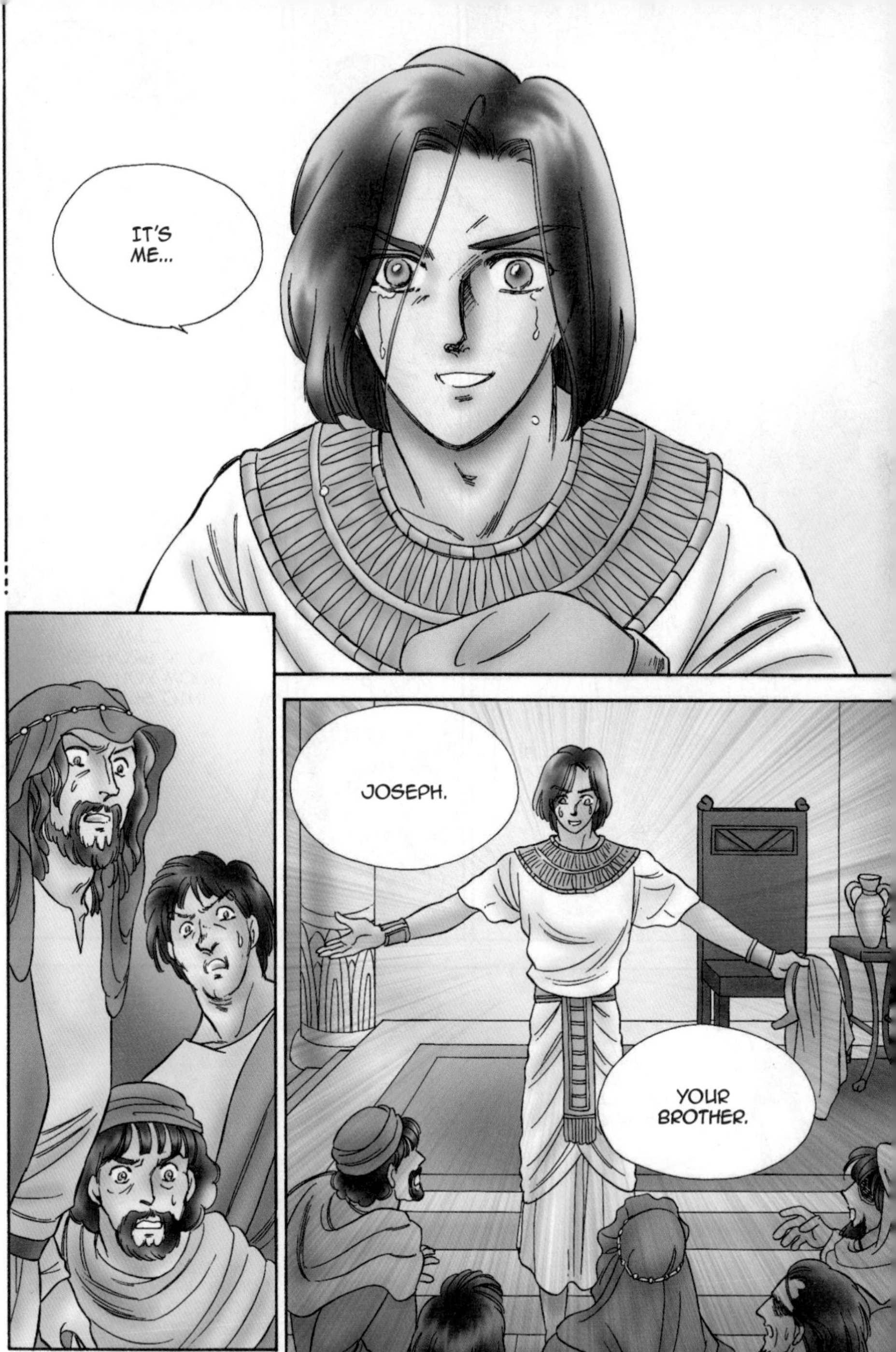
IT'S ME...
JOSEPH.
YOUR BROTHER.

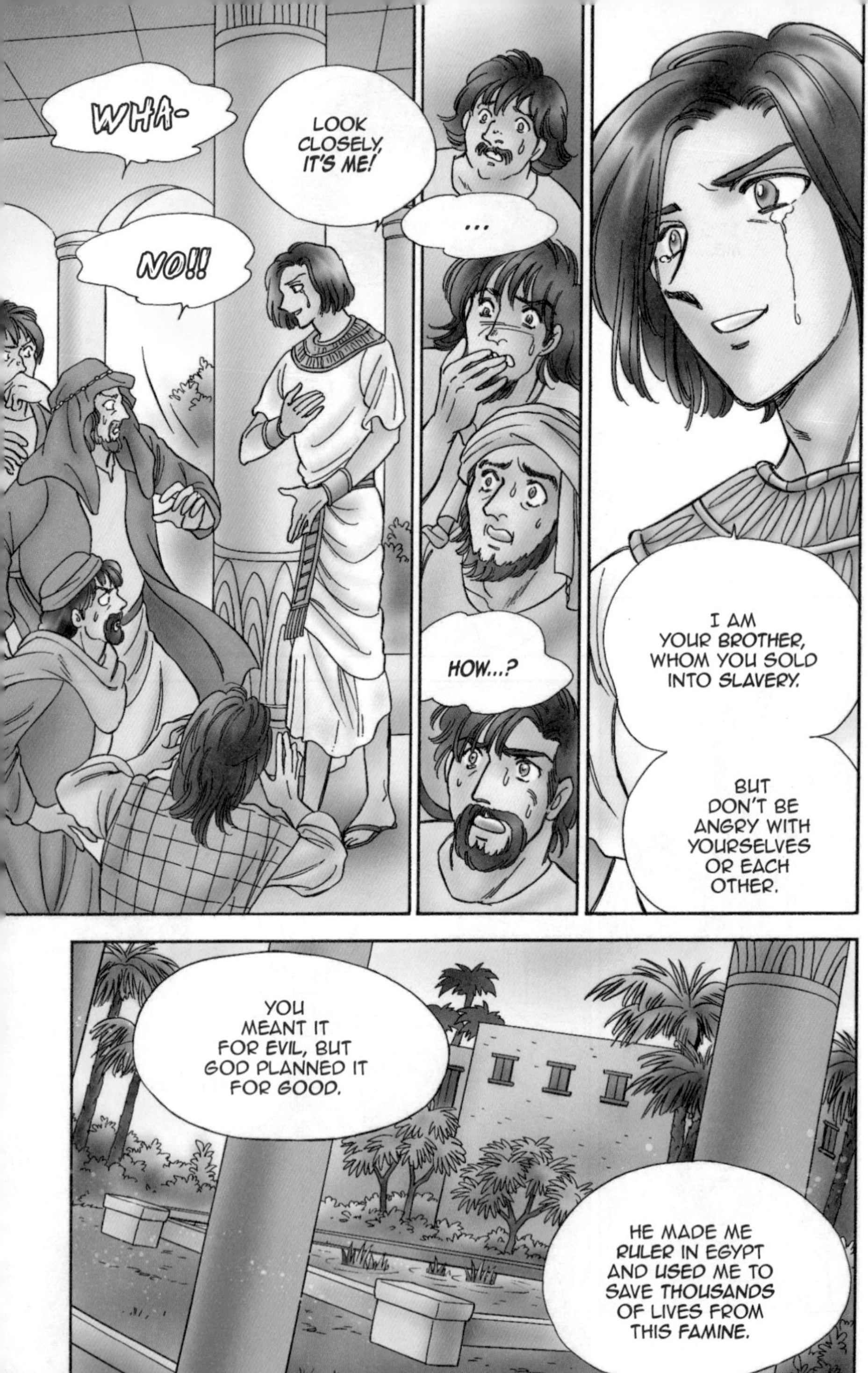
WHA-
NO!!
LOOK CLOSELY, IT'S ME!
...
HOW...?
I AM YOUR BROTHER, WHOM YOU SOLD INTO SLAVERY.
BUT DON'T BE ANGRY WITH YOURSELVES OR EACH OTHER.
YOU MEANT IT FOR EVIL, BUT GOD PLANNED IT FOR GOOD.
HE MADE ME RULER IN EGYPT AND USED ME TO SAVE THOUSANDS OF LIVES FROM THIS FAMINE.

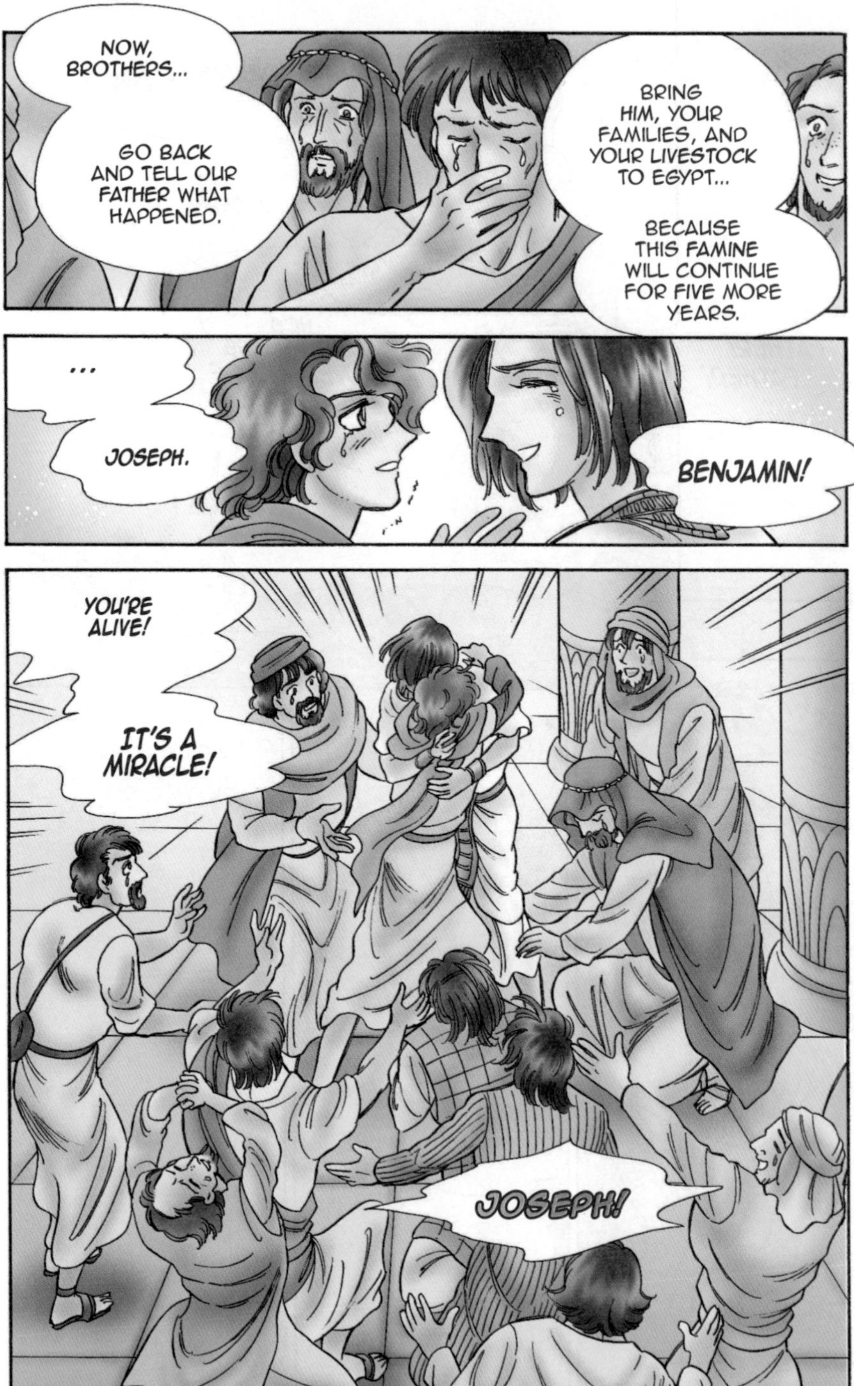

NOW, BROTHERS...
GO BACK AND TELL OUR FATHER WHAT HAPPENED.
BRING HIM, YOUR FAMILIES, AND YOUR LIVESTOCK TO EGYPT...
BECAUSE THIS FAMINE WILL CONTINUE FOR FIVE MORE YEARS.
...
JOSEPH.
BENJAMIN!
YOU'RE ALIVE!
IT'S A MIRACLE!
JOSEPH!

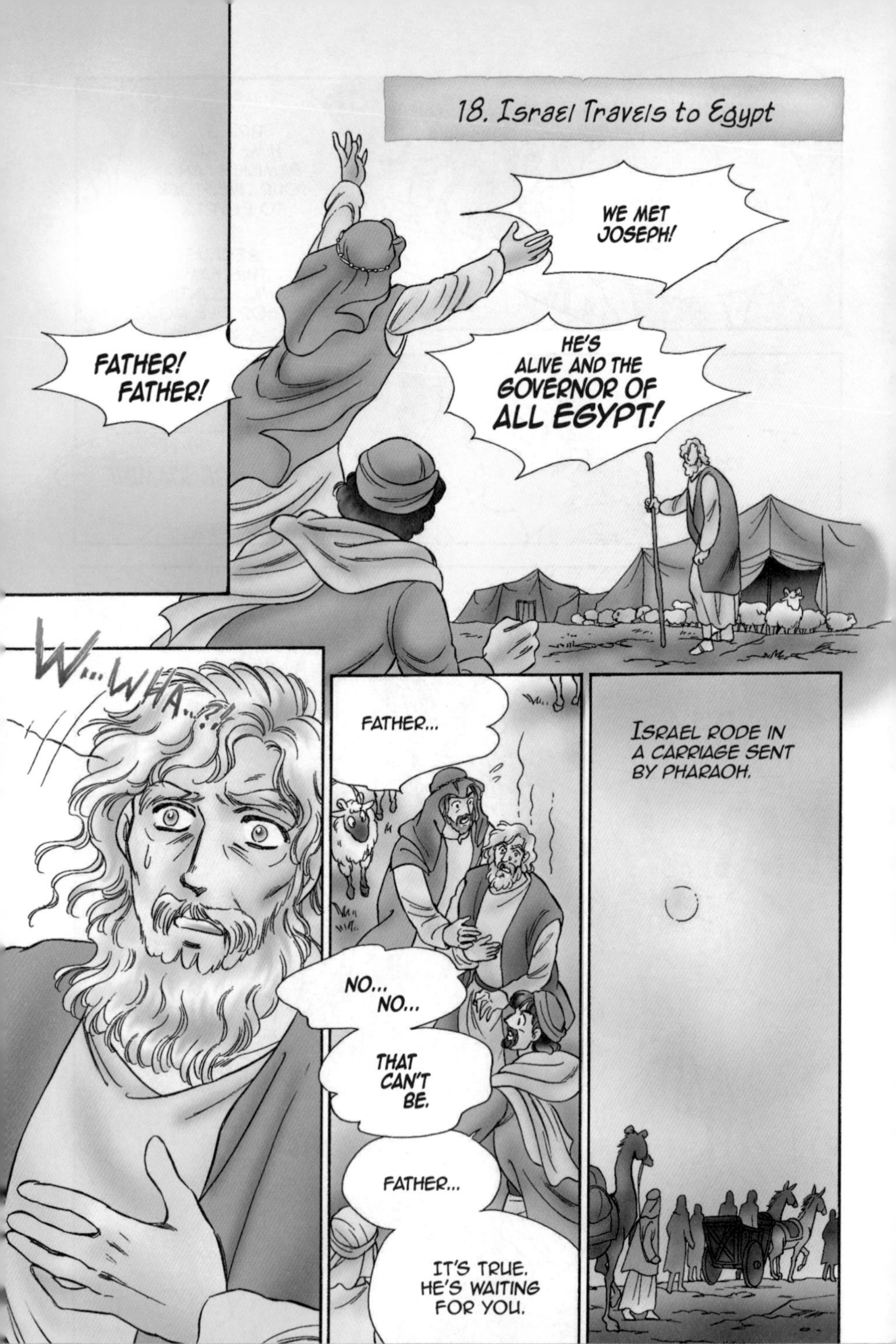
18. Israel Travels to Egypt
FATHER! FATHER!
WE MET JOSEPH!
HE'S ALIVE AND THE GOVERNOR OF ALL EGYPT!
W...WHA...?!
FATHER...
NO... NO...
THAT CAN'T BE.
FATHER...
IT'S TRUE. HE'S WAITING FOR YOU.
ISRAEL RODE IN A CARRIAGE SENT BY PHARAOH.

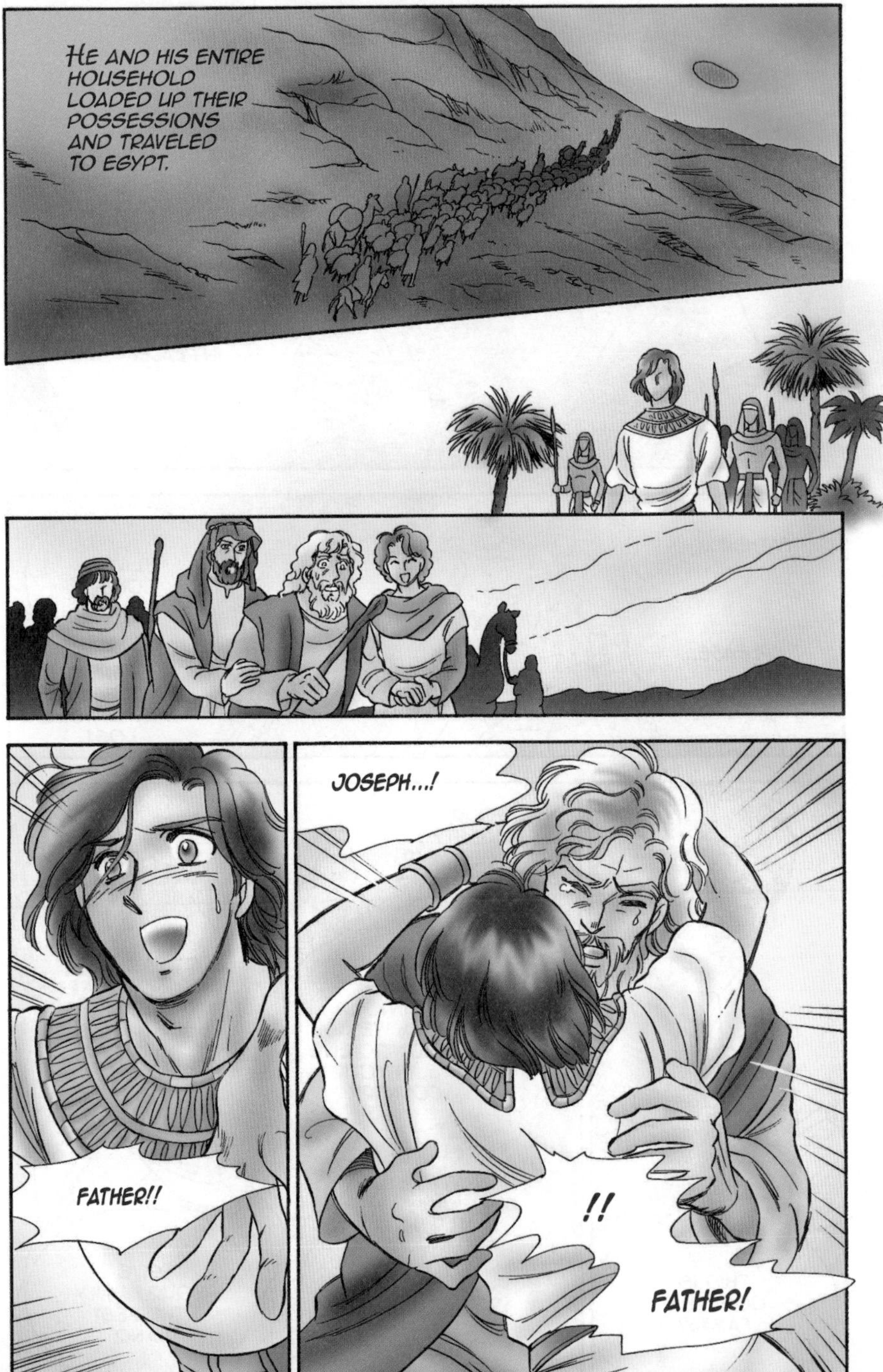
HE AND HIS ENTIRE HOUSEHOLD LOADED UP THEIR POSSESSIONS AND TRAVELED TO EGYPT.
FATHER!!
JOSEPH...!
!!
FATHER!

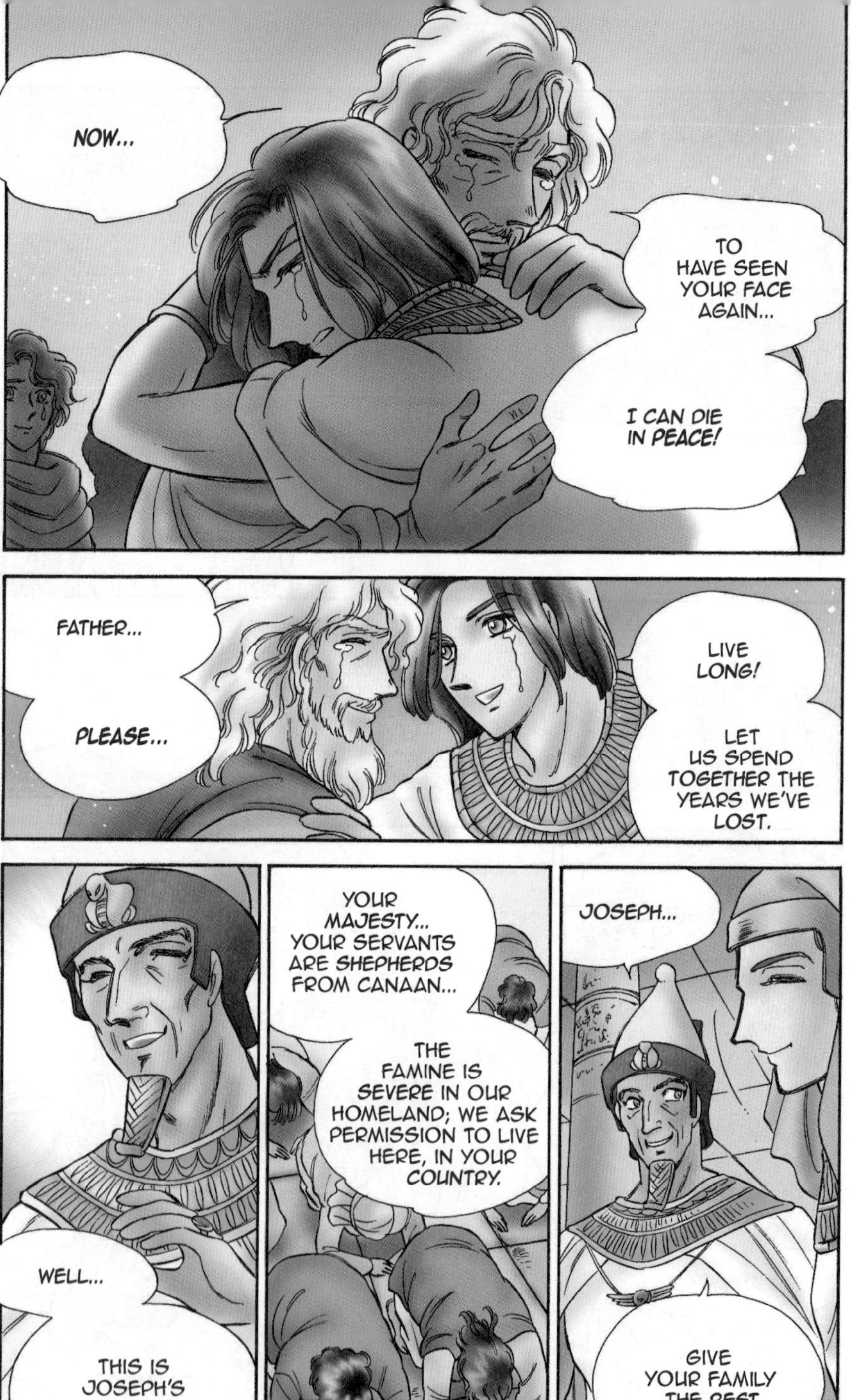
NOW...
TO HAVE SEEN YOUR FACE AGAIN...
I CAN DIE IN PEACE!
FATHER...
PLEASE...
LIVE LONG!
LET US SPEND TOGETHER THE YEARS WE'VE LOST.
WELL...
THIS IS JOSEPH'S FAMILY!
YOUR MAJESTY... YOUR SERVANTS ARE SHEPHERDS FROM CANAAN...
THE FAMINE IS SEVERE IN OUR HOMELAND; WE ASK PERMISSION TO LIVE HERE, IN YOUR COUNTRY.
JOSEPH...
GIVE YOUR FAMILY THE BEST LAND.

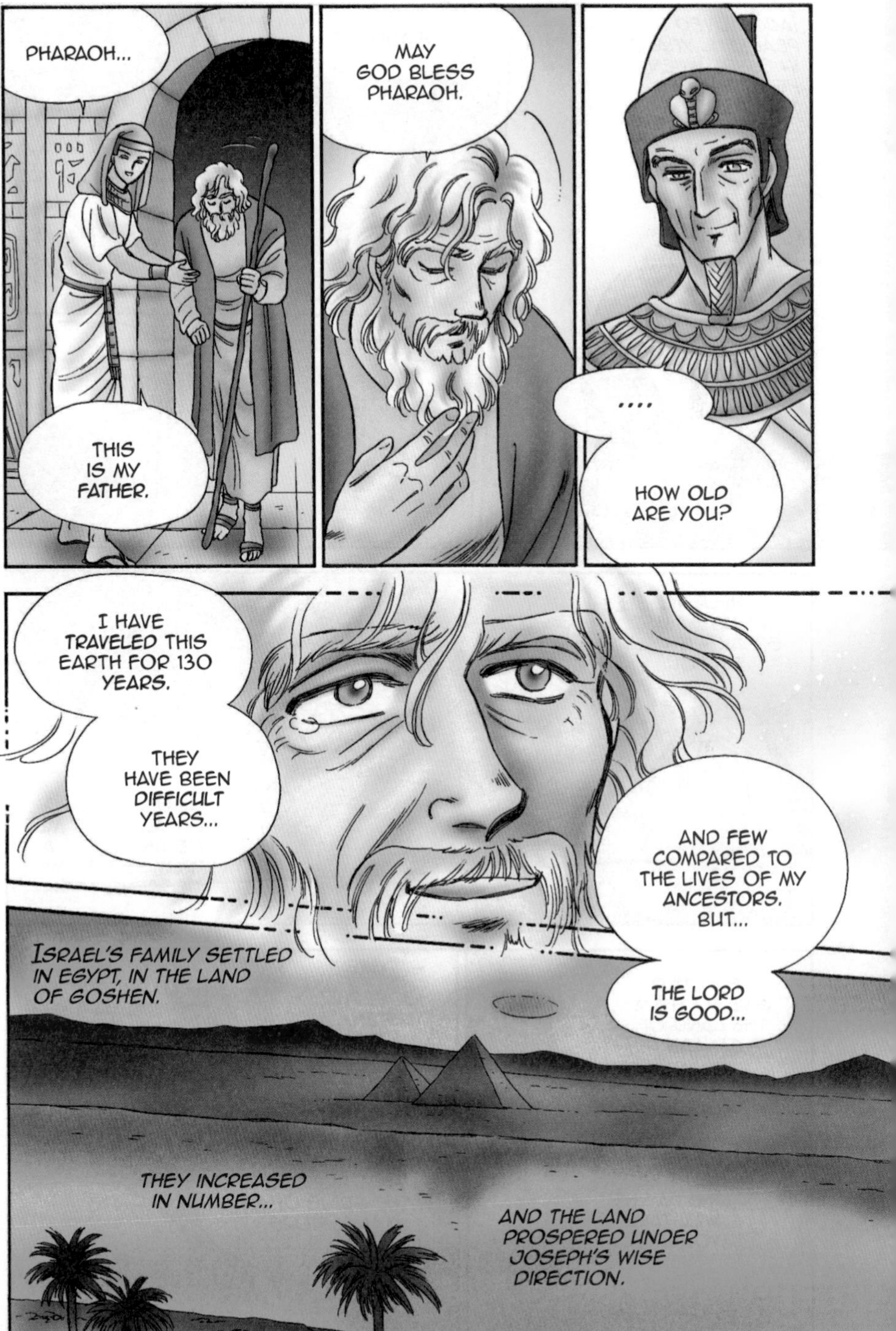
PHARAOH...
THIS IS MY FATHER.
MAY GOD BLESS PHARAOH.
....
HOW OLD ARE YOU?
I HAVE TRAVELED THIS EARTH FOR 130 YEARS.
THEY HAVE BEEN DIFFICULT YEARS...
AND FEW COMPARED TO THE LIVES OF MY ANCESTORS. BUT...
THE LORD IS GOOD...
ISRAEL'S FAMILY SETTLED IN EGYPT, IN THE LAND OF GOSHEN.
THEY INCREASED IN NUMBER...
AND THE LAND PROSPERED UNDER JOSEPH'S WISE DIRECTION.

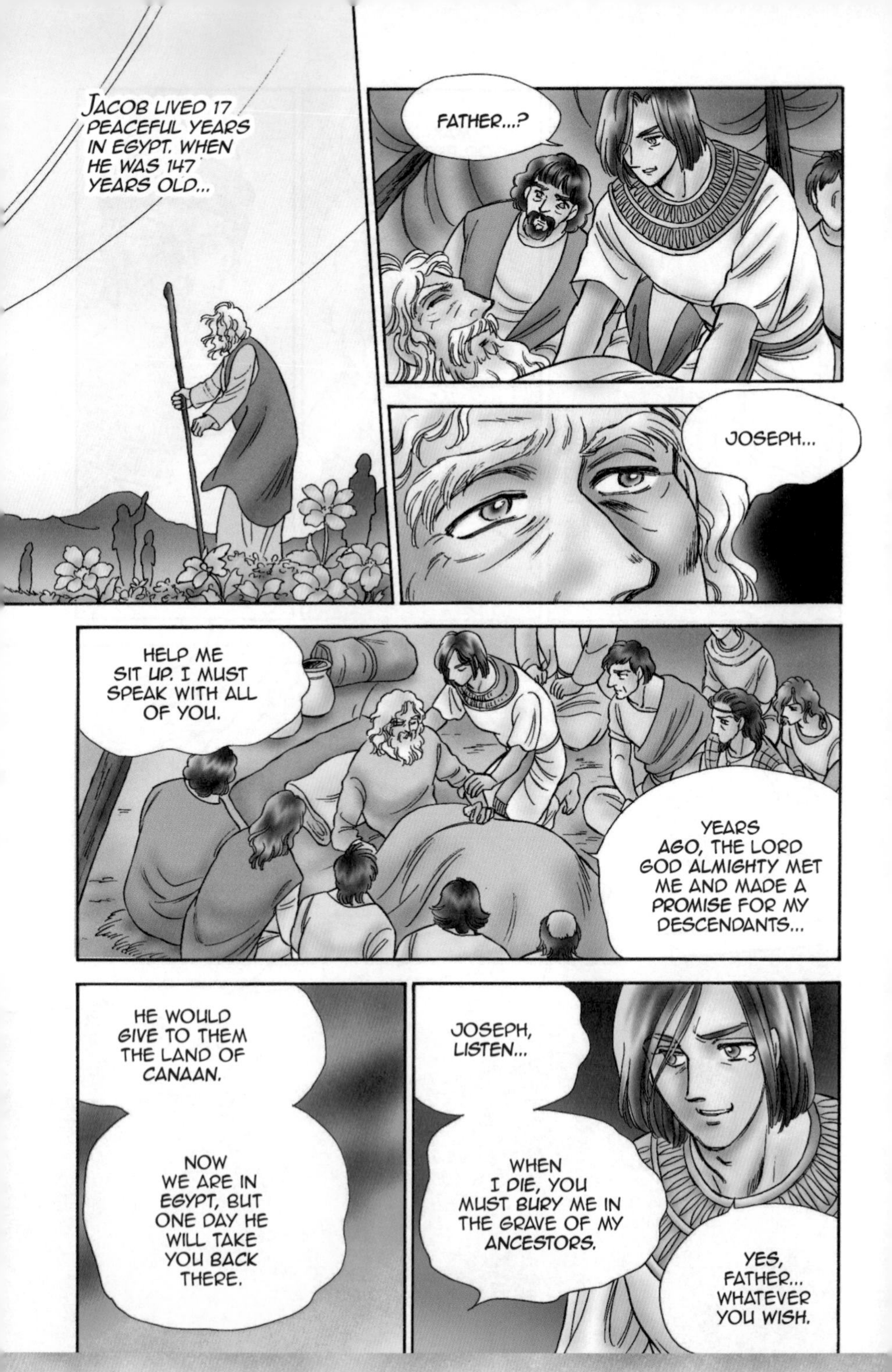
JACOB LIVED 17 PEACEFUL YEARS IN EGYPT. WHEN HE WAS 147 YEARS OLD...
FATHER...?
JOSEPH...
HELP ME SIT UP. I MUST SPEAK WITH ALL OF YOU.
YEARS AGO, THE LORD GOD ALMIGHTY MET ME AND MADE A PROMISE FOR MY DESCENDANTS...
HE WOULD GIVE TO THEM THE LAND OF CANAAN.
NOW WE ARE IN EGYPT, BUT ONE DAY HE WILL TAKE YOU BACK THERE.
JOSEPH, LISTEN...
WHEN I DIE, YOU MUST BURY ME IN THE GRAVE OF MY ANCESTORS.
YES, FATHER... WHATEVER YOU WISH.

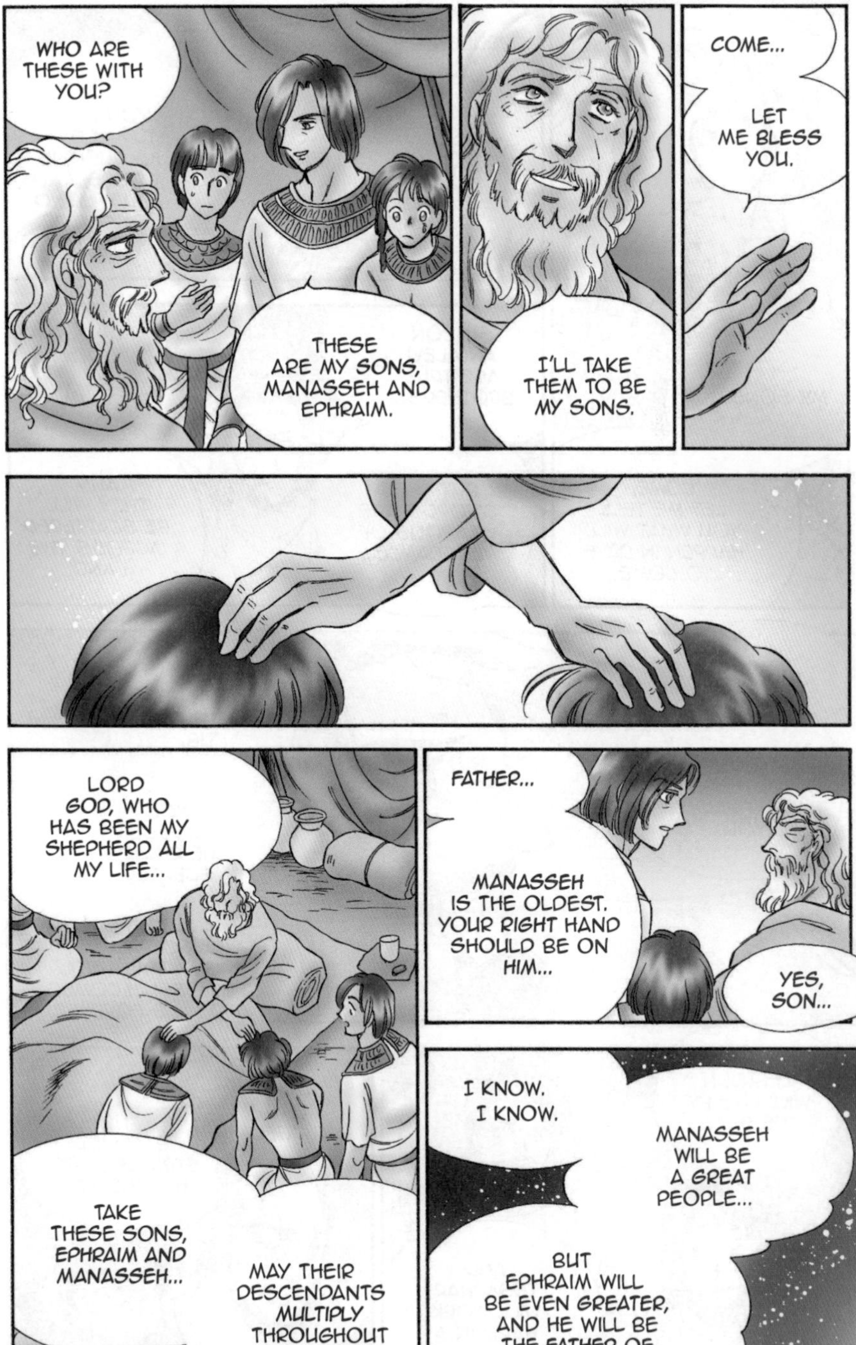
WHO ARE THESE WITH YOU?
THESE ARE MY SONS, MANASSEH AND EPHRAIM.
I'LL TAKE THEM TO BE MY SONS.
COME...
LET ME BLESS YOU.
LORD GOD, WHO HAS BEEN MY SHEPHERD ALL MY LIFE...
TAKE THESE SONS, EPHRAIM AND MANASSEH...
MAY THEIR DESCENDANTS MULTIPLY THROUGHOUT THE EARTH.
FATHER...
MANASSEH IS THE OLDEST. YOUR RIGHT HAND SHOULD BE ON HIM...
YES, SON...
I KNOW. I KNOW.
MANASSEH WILL BE A GREAT PEOPLE...
BUT EPHRAIM WILL BE EVEN GREATER, AND HE WILL BE THE FATHER OF NATIONS.

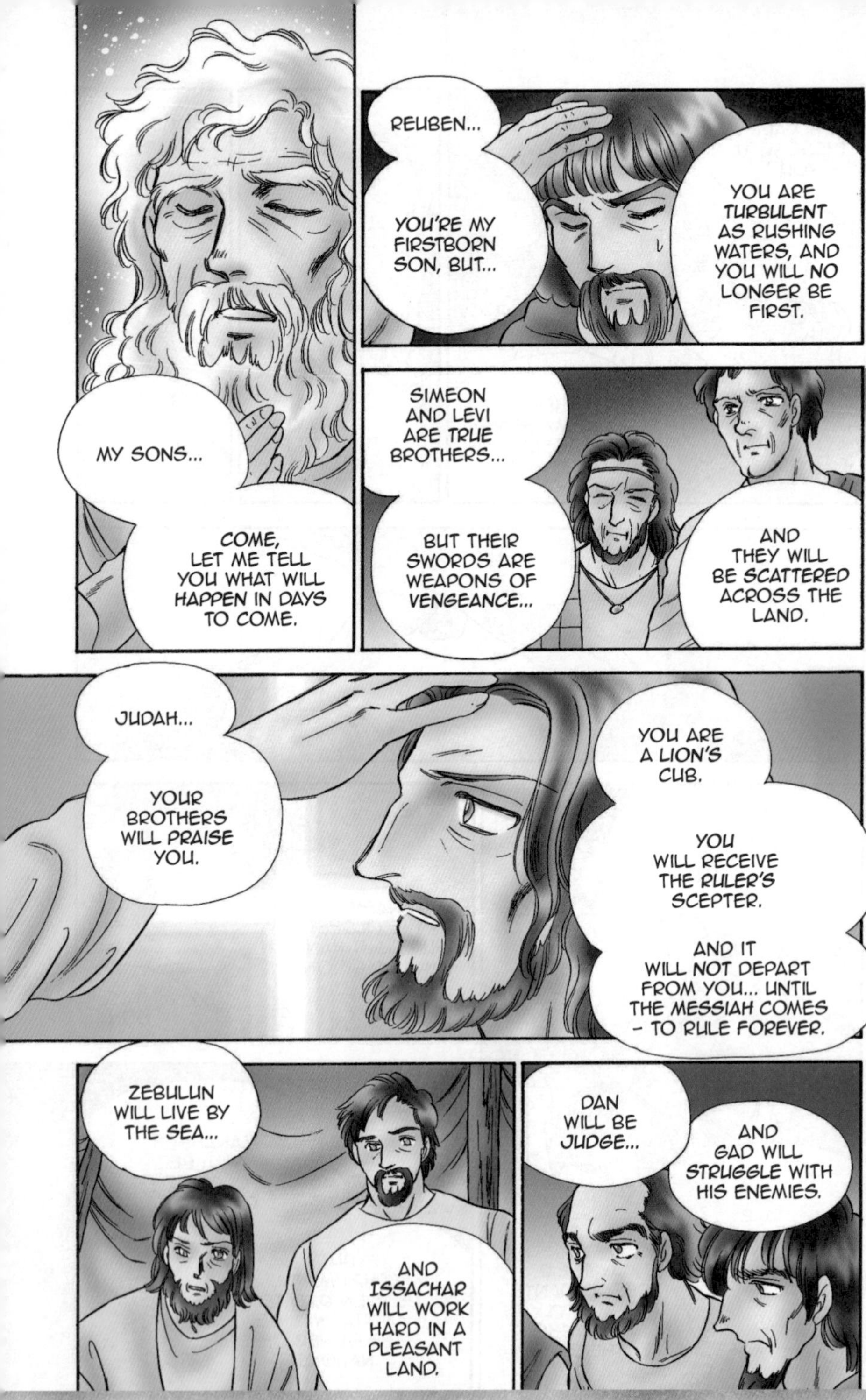
MY SONS...
COME, LET ME TELL YOU WHAT WILL HAPPEN IN DAYS TO COME.
REUBEN...
YOU'RE MY FIRSTBORN SON, BUT...
YOU ARE TURBULENT AS RUSHING WATERS, AND YOU WILL NO LONGER BE FIRST.
SIMEON AND LEVI ARE TRUE BROTHERS...
BUT THEIR SWORDS ARE WEAPONS OF VENGEANCE...
AND THEY WILL BE SCATTERED ACROSS THE LAND.
JUDAH...
YOUR BROTHERS WILL PRAISE YOU.
YOU ARE A LION'S CUB.
YOU WILL RECEIVE THE RULER'S SCEPTER.
AND IT WILL NOT DEPART FROM YOU... UNTIL THE MESSIAH COMES - TO RULE FOREVER.
ZEBULUN WILL LIVE BY THE SEA...
AND ISSACHAR WILL WORK HARD IN A PLEASANT LAND.
DAN WILL BE JUDGE...
AND GAD WILL STRUGGLE WITH HIS ENEMIES.

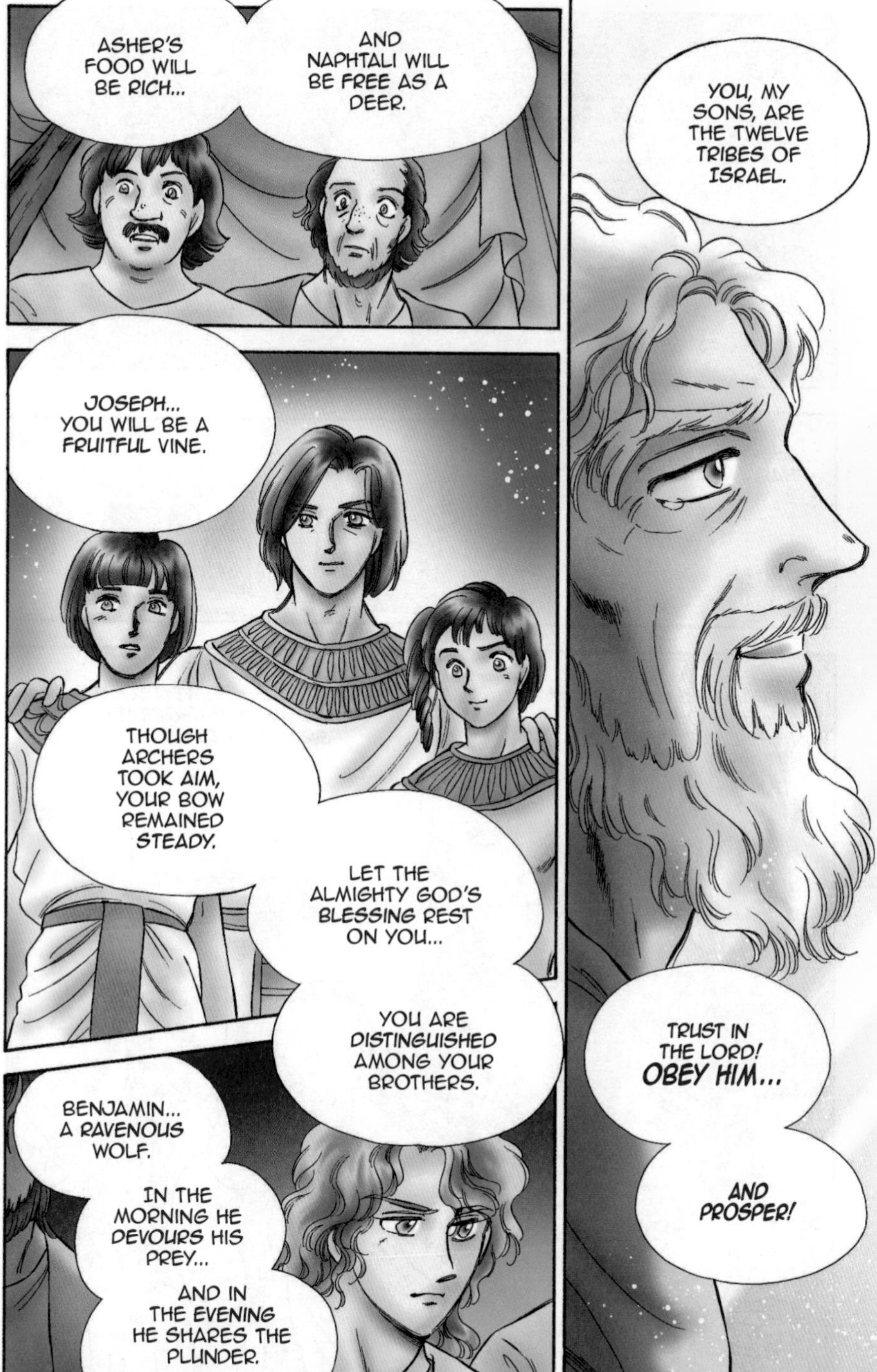
ASHER'S FOOD WILL BE RICH...
AND NAPHTALI WILL BE FREE AS A DEER.
JOSEPH... YOU WILL BE A FRUITFUL VINE.
THOUGH ARCHERS TOOK AIM, YOUR BOW REMAINED STEADY.
LET THE ALMIGHTY GOD'S BLESSING REST ON YOU...
YOU ARE DISTINGUISHED AMONG YOUR BROTHERS.
BENJAMIN... A RAVENOUS WOLF.
IN THE MORNING HE DEVOURS HIS PREY...
AND IN THE EVENING HE SHARES THE PLUNDER.
YOU, MY SONS, ARE THE TWELVE TRIBES OF ISRAEL.
TRUST IN THE LORD! **OBEY HIM...**
AND PROSPER!

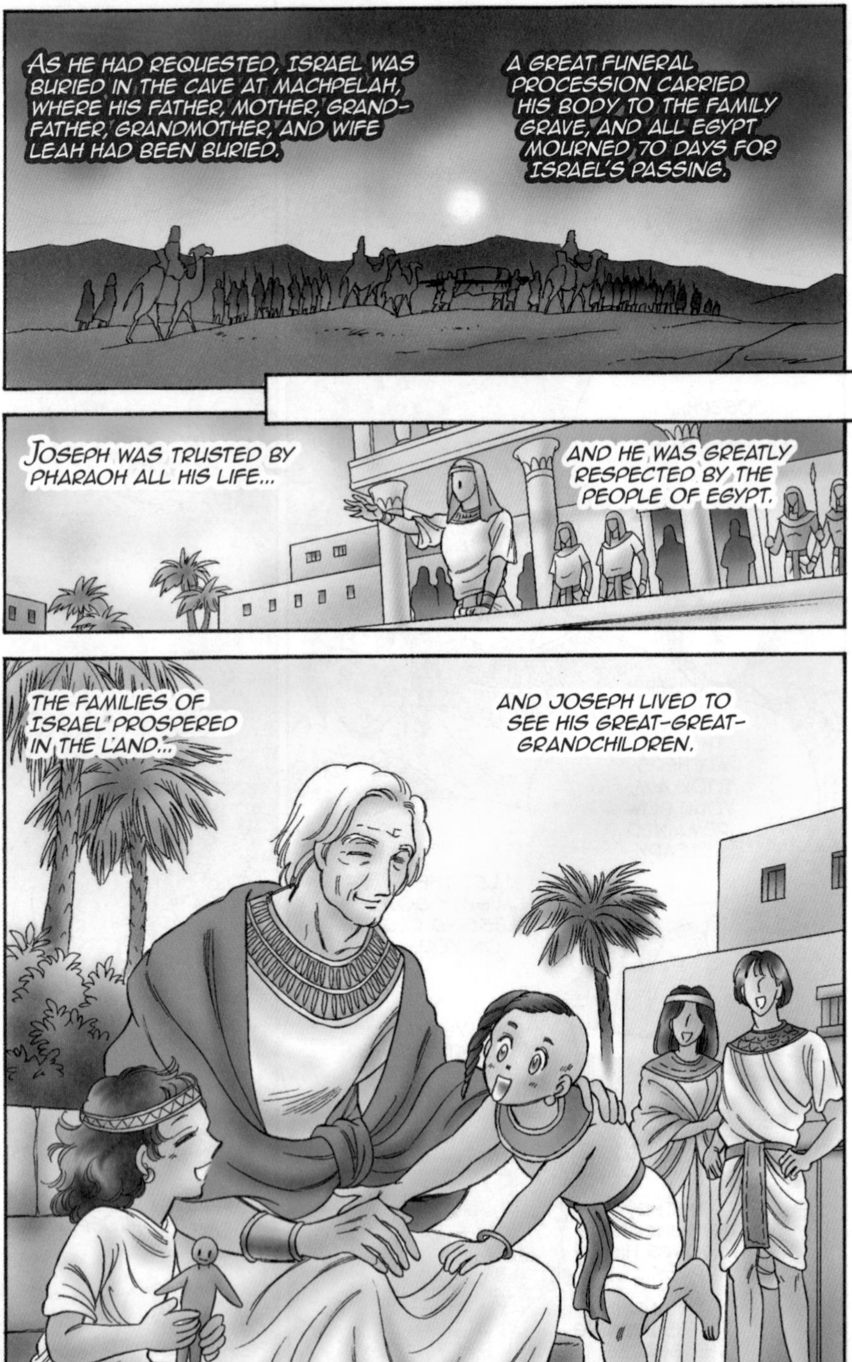
AS HE HAD REQUESTED, ISRAEL WAS BURIED IN THE CAVE AT MACHPELAH, WHERE HIS FATHER, MOTHER, GRAND-FATHER, GRANDMOTHER, AND WIFE LEAH HAD BEEN BURIED.
A GREAT FUNERAL PROCESSION CARRIED HIS BODY TO THE FAMILY GRAVE, AND ALL EGYPT MOURNED 70 DAYS FOR ISRAEL'S PASSING.
JOSEPH WAS TRUSTED BY PHARAOH ALL HIS LIFE...
AND HE WAS GREATLY RESPECTED BY THE PEOPLE OF EGYPT.
THE FAMILIES OF ISRAEL PROSPERED IN THE LAND...
AND JOSEPH LIVED TO SEE HIS GREAT-GREAT-GRANDCHILDREN.

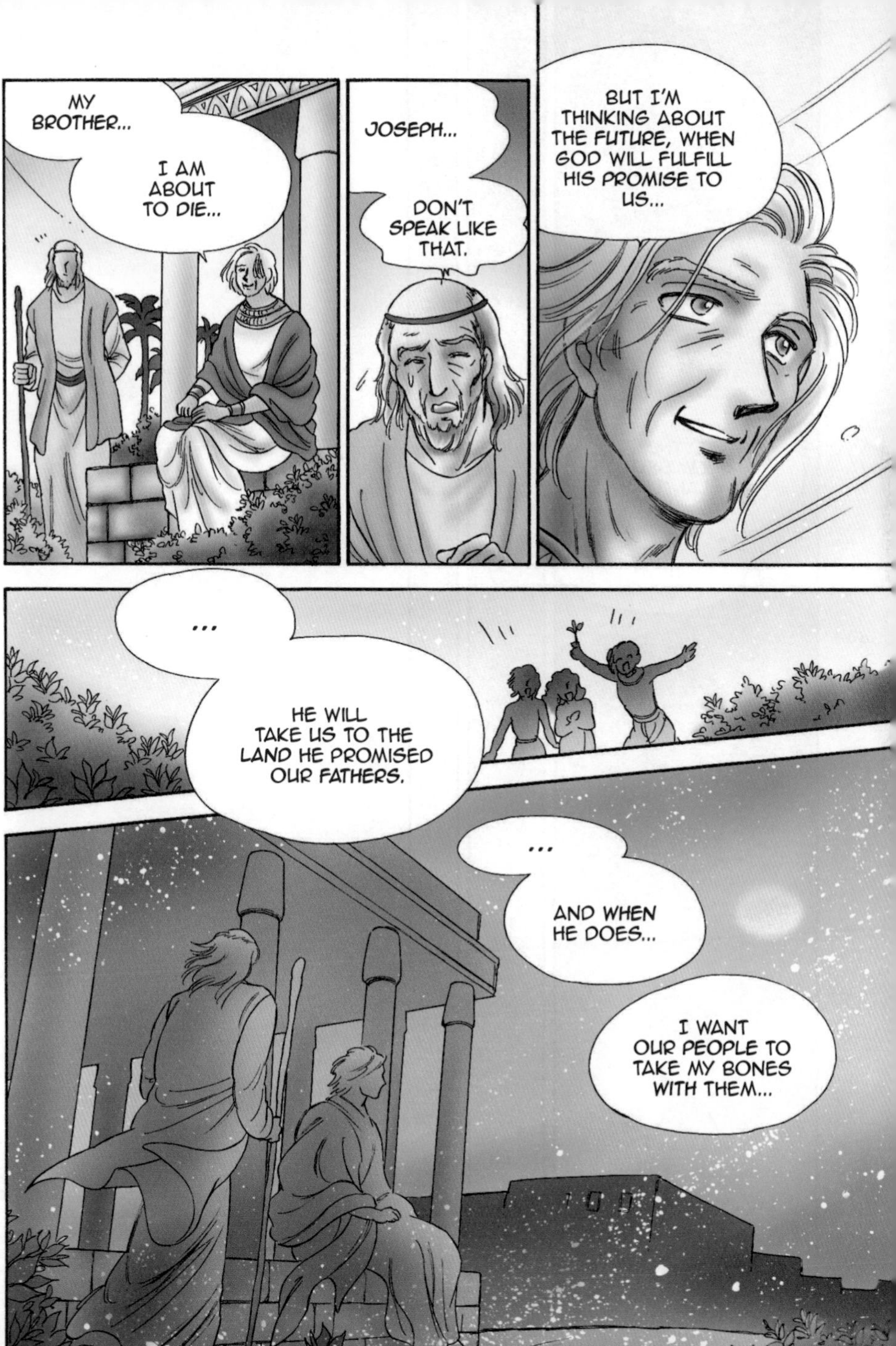
MY BROTHER...
I AM ABOUT TO DIE...
JOSEPH...
DON'T SPEAK LIKE THAT.
BUT I'M THINKING ABOUT THE FUTURE, WHEN GOD WILL FULFILL HIS PROMISE TO US...
...
HE WILL TAKE US TO THE LAND HE PROMISED OUR FATHERS.
...
AND WHEN HE DOES...
I WANT OUR PEOPLE TO TAKE MY BONES WITH THEM...

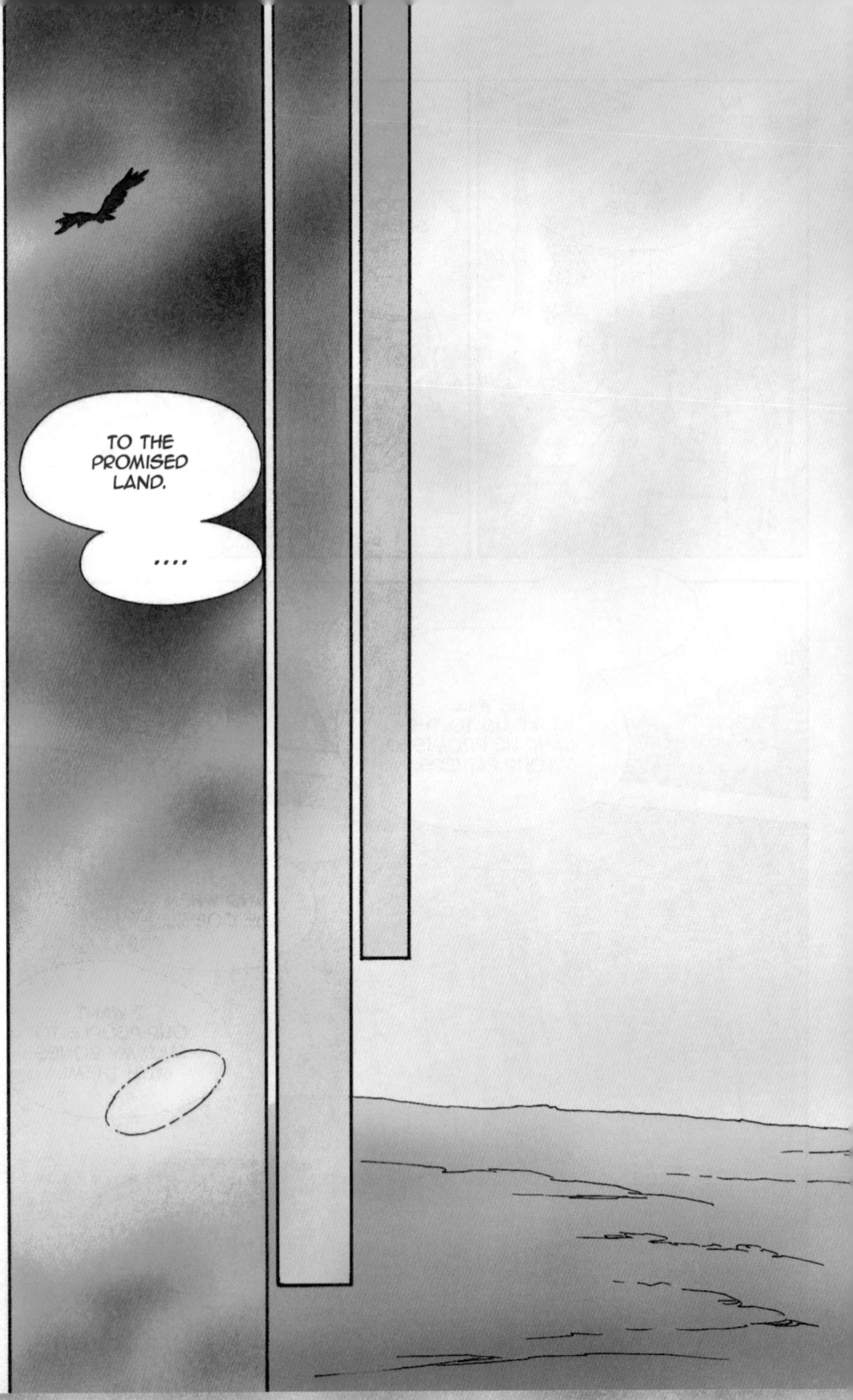
TO THE PROMISED LAND.
....

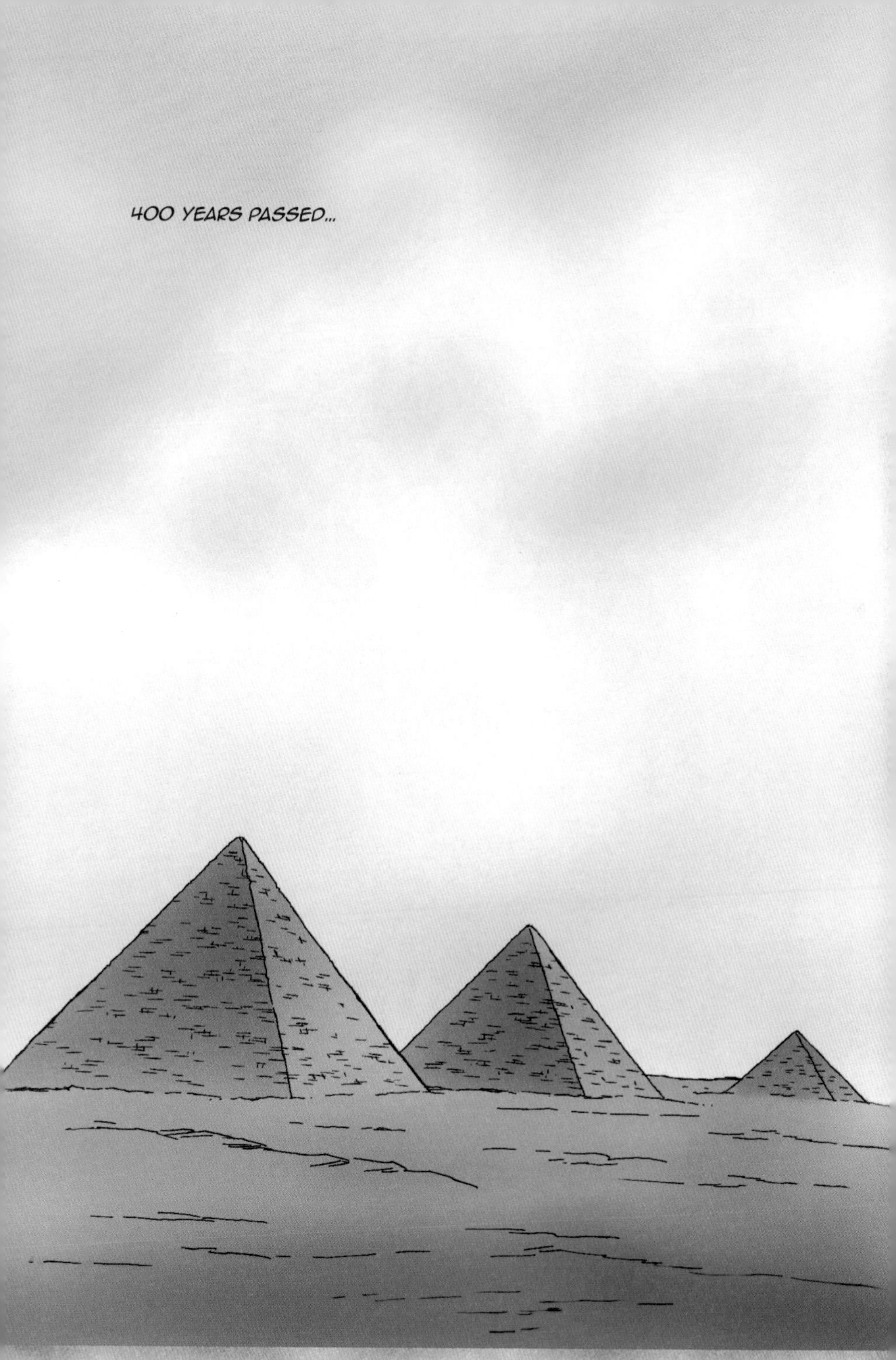
400 YEARS PASSED...

CHAPTER 4

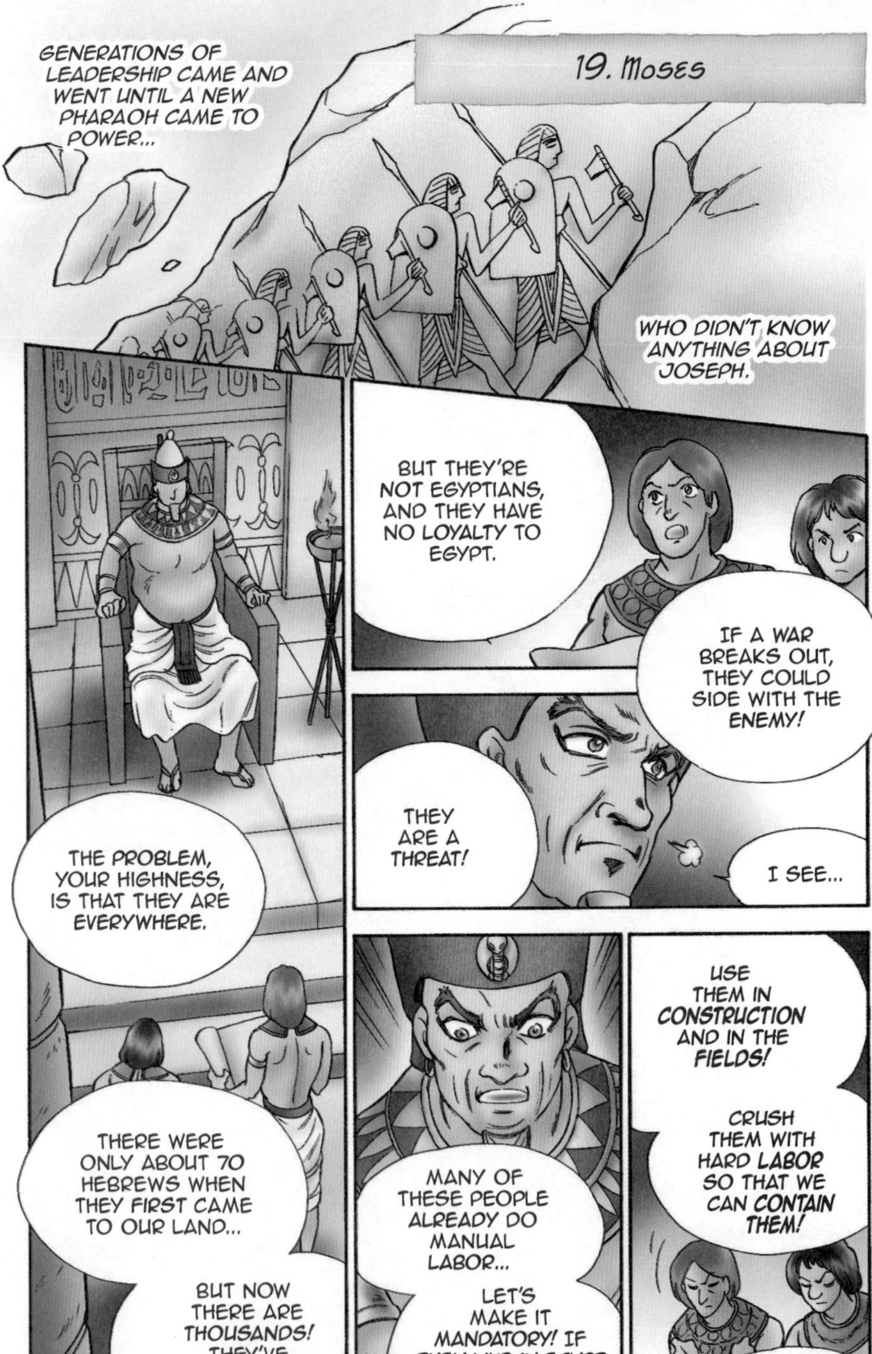

GENERATIONS OF LEADERSHIP CAME AND WENT UNTIL A NEW PHARAOH CAME TO POWER...
19. Moses
WHO DIDN'T KNOW ANYTHING ABOUT JOSEPH.
THE PROBLEM, YOUR HIGHNESS, IS THAT THEY ARE EVERYWHERE.
THERE WERE ONLY ABOUT 70 HEBREWS WHEN THEY FIRST CAME TO OUR LAND...
BUT NOW THERE ARE THOUSANDS! THEY'VE PROSPERED HERE...
BUT THEY'RE NOT EGYPTIANS, AND THEY HAVE NO LOYALTY TO EGYPT.
IF A WAR BREAKS OUT, THEY COULD SIDE WITH THE ENEMY!
THEY ARE A THREAT!
I SEE...
MANY OF THESE PEOPLE ALREADY DO MANUAL LABOR...
LET'S MAKE IT MANDATORY! IF THEY LIVE IN EGYPT, THEY MUST SERVE EGYPT!
USE THEM IN CONSTRUCTION AND IN THE FIELDS!
CRUSH THEM WITH HARD LABOR SO THAT WE CAN CONTAIN THEM!
YES SIR!

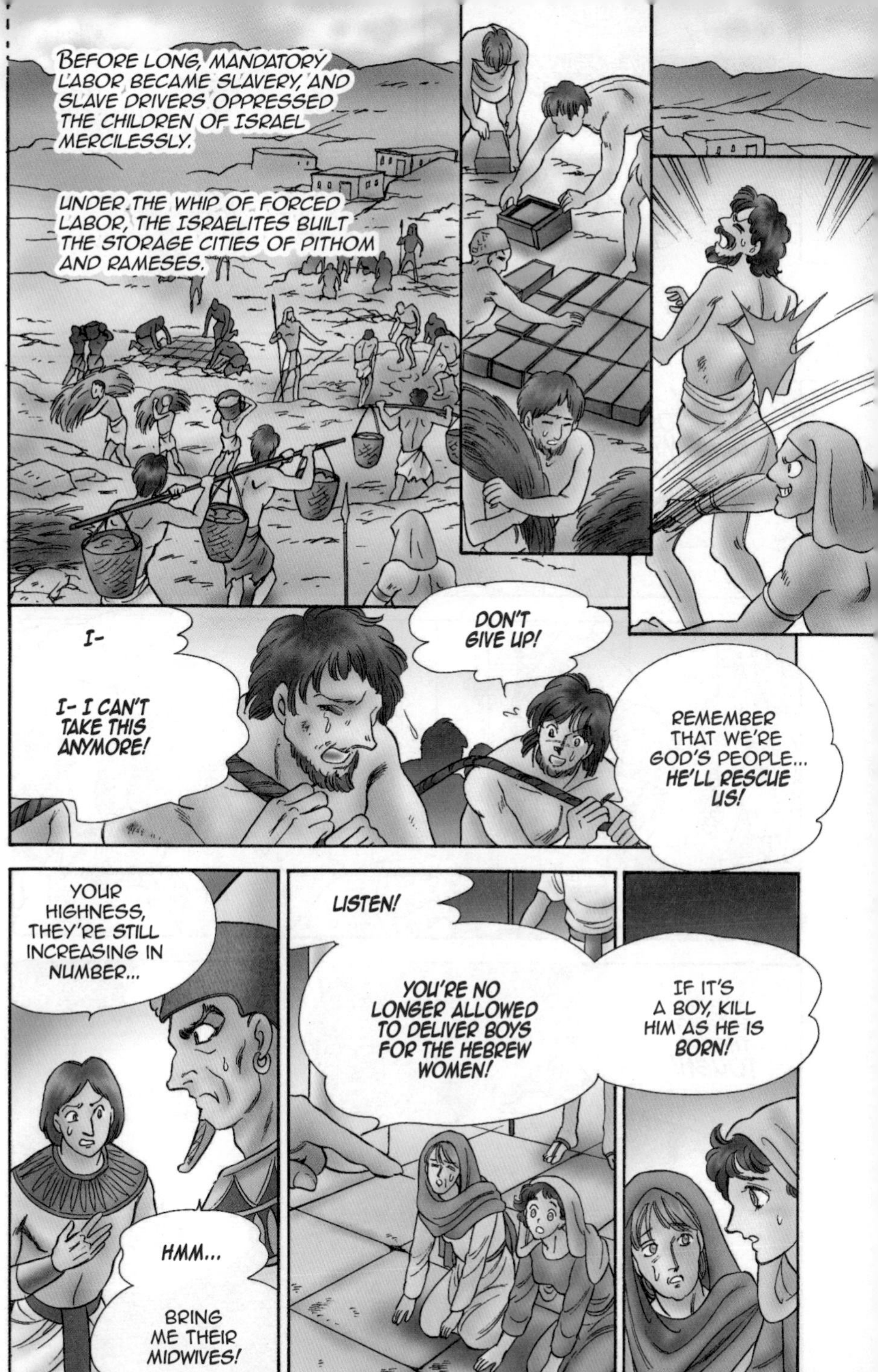
BEFORE LONG, MANDATORY LABOR BECAME SLAVERY, AND SLAVE DRIVERS OPPRESSED THE CHILDREN OF ISRAEL MERCILESSLY.
UNDER THE WHIP OF FORCED LABOR, THE ISRAELITES BUILT THE STORAGE CITIES OF PITHOM AND RAMESES.
I-
I- I CAN'T TAKE THIS ANYMORE!
DON'T GIVE UP!
REMEMBER THAT WE'RE GOD'S PEOPLE... HE'LL RESCUE US!
YOUR HIGHNESS, THEY'RE STILL INCREASING IN NUMBER...
HMM...
BRING ME THEIR MIDWIVES!
LISTEN!
YOU'RE NO LONGER ALLOWED TO DELIVER BOYS FOR THE HEBREW WOMEN!
IF IT'S A BOY, KILL HIM AS HE IS BORN!

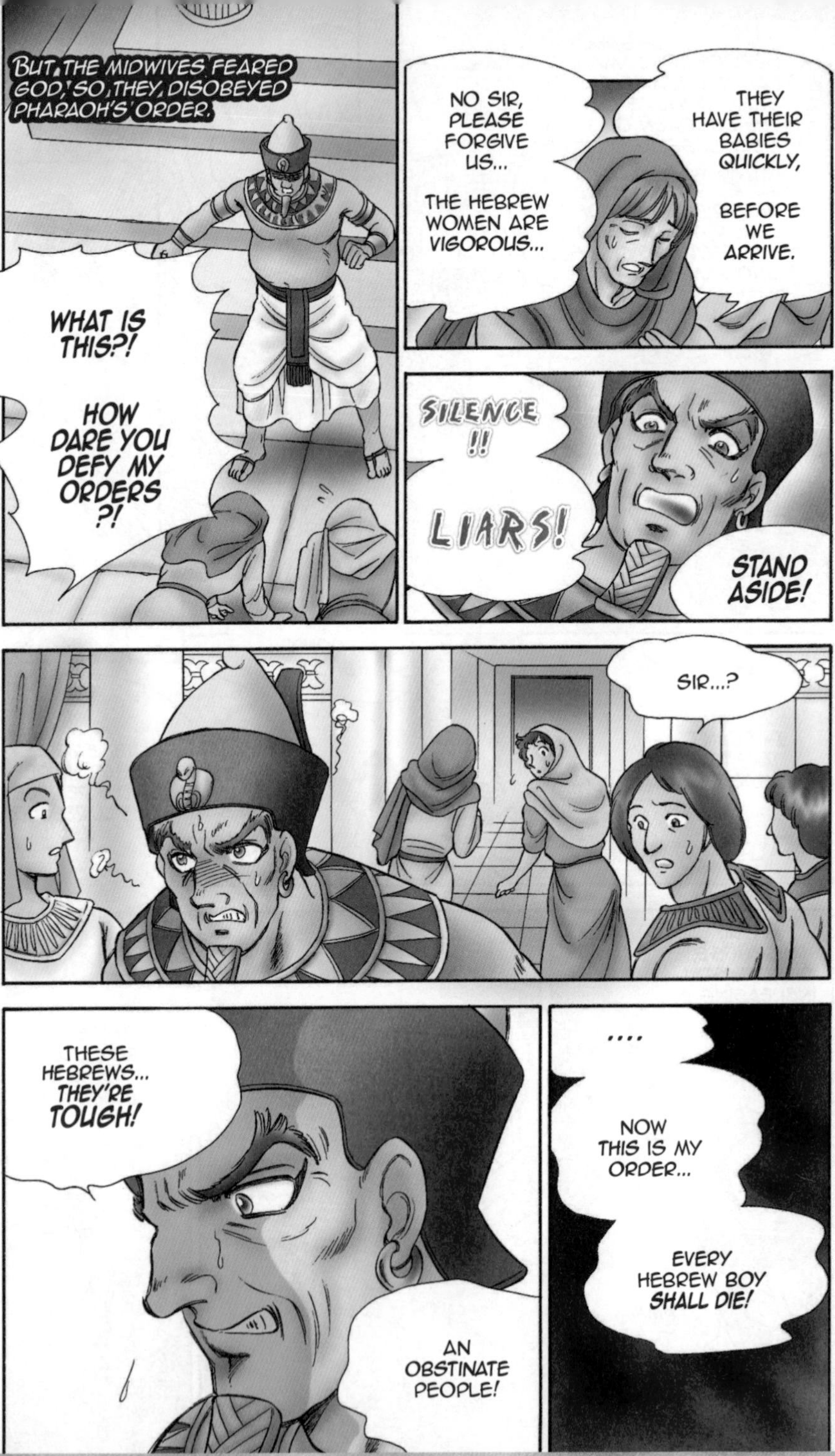

BUT THE MIDWIVES FEARED GOD, SO THEY DISOBEYED PHARAOH'S ORDER.
WHAT IS THIS?! HOW DARE YOU DEFY MY ORDERS?!
NO SIR, PLEASE FORGIVE US... THE HEBREW WOMEN ARE VIGOROUS...
THEY HAVE THEIR BABIES QUICKLY, BEFORE WE ARRIVE.
SILENCE!! LIARS!
STAND ASIDE!
SIR...?
THESE HEBREWS... THEY'RE TOUGH!
AN OBSTINATE PEOPLE!
....
NOW THIS IS MY ORDER...
EVERY HEBREW BOY SHALL DIE!

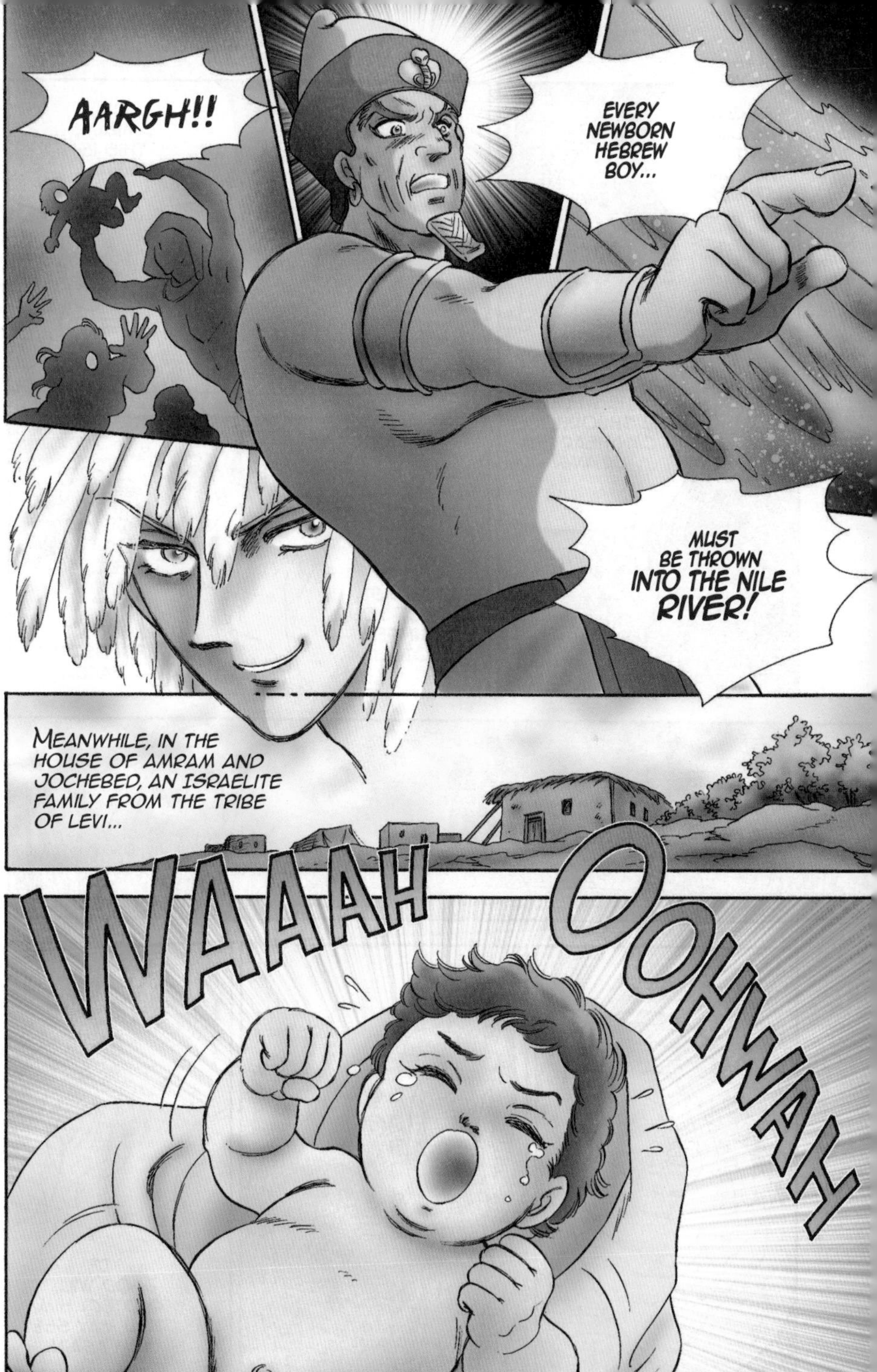
AARGH!!
EVERY NEWBORN HEBREW BOY...
MUST BE THROWN INTO THE NILE RIVER!
MEANWHILE, IN THE HOUSE OF AMRAM AND JOCHEBED, AN ISRAELITE FAMILY FROM THE TRIBE OF LEVI...
WAAAH
OOHWAAH

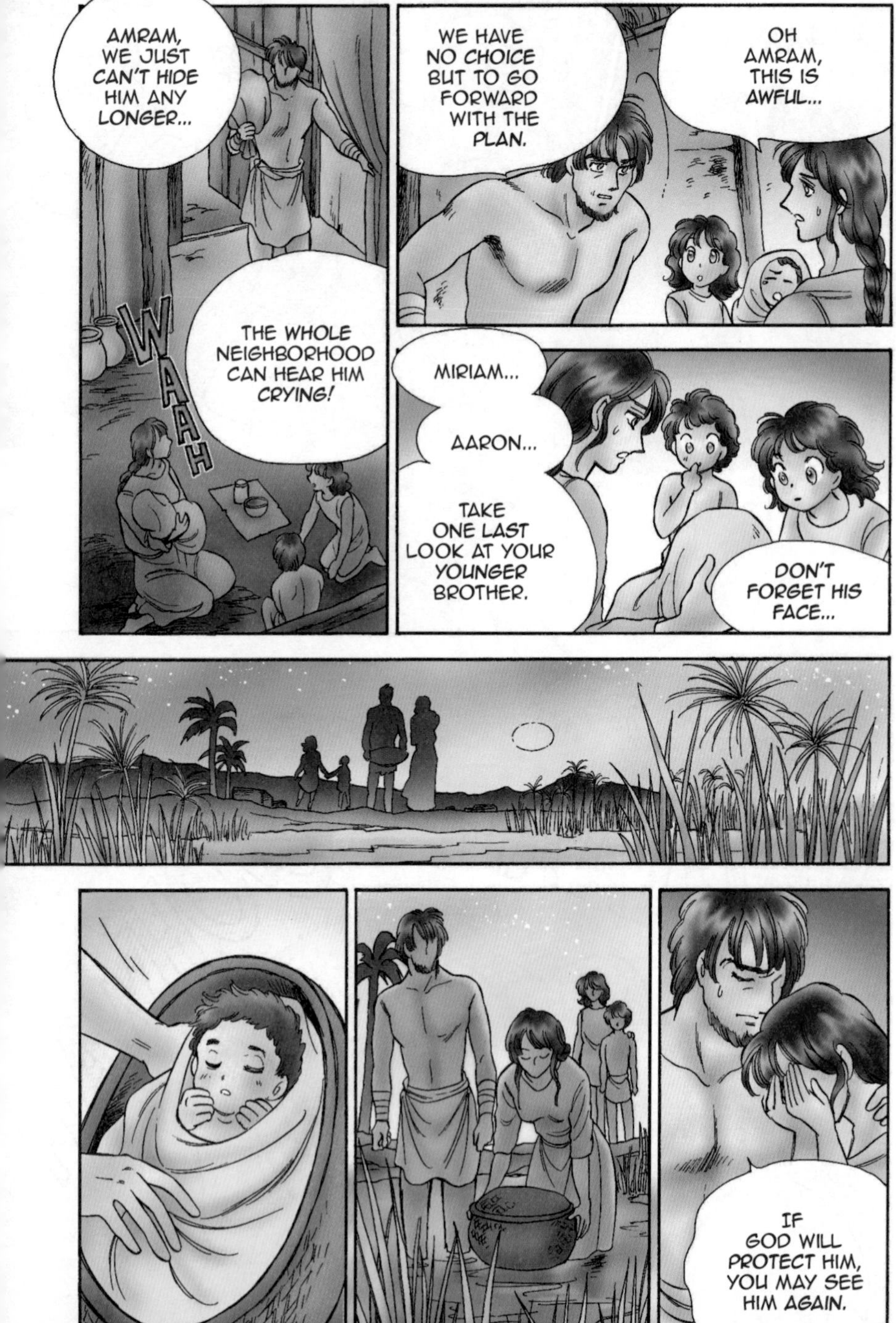
AMRAM, WE JUST CAN'T HIDE HIM ANY LONGER...
WAAAAH
THE WHOLE NEIGHBORHOOD CAN HEAR HIM CRYING!
WE HAVE NO CHOICE BUT TO GO FORWARD WITH THE PLAN.
OH AMRAM, THIS IS AWFUL...
MIRIAM...
AARON...
TAKE ONE LAST LOOK AT YOUR YOUNGER BROTHER.
DON'T FORGET HIS FACE...
IF GOD WILL PROTECT HIM, YOU MAY SEE HIM AGAIN.

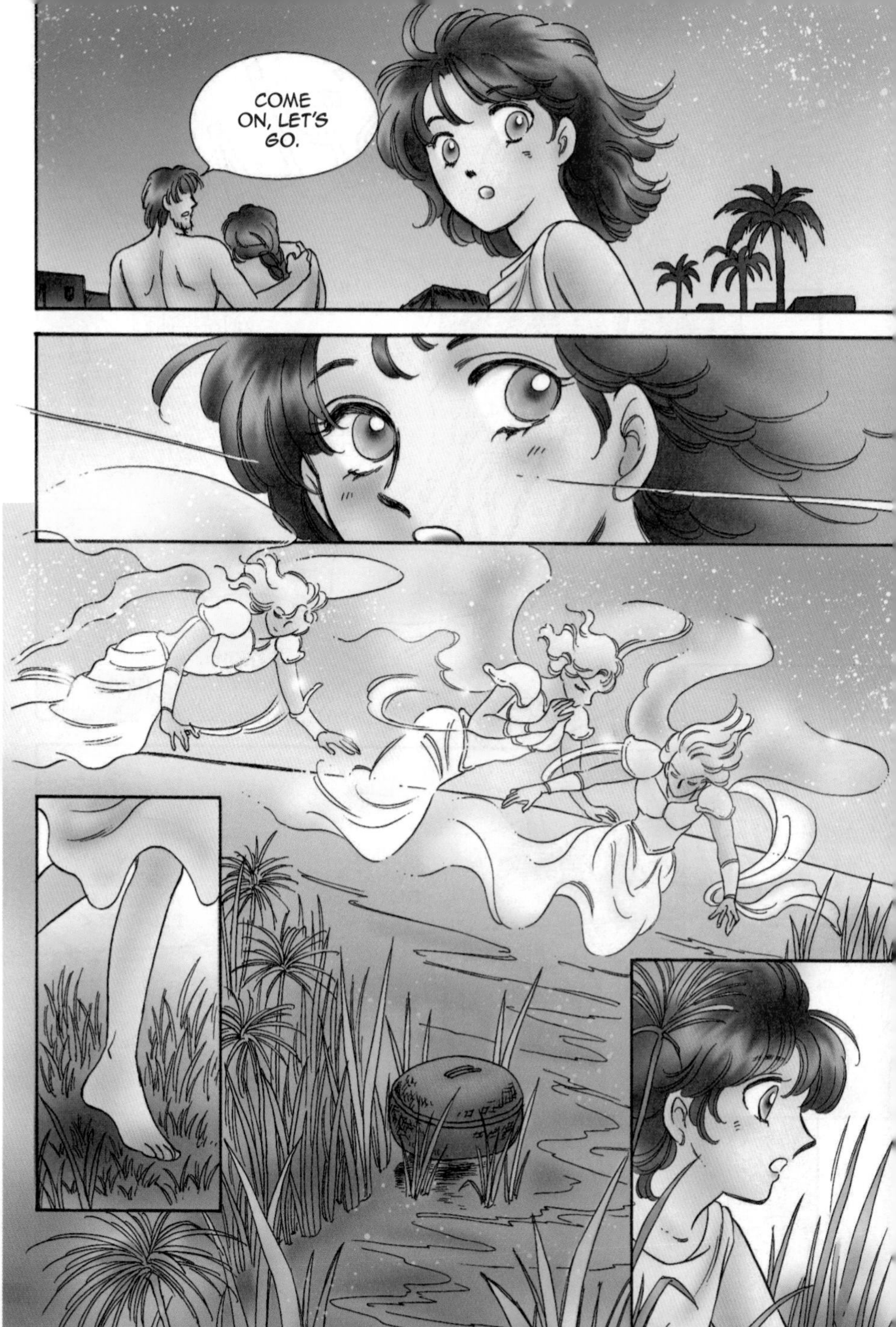
COME ON, LET'S GO.

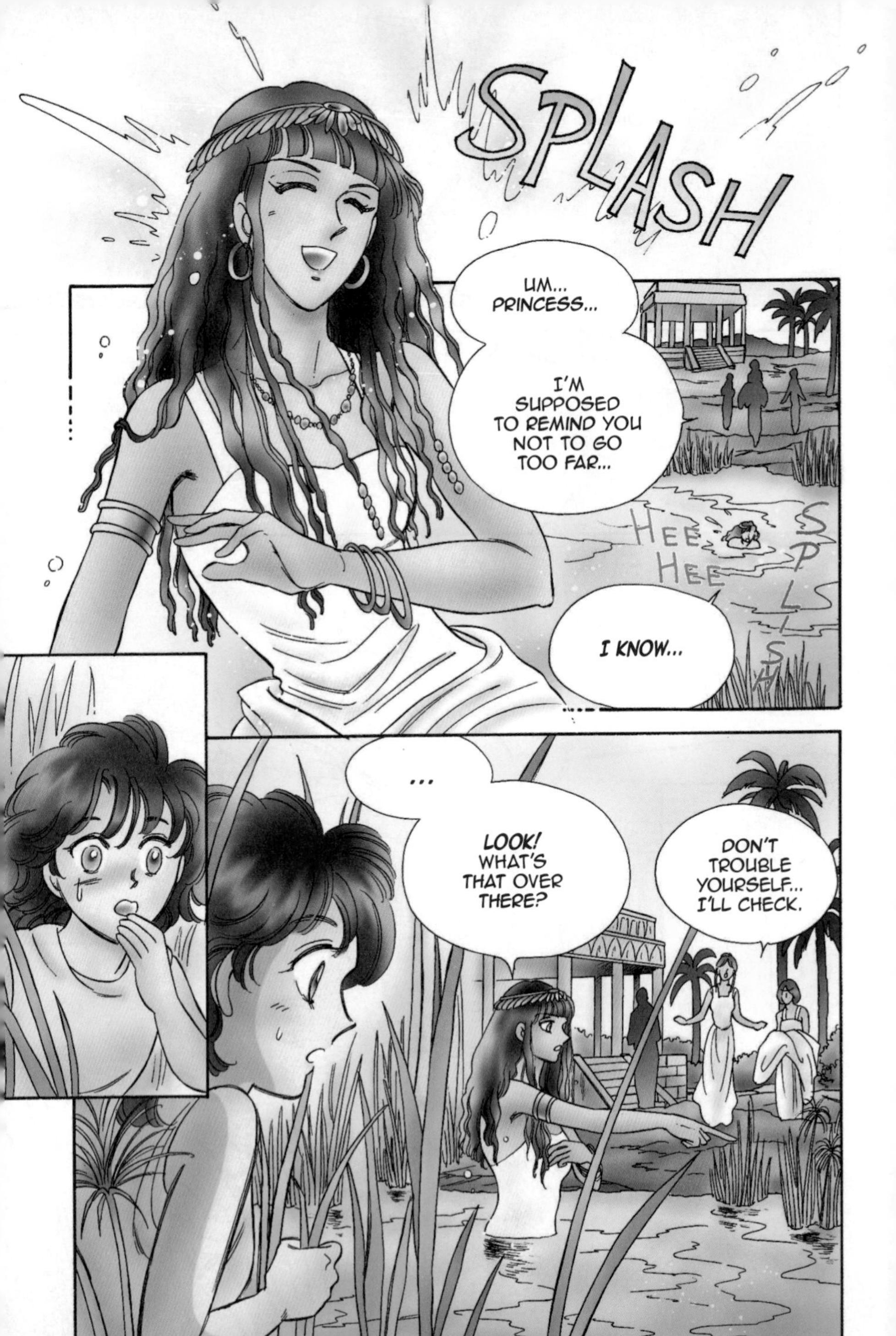
SPLASH
UM... PRINCESS...
I'M SUPPOSED TO REMIND YOU NOT TO GO TOO FAR...
HEE HEE
SPLISH
I KNOW...
...
LOOK! WHAT'S THAT OVER THERE?
DON'T TROUBLE YOURSELF... I'LL CHECK.

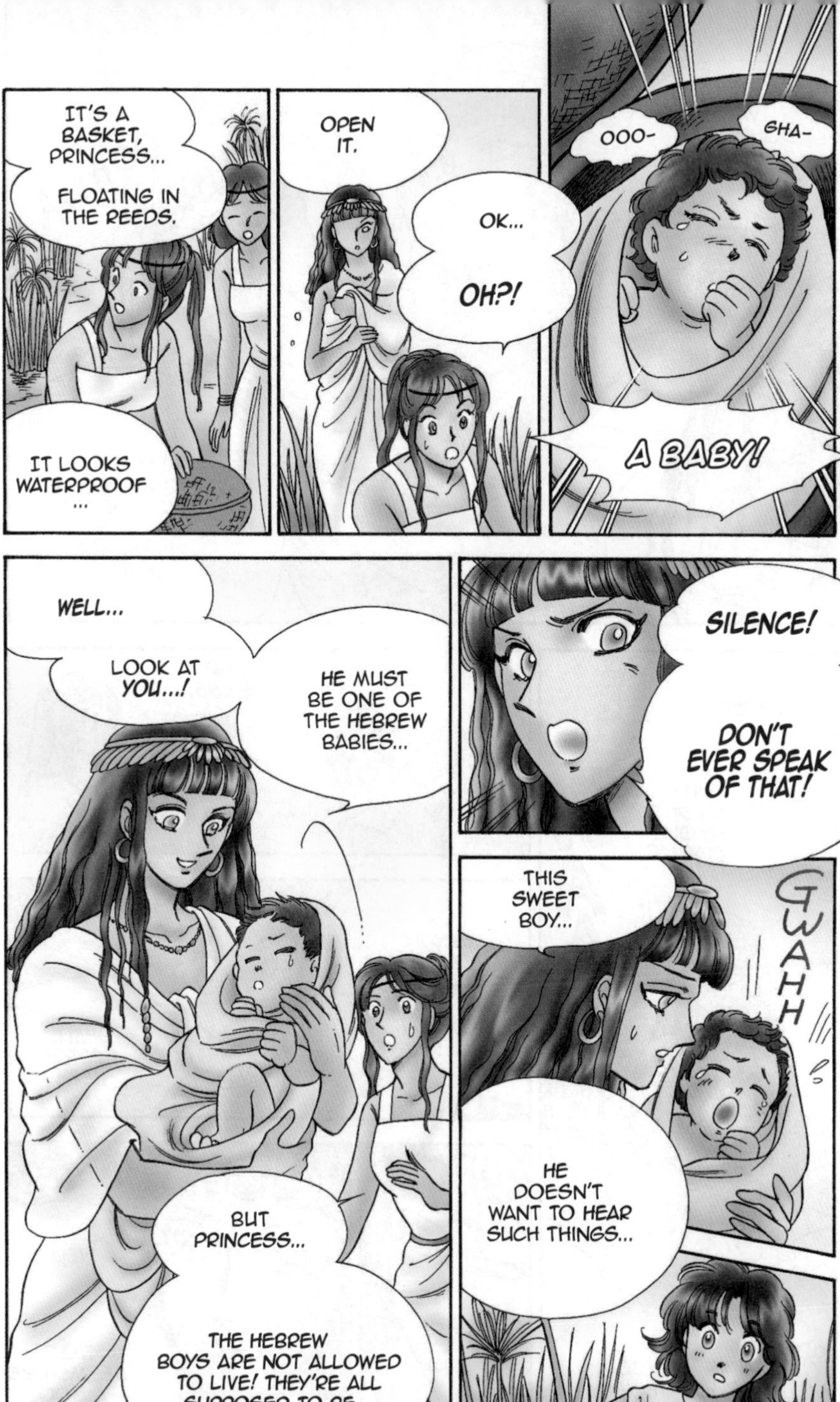

IT'S A BASKET, PRINCESS...
FLOATING IN THE REEDS.
IT LOOKS WATERPROOF ...
OPEN IT.
OK...
OH?!
OOO-
GHA-
A BABY!
WELL...
LOOK AT YOU...!
HE MUST BE ONE OF THE HEBREW BABIES...
BUT PRINCESS...
THE HEBREW BOYS ARE NOT ALLOWED TO LIVE! THEY'RE ALL SUPPOSED TO BE...
SILENCE!
DON'T EVER SPEAK OF THAT!
THIS SWEET BOY...
GWAHH
HE DOESN'T WANT TO HEAR SUCH THINGS...

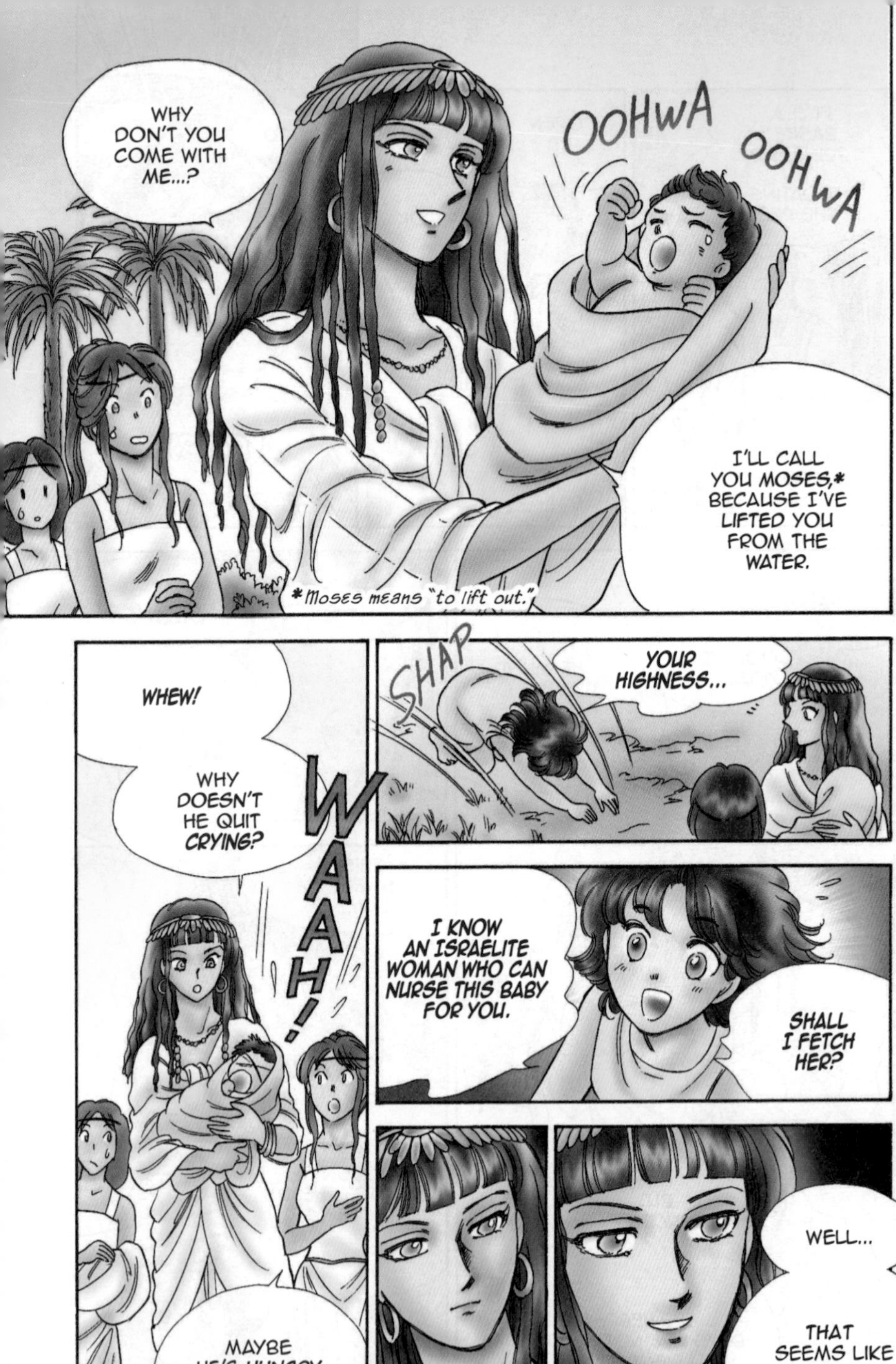
WHY DON'T YOU COME WITH ME...?
OOHWA
OOHWA
I'LL CALL YOU MOSES,* BECAUSE I'VE LIFTED YOU FROM THE WATER.
*Moses means "to lift out."
WHEW!
WHY DOESN'T HE QUIT CRYING?
WAAAH!!
SHAP
YOUR HIGHNESS...
I KNOW AN ISRAELITE WOMAN WHO CAN NURSE THIS BABY FOR YOU.
SHALL I FETCH HER?
MAYBE HE'S HUNGRY, PRINCESS?
WELL...
THAT SEEMS LIKE A GOOD IDEA...

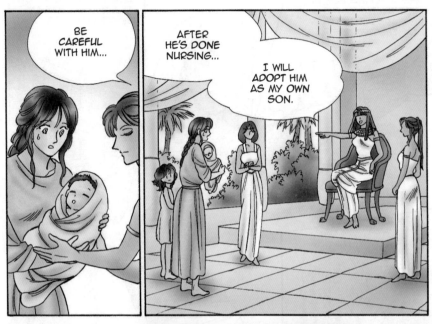

BE CAREFUL WITH HIM...

AFTER HE'S DONE NURSING...

I WILL ADOPT HIM AS MY OWN SON.

THAT'S ONE WAY FOR ME TO SEE THAT NOTHING BAD HAPPENS...

TO MY SWEET LITTLE MOSES.

YOUR HIGHNESS...

I WILL TAKE GOOD CARE OF HIM!

OH, MY LORD... MY LORD... THANK YOU!

THANK YOU!

SO MOSES SPENT THE FIRST SEVERAL YEARS OF HIS LIFE WITH HIS PARENTS.

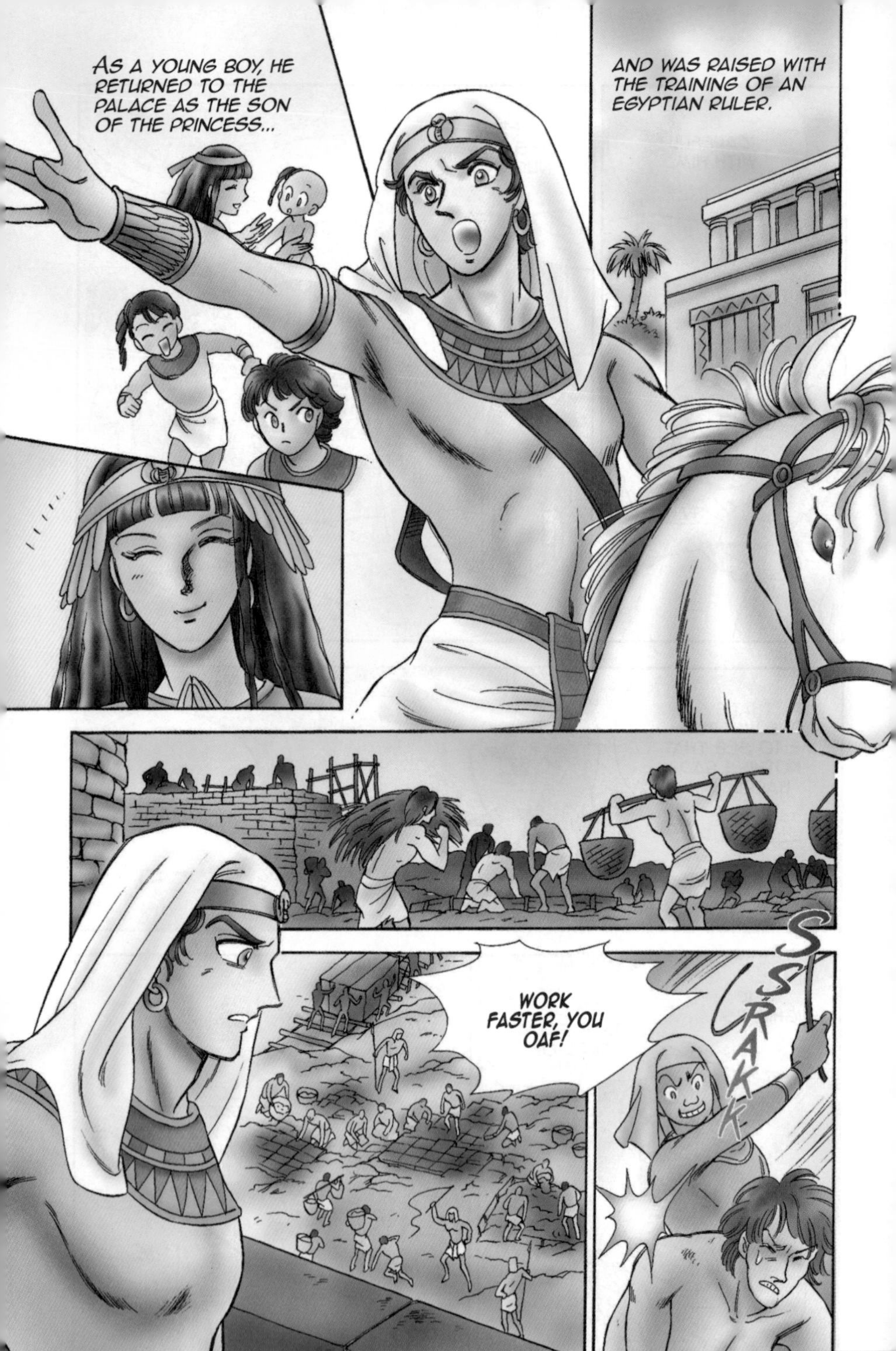
As a young boy, he returned to the palace as the son of the princess...
And was raised with the training of an Egyptian ruler.
Work faster, you oaf!
SSCRAKK

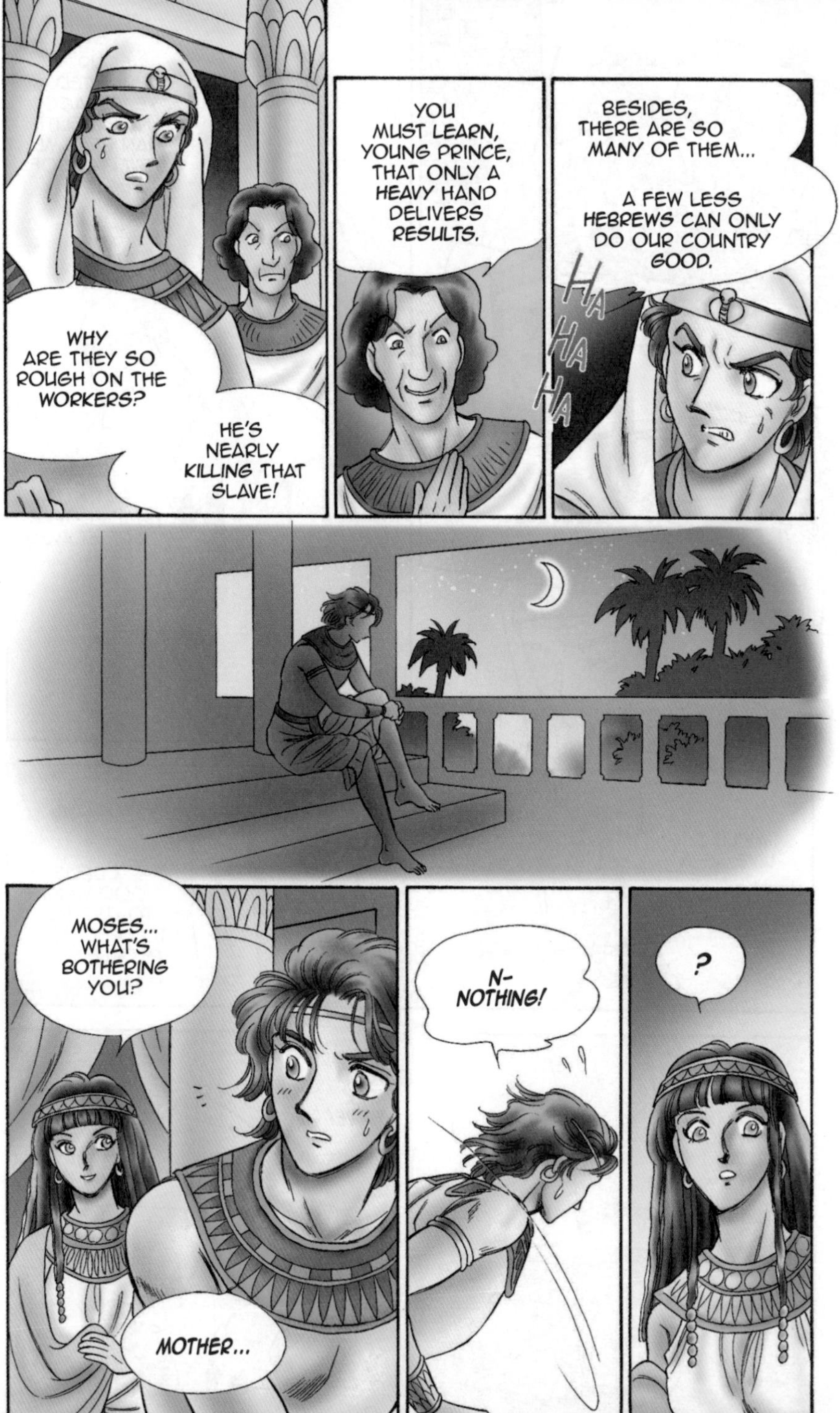
WHY ARE THEY SO ROUGH ON THE WORKERS?
HE'S NEARLY KILLING THAT SLAVE!
YOU MUST LEARN, YOUNG PRINCE, THAT ONLY A HEAVY HAND DELIVERS RESULTS.
BESIDES, THERE ARE SO MANY OF THEM...
A FEW LESS HEBREWS CAN ONLY DO OUR COUNTRY GOOD.
HA HA HA HA
MOSES... WHAT'S BOTHERING YOU?
MOTHER...
N- NOTHING!
?

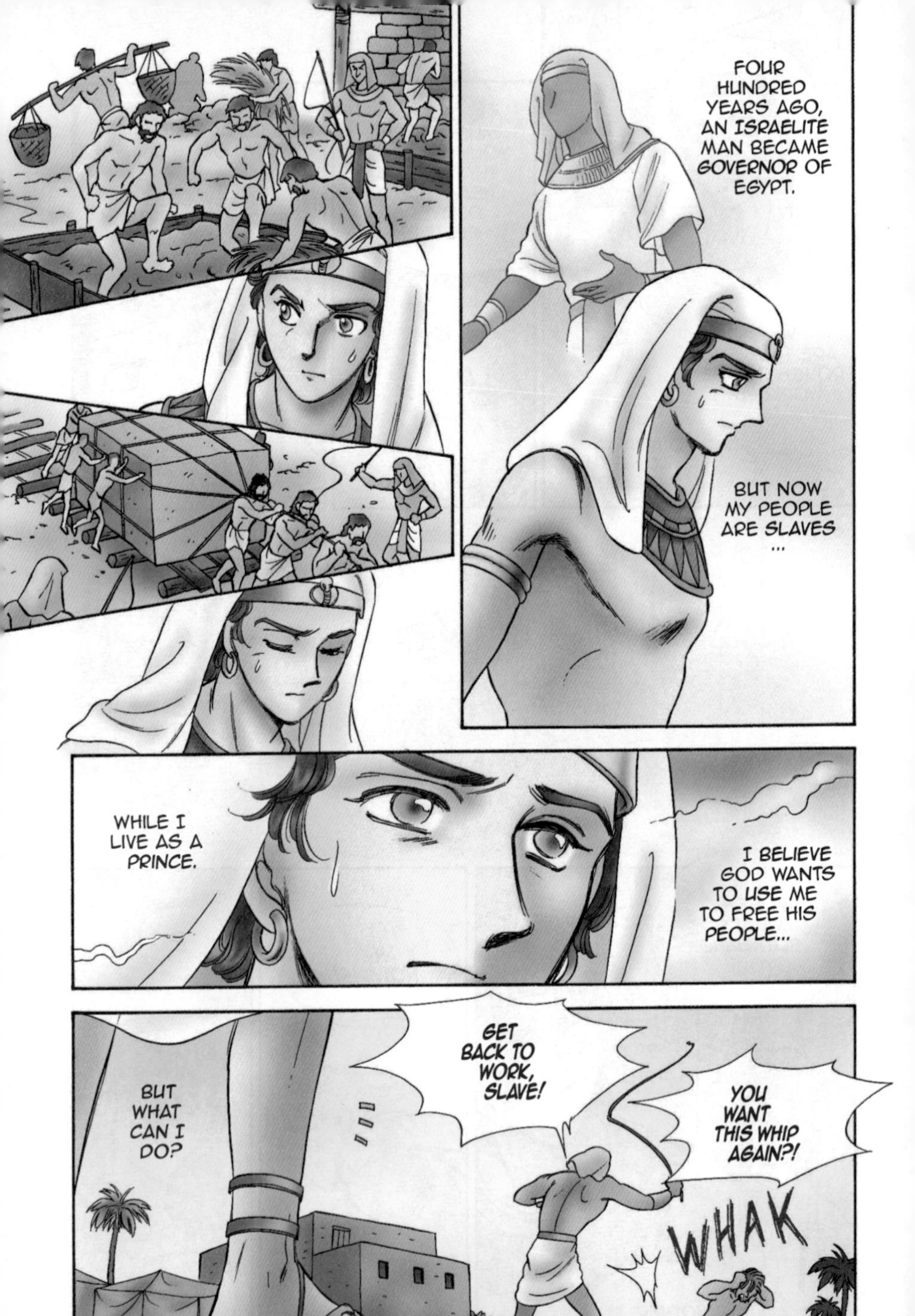
FOUR HUNDRED YEARS AGO, AN ISRAELITE MAN BECAME GOVERNOR OF EGYPT.
BUT NOW MY PEOPLE ARE SLAVES ...
WHILE I LIVE AS A PRINCE.
I BELIEVE GOD WANTS TO USE ME TO FREE HIS PEOPLE...
BUT WHAT CAN I DO?
GET BACK TO WORK, SLAVE!
YOU WANT THIS WHIP AGAIN?!
WHAK

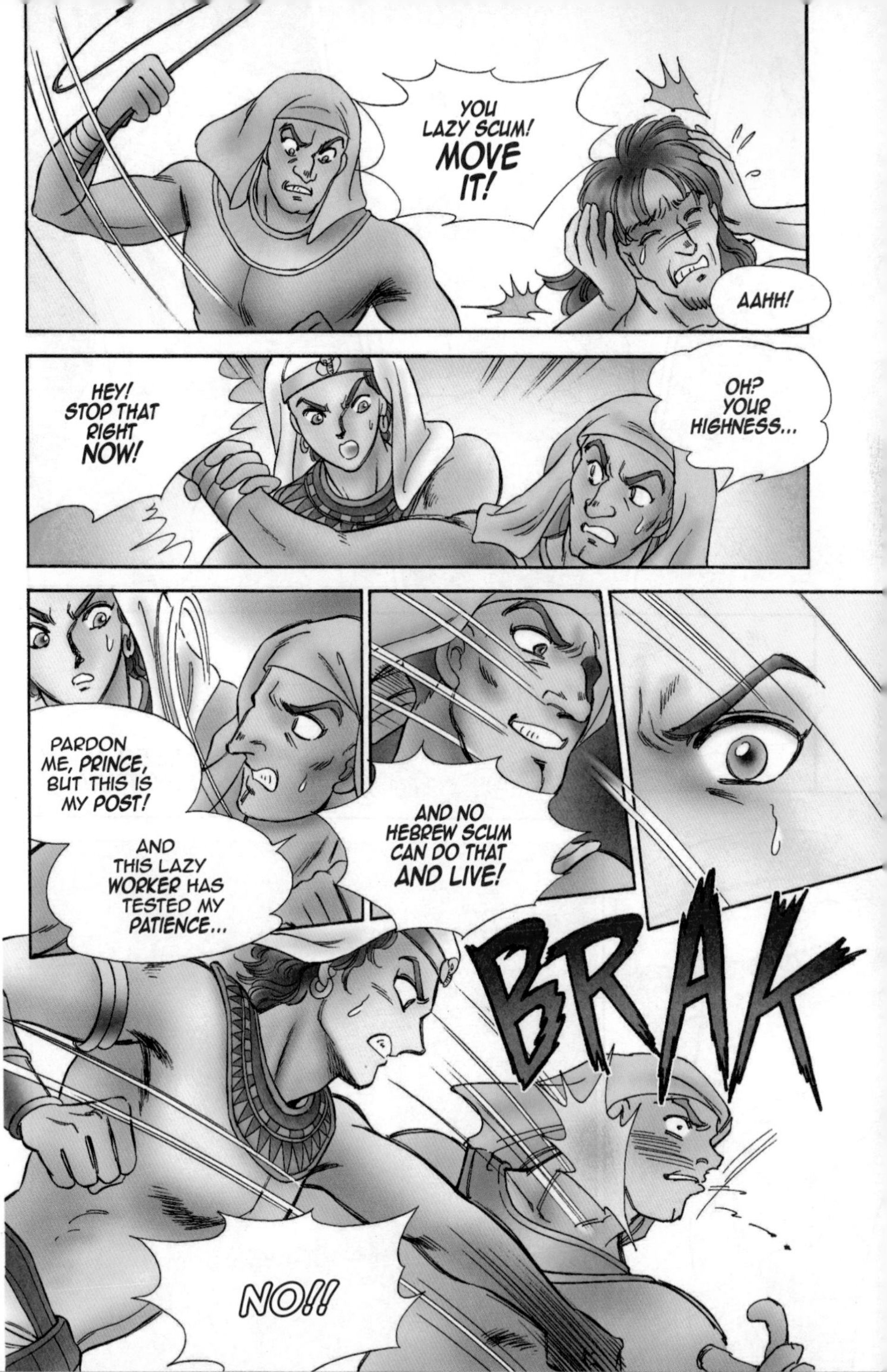

YOU LAZY SCUM! MOVE IT!
AAHH!
HEY! STOP THAT RIGHT NOW!
OH? YOUR HIGHNESS...
PARDON ME, PRINCE, BUT THIS IS MY POST!
AND THIS LAZY WORKER HAS TESTED MY PATIENCE...
AND NO HEBREW SCUM CAN DO THAT AND LIVE!
BRAK
NO!!

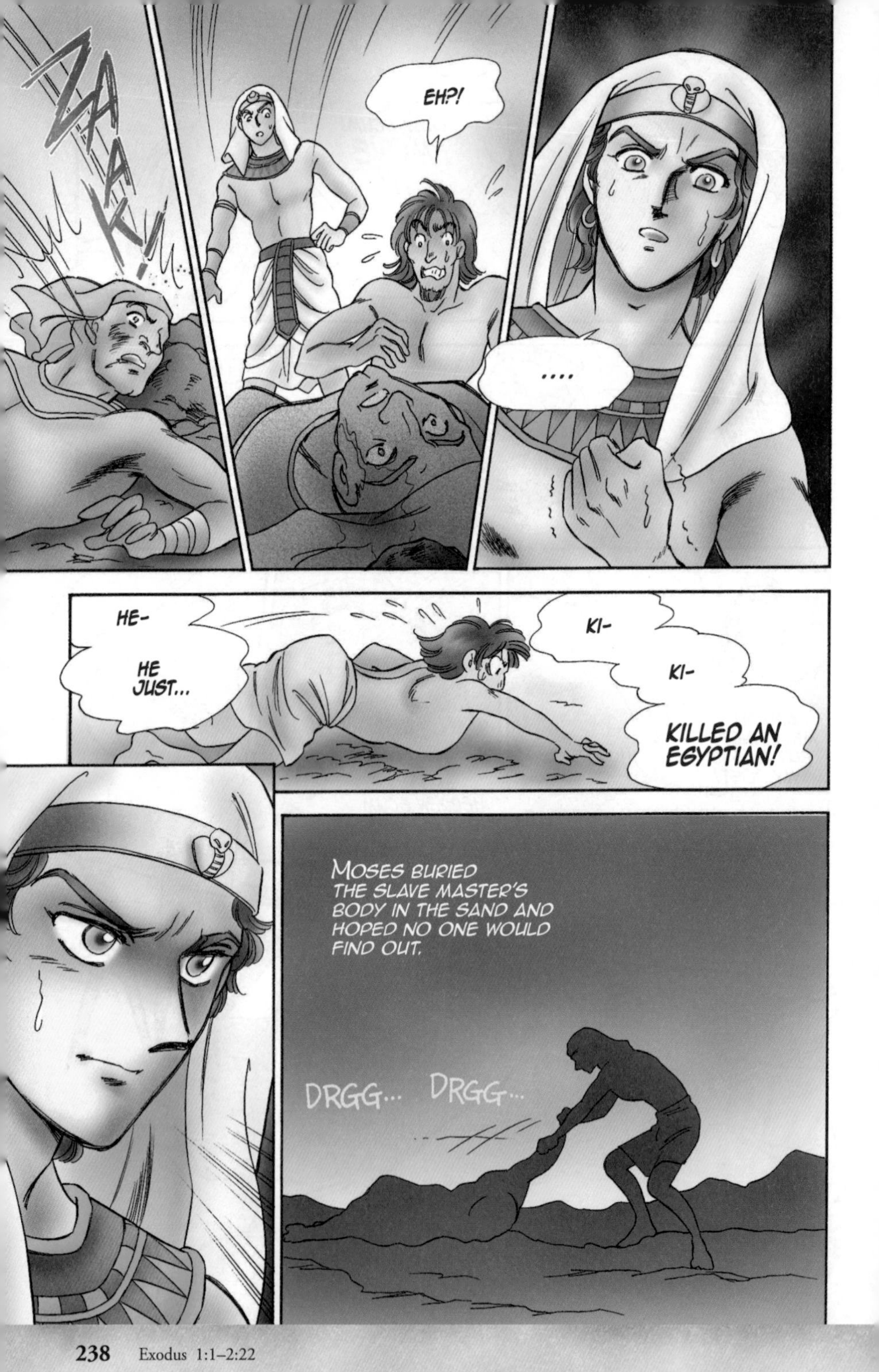
ZAAAK!
EH?!
....
HE-
HE JUST...
KI-
KI-
KILLED AN EGYPTIAN!
MOSES BURIED THE SLAVE MASTER'S BODY IN THE SAND AND HOPED NO ONE WOULD FIND OUT.
DRGG... DRGG...

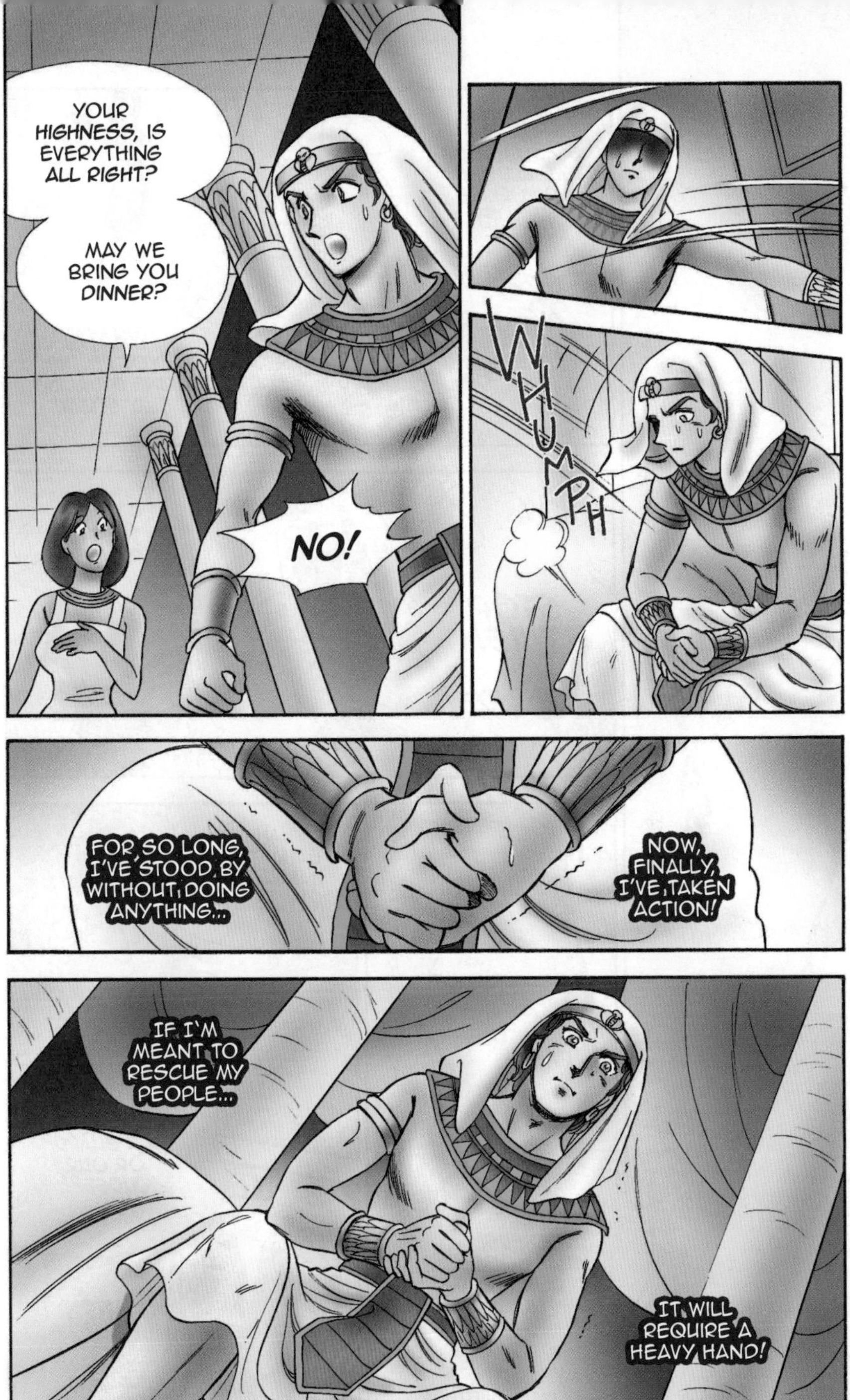
YOUR HIGHNESS, IS EVERYTHING ALL RIGHT?
MAY WE BRING YOU DINNER?
NO!
WHUMPH
FOR SO LONG, I'VE STOOD BY WITHOUT DOING ANYTHING...
NOW, FINALLY, I'VE TAKEN ACTION!
IF I'M MEANT TO RESCUE MY PEOPLE...
IT WILL REQUIRE A HEAVY HAND!

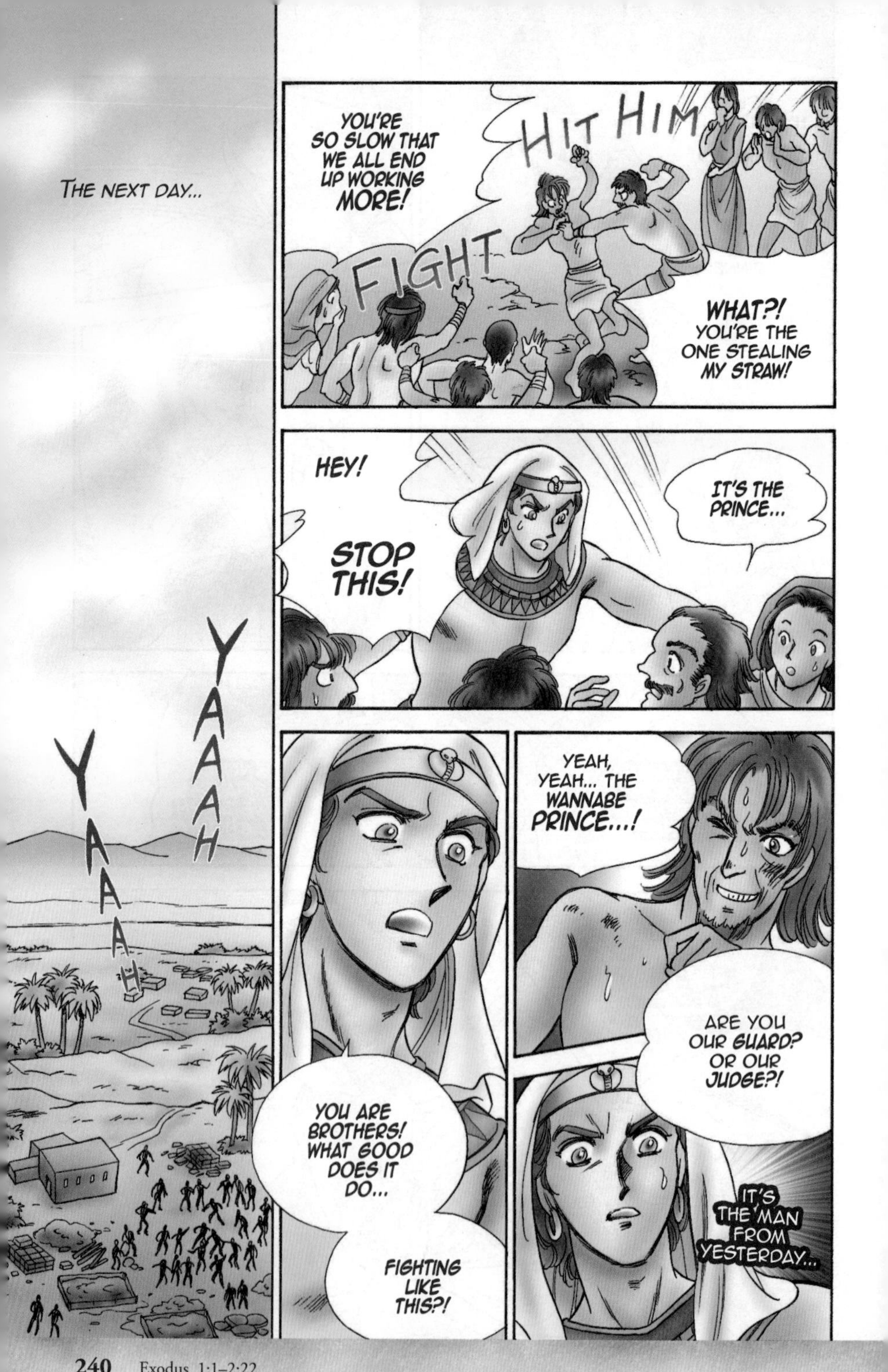
THE NEXT DAY...
YOU'RE SO SLOW THAT WE ALL END UP WORKING MORE!
HIT HIM
FIGHT
WHAT?! YOU'RE THE ONE STEALING MY STRAW!
HEY!
STOP THIS!
IT'S THE PRINCE...
YAAAAH
YAAAAH
YOU ARE BROTHERS! WHAT GOOD DOES IT DO...
FIGHTING LIKE THIS?!
YEAH, YEAH... THE WANNABE PRINCE...!
ARE YOU OUR GUARD? OR OUR JUDGE?!
IT'S THE MAN FROM YESTERDAY...

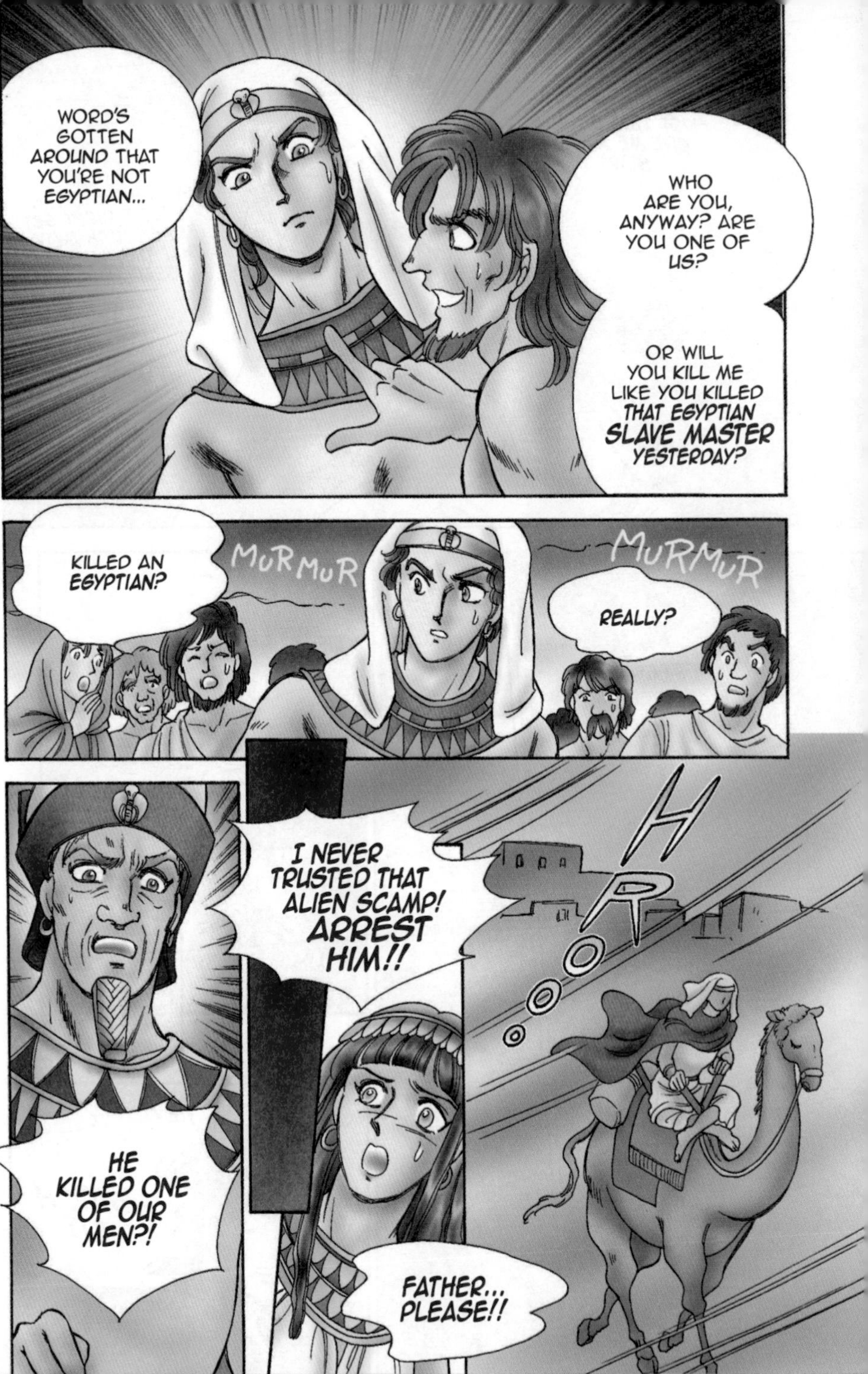
WORD'S GOTTEN AROUND THAT YOU'RE NOT EGYPTIAN...
WHO ARE YOU, ANYWAY? ARE YOU ONE OF US?
OR WILL YOU KILL ME LIKE YOU KILLED THAT EGYPTIAN SLAVE MASTER YESTERDAY?
KILLED AN EGYPTIAN?
MURMUR
MURMUR
REALLY?
HE KILLED ONE OF OUR MEN?!
I NEVER TRUSTED THAT ALIEN SCAMP! ARREST HIM!!
FATHER... PLEASE!!
HROOOO

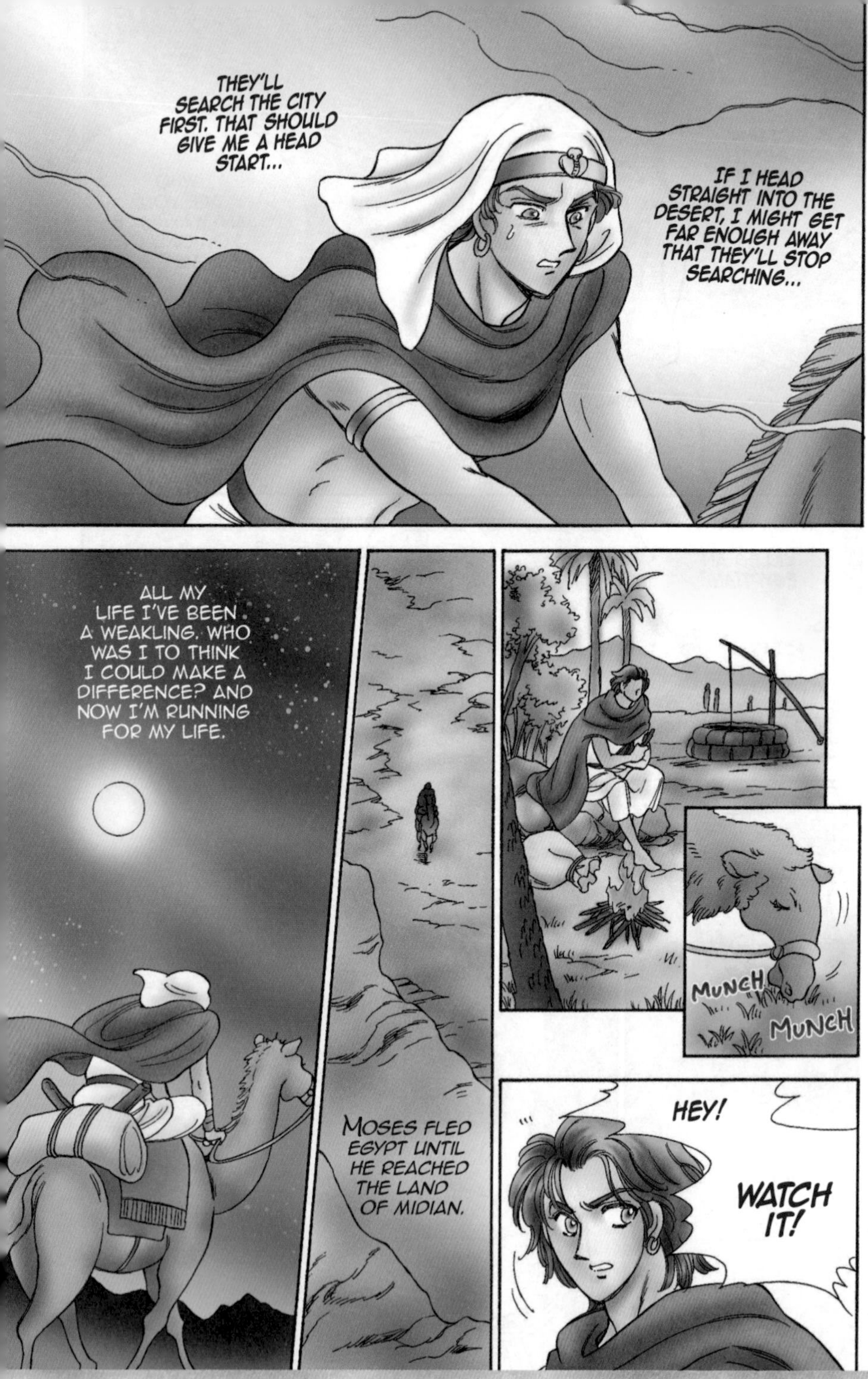
THEY'LL SEARCH THE CITY FIRST. THAT SHOULD GIVE ME A HEAD START...
IF I HEAD STRAIGHT INTO THE DESERT, I MIGHT GET FAR ENOUGH AWAY THAT THEY'LL STOP SEARCHING...
ALL MY LIFE I'VE BEEN A WEAKLING. WHO WAS I TO THINK I COULD MAKE A DIFFERENCE? AND NOW I'M RUNNING FOR MY LIFE.
MOSES FLED EGYPT UNTIL HE REACHED THE LAND OF MIDIAN.
MUNCH
MUNCH
HEY!
WATCH IT!

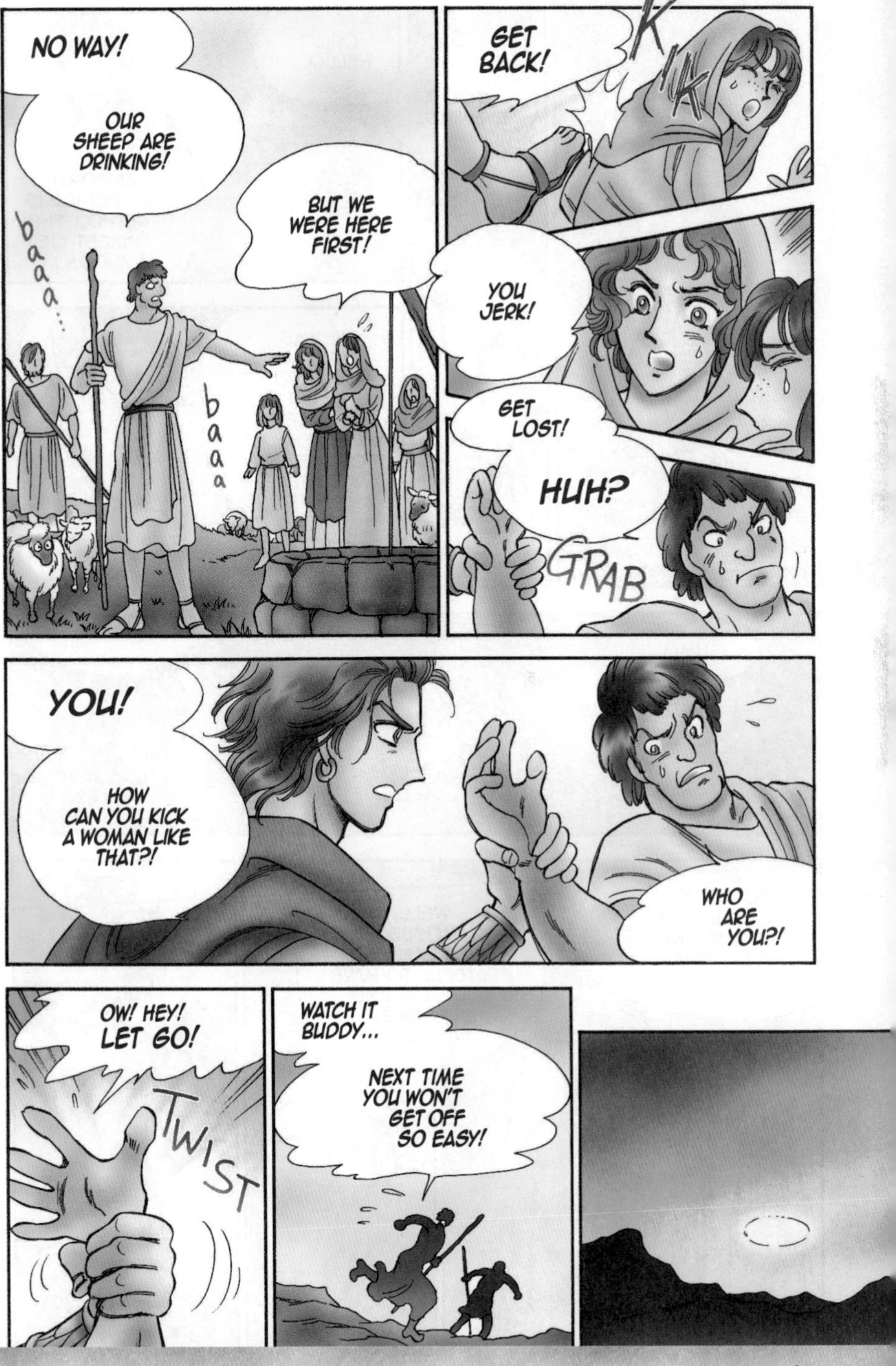
NO WAY!
OUR SHEEP ARE DRINKING!
baaa...
BUT WE WERE HERE FIRST!
baaa
GET BACK!
KIK
YOU JERK!
GET LOST!
HUH?
GRAB
YOU!
HOW CAN YOU KICK A WOMAN LIKE THAT?!
WHO ARE YOU?!
OW! HEY! LET GO!
TWIST
WATCH IT BUDDY...
NEXT TIME YOU WON'T GET OFF SO EASY!

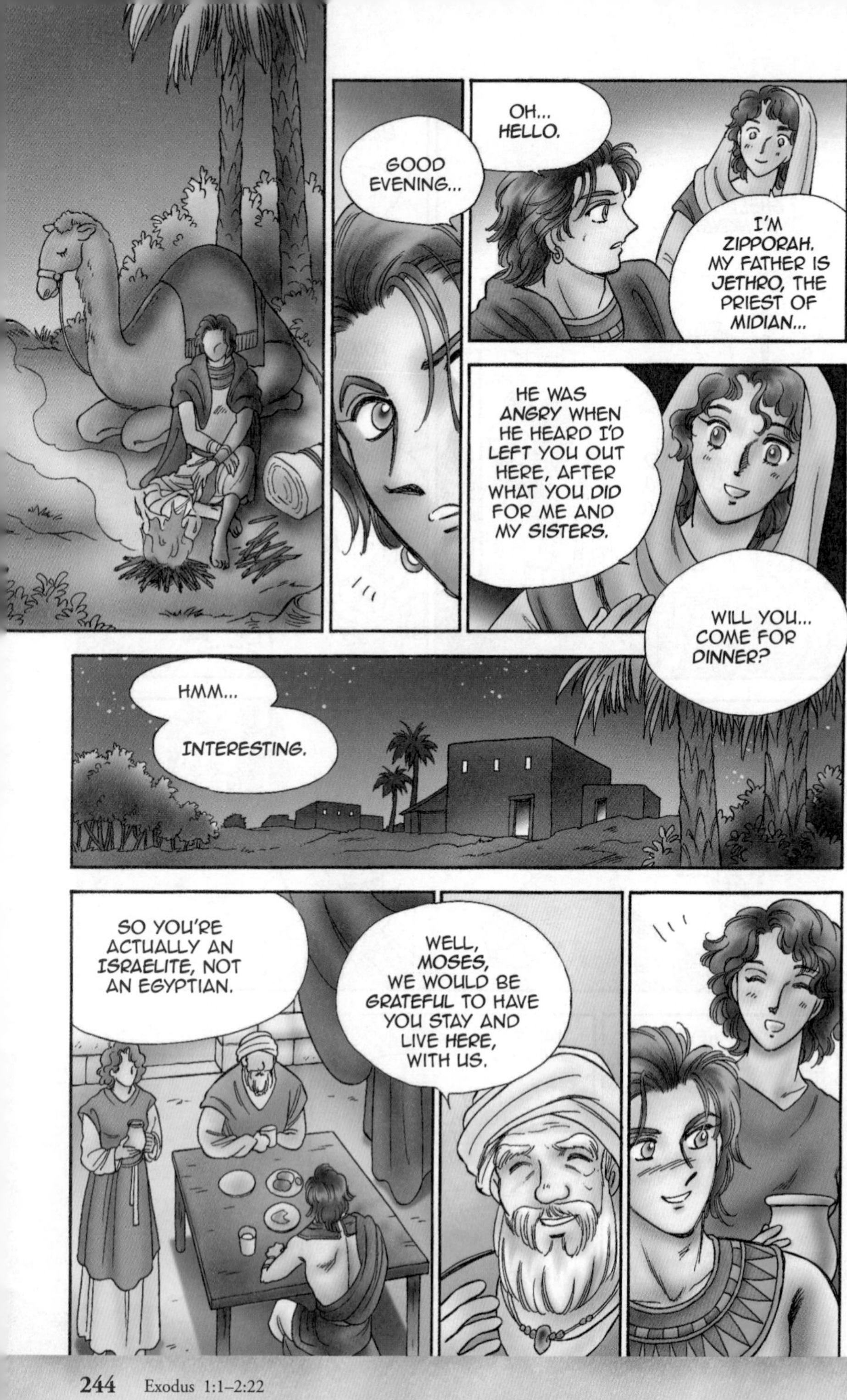
GOOD EVENING...
OH... HELLO.
I'M ZIPPORAH. MY FATHER IS JETHRO, THE PRIEST OF MIDIAN...
HE WAS ANGRY WHEN HE HEARD I'D LEFT YOU OUT HERE, AFTER WHAT YOU DID FOR ME AND MY SISTERS.
WILL YOU... COME FOR DINNER?
HMM...
INTERESTING.
SO YOU'RE ACTUALLY AN ISRAELITE, NOT AN EGYPTIAN.
WELL, MOSES, WE WOULD BE GRATEFUL TO HAVE YOU STAY AND LIVE HERE, WITH US.

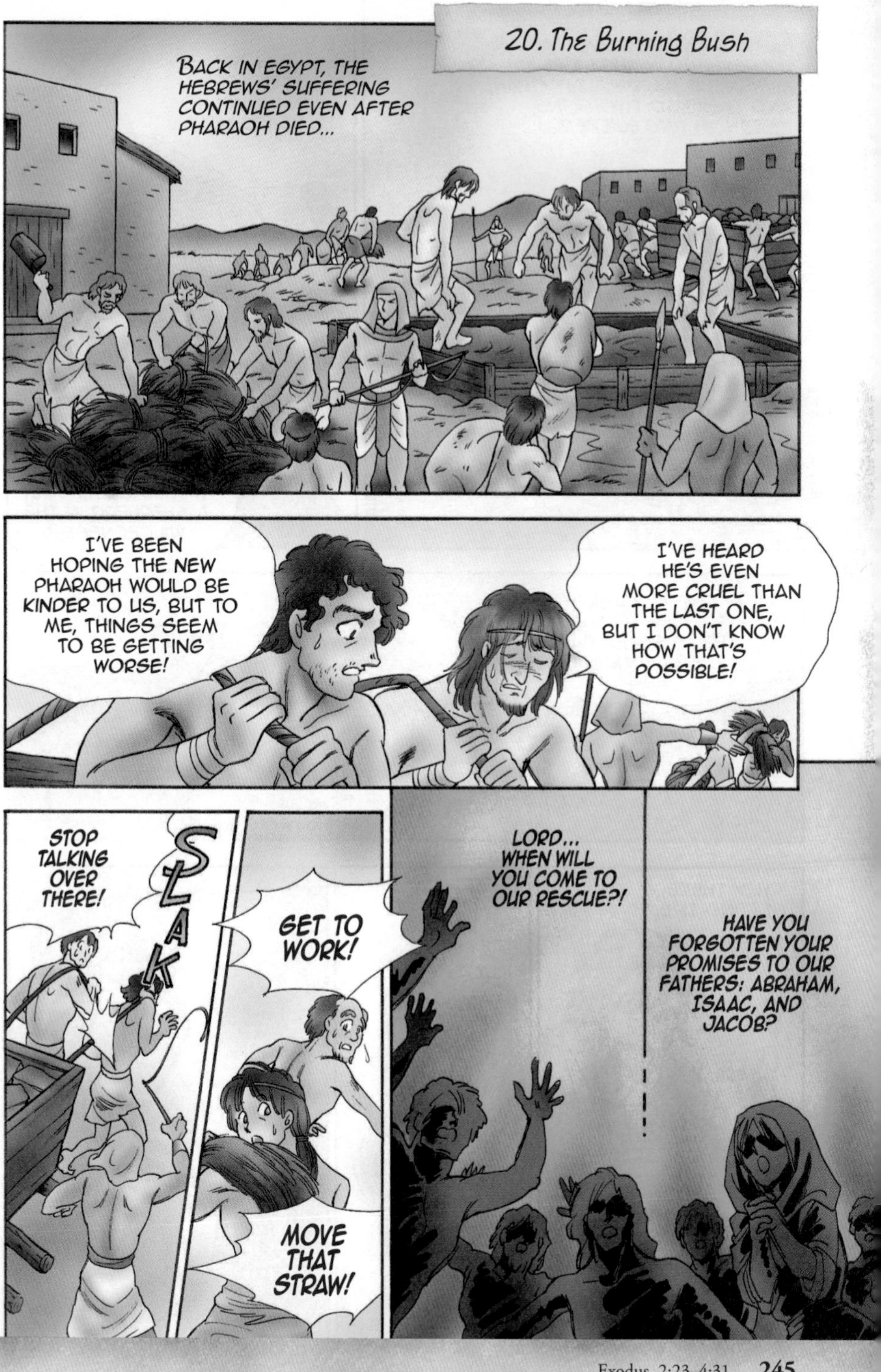
20. The Burning Bush
BACK IN EGYPT, THE HEBREWS' SUFFERING CONTINUED EVEN AFTER PHARAOH DIED...
I'VE BEEN HOPING THE NEW PHARAOH WOULD BE KINDER TO US, BUT TO ME, THINGS SEEM TO BE GETTING WORSE!
I'VE HEARD HE'S EVEN MORE CRUEL THAN THE LAST ONE, BUT I DON'T KNOW HOW THAT'S POSSIBLE!
STOP TALKING OVER THERE!
SLAK
GET TO WORK!
MOVE THAT STRAW!
LORD... WHEN WILL YOU COME TO OUR RESCUE?!
HAVE YOU FORGOTTEN YOUR PROMISES TO OUR FATHERS: ABRAHAM, ISAAC, AND JACOB?

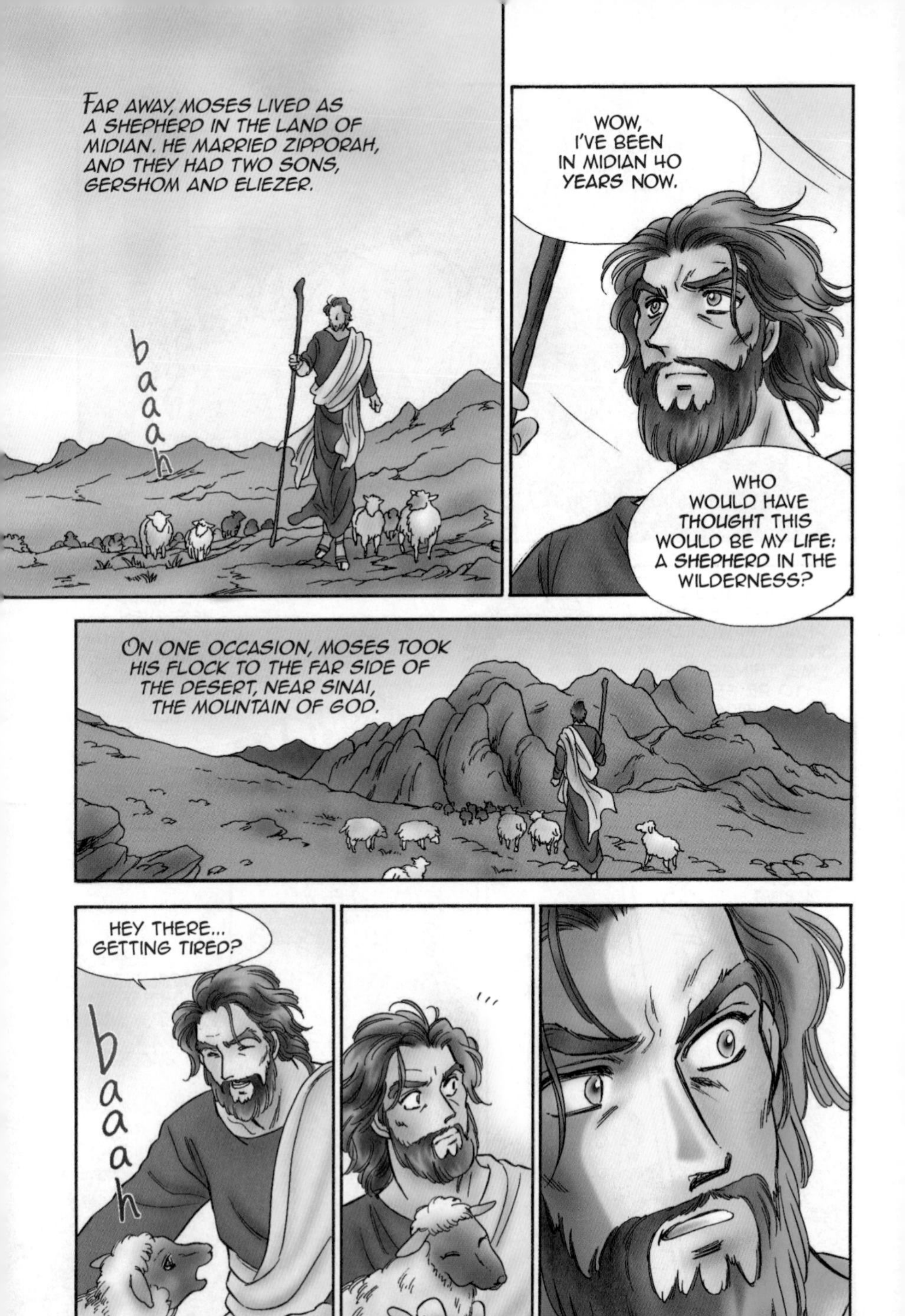
FAR AWAY, MOSES LIVED AS A SHEPHERD IN THE LAND OF MIDIAN. HE MARRIED ZIPPORAH, AND THEY HAD TWO SONS, GERSHOM AND ELIEZER.
baaah
WOW, I'VE BEEN IN MIDIAN 40 YEARS NOW.
WHO WOULD HAVE THOUGHT THIS WOULD BE MY LIFE: A SHEPHERD IN THE WILDERNESS?
ON ONE OCCASION, MOSES TOOK HIS FLOCK TO THE FAR SIDE OF THE DESERT, NEAR SINAI, THE MOUNTAIN OF GOD.
HEY THERE... GETTING TIRED?
baaah

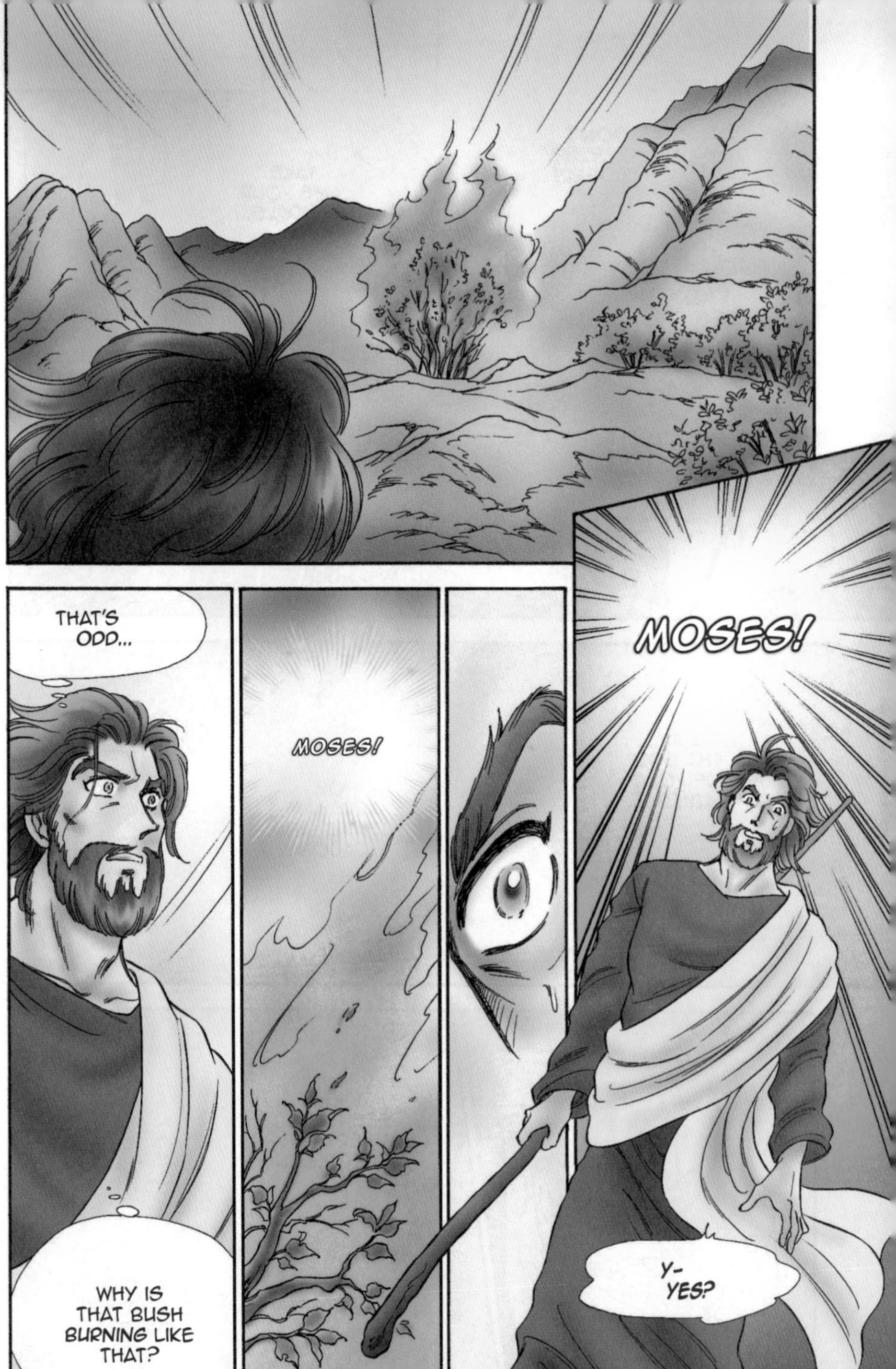
THAT'S ODD...
WHY IS THAT BUSH BURNING LIKE THAT?
MOSES!
MOSES!
Y- YES?

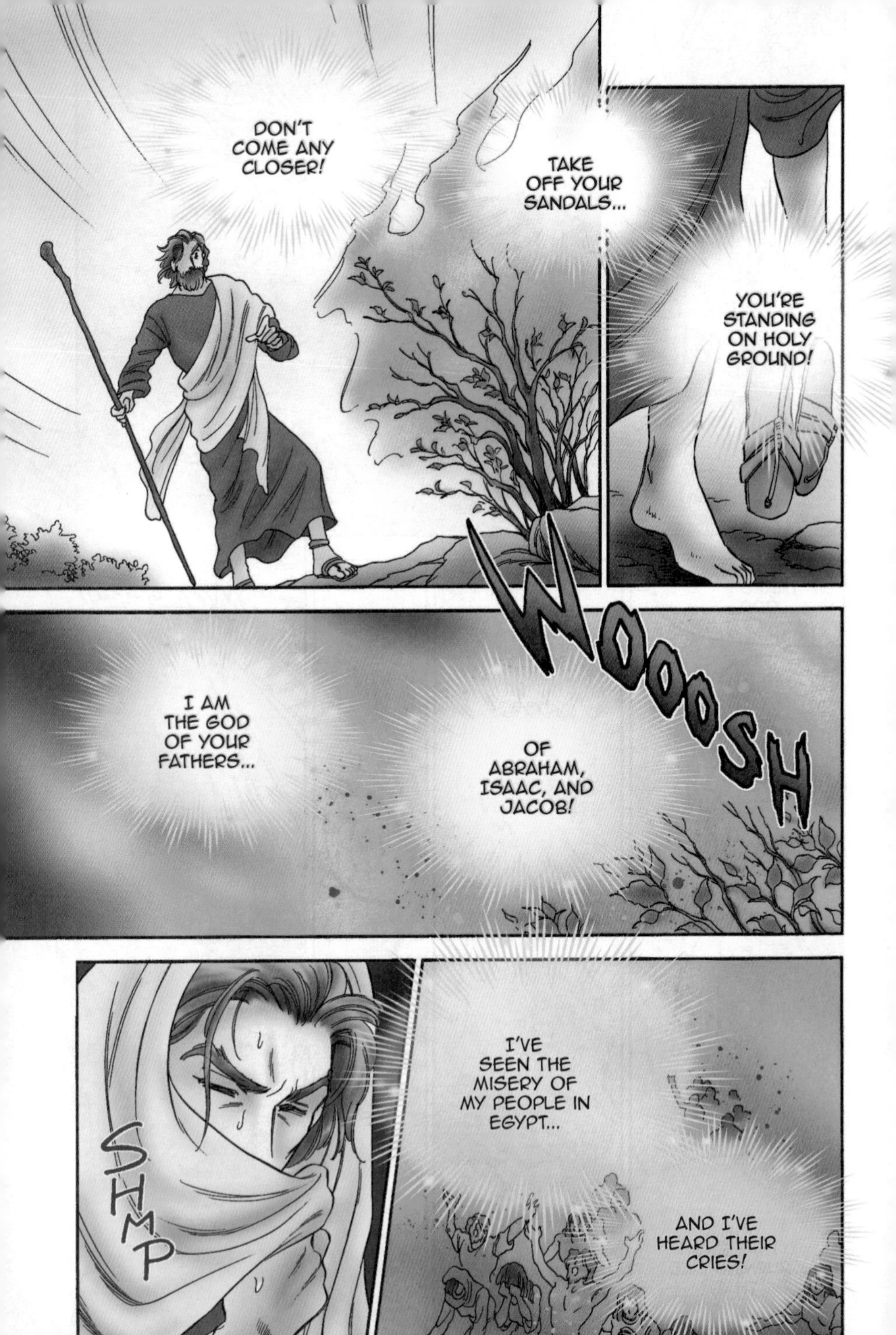
DON'T COME ANY CLOSER!
TAKE OFF YOUR SANDALS...
YOU'RE STANDING ON HOLY GROUND!
WOOOSH
I AM THE GOD OF YOUR FATHERS...
OF ABRAHAM, ISAAC, AND JACOB!
SHMP
I'VE SEEN THE MISERY OF MY PEOPLE IN EGYPT...
AND I'VE HEARD THEIR CRIES!

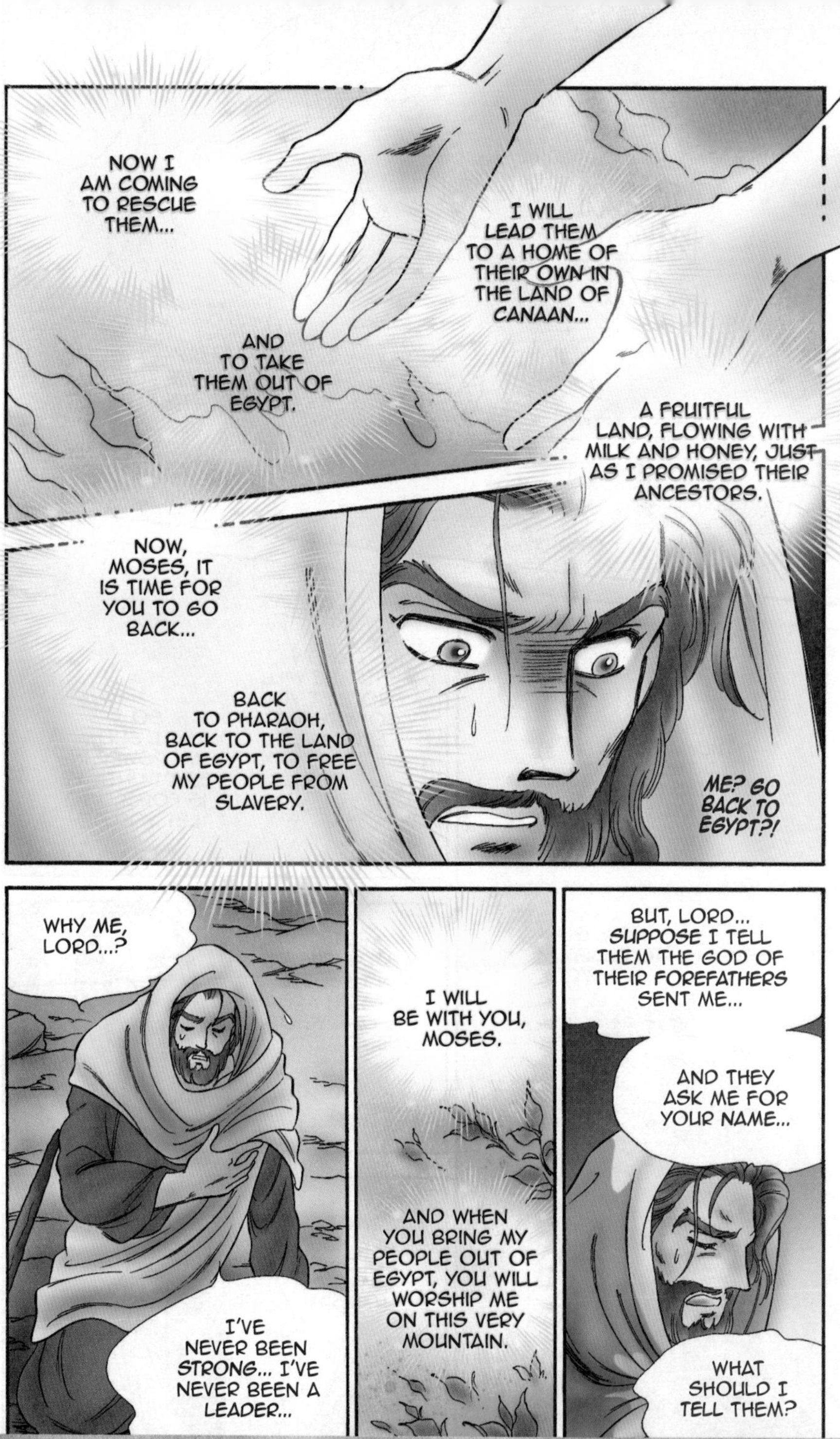
NOW I AM COMING TO RESCUE THEM...
AND TO TAKE THEM OUT OF EGYPT.
I WILL LEAD THEM TO A HOME OF THEIR OWN IN THE LAND OF CANAAN...
A FRUITFUL LAND, FLOWING WITH MILK AND HONEY, JUST AS I PROMISED THEIR ANCESTORS.
NOW, MOSES, IT IS TIME FOR YOU TO GO BACK...
BACK TO PHARAOH, BACK TO THE LAND OF EGYPT, TO FREE MY PEOPLE FROM SLAVERY.
ME? GO BACK TO EGYPT?!
WHY ME, LORD...?
I'VE NEVER BEEN STRONG... I'VE NEVER BEEN A LEADER...
I WILL BE WITH YOU, MOSES.
AND WHEN YOU BRING MY PEOPLE OUT OF EGYPT, YOU WILL WORSHIP ME ON THIS VERY MOUNTAIN.
BUT, LORD... SUPPOSE I TELL THEM THE GOD OF THEIR FOREFATHERS SENT ME...
AND THEY ASK ME FOR YOUR NAME...
WHAT SHOULD I TELL THEM?

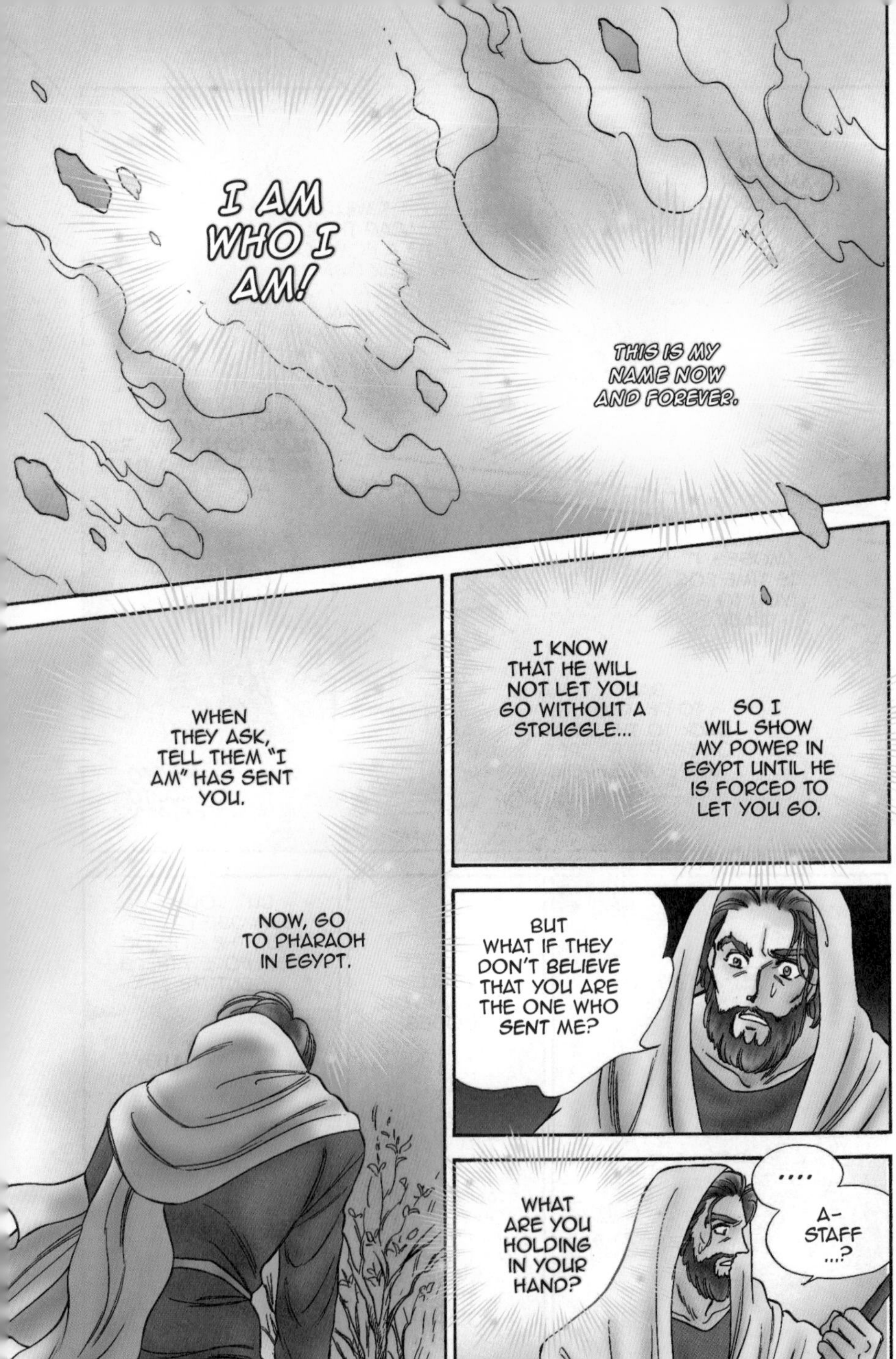
I AM WHO I AM!
THIS IS MY NAME NOW AND FOREVER.
WHEN THEY ASK, TELL THEM "I AM" HAS SENT YOU.
I KNOW THAT HE WILL NOT LET YOU GO WITHOUT A STRUGGLE...
SO I WILL SHOW MY POWER IN EGYPT UNTIL HE IS FORCED TO LET YOU GO.
NOW, GO TO PHARAOH IN EGYPT.
BUT WHAT IF THEY DON'T BELIEVE THAT YOU ARE THE ONE WHO SENT ME?
WHAT ARE YOU HOLDING IN YOUR HAND?
....
A- STAFF ...?

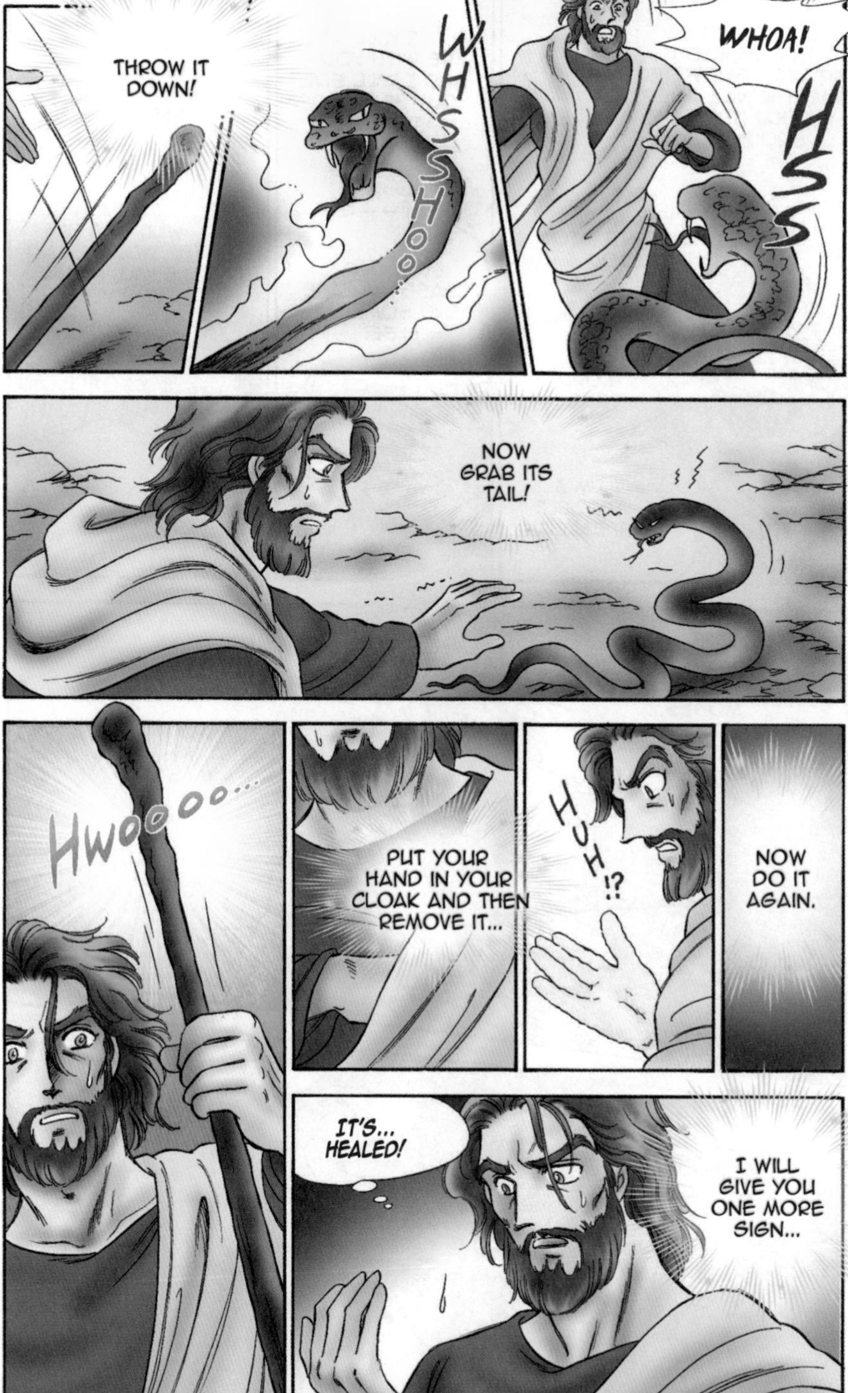
THROW IT DOWN!
WHSSHOO...
WHOA!
HSS
NOW GRAB ITS TAIL!
HWOOOO...
PUT YOUR HAND IN YOUR CLOAK AND THEN REMOVE IT...
HUH!?
NOW DO IT AGAIN.
IT'S... HEALED!
I WILL GIVE YOU ONE MORE SIGN...

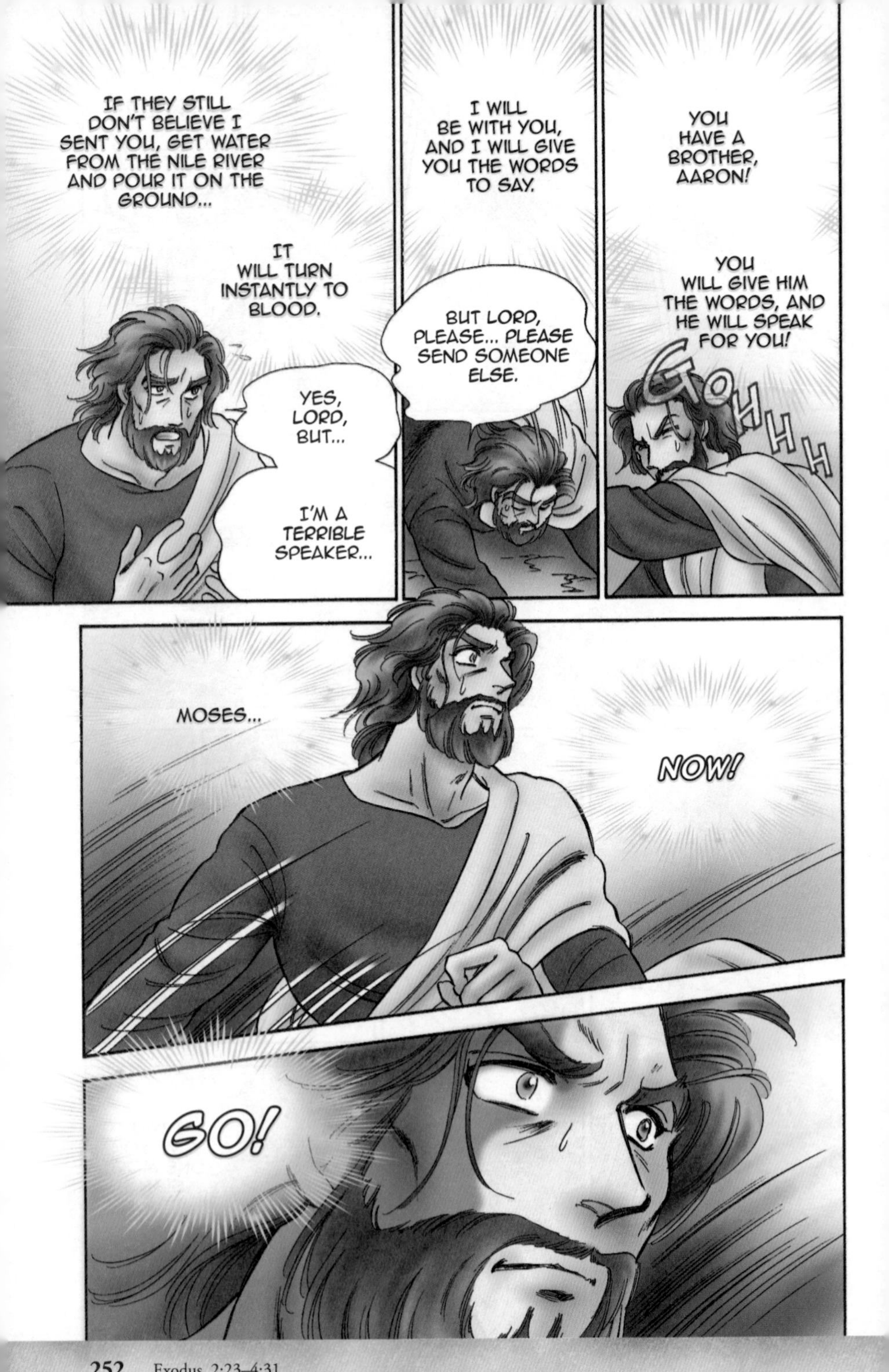
IF THEY STILL DON'T BELIEVE I SENT YOU, GET WATER FROM THE NILE RIVER AND POUR IT ON THE GROUND...
IT WILL TURN INSTANTLY TO BLOOD.
YES, LORD, BUT...
I'M A TERRIBLE SPEAKER...
I WILL BE WITH YOU, AND I WILL GIVE YOU THE WORDS TO SAY.
BUT LORD, PLEASE... PLEASE SEND SOMEONE ELSE.
YOU HAVE A BROTHER, AARON!
YOU WILL GIVE HIM THE WORDS, AND HE WILL SPEAK FOR YOU!
GOHHH
MOSES...
NOW!
GO!

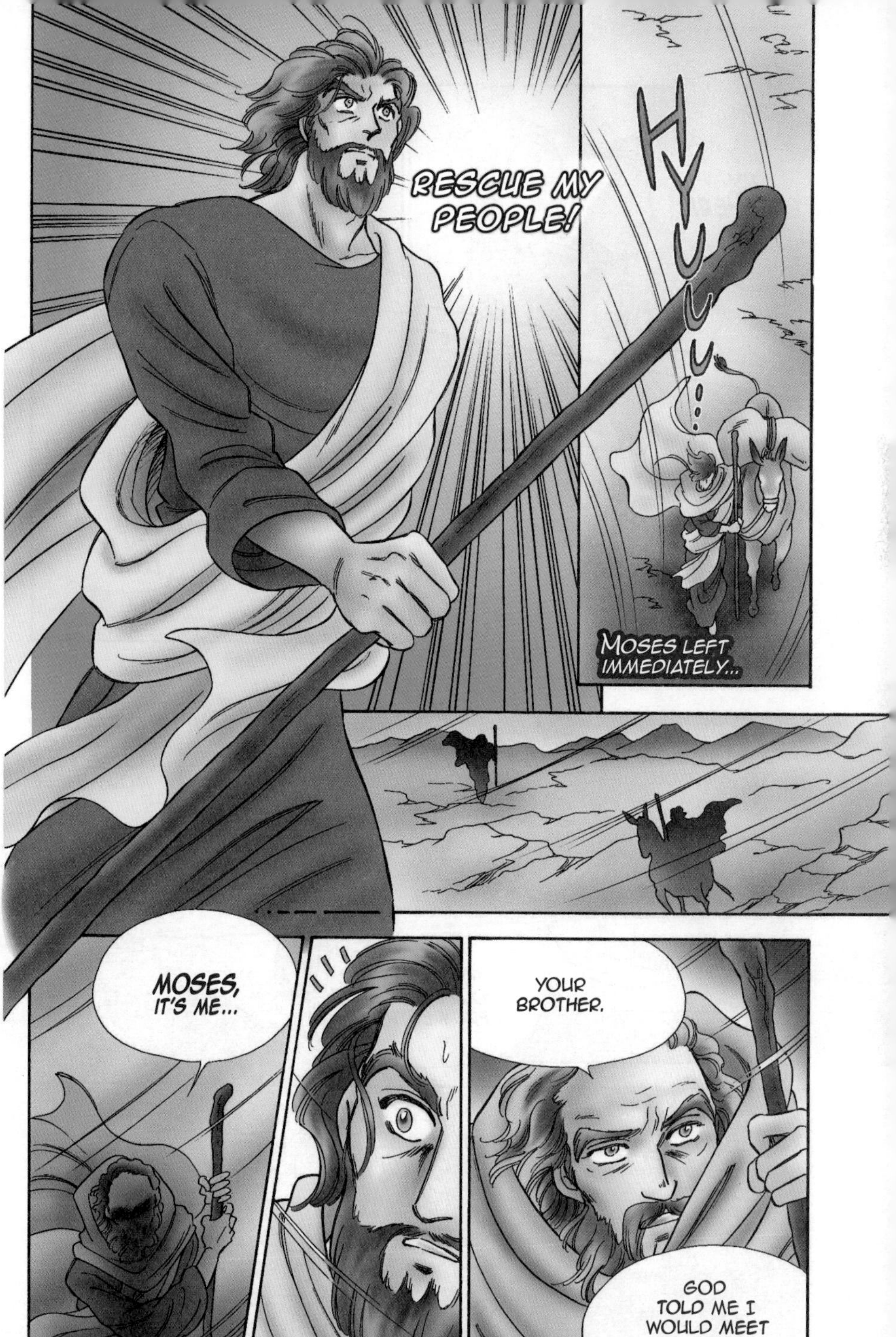
RESCUE MY PEOPLE!
HYUUUU...
MOSES LEFT IMMEDIATELY...
MOSES, IT'S ME...
YOUR BROTHER.
GOD TOLD ME I WOULD MEET YOU HERE.

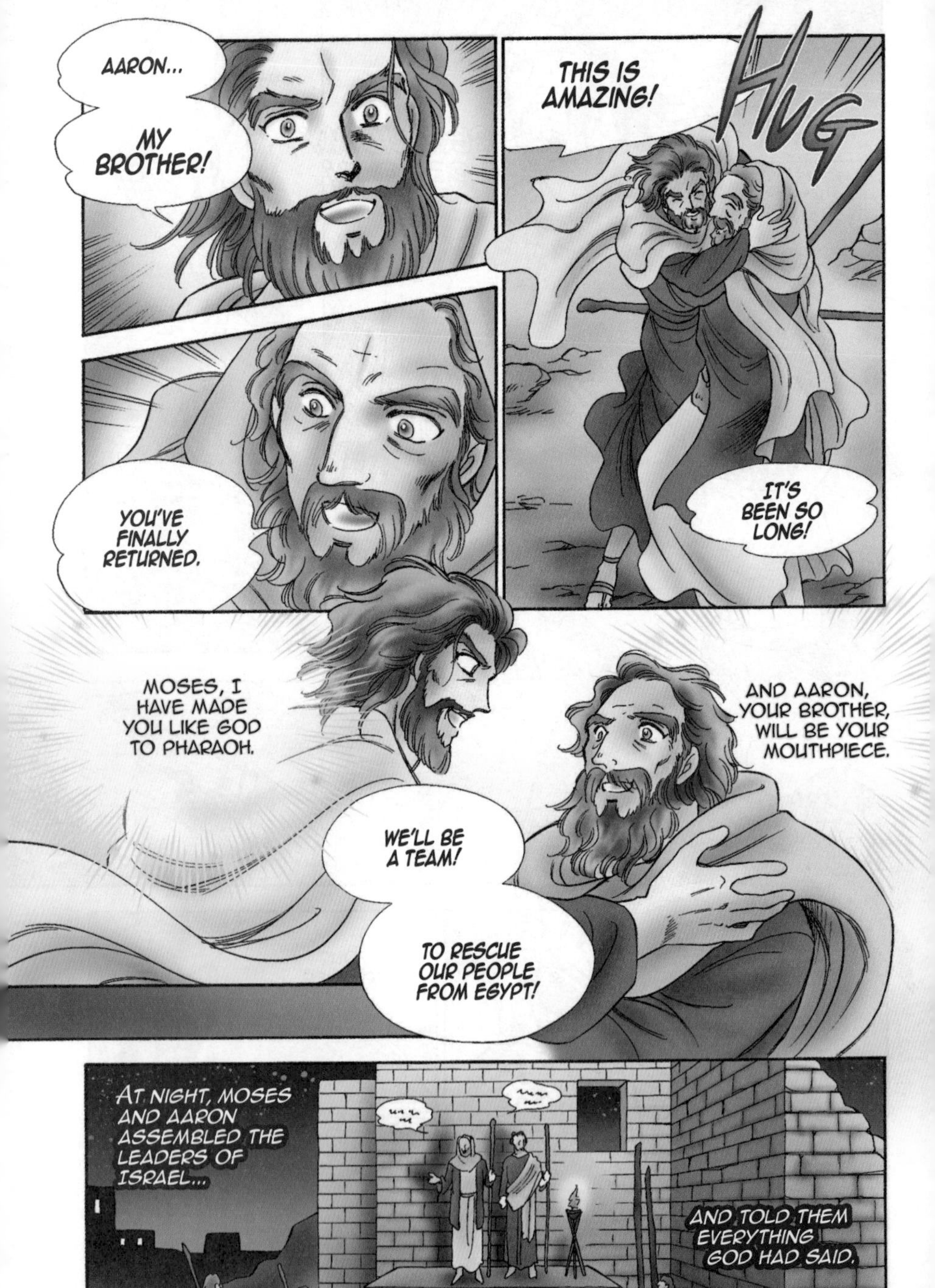
AARON...
MY BROTHER!
THIS IS AMAZING!
HUG
YOU'VE FINALLY RETURNED.
IT'S BEEN SO LONG!
MOSES, I HAVE MADE YOU LIKE GOD TO PHARAOH.
AND AARON, YOUR BROTHER, WILL BE YOUR MOUTHPIECE.
WE'LL BE A TEAM!
TO RESCUE OUR PEOPLE FROM EGYPT!
AT NIGHT, MOSES AND AARON ASSEMBLED THE LEADERS OF ISRAEL...
AND TOLD THEM EVERYTHING GOD HAD SAID.

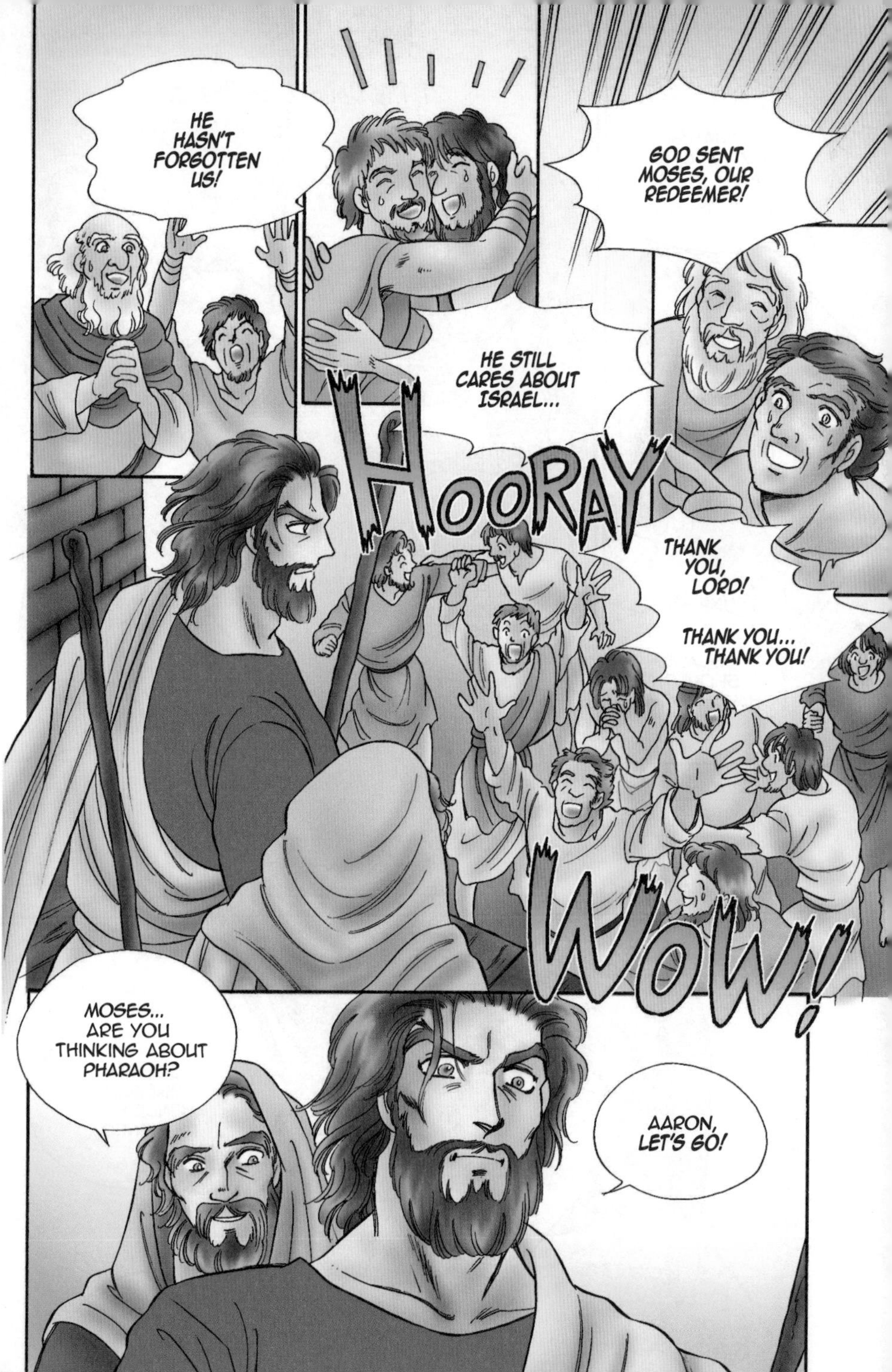
HE HASN'T FORGOTTEN US!
GOD SENT MOSES, OUR REDEEMER!
HE STILL CARES ABOUT ISRAEL...
HOORAY
THANK YOU, LORD!
THANK YOU... THANK YOU!
WOW!
MOSES... ARE YOU THINKING ABOUT PHARAOH?
AARON, LET'S GO!

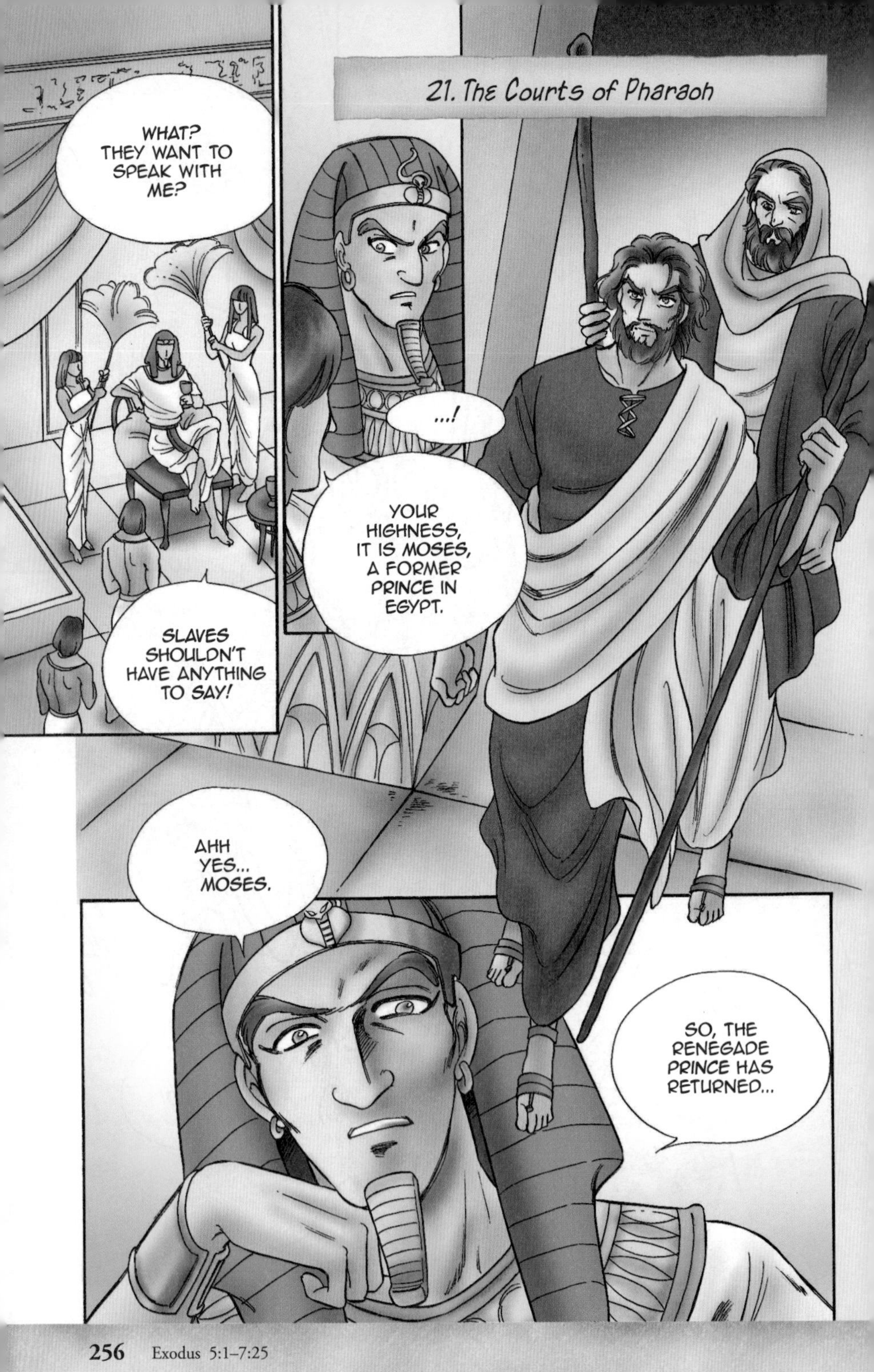
21. The Courts of Pharaoh
WHAT? THEY WANT TO SPEAK WITH ME?
SLAVES SHOULDN'T HAVE ANYTHING TO SAY!
...!
YOUR HIGHNESS, IT IS MOSES, A FORMER PRINCE IN EGYPT.
AHH YES... MOSES.
SO, THE RENEGADE PRINCE HAS RETURNED...

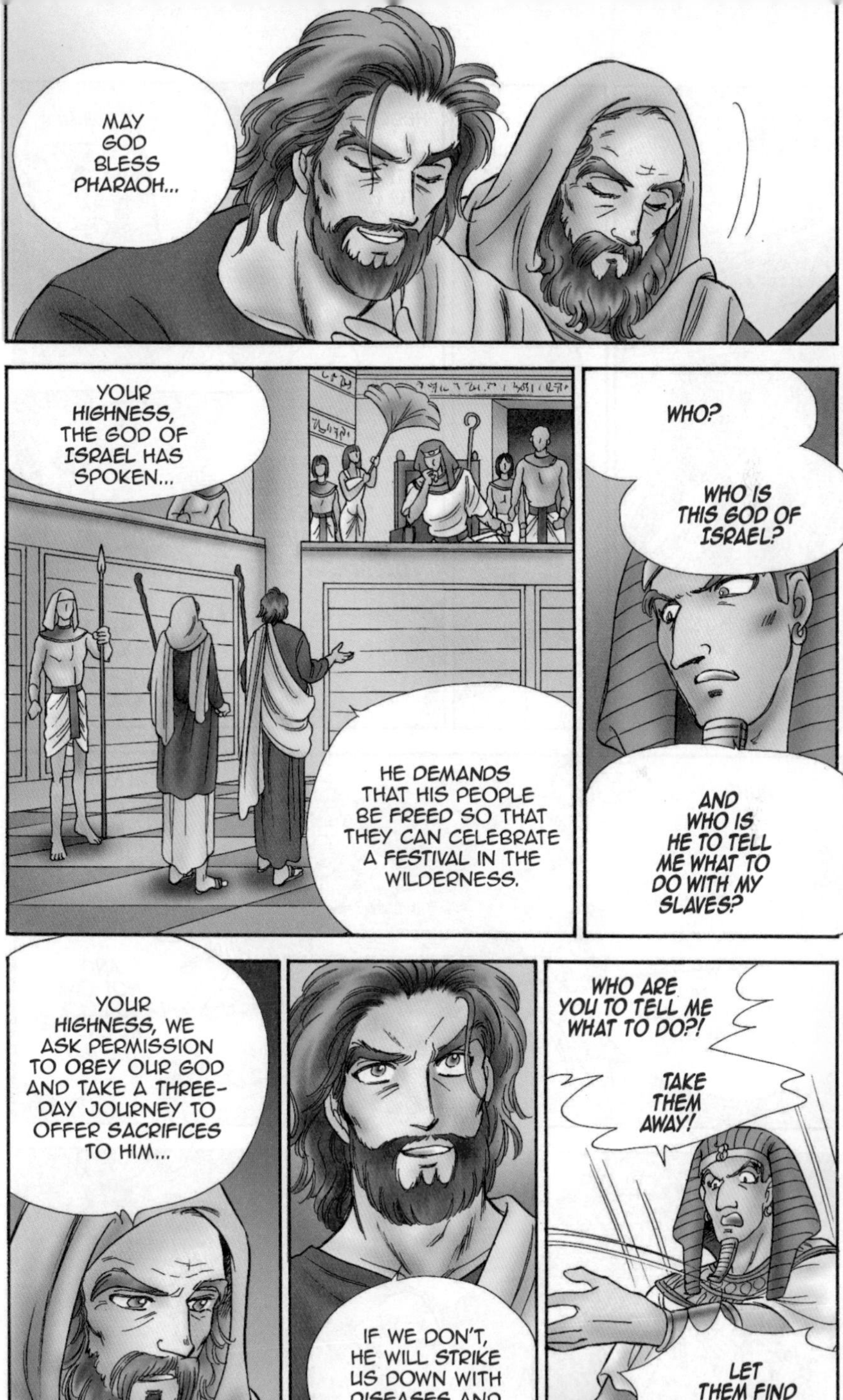
MAY GOD BLESS PHARAOH...
YOUR HIGHNESS, THE GOD OF ISRAEL HAS SPOKEN...
HE DEMANDS THAT HIS PEOPLE BE FREED SO THAT THEY CAN CELEBRATE A FESTIVAL IN THE WILDERNESS.
WHO?
WHO IS THIS GOD OF ISRAEL?
AND WHO IS HE TO TELL ME WHAT TO DO WITH MY SLAVES?
YOUR HIGHNESS, WE ASK PERMISSION TO OBEY OUR GOD AND TAKE A THREE-DAY JOURNEY TO OFFER SACRIFICES TO HIM...
IF WE DON'T, HE WILL STRIKE US DOWN WITH DISEASES AND DEATH!
WHO ARE YOU TO TELL ME WHAT TO DO?!
TAKE THEM AWAY!
LET THEM FIND SOME WORK TO DO!

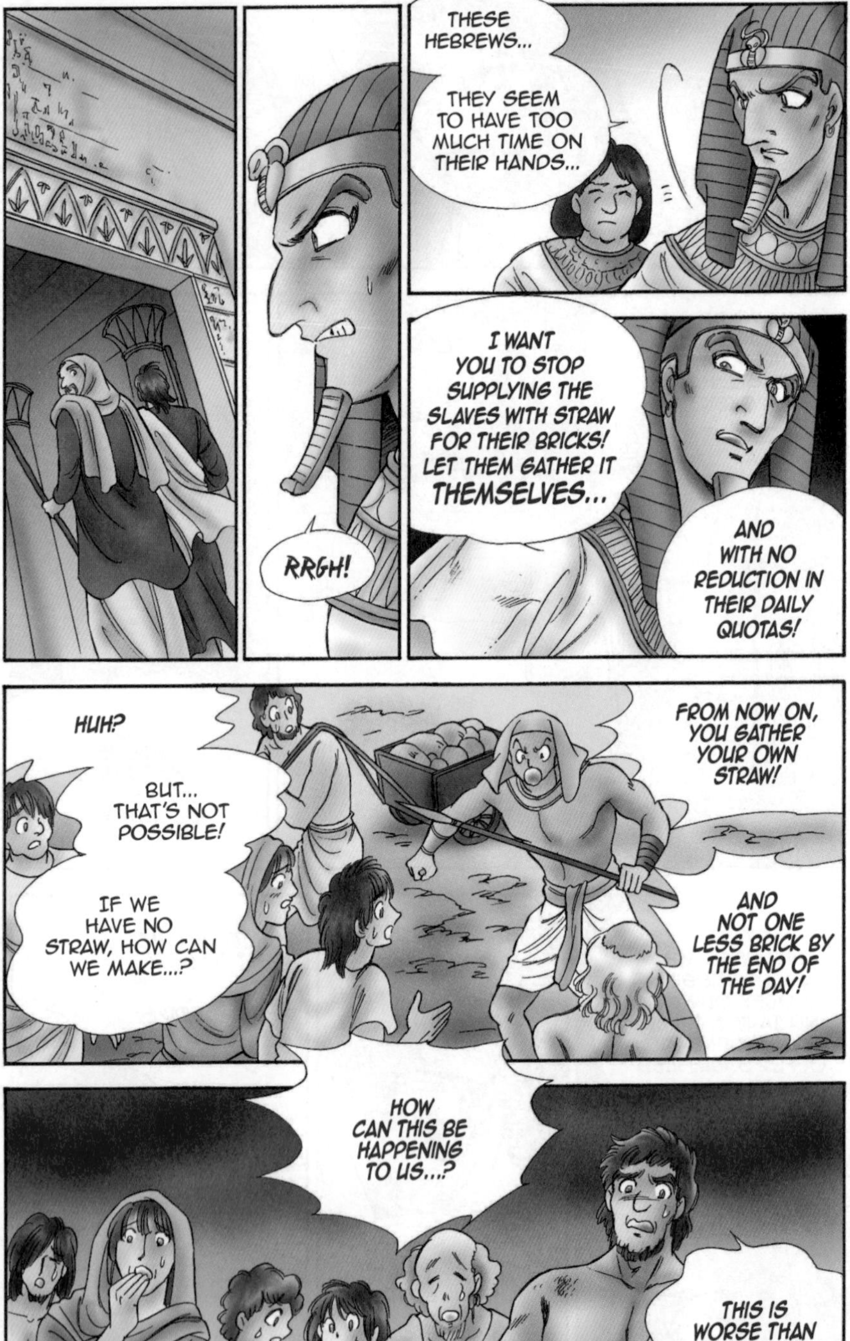

THESE HEBREWS...
THEY SEEM TO HAVE TOO MUCH TIME ON THEIR HANDS...
RRGH!
I WANT YOU TO STOP SUPPLYING THE SLAVES WITH STRAW FOR THEIR BRICKS! LET THEM GATHER IT THEMSELVES...
AND WITH NO REDUCTION IN THEIR DAILY QUOTAS!
FROM NOW ON, YOU GATHER YOUR OWN STRAW!
HUH?
BUT... THAT'S NOT POSSIBLE!
IF WE HAVE NO STRAW, HOW CAN WE MAKE...?
AND NOT ONE LESS BRICK BY THE END OF THE DAY!
HOW CAN THIS BE HAPPENING TO US...?
THIS IS WORSE THAN BEFORE!

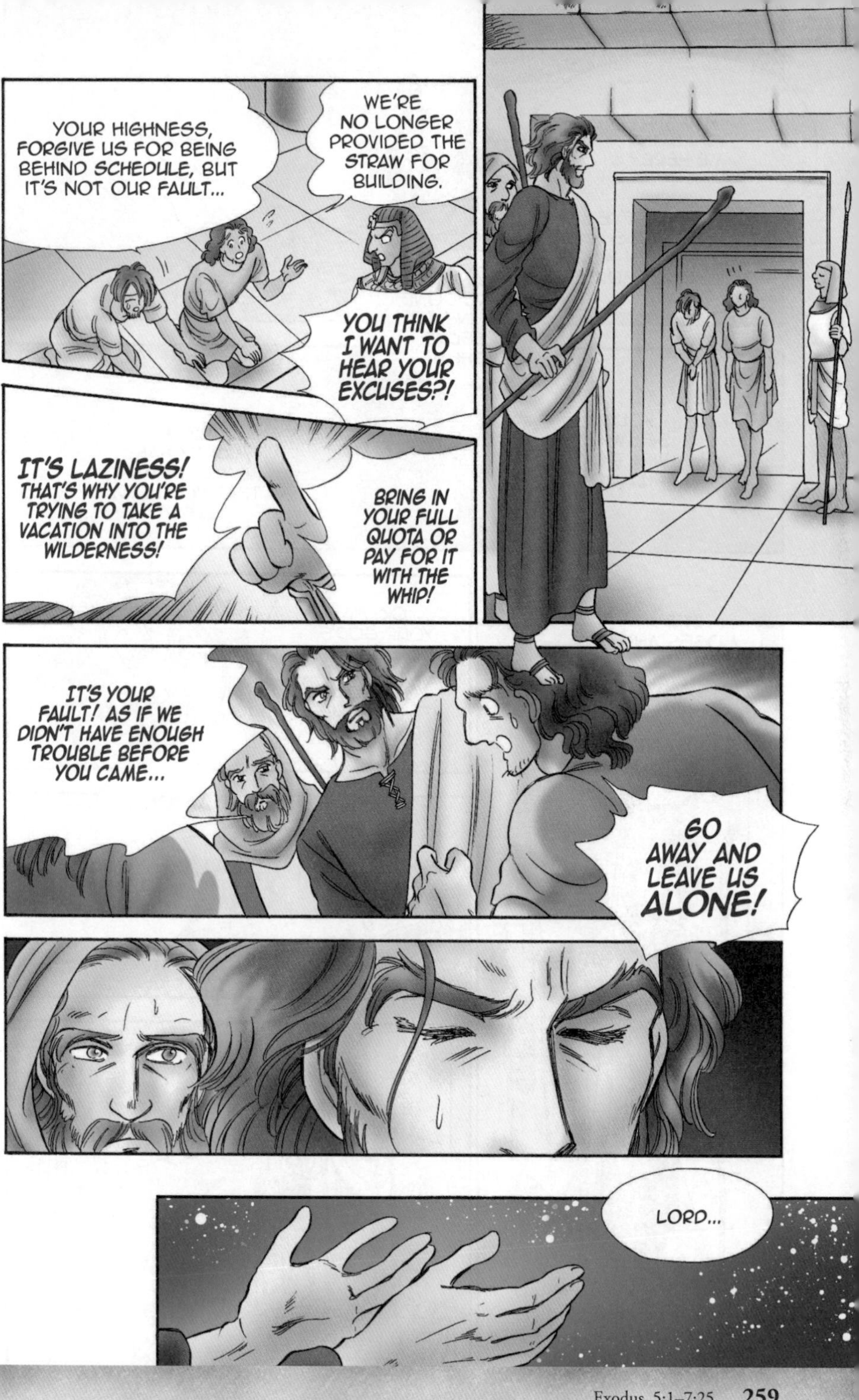
YOUR HIGHNESS, FORGIVE US FOR BEING BEHIND SCHEDULE, BUT IT'S NOT OUR FAULT...
WE'RE NO LONGER PROVIDED THE STRAW FOR BUILDING.
YOU THINK I WANT TO HEAR YOUR EXCUSES?!
IT'S LAZINESS! THAT'S WHY YOU'RE TRYING TO TAKE A VACATION INTO THE WILDERNESS!
BRING IN YOUR FULL QUOTA OR PAY FOR IT WITH THE WHIP!
IT'S YOUR FAULT! AS IF WE DIDN'T HAVE ENOUGH TROUBLE BEFORE YOU CAME...
GO AWAY AND LEAVE US ALONE!
LORD...

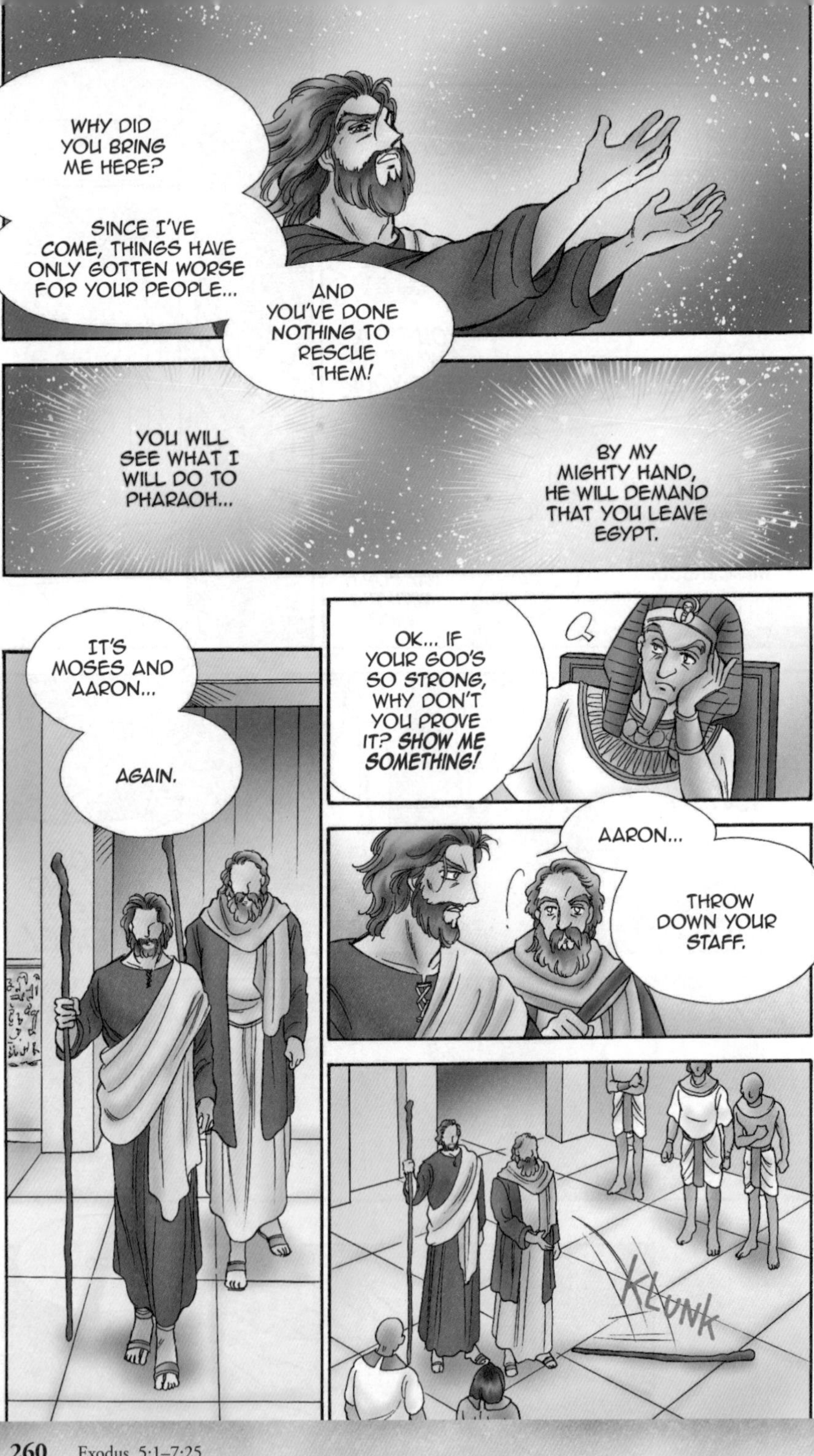
WHY DID YOU BRING ME HERE?
SINCE I'VE COME, THINGS HAVE ONLY GOTTEN WORSE FOR YOUR PEOPLE...
AND YOU'VE DONE NOTHING TO RESCUE THEM!
YOU WILL SEE WHAT I WILL DO TO PHARAOH...
BY MY MIGHTY HAND, HE WILL DEMAND THAT YOU LEAVE EGYPT.
IT'S MOSES AND AARON...
AGAIN.
OK... IF YOUR GOD'S SO STRONG, WHY DON'T YOU PROVE IT? SHOW ME SOMETHING!
AARON...
THROW DOWN YOUR STAFF.
KLUNK

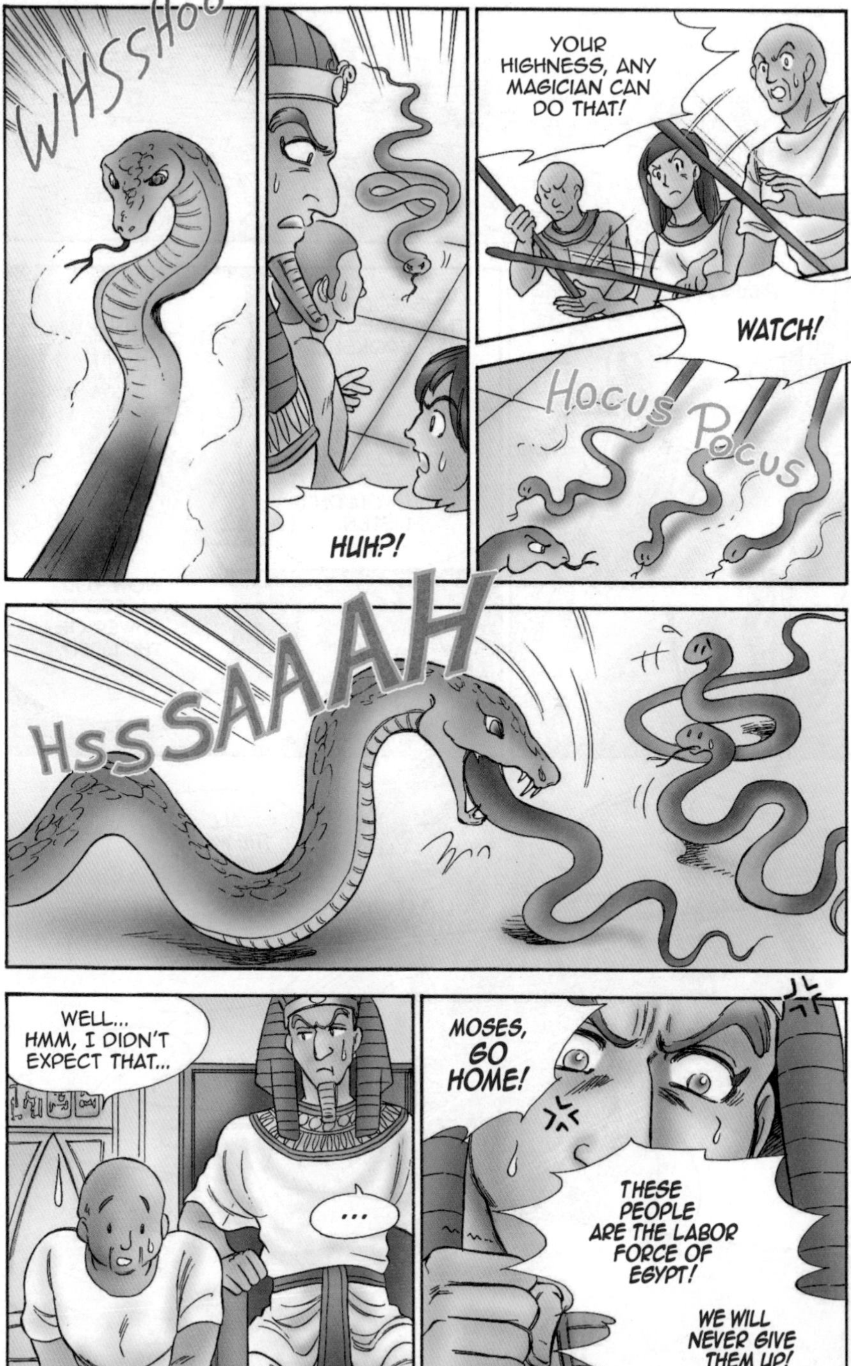
WHSSHOO
HUH?!
YOUR HIGHNESS, ANY MAGICIAN CAN DO THAT!
WATCH!
HOCUS POCUS
HSSSAAAH
WELL... HMM, I DIDN'T EXPECT THAT...
...
MOSES, GO HOME!
THESE PEOPLE ARE THE LABOR FORCE OF EGYPT!
WE WILL NEVER GIVE THEM UP!

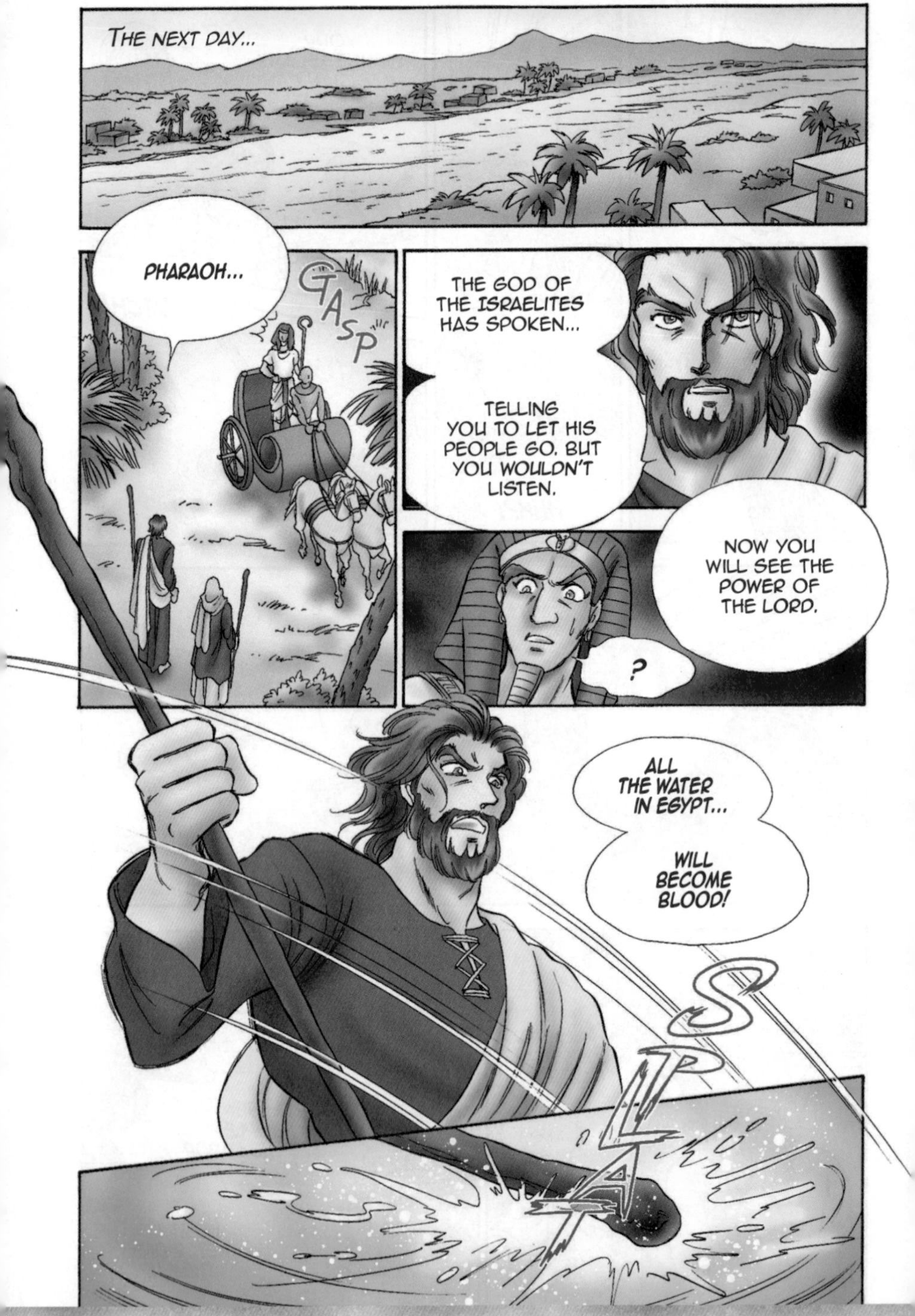
THE NEXT DAY...
PHARAOH...
GASP
THE GOD OF THE ISRAELITES HAS SPOKEN...
TELLING YOU TO LET HIS PEOPLE GO. BUT YOU WOULDN'T LISTEN.
NOW YOU WILL SEE THE POWER OF THE LORD.
?
ALL THE WATER IN EGYPT...
WILL BECOME BLOOD!
SPLAT

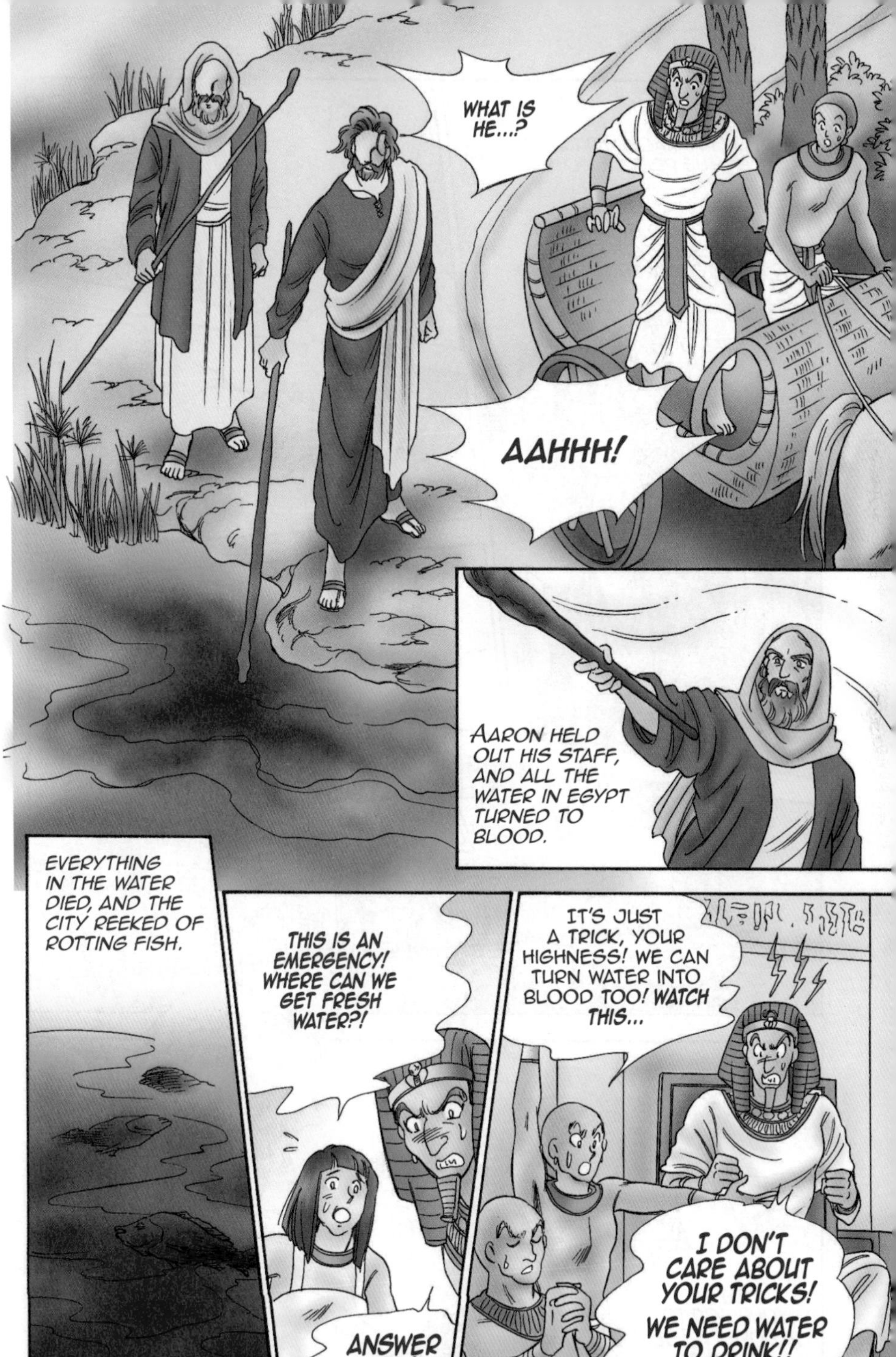

WHAT IS HE...?
AAHHH!
AARON HELD OUT HIS STAFF, AND ALL THE WATER IN EGYPT TURNED TO BLOOD.
EVERYTHING IN THE WATER DIED, AND THE CITY REEKED OF ROTTING FISH.
THIS IS AN EMERGENCY! WHERE CAN WE GET FRESH WATER?!
ANSWER ME!
IT'S JUST A TRICK, YOUR HIGHNESS! WE CAN TURN WATER INTO BLOOD TOO! WATCH THIS...
I DON'T CARE ABOUT YOUR TRICKS!
WE NEED WATER TO DRINK!!

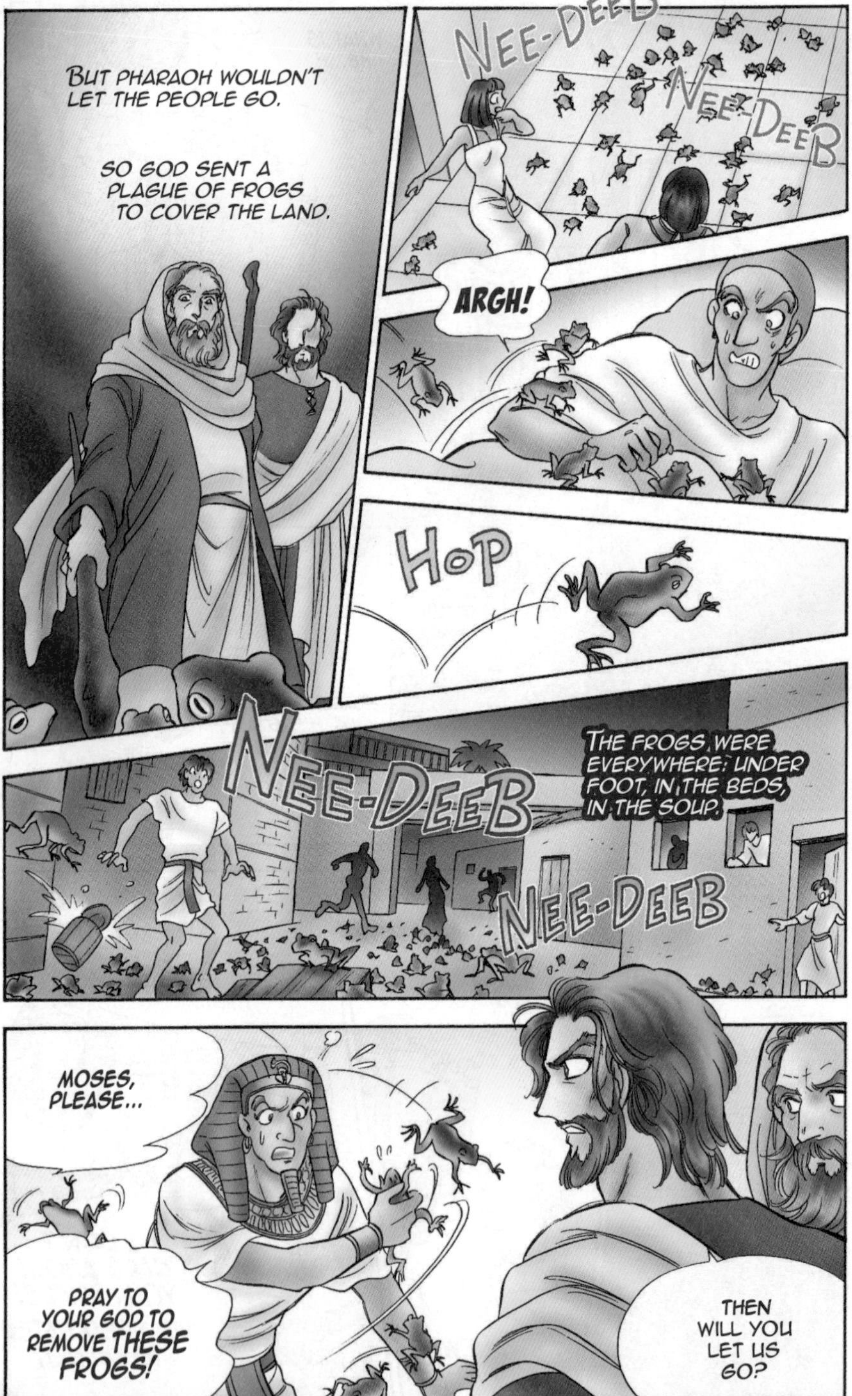
BUT PHARAOH WOULDN'T LET THE PEOPLE GO.
SO GOD SENT A PLAGUE OF FROGS TO COVER THE LAND.
NEE-DEEB
NEE-DEEB
ARGH!
HOP
NEE-DEEB
THE FROGS WERE EVERYWHERE: UNDER FOOT, IN THE BEDS, IN THE SOUP.
NEE-DEEB
MOSES, PLEASE...
PRAY TO YOUR GOD TO REMOVE THESE FROGS!
THEN WILL YOU LET US GO?

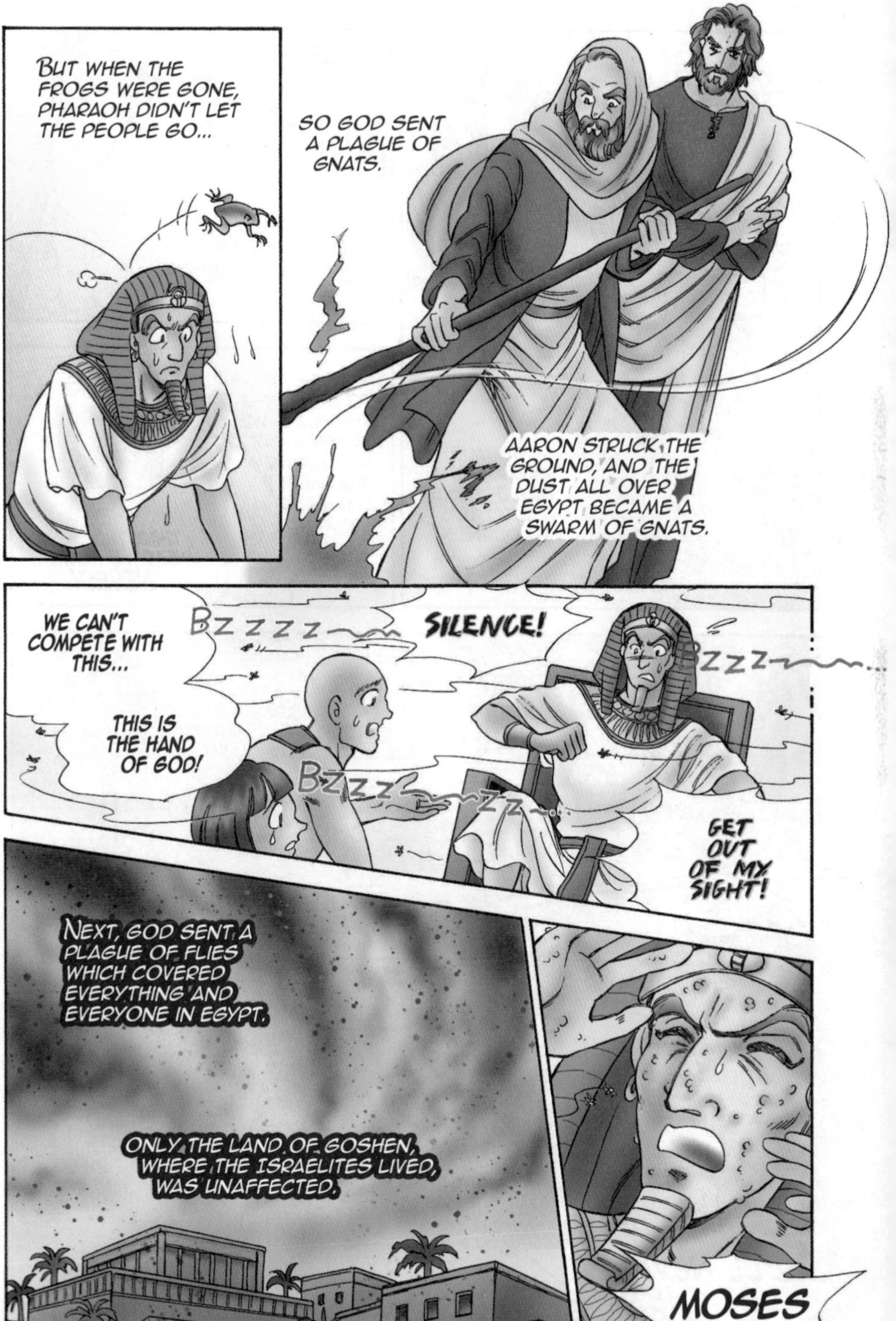
BUT WHEN THE FROGS WERE GONE, PHARAOH DIDN'T LET THE PEOPLE GO...
SO GOD SENT A PLAGUE OF GNATS.
AARON STRUCK THE GROUND, AND THE DUST ALL OVER EGYPT BECAME A SWARM OF GNATS.
WE CAN'T COMPETE WITH THIS...
BZZZZ
SILENCE!
BZZZ
THIS IS THE HAND OF GOD!
BZZZ ZZ
GET OUT OF MY SIGHT!
NEXT, GOD SENT A PLAGUE OF FLIES WHICH COVERED EVERYTHING AND EVERYONE IN EGYPT.
ONLY THE LAND OF GOSHEN, WHERE THE ISRAELITES LIVED, WAS UNAFFECTED.
MOSES !!

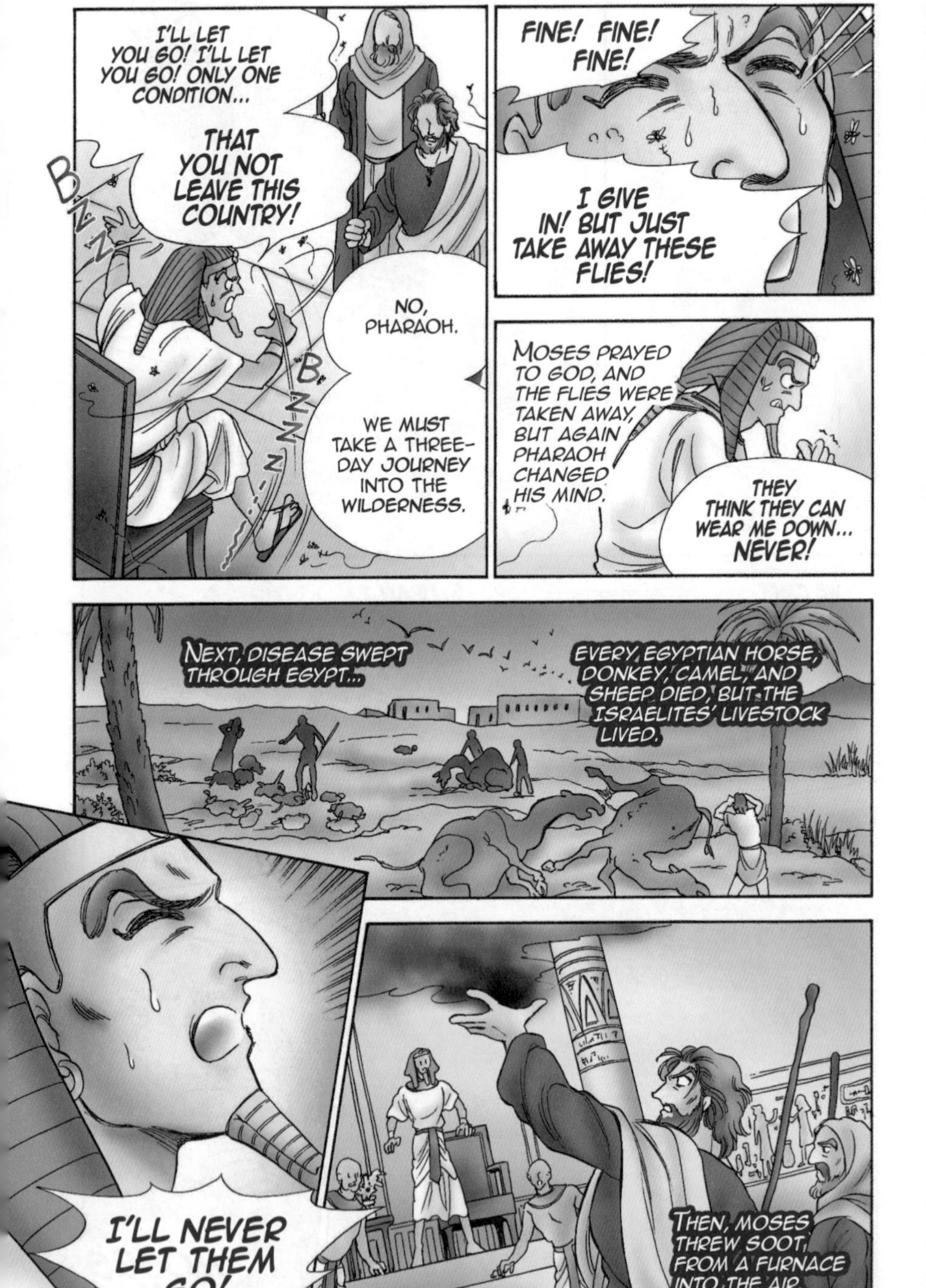
I'LL LET YOU GO! I'LL LET YOU GO! ONLY ONE CONDITION...
THAT YOU NOT LEAVE THIS COUNTRY!
BZZZ
NO, PHARAOH.
WE MUST TAKE A THREE-DAY JOURNEY INTO THE WILDERNESS.
BZZZ
FINE! FINE! FINE!
I GIVE IN! BUT JUST TAKE AWAY THESE FLIES!
MOSES PRAYED TO GOD, AND THE FLIES WERE TAKEN AWAY, BUT AGAIN PHARAOH CHANGED HIS MIND.
THEY THINK THEY CAN WEAR ME DOWN... NEVER!
NEXT, DISEASE SWEPT THROUGH EGYPT...
EVERY EGYPTIAN HORSE, DONKEY, CAMEL, AND SHEEP DIED, BUT THE ISRAELITES' LIVESTOCK LIVED.
I'LL NEVER LET THEM GO!
THEN, MOSES THREW SOOT FROM A FURNACE INTO THE AIR.

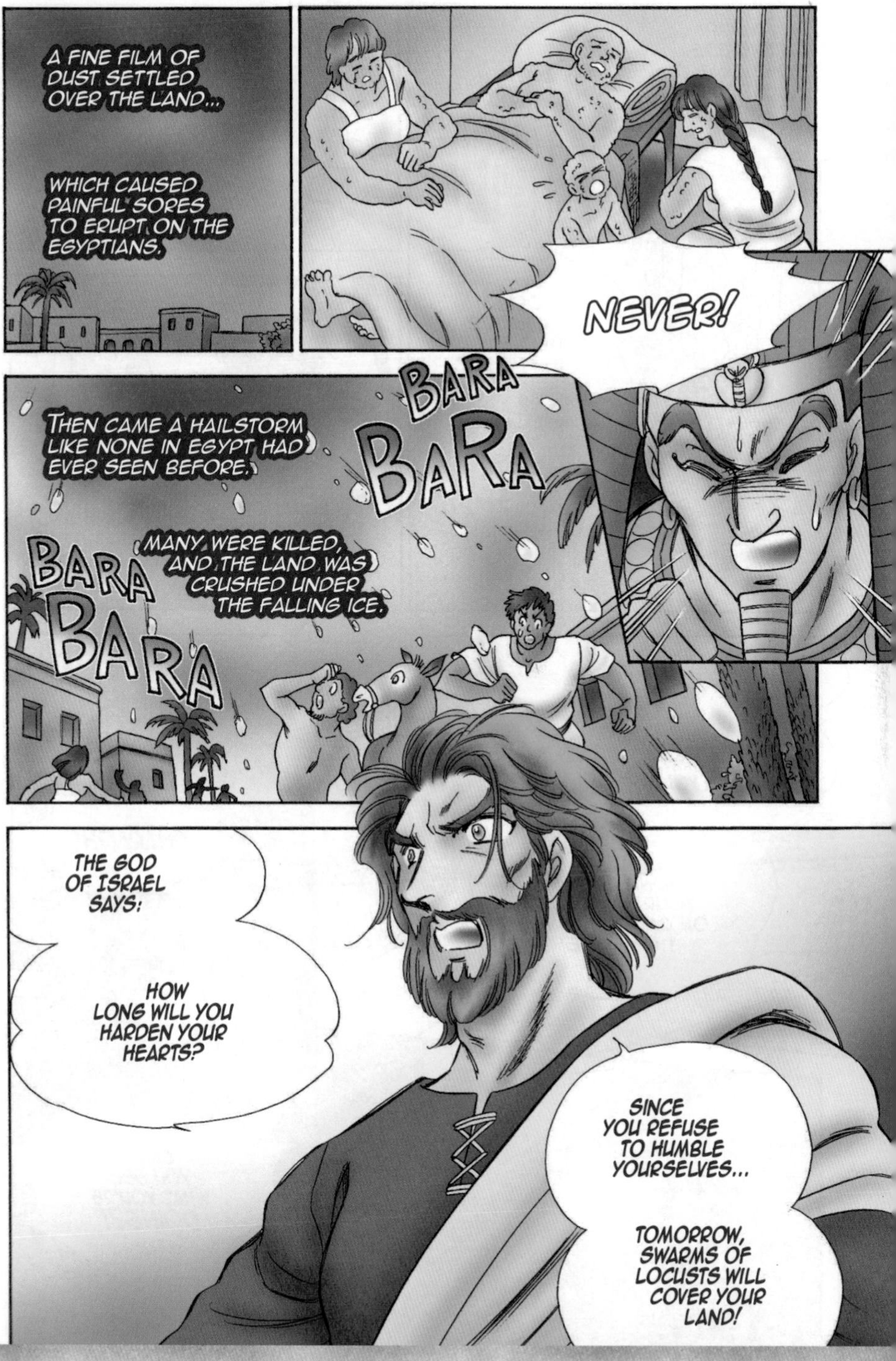

A FINE FILM OF DUST SETTLED OVER THE LAND...
WHICH CAUSED PAINFUL SORES TO ERUPT ON THE EGYPTIANS.
NEVER!
THEN CAME A HAILSTORM LIKE NONE IN EGYPT HAD EVER SEEN BEFORE.
BARA BARA
MANY WERE KILLED, AND THE LAND WAS CRUSHED UNDER THE FALLING ICE.
BARA BARA
THE GOD OF ISRAEL SAYS:
HOW LONG WILL YOU HARDEN YOUR HEARTS?
SINCE YOU REFUSE TO HUMBLE YOURSELVES...
TOMORROW, SWARMS OF LOCUSTS WILL COVER YOUR LAND!

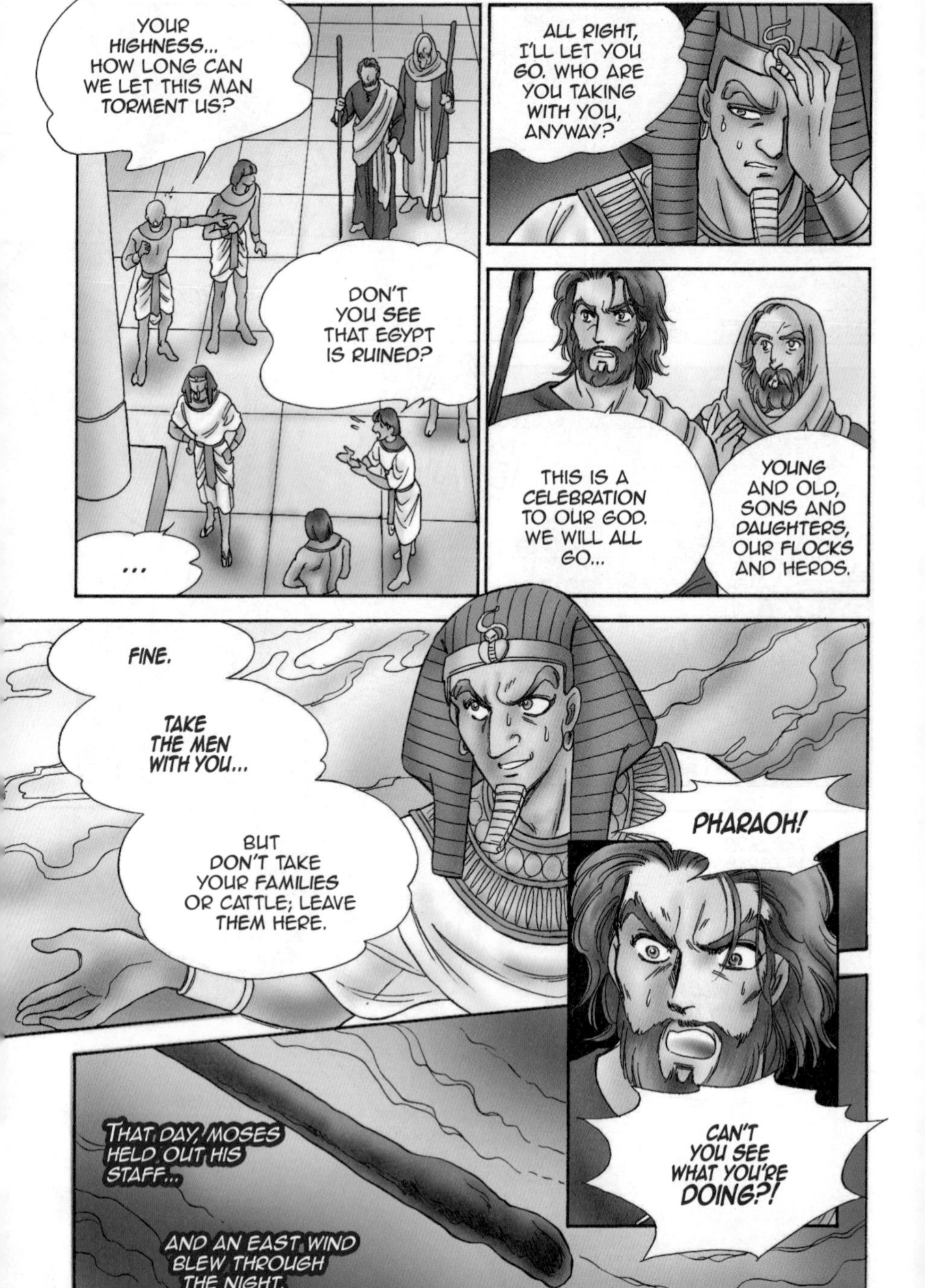
YOUR HIGHNESS... HOW LONG CAN WE LET THIS MAN TORMENT US?
DON'T YOU SEE THAT EGYPT IS RUINED?
...
ALL RIGHT, I'LL LET YOU GO. WHO ARE YOU TAKING WITH YOU, ANYWAY?
THIS IS A CELEBRATION TO OUR GOD. WE WILL ALL GO...
YOUNG AND OLD, SONS AND DAUGHTERS, OUR FLOCKS AND HERDS.
FINE.
TAKE THE MEN WITH YOU...
BUT DON'T TAKE YOUR FAMILIES OR CATTLE; LEAVE THEM HERE.
PHARAOH!
CAN'T YOU SEE WHAT YOU'RE DOING?!
THAT DAY, MOSES HELD OUT HIS STAFF...
AND AN EAST WIND BLEW THROUGH THE NIGHT.

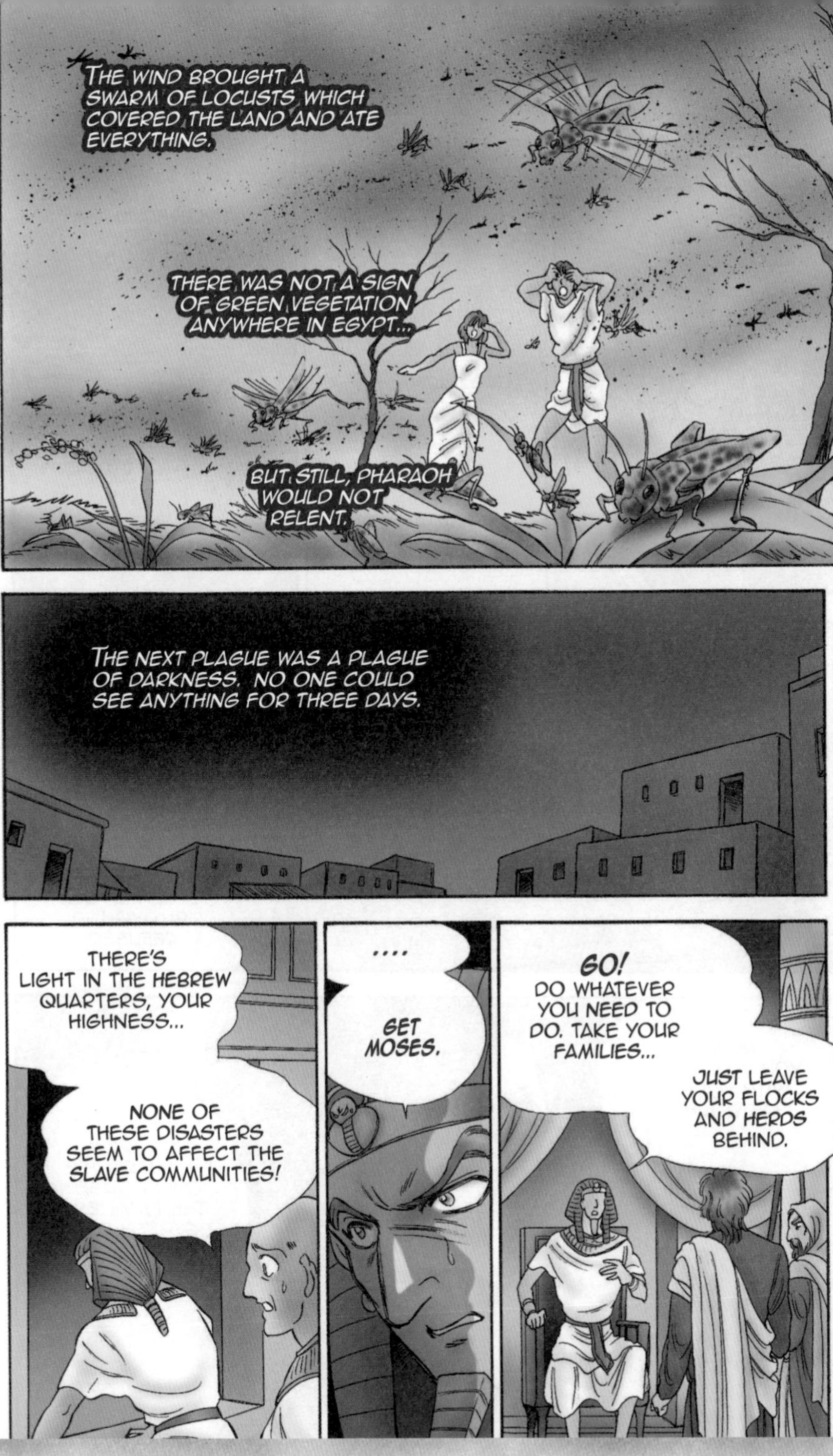
THE WIND BROUGHT A SWARM OF LOCUSTS WHICH COVERED THE LAND AND ATE EVERYTHING.
THERE WAS NOT A SIGN OF GREEN VEGETATION ANYWHERE IN EGYPT...
BUT STILL, PHARAOH WOULD NOT RELENT.
THE NEXT PLAGUE WAS A PLAGUE OF DARKNESS. NO ONE COULD SEE ANYTHING FOR THREE DAYS.
THERE'S LIGHT IN THE HEBREW QUARTERS, YOUR HIGHNESS...
NONE OF THESE DISASTERS SEEM TO AFFECT THE SLAVE COMMUNITIES!
....
GET MOSES.
GO! DO WHATEVER YOU NEED TO DO. TAKE YOUR FAMILIES...
JUST LEAVE YOUR FLOCKS AND HERDS BEHIND.

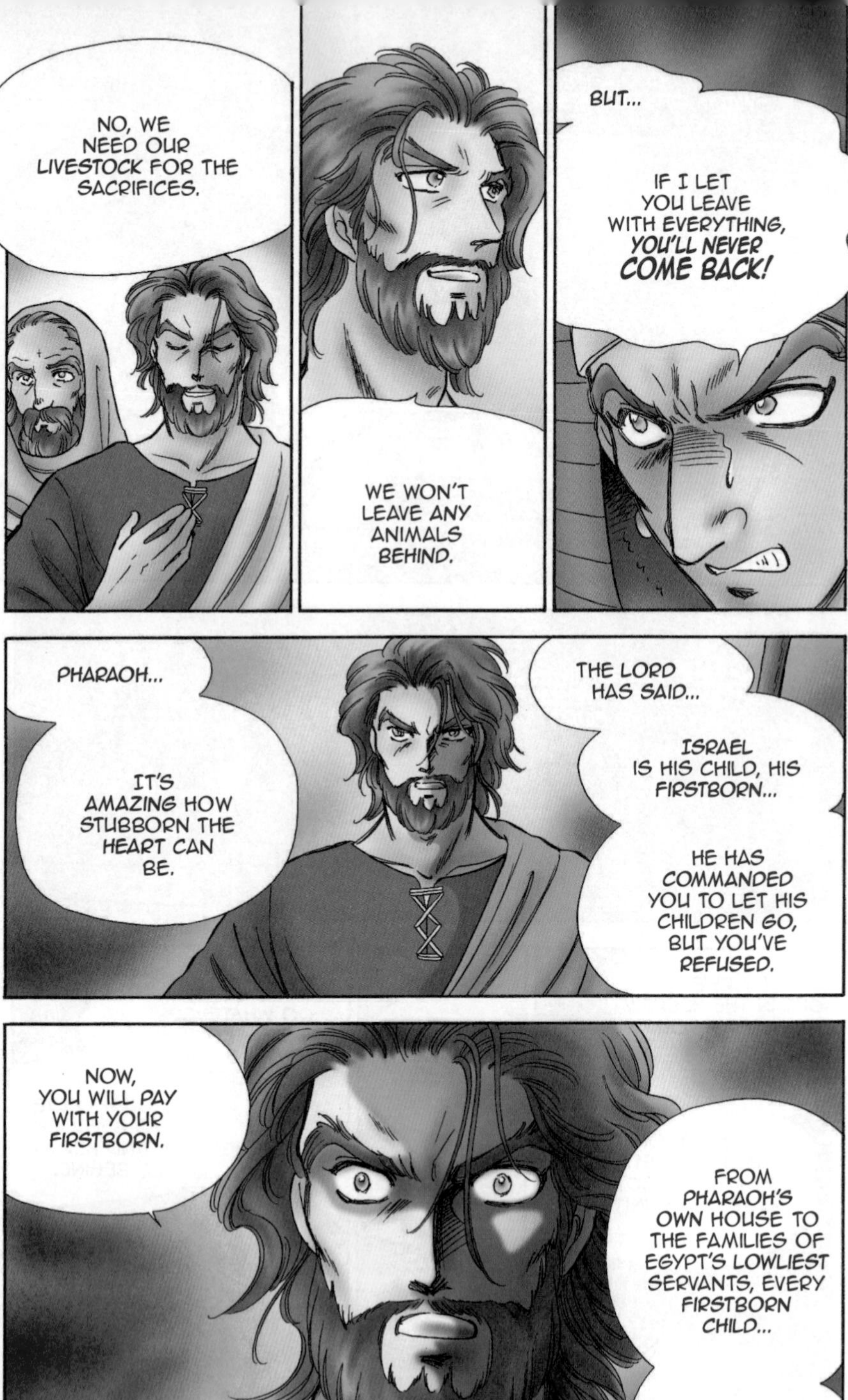
NO, WE NEED OUR LIVESTOCK FOR THE SACRIFICES.
WE WON'T LEAVE ANY ANIMALS BEHIND.
BUT...
IF I LET YOU LEAVE WITH EVERYTHING, *YOU'LL NEVER COME BACK!*
PHARAOH...
IT'S AMAZING HOW STUBBORN THE HEART CAN BE.
THE LORD HAS SAID...
ISRAEL IS HIS CHILD, HIS FIRSTBORN...
HE HAS COMMANDED YOU TO LET HIS CHILDREN GO, BUT YOU'VE REFUSED.
NOW, YOU WILL PAY WITH YOUR FIRSTBORN.
FROM PHARAOH'S OWN HOUSE TO THE FAMILIES OF EGYPT'S LOWLIEST SERVANTS, EVERY FIRSTBORN CHILD...
WILL DIE!

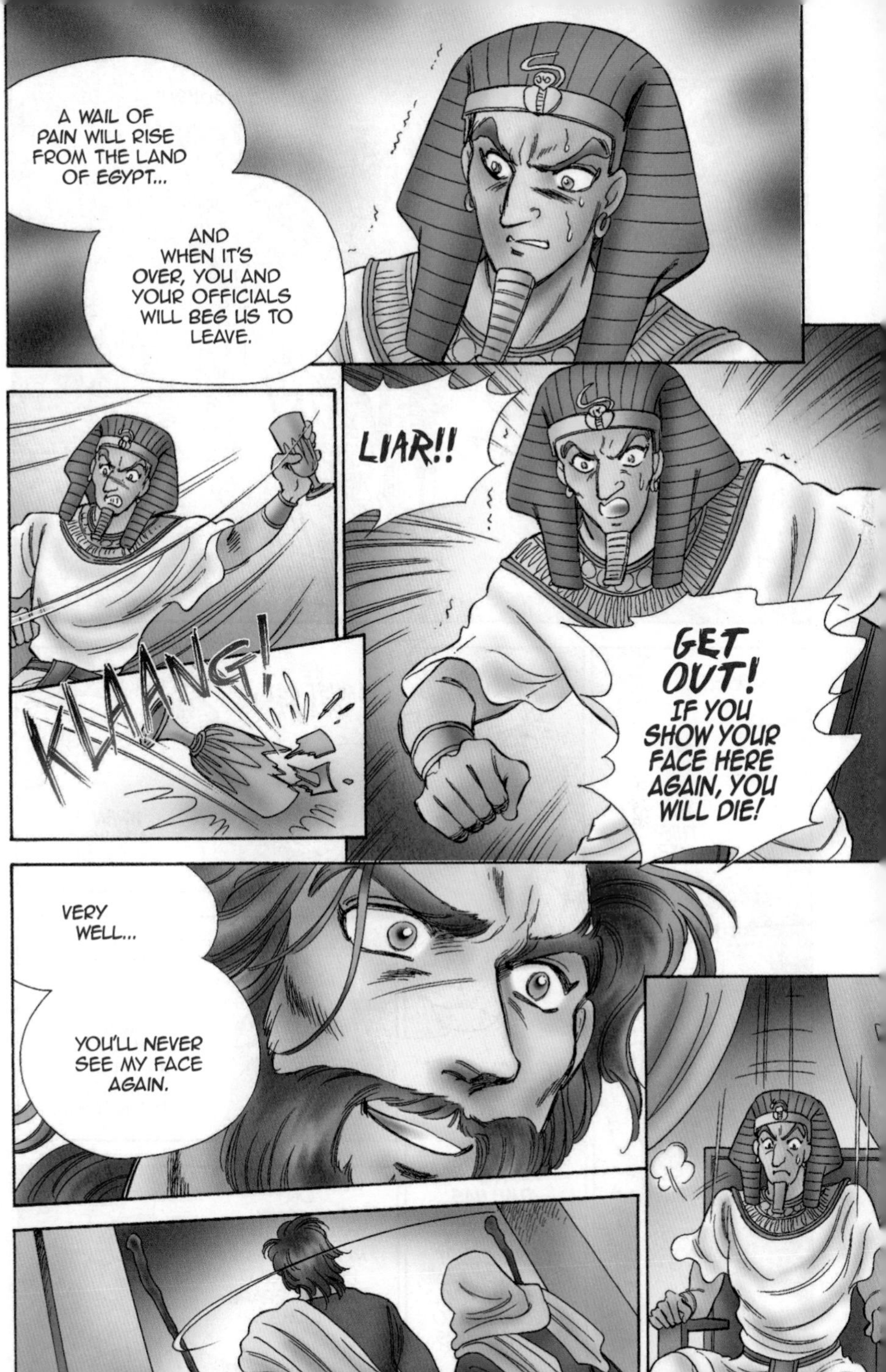
A WAIL OF PAIN WILL RISE FROM THE LAND OF EGYPT...
AND WHEN IT'S OVER, YOU AND YOUR OFFICIALS WILL BEG US TO LEAVE.
LIAR!!
KLAANG!
GET OUT! IF YOU SHOW YOUR FACE HERE AGAIN, YOU WILL DIE!
VERY WELL...
YOU'LL NEVER SEE MY FACE AGAIN.

22. Passover

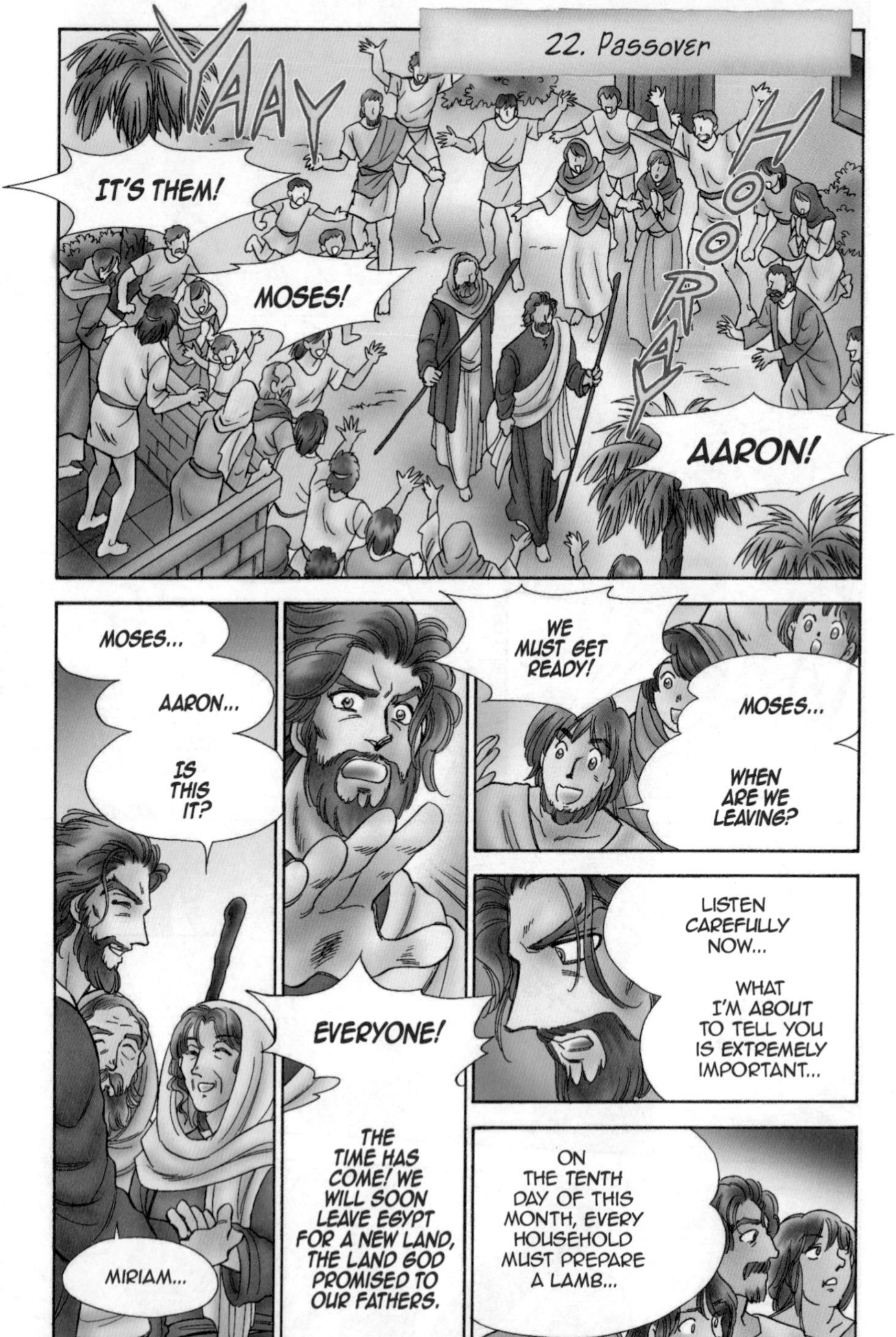
YAAY
HOORAY
IT'S THEM!
MOSES!
AARON!
MOSES...
AARON...
IS THIS IT?
MIRIAM...
WE MUST GET READY!
EVERYONE!
THE TIME HAS COME! WE WILL SOON LEAVE EGYPT FOR A NEW LAND, THE LAND GOD PROMISED TO OUR FATHERS.
MOSES...
WHEN ARE WE LEAVING?
LISTEN CAREFULLY NOW...
WHAT I'M ABOUT TO TELL YOU IS EXTREMELY IMPORTANT...
ON THE TENTH DAY OF THIS MONTH, EVERY HOUSEHOLD MUST PREPARE A LAMB...

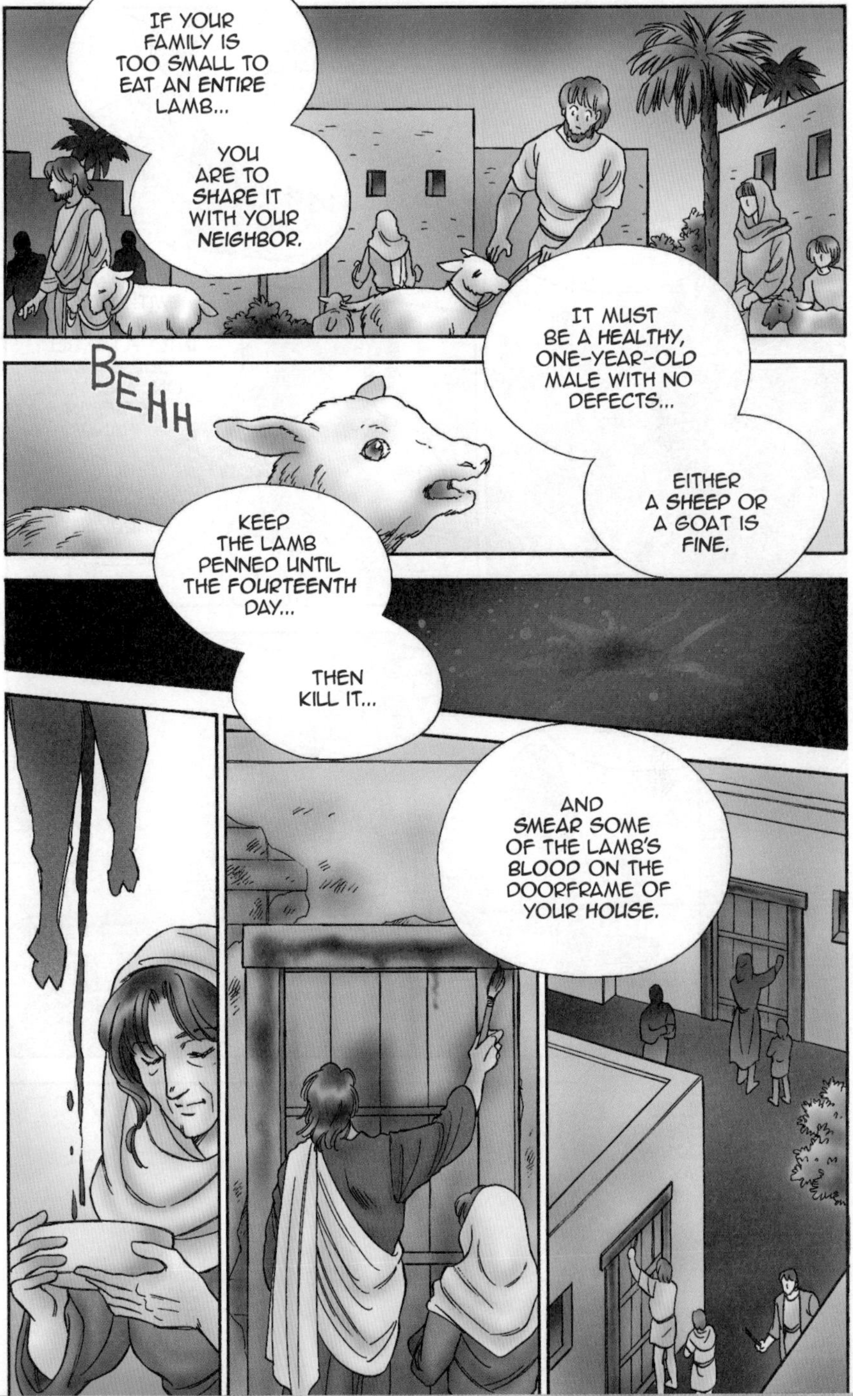
IF YOUR FAMILY IS TOO SMALL TO EAT AN ENTIRE LAMB...
YOU ARE TO SHARE IT WITH YOUR NEIGHBOR.
IT MUST BE A HEALTHY, ONE-YEAR-OLD MALE WITH NO DEFECTS...
BEHH
EITHER A SHEEP OR A GOAT IS FINE.
KEEP THE LAMB PENNED UNTIL THE FOURTEENTH DAY...
THEN KILL IT...
AND SMEAR SOME OF THE LAMB'S BLOOD ON THE DOORFRAME OF YOUR HOUSE.

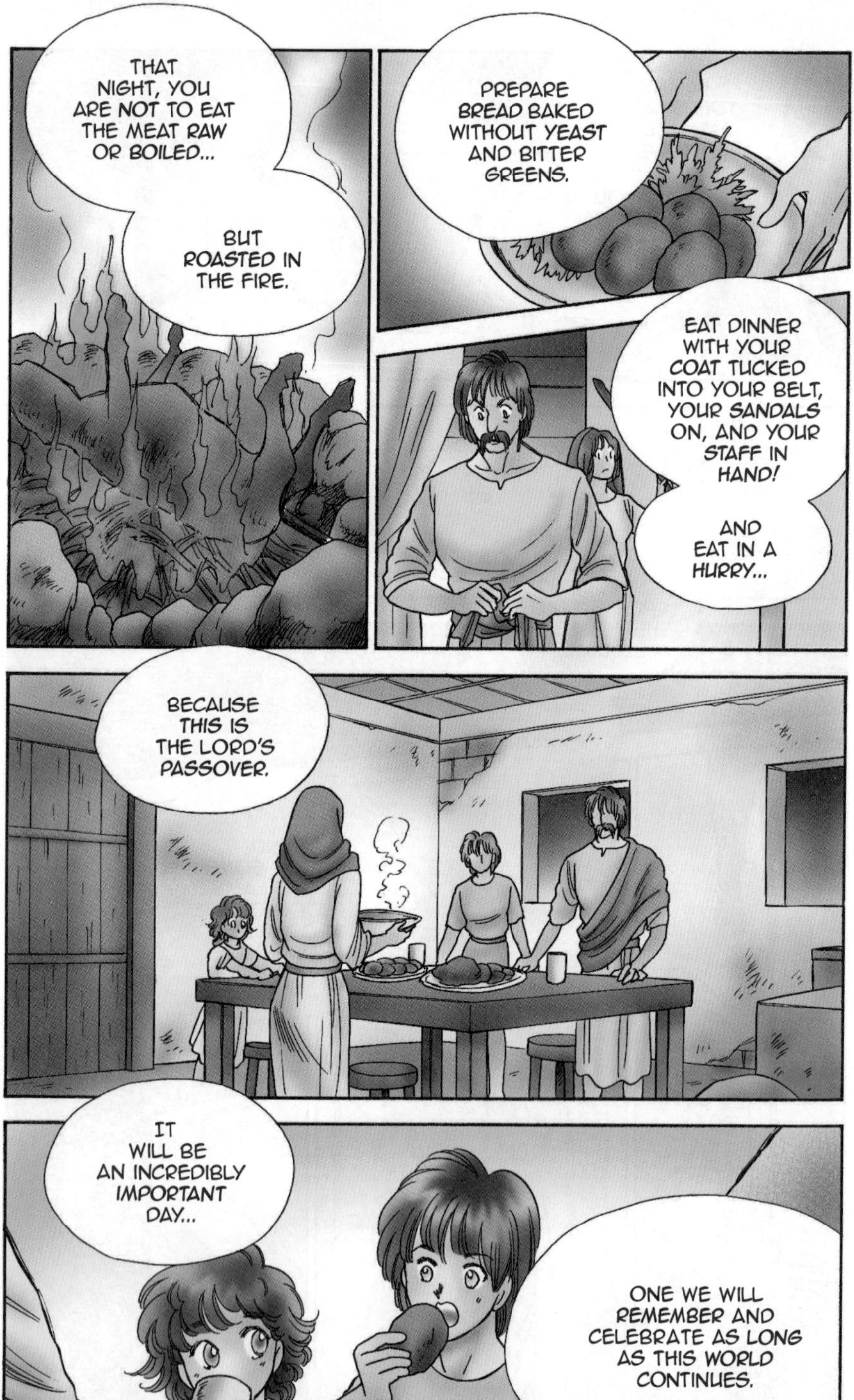
THAT NIGHT, YOU ARE NOT TO EAT THE MEAT RAW OR BOILED...
BUT ROASTED IN THE FIRE.
PREPARE BREAD BAKED WITHOUT YEAST AND BITTER GREENS.
EAT DINNER WITH YOUR COAT TUCKED INTO YOUR BELT, YOUR SANDALS ON, AND YOUR STAFF IN HAND!
AND EAT IN A HURRY...
BECAUSE THIS IS THE LORD'S PASSOVER.
IT WILL BE AN INCREDIBLY IMPORTANT DAY...
ONE WE WILL REMEMBER AND CELEBRATE AS LONG AS THIS WORLD CONTINUES.

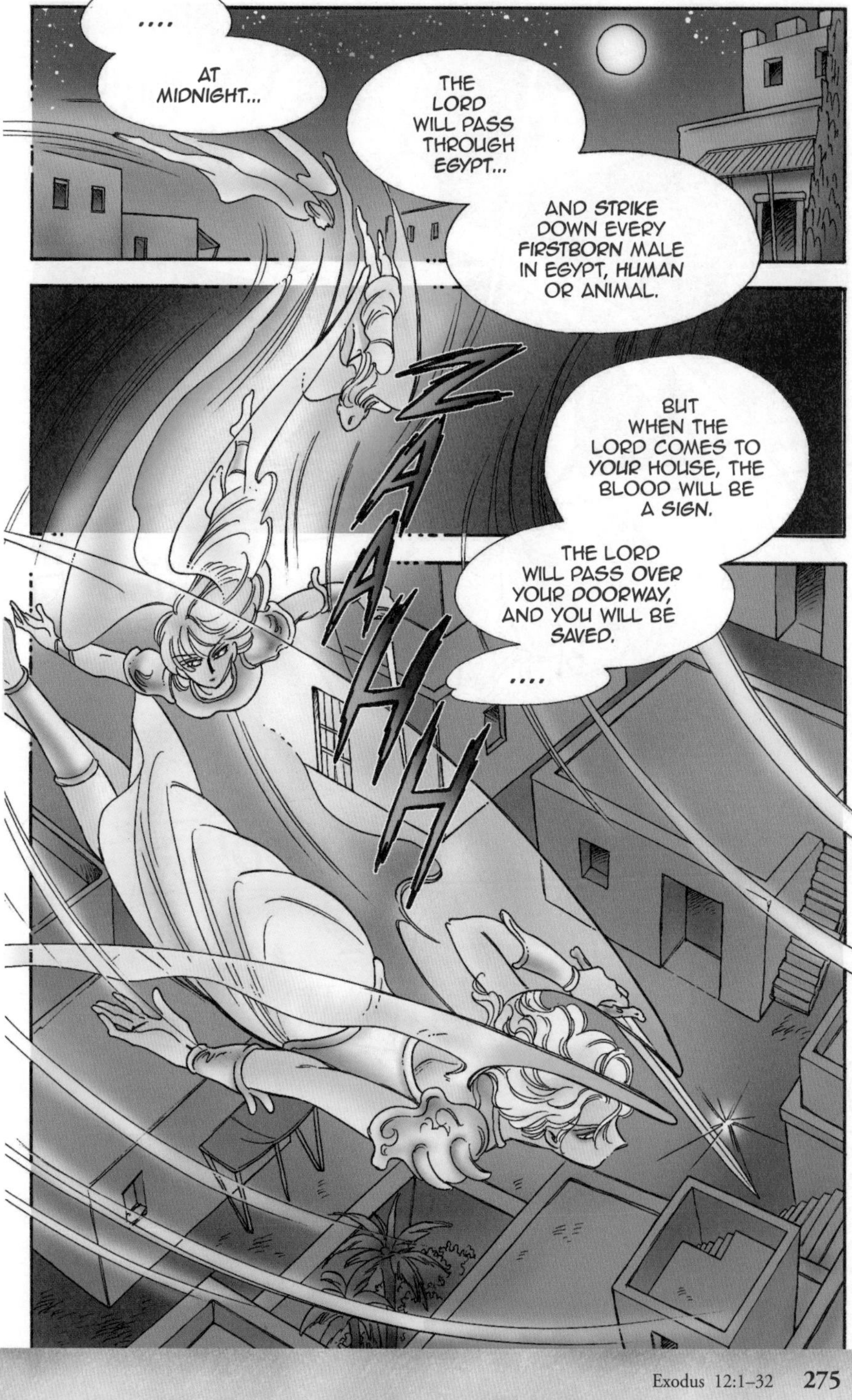
....
AT MIDNIGHT...
THE LORD WILL PASS THROUGH EGYPT...
AND STRIKE DOWN EVERY FIRSTBORN MALE IN EGYPT, HUMAN OR ANIMAL.
ZAAAHH
BUT WHEN THE LORD COMES TO YOUR HOUSE, THE BLOOD WILL BE A SIGN.
THE LORD WILL PASS OVER YOUR DOORWAY, AND YOU WILL BE SAVED.
....

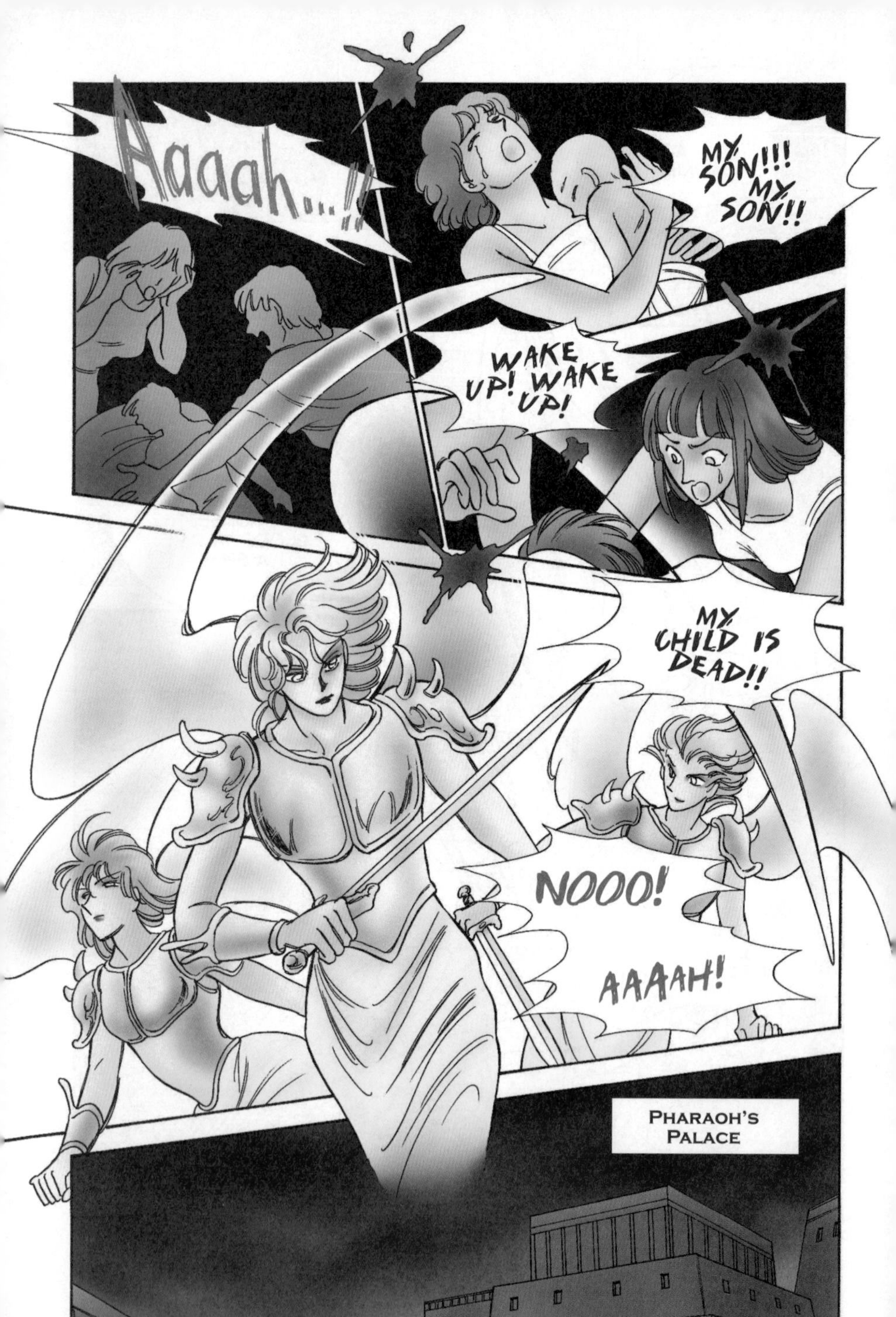
Aaaah...!!
MY SON!!! MY SON!!
WAKE UP! WAKE UP!
MY CHILD IS DEAD!!
NOOO!
AAAAH!
PHARAOH'S PALACE

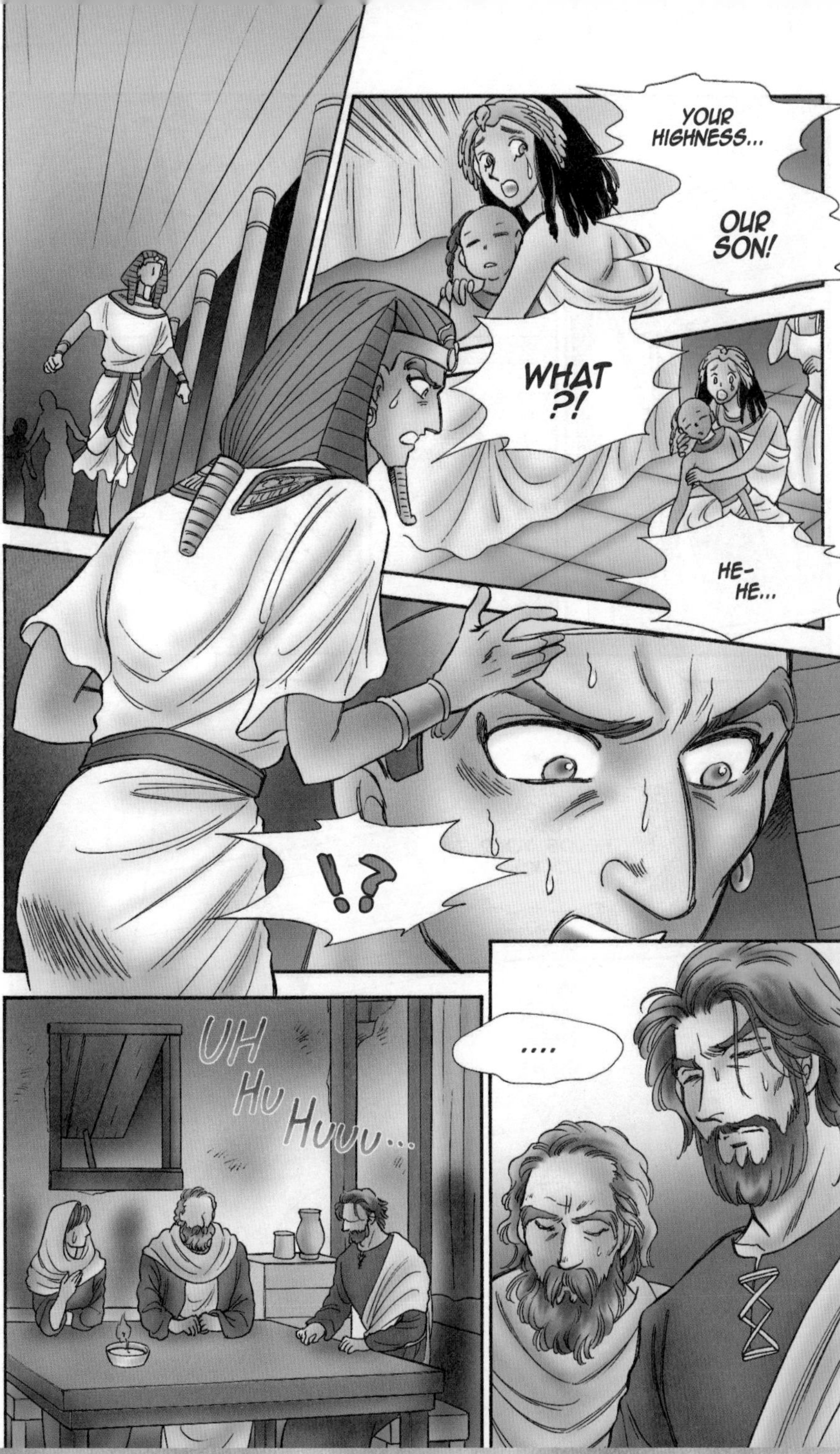
YOUR HIGHNESS...
OUR SON!
WHAT ?!
HE- HE...
!?
UH Hu Huuu...
....

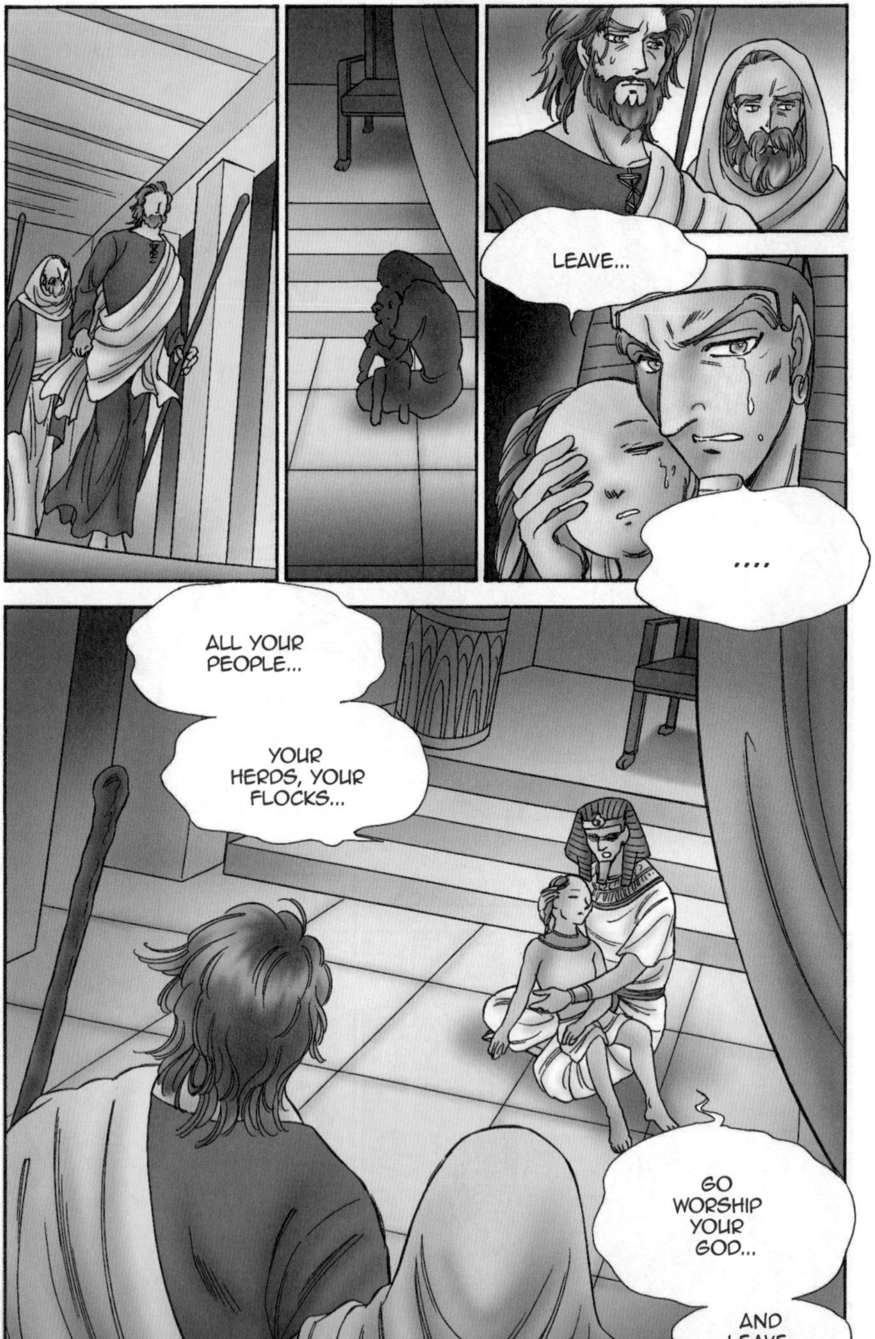
LEAVE...
....
ALL YOUR PEOPLE...
YOUR HERDS, YOUR FLOCKS...
GO WORSHIP YOUR GOD...
AND LEAVE.

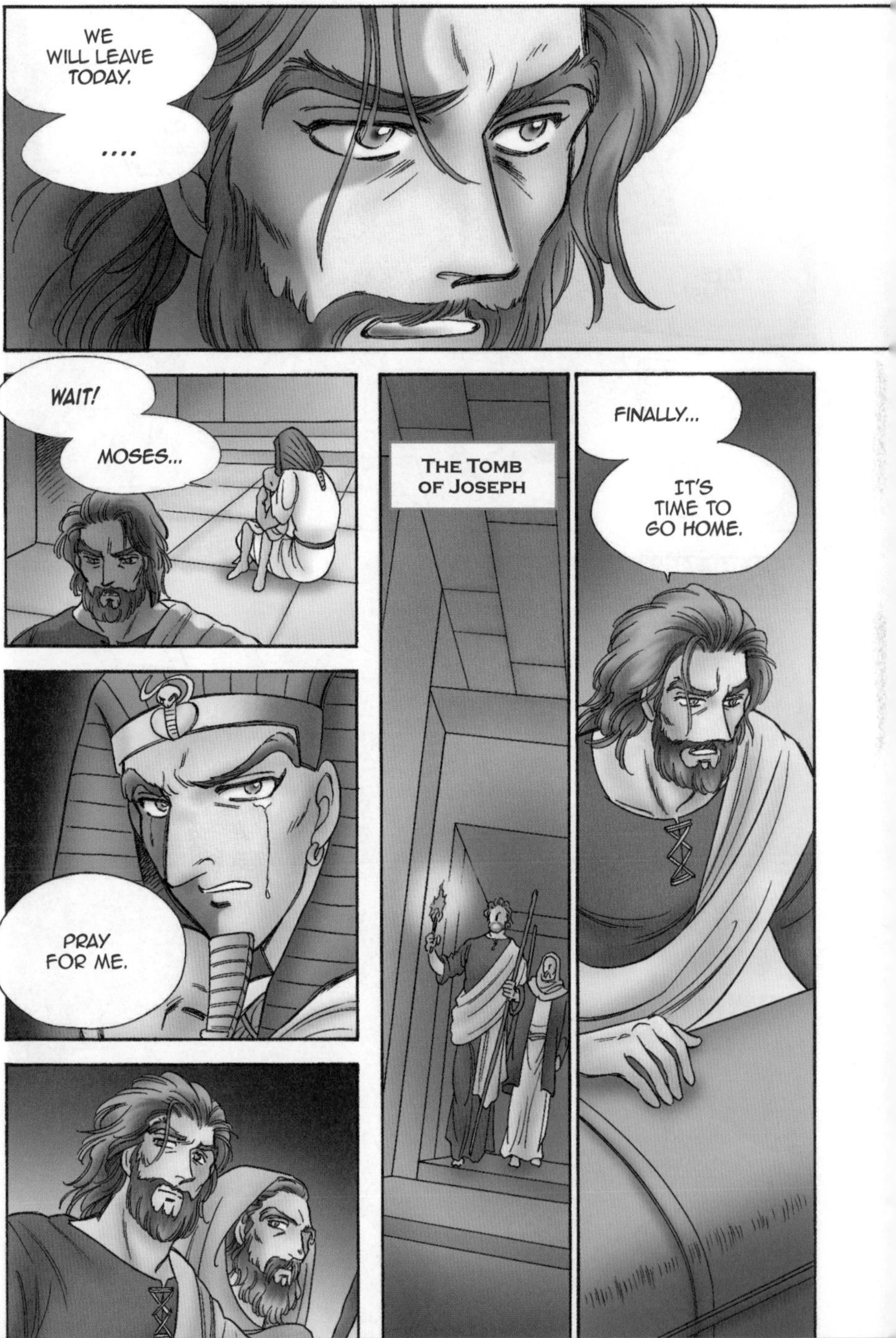
WE WILL LEAVE TODAY.
....
WAIT!
MOSES...
PRAY FOR ME.
THE TOMB OF JOSEPH
FINALLY...
IT'S TIME TO GO HOME.

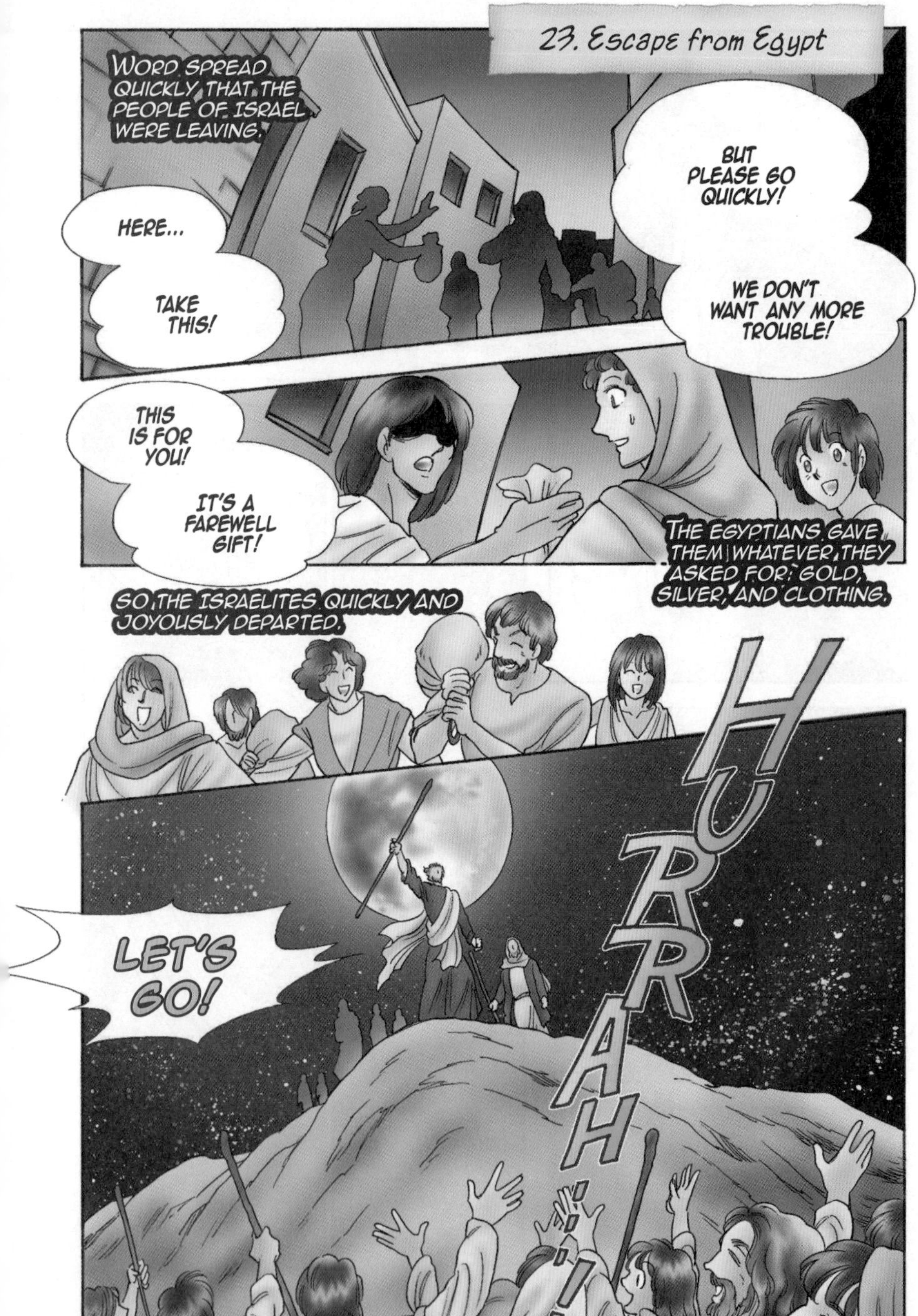
23. Escape from Egypt
Word spread quickly that the people of Israel were leaving.
Here...
Take this!
But please go quickly!
We don't want any more trouble!
This is for you!
It's a farewell gift!
The Egyptians gave them whatever they asked for: gold, silver, and clothing.
So the Israelites quickly and joyously departed.
Hurrah!
Let's go!

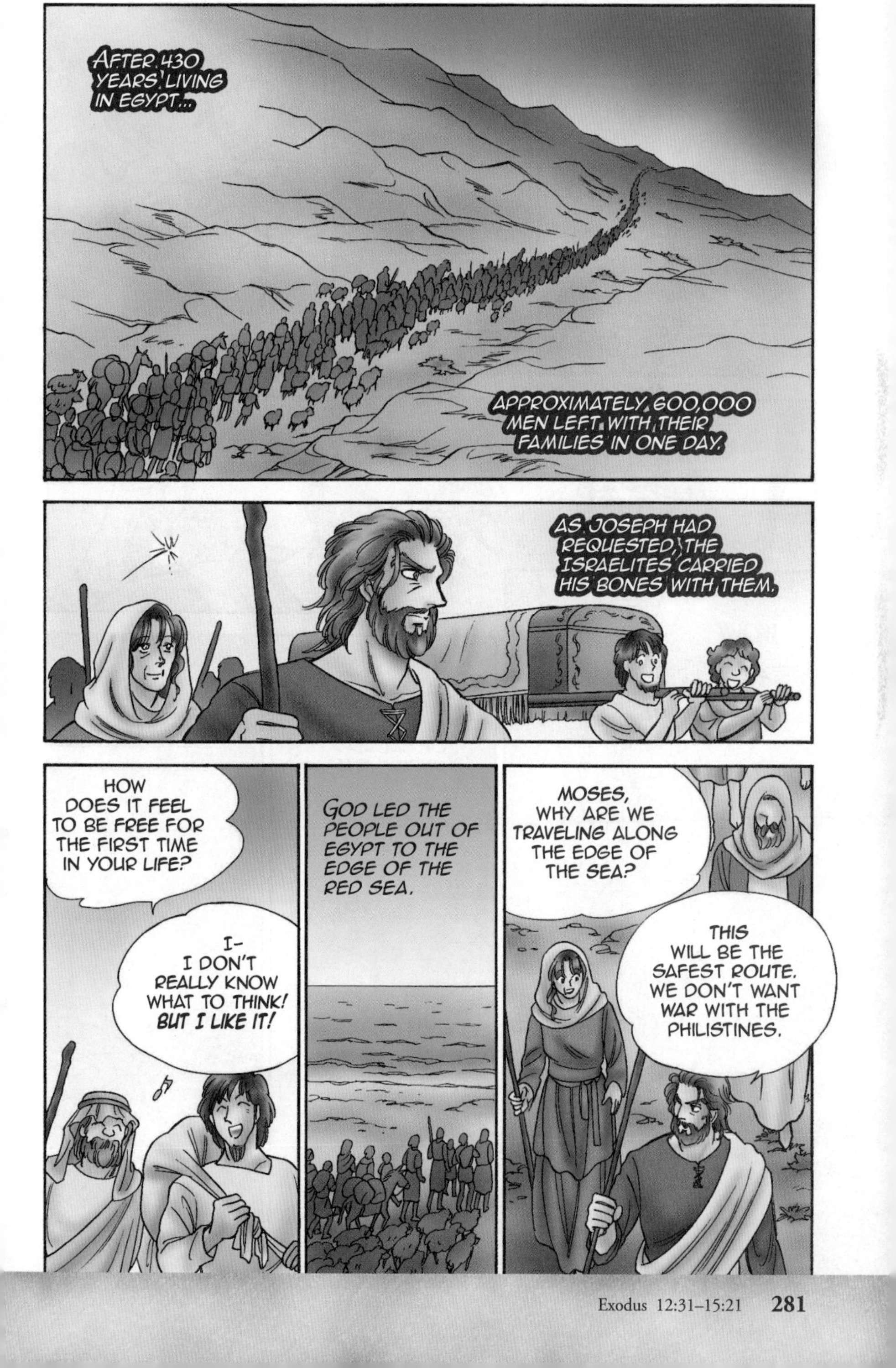
AFTER 430 YEARS LIVING IN EGYPT...
APPROXIMATELY 600,000 MEN LEFT WITH THEIR FAMILIES IN ONE DAY.
AS JOSEPH HAD REQUESTED, THE ISRAELITES CARRIED HIS BONES WITH THEM.
HOW DOES IT FEEL TO BE FREE FOR THE FIRST TIME IN YOUR LIFE?
I- I DON'T REALLY KNOW WHAT TO THINK! BUT I LIKE IT!
GOD LED THE PEOPLE OUT OF EGYPT TO THE EDGE OF THE RED SEA.
MOSES, WHY ARE WE TRAVELING ALONG THE EDGE OF THE SEA?
THIS WILL BE THE SAFEST ROUTE. WE DON'T WANT WAR WITH THE PHILISTINES.

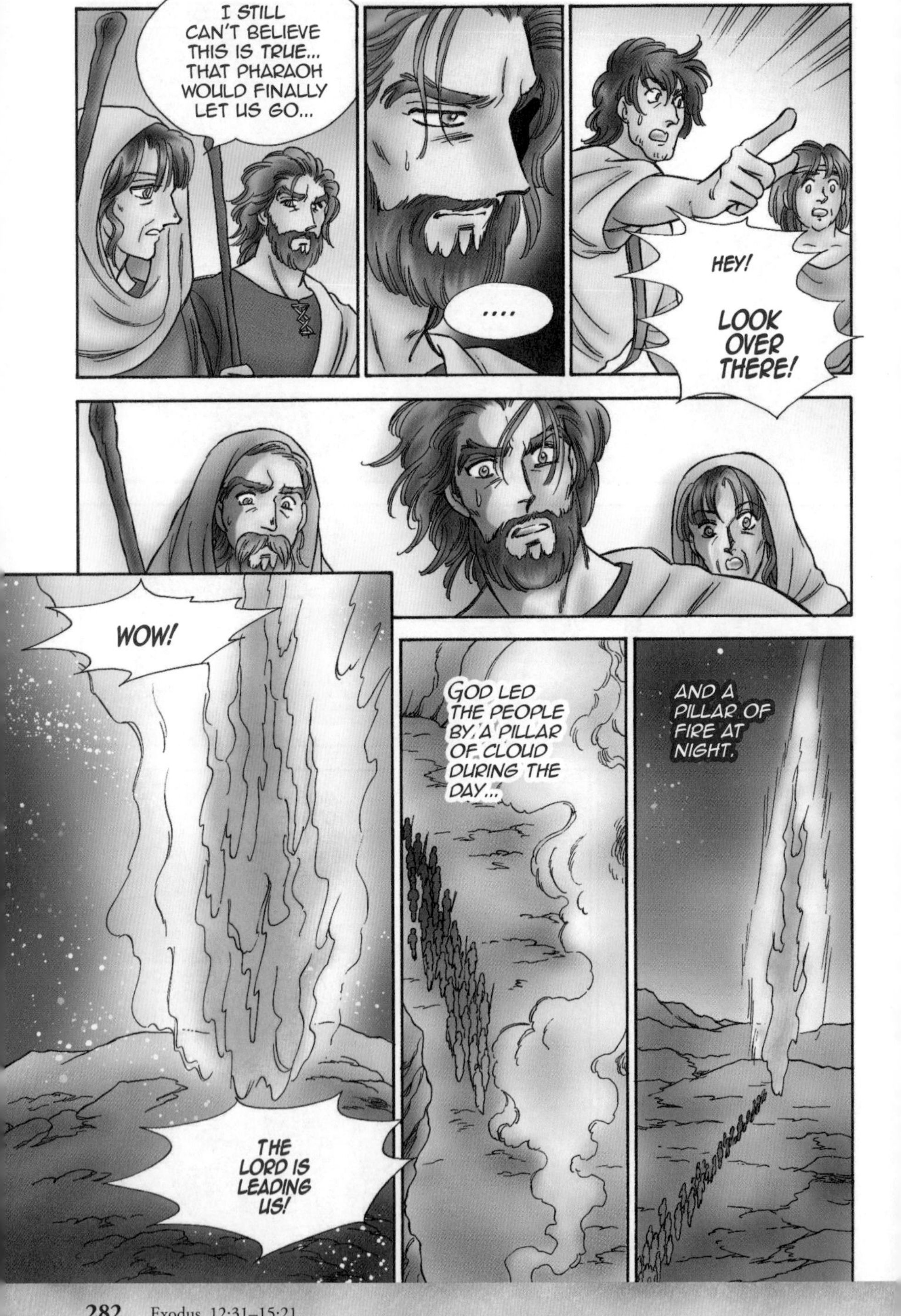
I STILL CAN'T BELIEVE THIS IS TRUE... THAT PHARAOH WOULD FINALLY LET US GO...
....
HEY!
LOOK OVER THERE!
WOW!
THE LORD IS LEADING US!
GOD LED THE PEOPLE BY A PILLAR OF CLOUD DURING THE DAY...
AND A PILLAR OF FIRE AT NIGHT.

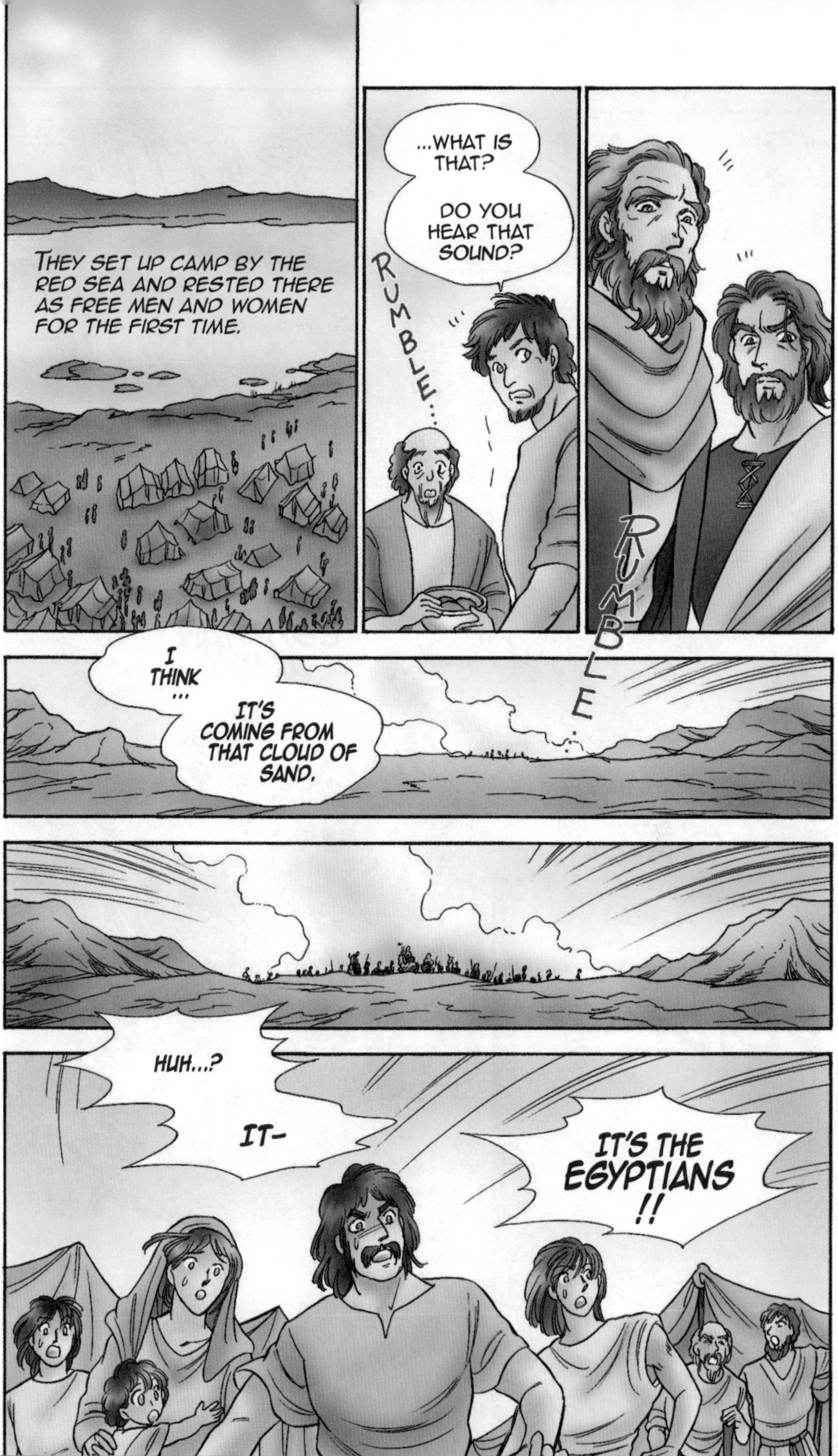
THEY SET UP CAMP BY THE RED SEA AND RESTED THERE AS FREE MEN AND WOMEN FOR THE FIRST TIME.
...WHAT IS THAT?
DO YOU HEAR THAT SOUND?
RUMBLE...
RUMBLE...
I THINK ...
IT'S COMING FROM THAT CLOUD OF SAND.
HUH...?
IT-
IT'S THE EGYPTIANS !!

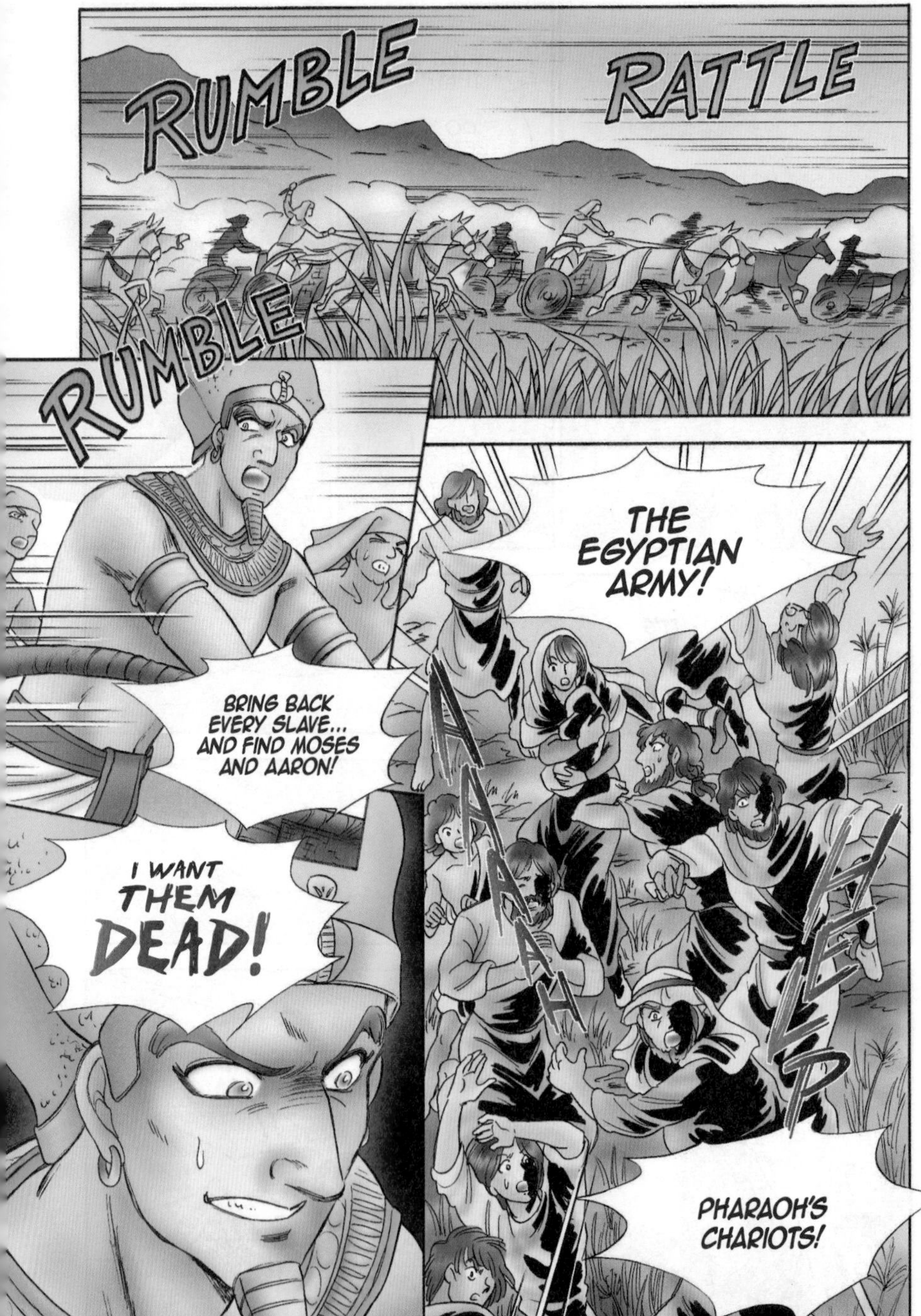
RUMBLE
RATTLE
RUMBLE
BRING BACK EVERY SLAVE... AND FIND MOSES AND AARON!
I WANT THEM DEAD!
THE EGYPTIAN ARMY!
AAAAH
HELP
PHARAOH'S CHARIOTS!

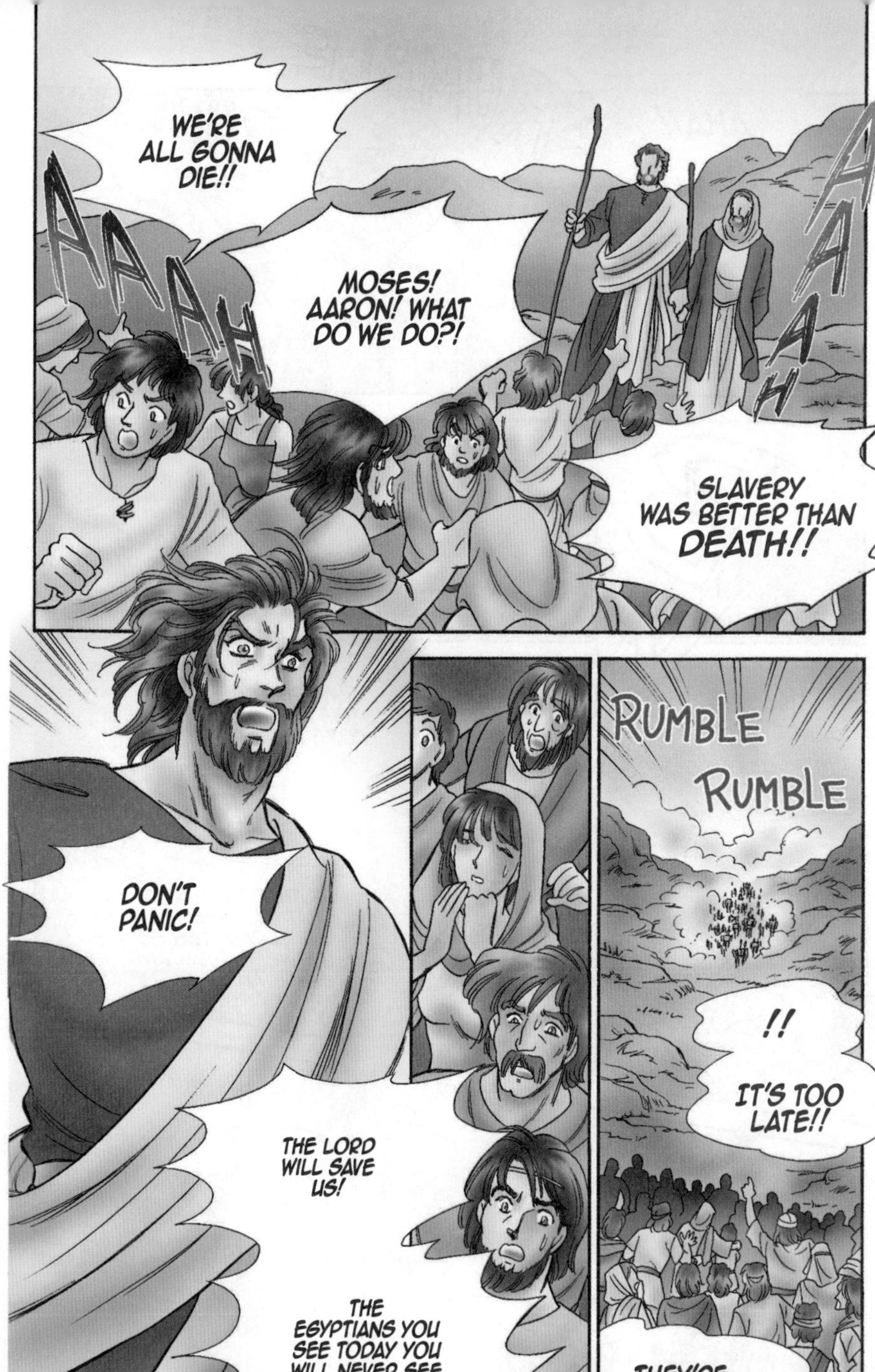
WE'RE ALL GONNA DIE!!
AAAAH
MOSES! AARON! WHAT DO WE DO?!
AAAAH
SLAVERY WAS BETTER THAN DEATH!!
DON'T PANIC!
THE LORD WILL SAVE US!
THE EGYPTIANS YOU SEE TODAY YOU WILL NEVER SEE AGAIN!
RUMBLE
RUMBLE
!!
IT'S TOO LATE!!
THEY'RE ALMOST HERE!!

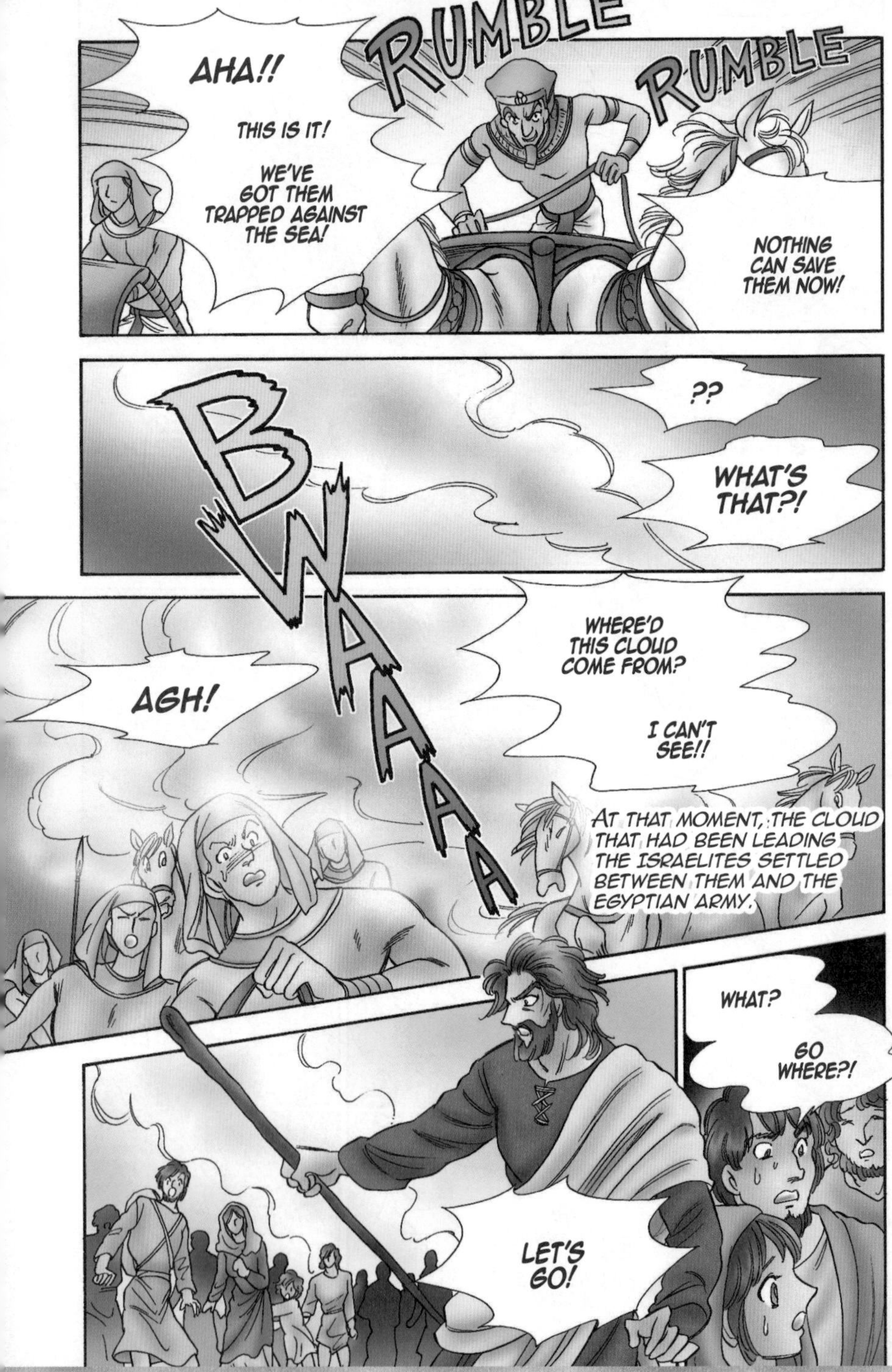
AHA!!
THIS IS IT!
WE'VE GOT THEM TRAPPED AGAINST THE SEA!
RUMBLE
RUMBLE
NOTHING CAN SAVE THEM NOW!
??
WHAT'S THAT?!
BWAAAA
AGH!
WHERE'D THIS CLOUD COME FROM?
I CAN'T SEE!!
AT THAT MOMENT, THE CLOUD THAT HAD BEEN LEADING THE ISRAELITES SETTLED BETWEEN THEM AND THE EGYPTIAN ARMY.
LET'S GO!
WHAT?
GO WHERE?!

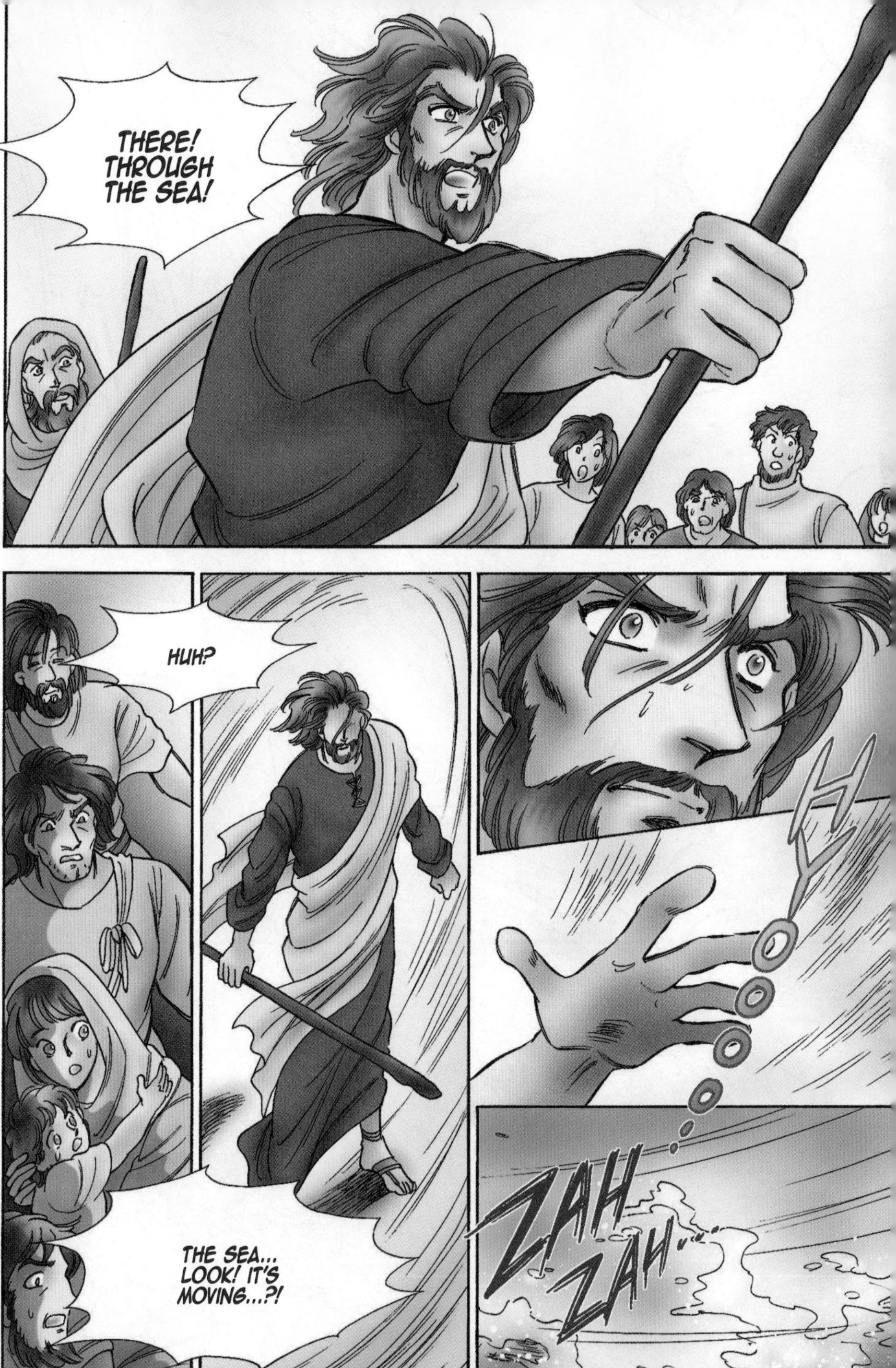
THERE! THROUGH THE SEA!
HUH?
THE SEA... LOOK! IT'S MOVING...?!
ZAH ZAH...

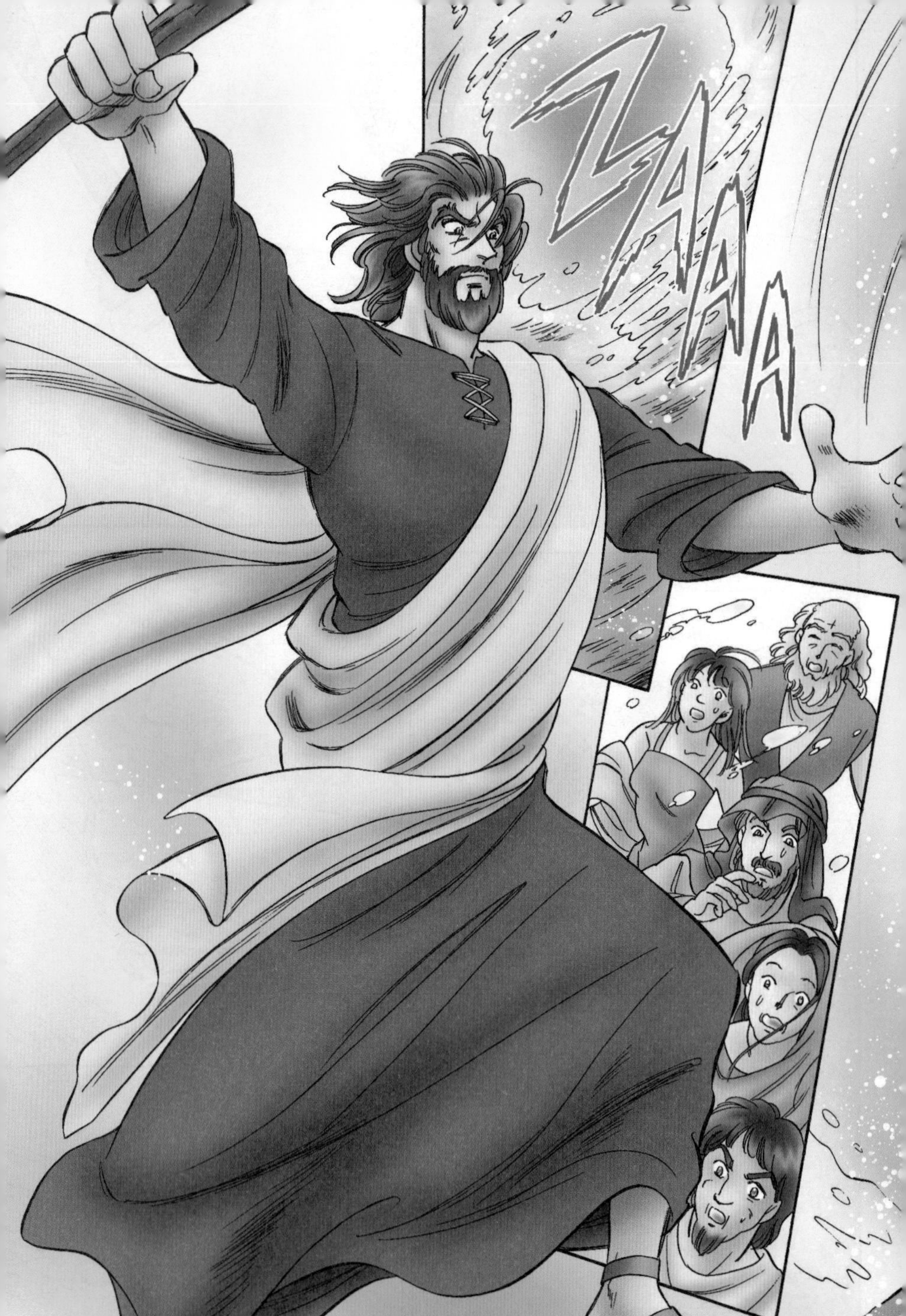
ZAAAA

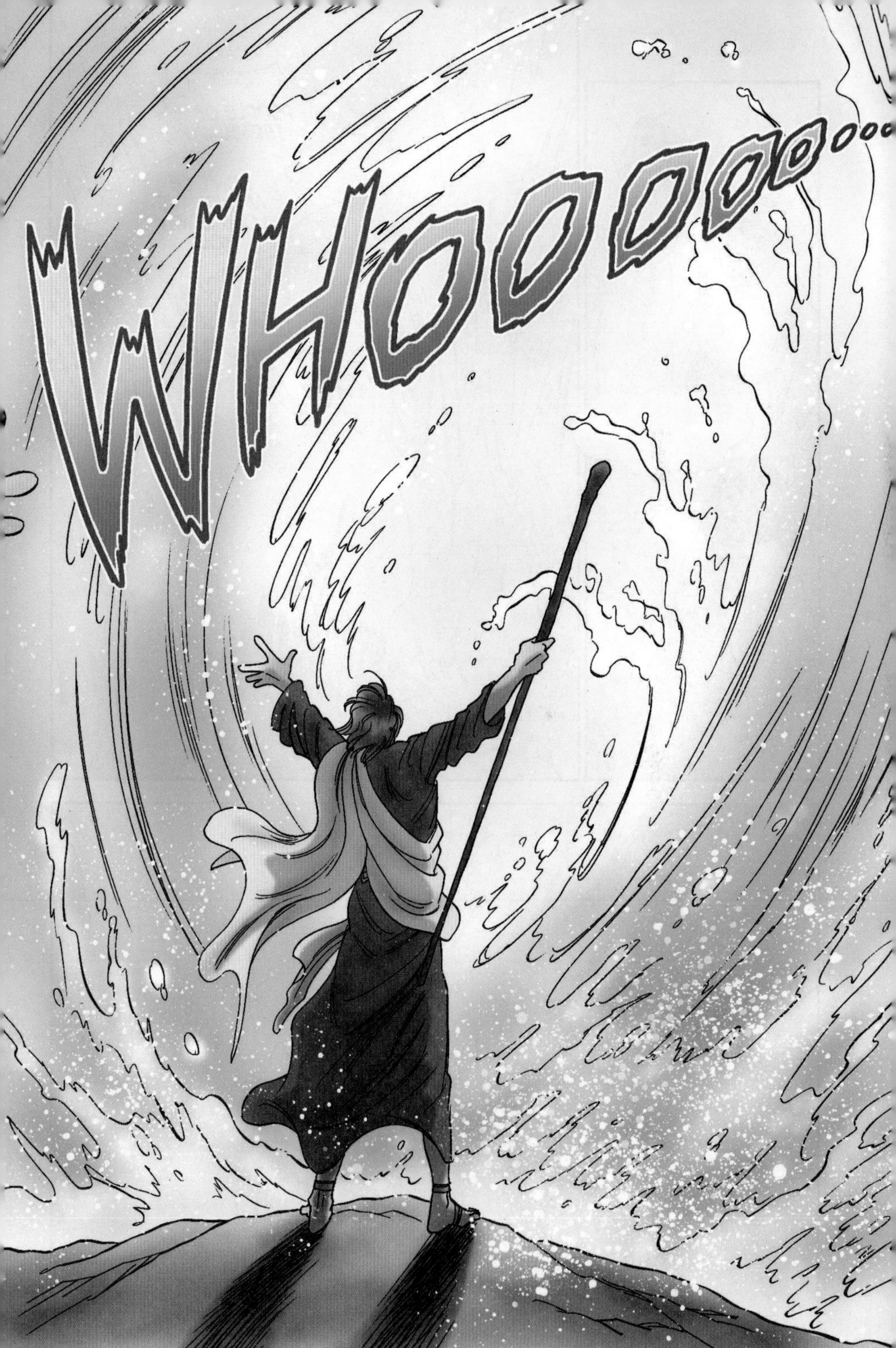
WHOOOOOOOOOO

...
...
PEOPLE OF ISRAEL...
DON'T BE AFRAID! THE LORD IS WITH YOU!
WHOOSH

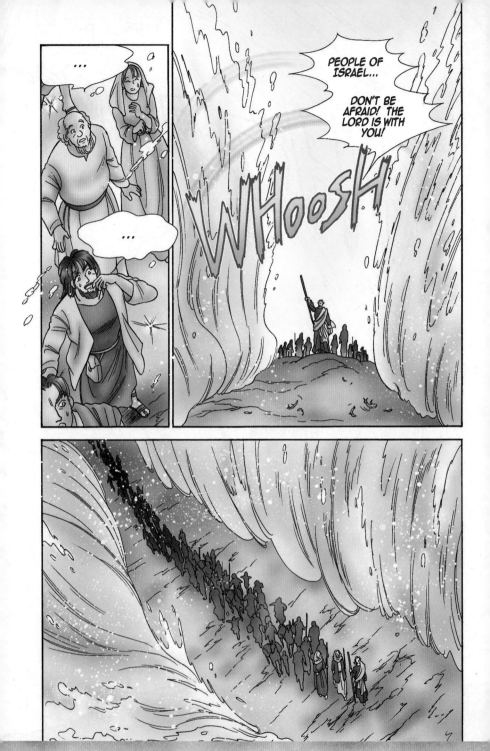

HOW IS THAT POSSIBLE...?
THE SEA SPLIT IN TWO!
WHAT ARE YOU WAITING FOR?!
AFTER THEM!!
RUMBLE
RUMBLE
THEY'RE COMING!
HURRY!
KRAK
ARGH! MY WHEELS ARE WOBBLING!
YOUR HIGHNESS, THIS SEEMS RISKY!
ISRAEL'S GOD IS FIGHTING AGAINST US!

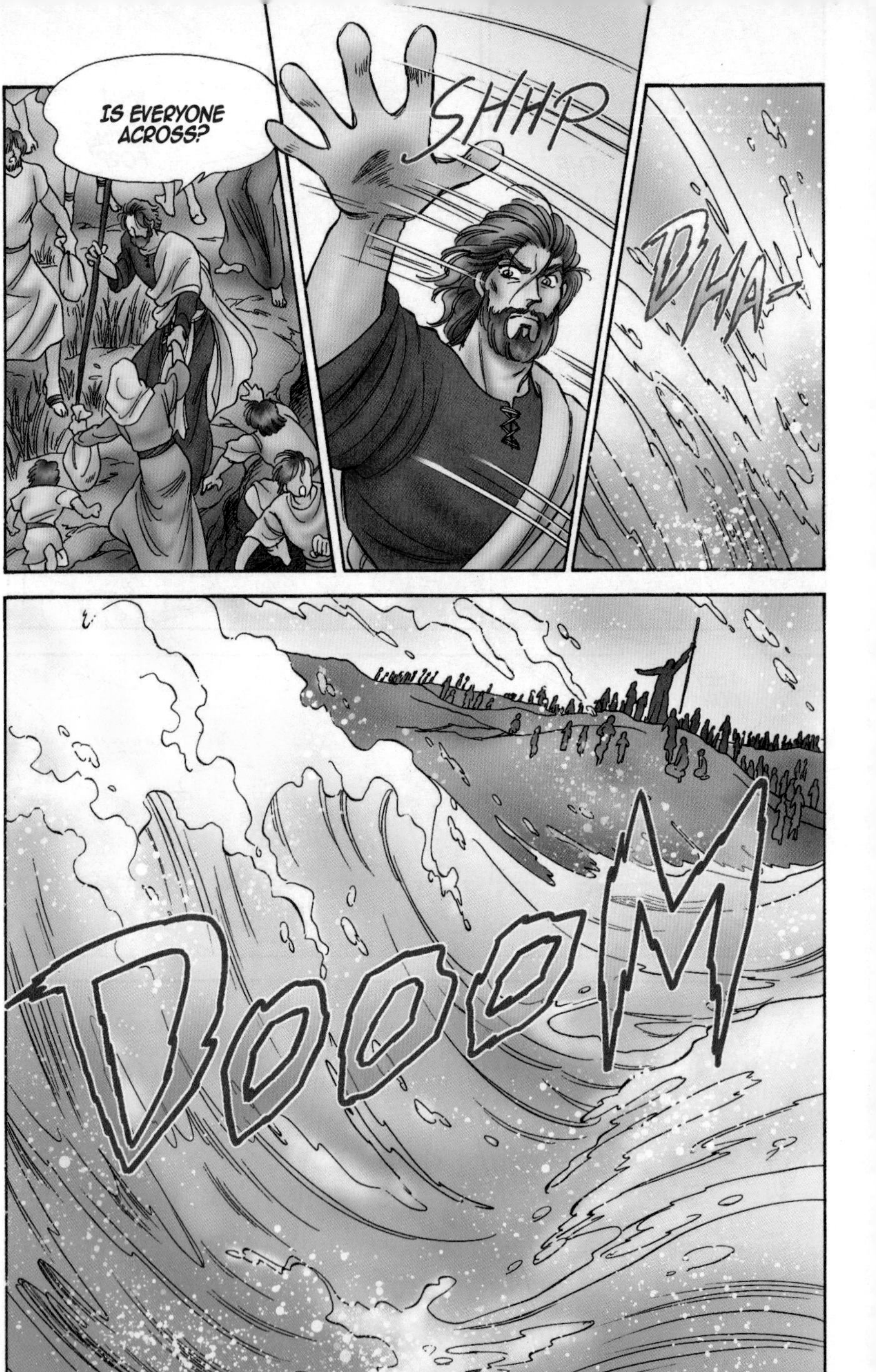
IS EVERYONE ACROSS?
SHHP
DWA-
DOOOOM

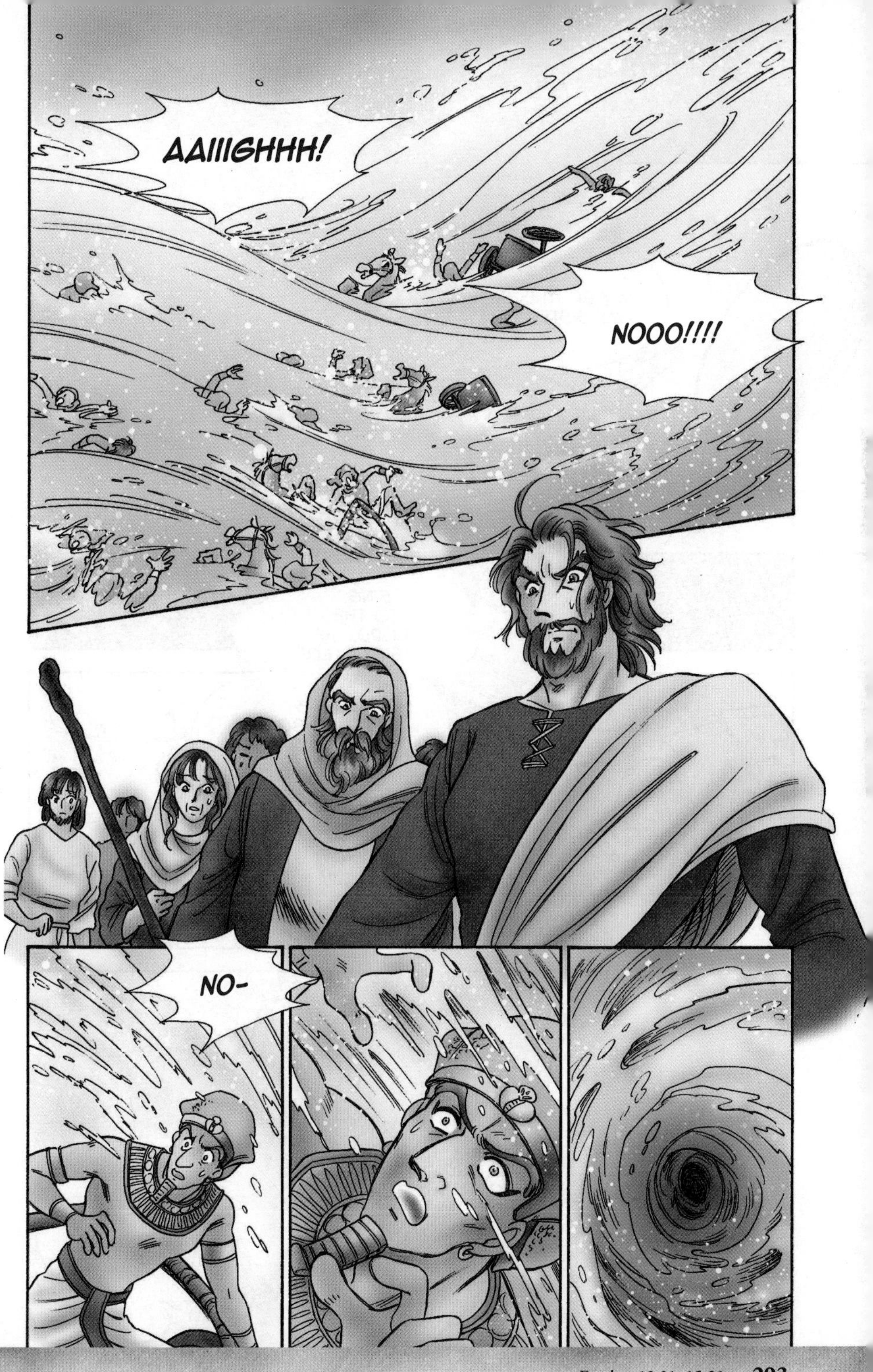
AAIIIGHHH!
NOOO!!!!
NO-

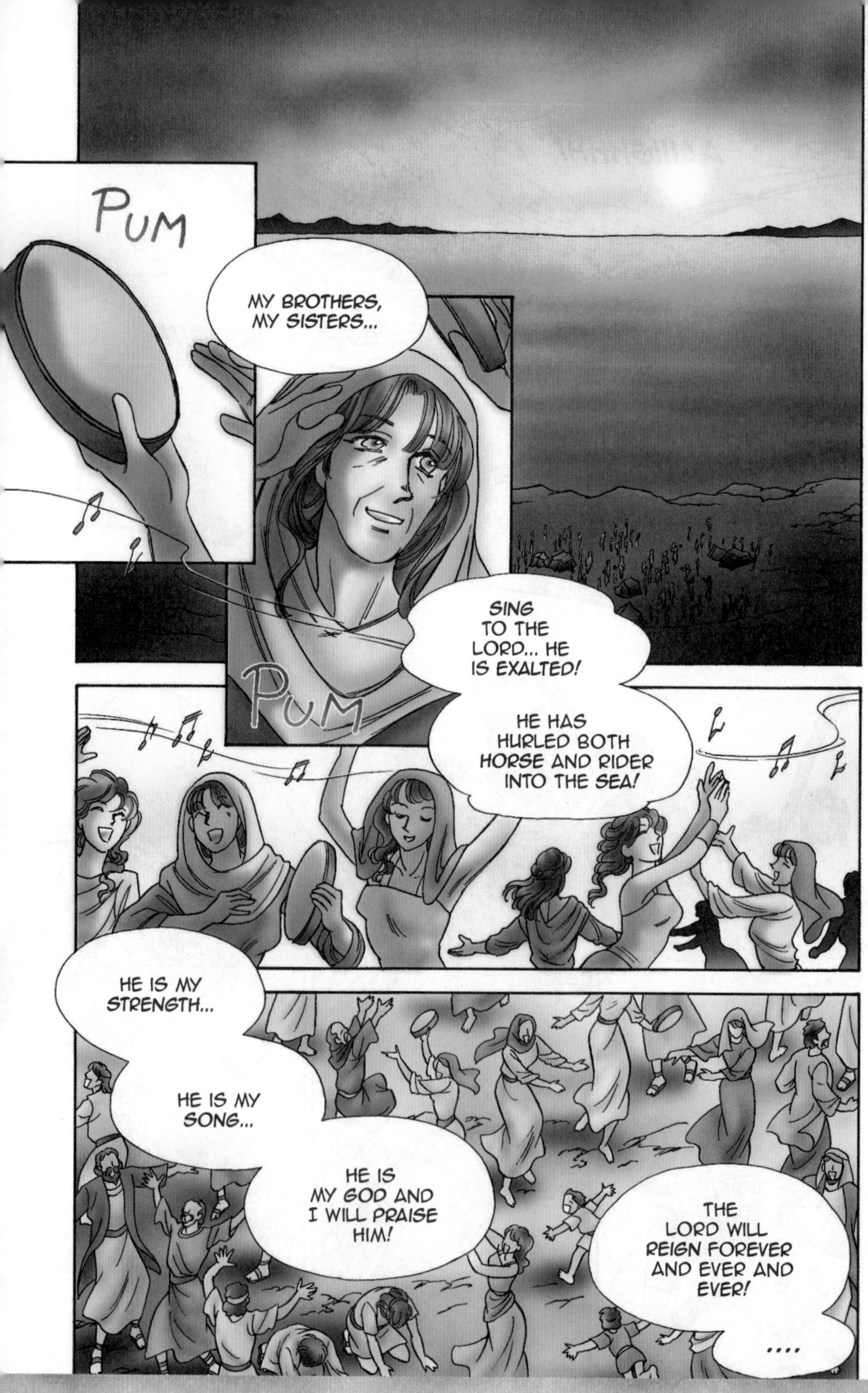
PUM
MY BROTHERS, MY SISTERS...
SING TO THE LORD... HE IS EXALTED!
PUM
HE HAS HURLED BOTH HORSE AND RIDER INTO THE SEA!
HE IS MY STRENGTH...
HE IS MY SONG...
HE IS MY GOD AND I WILL PRAISE HIM!
THE LORD WILL REIGN FOREVER AND EVER AND EVER!
....

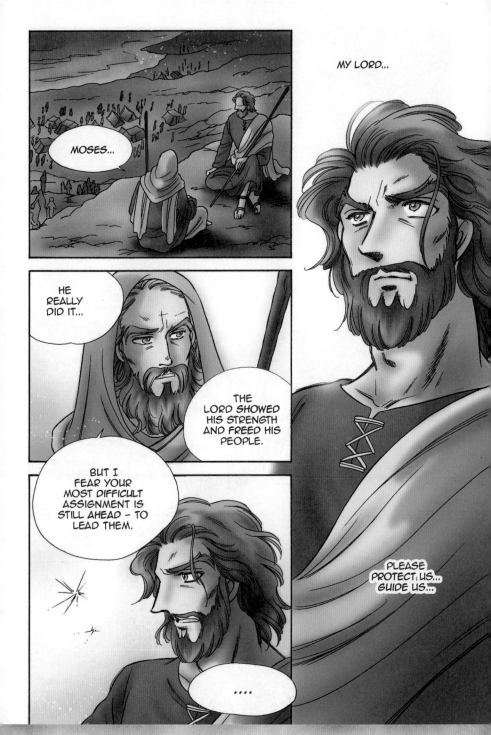

MY LORD...

MOSES...

HE REALLY DID IT...

THE LORD SHOWED HIS STRENGTH AND FREED HIS PEOPLE.

BUT I FEAR YOUR MOST DIFFICULT ASSIGNMENT IS STILL AHEAD — TO LEAD THEM.

PLEASE PROTECT US... GUIDE US...

....

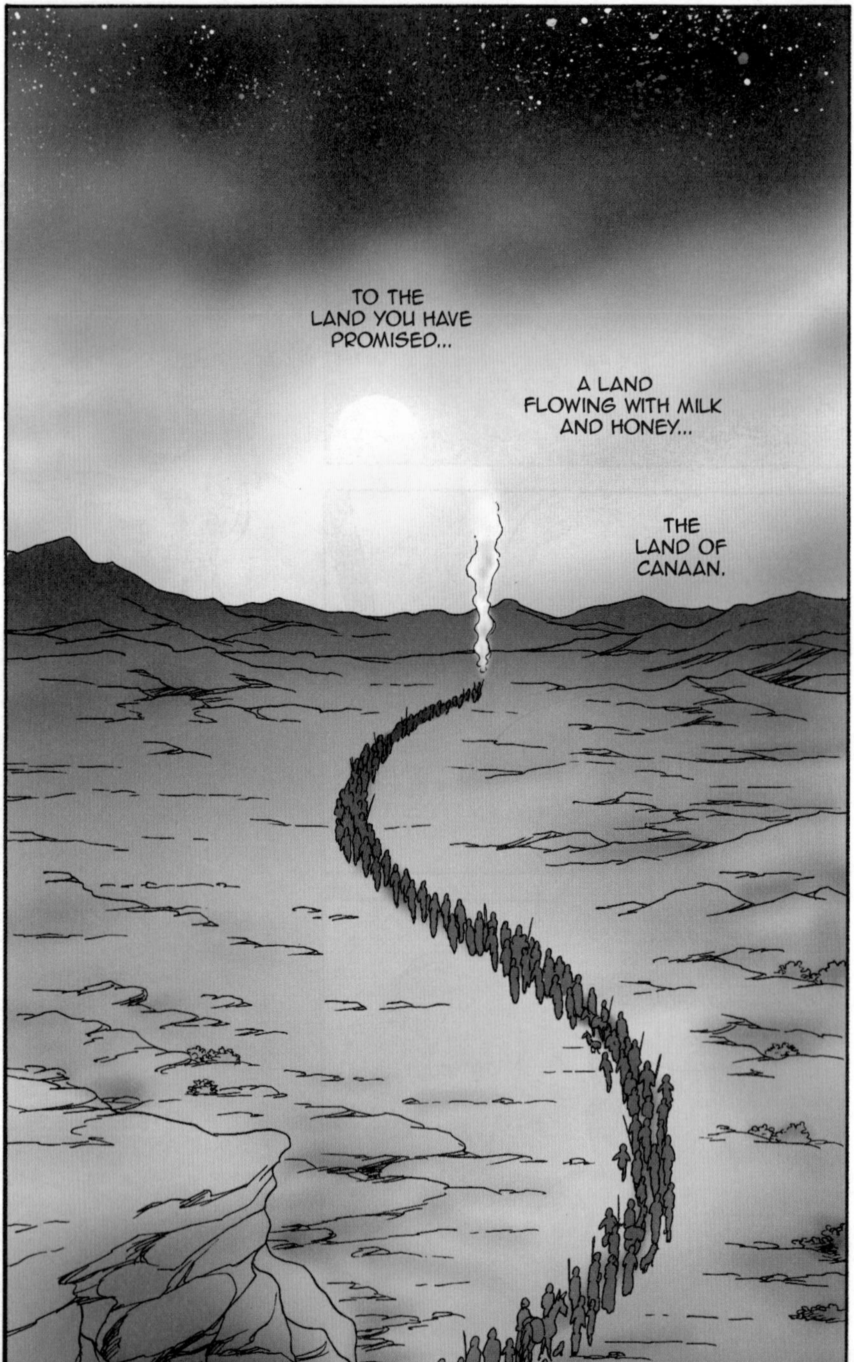
TO THE LAND YOU HAVE PROMISED...
A LAND FLOWING WITH MILK AND HONEY...
THE LAND OF CANAAN.